BERNARD SHAW'S PLAYS

MAJOR BARBARA

HEARTBREAK HOUSE

SAINT JOAN

TOO TRUE TO BE GOOD

With Backgrounds and Criticism

AUSTEN *Pride and Prejudice* edited by Donald Gray

BRONTË, CHARLOTTE *Jane Eyre* edited by Richard J. Dunn

BRONTË, EMILY *Wuthering Heights* edited by William M. Sale, Jr.

CLEMENS *Adventures of Huckleberry Finn* edited by Sculley Bradley,
Richmond Croom Beatty, and E. Hudson Long

CONRAD *Heart of Darkness* edited by Robert Kimbrough

CONRAD *Lord Jim* edited by Thomas Moser

CRANE *The Red Badge of Courage* edited by Sculley Bradley,
Richmond Croom Beatty, and E. Hudson Long

Darwin edited by Philip Appleman

DICKENS *Hard Times* edited by George Ford and Sylvère Monod

John Donne's Poetry selected and edited by A. L. Clements

DOSTOEVSKY *Crime and Punishment* (the Coulson translation)
edited by George Gibian

DREISER *Sister Carrie* edited by Donald Pizer

FLAUBERT *Madame Bovary* edited with a substantially new
translation by Paul de Man

HARDY *The Return of the Native* edited by James Gindin

HARDY *Tess of the D'Urbervilles* edited by Scott Elledge

HAWTHORNE *The House of the Seven Gables* edited by
Seymour L. Gross

HAWTHORNE *The Scarlet Letter* edited by Sculley Bradley,
Richmond Croom Beatty, and E. Hudson Long

IBSEN *The Wild Duck* translated and edited by Dounia B. Christiani

JAMES *The Ambassadors* edited by S. P. Rosenbaum

JAMES *The Turn of the Screw* edited by Robert Kimbrough

MELVILLE *The Confidence-Man* edited by Hershel Parker

MELVILLE *Moby-Dick* edited by Harrison Hayford
and Hershel Parker

NEWMAN *Apologia Pro Vita Sua* edited by David J. De Laura

SHAKESPEARE *Hamlet* edited by Cyrus Hoy

SHAKESPEARE *Henry IV, Part I*, Revised edited by
James L. Sanderson

Bernard Shaw's Plays edited by Warren Sylvester Smith

Edmund Spenser's Poetry selected and edited by Hugh Maclean

SOPHOCLES *Oedipus Tyrannus* translated and edited by
Luci Berkowitz and Theodore F. Brunner

STENDHAL *Red and Black* translated and edited by Robert M. Adams

SWIFT *Gulliver's Travels*, Revised edited by Robert A. Greenberg

Tennyson's Poetry selected and edited by Robert W. Hill, Jr.

THOREAU *Walden and Civil Disobedience* edited by Owen Thomas

TOLSTOY *Anna Karenina* (the Maude translation)
edited by George Gibian

TOLSTOY *War and Peace* (the Maude translation)
edited by George Gibian

TURGENEV *Fathers and Sons* edited with a substantially new
translation by Ralph E. Matlaw

VOLTAIRE *Candide* translated and edited by Robert M. Adams

A Norton Critical Edition of Modern Drama
edited by Anthony Caputi

BERNARD SHAW'S PLAYS

MAJOR BARBARA
HEARTBREAK HOUSE
SAINT JOAN
TOO TRUE TO BE GOOD

With Backgrounds and Criticism

➤➤ ◄◄

Edited by

WARREN SYLVESTER SMITH

THE PENNSYLVANIA STATE UNIVERSITY

W · W · NORTON & COMPANY · INC · *New York*

Copyright © 1970 by W. W. Norton & Company, Inc.

FIRST EDITION

Bernard Shaw: *Major Barbara, Heartbreak House, Saint Joan,* and *Too True to Be Good* are reprinted with the kind permission of Dodd, Mead & Company, Inc., and The Public Trustee; and The Society of Authors for the Bernard Shaw Estate. *Heartbreak House,* copyright © 1919, 1930, 1948 by George Bernard Shaw; copyright © 1957 by The Public Trustee as Executor of the Estate of George Bernard Shaw. *Saint Joan,* copyright © 1924, 1930 by George Bernard Shaw; copyright © 1951, 1957 by The Public Trustee as Executor of the Estate of George Bernard Shaw. *Too True to Be Good,* copyright © 1933, 1934 by George Bernard Shaw, copyright © 1960, 1961 by The Public Trustee as Executor of the Estate of George Bernard Shaw.

John Gassner, "Bernard Shaw and the Making of the Modern Mind": From *College English,* XXIII (April, 1962), pp. 517–525. Reprinted by permission of the publisher.

From Martin Meisel, *Shaw and the Nineteenth-Century Theater* (Princeton: Princeton University Press, 1963), pp. 38–61. Copyright © 1963 by Princeton University Press. Reprinted by permission of Princeton University Press and Oxford University Press.

From Julian B. Kaye, *Bernard Shaw and the Nineteenth-Century Tradition* (Norman: University of Oklahoma Press, 1958), pp. 132–152. Copyright © 1958 by the University of Oklahoma Press. Reprinted by permission of the publisher.

From Warren S. Smith, *The London Heretics* (New York: Dodd, Mead & Company, Inc., 1968), pp. 270–279. Reprinted by permission of the publisher.

Stanley Weintraub, "The Avant-Garde Shaw": From *Shaw Seminar Papers of 1965* (Toronto: Copp Clark Ltd., 1966), pp. 33–52. Reprinted by permission of the author and the publisher.

From G. K. Chesterton, *George Bernard Shaw* (New York: Devin-Adair Co., 1909). Reprinted by permission of the publisher.

Barbara Bellow Watson, "Sainthood for Millionaires": From *Modern Drama,* XI (December, 1968), pp. 227–244. Reprinted by permission of the publisher.

Sidney P. Albert, " 'In More Ways Than One': *Major Barbara's* Debt to Gilbert Murray": From *Educational Theatre Journal,* XX (May, 1968), pp. 123–140. Reprinted by permission of the publisher. The Gilbert Murray letters to Shaw, including the dialogue passages, published by permission of the copyright owners, George Allen & Unwin Ltd. and of their present holder, the Academic Center Library, the University of Texas.

Michael J. Mendelsohn, "The Heartbreak Houses of Shaw and Chekhov": From *The Shaw Review,* VI (September, 1963), pp. 89–95. Reprinted by permission of the author and the publisher.

Harold Clurman, "Notes for a Production of *Heartbreak House*": From *The Tulane Drama Review,* V (Spring, 1961), pp. 58–67. Copyright © 1961, The Tulane Drama Review; copyright © 1967, The Drama Review. Reprinted by permission. All rights reserved.

From Louis Crompton, *Shaw the Dramatist* (Lincoln: The University of Nebraska Press, 1969), pp. 153–168; 251–252. Copyright © 1969 by the University of Nebraska Press. Reprinted by permission of the publisher and the author.

Arthur H. Nethercot, "Zeppelins Over *Heartbreak House*": From *The Shaw Review,* IX (May, 1966), pp. 46–57. Reprinted by permission of the author and the publisher.

From *The Trial of Jeanne d'Arc,* trans. W. P. Barrett (London: Routledge & Kegan Paul Ltd., 1931), pp. 48–56, 341–351. Reprinted by permission of the publisher.

Luigi Pirandello, "Bernard Shaw's *Saint Joan*": From *The New York Times,* January 13, 1924. Copyright © 1924 by The New York Times Company. Reprinted by permission.

Alice Griffin, "The New York Critics and *Saint Joan*": From *Shaw Bulletin* (January, 1955), pp. 10–15. Reprinted by permission of the author and the publisher.

Katherine Haynes Gatch, "Bernard Shaw's Last Plays": From *English Stage Comedy,* ed. W. K. Wimsatt, Jr. (New York: Columbia University Press English Institute Essays, 1954), pp. 126–142. Reprinted by permission of the author and the publisher.

Stanley Weintraub, "The Two Sides of 'Lawrence of Arabia': Aubrey and Meek": From *The Shaw Review,* VII (May, 1964), pp. 54–57. Reprinted by permission of the author and the publisher.

Frederick P. W. McDowell, "The 'Pentecostal Flame' and the 'Lower Centers' ": From *The Shaw Review,* II (September, 1959), pp. 27–38. Reprinted by permission of the author and the publisher.

SBN 393 04323 1 (Cloth Edition)   SBN 393 09942 3 (Paper Edition)
Library of Congress Catalog Card No. 79–116119

PRINTED IN THE UNITED STATES OF AMERICA

1   2   3   4   5   6   7   8   9   0

Contents

Preface

The choice of plays for this volume may not be quite the same as it would have been ten or fifteen years ago. The times have altered our values. And more than any other modern playwright, Shaw has furnished us a large and varied selection. The tighter structuring of the earlier plays delights us less than it once did. The lack of step-by-step character motivation in the later ones no longer seems consequential enough to disturb us. In our slower and more pedestrian manner we have recently been traveling much of the same territory through which Shaw himself moved during the first half of this century. Since the beginning of the fifties our theater has become more and more restive about the old forms; but Shaw was ill at ease with them before World War I, and (as both Katherine Gatch and Stanley Weintraub give evidence in this volume) was even then impatient to cast them off.

Not that he was ever a "formless" playwright. A sense of form was an inherent element of his nature and a necessary lodestone in the seemingly aimless household of his early youth. Aesthetic form became, and remained, essential to his sanity. (Even his childhood prayers, he tells us, were in three movements, like a sonata!) When he determined, at nearly the age of forty, to take the art of play-writing seriously, he seems to have had little trouble adapting the structures of the standard French melodramatists, and of Henrik Ibsen and Charles Dickens, to his own purposes. But there are many indications that they never really fit him perfectly; that they were ready-made garments, good enough if altered here and there to find him an audience, but too innocently tailored for his more lasting and outrageous purposes.

Since Shaw grew up in a household of music, the traditional musical forms were closest to him and came most naturally to him. The chapter from Martin Meisel's *Shaw and the Nineteenth-Century Theater* included here asks you to consider Shaw's plays in the framework of opera. Indeed, Meisel's excellent study demonstrates that the idea of musical motifs and musical structure pervades all of Shaw's work. He himself quite often cited Mozart as his teacher in composition. And as he grew beyond the inordinate need to be heard, the Shaw who emerged, supremely confident of his own craftsmanship, was a Mozartian Shaw.

Beyond such musical analogies it has been most difficult to

devise accurate labels to cover the bulk of the Shaw plays, by calling them, for example, "discussion plays" or "Shavian extravaganzas." Though the style is always individual enough to be recognizable, each play is a unique experience. Where did the idea ever
come from that all the Shaw plays were alike, or were at best
entertaining variations on a simple Shavian theme? In any case,
even this small sampling should be enough to counter such an
impression. A far more profitable question would ask why he
should feel the need to break from the mold that seemed good
enough for such notable contemporaries as Arthur Wing Pinero,
Henry Arthur Jones, and John Galsworthy—or good enough, for
that matter, for his own seven *Plays Pleasant and Unpleasant* and
Three Plays for Puritans.

The answer to this lies in the complexity of the writer himself, as
evidenced in small part by the variety of the supporting critical
articles included in this volume. Without formal education of any
kind, almost without intellectual guidance, Shaw put together, with
a strange mixture of innocence and sophistication, an intricate and
formidable assemblage of knowledge. The barriers that centuries of
scholarship have erected between disciplines did not exist for him.
There was no reason why biology should not be a part of political
science, for example, or economics unified with philosophy. By the
turn of the century it had become clear that any work of Shaw's
would embody, at the very least, something of his own brand of
socialism and something of his own brand of mystical-rational religion. Accordingly, these two areas also receive special treatment in
the supplementary readings.

To integrate all this with his well-known passion for world-
betterment required some uses of the theater not provided for in
the formulas of Eugene Scribe or William Archer. He never denied
the efficacy of the "well-made play." Indeed, he continued to use it
whenever it suited him. The first act of *Major Barbara* is a model
of Scribean exposition, and the second act is a neatly structured
short play in itself. *Saint Joan*, based largely on the records of the
trial, falls into a fairly conventional pattern of storytelling. The last
act of *Major Barbara*, however, returns to the overall pattern of *A
Doll's House* (exposition–development–discussion). And the Epilogue to *Saint Joan*, originally criticized as an unfortunate Shavian
afterthought, provides both an emotional resolution and a dialectical summary of great brilliance. On the other hand, for *Heartbreak
House*, written before *Saint Joan*, Shaw turned first to Chekhov,
then, as the director Harold Clurman observes in his notes, turned
away again, baffling scholars in search of a prototype. In *Too True
to Be Good* we have an early use of the "serious farce," a format
which the absurdists found so useful twenty or thirty years later.

Here the blend of fantasy and reality, of laughter and frightening surrealism, seems less puzzling than it did in 1932. By now we may likely find it closer to the reality of our existence than we would find *Candida* or *The Devil's Disciple*.

Each of the plays, then, has its own sense of structure. Each is held together by a centrality of theme or of issue, not always by a story line. (Note Harold Clurman's use of the term *spine* in his analysis of *Heartbreak House*.) Each is given variety and coherence by recurring patterns of tempo; by alternations of solo, duet, and chorus; by balancing action against dialectics; by the ingenious shifts from detached laughter to emotional involvement. Only the playgoer with doctrinaire preconceptions as to what form is will find these plays "formless."

Individual as the plays are, there *is* one similarity that is noteworthy. They all end looking toward the future. Is this testimony to what many regard as Shaw's optimism? Only in the sense that a future is at least assumed. It is by no means a belief that "everything will turn out for the best." In 1906 it is, at most, a challenge. "Six o'clock tomorrow morning, Euripides," the cannon-maker says to the professor of Greek. But there is no evidence that Cusins and Barbara will do better by the world than Undershaft and Bodger have done. After World War I the view darkens, and there are palpable suspicions that things are, indeed, turning out for the worst. In Hesione's and Ellie's hope for the air raids to return the next night at the final curtain of *Heartbreak House*, in Aubrey's compulsive preaching as he searches for a way of life at the end of *Too True to Be Good*, and most of all in Joan's final Biblical cry of "How long, O Lord, how long?" despair lies close to the surface. Still the challenge has not completely disappeared. Nor has Shaw's sense of direction, pointing the way in which we must go to rescue a tottering civilization.

WARREN SYLVESTER SMITH

The Texts of
The Plays

A Note on the Texts

The texts of the plays are those of the Standard Edition, Constable & Co., London; Dodd, Mead, New York. Shaw's orthography and punctuation have been carefully preserved, as he considered them an integral part of his style. He used the apostrophe in contractions only where he felt its absence would cause confusion; he held on to a few older and variant spellings (Shakespear, shew); and he used spaced letters rather than italics to indicate emphasis in the actors' lines.

N.B. The Euripidean verses in the second act of Major Barbara are not by me, nor even directly by Euripides. They are by Professor Gilbert Murray, whose English version of the Bacchæ came into our dramatic literature with all the impulsive power of an original work shortly before Major Barbara was begun. The play, indeed, stands indebted to him in more ways than one.

G. B. S.

Major Barbara

Act I

*It is after dinner in January 1906, in the library in Lady Brito-
mart Undershaft's house in Wilton Crescent. A large and comfortable settee is in the middle of the room, upholstered in dark
leather. A person sitting on it (it is vacant at present) would have,
on his right, Lady Britomart's writing table, with the lady herself
busy at it; a smaller writing table behind him on his left; the door
behind him on Lady Britomart's side; and a window with a window
seat directly on his left. Near the window is an armchair.*

*Lady Britomart is a woman of fifty or thereabouts, well dressed
and yet careless of her dress, well bred and quite reckless of her
breeding, well mannered and yet appallingly outspoken and
indifferent to the opinion of her interlocutors, amiable and yet per-
emptory, arbitrary, and high-tempered to the last bearable degree,
and withal a very typical managing matron of the upper class,
treated as a naughty child until she grew into a scolding mother,
and finally settling down with plenty of practical ability and
worldly experience, limited in the oddest way with domestic and
class limitations, conceiving the universe exactly as if it were a large
house in Wilton Crescent, though handling her corner of it very effectively on that assumption, and being quite enlightened and liberal as to the books in the library, the pictures on the walls, the
music in the portfolios, and the articles in the papers.*

*Her son, Stephen, comes in. He is a gravely correct young man
under 25, taking himself very seriously, but still in some awe of his
mother, from childish habit and bachelor shyness rather than from
any weakness of character.*

STEPHEN. Whats the matter?

LADY BRITOMART. Presently, Stephen.

> *Stephen submissively walks to the settee and sits down. He
> takes up a Liberal weekly called The Speaker.*

LADY BRITOMART. Dont begin to read, Stephen. I shall require all
your attention.

STEPHEN. It was only while I was waiting—

LADY BRITOMART. Dont make excuses, Stephen. [*He puts down
The Speaker*]. Now! [*She finishes her writing; rises; and comes
to the settee*]. I have not kept you waiting very long, I think.

STEPHEN. Not at all, mother.

LADY BRITOMART. Bring me my cushion. [*He takes the cushion
from the chair at the desk and arranges it for her as she sits
down on the settee*]. Sit down. [*He sits down and fingers his*

tie nervously]. Dont fiddle with your tie, Stephen: there is nothing the matter with it.

STEPHEN. I beg your pardon. [*He fiddles with his watch chain instead*].

LADY BRITOMART. Now are you attending to me, Stephen?

STEPHEN. Of course, mother.

LADY BRITOMART. No: it's not of course. I want something much more than your everyday matter-of-course attention. I am going to speak to you very seriously, Stephen. I wish you would let that chain alone.

STEPHEN [*hastily relinquishing the chain*] Have I done anything to annoy you, mother? If so, it was quite unintentional.

LADY BRITOMART [*astonished*] Nonsense! [*With some remorse*] My poor boy, did you think I was angry with you?

STEPHEN. What is it, then, mother? You are making me very uneasy.

LADY BRITOMART [*squaring herself at him rather aggressively*] Stephen: may I ask how soon you intend to realize that you are a grown-up man, and that I am only a woman?

STEPHEN [*amazed*] Only a—

LADY BRITOMART. Dont repeat my words, please: it is a most aggravating habit. You must learn to face life seriously, Stephen. I really cannot bear the whole burden of our family affairs any longer. You must advise me; you must assume the responsibility.

STEPHEN. I!

LADY BRITOMART. Yes, you, of course. You were 24 last June. Youve been at Harrow and Cambridge. Youve been to India and Japan. You must know a lot of things, now; unless you have wasted your time most scandalously. Well, advise me.

STEPHEN [*much perplexed*] You know I have never interfered in the household—

LADY BRITOMART. No: I should think not. I dont want you to order the dinner.

STEPHEN. I mean in our family affairs.

LADY BRITOMART. Well, you must interfere now; for they are getting quite beyond me.

STEPHEN [*troubled*] I have thought sometimes that perhaps I ought; but really, mother, I know so little about them; and what I do know is so painful! it is so impossible to mention some things to you— [*he stops, ashamed*].

LADY BRITOMART. I suppose you mean your father.

STEPHEN [*almost inaudibly*] Yes.

LADY BRITOMART. My dear: we cant go on all our lives not mentioning him. Of course you were quite right not to open the subject until I asked you to; but you are old enough now to be taken into my confidence, and to help me to deal with him about the girls.

STEPHEN. But the girls are all right. They are engaged.

LADY BRITOMART [*complacently*] Yes: I have made a very good match for Sarah. Charles Lomax will be a millionaire at 35. But that is ten years ahead; and in the meantime his trustees cannot under the terms of his father's will allow him more than £800 a year.

STEPHEN. But the will says also that if he increases his income by his own exertions, they may double the increase.

LADY BRITOMART. Charles Lomax's exertions are much more likely to decrease his income than to increase it. Sarah will have to find at least another £800 a year for the next ten years; and even then they will be as poor as church mice. And what about Barbara? I thought Barbara was going to make the most brilliant career of all of you. And what does she do? Joins the Salvation Army; discharges her maid: lives on a pound a week; and walks in one evening with a professor of Greek whom she has picked up in the street, and who pretends to be a Salvationist, and actually plays the big drum for her in public because he has fallen head over ears in love with her.

STEPHEN. I was certainly rather taken aback when I heard they were engaged. Cusins is a very nice fellow, certainly: nobody would ever guess that he was born in Australia; but—

LADY BRITOMART. Oh, Adolphus Cusins will make a very good husband. After all, nobody can say a word against Greek: it stamps a man at once as an educated gentleman. And my family, thank Heaven, is not a pig-headed Tory one. We are Whigs, and believe in liberty. Let snobbish people say what they please: Barbara shall marry, not the man they like, but the man *I* like.

STEPHEN. Of course I was thinking only of his income. However, he is not likely to be extravagant.

LADY BRITOMART. Dont be too sure of that, Stephen. I know your quiet, simple, refined, poetic people like Adolphus: quite content with the best of everything! They cost more than your extravagant people, who are always as mean as they are second rate. No: Barbara will need at least £2000 a year. You see it means two additional households. Besides, my dear, you must marry soon. I dont approve of the present fashion of philandering bachelors and late marriages; and I am trying to arrange something for you.

STEPHEN. It's very good of you, mother; but perhaps I had better arrange that for myself.

LADY BRITOMART. Nonsense! you are much too young to begin matchmaking: you would be taken in by some pretty little nobody. Of course I dont mean that you are not to be consulted: you know that as well as I do. [*Stephen closes his lips and is silent*]. Now dont sulk, Stephen.

STEPHEN. I am not sulking, mother. What has all this got to do with—with—with my father?

LADY BRITOMART. My dear Stephen: where is the money to come from? It is easy enough for you and the other children to live on my income as long as we are in the same house; but I cant keep four families in four separate houses. You know how poor my father is: he has barely seven thousand a year now; and really, if he were not the Earl of Stevenage, he would have to give up society. He can do nothing for us. He says, naturally enough, that it is absurd that he should be asked to provide for the children of a man who is rolling in money. You see, Stephen, your father must be fabulously wealthy, because there is always a war going on somewhere.

STEPHEN. You need not remind me of that, mother. I have hardly ever opened a newspaper in my life without seeing our name in it. The Undershaft torpedo! The Undershaft quick firers! The Undershaft ten inch! the Undershaft disappearing rampart gun! the Undershaft submarine! and now the Undershaft aerial battleship! At Harrow they called me the Woolwich Infant. At Cambridge it was the same. A little brute at King's who was always trying to get up revivals, spoilt my Bible—your first birthday present to me—by writing under my name, "Son and heir to Undershaft and Lazarus, Death and Destruction Dealers: address, Christendom and Judea." But that was not so bad as the way I was kowtowed to everywhere because my father was making millions by selling cannons.

LADY BRITOMART. It is not only the cannons, but the war loans that Lazarus arranges under cover of giving credit for the cannons. You know, Stephen, it's perfectly scandalous. Those two men, Andrew Undershaft and Lazarus, positively have Europe under their thumbs. That is why your father is able to behave as he does. He is above the law. Do you think Bismarck or Gladstone or Disraeli could have openly defied every social and moral obligation all their lives as your father has? They simply wouldnt have dared. I asked Gladstone to take it up. I asked The Times to take it up. I asked the Lord Chamberlain to take it up. But it was just like asking them to declare war on the Sultan. They wouldnt. They said they couldnt touch him. I believe they were afraid.

STEPHEN. What could they do? He does not actually break the law.

LADY BRITOMART. Not break the law! He is always breaking the law. He broke the law when he was born: his parents were not married.

STEPHEN. Mother! Is that true?

LADY BRITOMART. Of course it's true: that was why we separated.

STEPHEN. He married without letting you know this!

LADY BRITOMART [*rather taken aback by this inference*] Oh no. To do Andrew justice, that was not the sort of thing he did. Besides, you know the Undershaft motto: Unashamed. Everybody knew.

STEPHEN. But you said that was why you separated.

LADY BRITOMART. Yes, because he was not content with being a foundling himself: he wanted to disinherit you for another foundling. That was what I couldnt stand.

STEPHEN [*ashamed*] Do you mean for—for—for—

LADY BRITOMART. Dont stammer, Stephen. Speak distinctly.

STEPHEN. But this is so frightful to me, mother. To have to speak to you about such things!

LADY BRITOMART. It's not pleasant for me, either, especially if you are still so childish that you must make it worse by a display of embarrassment. It is only in the middle classes, Stephen, that people get into a state of dumb helpless horror when they find that there are wicked people in the world. In our class, we have to decide what is to be done with wicked people; and nothing should disturb our self-possession. Now ask your question properly.

STEPHEN. Mother: have you no consideration for me? For Heaven's sake either treat me as a child, as you always do, and tell me nothing at all; or tell me everything and let me take it as best I can.

LADY BRITOMART. Treat you as a child! What do you mean? It is most unkind and ungrateful of you to say such a thing. You know I have never treated any of you as children. I have always made you my companions and friends, and allowed you perfect freedom to do and say whatever you liked, so long as you liked what I could approve of.

STEPHEN [*desperately*] I daresay we have been the very imperfect children of a very perfect mother; but I do beg you to let me alone for once, and tell me about this horrible business of my father wanting to set me aside for another son.

LADY BRITOMART [*amazed*] Another son! I never said anything of the kind. I never dreamt of such a thing. This is what comes of interrupting me.

STEPHEN. But you said—

LADY BRITOMART [*cutting him short*] Now be a good boy, Stephen, and listen to me patiently. The Undershafts are descended from a foundling in the parish of St Andrew Undershaft in the city. That was long ago, in the reign of James the First. Well, this foundling was adopted by an armorer and gun-maker. In the course of time the foundling succeeded to the business; and from some notion of gratitude, or some vow or something, he adopted another foundling, and left the business to him. And that foundling did the same. Ever since that, the cannon business has always been left to an adopted foundling named Andrew Undershaft.

STEPHEN. But did they never marry? Were there no legitimate sons?

LADY BRITOMART. Oh yes: they married just as your father did; and they were rich enough to buy land for their own children and leave them well provided for. But they always adopted and trained some foundling to succeed them in the business; and of course they always quarrelled with their wives furiously over it. Your father was adopted in that way; and he pretends to consider himself bound to keep up the tradition and adopt somebody to leave the business to. Of course I was not going to stand that. There may have been some reason for it when the Under-

shafts could only marry women in their own class, whose sons
were not fit to govern great estates. But there could be no excuse
for passing over my son.

STEPHEN [*dubiously*] I am afraid I should make a poor hand of
managing a cannon foundry.

LADY BRITOMART. Nonsense! you could easily get a manager and
pay him a salary.

STEPHEN. My father evidently had no great opinion of my capacity.

LADY BRITOMART. Stuff, child! you were only a baby: it had nothing to do with your capacity. Andrew did it on principle, just as
he did every perverse and wicked thing on principle. When my
father remonstrated, Andrew actually told him to his face that
history tells us of only two successful institutions: one the Undershaft firm, and the other the Roman Empire under the Anto-
nines. That was because the Antonine emperors all adopted their
successors. Such rubbish! The Stevenages are as good as the An-
tonines, I hope; and you are a Stevenage. But that was Andrew
all over. There you have the man! Always clever and unanswera-
ble when he was defending nonsense and wickedness: always
awkward and sullen when he had to behave sensibly and decently!

STEPHEN. Then it was on my account that your home life was broken up, mother. I am sorry.

LADY BRITOMART. Well, dear, there were other differences. I really
cannot bear an immoral man. I am not a Pharisee, I hope; and I
should not have minded his merely doing wrong things: we are
none of us perfect. But your father didnt exactly do wrong
things: he said them and thought them: that was what was so
dreadful. He really had a sort of religion of wrongness. Just as
one doesnt mind men practising immorality so long as they own
that they are in the wrong by preaching morality; so I couldnt
forgive Andrew for preaching immorality while he practised morality. You would all have grown up without principles, without
any knowledge of right and wrong, if he had been in the house.
You know, my dear, your father was a very attractive man in
some ways. Children did not dislike him; and he took advantage
of it to put the wickedest ideas into their heads, and make them
quite unmanageable. I did not dislike him myself: very far from
it; but nothing can bridge over moral disagreement.

STEPHEN. All this simply bewilders me, mother. People may differ
about matters of opinion, or even about religion; but how can
they differ about right and wrong? Right is right; and wrong is
wrong; and if a man cannot distinguish them properly, he is either a fool or a rascal: thats all.

LADY BRITOMART [*touched*] Thats my own boy [*she pats his
cheek*]! Your father never could answer that: he used to laugh
and get out of it under cover of some affectionate nonsense. And
now that you understand the situation, what do you advise me to
do?

STEPHEN. Well, what can you do?

LADY BRITOMART. I must get the money somehow.

STEPHEN. We cannot take money from him. I had rather go and live in some cheap place like Bedford Square or even Hampstead[1] than take a farthing of his money.

LADY BRITOMART. But after a!l, Stephen, our present income comes from Andrew.

STEPHEN [*shocked*] I never knew that.

LADY BRITOMART. Well, you surely didnt suppose your grandfather had anything to give me. The Stevenages could not do everything for you. We gave you social position. Andrew had to contribute something. He had a very good bargain, I think.

STEPHEN [*bitterly*] We are utterly dependent on him and his cannons, then?

LADY BRITOMART. Certainly not: the money is settled. But he provided it. So you see it is not a question of taking money from him or not: it is simply a question of how much. I dont want any more for myself.

STEPHEN. Nor do I.

LADY BRITOMART. But Sarah does; and Barbara does. That is, Charles Lomax and Adolphus Cusins will cost them more. So I must put my pride in my pocket and ask for it, I suppose. That is your advice, Stephen, is it not?

STEPHEN. No.

LADY BRITOMART [*sharply*] Stephen!

STEPHEN. Of course if you are determined—

LADY BRITOMART. I am not determined: I ask your advice; and I am waiting for it. I will not have all the responsibility thrown on my shoulders.

STEPHEN [*obstinately*] I would die sooner than ask him for another penny.

LADY BRITOMART [*resignedly*] You mean that I must ask him. Very well, Stephen: it shall be as you wish. You will be glad to know that your grandfather concurs. But he thinks I ought to ask Andrew to come here and see the girls. After all, he must have some natural affection for them.

STEPHEN. Ask him here!!!

LADY BRITOMART. Do not repeat my words, Stephen. Where else can I ask him?

STEPHEN. I never expected you to ask him at all.

LADY BRITOMART. Now dont tease, Stephen. Come! you see that it is necessary that he should pay us a visit, dont you?

STEPHEN [*reluctantly*] I suppose so, if the girls cannot do without his money.

LADY BRITOMART. Thank you, Stephen: I knew you would give me the right advice when it was properly explained to you. I have asked your father to come this evening. [*Stephen bounds from his seat*] Dont jump, Stephen: it fidgets me.

---

1. By no means undesirable neighborhoods!

STEPHEN [*in utter consternation*] Do you mean to say that my father is coming here tonight—that he may be here at any moment?

LADY BRITOMART [*looking at her watch*] I said nine. [*He gasps. She rises*]. Ring the bell, please. [*Stephen goes to the smaller writing table; presses a button on it; and sits at it with his elbows on the table and his head in his hands, outwitted and overwhelmed*]. It is ten minutes to nine yet; and I have to prepare the girls. I asked Charles Lomax and Adolphus to dinner on purpose that they might be here. Andrew had better see them in case he should cherish any delusions as to their being capable of supporting their wives. [*The butler enters: Lady Britomart goes behind the settee to speak to him*]. Morrison: go up to the drawing room and tell everybody to come down here at once. [*Morrison withdraws. Lady Britomart turns to Stephen*]. Now remember, Stephen: I shall need all your countenance and authority. [*He rises and tries to recover some vestige of these attributes*]. Give me a chair, dear. [*He pushes a chair forward from the wall to where she stands, near the smaller writing table. She sits down; and he goes to the armchair, into which he throws himself*]. I dont know how Barbara will take it. Ever since they made her a major in the Salvation Army she has developed a propensity to have her own way and order people about which quite cows me sometimes. It's not ladylike: I'm sure I dont know where she picked it up. Anyhow, Barbara shant bully me; but still it's just as well that your father should be here before she has time to refuse to meet him or make a fuss. Dont look nervous, Stephen: it will only encourage Barbara to make difficulties. I am nervous enough, goodness knows; but I dont shew it.

Sarah and Barbara come in with their respective young men, Charles Lomax and Adolphus Cusins. Sarah is slender, bored, and mundane. Barbara is robuster, jollier, much more energetic. Sarah is fashionably dressed: Barbara is in Salvation Army uniform. Lomax, a young man about town, is like many other young men about town. He is afflicted with a frivolous sense of humor which plunges him at the most inopportune moments into paroxysms of imperfectly suppressed laughter. Cusins is a spectacled student, slight, thin haired, and sweet voiced, with a more complex form of Lomax's complaint. His sense of humor is intellectual and subtle, and is complicated by an appalling temper. The lifelong struggle of a benevolent temperament and a high conscience against impulses of inhuman ridicule and fierce impatience has set up a chronic strain which has visibly wrecked his constitution. He is a most implacable, determined, tenacious, intolerant person who by mere force of character presents himself as—and indeed actually is—considerate, gentle, explanatory, even mild and apologetic, capable possibly of murder, but not of cruelty or coarseness. By the operation of some instinct which is not merciful enough to blind him with the illusions of love, he is obstinately bent on marrying Bar-

bara. Lomax likes Sarah and thinks it will be rather a lark to marry her. Consequently he has not attempted to resist Lady Britomart's arrangements to that end.

All four look as if they had been having a good deal of fun in the drawing room. The girls enter first, leaving the swains outside. Sarah comes to the settee. Barbara comes in after her and stops at the door.

BARBARA. Are Cholly and Dolly to come in?

LADY BRITOMART [*forcibly*] Barbara: I will not have Charles called Cholly: the vulgarity of it positively makes me ill.

BARBARA. It's all right, mother: Cholly is quite correct nowadays. Are they to come in?

LADY BRITOMART. Yes, if they will behave themselves.

BARBARA [*through the door*] Come in, Dolly; and behave yourself.
Barbara comes to her mother's writing table. Cusins enters smiling, and wanders towards Lady Britomart.

SARAH [*calling*] Come in, Cholly. [*Lomax enters, controlling his features very imperfectly, and places himself vaguely between Sarah and Barbara*].

LADY BRITOMART [*peremptorily*] Sit down, all of you. [*They sit. Cusins crosses to the window and seats himself there. Lomax takes a chair. Barbara sits at the writing table and Sarah on the settee*]. I dont in the least know what you are laughing at, Adolphus. I am surprised at you, though I expected nothing better from Charles Lomax.

CUSINS [*in a remarkably gentle voice*] Barbara has been trying to teach me the West Ham Salvation March.

LADY BRITOMART. I see nothing to laugh at in that; nor should you if you are really converted.

CUSINS [*sweetly*] You were not present. It was really funny, I believe.

LOMAX. Ripping.

LADY BRITOMART. Be quiet, Charles. Now listen to me, children. Your father is coming here this evening.
General stupefaction. Lomax, Sarah, and Barbara rise: Sarah scared, and Barbara amused and expectant.

LOMAX [*remonstrating*] Oh I say!

LADY BRITOMART. You are not called on to say anything, Charles.

SARAH. Are you serious, mother?

LADY BRITOMART. Of course I am serious. It is on your account, Sarah, and also on Charles's. [*Silence. Sarah sits, with a shrug. Charles looks painfully unworthy*]. I hope you are not going to object, Barbara.

BARBARA. I! why should I? My father has a soul to be saved like anybody else. He's quite welcome as far as I am concerned. [*She sits on the table, and softly whistles 'Onward, Christian Soldiers'*].

LOMAX [*still remonstrant*] But really, dont you know! Oh I say!

LADY BRITOMART. [*frigidly*] What do you wish to convey, Charles?

LOMAX. Well, you must admit that this is a bit thick.

LADY BRITOMART [*turning with ominous suavity to Cusins*] Adolphus: you are a professor of Greek. Can you translate Charles Lomax's remarks into reputable English for us?

CUSINS [*cautiously*] If I may say so, Lady Brit, I think Charles has rather happily expressed what we all feel. Homer, speaking of Autolycus, uses the same phrase. πυκινὸν δόμον ἐλθεῖν² means a bit thick.

LOMAX [*handsomely*] Not that I mind, you know, if Sarah dont. [*He sits*].

LADY BRITOMART [*crushingly*] Thank you. Have I your permission, Adolphus, to invite my own husband to my own house?

CUSINS [*gallantly*] You have my unhesitating support in everything you do.

LADY BRITOMART. Tush! Sarah: have you nothing to say?

SARAH. Do you mean that he is coming regularly to live here?

LADY BRITOMART. Certainly not. The spare room is ready for him if he likes to stay for a day or two and see a little more of you; but there are limits.

SARAH. Well, he cant eat us, I suppose. *I* dont mind.

LOMAX [*chuckling*] I wonder how the old man will take it.

LADY BRITOMART. Much as the old woman will, no doubt, Charles.

LOMAX [*abashed*] I didnt mean—at least—

LADY RBITOMART. You didnt think, Charles. You never do; and the result is, you never mean anything. And now please attend to me, children. Your father will be quite a stranger to us.

LOMAX. I suppose he hasnt seen Sarah since she was a little kid.

LADY BRITOMART. Not since she was a little kid, Charles, as you express it with that elegance of diction and refinement of thought that seem never to desert you. Accordingly—er— [*impatiently*] Now I have forgotten what I was going to say. That comes of your provoking me to be sarcastic, Charles. Adolphus: will you kindly tell me where I was.

CUSINS [*sweetly*] You were saying that as Mr Undershaft has not seen his children since they were babies, he will form his opinion of the way you have brought them up from their behavior tonight, and that therefore you wish us all to be particularly careful to conduct ourselves well, especially Charles.

LADY BRITOMART [*with emphatic approval*] Precisely.

LOMAX. Look here, Dolly: Lady Brit didnt say that.

LADY BRITOMART [*vehemently*] I did, Charles. Adolphus's recollection is perfectly correct. It is most important that you should be good; and I do beg you for once not to pair off into opposite corners and giggle and whisper while I am speaking to your father.

BARBARA. All right, mother. We'll do you credit. [*She comes off the table, and sits in her chair with ladylike elegance*].

LADY BRITOMART. Remember, Charles, that Sarah will want to feel proud of you instead of ashamed of you.

2. "Pukinon domon elthein." See the article by Sidney P. Albert in this book.

LOMAX.   Oh I say! theres nothing to be exactly proud of, dont you know.

LADY BRITOMART.   Well, try and look as if there was.

> *Morrison, pale and dismayed, breaks into the room in unconcealed disorder.*

MORRISON.   Might I speak a word to you, my lady?

LADY BRITOMART.   Nonsense! Shew him up.

MORRISON.   Yes, my lady. [*He goes*].

LOMAX.   Does Morrison know who it is?

LADY BRITOMART.   Of course. Morrison has always been with us.

LOMAX.   It must be a regular corker for him, dont you know.

LADY BRITOMART.   Is this a moment to get on my nerves, Charles, with your outrageous expressions?

LOMAX.   But this is something out of the ordinary, really—

MORRISON [*at the door*] The—er—Mr Undershaft. [*He retreats in confusion*].

> *Andrew Undershaft comes in. All rise. Lady Britomart meets him in the middle of the room behind the settee.*
>
> *Andrew is, on the surface, a stoutish, easygoing elderly man, with kindly patient manners, and an engaging simplicity of character. But he has a watchful, deliberate, waiting, listening face, and formidable reserves of power, both bodily and mental, in his capacious chest and long head. His gentleness is partly that of a strong man who has learnt by experience that his natural grip hurts ordinary people unless he handles them very carefully, and partly the mellowness of age and success. He is also a little shy in his present very delicate situation.*

LADY BRITOMART.   Good evening, Andrew.

UNDERSHAFT.   How d'ye do, my dear.

LADY BRITOMART.   You look a good deal older.

UNDERSHAFT [*apologetically*]   I a m somewhat older. [*Taking her hand with a touch of courtship*] Time has stood still with you.

LADY BRITOMART [*throwing away his hand*] Rubbish! This is your family.

UNDERSHAFT [*surprised*] Is it so large? I am sorry to say my memory is failing very badly in some things. [*He offers his hand with paternal kindness to Lomax*].

LOMAX [*jerkily shaking his hand*] Ahdedoo.

UNDERSHAFT.   I can see you are my eldest. I am very glad to meet you again, my boy.

LOMAX [*remonstrating*] No, but look here dont you know— [*Overcome*] Oh I say!

LADY BRITOMART [*recovering from momentary speechlessness*] Andrew: do you mean to say that you dont remember how many children you have?

UNDERSHAFT.   Well, I am afraid I—. They have grown so much—er. Am I making any ridiculous mistake? I may as well confess: I recollect only one son. But so many things have happened since, of course—er—

LADY BRITOMART [*decisively*] Andrew: you are talking nonsense. Of course you have only one son.

UNDERSHAFT. Perhaps you will be good enough to introduce me, my dear.

LADY BRITOMART. That is Charles Lomax, who is engaged to Sarah.

UNDERSHAFT. My dear sir, I beg your pardon.

LOMAX. Notatall. Delighted, I assure you.

LADY BRITOMART. This is Stephen.

UNDERSHAFT [*bowing*] Happy to make your acquaintance, Mr Stephen. Then [*going to Cusins*] you must be my son. [*Taking Cusins' hands in his*] How are you, my young friend? [*To Lady Britomart*] He is very like you, my love.

CUSINS. You flatter me, Mr Undershaft. My name is Cusins: engaged to Barbara. [*Very explicitly*] That is Major Barbara Undershaft, of the Salvation Army. That is Sarah, your second daughter. This is Stephen Undershaft, your son.

UNDERSHAFT. My dear Stephen, I beg your pardon.

STEPHEN. Not at all.

UNDERSHAFT. Mr Cusins: I am much indebted to you for explaining so precisely. [*Turning to Sarah*] Barbara, my dear—

SARAH [*prompting him*] Sarah.

UNDERSHAFT. Sarah, of course. [*They shake hands. He goes over to Barbara*] Barbara—I am right this time, I hope?

BARBARA. Quite right. [*They shake hands*].

LADY BRITOMART [*resuming command*] Sit down, all of you. Sit down, Andrew. [*She comes forward and sits on the settee. Cusins also brings his chair forward on her left. Barbara and Stephen resume their seats. Lomax gives his chair to Sarah and goes for another*].

UNDERSHAFT. Thank you, my love.

LOMAX [*conversationally, as he brings a chair forward between the writing table and the settee, and offers it to Undershaft*] Takes you some time to find out exactly where you are, dont it?

UNDERSHAFT [*accepting the chair, but remaining standing*] That is not what embarrasses me, Mr Lomax. My difficulty is that if I play the part of a father, I shall produce the effect of an intrusive stranger; and if I play the part of a discreet stranger, I may appear a callous father.

LADY BRITOMART. There is no need for you to play any part at all, Andrew. You had much better be sincere and natural.

UNDERSHAFT [*submissively*] Yes, my dear: I daresay that will be best. [*He sits down comfortably*]. Well, here I am. Now what can I do for you all?

LADY BRITOMART. You need not do anything, Andrew. You are one of the family. You can sit with us and enjoy yourself.

> *A painfully conscious pause. Barbara makes a face at Lomax, whose too long suppressed mirth immediately explodes in agonized neighings.*

LADY BRITOMART [*outraged*] Charles Lomax: if you can behave yourself, behave yourself. If not, leave the room.

LOMAX. I'm awfully sorry, Lady Brit; but really you know, upon my soul! [*He sits on the settee between Lady Britomart and Undershaft, quite overcome*].

BARBARA. Why dont you laugh if you want to, Cholly? It's good for your inside.

LADY BRITOMART. Barbara: you have had the education of a lady. Please let your father see that; and dont talk like a street girl.

UNDERSHAFT. Never mind me, my dear. As you know, I am not a gentleman; and I was never educated.

LOMAX [*encouragingly*] Nobody'd know it, I assure you. You look all right, you know.

CUSINS. Let me advise you to study Greek, Mr Undershaft. Greek scholars are privileged men. Few of them know Greek; and none of them know anything else; but their position is unchallengeable. Other languages are the qualifications of waiters and commercial travellers: Greek is to a man of position what the hallmark is to silver.

BARBARA. Dolly: dont be insincere. Cholly: fetch your concertina and play something for us.

LOMAX [*jumps up eagerly, but checks himself to remark doubtfully to Undershaft*] Perhaps that sort of thing isnt in your line, eh?

UNDERSHAFT. I am particularly fond of music.

LOMAX [*delighted*] Are you? Then I'll get it. [*He goes upstairs for the instrument*].

UNDERSHAFT. Do you play, Barbara?

BARBARA. Only the tambourine. But Cholly's teaching me the concertina.

UNDERSHAFT. Is Cholly also a member of the Salvation Army?

BARBARA. No: he says it's bad form to be a dissenter. But I dont despair of Cholly. I made him come yesterday to a meeting at the dock gates, and take the collection in his hat.

UNDERSHAFT [*looks whimsically at his wife*]!!

LADY BRITOMART. It is not my doing, Andrew. Barbara is old enough to take her own way. She has no father to advise her.

BARBARA. Oh yes she has. There are no orphans in the Salvation Army.

UNDERSHAFT. Your father there has a great many children and plenty of experience, eh?

BARBARA [*looking at him with quick interest and nodding*] Just so. How did you come to understand that? [*Lomax is heard at the door trying the concertina*].

LADY BRITOMART. Come in, Charles. Play us something at once.

LOMAX. Righto! [*He sits down in his former place, and preludes*].

UNDERSHAFT. One moment, Mr Lomax. I am rather interested in the Salvation Army. Its motto might be my own: Blood and Fire.

LOMAX [*shocked*] But not your sort of blood and fire, you know.

UNDERSHAFT. My sort of blood cleanses: my sort of fire purifies.

BARBARA. So do ours. Come down tomorrow to my shelter—the West Ham shelter—and see what we're doing. We're going to march to a great meeting in the Assembly Hall at Mile End. Come and see the shelter and then march with us: it will do you a lot of good. Can you play anything?

UNDERSHAFT. In my youth I earned pennies, and even shillings occasionally, in the streets and in public house parlors by my natural talent for stepdancing. Later on, I became a member of the Undershaft orchestral society, and performed passably on the tenor trombone.

LOMAX [*scandalized—putting down the concertina*] Oh I say!

BARBARA. Many a sinner has played himself into heaven on the trombone, thanks to the Army.

LOMAX [*to Barbara, still rather shocked*] Yes; but what about the cannon business, dont you know? [*To Undershaft*] Getting into heaven is not exactly in your line, is it?

LADY BRITOMART. Charles!!!

LOMAX. Well; but it stands to reason, dont it? The cannon business may be necessary and all that: we cant get on without cannons; but it isnt right, you know. On the other hand, there may be a certain amount of tosh about the Salvation Army—I belong to the Established Church myself—but still you cant deny that it's religion; and you cant go against religion, can you? At least unless youre downright immoral, dont you know.

UNDERSHAFT. You hardly appreciate my position, Mr Lomax—

LOMAX [*hastily*] I'm not saying anything against you personally—

UNDERSHAFT. Quite so, quite so. But consider for a moment. Here I am, a profiteer in mutilation and murder. I find myself in a specially amiable humor just now because, this morning, down at the foundry, we blew twenty-seven dummy soldiers into fragments with a gun which formerly destroyed only thirteen.

LOMAX [*leniently*] Well, the more destructive war becomes, the sooner it will be abolished, eh?

UNDERSHAFT. Not at all. The more destructive war becomes the more fascinating we find it. No, Mr Lomax: I am obliged to you for making the usual excuse for my trade; but I am not ashamed of it. I am not one of those men who keep their morals and their business in water-tight compartments. All the spare money my trade rivals spend on hospitals, cathedrals, and other receptacles for conscience money, I devote to experiments and researches in improved methods of destroying life and property. I have always done so; and I always shall. Therefore your Christmas card moralities of peace on earth and goodwill among men are of no use to me. Your Christianity, which enjoins you to resist not evil, and to turn the other cheek, would make me a bankrupt. My morality—my religion—must have a place for cannons and torpedoes in it.

STEPHEN [*coldly—almost sullenly*] You speak as if there were half a dozen moralities and religions to choose from, instead of one true morality and one true religion.

UNDERSHAFT. For me there is only one true morality; but it might not fit you, as you do not manufacture aerial battleships. There is only one true morality for every man; but every man has not the same true morality.

LOMAX [*overtaxed*] Would you mind saying that again? I didnt quite follow it.

CUSINS. It's quite simple. As Euripides says, one man's meat is another man's poison morally as well as physically.

UNDERSHAFT. Precisely.

LOMAX. Oh, that! Yes, yes, yes. True. True.

STEPHEN. In other words, some men are honest and some are scoundrels.

BARBARA. Bosh! There are no scoundrels.

UNDERSHAFT. Indeed? Are there any good men?

BARBARA. No. Not one. There are neither good men nor scoundrels: there are just children of one Father; and the sooner they stop calling one another names the better. You neednt talk to me: I know them. Ive had scores of them through my hands: scoundrels, criminals, infidels, philanthropists, missionaries, county councillors, all sorts. Theyre all just the same sort of sinner; and theres the same salvation ready for them all.

UNDERSHAFT. May I ask have you ever saved a maker of cannons?

BARBARA. No. Will you let me try?

UNDERSHAFT. Well, I will make a bargain with you. If I go to see you tomorrow in your Salvation Shelter, will you come the day after to see me in my cannon works?

BARBARA. Take care. It may end in your giving up the cannons for the sake of the Salvation Army.

UNDERSHAFT. Are you sure it will not end in your giving up the Salvation Army for the sake of the cannons?

BARBARA. I will take my chance of that.

UNDERSHAFT. And I will take my chance of the other. [*They shake hands on it*]. Where is your shelter?

BARBARA. In West Ham. At the sign of the cross. Ask anybody in Canning Town. Where are your works?

UNDERSHAFT. In Perivale St Andrews. At the sign of the sword. Ask anybody in Europe.

LOMAX. Hadnt I better play something?

BARBARA. Yes. Give us Onward, Christian Soldiers.

LOMAX. Well, thats rather a strong order to begin with, dont you know. Suppose I sing Thourt passing hence, my brother. It's much the same tune.

BARBARA. It's too melancholy. You get saved, Cholly; and youll pass hence, my brother, without making such a fuss about it.

LADY BRITOMART. Really, Barbara, you go on as if religion were a pleasant subject. Do have some sense of propriety.

UNDERSHAFT. I do not find it an unpleasant subject, my dear. It is the only one that capable people really care for.

LADY BRITOMART [*looking at her watch*] Well, if you are determined to have it, I insist on having it in a proper and respectable way. Charles: ring for prayers.

> *General amazement. Stephen rises in dismay.*

LOMAX [*rising*] Oh I say!

UNDERSHAFT [*rising*] I am afraid I must be going.

LADY BRITOMART. You cannot go now, Andrew: it would be most improper. Sit down. What will the servants think?

UNDERSHAFT. My dear: I have conscientious scruples. May I suggest a compromise? If Barbara will conduct a little service in the drawing room, with Mr Lomax as organist, I will attend it willingly. I will even take part, if a trombone can be procured.

LADY BRITOMART. Dont mock, Andrew.

UNDERSHAFT [*shocked—to Barbara*] You dont think I am mocking, my love, I hope.

BARBARA. No, of course not; and it wouldnt matter if you were: half the Army came to their first meeting for a lark. [*Rising*] Come along. [*She throws her arm round her father and sweeps him out, calling to the others from the threshold*] Come, Dolly. Come, Cholly.

> *Cusins rises.*

LADY BRITOMART. I will not be disobeyed by everybody. Adolphus: sit down. [*He does not*]· Charles: you may go. You are not fit for prayers: you cannot keep your countenance.

LOMAX. Oh I say! [*He goes out*].

LADY BRITOMART [*continuing*] But you, Adolphus, can behave yourself if you choose to. I insist on your staying.

CUSINS. My dear Lady Brit: there are things in the family prayer book that I couldnt bear to hear you say.

LADY BRITOMART. What things, pray?

CUSINS. Well, you would have to say before all the servants that we have done things we ought not to have done, and left undone things we ought to have done, and that there is no health in us. I cannot bear to hear you doing yourself such an injustice, and Barbara such an injustice. As for myself, I flatly deny it: I have done my best. I shouldnt dare to marry Barbara—I couldnt look you in the face—if it were true. So I must go to the drawing room.

LADY BRITOMART [*offended*] Well, go. [*He starts for the door*]. And remember this, Adolphus [*he turns to listen*]: I have a very strong suspicion that you went to the Salvation Army to worship Barbara and nothing else. And I quite appreciate the very clever way in which you systematically humbug me. I have found you out. Take care Barbara doesnt. Thats all.

CUSINS [*with unruffled sweetness*] Dont tell on me. [*He steals out*].

LADY BRITOMART. Sarah: if you want to go, go. Anything's better than to sit there as if you wished you were a thousand miles away.

SARAH [*languidly*] Very well, mamma. [*She goes*].

Lady Britomart, with a sudden flounce, gives way to a little gust of tears.

STEPHEN [*going to her*] Mother: whats the matter?

LADY BRITOMART [*swishing away her tears with her handkerchief*] Nothing. Foolishness. You can go with him, too, if you like, and leave me with the servants.

STEPHEN. Oh, you mustnt think that, mother. I—I dont like him.

LADY BRITOMART. The others do. That is the injustice of a woman's lot. A woman has to bring up her children; and that means to restrain them, to deny them things they want, to set them tasks, to punish them when they do wrong, to do all the unpleasant things. And then the father, who has nothing to do but pet them and spoil them, comes in when all her work is done and steals their affection from her.

STEPHEN. He has not stolen our affection from you. It is only curiosity.

LADY BRITOMART [*violently*] I wont be consoled, Stephen. There is nothing the matter with me. [*She rises and goes towards the door*].

STEPHEN. Where are you going, mother?

LADY BRITOMART. To the drawing room, of course. [*She goes out. Onward, Christian Soldiers, on the concertina, with tambourine accompaniment, is heard when the door opens*]. Are you coming, Stephen?

STEPHEN. No. Certainly not. [*She goes. He sits down on the settee, with compressed lips and an expression of strong dislike*].

Act II

*The yard of the West Ham shelter of the Salvation Army is a
cold place on a January morning. The building itself, an old ware-
house, is newly whitewashed. Its gabled end projects into the yard
in the middle, with a door on the ground floor, and another in the
loft above it without any balcony or ladder, but with a pulley
rigged over it for hoisting sacks. Those who come from this central
gable end into the yard have the gateway leading to the street on
their left, with a stone horse-trough just beyond it, and, on the
right, a penthouse shielding a table from the weather. There are
forms at the table; and on them are seated a man and a woman,
both much down on their luck, finishing a meal of bread (one
thick slice each, with margarine and golden syrup) and diluted
milk.*

*The man, a workman out of employment, is young, agile, a
talker, a poser, sharp enough to be capable of anything in reason
except honesty or altruistic considerations of any kind. The woman
is a commonplace old bundle of poverty and hard-worn humanity.
She looks sixty and probably is forty-five. If they were rich people,
gloved and muffed and well wrapped up in furs and overcoats, they
would be numbed and miserable; for it is a grindingly cold raw January day; and a glance at the background of grimy warehouses and
leaden sky visible over the whitewashed walls of the yard would
drive any idle rich person straight to the Mediterranean. But these
two, being no more troubled with visions of the Mediterranean
than of the moon, and being compelled to keep more of their
clothes in the pawnshop, and less on their persons, in winter than
in summer, are not depressed by the cold: rather are they stung
into vivacity, to which their meal has just now given an almost jolly
turn. The man takes a pull at his mug, and then gets up and moves
about the yard with his hands deep in his pockets, occasionally
breaking into a stepdance.*

THE WOMAN. Feel better arter your meal, sir?

THE MAN. No. Call that a meal! Good enough for you, praps; but
wot is it to me, an intelligent workin man.

THE WOMAN. Workin man! Wot are you?

THE MAN. Painter.

THE WOMAN [*sceptically*] Yus, I dessay.

THE MAN. Yus, you dessay! I know. Every loafer that cant do noth-
ink calls isself a painter. Well, I'm a real painter: grainer,
finisher, thirty-eight bob a week when I can get it.

THE WOMAN. Then why dont you go and get it?

THE MAN. I'll tell you why. Fust: I'm intelligent—fffff! it's rotten
cold here [*he dances a step or two*]—yes: intelligent beyond the
station o life into which it has pleased the capitalists to call me;

and they dont like a man that sees through em. Second, an intelligent bein needs a doo share of appiness; so I drink somethink
cruel when I get the chawnce. Third, I stand by my class and do
as little as I can so's to leave arf the job for me fellow workers.
Fourth, I'm fly enough to know wots inside the law and wots
outside it; and inside it I do as the capitalists do: pinch wot I
can lay me ands on. In a proper state of society I am sober,
industrious and honest: in Rome, so to speak, I do as the
Romans do. Wots the consequence? When trade is bad—and
it's rotten bad just now—and the employers az to sack arf their
men, they generally start on me.

THE WOMAN. Whats your name?

THE MAN. Price. Bronterre O'Brien Price. Usually called Snobby
Price, for short.

THE WOMAN. Snobby's a carpenter, aint it? You said you was a
painter.

PRICE. Not that kind of snob, but the genteel sort. I'm too uppish,
owing to my intelligence, and my father being a Chartist[3] and a
reading, thinking man: a stationer, too. I'm none of your
common hewers of wood and drawers of water; and dont you
forget it. [*He returns to his seat at the table, and takes up his
mug*]. Wots your name?

THE WOMAN. Rummy Mitchens, sir.

PRICE [*quaffing the remains of his milk to her*] Your elth, Miss
Mitchens.

RUMMY [*correcting him*] Missis Mitchens.

PRICE. Wot! Oh Rummy, Rummy! Respectable married woman,
Rummy, gittin rescued by the Salvation Army by pretendin to
be a bad un. Same old game!

RUMMY. What am I to do? I cant starve. Them Salvation lasses is
dear good girls; but the better you are, the worse they likes to
think you were before they rescued you. Why shouldnt they av
a bit o credit, poor loves? theyre worn to rags by their work. And
where would they get the money to rescue us if we was to let on
we're no worse than other people? You know what ladies and
gentlemen are.

PRICE. Thievin swine! Wish I ad their job, Rummy, all the same.
Wot does Rummy stand for? Pet name praps?

RUMMY. Short for Romola.[4]

PRICE. For wot!?

RUMMY. Romola. It was out of a new book. Somebody me mother
wanted me to grow up like.

PRICE. We're companions in misfortune, Rummy. Both on us got
names that nobody cawnt pronounce. Consequently I'm Snobby
and youre Rummy because Bill and Sally wasnt good enough for
our parents. Such is life!

3. An English workers' reform movement of the 1840's.

4. The idealistic heroine of George
Eliot's novel, 1863.

RUMMY. Who saved you, Mr Price? Was it Major Barbara?

PRICE. No: I come here on my own. I'm going to be Bronterre O'Brien Price, the converted painter. I know wot they like. I'll tell em how I blasphemed and gambled and wopped my poor old mother—

RUMMY [*shocked*] Used you to beat your mother?

PRICE. Not likely. She used to beat me. No matter: you come and listen to the converted painter, and youll hear how she was a pious woman that taught me me prayers at er knee, an how I used to come home drunk and drag her out o bed be er snow white airs, an lam into er with the poker.

RUMMY. That whats so unfair to us women. Your confessions is just as big lies as ours: you dont tell what you really done no more than us; but you men can tell your lies right out at the meetins and be made much of for it; while the sort o confessions we az to make az to be wispered to one lady at a time. It aint right, spite of all their piety.

PRICE. Right! Do you spose the Army'd be allowed if it went and did right? Not much. It combs our air and makes us good little blokes to be robbed and put upon. But I'll play the game as good as any of em. I'll see somebody struck by lightnin, or hear a voice sayin "Snobby Price: where will you spend eternity?" I'll av a time of it, I tell you.

RUMMY. You wont be let drink, though.

PRICE. I'll take it out in gorspellin, then. I dont want to drink if I can get fun enough any other way.

> *Jenny Hill, a pale, overwrought, pretty Salvation lass of 18, comes in through the yard gate, leading Peter Shirley, a half hardened, half worn-out elderly man, weak with hunger.*

JENNY [*supporting him*] Come! pluck up. I'll get you something to eat. Youll be all right then.

PRICE [*rising and hurrying officiously to take the old man off Jenny's hands*] Poor old man! Cheer up, brother: youll find rest and peace and appiness ere. Hurry up with the food, miss: e's fair done [*Jenny hurries into the shelter*]. Ere, buck up, daddy! she's fetchin y'a thick slice o breadn treacle,[5] an a mug o skyblue. [*He seats him at the corner of the table*].

RUMMY [*gaily*] Keep up your old art! Never say die!

SHIRLEY. I'm not an old man. I'm only 46. I'm as good as ever I was. The grey patch come in my hair before I was thirty. All it wants is three pennorth o hair dye: am I to be turned on the streets to starve for it? Holy God! Ive worked ten to twelve hours a day since I was thirteen, and paid my way all through; and now am I to be thrown into the gutter and my job given to a young man that can do it no better than me because Ive black hair that goes white at the first change?

PRICE [*cheerfully*] No good jawrin about it. Youre ony a

5. Molasses.

jumped-up, jerked-off, orspittle-turned-out incurable of an ole workin man: who cares about you? Eh? Make the thievin swine give you a meal: theyve stole many a one from you. Get a bit o your own back [*Jenny returns with the usual meal*].There you are, brother. Awsk a blessin an tuck that into you.

SHIRLEY [*looking at it ravenously but not touching it, and crying like a child*] I never took anything before.

JENNY [*petting him*] Come, come! the Lord sends it to you: he wasnt above taking bread from his friends; and why should you be? Besides, when we find you a job you can pay us for it if you like.

SHIRLEY [*eagerly*] Yes, yes: thats true. I can pay you back: it's only a loan. [*Shivering*] Oh Lord! oh Lord! [*He turns to the table and attacks the meal ravenously*].

JENNY. Well, Rummy, are you more comfortable now?

RUMMY. God bless you, lovey! youve fed my body and saved my soul, havnt you? [*Jenny, touched, kisses her*]. Sit down and rest a bit: you must be ready to drop.

JENNY. Ive been going hard since morning. But theres more work than we can do. I mustnt stop.

RUMMY. Try a prayer for just two minutes. Youll work all the better after.

JENNY [*her eyes lighting up*] Oh isnt it wonderful how a few minutes prayer revives you! I was quite lightheaded at twelve o'clock, I was so tired; but Major Barbara just sent me to pray for five minutes; and I was able to go on as if I had only just begun. [*To Price*] Did you have a piece of bread?

PRICE [*with unction*] Yes, miss; but Ive got the piece that I value more; and thats the peace that passeth hall hannerstennin.

RUMMY [*fervently*] Glory Hallelujah!

> *Bill Walker, a rough customer of about 25, appears at the yard gate and looks malevolently at Jenny.*

JENNY. That makes me so happy. When you say that, I feel wicked for loitering here. I must get to work again.

> *She is hurrying to the shelter, when the new-comer moves quickly up to the door and intercepts her. His manner is so threatening that she retreats as he comes at her truculently, driving her down the yard.*

BILL. Aw knaow you. Youre the one that took awy maw girl. Youre the one that set er agen me. Well, I'm gowin to ev er aht. Not that Aw care a carse for er or you: see? Bat Aw'll let er knaow; and Aw'll let you knaow. Aw'm gowing to give her a doin thatll teach er to cat awy from me. Nah in wiv you and tell er to cam aht afore Aw cam in and kick er aht. Tell er Bill Walker wants er. She'll knaow wot thet means; and if she keeps me witin itll be worse. You stop to jawr beck at me; and Aw'll stawt on you: d'ye eah? Theres your wy. In you gow. [*He takes her by the arm and slings her towards the door of the shelter. She falls on her hand and knee. Rummy helps her up again*].

PRICE [*rising, and venturing irresolutely towards Bill*] Easy there, mate. She aint doin you no arm.

BILL. Oo are you callin mite? [*Standing over him threateningly*] Youre gowin to stend ap for er, aw yer? Put ap your ends.

RUMMY [*running indignantly to him to scold him*] Oh, you great brute—[*He instantly swings his left hand back against her face. She screams and reels back to the trough, where she sits down, covering her bruised face with her hands and rocking herself and moaning with pain*].

JENNY [*going to her*] Oh, God forgive you! How could you strike an old woman like that?

BILL [*seizing her by the hair so violently that she also screams, and tearing her away from the old woman*] You Gawd forgimme again an Aw'll Gawd forgive you one on the jawr thetll stop you pryin for a week. [*Holding her and turning fiercely on Price*] Ev you ennything to sy agen it?

PRICE [*intimidated*] No, matey: she aint anything to do with me.

BILL. Good job for you! Aw'd pat two meals into you and fawt you with one finger arter, you stawved cur. [*To Jenny*] Nah are you gowin to fetch aht Mog Ebbijem; or em Aw to knock your fice off you and fetch her meself?

JENNY [*writhing in his grasp*] Oh please someone go in and tell Major Barbara—[*she screams again as he wrenches her head down; and Price and Rummy flee into the shelter*].

BILL. You want to gow in and tell your Mijor of me, do you?

JENNY. Oh please dont drag my hair. Let me go.

BILL. Do you or downt you? [*She stifles a scream*]. Yus or nao?

JENNY. God give me strength—

BILL [*striking her with his fist in the face*] Gow an shaow her thet, and tell her if she wants one lawk it to cam and interfere with me. [*Jenny, crying with pain, goes into the shed. He goes to the form and addresses the old man*]. Eah: finish your mess; an git aht o maw wy.

SHIRLEY [*springing up and facing him fiercely, with the mug in his hand*] You take a liberty with me, and I'll smash you over the face with the mug and cut your eye out. Aint you satisfied—young whelps like you—with takin the bread out o the mouths of your elders that have brought you up and slaved for you, but you must come shovin and cheekin and bullyin in here, where the bread o charity is sickenin in our stummicks?

BILL [*contemptuously, but backing a little*] Wot good are you, you aold palsy mag?[6] Wot good are you?

SHIRLEY. As good as you and better. I'll do a day's work agen you or any fat young soaker of your age. Go and take my job at Horrockses, where I worked for ten year. They want young men there: they cant afford to keep men over forty-five. Theyre very sorry—give you a character and happy to help you to get anything suited to your years—sure a steady man wont be long out

6. Drunkard.

of a job. Well, let em try you. Theyll find the differ. What do you know? Not as much as how to beeyave yourself—layin your dirty fist across the mouth of a respectable woman!

BILL. Downt provowk me to ly it acrost yours: d'ye eah?

SHIRLEY [*with blighting contempt*] Yes: you like an old man to hit, dont you, when youve finished with the women. I aint seen you hit a young one yet.

BILL [*stung*] You loy, you aold soupkitchener, you. There was a yang menn eah. Did Aw offer to itt him or did Aw not?

SHIRLEY. Was he starvin or was he not? Was he a man or only a crosseyed thief an a loafer? Would you hit my son-in-law's brother?

BILL. Oo's ee?

SHIRLEY. Todger Fairmile o Balls Pond. Him that won £20 off the Japanese wrastler at the music hall by standin out 17 minutes 4 seconds agen him.

BILL [*sullenly*] Aw'm nao music awl wrastler. Ken he box?

SHIRLEY Yes: an you cant.

BILL. Wot! Aw cawnt, cawnt Aw? Wots thet you sy [*threatening him*]?

SHIRLEY [*not budging an inch*] Will you box Todger Fairmile if I put him on to you? Say the word.

BILL [*subsiding with a slouch*] Aw'll stend ap to enny menn alawv, if he was ten Todger Fairmawls. But Aw dont set ap to be a perfeshnal.

SHIRLEY [*looking down on him with unfathomable disdain*] You box! Slap an old woman with the back o your hand! You hadnt even the sense to hit her where a magistrate couldnt see the mark of it, you silly young lump of conceit and ignorance. Hit a girl in the jaw and ony make her cry! If Todger Fairmile'd done it, she wouldnt a got up inside o ten minutes, no more than you would if he got on to you. Yah! I'd set about you myself if I had a week's feedin in me instead o two months' starvation. [*He turns his back on him and sits down moodily at the table*].

BILL [*following him and stooping over him to drive the taunt in*] You loy! youve the bread and treacle in you that you cam eah to beg.

SHIRLEY [*bursting into tears*] Oh God! it's true: I'm only an old pauper on the scrap heap. [*Furiously*] But youll come to it yourself; and then youll know. Youll come to it sooner than a teetotaller like me, fillin yourself with gin at this hour o the mornin!

BILL. Aw'm nao gin drinker, you oald lawr; bat wen Aw want to give my girl a bloomin good awdin Aw lawk to ev a bit o devil in me: see? An eah Aw emm, talkin to a rotten aold blawter like you sted o givin her wot for. [*Working himself into a rage*] Aw'm gowin in there to fetch her aht. [*He makes vengefully for the shelter door*].

SHIRLEY. Youre goin to the station on a stretcher, more likely; and theyll take the gin and the devil out of you there when they get you inside. You mind what youre about: the major here is the Earl o Stevenage's granddaughter.

BILL [*checked*] Garn!

SHIRLEY. Youll see.

BILL [*his resolution oozing*] Well, Aw aint dan nathin to er.

SHIRLEY. Spose she said you did! who'd believe you?

BILL [*very uneasy, skulking back to the corner of the penthouse*] Gawd! theres no jastice in this cantry. To think wot them people can do! Aw'm as good as er.

SHIRLEY. Tell her so. It's just what a fool like you would do.

> Barbara, brisk and businesslike, comes from the shelter with a note book, and addresses herself to Shirley. Bill, cowed, sits down in the corner on a form, and turns his back on them.

BARBARA. Good morning.

SHIRLEY [*standing up and taking off his hat*] Good morning, miss.

BARBARA. Sit down: make yourself at home. [*He hesitates; but she puts a friendly hand on his shoulder and makes him obey*]. Now then! since youve made friends with us, we want to know all about you. Names and addresses and trades.

SHIRLEY. Peter Shirley. Fitter. Chucked out two months ago because I was too old.

BARBARA [*not at all surprised*] Youd pass still. Why didnt you dye your hair?

SHIRLEY. I did. Me age come out at a coroner's inquest on me daughter.

BARBARA. Steady?

SHIRLEY. Teetotaller. Never out of a job before. Good worker. And sent to the knackers[7] like an old horse!

BARBARA. No matter: if you did your part God will do his.

SHIRLEY [*suddenly stubborn*] My religion's no concern of anybody but myself.

BARBARA [*guessing*] I know. Secularist?[8]

SHIRLEY [*hotly*] Did I offer to deny it?

BARBARA. Why should you? My own father's a Secularist, I think. Our Father—yours and mine—fulfils himself in many ways; and I daresay he knew what he was about when he made a Secularist of you. So buck up, Peter! we can always find a job for a steady man like you. [*Shirley, disarmed and a little bewildered, touches his hat. She turns from him to Bill*]. Whats your name?

BILL [*insolently*] Wots thet to you?

BARBARA [*calmly making a note*] Afraid to give his name. Any trade?

BILL. Oo's afride to give is nime? [*Doggedly, with a sense of heroically defying the House of Lords in the person of Lord Stevenage*] If you want to bring a chawge agen me, bring it. [*She waits, unruffled*]. Moy nime's Bill Walker.

BARBARA [*as if the name were familiar: trying to remember how*]

---

7. Buyers and slaughterers of old animals.

8. Secularism, as a kind of organized atheism, was a thriving movement in London of the time.

Bill Walker? [*Recollecting*] Oh, I know: youre the man that
Jenny Hill was praying for inside just now. [*She enters his name
in her note book*].

BILL. Oo's Jenny Ill? And wot call as she to pry for me?

BARBARA. I dont know. Perhaps it was you that cut her lip.

BILL [*defiantly*] Yus, it was me that cat her lip. Aw aint afride o
you.

BARBARA. How could you be, since youre not afraid of God? Youre
a brave man, Mr Walker. It takes some pluck to do our work
here; but none of us dare lift our hand against a girl like that, for
fear of her father in heaven.

BILL [*sullenly*] I want nan o your kentin jawr. I spowse you think
Aw cam eah to beg from you, like this demmiged lot eah. Not
me. Aw downt want your bread and scripe and ketlep.[9] Aw dont
blieve in your Gawd, no more than you do yourself.

BARBARA [*sunnily apologetic and ladylike, as on a new footing with
him*] Oh, I beg your pardon for putting your name down, Mr
Walker. I didnt understand. I'll strike it out.

BILL [*taking this as a slight, and deeply wounded by it*] Eah! you
let maw nime alown. Aint it good enaff to be in your book?

BARBARA [*considering*] Well, you see, theres no use putting down
your name unless I can do something for you, is there? Whats
your trade?

BILL [*still smarting*] Thets nao concern o yours.

BARBARA. Just so. [*Very businesslike*] I'll put you down as
[*writing*] the man who—struck—poor little Jenny Hill—in the
mouth.

BILL [*rising threateningly*] See eah. Awve ed enaff o this.

BARBARA [*quite sunny and fearless*] What did you come to us for?

BILL. Aw cam for maw gel, see? Aw cam to tike her aht o this and
to brike er jawr for er.

BARBARA [*complacently*] You see I was right about your trade.
[*Bill, on the point of retorting furiously, finds himself, to his
great shame and terror, in danger of crying instead. He sits down
again suddenly*]. Whats her name?

BILL [*dogged*] Er nime's Mog Ebbijem: thets wot her nime is.

BARBARA. Mog Habbijam! Oh, she's gone to Canning Town,
to our barracks there.

BILL [*fortified by his resentment of Mog's perfidy*] Is she?
[*Vindictively*] Then Aw'm gowin to Kennintahn arter her.
[*He crosses to the gate; hesitates; finally comes back at Barbara*].
Are you loyin to me to git shat o me?

BARBARA. I dont want to get shut of you. I want to keep you here
and save your soul. Youd better stay: youre going to have a bad
time today, Bill.

BILL. Oo's gowin to give it to me? You, preps?

BARBARA. Someone you dont believe in. But youll be glad afterwards.

BILL [*slinking off*] Aw'll gow to Kennintahn to be aht o reach o

9. "Scrape," that is, thinly spread butter, and "catlap," a diluted drink.

your tangue. [*Suddenly turning on her with intense malice*] And if Aw downt fawnd Mog there, Aw'll cam beck and do two years for you, selp me Gawd if Aw downt!

BARBARA [*a shade kindlier, if possible*] It's no use, Bill. She's got another bloke.

BILL. Wot!

BARBARA. One of her own converts. He fell in love with her when he saw her with her soul saved, and her face clean, and her hair washed.

BILL [*surprised*] Wottud she wash it for, the carroty slat? It's red.

BARBARA. It's quite lovely now, because she wears a new look in her eyes with it. It's a pity youre too late. The new bloke has put your nose out of joint, Bill.

BILL. Aw'll put his nowse aht o joint for him. Not that Aw care a carse for er, mawnd thet. But Aw'll teach her to drop me as if Aw was dirt. And Aw'll teach him to meddle with maw judy. Wots iz bleedin nime?

BARBARA. Sergeant Todger Fairmile.

SHIRLEY [*rising with grim joy*] I'll go with him, miss. I want to see them two meet. I'll take him to the infirmary when it's over.

BILL [*to Shirley, with undissembled misgiving*] Is thet im you was speakin on?

SHIRLEY. Thats him.

BILL. Im that wrastled in the music awl?

SHIRLEY. The competitions at the National Sportin Club was worth nigh a hundred a year to him. He's gev em up now for religion; so he's a bit fresh for want of the exercise he was accustomed to. He'll be glad to see you. Come along.

BILL. Wots is wight?

SHIRLEY. Thirteen four.[1] [*Bill's last hope expires*].

BARBARA. Go and talk to him, Bill. He'll convert you.

SHIRLEY. He'll convert your head into a mashed potato.

BILL [*sullenly*] Aw aint afride of im. Aw aint afride of ennybody. Bat e can lick me. She's dan me. [*He sits down moodily on the edge of the horse trough*].

SHIRLEY. You aint goin. I thought not. [*He resumes his seat*].

BARBARA [*calling*] Jenny!

JENNY [*appearing at the shelter door with a plaster on the corner of her mouth*] Yes, Major.

BARBARA. Send Rummy Mitchens out to clear away here.

JENNY. I think she's afraid.

BARBARA [*her resemblance to her mother flashing out for a moment*] Nonsense! she must do as she's told.

JENNY [*calling into the shelter*] Rummy: the Major says you must come.

> Jenny comes to Barbara, purposely keeping on the side next Bill, lest he should suppose that she shrank from him or bore malice.

1. Thirteen stone, four pounds equal 186 pounds.

BARBARA. Poor little Jenny! Are you tired? [*Looking at the wounded cheek*] Does it hurt?

JENNY. No: it's all right now. It was nothing.

BARBARA [*critically*] It was as hard as he could hit, I expect. Poor Bill! You dont feel angry with him, do you?

JENNY. Oh no, no, no: indeed I dont, Major, bless his poor heart! [*Barbara kisses her; and she runs away merrily into the shelter. Bill writhes with an agonizing return of his new and alarming symptoms, but says nothing. Rummy Mitchens comes from the shelter*].

BARBARA [*going to meet Rummy*] Now Rummy, bustle. Take in those mugs and plates to be washed; and throw the crumbs about for the birds.

> Rummy takes the three plates and mugs; but Shirley takes back his mug from her, as there is still some milk left in it.

RUMMY. There aint any crumbs. This aint a time to waste good bread on birds.

PRICE [*appearing at the shelter door*] Gentleman come to see the shelter, Major. Says he's your father.

BARBARA. All right. Coming. [*Snobby goes back into the shelter, followed by Barbara*].

RUMMY [*stealing across to Bill and addressing him in a subdued voice, but with intense conviction*] I'd av the lor of you, you flat eared pignosed potwalloper,[2] if she'd let me. Youre no gentleman, to hit a lady in the face. [*Bill, with greater things moving in him, takes no notice*].

SHIRLEY [*following her*] Here! in with you and dont get yourself into more trouble by talking.

RUMMY [*with hauteur*] I aint ad the pleasure o being hintroduced to you, as I can remember. [*She goes into the shelter with the plates*].

SHIRLEY. Thats the—

BILL [*savagely*] Downt you talk to me, d'ye eah? You lea me alown, or Aw'll do you a mischief. Aw'm not dirt under y o u r feet, ennywy.

SHIRLEY [*calmly*] Dont you be afeerd. You aint such prime company that you need expect to be sought after. [*He is about to go into the shelter when Barbara comes out, with Undershaft on her right*].

BARBARA. Oh, there you are, Mr Shirley! [*Between them*] This is my father: I told you he was a Secularist, didnt I? Perhaps youll be able to comfort one another.

UNDERSHAFT [*startled*] A Secularist! Not the least in the world: on the contrary, a confirmed mystic.

BARBARA. Sorry, I'm sure. By the way, papa, what is your religion? in case I have to introduce you again.

UNDERSHAFT. My religion? Well, my dear, I am a Millionaire. That is my religion.

2. A pot-washer, a menial servant.

BARBARA. Then I'm afraid you and Mr Shirley wont be able to comfort one another after all. Youre not a Millionaire, are you, Peter?

SHIRLEY. No; and proud of it.

UNDERSHAFT [*gravely*] Poverty, my friend, is not a thing to be proud of.

SHIRLEY [*angrily*] Who made your millions for you? Me and my like. Whats kep us poor? Keepin you rich. I wouldnt have your conscience, not for all your income.

UNDERSHAFT. I wouldnt have your income, not for all your conscience, Mr Shirley. [*He goes to the penthouse and sits down on a form*].

BARBARA [*stopping Shirley adroitly as he is about to retort*] You wouldnt think he was my father, would you, Peter? Will you go into the shelter and lend the lasses a hand for a while: we're worked off our feet.

SHIRLEY [*bitterly*] Yes: I'm in their debt for a meal, aint I?

BARBARA. Oh, not because youre in their debt, but for love of them, Peter, for love of them. [*He cannot understand, and is rather scandalized*] There! dont stare at me. In with you; and give that conscience of yours a holiday [*bustling him into the shelter*].

SHIRLEY [*as he goes in*] Ah! it's a pity you never was trained to use your reason, miss. Youd have been a very taking lecturer on Secularism.

> *Barbara turns to her father.*

UNDERSHAFT. Never mind me, my dear. Go about your work; and let me watch it for a while.

BARBARA. All right.

UNDERSHAFT. For instance, whats the matter with that out-patient over there?

BARBARA [*looking at Bill, whose attitude has never changed, and whose expression of brooding wrath has deepened*] Oh, we shall cure him in no time. Just watch. [*She goes over to Bill and waits. He glances up at her and casts his eyes down again, uneasy, but grimmer than ever*]. It would be nice to just stamp on Mog Habbijam's face, wouldnt it, Bill?

BILL [*starting up from the trough in consternation*] It's a loy: Aw never said so. [*She shakes her head*]. Oo taold you wot was in moy mawnd?

BARBARA. Only your new friend.

BILL. Wot new friend?

BARBARA. The devil, Bill. When he gets round people they get miserable, just like you.

BILL [*with a heartbreaking attempt at devil-may-care cheerfulness*] Aw aint miserable. [*He sits down again, and stretches his legs in an attempt to seem indifferent*].

BARBARA. Well, if youre happy, why dont you look happy, as we do?

BILL [*his legs curling back in spite of him*] Aw'm eppy enaff, Aw tell you. Woy cawnt you lea me alown? Wot ev I dan to y o u? Aw aint smashed y o u r fice, ev Aw?

BARBARA [*softly: wooing his soul*] It's not me thats getting at you, Bill.

BILL. Oo else is it?

BARBARA. Somebody that doesn't intend you to smash women's faces, I suppose. Somebody or something that wants to make a man of you.

BILL [*blustering*] Mike a menn o m e! Aint Aw a menn? eh? Oo sez Aw'm not a menn?

BARBARA. Theres a man in you somewhere, I suppose. But why did he let you hit poor little Jenny Hill? That wasnt very manly of him, was it?

BILL [*tormented*] Ev dan wiv it, Aw tell you. Chack it. Aw'm sick o your Jenny Ill and er silly little fice.

BARBARA. Then why do you keep thinking about it? Why does it keep coming up against you in your mind? Youre not getting converted, are you?

BILL [*with conviction*] Not ME. Not lawkly.

BARBARA. Thats right, Bill. Hold out against it. Put out your strength. Dont lets get you cheap. Todger Fairmile said he wrestled for three nights against his salvation harder than he ever wrestled with the Jap at the music hall. He gave in to the Jap when his arm was going to break. But he didnt give in to his salvation until his heart was going to break. Perhaps youll escape that. You havnt any heart, have you?

BILL. Wot d'ye mean? Woy aint Aw got a awt the sime as ennybody else?

BARBARA. A man with a heart wouldnt have bashed poor little Jenny's face, would he?

BILL [*almost crying*] Ow, will you lea me alown? Ev Aw ever offered to meddle with you, that you cam neggin and provowkin me lawk this? [*He writhes convulsively from his eyes to his toes*].

BARBARA [*with a steady soothing hand on his arm and a gentle voice that never lets him go*] It's your soul thats hurting you, Bill, and not me. Weve been through it all ourselves. Come with us, Bill. [*He looks wildly round*]. To brave manhood on earth and eternal glory in heaven. [*He is on the point of breaking down*]. Come. [*A drum is heard in the shelter; and Bill, with a gasp, escapes from the spell as Barbara turns quickly. Adolphus enters from the shelter with a big drum*]. Oh! there you are, Dolly. Let me introduce a new friend of mine, Mr Bill Walker. This is my bloke, Bill: Mr Cusins. [*Cusins salutes with his drumstick*].

BILL. Gowin to merry im?

BARBARA. Yes.

BILL [*fervently*] Gawd elp im! Gaw-aw-aw-awd elp im!

BARBARA. Why? Do you think he wont be happy with me?

BILL. Awve aony ed to stend it for a mawnin: e'll ev to stend it for a lawftawm.

CUSINS. That is a frightful reflection, Mr Walker. But I cant tear myself away from her.

BILL. Well, Aw ken. [*To Barbara*] Eah! do you knaow where Aw'm gowin to, and wot Aw'm gowin to do?

BARBARA. Yes: youre going to heaven; and youre coming back here before the week's out to tell me so.

BILL. You loy. Aw'm gowin to Kennintahn, to spit in Todger Fairmawl's eye. Aw beshed Jenny Ill's fice; an nar Aw'll git me aown fice beshed and cam beck and shaow it to er. Ee'll itt me ardern Aw itt er. Thatll mike us square. [*To Adolphus*] Is thet fair or is it not? Youre a genlmn: you oughter knaow.

BARBARA. Two black eyes wont make one white one, Bill.

BILL. Aw didnt awst you. Cawnt you never keep your mahth shat? Oy awst the genlmn.

CUSINS [*reflectively*] Yes: I think youre right, Mr Walker. Yes: I should do it. It's curious: it's exactly what an ancient Greek would have done.

BARBARA. But what good will it do?

CUSINS. Well, it will give Mr Fairmile some exercise; and it will satisfy Mr Walker's soul.

BILL. Rot! there aint nao sach a thing as a saoul. Ah kin you tell wevver Awve a saoul or not? You never seen it.

BARBARA. Ive seen it hurting you when you went against it.

BILL [*with compressed aggravation*] If you was maw gel and took the word aht o me mahth lawk thet, Aw'd give you sathink youd feel urtin, Aw would. [*To Adolphus*] You tike maw tip, mite. Stop er jawr; or youll doy afoah your tawm [*With intense expression*] Wore aht: thets wot youll be: wore aht. [*He goes away through the gate*].

CUSINS [*looking after him*] I wonder!

BARBARA. Dolly! [*indignant, in her mother's manner*].

CUSINS. Yes, my dear, it's very wearing to be in love with you. If it lasts, I quite think I shall die young.

BARBARA. Should you mind?

CUSINS. Not at all. [*He is suddenly softened, and kisses her over the drum, evidently not for the first time, as people cannot kiss over a big drum without practice. Undershaft coughs*].

BARBARA. It's all right, papa, weve not forgotten you. Dolly: explain the place to papa: I havnt time. [*She goes busily into the shelter*].

> Undershaft and Adolphus now have the yard to themselves. Undershaft, seated on a form, and still keenly attentive, looks hard at Adolphus. Adolphus looks hard at him.

UNDERSHAFT. I fancy you guess something of what is in my mind, Mr Cusins. [*Cusins flourishes his drumsticks as if in the act of beating a lively rataplan, but makes no sound*]. Exactly so. But suppose Barbara finds you out!

CUSINS. You know, I do not admit that I am imposing on Barbara. I am quite genuinely interested in the views of the Salvation Army. The fact is, I am a sort of collector of religions; and the curious thing is that I find I can believe them all. By the way, have you any religion?

UNDERSHAFT. Yes.

CUSINS. Anything out of the common?

UNDERSHAFT. Only that there are two things necessary to Salvation.

CUSINS [*disappointed, but polite*] Ah, the Church Catechism. Charles Lomax also belongs to the Established Church.

UNDERSHAFT. The two things are—

CUSINS. Baptism and—

UNDERSHAFT. No. Money and gunpowder.

CUSINS [*surprised, but interested*] That is the general opinion of our governing classes. The novelty is in hearing any man confess it.

UNDERSHAFT. Just so.

CUSINS. Excuse me: is there any place in your religion for honor, justice, truth, love, mercy and so forth?

UNDERSHAFT. Yes: they are the graces and luxuries of a rich, strong, and safe life.

CUSINS. Suppose one is forced to choose between them and money or gunpowder?

UNDERSHAFT. Choose money and gunpowder; for without enough of both you cannot afford the others.

CUSINS. That is your religion?

UNDERSHAFT. Yes.

> *The cadence of this reply makes a full close in the conversation. Cusins twists his face dubiously and contemplates Undershaft. Undershaft contemplates him.*

CUSINS. Barbara wont stand that. You will have to choose between your religion and Barbara.

UNDERSHAFT. So will you, my friend. She will find out that that drum of yours is hollow.

CUSINS. Father Undershaft: you are mistaken: I am a sincere Salvationist. You do not understand the Salvation Army. It is the army of joy, of love, of courage: it has banished the fear and remorse and despair of the old hell-ridden evangelical sects: it marches to fight the devil with trumpet and drum, with music and dancing, with banner and palm, as becomes a sally from heaven by its happy garrison. It picks the waster out of the public house and makes a man of him: it finds a worm wriggling in a back kitchen, and lo! a woman! Men and women of rank too, sons and daughters of the Highest. It takes the poor professor of Greek, the most artificial and self-suppressed of human creatures, from his meal of roots, and lets loose the rhapsodist in him; reveals the true worship of Dionysos to him; sends him down the public street drumming dithyrambs [*he plays a thundering flourish on the drum*].

UNDERSHAFT. You will alarm the shelter.

CUSINS. Oh, they are accustomed to these sudden ecstasies. However, if the drum worries you—[*he pockets the drumsticks; unhooks the drum; and stands it on the ground opposite the gateway*].

UNDERSHAFT. Thank you.

CUSINS. You remember what Euripides says about your money and gunpowder?

UNDERSHAFT. No.

CUSINS [*declaiming*]

> One and another
> In money and guns may outpass his brother;
> And men in their millions float and flow
> And seethe with a million hopes as leaven;
> And they win their will; or they miss their will;
> And their hopes are dead or are pined for still;
> But who'er can know
> As the long days go
> That to live is happy, has found his heaven.

My translation: what do you think of it?

UNDERSHAFT. I think, my friend, that if you wish to know, as the long days go, that to live is happy, you must first acquire money enough for a decent life, and power enough to be your own master.

CUSINS. You are damnably discouraging. [*He resumes his declamation*].

> Is it so hard a thing to see
> That the spirit of God—whate'er it be—
> The law that abides and changes not, ages long,
> The Eternal and Nature-born: these things be strong?
> What else is Wisdom? What of Man's endeavor,
> Or God's high grace so lovely and so great?
> To stand from fear set free? to breathe and wait?
> To hold a hand uplifted over Fate?
> And shall not Barbara be loved for ever?

UNDERSHAFT. Euripides mentions Barbara, does he?

CUSINS. It is a fair translation. The word means Loveliness.

UNDERSHAFT. May I ask—as Barbara's father—how much a year she is to be loved for ever on?

CUSINS. As Barbara's father, that is more your affair than mine. I can feed her by teaching Greek: that is about all.

UNDERSHAFT. Do you consider it a good match for her?

CUSINS [*with polite obstinacy*] Mr Undershaft: I am in many ways a weak, timid, ineffectual person; and my health is far from satisfactory. But whenever I feel that I must have anything, I get it, sooner or later. I feel that way about Barbara. I dont like marriage: I feel intensely afraid of it; and I dont know what I shall do with Barbara or what she will do with me. But I feel that I and nobody else must marry her. Please regard that as settled.—Not that I wish to be arbitrary; but why should I waste your time in discussing what is inevitable?

UNDERSHAFT. You mean that you will stick at nothing: not even the conversion of the Salvation Army to the worship of Dionysos?

CUSINS. The business of the Salvation Army is to save, not to wrangle about the name of the pathfinder. Dionysos or another: what does it matter?

UNDERSHAFT [*rising and approaching him*] Professor Cusins: you are a young man after my own heart.

CUSINS. Mr Undershaft: you are, as far as I am able to gather, a most infernal old rascal; but you appeal very strongly to my sense of ironic humor.

Undershaft mutely offers his hand. They shake.

UNDERSHAFT [*suddenly concentrating himself*] And now to business.

CUSINS. Pardon me. We are discussing religion. Why go back to such an uninteresting and unimportant subject as business?

UNDERSHAFT. Religion is our business at present, because it is through religion alone that we can win Barbara.

CUSINS. Have you, too, fallen in love with Barbara?

UNDERSHAFT. Yes, with a father's love.

CUSINS. A father's love for a grown-up daughter is the most dangerous of all infatuations. I apologize for mentioning my own pale, coy, mistrustful fancy in the same breath with it.

UNDERSHAFT. Keep to the point. We have to win her; and we are neither of us Methodists.

CUSINS. That doesnt matter. The power Barbara wields here—the power that wields Barbara herself—is not Calvinism, not Presbyterianism, not Methodism—

UNDERSHAFT. Not Greek Paganism either, eh?

CUSINS. I admit that. Barbara is quite original in her religion.

UNDERSHAFT [*triumphantly*] Aha! Barbara Undershaft would be. Her inspiration comes from within herself.

CUSINS. How do you suppose it got there?

UNDERSHAFT [*in towering excitement*] It is the Undershaft inheritance. I shall hand on my torch to my daughter. She shall make my converts and preach my gospel—

CUSINS. What! Money and gunpowder!

UNDERSHAFT. Yes, money and gunpowder. Freedom and power. Command of life and command of death.

CUSINS [*urbanely: trying to bring him down to earth*] This is extremely interesting, Mr Undershaft. Of course you know that you are mad.

UNDERSHAFT [*with redoubled force*] And you?

CUSINS. Oh, mad as a hatter. You are welcome to my secret since I have discovered yours. But I am astonished. Can a madman make cannons?

UNDERSHAFT. Would anyone else than a madman make them? And now [*with surging energy*] question for question. Can a sane man translate Euripides?

CUSINS. No.

UNDERSHAFT [*seizing him by the shoulder*] Can a sane woman make a man of a waster or a woman of a worm?

CUSINS [*reeling before the storm*] Father Colossus—Mammoth Millionaire—

UNDERSHAFT [*pressing him*] Are there two mad people or three in this Salvation shelter today?

CUSINS. You mean Barbara is as mad as we are?

UNDERSHAFT [*pushing him lightly off and resuming his equanimity suddenly and completely*] Pooh, Professor! let us call things by their proper names. I am a millionaire; you are a poet; Barbara is a savior of souls. What have we three to do with the common mob of slaves and idolaters? [*He sits down again with a shrug of contempt for the mob*].

CUSINS. Take care! Barbara is in love with the common people. So am I. Have you never felt the romance of that love?

UNDERSHAFT [*cold and sardonic*] Have you ever been in love with Poverty, like St Francis? Have you ever been in love with Dirt, like St Simeon! Have you ever been in love with disease and suffering, like our nurses and philanthropists? Such passions are not virtues, but the most unnatural of all the vices. This love of the common people may please an earl's granddaughter and a university professor; but I have been a common man and a poor man; and it has no romance for me. Leave it to the poor to pretend that poverty is a blessing: leave it to the coward to make a religion of his cowardice by preaching humility: we know better than that. We three must stand together above the common people: how else can we help their children to climb up beside us? Barbara must belong to us, not to the Salvation Army.

CUSINS. Well, I can only say that if you think you will get her away from the Salvation Army by talking to her as you have been talking to me, you dont know Barbara.

UNDERSHAFT. My friend: I never ask for what I can buy.

CUSINS [*in a white fury*] Do I understand you to imply that you can buy Barbara?

UNDERSHAFT. No; but I can buy the Salvation Army.

CUSINS. Quite impossible.

UNDERSHAFT. You shall see. All religious organizations exist by selling themselves to the rich.

CUSINS. Not the Army. That is the Church of the poor.

UNDERSHAFT. All the more reason for buying it.

CUSINS. I dont think you quite know what the Army does for the poor.

UNDERSHAFT. Oh yes I do. It draws their teeth: that is enough for me as a man of business.

CUSINS. Nonsense! It makes them sober—

UNDERSHAFT. I prefer sober workmen. The profits are larger.

CUSINS—honest—

UNDERSHAFT. Honest workmen are the most economical.

CUSINS—attached to their homes—

UNDERSHAFT. So much the better: they will put up with anything sooner than change their shop.

CUSINS—happy—

UNDERSHAFT. An invaluable safeguard against revolution.

CUSINS—unselfish—

UNDERSHAFT. Indifferent to their own interests, which suits me exactly.

CUSINS—with their thoughts on heavenly things—

UNDERSHAFT [*rising*] And not on Trade Unionism nor Socialism. Excellent.

CUSINS [*revolted*] You really are an infernal old rascal.

UNDERSHAFT [*indicating Peter Shirley, who has just come from the shelter and strolled dejectedly down the yard between them*] And this is an honest man!

SHIRLEY. Yes; and what av I got by it? [*he passes on bitterly and sits on the form, in the corner of the penthouse*].

> Snobby Price, beaming sanctimoniously, and Jenny Hill, with a tambourine full of coppers, come from the shelter and go to the drum, on which Jenny begins to count the money.

UNDERSHAFT [*replying to Shirley*] Oh, your employers must have got a good deal by it from first to last. [*He sits on the table, with one foot on the side form. Cusins, overwhelmed, sits down on the same form nearer the shelter. Barbara comes from the shelter to the middle of the yard. She is excited and a little overwrought*].

BARBARA. Weve just had a splendid experience meeting at the other gate in Cripps's lane. Ive hardly ever seen them so much moved as they were by your confession, Mr Price.

PRICE. I could almost be glad of my past wickedness if I could believe that it would elp to keep hathers stright.

BARBARA. So it will, Snobby. How much, Jenny?

JENNY. Four and tenpence, Major.

BARBARA. Oh Snobby, if you had given your poor mother just one more kick, we should have got the whole five shillings!

PRICE. If she heard you say that, miss, she'd be sorry I didnt. But I'm glad. Oh what a joy it will be to her when she hears I'm saved!

UNDERSHAFT. Shall I contribute the odd twopence, Barbara? The millionaire's mite, eh? [*He takes a couple of pennies from his pocket*].

BARBARA. How did you make that twopence?

UNDERSHAFT. As usual. By selling cannons, torpedoes, submarines, and my new patent Grand Duke hand grenade.

BARBARA. Put it back in your pocket. You cant buy your salvation here for twopence: you must work it out.

UNDERSHAFT. Is twopence not enough? I can afford a little more, if you press me.

BARBARA. Two million millions would not be enough. There is bad blood on your hands; and nothing but good blood can cleanse them. Money is no use. Take it away. [*She turns to Cusins*]. Dolly: you must write another letter for me to the papers. [*He makes a wry face*]. Yes: I know you dont like it; but it must be done. The starvation this winter is beating us: everybody is unemployed. The General says we must close this shelter if we cant get more money. I force the collections at the meetings until I am ashamed: dont I, Snobby?

PRICE. It's a fair treat to see you work it, miss. The way you got them up from three-and-six to four-and-ten with that hymn, penny by penny and verse by verse, was a caution. Not a Cheap Jack on Mile End Waste[3] could touch you at it.

BARBARA. Yes; but I wish we could do without it. I am getting at last to think more of the collection than of the people's souls. And what are those hatfuls of pence and halfpence? We want thousands! tens of thousands! hundreds of thousands! I want to convert people, not to be always begging for the Army in a way I'd die sooner than beg for myself.

UNDERSHAFT [*in profound irony*] Genuine unselfishness is capable of anything, my dear.

BARBARA [*unsuspectingly, as she turns away to take the money from the drum and put it in a bag she carries*] Yes, isnt it? [*Undershaft looks sardonically at Cusins*].

CUSINS [*aside to Undershaft*] Mephistopheles! Machiavelli!

BARBARA [*tears coming into her eyes as she ties the bag and pockets it*] How are we to feed them? I cant talk religion to a man with bodily hunger in his eyes. [*Almost breaking down*] It's frightful.

JENNY [*running to her*] Major, dear—

BARBARA [*rebounding*] No: dont comfort me. It will be all right. We shall get the money.

UNDERSHAFT. How?

JENNY. By praying for it, of course. Mrs Baines says she prayed for it last night; and she has never prayed for it in vain: never once. [*She goes to the gate and looks out into the street*].

BARBARA [*who has dried her eyes and regained her composure*] By the way, dad, Mrs Baines has come to march with us to our big meeting this afternoon; and she is very anxious to meet you, for some reason or other. Perhaps she'll convert you.

UNDERSHAFT. I shall be delighted, my dear.

3. A peddler of the bargaining kind, at a familiar spot for gatherings and fairs.

JENNY [*at the gate: excitedly*] Major! Major! heres that man back again.

BARBARA. What man?

JENNY. The man that hit me. Oh, I hope he's coming back to join us.

> *Bill Walker, with frost on his jacket, comes through the gate, his hands deep in his pockets and his chin sunk between his shoulders, like a cleaned-out gambler. He halts between Barbara and the drum.*

BARBARA. Hullo, Bill! Back already!

BILL [*nagging at her*] Bin talkin ever sence, ev you?

BARBARA. Pretty nearly. Well, has Todger paid you out for poor Jenny's jaw?

BILL. Nao e aint.

BARBARA. I thought your jacket looked a bit snowy.

BILL.. Sao it is snaowy. You want to knaow where the snaow cam from, downt you?

BARBARA. Yes.

BILL. Well, it cam from orf the grahnd in Pawkinses Corner in Kennintahn. It got rabbed orf be maw shaoulders: see?

BARBARA. Pity you didnt rub some off with your knees, Bill! That would have done you a lot of good.

BILL [*with sour mirthless humor*] Aw was sivin anather menn's knees at the tawm. E was kneelin on moy ed, e was.

JENNY. Who was kneeling on your head?

BILL.. Todger was. E was pryin for me: pryin camfortable wiv me as a cawpet. Sow was Mog. Sao was the aol bloomin meetin. Mog she sez "Ow Lawd brike is stabborn sperrit; bat downt urt is dear art." Thet was wot she said. "Downt urt is dear art"! An er blowk—thirteen stun four!—kneelin wiv all is wight on me. Fanny, aint it?

JENNY. Oh no. We're sorry, Mr Walker.

BARBARA [*enjoying it frankly*] Nonsense! of course it's funny. Served you right, Bill! You must have done something to him first.

BILL [*doggedly*] Aw did wot Aw said Aw'd do. Aw spit in is eye. E looks ap at the skoy and sez, "Ow that Aw should be fahnd worthy to be spit upon for the gospel's sike!" e sez; an Mog sez "Glaory Allelloolier!"; an then e called me Braddher, an dahned me as if Aw was a kid and e was me mather worshin me a Setterda nawt. Aw ednt jast nao shaow wiv im at all. Arf the street pryed; an the tather arf larfed fit to split theirselves. [*To Barbara*] There! are you settisfawd nah?

BARBARA [*her eyes dancing*] Wish I'd been there, Bill.

BILL. Yus: youd a got in a hextra bit o talk on me, wouldnt you?

JENNY. I'm so sorry, Mr Walker.

BILL [*fiercely*] Downt you gow bein sorry for me: youve no call. Listen eah. Aw browk your jawr.

JENNY. No, it didnt hurt me: indeed it didnt, except for a moment. It was only that I was frightened.

BILL. Aw downt want to be forgive be you, or be ennybody. Wot Aw did Aw'll py for. Aw trawd to gat me aown jawr browk to settisfaw you—

JENNY [*distressed*] Oh no—

BILL [*impatiently*] Tell y' Aw did: cawnt you listen to wots bein taold you? All Aw got be it was being mide a sawt of in the public street for me pines. Well, if Aw cawnt settisfaw you one wy, Aw ken anather. Listen eah! Aw ed two quid[4] sived agen the frost; an Awve a pahnd of it left. A mite o mawn last week ed words with the judy e's gowin to merry. E give er wot-for; an e's bin fawnd fifteen bob.[5] E ed a rawt to itt er cause they was gowin to be merrid; but Aw ednt nao rawt to itt you; sao put anather fawv bob on an call it a pahnd's worth. [*He produces a sovereign*].[6] Eahs the manney. Tike it; and lets ev no more o your forgivin an pryin and your Mijor jawrin me. Let wot Aw dan be dan an pide for; and let there be a end of it.

JENNY. Oh, I couldnt take it, Mr Walker. But if you would give a shilling or two to poor Rummy Mitchens! you really did hurt her; and she's old.

BILL [*contemptuously*] Not lawkly. Aw'd give her anather as soon as look at er. Let her ev the lawr o me as she threatened! She aint forgiven me: not mach. Wot Aw dan to er is not on me mawnd—wot she [*indicating Barbara*] mawt call on me conscience—no more than stickin a pig. It's this Christian gime o yours that Aw wownt ev plyed agen me: this bloomin forgivin an neggin an jawrin that mikes a menn thet sore that iz lawf's a burdn to im. Aw wownt ev it, Aw tell you; sao tike your manney and stop thraowin your silly beshed fice hap agen me.

JENNY. Major: may I take a little of it for the Army?

BARBARA. No: the Army is not to be bought. We want your soul, Bill; and we'll take nothing less.

BILL [*bitterly*] Aw knaow. Me an maw few shillins is not good enaff for you. Youre a earl's grendorter, you are. Nathink less than a anderd pahnd for you.

UNDERSHAFT. Come, Barbara! you could do a great deal of good with a hundred pounds. If you will set this gentleman's mind at ease by taking his pound, I will give the other ninety-nine.

Bill, dazed by such opulence, instinctively touches his cap.

BARBARA. Oh, youre too extravagant, papa. Bill offers twenty pieces of silver. All you need offer is the other ten.[7] That will make the standard price to buy anybody who's for sale. I'm not; and the Army's not. [*To Bill*] Youll never have another quiet moment, Bill, until you come round to us. You cant stand out against your salvation.

4. "Quid" is slang for a pound note.
5. A "bob" is a shilling, or 1/20 of a pound.
6. A sovereign is a gold coin worth a pound.
7. Bill's sovereign is twenty silver shillings; the thirty "pieces of silver" was Judas' reward for betraying Jesus.

BILL [*sullenly*] Aw cawnt stand aht agen music awl wrastlers and awtful tangued women. Awve offered to py. Aw can do no more. Tike it or leave it. There it is. [*He throws the sovereign on the drum, and sits down on the horse-trough. The coin fascinates Snobby Price, who takes an early opportunity of dropping his cap on it*].

Mrs Baines comes from the shelter. She is dressed as a Salvation Army Commissioner. She is an earnest looking woman of about 40, with a caressing, urgent voice, and an appealing manner.

BARBARA. This is my father, Mrs Baines [*Undershaft comes from the table, taking his hat off with marked civility*]. Try what you can do with him. He wont listen to me, because he remembers what a fool I was when I was a baby. [*She leaves them together and chats with Jenny*].

MRS BAINES. Have you been shewn over the shelter, Mr Undershaft? You know the work we're doing, of course.

UNDERSHAFT [*very civilly*] The whole nation knows it, Mrs Baines.

MRS BAINES. No, sir: the whole nation does not know it, or we should not be crippled as we are for want of money to carry our work through the length and breadth of the land. Let me tell you that there would have been rioting this winter in London but for us.

UNDERSHAFT. You really think so?

MRS BAINES. I know it. I remember 1886, when you rich gentlemen hardened your hearts against the cry of the poor. They broke the windows of your clubs in Pall Mall.

UNDERSHAFT [*gleaming with approval of their method*] And the Mansion House Fund went up next day from thirty thousand pounds to seventy-nine thousand! I remember quite well.

MRS BAINES. Well, wont you help me to get at the people? They wont break windows then. Come here, Price. Let me shew you to this gentleman [*Price comes to be inspected*]. Do you remember the window breaking?

PRICE. My ole father thought it was the revolution, maam.

MRS BAINES. Would you break windows now?

PRICE. Oh no, maam. The windows of eaven av bin opened to me. I know now that the rich man is a sinner like myself.

RUMMY [*appearing above at the loft door*] Snobby Price!

SNOBBY. Wot is it?

RUMMY. Your mother's askin for you at the other gate in Cripps's Lane. She's heard about your confession [*Price turns pale*].

MRS BAINES. Go, Mr Price; and pray with her.

JENNY. You can go through the shelter, Snobby.

PRICE [*to Mrs Baines*] I couldnt face her now, maam, with all the weight of my sins fresh on me. Tell her she'll find her son at ome, waitin for her in prayer. [*He skulks off through the gate, incidentally stealing the sovereign on his way out by picking up his cap from the drum*].

MRS BAINES [*with swimming eyes*] You see how we take the anger and the bitterness against you out of their hearts, Mr Undershaft.

UNDERSHAFT. It is certainly most convenient and gratifying to all large employers of labor, Mrs Baines.

MRS BAINES. Barbara: Jenny: I have good news: most wonderful news. [*Jenny runs to her*]. My prayers have been answered. I told you they would, Jenny, didnt I?

JENNY. Yes, yes.

BARBARA [*moving nearer to the drum*] Have we got money enough to keep the shelter open?

MRS BAINES. I hope we shall have enough to keep all the shelters open. Lord Saxmundham has promised us five thousand pounds—

BARBARA. Hooray!

JENNY. Glory!

MRS BAINES. —if—

BARBARA. "If!" If what?

MRS BAINES. —if five other gentlemen will give a thousand each to make it up to ten thousand.

BARBARA. Who is Lord Saxmundham? I never heard of him.

UNDERSHAFT [*who has pricked up his ears at the peer's name, and is now watching Barbara curiously*] A new creation, my dear. You have heard of Sir Horace Bodger?

BARBARA. Bodger! Do you mean the distiller? Bodger's whisky!

UNDERSHAFT. That is the man. He is one of the greatest of our public benefactors. He restored the cathedral at Hakington. They made him a baronet for that. He gave half a million to the funds of his party: they made him a baron for that.

SHIRLEY. What will they give him for the five thousand?

UNDERSHAFT. There is nothing left to give him. So the five thousand, I should think, is to save his soul.

MRS BAINES. Heaven grant it may! Oh Mr Undershaft, you have some very rich friends. Cant you help us towards the other five thousand? We are going to hold a great meeting this afternoon at the Assembly Hall in the Mile End Road. If I could only announce that one gentleman had come forward to support Lord Saxmundham, others would follow. Dont you know somebody? couldnt you? wouldnt you? [*her eyes fill with tears*] oh, think of those poor people, Mr Undershaft: think of how much it means to them, and how little to a great man like you.

UNDERSHAFT [*sardonically gallant*] Mrs Baines: you are irresistible. I cant disappoint you; and I cant deny myself the satisfaction of making Bodger pay up. You shall have your five thousand pounds.

MRS BAINES. Thank God!

UNDERSHAFT. You dont thank m e?

MRS BAINES. Oh sir, dont try to be cynical: dont be ashamed of being a good man. The Lord will bless you abundantly; and our prayers will be like a strong fortification round you all the days of your life. [*With a touch of caution*] You will let me have the cheque to shew at the meeting, wont you? Jenny: go in and fetch a pen and ink. [*Jenny runs to the shelter door*].

UNDERSHAFT. Do not disturb Miss Hill: I have a fountain pen [*Jenny halts. He sits at the table and writes the cheque. Cusins rises to make room for him. They all watch him silently*].

BILL [*cynically, aside to Barbara, his voice and accent horribly debased*] Wot prawce selvytion nah?

BARBARA. Stop. [*Undershaft stops writing: they all turn to her in surprise*]. Mrs Baines: are you really going to take this money?

MRS BAINES [*astonished*] Why not, dear?

BARBARA. Why not! Do you know what my father is? Have you forgotten that Lord Saxmundham is Bodger the whisky man? Do you remember how we implored the County Council to stop him from writing Bodger's Whisky in letters of fire against the sky; so that the poor drink-ruined creatures on the Embankment could not wake up from their snatches of sleep without being reminded of their deadly thirst by that wicked sky sign? Do you know that the worst thing I have had to fight here is not the devil, but Bodger, Bodger, Bodger, with his whisky, his distilleries, and his tied houses?[8] Are you going to make our shelter another tied house for him, and ask me to keep it?

BILL. Rotten dranken whisky it is too.

MRS BAINES. Dear Barbara: Lord Saxmundham has a soul to be saved like any of us. If heaven has found the way to make a good use of his money, are we to set ourselves up against the answer to our prayers?

BARBARA. I know he has a soul to be saved. Let him come down here; and I'll do my best to help him to his salvation. But he wants to send his cheque down to buy us, and go on being as wicked as ever.

UNDERSHAFT [*with a reasonableness which Cusins alone perceives to be ironical*] My dear Barbara: alcohol is a very necessary article. It heals the sick—

BARBARA. It does nothing of the sort.

UNDERSHAFT. Well, it assists the doctor: that is perhaps a less questionable way of putting it. It makes life bearable to millions of people who could not endure their existence if they were quite sober. It enables Parliament to do things at eleven at night that no sane person would do at eleven in the morning. Is it Bodger's fault that this inestimable gift is deplorably abused by less than one per cent of the poor? [*He turns again to the table; signs the cheque; and crosses it*].

MRS BAINES. Barbara: will there be less drinking or more if all those poor souls we are saving come tomorrow and find the doors of our shelters shut in their faces? Lord Saxmundham gives us

---

8. Taverns owned by brewing firms which require the manager to handle only their whiskey.

the money to stop drinking—to take his own business from him.

CUSINS [*impishly*] Pure self-sacrifice on Bodger's part, clearly! Bless dear Bodger! [*Barbara almost breaks down as Adolphus, too, fails her*].

UNDERSHAFT [*tearing out the cheque and pocketing the book as he rises and goes past Cusins to Mrs Baines*] I also, Mrs Baines, may claim a little disinterestedness. Think of my business! think of the widows and orphans! the men and lads torn to pieces with shrapnel and poisoned with lyddite![9] [*Mrs Baines shrinks; but he goes on remorselessly*] the oceans of blood, not one drop of which is shed in a really just cause! the ravaged crops! the peaceful peasant forced, women and men, to till their fields, under the fire of opposing armies on pain of starvation! the bad blood of the fierce little cowards at home who egg on others to fight for the gratification of their national vanity! All this makes money for me: I am never richer, never busier than when the papers are full of it. Well, it is your work to preach peace on earth and goodwill to men. [*Mrs Baines's face lights up again*]. Every convert you make is a vote against war. [*Her lips move in prayer*]. Yet I give you this money to help you to hasten my own commercial ruin. [*He gives her the cheque*].

CUSINS [*mounting the form in an ecstasy of mischief*] The millennium will be inaugurated by the unselfishness of Undershaft and Bodger. Oh be joyful! [*He takes the drum-sticks from his pocket and flourishes them*].

MRS BAINES [*taking the cheque*] The longer I live the more proof I see that there is an Infinite Goodness that turns everything to the work of salvation sooner or later. Who would have thought that any good could have come out of war and drink? And yet their profits are brought today to the feet of salvation to do its blessed work. [*She is affected to tears*].

JENNY [*running to Mrs Baines and throwing her arms around her*] Oh dear! how blessed, how glorious it all is!

CUSINS [*in a convulsion of irony*] Let us seize this unspeakable moment. Let us march to the great meeting at once. Excuse me just an instant. [*He rushes into the shelter. Jenny takes her tambourine from the drum head*].

MRS BAINES. Mr Undershaft: have you ever seen a thousand people fall on their knees with one impulse and pray? Come with us to the meeting. Barbara shall tell them that the Army is saved, and saved through you.

CUSINS [*returning impetuously from the shelter with a flag and a trombone, and coming between Mrs Baines and Undershaft*] You shall carry the flag down the first street, Mrs Baines [*he gives her the flag*]. Mr Undershaft is a gifted trombonist: he shall intone an Olympian diapason to the West Ham Salvation March. [*Aside to Undershaft, as he forces the trombone on him*] Blow, Machiavelli, blow.

9. An explosive.

UNDERSHAFT [*aside to him, as he takes the trombone*] The trumpet in Zion! [*Cusins rushes to the drum, which he takes up and puts on. Undershaft continues, aloud*] I will do my best. I could vamp a bass if I knew the tune.

CUSINS. It is a wedding chorus from one of Donizetti's operas; but we have converted it. We convert everything to good here, including Bodger. You remember the chorus. "For thee immense rejoicing—immenso giubilo—immenso giubilo." [*With drum obbligato*] Rum tum ti tum, tum tum ti ta—

BARBARA. Dolly: you are breaking my heart.

CUSINS. What is a broken heart more or less here? Dionysos Undershaft has descended. I am possessed.

MRS BAINES. Come, Barbara: I must have my dear Major to carry the flag with me.

JENNY. Yes, yes, Major darling.

CUSINS [*snatches the tambourine out of Jenny's hand and mutely offers it to Barbara*].

BARBARA [*coming forward a little as she puts the offer behind her with a shudder, whilst Cusins recklessly tosses the tambourine back to Jenny and goes to the gate*] I cant come.

JENNY. Not come!

MRS BAINES [*with tears in her eyes*] Barbara: do you think I am wrong to take the money?

BARBARA [*impulsively going to her and kissing her*] No, no: God help you, dear, you must: you are saving the Army. Go; and may you have a great meeting!

JENNY. But arnt you coming?

BARBARA. No. [*She begins taking off the silver S brooch from her collar*].

MRS BAINES. Barbara: what are you doing?

JENNY. Why are you taking your badge off? You cant be going to leave us, Major.

BARBARA [*quietly*] Father: come here.

UNDERSHAFT [*coming to her*] My dear! [*Seeing that she is going to pin the badge on his collar, he retreats to the penthouse in some alarm*].

BARBARA [*following him*] Dont be frightened. [*She pins the badge on and steps back towards the table, shewing him to the others*] There! It's not much for £5000, is it?

MRS BAINES. Barbara: if you wont come and pray with us, promise me you will pray for us.

BARBARA. I cant pray now. Perhaps I shall never pray again.

MRS BAINES. Barbara!

JENNY. Major!

BARBARA [*almost delirious*] I cant bear any more. Quick march!

CUSINS [*calling to the procession in the street outside*] Off we go. Play up, there! I m m e n s o   g i u b i l o. [*He gives the time with his drum; and the band strikes up the march, which rapidly becomes more distant as the procession moves briskly away*].

MRS BAINES. I must go, dear. Youre overworked: you will be all right tomorrow. We'll never lose you. Now Jenny: step out with the old flag. Blood and Fire! [*She marches out through the gate with her flag*].

JENNY. Glory Hallelujah! [*flourishing her tambourine and marching*].

UNDERSHAFT [*to Cusins, as he marches out past him easing the slide of his trombone*] "My ducats and my daughter"!

CUSINS [*following him out*] Money and gunpowder!

BARBARA. Drunkenness and Murder! My God: why hast thou forsaken me?

> *She sinks on the form with her face buried in her hands. The march passes away into silence. Bill Walker steals across to her.*

BILL [*taunting*] Wot prawce selvytion nah?

SHIRLEY. Dont you hit her when she's down.

BILL. She itt me wen aw wiz dahn. Waw shouldnt Aw git a bit o me aown beck?

BARBARA [*raising her head*] I didnt take your money, Bill. [*She crosses the yard to the gate and turns her back on the two men to hide her face from them*].

BILL [*sneering after her*] Naow, it warnt enaff for you. [*Turning to the drum, he misses the money*] Ellow! If you aint took it sammun else ez. Weres it gorn? Bly me if Jenny Ill didnt tike it arter all!

RUMMY [*screaming at him from the loft*] You lie, you dirty blackguard! Snobby Price pinched it off the drum when he took up his cap. I was up here all the time an see im do it.

BILL. Wot! Stowl maw manney! Waw didnt you call thief on him, you silly aold macker you?

RUMMY. To serve you aht for ittin me acrost the fice. It's cost y'pahnd, that az. [*Raising a pæan of squalid triumph*] I done you. I'm even with you. Ive ad it aht o y— [*Bill snatches up Shirley's mug and hurls it at her. She slams the loft door and vanishes. The mug smashes against the door and falls in fragments*].

BILL [*beginning to chuckle*] Tell us, aol menn, wot o'clock this mawnin was it wen im as they call Snobby Prawce was sived?

BARBARA [*turning to him more composedly, and with unspoiled sweetness*] About half past twelve, Bill. And he pinched your pound at a quarter to two. I know. Well, you cant afford to lose it. I'll send it to you.

BILL [*his voice and accent suddenly improving*] Not if Aw wiz to stawve for it. Aw aint to be bought.

SHIRLEY. Aint you? Youd sell yourself to the devil for a pint o beer; only there aint no devil to make the offer.

BILL [*unshamed*] Sao Aw would, mite, and often ev, cheerful. But she cawnt baw me. [*Approaching Barbara*] You wanted maw saoul, did you? Well, you aint got it.

BARBARA. I nearly got it, Bill. But weve sold it back to you for ten thousand pounds.

SHIRLEY. And dear at the money!

BARBARA. No, Peter: it was worth more than money.

BILL [*salvationproof*] It's nao good: you cawnt get rahnd me nah. Aw downt blieve in it; and Awve seen tody that Aw was rawt. [*Going*] Sao long, aol soupkitchener! Ta, ta, Mijor Earl's Grendorter! [*Turning at the gate*] Wot prawce selvytion nah? Snobby Prawce! Ha! ha!

BARBARA [*offering her hand*] Goodbye, Bill.

BILL [*taken aback, half plucks his cap off; then shoves it on again defiantly*] Git aht. [*Barbara drops her hand, discouraged. He has a twinge of remorse*]. But thets aw rawt, you knaow. Nathink pasnl. Naow mellice. Sao long, Judy. [*He goes*].

BARBARA. No malice. So long, Bill.

SHIRLEY [*shaking his head*] You make too much of him, miss, in your innocence.

BARBARA [*going to him*] Peter: I'm like you now. Cleaned out, and lost my job.

SHIRLEY. Youve youth an hope. Thats two better than me.

BARBARA. I'll get you a job, Peter. Thats hope for you: the youth will have to be enough for me. [*She counts her money*]. I have just enough left for two teas at Lockharts, a Rowton doss[1] for you, and my tram and bus home. [*He frowns and rises with offended pride. She takes his arm*]. Dont be proud, Peter: it's sharing between friends. And promise me youll talk to me and not let me cry. [*She draws him towards the gate*].

SHIRLEY. Well, I'm not accustomed to talk to the like of you—

BARBARA [*urgently*] Yes, yes: you must talk to me. Tell me about Tom Paine's books and Bradlaugh's lectures.[2] Come along.

SHIRLEY. Ah, if you would only read Tom Paine in the proper spirit, miss! [*They go out through the gate together*].

1. A bed in one of Rowton's cheap rooming houses.
2. A slight anachronism: Charles Bradlaugh, the great secularist, died in 1891.

Act III

Next day after lunch Lady Britomart is writing in the library in
Wilton Crescent. Sarah is reading in the armchair near the window.
Barbara, in ordinary fashionable dress, pale and brooding, is on the
settee. Charles Lomax enters. He starts on seeing Barbara fashion-
ably attired and in low spirits.

LOMAX. Youve left off your uniform!
> *Barbara says nothing; but an expression of pain passes over*
> *her face.*

LADY BRITOMART [*warning him in low tones to be careful*] Charles!

LOMAX [*much concerned, coming behind the settee and bending*
sympathetically over Barbara] I'm awfully sorry, Barbara. You
know I helped you all I could with the concertina and so forth.
[*Momentously*] Still, I have never shut my eyes to the fact that
there is a certain amount of tosh about the Salvation Army. Now
the claims of the Church of England—

LADY BRITOMART. Thats enough, Charles. Speak of something
suited to your mental capacity.

LOMAX. But surely the Church of England is suited to all our
capacities.

BARBARA [*pressing his hand*] Thank you for your sympathy,
Cholly. Now go and spoon with Sarah.

LOMAX [*dragging a chair from the writing table and seating himself*
affectionately by Sarah's side] How is my ownest today?

SARAH. I wish you wouldnt tell Cholly to do things, Barbara. He
always comes straight and does them. Cholly: we're going to the
works this afternoon.

LOMAX. What works?

SARAH. The cannon works.

LOMAX. What? your governor's shop!

SARAH. Yes.

LOMAX. Oh I say!
> *Cusins enters in poor condition. He also starts visibly when*
> *he sees Barbara without her uniform.*

BARBARA. I expected you this morning, Dolly. Didnt you guess
that?

CUSINS [*sitting down beside her*] I'm sorry. I have only just break-
fasted.

SARAH. But weve just finished lunch.

BARBARA. Have you had one of your bad nights?

CUSINS. No: I had rather a good night: in fact, one of the most
remarkable nights I have ever passed.

BARBARA. The meeting?

CUSINS. No: after the meeting.

LADY BRITOMART. You should have gone to bed after the meeting. What were you doing?

CUSINS. Drinking.

LADY BRITOMART.	Adolphus!
SARAH.	Dolly!
BARBARA.	Dolly!
LOMAX.	Oh I say!

LADY BRITOMART. What were you drinking, may I ask?

CUSINS. A most devilish kind of Spanish burgundy, warranted free from added alcohol: a Temperance burgundy in fact. Its richness in natural alcohol made any addition superfluous.

BARBARA. Are you joking, Dolly?

CUSINS [*patiently*] No. I have been making a night of it with the nominal head of this household: that is all.

LADY BRITOMART. Andrew made you drunk!

CUSINS. No: he only provided the wine. I think it was Dionysos who made me drunk. [*To Barbara*] I told you I was possessed.

LADY BRITOMART. Youre not sober yet. Go home to bed at once.

CUSINS. I have never before ventured to reproach you, Lady Brit; but how could you marry the Prince of Darkness?

LADY BRITOMART. It was much more excusable to marry him than to get drunk with him. That is a new accomplishment of Andrew's, by the way. He usent to drink.

CUSINS. He doesnt now. He only sat there and completed the wreck of my moral basis, the rout of my convictions, the purchase of my soul. He cares for you, Barbara. That is what makes him so dangerous to me.

BARBARA. That has nothing to do with it, Dolly. There are larger loves and diviner dreams than the fireside ones. You know that, dont you?

CUSINS. Yes: that is our understanding. I know it. I hold to it. Unless he can win me on that holier ground he may amuse me for a while; but he can get no deeper hold, strong as he is.

BARBARA. Keep to that; and the end will be right. Now tell me what happened at the meeting?

CUSINS. It was an amazing meeting. Mrs Baines almost died of emotion. Jenny Hill simply gibbered with hysteria. The Prince of Darkness played his trombone like a madman: its brazen roarings were like the laughter of the damned. 117 conversions took place then and there. They prayed with the most touching sincerity and gratitude for Bodger, and for the anonymous donor of the £5000. Your father would not let his name be given.

LOMAX. That was rather fine of the old man, you know. Most chaps would have wanted the advertisement.

CUSINS. He said all the charitable institutions would be down on him like kites on a battle-field if he gave his name.

LADY BRITOMART. Thats Andrew all over. He never does a proper thing without giving an improper reason for it.

CUSINS. He convinced me that I have all my life been doing improper things for proper reasons.

LADY BRITOMART. Adolphus: now that Barbara has left the Salvation Army, you had better leave it too. I will not have you playing that drum in the streets.

CUSINS. Your orders are already obeyed, Lady Brit.

BARBARA. Dolly: were you ever really in earnest about it? Would you have joined if you had never seen me?

CUSINS [*disingenuously*] Well—er—well, possibly, as a collector of religions—

LOMAX [*cunningly*] Not as a drummer, though, you know. You are a very clearheaded brainy chap, Dolly; and it must have been apparent to you that there is a certain amount of tosh about—

LADY BRITOMART. Charles: if you must drivel, drivel like a grown-up man and not like a schoolboy.

LOMAX [*out of countenance*] Well, drivel is drivel, dont you know, whatever a man's age.

LADY BRITOMART. In good society in England, Charles, men drivel at all ages by repeating silly formulas with an air of wisdom. Schoolboys make their own formulas out of slang, like you. When they reach your age, and get political private secretaryships and things of that sort, they drop slang and get their formulas out of The Spectator or The Times. You had better confine yourself to The Times. You will find that there is a certain amount of tosh about The Times; but at least its language is reputable.

LOMAX [*overwhelmed*] You are so awfully strong-minded, Lady Brit—

LADY BRITOMART. Rubbish! [*Morrison comes in*]. What is it?

MORRISON. If you please, my lady, Mr Undershaft has just drove up to the door.

LADY BRITOMART. Well, let him in. [*Morrison hesitates*]. Whats the matter with you?

MORRISON. Shall I announce him, my lady; or is he at home here, so to speak, my lady?

LADY BRITOMART. Announce him.

MORRISON. Thank you, my lady. You wont mind my asking, I hope. The occasion is in a manner of speaking new to me.

LADY BRITOMART. Quite right. Go and let him in.

MORRISON. Thank you, my lady. [*He withdraws*].

LADY BRITOMART. Children: go and get ready. [*Sarah and Barbara go upstairs for their out-of-door wraps*]. Charles: go and tell Stephen to come down here in five minutes: you will find him in the drawing room. [*Charles goes*]. Adolphus: tell them to send round the carriage in about fifteen minutes. [*Adolphus goes*].

MORRISON [*at the door*] Mr Undershaft.

Undershaft comes in. Morrison goes out.

UNDERSHAFT. Alone! How fortunate!

LADY BRITOMART [*rising*] Dont be sentimental, Andrew. Sit down.

[*She sits on the settee: he sits beside her, on her left. She comes to the point before he has time to breathe*]. Sarah must have £800 a year until Charles Lomax comes into his property. Barbara will need more, and need it permanently, because Adolphus hasnt any property.

UNDERSHAFT [*resignedly*] Yes, my dear: I will see to it. Anything else? for yourself, for instance?

LADY BRITOMART. I want to talk to you about Stephen.

UNDERSHAFT [*rather wearily*] Dont, my dear. Stephen doesnt interest me.

LADY BRITOMART. He does interest me. He is our son.

UNDERSHAFT. Do you really think so? He has induced us to bring him into the world; but he chose his parents very incongruously, I think. I see nothing of myself in him, and less of you.

LADY BRITOMART. Andrew: Stephen is an excellent son, and a most steady, capable, highminded young man. You are simply trying to find an excuse for disinheriting him.

UNDERSHAFT. My dear Biddy: the Undershaft tradition disinherits him. It would be dishonest of me to leave the cannon foundry to my son.

LADY BRITOMART. It would be most unnatural and improper of you to leave it to anyone else, Andrew. Do you suppose this wicked and immoral tradition can be kept up for ever? Do you pretend that Stephen could not carry on the foundry just as well as all the other sons of the big business houses?

UNDERSHAFT. Yes: he could learn the office routine without understanding the business, like all the other sons; and the firm would go on by its own momentum until the real Undershaft—probably an Italian or a German—would invent a new method and cut him out.

LADY BRITOMART. There is nothing that any Italian or German could do that Stephen could not do. And Stephen at least has breeding.

UNDERSHAFT. The son of a foundling! Nonsense!

LADY BRITOMART. My son, Andrew! And even you may have good blood in your veins for all you know.

UNDERSHAFT. True. Probably I have. That is another argument in favor of a foundling.

LADY BRITOMART. Andrew: dont be aggravating. And dont be wicked. At present you are both.

UNDERSHAFT. This conversation is part of the Undershaft tradition, Biddy. Every Undershaft's wife has treated him to it ever since the house was founded. It is a mere waste of breath. If the tradition be ever broken it will be for an abler man than Stephen.

LADY BRITOMART [*pouting*] Then go away.

UNDERSHAFT [*deprecatory*] Go away!

LADY BRITOMART. Yes: go away. If you will do nothing for Stephen, you are not wanted here. Go to your foundling, whoever he is; and look after him.

UNDERSHAFT. The fact is, Biddy—

LADY BRITOMART. Dont call me Biddy. I dont call you Andy.

UNDERSHAFT. I will not call my wife Britomart: it is not good sense. Seriously, my love, the Undershaft tradition has landed me in a difficulty. I am getting on in years; and my partner Lazarus has at last made a stand and insisted that the succession must be settled one way or the other; and of course he is quite right. You see, I havnt found a fit successor yet.

LADY BRITOMART. [*obstinately*] There is Stephen.

UNDERSHAFT. Thats just it: all the foundlings I can find are exactly like Stephen.

LADY BRITOMART. Andrew!!

UNDERSHAFT. I want a man with no relations and no schooling: that is, a man who would be out of the running altogether if he were not a strong man. And I cant find him. Every blessed foundling nowadays is snapped up in his infancy by Barnardo homes, or School Board officers, or Boards of Guardians; and if he shews the least ability he is fastened on by schoolmasters; trained to win scholarships like a racehorse; crammed with secondhand ideas; drilled and disciplined in docility and what they call good taste; and lamed for life so that he is fit for nothing but teaching. If you want to keep the foundry in the family, you had better find an eligible foundling and marry him to Barbara.

LADY BRITOMART. Ah! Barbara! Your pet! You would sacrifice Stephen to Barbara.

UNDERSHAFT. Cheerfully. And you, my dear, would boil Barbara to make soup for Stephen.

LADY BRITOMART. Andrew: this is not a question of our likings and dislikings: it is a question of duty. It is your duty to make Stephen your successor.

UNDERSHAFT. Just as much as it is your duty to submit to your husband. Come, Biddy! these tricks of the governing class are of no use with me. I am one of the governing class myself; and it is a waste of time giving tracts to a missionary. I have the power in this matter; and I am not to be humbugged into using it for your purposes.

LADY BRITOMART. Andrew: you can talk my head off; but you cant change wrong into right. And your tie is all on one side. Put it straight.

UNDERSHAFT [*disconcerted*] It wont stay unless it's pinned [*he fumbles at it with childish grimaces*]—
    Stephen comes in.

STEPHEN [*at the door*] I beg your pardon [*about to retire*].

LADY BRITOMART. No: come in, Stephen. [*Stephen comes forward to his mother's writing table*].

UNDERSHAFT [*not very cordially*] Good afternoon.

STEPHEN [*coldly*] Good afternoon.

UNDERSHAFT [*to Lady Britomart*] He knows all about the tradition, I suppose?

LADY BRITOMART. Yes. [*To Stephen*] It is what I told you last night, Stephen.

UNDERSHAFT [*sulkily*] I understand you want to come into the cannon business.

STEPHEN. *I* go into trade! Certainly not.

UNDERSHAFT [*opening his eyes, greatly eased in mind and manner*] Oh! in that case—

LADY BRITOMART. Cannons are not trade, Stephen. They are enterprise.

STEPHEN. I have no intention of becoming a man of business in any sense. I have no capacity for business and no taste for it. I intend to devote myself to politics.

UNDERSHAFT [*rising*] My dear boy: this is an immense relief to me. And I trust it may prove an equally good thing for the country. I was afraid you would consider yourself disparaged and slighted. [*He moves towards Stephen as if to shake hands with him*].

LADY BRITOMART [*rising and interposing*] Stephen: I cannot allow you to throw away an enormous property like this.

STEPHEN [*stiffly*] Mother: there must be an end of treating me as a child, if you please [*Lady Britomart recoils, deeply wounded by his tone*]. Until last night I did not take your attitude seriously, because I did not think you meant it seriously. But I find now that you left me in the dark as to matters which you should have explained to me years ago. I am extremely hurt and offended. Any further discussion of my intentions had better take place with my father, as between one man and another.

LADY BRITOMART. Stephen! [*She sits down again, her eyes filling with tears*].

UNDERSHAFT [*with grave compassion*] You see, my dear, it is only the big men who can be treated as children.

STEPHEN. I am sorry, mother, that you have forced me—

UNDERSHAFT [*stopping him*] Yes, yes, yes, yes: thats all right, Stephen. She wont interfere with you any more: your independence is achieved: you have won your latchkey. Dont rub it in; and above all, dont apologize. [*He resumes his seat*]. Now what about your future, as between one man and another—I beg your pardon, Biddy: as between two men and a woman.

LADY BRITOMART [*who has pulled herself together strongly*] I quite understand, Stephen. By all means go your own way if you feel strong enough. [*Stephen sits down magisterially in the chair at the writing table with an air of affirming his majority*].

UNDERSHAFT. It is settled that you do not ask for the succession to the cannon business.

STEPHEN. I hope it is settled that I repudiate the cannon business.

UNDERSHAFT. Come, come! dont be so devilishly sulky: it's boyish. Freedom should be generous. Besides, I owe you a fair start in life in exchange for disinheriting you. You cant become prime minister all at once. Havnt you a turn for something? What about literature, art, and so forth?

STEPHEN. I have nothing of the artist about me, either in faculty or character, thank Heaven!

UNDERSHAFT. A philosopher, perhaps? Eh?

STEPHEN. I make no such ridiculous pretension.

UNDERSHAFT. Just so. Well, there is the army, the navy, the Church, the Bar. The Bar requires some ability. What about the Bar?

STEPHEN. I have not studied law. And I am afraid I have not the necessary push—I believe that is the name barristers give to their vulgarity—for success in pleading.

UNDERSHAFT. Rather a difficult case, Stephen. Hardly anything left but the stage, is there? [*Stephen makes an impatient movement*]. Well, come! is there anything you know or care for?

STEPHEN [*rising and looking at him steadily*] I know the difference between right and wrong.

UNDERSHAFT [*hugely tickled*] You dont say so! What! no capacity for business, no knowledge of law, no sympathy with art, no pretension to philosophy; only a simple knowledge of the secret that has puzzled all the philosophers, baffled all the lawyers, muddled all the men of business, and ruined most of the artists: the secret of right and wrong. Why, man, youre a genius, a master of masters, a god! At twentyfour, too!

STEPHEN [*keeping his temper with difficulty*] You are pleased to be facetious. I pretend to nothing more than any honorable English gentleman claims as his birthright [*he sits down angrily*].

UNDERSHAFT. Oh, thats everybody's birthright. Look at poor little Jenny Hill, the Salvation lassie! she would think you were laughing at her if you asked her to stand up in the street and teach grammar or geography or mathematics or even drawing room dancing; but it never occurs to her to doubt that she can teach morals and religion. You are all alike, you respectable people. You cant tell me the bursting strain of a ten-inch gun, which is a very simple matter; but you all think you can tell me the bursting strain of a man under temptation. You darent handle high explosives; but youre all ready to handle honesty and truth and justice and the whole duty of man, and kill one another at that game. What a country! What a world!

LADY BRITOMART [*uneasily*] What do you think he had better do, Andrew?

UNDERSHAFT. Oh, just what he wants to do. He knows nothing and he thinks he knows everything. That points clearly to a political career. Get him a private secretaryship to someone who can get him an Under Secretaryship; and then leave him alone. He will find his natural and proper place in the end on the Treasury Bench.

STEPHEN [*springing up again*] I am sorry, sir, that you force me to forget the respect due to you as my father. I am an Englishman and I will not hear the Government of my country insulted. [*He thrusts his hands in his pockets, and walks angrily across to the window*].

UNDERSHAFT [*with a touch of brutality*] The government of your country! *I* am the government of your country: I, and Lazarus. Do you suppose that you and half a dozen amateurs like you, sitting in a row in that foolish gabble shop, can govern Undershaft and Lazarus? No, my friend: you will do what pays us. You will make war when it suits us, and keep peace when it doesnt. You will find out that trade requires certain measures when we have decided on those measures. When I want anything to keep my dividends up, you will discover that my want is a national need. When other people want something to keep my dividends down, you will call out the police and military. And in return you shall have the support and applause of my newspapers, and the delight of imagining that you are a great statesman. Government of your country! Be off with you, my boy, and play with your caucuses and leading articles and historic parties and great leaders and burning questions and the rest of your toys. *I* am going back to my counting-house to pay the piper and call the tune.

STEPHEN [*actually smiling, and putting his hand on his father's shoulder with indulgent patronage*] Really, my dear father, it is impossible to be angry with you. You dont know how absurd all this sounds to me. You are very properly proud of having been industrious enough to make money; and it is greatly to your credit that you have made so much of it. But it has kept you in circles where you are valued for your money and deferred to for it, instead of in the doubtless very old-fashioned and behind-the-times public school and university where I formed my habits of mind. It is natural for you to think that money governs England; but you must allow me to think I know better.

UNDERSHAFT. And what does govern England, pray?

STEPHEN. Character, father, character.

UNDERSHAFT. Whose character? Yours or mine?

STEPHEN. Neither yours nor mine, father, but the best elements in the English national character.

UNDERSHAFT. Stephen: Ive found your profession for you. Youre a born journalist. I'll start you with a high-toned weekly review. There!

Before Stephen can reply Sarah, Barbara, Lomax, and Cusins come in ready for walking. Barbara crosses the room to the window and looks out. Cusins drifts amiably to the armchair. Lomax remains near the door, whilst Sarah comes to her mother.

Stephen goes to the smaller writing table and busies himself with his letters.

SARAH. Go and get ready, mama: the carriage is waiting. [*Lady Britomart leaves the room*].

UNDERSHAFT [*to Sarah*] Good day, my dear. Good afternoon, Mr Lomax.

LOMAX [*vaguely*] Ahdedoo.

UNDERSHAFT [*to Cusins*] Quite well after last night, Euripides, eh?

CUSINS. As well as can be expected.

UNDERSHAFT. Thats right. [*To Barbara*] So you are coming to see my death and devastation factory, Barbara?

BARBARA [*at the window*] You came yesterday to see my salvation factory. I promised you a return visit.

LOMAX [*coming forward between Sarah and Undershaft*] Youll find it awfully interesting. Ive been through the Woolwich Arsenal; and it gives you a ripping feeling of security, you know, to think of the lot of beggars we could kill if it came to fighting. [*To Undershaft, with sudden solemnity*] Still, it must be rather an awful reflection for you, from the religious point of view as it were. Youre getting on, you know, and all that.

SARAH. You dont mind Cholly's imbecility, papa, do you?

LOMAX [*much taken aback*] Oh I say!

UNDERSHAFT. Mr Lomax looks at the matter in a very proper spirit, my dear.

LOMAX. Just so. Thats all I meant, I assure you.

SARAH. Are you coming, Stephen?

STEPHEN. Well, I am rather busy—er— [*Magnanimously*] Oh well, yes: I'll come. That is, if there is room for me.

UNDERSHAFT. I can take two with me in a little motor I am experimenting with for field use. You wont mind its being rather unfashionable. It's not painted yet; but it's bullet proof.

LOMAX [*appalled at the prospect of confronting Wilton Crescent in an unpainted motor*] Oh I say!

SARAH. The carriage for me, thank you. Barbara doesnt mind what she's seen in.

LOMAX. I say, Dolly, old chap: do you really mind the car being a guy? Because of course if you do I'll go in it. Still—

CUSINS. I prefer it.

LOMAX. Thanks awfully, old man. Come, my ownest. [*He hurries out to secure his seat in the carriage. Sarah follows him*]...

CUSINS [*moodily walking across to Lady Britomart's writing table*] Why are we two coming to this Works Department of Hell? that is what I ask myself.

BARBARA. I have always thought of it as a sort of pit where lost creatures with blackened faces stirred up smoky fires and were driven and tormented by my father? Is it like that, dad?

UNDERSHAFT [*scandalized*] My dear! It is a spotlessly clean and beautiful hillside town.

CUSINS. With a Methodist chapel? Oh do say theres a Methodist chapel.

UNDERSHAFT. There are two: a Primitive one and a sophisticated one. There is even an Ethical Society; but it is not much patronized, as my men are all strongly religious. In the High Explosives Sheds they object to the presence of Agnostics as unsafe.

CUSINS. And yet they dont object to you!

BARBARA. Do they obey all your orders?

UNDERSHAFT. I never give them any orders. When I speak to one of them it is "Well, Jones, is the baby doing well? and has Mrs

Jones made a good recovery?" "Nicely, thank you, sir." And thats all.

CUSINS. But Jones has to be kept in order. How do you maintain discipline among your men?

UNDERSHAFT. I dont. They do. You see, the one thing Jones wont stand is any rebellion from the man under him, or any assertion of social equality between the wife of the man with 4 shillings a week less than himself, and Mrs Jones! Of course they all rebel against me, theoretically. Practically, every man of them keeps the man just below him in his place. I never meddle with them. I never bully them. I dont even bully Lazarus. I say that certain things are to be done; but I dont order anybody to do them. I dont say, mind you, that there is no ordering about and snubbing and even bullying. The men snub the boys and order them about; the carmen snub the sweepers; the artisans snub the unskilled laborers; the foremen drive and bully both the laborers and artisans; the assistant engineers find fault with the foremen; the chief engineers drop on the assistants; the departmental managers worry the chiefs; and the clerks have tall hats and hymnbooks and keep up the social tone by refusing to associate on equal terms with anybody. The result is a colossal profit, which comes to me.

CUSINS [*revolted*] You really are a—well, what I was saying yesterday.

BARBARA. What was he saying yesterday?

UNDERSHAFT. Never mind, my dear. He thinks I have made you unhappy. Have I?

BARBARA. Do you think I can be happy in this vulgar silly dress? I! who have worn the uniform. Do you understand what you have done to me? Yesterday I had a man's soul in my hand. I set him in the way of life with his face to salvation. But when we took your money he turned back to drunkenness and derision. [*With intense conviction*] I will never forgive you that. If I had a child, and you destroyed its body with your explosives—if you murdered Dolly with your horrible guns—I could forgive you if my forgiveness would open the gates of heaven to you. But to take a human soul from me, and turn it into the soul of a wolf! that is worse than any murder.

UNDERSHAFT. Does my daughter despair so easily? Can you strike a man to the heart and leave no mark on him?

BARBARA [*her face lighting up*] Oh, you are right: he can never be lost now: where was my faith?

CUSINS. Oh, clever clever devil!

BARBARA. You may be a devil; but God speaks through you sometimes [*She takes her father's hands and kisses them*]. You have given me back my happiness: I feel it deep down now, though my spirit is troubled.

UNDERSHAFT. You have learnt something. That always feels at first as if you had lost something.

BARBARA. Well, take me to the factory of death; and let me learn something more. There must be some truth or other behind all this frightful irony. Come, Dolly. [*She goes out*].

CUSINS. My guardian angel! [*To Undershaft*] Avaunt! [*He follows Barbara*].

STEPHEN [*quietly, at the writing table*] You must not mind Cusins, father. He is a very amiable good fellow; but he is a Greek scholar and naturally a little eccentric.

UNDERSHAFT. Ah, quite so. Thank you, Stephen. Thank you. [*He goes out*].

 Stephen smiles patronizingly; buttons his coat responsibly; and crosses the room to the door. Lady Britomart, dressed for out-of-doors, opens it before he reaches it. She looks round for the others; looks at Stephen; and turns to go without a word.

STEPHEN [*embarrassed*] Mother—

LADY BRITOMART. Dont be apologetic, Stephen. And dont forget that you have outgrown your mother. [*She goes out*].

Perivale St Andrews lies between two Middlesex hills, half climbing the northern one. It is an almost smokeless town of white walls, roofs of narrow green slates or red tiles, tall trees, domes, campaniles, and slender chimney shafts, beautifully situated and beautiful in itself. The best view of it is obtained from the crest of a slope about half a mile to the east, where the high explosives are dealt with. The foundry lies hidden in the depths between, the tops of its chimneys sprouting like huge skittles into the middle distance. Across the crest runs an emplacement of concrete, with a firestep, and a parapet which suggests a fortification, because there is a huge cannon of the obsolete Woolwich Infant pattern peering across it at the town. The cannon is mounted on an experimental gun carriage: possibly the original model of the Undershaft disappearing rampart gun alluded to by Stephen. The firestep, being a convenient place to sit, is furnished here and there with straw disc cushions; and at one place there is the additional luxury of a fur rug.

Barbara is standing on the firestep, looking over the parapet towards the town. On her right is the cannon; on her left the end of a shed raised on piles, with a ladder of three or four steps up to the door, which opens outwards and has a little wooden landing at the threshold, with a fire bucket in the corner of the landing. Several dummy soldiers more or less mutilated, with straw protruding from their gashes, have been shoved out of the way under the landing. A few others are nearly upright against the shed; and one has fallen forward and lies, like a grotsque corpse, on the emplacement. The parapet stops short of the shed, leaving a gap which is the beginning of the path down the hill through the foundry to the town. The rug is on the firestep near this gap. Down on the emplacement behind the cannon is a trolley carrying a huge conical bombshell with a red band painted on it. Further to the right is the door of an office, which, like the sheds, is of the lightest possible construction.

Cusins arrives by the path from the town.

BARBARA. Well?

CUSINS. Not a ray of hope. Everything perfect! wonderful! real! It only needs a cathedral to be a heavenly city instead of a hellish one.

BARBARA. Have you found out whether they have done anything for old Peter Shirley?

CUSINS. They have found him a job as gatekeeper and timekeeper. He's frightfully miserable. He calls the time-keeping brainwork, and says he isnt used to it; and his gate lodge is so splendid that he's ashamed to use the rooms, and skulks in the scullery.

BARBARA. Poor Peter!

Stephen arrives from the town. He carries a fieldglass.

STEPHEN [*enthusiastically*] Have you two seen the place? Why did you leave us?

CUSINS. I wanted to see everything I was not intended to see; and Barbara wanted to make the men talk.

STEPHEN. Have you found anything discreditable?

CUSINS. No. They call him Dandy Andy and are proud of his being a cunning old rascal; but it's all horribly, frightfully, immorally, unanswerably perfect.

Sarah arrives.

SARAH. Heavens! what a place! [*She crosses to the trolley*]. Did you see the nursing home!? [*She sits down on the shell*].

STEPHEN. Did you see the libraries and schools!?

SARAH. Did you see the ball room and the banqueting chamber in the Town Hall!?

STEPHEN. Have you gone into the insurance fund, the pension fund, the building society, the various applications of co-operation!?

Undershaft comes from the office, with a sheaf of telegrams in his hand.

UNDERSHAFT. Well, have you seen everything? I'm sorry I was called away. [*Indicating the telegrams*] Good news from Manchuria.

STEPHEN. Another Japanese victory?

UNDERSHAFT. Oh, I dont know. Which side wins does not concern us here. No: the good news is that the aerial battleship is a tremendous success. At the first trial it has wiped out a fort with three hundred soldiers in it.

CUSINS [*from the platform*] Dummy soldiers?

UNDERSHAFT [*striding across to Stephen and kicking the prostrate dummy brutally out of his way*] No: the real thing.

Cusins and Barbara exchange glances. Then Cusins sits on the step and buries his face in his hands. Barbara gravely lays her hand on his shoulder. He looks up at her in whimsical desperation.

UNDERSHAFT. Well, Stephen, what do you think of the place?

STEPHEN. Oh, magnificent. A perfect triumph of modern industry. Frankly, my dear father, I have been a fool: I had no idea of what it all meant: of the wonderful forethought, the power of organization, the administrative capacity, the financial genius, the colossal capital it represents. I have been repeating to myself as I came through your streets "Peace hath her victories no less renowned than War." I have only one misgiving about it all.

UNDERSHAFT. Out with it.

STEPHEN. Well, I cannot help thinking that all this provision for every want of your workmen may sap their independence and weaken their sense of responsibility. And greatly as we enjoyed our tea at that splendid restaurant—how they gave us all that luxury and cake and jam and cream for threepence I really cannot imagine!—still you must remember that restaurants break up home life. Look at the continent, for instance! Are you sure so much pampering is really good for the men's characters?

UNDERSHAFT. Well you see, my dear boy, when you are organizing civilization you have to make up your mind whether trouble and anxiety are good things or not. If you decide that they are, then, I take it, you simply dont organize civilization; and there you are, with trouble and anxiety enough to make us all angels! But if you decide the other way, you may as well go through with it. However, Stephen, our characters are safe here. A sufficient dose of anxiety is always provided by the fact that we may be blown to smithereens at any moment.

SARAH. By the way, papa, where do you make the explosives?

UNDERSHAFT. In separate little sheds, like that one. When one of them blows up, it costs very little; and only the people quite close to it are killed.

> *Stephen, who is quite close to it, looks at it rather scaredly, and moves away quickly to the cannon. At the same moment the door of the shed is thrown abruptly open; and a foreman in overalls and list slippers[3] comes out on the little landing and holds the door for Lomax, who appears in the doorway.*

LOMAX [*with studied coolness*] My good fellow: you neednt get into a state of nerves. Nothing's going to happen to you; and I suppose it wouldnt be the end of the world if anything did. A little bit of British pluck is what you want, old chap. [*He descends and strolls across to Sarah*].

UNDERSHAFT [*to the foreman*] Anything wrong, Bilton?

BILTON [*with ironic calm*] Gentleman walked into the high explosives shed and lit a cigaret, sir: thats all.

UNDERSHAFT. Ah, quite so. [*Going over to Lomax*] Do you happen to remember what you did with the match?

LOMAX. Oh come! I'm not a fool. I took jolly good care to blow it out before I chucked it away.

BILTON. The top of it was red hot inside, sir.

---

3. Cloth overshoes.

LOMAX. Well, suppose it was! I didn't chuck it into any of your messes.

UNDERSHAFT. Think no more of it, Mr Lomax. By the way, would you mind lending me your matches.

LOMAX [*offering his box*] Certainly.

UNDERSHAFT. Thanks. [*He pockets the matches.*]

LOMAX [*lecturing to the company generally*] You know, these high explosives dont go off like gunpowder, except when theyre in a gun. When theyre spread loose, you can put a match to them without the least risk: they just burn quietly like a bit of paper. [*Warming to the scientific interest of the subject*] Did you know that, Undershaft? Have you ever tried?

UNDERSHAFT. Not on a large scale, Mr Lomax. Bilton will give you a sample of gun cotton when you are leaving if you ask him. You can experiment with it at home. [*Bilton looks puzzled*].

SARAH. Bilton will do nothing of the sort, papa. I suppose it's your business to blow up the Russians and Japs; but you might really stop short of blowing up poor Cholly. [*Bilton gives it up and retires into the shed*].

LOMAX. My ownest, there is no danger. [*He sits beside her on the shell*].

Lady Britomart arrives from the town with a bouquet.

LADY BRITOMART [*impetuously*] Andrew: you shouldnt have let me see this place.

UNDERSHAFT. Why, my dear?

LADY BRITOMART. Never mind why: you shouldnt have: thats all. To think of all that [*indicating the town*] being yours! and that you have kept it to yourself all these years!

UNDERSHAFT. It does not belong to me. I belong to it. It is the Undershaft inheritance.

LADY BRITOMART. It is not. Your ridiculous cannons and that noisy banging foundry may be the Undershaft inheritance; but all that plate and linen, all that furniture and those houses and orchards and gardens belong to us. They belong to me: they are not a man's business. I wont give them up. You must be out of your senses to throw them all away; and if you persist in such folly, I will call in a doctor.

UNDERSHAFT [*stooping to smell the bouquet*] Where did you get the flowers, my dear?

LADY BRITOMART. Your men presented them to me in your William Morris Labor Church.[4]

CUSINS. Oh! It needed only that. A Labor Church! [*he mounts the firestep distractedly, and leans with his elbows on the parapet, turning his back to them*].

LADY BRITOMART. Yes, with Morris's words in mosaic letters ten feet high round the dome. No MAN IS GOOD ENOUGH TO BE

4. The first Labor Church was founded by John Trevor in 1891 in an attempt to transform the Labor movement into a kind of religious organization. The movement did not survive World War I.

ANOTHER MAN'S MASTER. The cynicism of it!

UNDERSHAFT. It shocked the men at first, I am afraid. But now they take no more notice of it than of the ten commandments in church.

LADY BRITOMART. Andrew: you are trying to put me off the subject of the inheritance by profane jokes. Well, you shant. I dont ask it any longer for Stephen: he has inherited far too much of your perversity to be fit for it. But Barbara has rights as well as Stephen. Why should not Adolphus succeed to the inheritance? I could manage the town for him; and he can look after the cannons, if they are really necessary.

UNDERSHAFT. I should ask nothing better if Adolphus were a foundling. He is exactly the sort of new blood that is wanted in English business. But he's not a foundling; and theres an end of it .[*He makes for the office door*].

CUSINS [*turning to them*] Not quite. [*They all turn and stare at him*]. I think—Mind! I am not committing myself in any way as to my future course—but I think the foundling difficulty can be got over. [*He jumps down to the emplacement*].

UNDERSHAFT [*coming back to him*] What do you mean?

CUSINS. Well, I have something to say which is in the nature of a confession.

SARAH.
LADY BRITOMART.
BARBARA.
STEPHEN. } Confession!

LOMAX. Oh I say!

CUSINS. Yes, a confession. Listen, all. Until I met Barbara I thought myself in the main an honorable, truthful man, because I wanted the approval of my conscience more than I wanted anything else. But the moment I saw Barbara, I wanted her far more than the approval of my conscience.

LADY BRITOMART. Adolphus!

CUSINS. It is true. You accused me yourself, Lady Brit, of joining the Army to worship Barbara; and so I did. She bought my soul like a flower at a street corner; but she bought it for herself.

UNDERSHAFT. What! Not for Dionysos or another?

CUSINS. Dionysos and all the others are in herself. I adored what was divine in her, and was therefore a true worshipper. But I was romantic about her too. I thought she was a woman of the people, and that a marriage with a professor of Greek would be far beyond the wildest social ambitions of her rank.

LADY BRITOMART. Adolphus!!

LOMAX. Oh I say!!!

CUSINS. When I learnt the horrible truth—

LADY BRITOMART. What do you mean by the horrible truth, pray?

CUSINS. That she was enormously rich; that her grandfather was an earl; that her father was the Prince of Darkness—

UNDERSHAFT. Chut!

CUSINS. —and that I was only an adventurer trying to catch a rich wife, then I stooped to deceive her about my birth.

BARBARA [*rising*] Dolly!

LADY BRITOMART. Your birth! Now Adolphus, dont dare to make up a wicked story for the sake of these wretched cannons. Remember: I have seen photographs of your parents; and the Agent General for South Western Australia knows them personally and has assured me that they are most respectable married people.

CUSINS. So they are in Australia; but here they are outcasts. Their marriage is legal in Australia, but not in England. My mother is my father's deceased wife's sister; and in this island I am consequently a foundling. [*Sensation*].[5]

BARBARA. Silly! [*She climbs to the cannon, and leans, listening, in the angle it makes with the parapet*].

CUSINS. Is the subterfuge good enough, Machiavelli?

UNDERSHAFT [*thoughtfully*] Biddy: this may be a way out of the difficulty.

LADY BRITOMART. Stuff! A man cant make cannons any the better for being his own cousin instead of his proper self [*she sits down on the rug with a bounce that expresses her downright contempt for their casuistry*].

UNDERSHAFT [*to Cusins*] You are an educated man. That is against the tradition.

CUSINS. Once in ten thousand times it happens that the schoolboy is a born master of what they try to teach him. Greek has not destroyed my mind: it has nourished it. Besides, I did not learn it at an English public school.

UNDERSHAFT. Hm! Well, I cannot afford to be too particular: you have cornered the foundling market. Let it pass. You are eligible, Euripides: you are eligible.

BARBARA. Dolly: yesterday morning, when Stephen told us all about the tradition, you became very silent; and you have been strange and excited ever since. Were you thinking of your birth then?

CUSINS. When the finger of Destiny suddenly points at a man in the middle of his breakfast, it makes him thoughtful.

UNDERSHAFT. Aha! You have had your eye on the business, my young friend, have you?

CUSINS. Take care! There is an abyss of moral horror between me and your accursed aerial battleships.

UNDERSHAFT. Never mind the abyss for the present. Let us settle the practical details and leave your final decision open. You know that you will have to change your name. Do you object to that?

CUSINS. Would any man named Adolphus—any man called Dolly!—object to be called something else?

UNDERSHAFT. Good. Now, as to money! I propose to treat you

5. The Deceased Wife's Sister Act, later repealed, forbade marriage of a widower with his late wife's sister.

handsomely from the beginning. You shall start at a thousand a year.

CUSINS [*with sudden heat, his spectacles twinkling with mischief*] A thousand! You dare offer a miserable thousand to the son-in-law of a millionaire! No, by Heavens, Machiavelli! you shall not cheat me. You cannot do without me; and I can do without you. I must have two thousand five hundred a year for two years. At the end of that time, if I am a failure, I go. But if I am a success, and stay on, you must give me the other five thousand.

UNDERSHAFT. What other five thousand?

CUSINS. To make the two years up to five thousand a year. The two thousand five hundred is only half pay in case I should turn out a failure. The third year I must have ten per cent on the profits.

UNDERSHAFT [*taken aback*] Ten per cent! Why, man, do you know what my profits are?

CUSINS. Enormous, I hope: otherwise I shall require twentyfive per cent.

UNDERSHAFT. But, Mr Cusins, this is a serious matter of business. You are not bringing any capital into the concern.

CUSINS. What! no capital! Is my mastery of Greek no capital? Is my access to the subtlest thought, the loftiest poetry yet attained by humanity, no capital? My character! my intellect! my life! my career! what Barbara calls my soul! are these no capital? Say another word; and I double my salary.

UNDERSHAFT. Be reasonable—

CUSINS [*permptorily*] Mr Undershaft: you have my terms. Take them or leave them.

UNDERSHAFT [*recovering himself*] Very well. I note your terms; and I offer you half.

CUSINS [*disgusted*] Half!

UNDERSHAFT [*firmly*] Half.

CUSINS. You call yourself a gentleman; and you offer me half!!

UNDERSHAFT. I do not call myself a gentleman; but I offer you half.

CUSINS. This to your future partner! your successor! your son-in-law!

BARBARA. You are selling your own soul, Dolly, not mine. Leave me out of the bargain, please.

UNDERSHAFT. Come! I will go a step further for Barbara's sake. I will give you three fifths; but that is my last word.

CUSINS. Done!

LOMAX. Done in the eye! Why, *I* get only eight hundred, you know.

CUSINS. By the way, Mac, I am a classical scholar, not an arithmetical one. Is three fifths more than half or less?

UNDERSHAFT. More, of course.

CUSINS. I would have taken two hundred and fifty. How you can succeed in business when you are willing to pay all that money to a University don who is obviously not worth a junior clerk's wages!—well! What will Lazarus say?

UNDERSHAFT. Lazarus is a gentle romantic Jew who cares for nothing but string quartets and stalls at fashionable theatres. He will be blamed for your rapacity in money matters, poor fellow! as he has hitherto been blamed for mine. You are a shark of the first order, Euripides. So much the better for the firm!

BARBARA. Is the bargain closed, Dolly? Does your soul belong to him now?

CUSINS. No: the price is settled: that is all. The real tug of war is still to come. What about the moral question?

LADY BRITOMART. There is no moral question in the matter at all, Adolphus. You must simply sell cannons and weapons to people whose cause is right and just, and refuse them to foreigners and criminals.

UNDERSHAFT [*determinedly*] No: none of that. You must keep the true faith of an Armorer, or you dont come in here.

CUSINS. What on earth is the true faith of an Armorer?

UNDERSHAFT. To give arms to all men who offer an honest price for them, without respect of persons or principles: to aristocrat and republican, to Nihilist and Tsar, to Capitalist and Socialist, to Protestant and Catholic, to burglar and policeman, to black man, white man and yellow man, to all sorts and conditions, all nationalities, all faiths, all follies, all causes and all crimes. The first Undershaft wrote up in his shop IF GOD GAVE THE HAND, LET NOT MAN WITHHOLD THE SWORD. The second wrote up ALL HAVE THE RIGHT TO FIGHT: NONE HAVE THE RIGHT TO JUDGE. The third wrote up TO MAN THE WEAPON: TO HEAVEN THE VICTORY. The fourth had no literary turn; so he did not write up anything; but he sold cannons to Napoleon under the nose of George the Third. The fifth wrote up PEACE SHALL NOT PREVAIL SAVE WITH A SWORD IN HER HAND. The sixth, my master, was the best of all. He wrote up NOTHING IS EVER DONE IN THIS WORLD UNTIL MEN ARE PREPARED TO KILL ONE ANOTHER IF IT IS NOT DONE. After that, there was nothing left for the seventh to say. So he wrote up, simply, UNASHAMED.

CUSINS. My good Machiavelli, I shall certainly write something up on the wall; only, as I shall write it in Greek, you wont be able to read it. But as to your Armorer's faith, if I take my neck out of the noose of my own morality I am not going to put it into the noose of yours. I shall sell cannons to whom I please and refuse them to whom I please. So there!

UNDERSHAFT. From the moment when you become Andrew Undershaft, you will never do as you please again. Dont come here lusting for power, young man.

CUSINS. If power were my aim I should not come here for it. You have no power.

UNDERSHAFT. None of my own, certainly.

CUSINS. I have more power than you, more will. You do not drive this place: it drives you. And what drives the place?

UNDERSHAFT [*enigmatically*] A will of which I am a part.

BARBARA [*startled*] Father! Do you know what you are saying; or are you laying a snare for my soul?

CUSINS. Dont listen to his metaphysics, Barbara. The place is driven by the most rascally part of society, the money hunters, the pleasure hunters, the military promotion hunters; and he is their slave.

UNDERSHAFT. Not necessarily. Remember the Armorer's Faith. I will take an order from a good man as cheerfully as from a bad one. If you good people prefer preaching and shirking to buying my weapons and fighting the rascals, dont blame me. I can make cannons: I cannot make courage and conviction. Bah! you tire me, Euripides, with your morality mongering. Ask Barbara: she understands. [*He suddenly reaches up and takes Barbara's hands, looking powerfully into her eyes*] Tell him, my love, what power really means.

BARBARA [*hypnotized*] Before I joined the Salvation Army, I was in my own power; and the consequence was that I never knew what to do with myself. When I joined it, I had not time enough for all the things I had to do.

UNDERSHAFT [*approvingly*] Just so. And why was that, do you suppose?

BARBARA. Yesterday I should have said, because I was in the power of God. [*She resumes her self-possession, withdrawing her hands from his with a power equal to his own*]. But you came and shewed me that I was in the power of Bodger and Undershaft. Today I feel—oh! how can I put it into words? Sarah: do you remember the earthquake at Cannes, when we were little children?—how little the surprise of the first shock mattered compared to the dread and horror of waiting for the second? That is how I feel in this place today. I stood on the rock I thought eternal; and without a word of warning it reeled and crumbled under me. I was safe with an infinite wisdom watching me, an army marching to Salvation with me; and in a moment, at a stroke of your pen in a cheque book, I stood alone; and the heavens were empty. That was the first shock of the earthquake: I am waiting for the second.

UNDERSHAFT. Come, come, my daughter! dont make too much of your little tinpot tragedy. What do we do here when we spend years of work and thought and thousands of pounds of solid cash on a new gun or an aerial battleship that turns out just a hairsbreadth wrong after all? Scrap it. Scrap it without wasting another hour or another pound on it. Well, you have made for yourself something that you call a morality or a religion or what not. It doesnt fit the facts. Well, scrap it. Scrap it and get one that does fit. That is what is wrong with the world at present. It scraps its obsolete steam engines and dynamos; but it wont scrap its old prejudices and its old moralities and its old religions and its old political constitutions. Whats the result? In machinery it does very well; but in morals and religion and politics it is working at a loss that brings it nearer bankruptcy every year. Dont persist in that folly. If your old religion broke down yesterday, get a newer and a better one for tomorrow.

BARBARA. Oh how gladly I would take a better one to my soul! But you offer me a worse one. [*Turning on him with sudden vehemence*]. Justify yourself: shew me some light through the darkness of this dreadful place, with its beautifully clean workshops, and respectable workmen, and model homes.

UNDERSHAFT. Cleanliness and respectability do not need justification, Barbara: they justify themselves. I see no darkness here, no dreadfulness. In your Salvation shelter I saw poverty, misery, cold and hunger. You gave them bread and treacle and dreams of heaven. I give them thirty shillings a week to twelve thousand a year. They find their own dreams; but I look after the drainage.

BARBARA. And their souls?

UNDERSHAFT. I save their souls just as I saved yours.

BARBARA [*revolted*] You saved my soul! What do you mean?

UNDERSHAFT. I fed you and clothed you and housed you. I took care that you should have money enough to live handsomely— more than enough; so that you could be wasteful, careless, generous. That saved your soul from the seven deadly sins.

BARBARA [*bewildered*] The seven deadly sins!

UNDERSHAFT. Yes, the deadly seven. [*Counting on his fingers*] Food, clothing, firing, rent, taxes, respectability and children. Nothing can lift those seven millstones from Man's neck but money; and the spirit cannot soar until the millstones are lifted. I lifted them from your spirit. I enabled Barbara to become Major Barbara; and I saved her from the crime of poverty.

CUSINS. Do you call poverty a crime?

UNDERSHAFT. The worst of crimes. All the other crimes are virtues beside it: all the other dishonors are chivalry itself by comparison. Poverty blights whole cities; spreads horrible pestilences; strikes dead the very souls of all who come within sight, sound, or smell of it. What you call crime is nothing: a murder here and a theft there, a blow now and a curse then: what do they matter? they are only the accidents and illnesses of life: there are not fifty genuine professional criminals in London. But there are millions of poor people, abject people, dirty people, ill fed, ill clothed people. They poison us morally and physically: they kill the happiness of society: they force us to do away with our own liberties and to organize unnatural cruelties for fear they should rise against us and drag us down into their abyss. Only fools fear crime: we all fear poverty. Pah! [*turning on Barbara*] you talk of your half-saved ruffian in West Ham: you accuse me of dragging his soul back to perdition. Well, bring him to me here; and I will drag his soul back again to salvation for you. Not by words and dreams; but by thirtyeight shillings a week, a sound house in a handsome street, and a permanent job. In three weeks he will have a fancy waistcoat; in three months a tall hat and a chapel sitting; before the end of the year he will shake hands with a duchess at a Primrose League meeting, and join the Conservative Party.

BARBARA. And will he be the better for that?

UNDERSHAFT. You know he will. Dont be a hypocrite, Barbara. He will be better fed, better housed, better clothed, better behaved; and his children will be pounds heavier and bigger. That will be better than an American cloth mattress in a shelter, chopping firewood, eating bread and treacle, and being forced to kneel down from time to time to thank heaven for it: knee drill, I think you call it. It is cheap work converting starving men with a Bible in one hand and a slice of bread in the other. I will undertake to convert West Ham to Mahometanism on the same terms. Try your hand on my men: their souls are hungry because their bodies are full.

BARBARA. And leave the east end to starve?

UNDERSHAFT [*his energetic tone dropping into one of bitter and brooding remembrance*] I was an east ender. I moralized and starved until one day I swore that I would be a full-fed free man at all costs; that nothing should stop me except a bullet, neither reason nor morals nor the lives of other men. I said "Thou shalt starve ere I starve"; and with that word I became free and great. I was a dangerous man until I had my will: now I am a useful, beneficent, kindly person. That is the history of most self-made millionaires, I fancy. When it is the history of every Englishman we shall have an England worth living in.

LADY BRITOMART. Stop making speeches, Andrew. This is not the place for them.

UNDERSHAFT [*punctured*] My dear: I have no other means of conveying my ideas.

LADY BRITOMART. Your ideas are nonsense. You got on because you were selfish and unscrupulous.

UNDERSHAFT. Not at all. I had the strongest scruples about poverty and starvation. Your moralists are quite unscrupulous about both: they make virtues of them. I had rather be a thief than a pauper. I had rather be a murderer than a slave. I dont want to be either; but if you force the alternative on me, then, by Heaven, I'll choose the braver and more moral one. I hate poverty and slavery worse than any other crimes whatsoever. And let me tell you this. Poverty and slavery have stood up for centuries to your sermons and leading articles: they will not stand up to my machine guns. Dont preach at them: dont reason with them. Kill them.

BARBARA. Killing. Is that your remedy for everything?

UNDERSHAFT. It is the final test of conviction, the only lever strong enough to overturn a social system, the only way of saying Must. Let six hundred and seventy fools loose in the streets; and three policemen can scatter them. But huddle them together in a certain house in Westminster; and let them go through certain ceremonies and call themselves certain names until at last they get the courage to kill; and your six hundred and seventy fools become a government. Your pious mob fills up ballot papers and imagines it is governing its masters; but the ballot paper that really governs is the paper that has a bullet wrapped up in it.

CUSINS. That is perhaps why, like most intelligent people, I never vote.

UNDERSHAFT. Vote! Bah! When you vote, you only change the names of the cabinet. When you shoot, you pull down governments, inaugurate new epochs, abolish old orders and set up new. Is that historically true, Mr Learned Man, or is it not?

CUSINS. It is historically true. I loathe having to admit it. I repudiate your sentiments. I abhor your nature. I defy you in every possible way. Still, it is true. But it ought not to be true.

UNDERSHAFT. Ought! ought! ought! ought! ought! Are you going to spend your life saying ought, like the rest of our moralists? Turn your oughts into shalls, man. Come and make explosives with me. Whatever can blow men up can blow society up. The history of the world is the history of those who had courage enough to embrace this truth. Have you the courage to embrace it, Barbara?

LADY BRITOMART. Barbara: I positively forbid you to listen to your father's abominable wickedness. And you, Adolphus, ought to know better than to go about saying that wrong things are true. What does it matter whether they are true if they are wrong?

UNDERSHAFT. What does it matter whether they are wrong if they are true?

LADY BRITOMART [*rising*] Children: come home instantly. Andrew: I am exceedingly sorry I allowed you to call on us. You are wickeder than ever. Come at once.

BARBARA [*shaking her head*] It's no use running away from wicked people, mamma.

LADY BRITOMART. It is every use. It shews your disapprobation of them.

BARBARA. It does not save them.

LADY BRITOMART. I can see that you are going to disobey me. Sarah: are you coming home or are you not?

SARAH. I daresay it's very wicked of papa to make cannons; but I dont think I shall cut him on that account.

LOMAX [*pouring oil on the troubled waters*] The fact is, you know, there is a certain amount of tosh about this notion of wickedness. It doesnt work. You must look at facts. Not that I would say a word in favor of anything wrong; but then, you see, all sorts of chaps are always doing all sorts of things; and we have to fit them in somehow, dont you know. What I mean is that you cant go cutting everybody; and thats about what it comes to. [*Their rapt attention to his eloquence makes him nervous*]. Perhaps I dont make myself clear.

LADY BRITOMART. You are lucidity itself, Charles. Because Andrew is successful and has plenty of money to give to Sarah, you will flatter him and encourage him in his wickedness.

LOMAX [*unruffled*] Well, where the carcase is, there will the eagles be gathered, dont you know. [*To Undershaft*] Eh? What?

UNDERSHAFT. Precisely. By the way, may I call you Charles?

LOMAX. Delighted. Cholly is the usual ticket.

UNDERSHAFT [*to Lady Britomart*] Biddy—

LADY BRITOMART [*violently*] Dont dare call me Biddy. Charles Lomax: you are a fool. Adolphus Cusins: you are a Jesuit. Stephen: you are a prig. Barbara: you are a lunatic. Andrew: you are a vulgar tradesman. Now you all know my opinion; and my conscience is clear, at all events [*she sits down with a vehemence that the rug fortunately softens*].

UNDERSHAFT. My dear: you are the incarnation of morality. [*She snorts*]. Your conscience is clear and your duty done when you have called everybody names. Come, Euripides! it is getting late; and we all want to go home. Make up your mind.

CUSINS. Understand this, you old demon—

LADY BRITOMART. Adolphus!

UNDERSHAFT. Let him alone, Biddy. Proceed, Euripides.

CUSINS. You have me in a horrible dilemma. I want Barbara.

UNDERSHAFT. Like all young men, you greatly exaggerate the difference between one young woman and another.

BARBARA. Quite true, Dolly.

CUSINS. I also want to avoid being a rascal.

UNDERSHAFT [*with biting contempt*] You lust for personal righteousness, for self-approval, for what you call a good conscience, for what Barbara calls salvation, for what I call patronizing people who are not so lucky as yourself.

CUSINS. I do not: all the poet in me recoils from being a good man. But there are things in me that I must reckon with. Pity—

UNDERSHAFT. Pity! The scavenger of misery.

CUSINS. Well, love.

UNDERSHAFT. I know. You love the needy and the outcast: you love the oppressed races, the negro, the Indian ryot,[6] the underdog everywhere. Do you love the Japanese? Do you love the French? Do you love the English?

CUSINS. No. Every true Englishman detests the English. We are the wickedest nation on earth; and our success is a moral horror.

UNDERSHAFT. That is what comes of your gospel of love, is it?

CUSINS. May I not love even my father-in-law?

UNDERSHAFT. Who wants your love, man? By what right do you take the liberty of offering it to me? I will have your due heed and respect, or I will kill you. But your love! Damn your impertinence!

CUSINS [*grinning*] I may not be able to control my affections, Mac.

UNDERSHAFT. You are fencing, Euripides. You are weakening: your

6. Tenant farmer.

grip is slipping. Come! try your last weapon. Pity and love have broken in your hand: forgiveness is still left.

CUSINS. No: forgiveness is a beggar's refuge. I am with you there: we must pay our debts.

UNDERSHAFT. Well said. Come! you will suit me. Remember the words of Plato.

CUSINS [*starting*] Plato! You dare quote Plato to me!

UNDERSHAFT. Plato says, my friend, that society cannot be saved until either the Professors of Greek take to making gunpowder, or else the makers of gunpowder become Professors of Greek.

CUSINS. Oh, tempter, cunning tempter!

UNDERSHAFT. Come! choose, man, choose.

CUSINS. But perhaps Barbara will not marry me if I make the wrong choice.

BARBARA. Perhaps not.

CUSINS [*desperately perlexed*] You hear!

BARBARA. Father: do you love nobody?

UNDERSHAFT. I love my best friend.

LADY BRITOMART. And who is that, pray?

UNDERSHAFT. My bravest enemy. That is the man who keeps me up to the mark.

CUSINS. You know, the creature is really a sort of poet in his way. Suppose he is a great man, after all!

UNDERSHAFT. Suppose you stop talking and make up your mind, my young friend.

CUSINS. But you are driving me against my nature. I hate war.

UNDERSHAFT. Hatred is the coward's revenge for being intimidated. Dare you make war on war? Here are the means: my friend Mr. Lomax is sitting on them.

LOMAX [*springing up*] Oh I say! You dont mean that this thing is loaded, do you? My ownest: come off it.

SARAH [*sitting placidly on the shell*] If I am to be blown up, the more thoroughly it is done the better. Dont fuss, Cholly.

LOMAX [*to Undershaft, strongly remonstrant*] Your own daughter, you know!

UNDERSHAFT. So I see. [*To Cusins*] Well, my friend, may we expect you here at six tomorrow morning?

CUSINS [*firmly*] Not on any account. I will see the whole establishment blown up with its own dynamite before I will get up at five. My hours are healthy, rational hours: eleven to five.

UNDERSHAFT. Come when you please: before a week you will come at six and stay until I turn you out for the sake of your health. [*Calling*] Bilton! [*He turns to Lady Britomart, who rises*]. My dear: let us leave these two young people to themselves for a moment. [*Bilton comes from the shed*]. I am going to take you through the gun cotton shed.

BILTON [*barring the way*] You cant take anything explosive in here, sir.

LADY BRITOMART. What do you mean? Are you alluding to me?

BILTON [*unmoved*] No, maam. Mr Undershaft has the other gentleman's matches in his pocket.

LADY BRITOMART [*abruptly*] Oh! I beg your pardon. [*She goes into the shed*].

UNDERSHAFT. Quite right, Bilton, quite right: here you are. [*He gives Bilton the box of matches*]. Come, Stephen. Come, Charles. Bring Sarah. [*He passes into the shed*].

    Bilton opens the box and deliberately drops the matches into the fire-bucket.

LOMAX. Oh! I say [*Bilton stolidly hands him the empty box*]. Infernal nonsense! Pure scientific ignorance! [*He goes in*].

SARAH. Am I all right, Bilton?

BILTON. Youll have to put on list slippers, miss: thats all. Weve got em inside [*She goes in*].

STEPHEN [*very seriously to Cusins*] Dolly, old fellow, think. Think before you decide. Do you feel that you are a sufficiently practical man? It is a huge undertaking, an enormous responsibility. All this mass of business will be Greek to you.

CUSINS. Oh, I think it will be much less difficult than Greek.

STEPHEN. Well, I just want to say this before I leave you to yourselves. Dont let anything I have said about right and wrong prejudice you against this great chance in life. I have satisfied myself that the business is one of the highest character and a credit to our country. [*Emotionally*] I am very proud of my father. I— [*Unable to proceed, he presses Cusins' hand and goes hastily into the shed, followed by Bilton*].

    Barbara and Cusins, left alone together, look at one another silently.

CUSINS. Barbara: I am going to accept this offer.

BARBARA. I thought you would.

CUSINS. You understand, dont you, that I had to decide without consulting you. If I had thrown the burden of the choice on you, you would sooner or later have despised me for it.

BARBARA. Yes; I did not want you to sell your soul for me any more than for this inheritance.

CUSINS. It is not the sale of my soul that troubles me: I have sold it too often to care about that. I have sold it for a professorship. I have sold it for an income. I have sold it to escape being imprisoned for refusing to pay taxes for hangmen's ropes and unjust wars and things that I abhor. What is all human conduct but the daily and hourly sale of our souls for trifles? What I am now selling it for is neither money nor position nor comfort, but for reality and for power.

BARBARA. You know that you will have no power, and that he has none.

CUSINS. I know. It is not for myself alone. I want to make power for the world.

BARBARA. I want to make power for the world too; but it must be spiritual power.

CUSINS. I think all power is spiritual: these cannons will not go off by themselves. I have tried to make spiritual power by teaching Greek. But the world can never be really touched by a dead language and a dead civilization. The people must have power; and the people cannot have Greek. Now the power that is made here can be wielded by all men.

BARBARA. Power to burn women's houses down and kill their sons and tear their husbands to pieces.

CUSINS. You cannot have power for good without having power for evil too. Even mother's milk nourishes murderers as well as heroes. This power which only tears men's bodies to pieces has never been so horribly abused as the intellectual power, the imaginative power, the poetic, religious power that can enslave men's souls. As a teacher of Greek I gave the intellectual man weapons against the common man. I now want to give the common man weapons against the inellectual man. I love the common people. I want to arm them against the lawyers, the doctors, the priests, the literary men, the professors, the artists, and the politicians, who, once in authority, are more disastrous and tyrannical than all the fools, rascals, and impostors. I want a power simple enough for common men to use, yet strong enough to force the intellectual oligarchy to use its genius for the general good.

BARBARA. Is there no higher power than that [*pointing to the shell*]?

CUSINS. Yes; but that power can destroy the higher powers just as a tiger can destroy a man: therefore Man must master that power first. I admitted this when the Turks and Greeks were last at war. My best pupil went out to fight for Hellas. My parting gift to him was not a copy of Plato's Republic, but a revolver and a hundred Undershaft cartridges. The blood of every Turk he shot—if he shot any—is on my head as well as on Undershaft's. That act committed me to this place for ever. Your father's challenge has beaten me. Dare I make war on war? I dare. I must. I will. And now, is it all over between us?

BARBARA [*touched by his evident dread of her answer*] Silly baby Dolly! How could it be!

CUSINS [*overjoyed*] Then you—you—you— Oh for my drum! [*He flourishes imaginary drumsticks*].

BARBARA [*angered by his levity*] Take care, Dolly, take care. Oh, if only I could get away from you and from father and from it all! if I could have the wings of a dove and fly away to heaven!

CUSINS. And leave me!

BARBARA. Yes, you, and all the other naughty mischievous children of men. But I cant. I was happy in the Salvation Army for a moment. I escaped from the world into a paradise of enthusiasm and prayer and soul saving; but the moment our money ran short, it all came back to Bodger: it was he who saved our people: he, and the Prince of Darkness, my papa. Undershaft and Bodger: their hands stretch everywhere: when we feed a starving fellow creature, it is with their bread, because there is no other bread; when we tend the sick, it is in the hospitals they endow; if we turn from the churches they build, we must kneel on the stones of the streets they pave. As long as that lasts, there is no getting away from them. Turning our backs on Bodger and Undershaft is turning our backs on life.

CUSINS. I thought you were determined to turn your back on the wicked side of life.

BARBARA. There is no wicked side: life is all one. And I never wanted to shirk my share in whatever evil must be endured, whether it be sin or suffering. I wish I could cure you of middle-class ideas, Dolly.

CUSINS [*gasping*] Middle cl—! A snub! A social snub to me! from the daughter of a foundling!

BARBARA. That is why I have no class, Dolly: I come straight out of the heart of the whole people. If I were middle-class I should turn my back on my father's business; and we should both live in an artistic drawing room, with you reading the reviews in one corner, and I in the other at the piano, playing Schumann: both very superior persons, and neither of us a bit of use. Sooner than that, I would sweep out the guncotton shed, or be one of Bodger's barmaids. Do you know what would have happened if you had refused papa's offer?

CUSINS. I wonder!

BARBARA. I should have given you up and married the man who accepted it. After all, my dear old mother has more sense than any of you. I felt like her when I saw this place—felt that I must have it—that never, never, never could I let it go; only she thought it was the houses and the kitchen ranges and the linen and china, when it was really all the human souls to be saved: not weak souls in starved bodies, sobbing with gratitude for a scrap of bread and treacle, but fullfed, quarrelsome, snobbish, uppish creatures, all standing on their little rights and dignities, and thinking that my father ought to be greatly obliged to them for making so much money for him—and so he ought. That is where salvation is really wanted. My father shall never throw it in my teeth again that my converts were bribed with bread. [*She is transfigured*]. I have got rid of the bribe of bread. I have got rid of the bribe of heaven. Let God's work be done for its own sake: the work he had to create us to do because it cannot be done except by living men and women. When I die, let him be in my debt, not I in his; and let me forgive him as becomes a woman of my rank.

CUSINS. Then the way of life lies through the factory of death?

BARBARA. Yes, through the raising of hell to heaven and of man to God, through the unveiling of an eternal light in the Valley of The Shadow. [*Seizing him with both hands*] Oh, did you think my courage would never come back? did you believe that I was a deserter? that I, who have stood in the streets, and taken my people to my heart, and talked of the holiest and greatest things with them, could ever turn back and chatter foolishly to fashionable people about nothing in a drawing room? Never, never, never, never: Major Barbara will die with the colors. Oh! and I have my dear little Dolly boy still; and he has found me my place and my work. Glory Hallelujah! [*She kisses him*].

CUSINS. My dearest: consider my delicate health. I cannot stand as much happiness as you can.

BARBARA. Yes: it is not easy work being in love with me, is it? But it's good for you. [*She runs to the shed, and calls, childlike*] Mamma! Mamma! [*Bilton comes out of the shed, followed by Undershaft*]. I want Mamma.

UNDERSHAFT. She is taking off her list slippers, dear. [*He passes on to Cusins*]. Well? What does she say?

CUSINS. She has gone right up into the skies.

LADY BRITOMART [*coming from the shed and stopping on the steps, obstructing Sarah, who follows with Lomax. Barbara clutches like a baby at her mother's skirt*] Barbara: when will you learn to be independent and to act and think for yourself? I know as well as possible what that cry of "Mamma, Mamma," means. Always running to me!

SARAH [*touching Lady Britomart's ribs with her finger tips and imitating a bicycle horn*] Pip! pip!

LADY BRITOMART [*highly indignant*] How dare you say Pip! pip! to me, Sarah? You are both very naughty children. What do you want, Barbara?

BARBARA. I want a house in the village to live in with Dolly. [*Dragging at the skirt*] Come and tell me which one to take.

UNDERSHAFT [*to Cusins*] Six o'clock tomorrow morning, Euripides.

THE END

Heartbreak House

Act I

*The hilly country in the middle of the north edge of Sussex,
looking very pleasant on a fine evening at the end of September, is
seen through the windows of a room which has been built so as to
resemble the after part of an old-fashioned high-pooped ship with a
stern gallery; for the windows are ship built with heavy timbering,
and run right across the room as continuously as the stability of the
wall allows. A row of lockers under the windows provides an unup-
holstered window-seat interrupted by twin glass doors, respectively
halfway between the stern post and the sides. Another door strains
the illusion a little by being apparently in the ship's port side, and
yet leading, not to the open sea, but to the entrance hall of the
house. Between this door and the stern gallery are bookshelves.
There are electric light switches beside the door leading to the hall
and the glass doors in the stern gallery. Against the starboard wall
is a carpenter's bench. The vice has a board in its jaws; and the
floor is littered with shavings, overflowing from a waste-paper basket. A couple of planes and a centrebit are on the bench. In the
same wall, between the bench and the windows, is a narrow doorway with a half door, above which a glimpse of the room beyond
shews that it is a shelved pantry with bottles and kitchen crockery.*

*On the starboard side, but close to the middle, is a plain oak
drawing-table with drawing-board, T-square, straightedges, set
squares, mathematical instruments, saucers of water color, a tum-
bler of discolored water, Indian ink, pencils, and brushes on it. The
drawing-board is set so that the draughtsman's chair has the window on its left hand. On the floor at the end of the table, on his
right, is a ship's fire bucket. On the port side of the room, near the
bookshelves, is a sofa with its back to the windows. It is a sturdy
mahogany article, oddly upholstered in sailcloth, including the bol-
ster, with a couple of blankets hanging over the back. Between the
sofa and the drawing-table is a big wicker chair, with broad arms
and a low sloping back, with its back to the light. A small but stout
table of teak, with a round top and gate legs, stands against the
port wall between the door and the bookcase. It is the only article
in the room that suggests (not at all convincingly) a woman's hand
in the furnishing. The uncarpeted floor of narrow boards is caulked
and holystoned like a deck.*

*The garden to which the glass doors lead dips to the south be-
fore the landscape rises again to the hills. Emerging from the hollow is the cupola of an observatory. Between the observatory and*

the house is a flagstaff on a little esplanade, with a hammock on the east side and a long garden seat on the west.

A young lady, gloved and hatted, with a dust coat on, is sitting in the window-seat with her body twisted to enable her to look out at the view. One hand props her chin: the other hangs down with a volume of the Temple Shakespear in it, and her finger stuck in the page she has been reading.

A clock strikes six.

The young lady turns and looks at her watch. She rises with an air of one who waits and is almost at the end of her patience. She is a pretty girl, slender, fair, and intelligent looking, nicely but not expensively dressed, evidently not a smart idler.

With a sigh of weary resignation she comes to the draughtsman's chair; sits down; and begins to read Shakespear. Presently the book sinks to her lap; her eyes close; and she dozes into a slumber.

An elderly womanservant comes in from the hall with three unopened bottles of rum on a tray. She passes through and disappears in the pantry without noticing the young lady. She places the bottles on the shelf and fills her tray with empty bottles. As she returns with these, the young lady lets her book drop, awakening herself, and startling the womanservant so that she all but lets the tray fall.

THE WOMANSERVANT. God bless us! [The young lady picks up the book and places it on the table]. Sorry to wake you, miss, I'm sure; but you are a stranger to me. What might you be waiting here for now?

THE YOUNG LADY. Waiting for somebody to shew some signs of knowing that I have been invited here.

THE WOMANSERVANT. Oh, youre invited, are you? And has nobody come? Dear! dear!

THE YOUNG LADY. A wild-looking old gentleman came and looked in at the window; and I heard him calling out "Nurse: there is a young and attractive female waiting in the poop. Go and see what she wants." Are you the nurse?

THE WOMANSERVANT. Yes, miss: I'm Nurse Guinness. That was old Captain Shotover, Mrs Hushabye's father. I heard him roaring; but I thought it was for something else. I suppose it was Mrs Hushabye that invited you, ducky?

THE YOUNG LADY. I understood her to do so. But really I think I'd better go.

NURSE GUINNESS. Oh, dont think of such a thing, miss. If Mrs Hushabye has forgotten all about it, it will be a pleasant surprise for her to see you, wont it?

THE YOUNG LADY. It has been a very unpleasant surprise to me to find that nobody expects me.

NURSE GUINNESS. Youll get used to it, miss: this house is full of surprises for them that dont know our ways.

CAPTAIN SHOTOVER [looking in from the hall suddenly: an ancient *but still hardy man with an immense white beard in a reefer jacket with a whistle hanging from his neck*] Nurse: there is a hold-all and a handbag on the front steps for everybody to fall over. Also a tennis racquet. Who the devil left them there?

THE YOUNG LADY. They are mine, I'm afraid.

THE CAPTAIN [*advancing to the drawing-table*] Nurse: who is this misguided and unfortunate young lady?

NURSE GUINNESS. She says Miss Hessy invited her, sir.

THE CAPTAIN. And had she no friend, no parents, to warn her against my daughter's invitations? This is a pretty sort of house, by heavens! A young and attractive lady is invited here. Her luggage is left on the steps for hours; and she herself is deposited in the poop and abandoned, tired and starving. This is our hospitality. These are our manners. No room ready. No hot water. No welcoming hostess. Our visitor is to sleep in the toolshed, and to wash in the duckpond.

NURSE GUINNESS. Now it's all right, Captain: I'll get the lady some tea; and her room shall be ready before she has finished it. [*To the young lady*] Take off your hat, ducky; and make yourself at home [*She goes to the door leading to the hall*].

THE CAPTAIN [*as she passes him*] Ducky! Do you suppose, woman, that because this young lady has been insulted and neglected, you have the right to address her as you address my wretched children, whom you have brought up in ignorance of the commonest decencies of social intercourse?

NURSE GUINNESS. Never mind him, doty. [*Quite unconcerned, she goes out into the hall on her way to the kitchen*].

THE CAPTAIN. Madam: will you favor me with your name? [*He sits down in the big wicker chair*].

THE YOUNG LADY. My name is Ellie Dunn.

THE CAPTAIN. Dunn! I had a boatswain whose name was Dunn. He was originally a pirate in China. He set up as a ship's chandler with stores which I have every reason to believe he stole from me. No doubt he became rich. Are you his daughter?

ELLIE [*indignant*] No: certainly not. I am proud to be able to say that though my father has not been a successful man, nobody has ever had one word to say against him. I think my father is the best man I have ever known.

THE CAPTAIN. He must be greatly changed. Has he attained the seventh degree of concentration?

ELLIE. I dont understand.

THE CAPTAIN. But how could he, with a daughter? I, madam, have two daughters. One of them is Hesione Hushabye, who invited you here. I keep this house: she upsets it. I desire to attain the seventh degree of concentration: she invites visitors and leaves me to entertain them. [*Nurse Guinness returns with the tea-tray, which she places on the teak table*]. I have a second daughter who is, thank God, in a remote part of the Empire with her numskull of a husband. As a child she thought the figure-head of my ship, the Dauntless, the most beautiful thing on earth. He resembled it. He had the same expression: wooden yet enterprising. She married him, and will never set foot in this house again.

NURSE GUINNESS [*carrying the table, with the tea-things on it, to Ellie's side*] Indeed you never were more mistaken. She is in England this very moment. You have been told three times this week that she is coming home for a year for her health. And very glad you should be to see your own daughter again after all these years.

THE CAPTAIN. I am not glad. The natural term of the affection of the human animal for its offspring is six years. My daughter Ariadne was born when I was forty-six. I am now eighty-eight. If she comes, I am not at home. If she wants anything, let her take it. If she asks for me, let her be informed that I am extremely old, and have totally forgotten her.

NURSE GUINNESS. Thats no talk to offer to a young lady. Here, ducky, have some tea; and dont listen to him. [*She pours out a cup of tea*].

THE CAPTAIN [*rising wrathfully*] Now before high heaven they have given this innocent child Indian tea: the stuff they tan their own leather insides with. [*He seizes the cup and the tea-pot and empties both into the leathern bucket*].

ELLIE [*almost in tears*] Oh, please! I am so tired. I should have been glad of anything.

NURSE GUINNESS. Oh, what a thing to do! The poor lamb is ready to drop.

THE CAPTAIN. You shall have some of my tea. Do not touch that fly-blown cake: nobody eats it here except the dogs. [*He disappears into the pantry*].

NURSE GUINNESS. Theres a man for you! They say he sold himself to the devil in Zanzibar before he was a captain; and the older he grows the more I believe them.

A WOMAN'S VOICE [*in the hall*] Is anyone at home? Hesione! Nurse! Papa! Do come, somebody; and take in my luggage.

Thumping heard, as of an umbrella, on the wainscot.

NURSE GUINNESS. My gracious! It's Miss Addy, Lady Utterword, Mrs Hushabye's sister: the one I told the Captain about. [*Calling*] Coming, Miss, coming.

She carries the table back to its place by the door, and is hurrying out when she is intercepted by Lady Utterword, who bursts in much flustered. Lady Utterword, a blonde, is very handsome, very well dressed, and so precipitate in speech and action that the first impression (erroneous) is one of comic silliness.

LADY UTTERWORD. Oh, is that you, Nurse? How are you? You dont look a day older. Is nobody at home? Where is Hesione? Doesnt she expect me? Where are the servants? Whose luggage is that on the steps? Where's papa? Is everybody asleep? [*Seeing Ellie*]

Oh! I beg your pardon. I suppose you are one of my nieces. [*Approaching her with outstretched arms*] Come and kiss your aunt, darling.

ELLIE. I'm only a visitor. It is my luggage on the steps.

NURSE GUINNESS. I'll go get you some fresh tea, ducky. [*She takes up the tray*].

ELLIE. But the old gentleman said he would make some himself.

NURSE GUINNESS. Bless you! he's forgotten what he went for already. His mind wanders from one thing to another.

LADY UTTERWORD. Papa, I suppose.

NURSE GUINNESS. Yes, Miss.

LADY UTTERWOOD [*vehemently*] Dont be silly, Nurse. Dont call me Miss.

NURSE GUINNESS [*placidly*] No, lovey. [*She goes out with the tea tray*].

LADY UTTERWORD [*sitting down with a flounce on the sofa*] I know what you must feel. Oh, this house, this house! I come back to it after twenty-three years; and it is just the same: the luggage lying on the steps, the servants spoilt and impossible, nobody at home to receive anybody, no regular meals, nobody ever hungry because they are always gnawing bread and butter or munching apples, and, what is worse, the same disorder in ideas, in talk, in feeling. When I was a child I was used to it: I had never known anything better, though I was unhappy, and longed all the time—oh, how I longed!—to be respectable, to be a lady, to live as others did, not to have to think of everything for myself. I married at nineteen to escape from it. My husband is Sir Hastings Utterword, who has been governor of all the crown colonies in succession. I have always been the mistress of Government House. I have been so happy: I had forgotten that people could live like this. I wanted to see my father, my sister, my nephews and nieces (one ought to, you know), and I was looking forward to it. And now the state of the house! the way I'm received! the casual impudence of that woman Guinness, our old nurse! really Hesione might at least have been here: s o m e preparation might have been made for me. You must excuse my going on in this way; but I am really very much hurt and annoyed and disillusioned: and if I had realized it was to be like this, I wouldnt have come. I have a great mind to go away without another word. [*She is on the point of weeping*].

ELLIE [*also very miserable*] Nobody has been here to receive me either. I thought I ought to go away too. But how can I, Lady Utterword? My luggage is on the steps; and the station fly has gone.

The Captain emerges from the pantry with a tray of Chinese lacquer and a very fine tea-set on it. He rests it provisionally on the end of the table; snatches away the drawing-board, which he stands on the floor against the table legs; and puts the tray in the space thus cleared. Ellie pours out a cup greedily.

fetch another cup. [*He makes for the pantry*].

THE CAPTAIN. Your tea, young lady. What! another lady! I must

LADY UTTERWORD [*rising from the sofa, suffused with emotion*] Papa! Dont you know me? I'm your daughter.

THE CAPTAIN. Nonsense! my daughter's upstairs asleep. [*He vanishes through the half door*].

Lady Utterword retires to the window to conceal her tears.

ELLIE [*going to her with the cup*] Dont be so distressed. Have this cup of tea. He is very old and very strange: he has been just like that to me. I know how dreadful it must be: my own father is all the world to me. Oh, I'm sure he didnt mean it.

The Captain returns with another cup.

THE CAPTAIN. Now we are complete. [*He places it on the tray*].

LADY UTTERWORD [*hysterically*] Papa: you cant have forgotten me. I am Ariadne. I'm little Paddy Patkins. Wont you kiss me? [*She goes to him and throws her arms around his neck*].

THE CAPTAIN [*woodenly enduring her embrace*] How can you be Ariadne? You are a middle-aged woman: well preserved, madam, but no longer young.

LADY UTTERWORD. But think of all the years and years I have been away, papa. I have had to grow old, like other people.

THE CAPTAIN [*disengaging himself*] You should grow out of kissing strange men: they may be striving to attain the seventh degree of concentration.

LADY UTTERWORD. But I'm your daughter. You havnt seen me for years.

THE CAPTAIN. So much the worse! When our relatives are at home, we have to think of all their good points or it would be impossible to endure them. But when they are away, we console ourselves for their absence by dwelling on their vices. That is how I have come to think my absent daughter Ariadne a perfect fiend; so do not try to ingratiate yourself here by impersonating her [*He walks firmly away to the other side of the room*].

LADY UTTERWORD. Ingratiating myself indeed! [*With dignity*] Very well, papa. [*She sits down at the drawing-table and pours out tea for herself*].

THE CAPTAIN. I am neglecting my social duties. You remember Dunn? Billy Dunn?

LADY UTTERWORD. Do you mean that villainous sailor who robbed you?

THE CAPTAIN [*introducing Ellie*] His daughter. [*He sits down on the sofa*].

ELLIE [*protesting*] No—

Nurse Guinness returns with fresh tea.

THE CAPTAIN. Take that hogwash away. Do you hear?

NURSE. Youve actually remembered about the tea! [*To Ellie*] O, miss, he didnt forget you after all! You h a v e made an impression.

THE CAPTAIN [*gloomily*] Youth! beauty! novelty! They are badly wanted in this house. I am excessively old. Hesione is only moderately young. Her children are not youthful.

LADY UTTERWORD. How can children be expected to be youthful in this house? Almost before we could speak we were filled with notions that might have been all very well for pagan philosophers of fifty, but were certainly quite unfit for respectable people of any age.

NURSE. You were always for respectability, Miss Addy.

LADY UTTERWORD. Nurse: will you please remember that I am Lady Utterword, and not Miss Addy, nor lovey, nor darling, nor doty? Do you hear?

NURSE. Yes, ducky: all right. I'll tell them all they must call you my lady. [*She takes her tray out with undisturbed placidity*].

LADY UTTERWORD. What comfort? what sense is there in having servants with no manners?

ELLIE [*rising and coming to the table to put down her empty cup*] Lady Utterword: do you think Mrs Hushabye really expects me?

LADY UTTERWORD. Oh, dont ask me. You can see for yourself that Ive just arrived; her only sister, after twenty-three years absence! and it seems that *I* am not expected.

THE CAPTAIN. What does it matter whether the young lady is expected or not? She is welcome. There are beds: there is food. I'll find a room for her myself [*He makes for the door*].

ELLIE [*following him to stop him*] Oh please— [*He goes out*]. Lady Utterword: I dont know what to do. Your father persists in believing that my father is some sailor who robbed him.

LADY UTTERWORD. You had better pretend not to notice it. My father is a very clever man; but he always forgot things; and now that he is old, of course he is worse. And I must warn you that it is sometimes very hard to feel quite sure that he really forgets.

> *Mrs Hushabye bursts into the room tempestuously, and embraces Ellie. She is a couple of years older than Lady Utterword, and even better looking. She has magnificent black hair, eyes like the fishpools of Heshbon, and a nobly modelled neck, short at the back and low between her shoulders in front. Unlike her sister she is uncorseted and dressed anyhow in a rich robe of black pile that shews off her white skin and statuesque contour.*

MRS HUSHABYE. Ellie, my darling, my pettikins [*kissing her*]: how long have you been here? Ive been at home all the time: I was putting flowers and things in your room; and when I just sat down for a moment to try how comfortable the armchair was I went off to sleep. Papa woke me and told me you were here. Fancy your finding no one, and being neglected and abandoned. [*Kissing her again*]. My poor love! [*She deposits Ellie on the sofa. Meanwhile Ariadne has left the table and come over to claim her share of attention*]. Oh! youve brought someone with you. Introduce me.

LADY UTTERWORD. Hesione: is it possible that y o u dont know me?

MRS HUSHABYE [*conventionally*] Of course I remember your face quite well. Where have we met?

LADY UTTERWORD. Didnt papa tell you I was here? Oh! this is really too much. [*She throws herself sulkily into the big chair*].

MRS HUSHABYE. Papa!

LADY UTTERWORD. Yes: Papa. O u r papa, you unfeeling wretch. [*Rising angrily*] I'll go straight to a hotel.

MRS HUSHABYE [*seizing her by the shoulders*] My goodness gracious goodness, you dont mean to say that youre Addy!

LADY UTTERWORD. I certainly am Addy; and I dont think I can be so changed that you would not have recognized me if you had any real affection for me. And papa didnt think me even worth mentioning.

MRS HUSHABYE. What a lark! Sit down. [*She pushes her back into the chair instead of kissing her, and posts herself behind it*]. You d o look a swell. Youre much handsomer than you used to be. Youve made the acquaintance of Ellie, of course. She is going to marry a perfect hog of a millionaire for the sake of her father, who is as poor as a church mouse; and you must help me to stop her.

ELLIE. Oh p l e a s e Hesione.

MRS HUSHABYE. My pettikins, the man's coming here today with your father to begin persecuting you; and everybody will see the state of the case in ten minutes; so whats the use of making a secret of it?

ELLIE. He is not a hog, Hesione. You dont know how wonderfully good he was to my father, and how deeply grateful I am to him.

MRS HUSHABYE [*to Lady Utterword*] Her father is a very remarkable man, Addy. His name is Mazzini Dunn. Mazzini was a celebrity of some kind who knew Ellie's grandparents. They were both poets, like the Brownings; and when her father came into the world Mazzini said "Another soldier born for freedom!" So they christened him Mazzini; and he has been fighting for freedom in his quiet way ever since. Thats why he is so poor.

ELLIE. I am proud of his poverty.

MRS HUSHABYE. Of course you are, pettikins. Why not leave him in it, and marry someone you love?

LADY UTTERWORD [*rising suddenly and explosively*] Hesione: are you going to kiss me or are you not?

MRS HUSHABYE. What do you want to be kissed for?

LADY UTTERWORD. I d o n t want to be kissed; but I do want you to behave properly and decently. We are sisters. We have been separated for twenty-three years. You o u g h t to kiss me.

MRS HUSHABYE. Tomorrow morning, dear, before you make up. I hate the smell of powder.

LADY UTTERWORD. Oh! you unfeeling— [*She is interrupted by the return of the captain*].

THE CAPTAIN [*to Ellie*] Your room is ready. [*Ellie rises*]. The sheets were damp; but I have changed them. [*He makes for the garden door on the port side*].

LADY UTTERWORD. Oh! What about m y sheets?

THE CAPTAIN [*halting at the door*] Take my advice: air them; or take them off and sleep in blankets. You shall sleep in Ariadne's old room.

LADY UTTERWORD. Indeed I shall do nothing of the sort. That little hole! I am entitled to the best spare room.

THE CAPTAIN [*continuing unmoved*] She married a numskull. She told me she would marry anyone to get away from home.

LADY UTTERWORD. You are pretending not to know me on purpose. I will leave the house.

    Mazzini Dunn enters from the hall. He is a little elderly man with bulging credulous eyes and earnest manners. He is dressed in a blue serge jacket suit with an unbuttoned mackintosh over it, and carries a soft black hat of clerical cut.

ELLIE. At last! Captain Shotover: here is my father.

THE CAPTAIN. This! Nonsense! not a bit like him [*He goes away through the garden, shutting the door sharply behind him*].

LADY UTTERWORD. I will not be ignored and pretended to be somebody else. I will have it out with papa now, this instant. [*To Mazzini*] Excuse me. [*She follows the Captain out, making a hasty bow to Mazzini, who returns it*].

MRS HUSHABYE [*hospitably, shaking hands*] How good of you to come, Mr Dunn! You dont mind papa, do you? He is as mad as a hatter, you know, but quite harmless, and extremely clever. You will have some delightful talks with him.

MAZZINI. I hope so. [*To Ellie*] So here you are, Ellie, dear. [*He draws her arm affectionately through his*]. I must thank you, Mrs Hushabye, for your kindness to my daughter. I'm afraid she would have had no holiday if you had not invited her.

MRS HUSHABYE. Not at all. Very nice of her to come and attract young people to the house for us.

MAZZINI [*smiling*] I'm afraid Ellie is not interested in young men, Mrs Hushabye. Her taste is on the graver, solider side.

MRS HUSHABYE [*with a sudden rather hard brightness in her manner*] Wont you take off your overcoat, Mr Dunn? You will find a cupboard for coats and hats and things in the corner of the hall.

MAZZINI [*hastily releasing Ellie*] Yes—thank you—I had better— [*He goes out*].

MRS HUSHABYE [*emphatically*] The old brute!

ELLIE. Who?

MRS HUSHABYE. Who! Him. He. It [*Pointing after Mazzini*]. "Graver, solider tastes," indeed!

ELLIE [*aghast*] You dont mean that you were speaking like that of my father!

MRS HUSHABYE. I was. You know I was.

ELLIE [*with dignity*] I will leave your house at once. [*She turns to the door*].

MRS HUSHABYE. If you attempt it, I'll tell your father why.

ELLIE [*turning again*] Oh! How can you treat a visitor like this, Mrs Hushabye?

MRS HUSHABYE. I thought you were going to call me Hesione.

ELLIE. Certainly not now?

MRS HUSHABYE. Very well: I'll tell your father.

ELLIE [*distressed*] Oh!

MRS HUSHABYE. If you turn a hair—if you take his part against me and against your own heart for a moment, I'll give that born soldier of freedom a piece of my mind that will stand him on his selfish old head for a week.

ELLIE. Hesione! My father selfish! How little you know—

She is interrupted by Mazzini, who returns, excited and perspiring.

MAZZINI. Ellie: Mangan has come: I thought youd like to know. Excuse me, Mrs Hushabye: the strange old gentleman—

MRS HUSHABYE. Papa. Quite so.

MAZZINI. Oh, I beg your pardon: of course: I was a little confused by his manner. He is making Mangan help him with something in the garden; and he wants me to—

A powerful whistle is heard.

THE CAPTAIN'S VOICE. Bosun ahoy! [*The whistle is repeated*].

MAZZINI [*flustered*] Oh dear! I believe he is whistling for me [*He hurries out*].

MRS HUSHABYE. Now m y father is a wonderful man if you like.

ELLIE. Hesione: listen to me. You dont understand. My father and Mr Mangan were boys together. Mr Ma—

MRS HUSHABYE. I dont care what they were: we must sit down if you are going to begin as far back as that [*She snatches at Ellie's waist, and makes her sit down on the sofa beside her*]. Now, pettikins: tell me all about Mr Mangan. They call him Boss Mangan, dont they? He is a Napoleon of industry and disgustingly rich, isnt he? Why isnt your father rich?

ELLIE. My poor father should never have been in business. His parents were poets; and they gave him the noblest ideas; but they could not afford to give him a profession.

MRS HUSHABYE. Fancy your grandparents, with their eyes in fine frenzy rolling! And so your poor father had to go into business. Hasnt he succeeded in it?

ELLIE. He always used to say he could succeed if he only had some capital. He fought his way along, to keep a roof over our heads and bring us up well; but it was always a struggle: always the same difficulty of not having capital enough. I dont know how to describe it to you.

MRS HUSHABYE. Poor Ellie! I know. Pulling the devil by the tail.

ELLIE [*hurt*] Oh no. Not like that. It was at least dignified.

MRS HUSHABYE. That made it all the harder, didnt it? *I* shouldn't have pulled the devil by the tail with dignity. I should have pulled hard—[*between her teeth*] h a r d. Well? Go on.

ELLIE. At last it seemed that all our troubles were at an end. Mr. Mangan did an extraordinarily noble thing out of pure friendship for my father and respect for his character. He asked him how much capital he wanted, and gave it to him. I dont mean that he lent it to him, or that he invested it in his business. He just simply made him a present of it. Wasnt that splendid of him?

MRS HUSHABYE. On condition that you married him?

ELLIE. Oh no, no, no. This was when I was a child. He had never even seen me: he never came to our house. It was absolutely disinterested. Pure generosity.

MRS HUSHABYE. Oh! I beg the gentleman's pardon. Well, what became of the money?

ELLIE. We all got new clothes and moved into another house. And I went to another school for two years.

MRS HUSHABYE. Only two years?

ELLIE. That was all; for at the end of two years my father was utterly ruined.

MRS HUSHABYE. How?

ELLIE. I dont know. I never could understand. But it was dreadful. When we were poor my father had never been in debt. But when he launched out into business on a large scale, he had to incur liabilities. When the business went into liquidation he owed more money than Mr Mangan had given him.

MRS HUSHABYE. Bit off more than he could chew, I suppose.

ELLIE. I think you are a little unfeeling about it.

MRS HUSHABYE. My pettikins: you mustnt mind my way of talking. I was quite as sensitive and particular as you once; but I have picked up so much slang from the children that I am really hardly presentable. I suppose your father had no head for business, and made a mess of it.

ELLIE. Oh, that just shews how entirely you are mistaken about him. The business turned out a great success. It now pays forty-four per cent after deducting the excess profits tax.

MRS HUSHABYE. Then why arnt you rolling in money?

ELLIE. I dont know. It seems very unfair to me. You see, my father was made bankrupt. It nearly broke his heart, because he had persuaded several of his friends to put money into the business. He was sure it would succeed; and events proved that he was quite right. But they all lost their money. It was dreadful. I dont know what we should have done but for Mr Mangan.

MRS HUSHABYE. What! Did the Boss come to the rescue again, after all his money being thrown away?

ELLIE. He did indeed, and never uttered a reproach to my father. He bought what was left of the business—the buildings and the machinery and things—from the official trustee for enough money to enable my father to pay six and eightpence in the pound and get his discharge. Everyone pitied papa so much, and saw so plainly that he was an honorable man, that they let him off at six-and-eightpence instead of ten shillings. Then Mr Mangan started a company to take up the business, and made my father a manager in it to save us from starvation; for I wasnt earning anything then.

MRS HUSHABYE. Quite a romance. And when did the Boss develop the tender passion?

ELLIE. Oh, that was years after, quite lately. He took the chair one night at a sort of people's concert. I was singing there. As an amateur, you know: half a guinea for expenses and three songs with three encores. He was so pleased with my singing that he asked might he walk home with me. I never saw anyone so taken aback as he was when I took him home and introduced him to my father: his own manager. It was then that my father told me how nobly he had behaved. Of course it was considered a great chance for me, as he is so rich. And—and—we drifted into a sort of understanding—I suppose I should call it an engagement—[*She is distressed and cannot go on*].

MRS HUSHABYE [*rising and marching about*] You may have drifted into it; but you will bounce out of it, my pettikins, if I am to have anything to do with it.

ELLIE [*hopelessly*] No: it's no use. I am bound in honor and gratitude. I will go through with it.

MRS HUSHABYE [*behind the sofa, scolding down at her*] You know, of course, that it's not honorable or grateful to marry a man you dont love. Do you love this Mangan man?

ELLIE. Yes. At least—

MRS HUSHABYE. I dont want to know about "the least": I want to know the worst. Girls of your age fall in love with all sorts of impossible people, especially old people.

ELLIE. I like Mr Mangan very much; and I shall always be—

MRS HUSHABYE [*impatiently completing the sentence and prancing away intolerantly to starboard*] —grateful to him for his kindness to dear father. I know. Anybody else?

ELLIE. What do you mean?

MRS HUSHABYE. Anybody else? Are you in love with anybody else?

ELLIE. Of course not.

MRS HUSHABYE. Humph! [*The book on the drawing-table catches her eye. She picks it up, and evidently finds the title very unexpected. She looks at Ellie, and asks, quaintly*]. Quite sure youre not in love with an actor?

ELLIE. No, no. Why? What put such a thing into your head?

MRS HUSHABYE. This is yours, isnt it? Why else should you be reading Othello?

ELLIE. My father taught me to love Shakespear.

MRS HUSHABYE [*flinging the book down on the table*] Really! your father does seem to be about the limit.

ELLIE [*naïvely*] Do you never read Shakespear, Hesione? That seems to me so extraordinary. I like Othello.

MRS HUSHABYE. Do you indeed? He was jealous, wasnt he?

ELLIE. Oh, not that. I think all the part about jealousy is horrible.
But dont you think it must have been a wonderful experience for
Desdemona, brought up so quietly at home, to meet a man who
had been out in the world doing all sorts of brave things and
having terrible adventures, and yet finding something in her that
made him love to sit and talk with her and tell her about them?

MRS HUSHABYE. Thats your idea of romance, is it?

ELLIE. Not romance, exactly. It might really happen.

*Ellie's eyes shew that she is not arguing, but in a day-
dream. Mrs. Hushabye, watching her inquisitively, goes deliberately back to the sofa and resumes her seat beside her.*

MRS HUSHABYE. Ellie darling: have you noticed that some of
those stories that Othello told Desdemona couldnt have happened?

ELLIE. Oh no. Shakespear thought they could have happened.

MRS HUSHABYE. Hm! Desdemona thought they could have happened. But they didnt.

ELLIE. Why do you look so enigmatic about it? You are such a
sphinx: I never know what you mean.

MRS HUSHABYE. Desdemona would have found him out if she had
lived, you know. I wonder was that why he strangled her!

ELLIE. Othello was not telling lies.

MRS HUSHABYE. How do you know?

ELLIE. Shakespear would have said if he was. Hesione: there are
men who have done wonderful things: men like Othello, only, of
course, white, and very handsome, and—

MRS HUSHABYE. Ah! Now we're coming to it. Tell me all about
him. I knew there must be somebody, or youd never have been
so miserable about Mangan: youd have thought it quite a lark to
marry him.

ELLIE [*blushing vividly*] Hesione: you are dreadful. But I dont
want to make a secret of it, though of course I dont tell everybody. Besides, I dont know him.

MRS HUSHABYE. Dont know him! What does that mean?

ELLIE. Well, of course I know him to speak to.

MRS HUSHABYE. But you want to know him ever so much more intimately, eh?

ELLIE. No no: I know him quite—almost intimately.

MRS HUSHABYE. You dont know him; and you know him almost intimately. How lucid!

ELLIE. I mean that he does not call on us. I—I got into conversation with him by chance at a concert.

MRS HUSHABYE. You seem to have rather a gay time at your concerts, Ellie.

ELLIE. Not at all: we talk to everyone in the green-room waiting
for our turns. I thought he was one of the artists: he looked so
splendid. But he was only one of the committee. I happened to
tell him that I was copying a picture at the National Gallery. I
make a little money that way. I cant paint much; but as it's al-

ways the same picture I can do it pretty quickly and get two or three pounds for it. It happened that he came to the National Gallery one day.

MRS HUSHABYE. One student's day. Paid sixpence to stumble about through a crowd of easels, when he might have come in next day for nothing and found the floor clear! Quite by accident?

ELLIE [*triumphantly*] No. On purpose. He liked talking to me. He knows lots of the most splendid people. Fashionable women who are all in love with him. But he ran away from them to see me at the National Gallery and persuade me to come with him for a drive round Richmond Park in a taxi.

MRS HUSHABYE. My pettikins, you have been going it. It's wonderful what you good girls can do without anyone saying a word.

ELLIE. I am not in society, Hesione. If I didnt make acquaintances in that way I shouldnt have any at all.

MRS HUSHABYE. Well, no harm if you know how to take care of yourself. May I ask his name?

ELLIE [*slowly and musically*] Marcus Darnley.

MRS HUSHABYE [*echoing the music*] Marcus Darnley! What a splendid name!

ELLIE. Oh, I'm so glad you think so. I think so too; but I was afraid it was only a silly fancy of my own.

MRS HUSHABYE. Hm! Is he one of the Aberdeen Darnleys?

ELLIE. Nobody knows. Just fancy! He was found in an antique chest—

MRS HUSHABYE. A what?

ELLIE. An antique chest, one summer morning in a rose garden, after a night of the most terrible thunderstorm.

MRS HUSHABYE. What on earth was he doing in the chest? Did he get into it because he was afraid of the lightning?

ELLIE. Oh no, no: he was a baby. The name Marcus Darnley was embroidered on his babyclothes. And five hundred pounds in gold.

MRS HUSHABYE [*looking hard at her*] Ellie!

ELLIE. The garden of the Viscount—

MRS HUSHABYE. —de Rougemont?

ELLIE [*innocently*] No: de Larochejaquelin. A French family. A vicomte. His life has been one long romance. A tiger—

MRS HUSHABYE. Slain by his own hand?

ELLIE. Oh no: nothing vulgar like that. He saved the life of the tiger from a hunting party: one of King Edward's hunting parties in India. The King was furious: that was why he never had his military services properly recognized. But he doesnt care. He is a Socialist and despises rank, and has been in three revolutions fighting on the barricades.

MRS HUSHABYE. How can you sit there telling me such lies? You, Ellie, of all people! And I thought you were a perfectly simple, straightforward, good girl.

ELLIE [*rising, dignified but very angry*] Do you mean to say you dont believe me?

MRS HUSHABYE. Of course I dont believe you. Youre inventing every word of it. Do you take me for a fool?

    Ellie stares at her. Her candor is so obvious that Mrs Hushabye is puzzled.

ELLIE. Goodbye, Hesione. I'm very sorry. I see now that it sounds very improbable as I tell it. But I cant stay if you think that way about me.

MRS HUSHABYE [*catching her dress*] You shant go. I couldnt be so mistaken: I know too well what liars are like. Somebody has really told you all this.

ELLIE [*flushing*] Hesione: dont say that you dont believe h i m. I couldnt bear that.

MRS HUSHABYE [*soothing her*] Of course I believe him, dearest. But you should have broken it to me by degrees. [*Drawing her back to her seat*] Now tell me all about him. Are you in love with him?

ELLIE. Oh no. I'm not so foolish. I dont fall in love with people. I'm not so silly as you think.

MRS HUSHABYE. I see. Only something to think about—to give some interest and pleasure to life.

ELLIE. Just so. Thats all, really.

MRS HUSHABYE. It makes the hours go fast, doesnt it? No tedious waiting to go to sleep at nights and wondering whether you will have a bad night. How delightful it makes waking up in the morning! How much better than the happiest dream! All life transfigured! No more wishing one had an interesting book to read, because life is so much happier than any book! No desire but to be alone and not to have to talk to anyone: to be alone and just think about it.

ELLIE [*embracing her*] Hesione: you are a witch. How do you know? Oh, you are the most sympathetic woman in the world.

MRS HUSHABYE [*caressing her*] Pettikins, my pettikins: how I envy you! and how I pity you!

ELLIE. Pity me! Oh, why?

    A very handsome man of fifty, with mousquetaire moustaches, wearing a rather dandified curly brimmed hat, and carrying an elaborate walking-stick, comes into the room from the hall, and stops short at sight of the women on the sofa.

ELLIE [*seeing him and rising in glad surprise*] Oh! Hesione: this is Mr Marcus Darnley.

MRS HUSHABYE [*rising*] What a lark! He is my husband.

ELLIE. But how— [*She stops suddenly; then turns pale and sways*].

MRS HUSHABYE [*catching her and sitting down with her on the sofa*] Steady, my pettikins.

THE MAN [*with a mixture of confusion and effrontery, depositing his hat and stick on the teak table*] My real name, Miss Dunn, is Hector Hushabye. I leave you to judge whether that is a name any sensitive man would care to confess to. I never use it when I can possibly help it. I have been away for nearly a month; and I had no idea you knew my wife, or that you were coming here. I am none the less delighted to find you in our little house.

ELLIE [*in great distress*] I dont know what to do. Please, may I speak to papa? Do leave me. I cant bear it.

MRS HUSHABYE. Be off, Hector.

HECTOR. I—

MRS HUSHABYE. Quick, quick. Get out.

HECTOR. If you think it better— [*He goes out, taking his hat with him but leaving the stick on the table*].

MRS HUSHABYE [*laying Ellie down at the end of the sofa*] Now, pettikins, he is gone. Theres nobody but me. You can let yourself go. Dont try to control yourself. Have a good cry.

ELLIE [*raising her head*] Damn!

MRS HUSHABYE. Splendid! Oh, what a relief! I thought you were going to be broken-hearted. Never mind me. Damn him again.

ELLIE. I am not damning him: I am damning myself for being such a fool. [*Rising*] How could I let myself be taken in so? [*She begins prowling to and fro, her bloom gone, looking curiously older and harder*].

MRS HUSHABYE [*cheerfully*] Why not, pettikins? Very few young women can resist Hector. I couldnt when I was your age. He is really rather splendid, you know.

ELLIE [*turning on her*] Splendid! Yes: splendid l o o k i n g, of course. But how can you love a liar?

MRS HUSHABYE. I dont know. But you can, fortunately. Otherwise there wouldnt be much love in the world.

ELLIE. But to lie like that! To be a boaster! a coward!

MRS HUSHABYE [*rising in alarm*] Pettikins: none of that, if you please. If you hint the slightest doubt of Hector's courage, he will go straight off and do the most horribly dangerous things to convince himself that he isnt a coward. He has a dreadful trick of getting out of one third-floor window and coming in at another, just to test his nerve. He has a whole drawerful of Albert Medals for saving people's lives.

ELLIE. He never told me that.

MRS HUSHABYE. He never boasts of anything he really did: he cant bear it; and it makes him shy if anyone else does. All his stories are made-up stories.

ELLIE [*coming to her*] Do you mean that he is really brave, and really has adventures, and yet tells lies about things that he never did and that never happened?

MRS HUSHABYE. Yes, pettikins, I do. People dont have their virtues and vices in sets: they have them anyhow: all mixed.

ELLIE [*staring at her thoughtfully*] Theres something odd about this house, Hesione, and even about you. I dont know why I'm talking to you so calmly. I have a horrible fear that my heart is broken, but that heartbreak is not like what I thought it must be.

MRS HUSHABYE [*fondling her*] It's only life educating you, pettikins. How do you feel about Boss Mangan now?

ELLIE [*disengaging herself with an expression of distaste*] Oh, how can you remind me of him, Hesione?

MRS HUSHABYE. Sorry, dear. I think I hear Hector coming back. You dont mind now, do you, dear?

ELLIE. Not in the least. I'm quite cured.

Mazzini Dunn and Hector come in from the hall.

HECTOR [*as he opens the door and allows Mazzini to pass in*] One second more, and she would have been a dead woman!

MAZZINI. Dear! dear! what an escape! Ellie, my love: Mr Hushabye has just been telling me the most extraordinary—

ELLIE. Yes: Ive heard it [*She crosses to the other side of the room*].

HECTOR [*following her*] Not this one: I'll tell it to you after dinner. I think youll like it. The truth is, I made it up for you, and was looking forward to the pleasure of telling it to you. But in a moment of impatience at being turned out of the room, I threw it away on your father.

ELLIE [*turning at bay with her back to the carpenter's bench, scornfully self-possessed*] It was not thrown away. He believes it. I should not have believed it.

MAZZINI [*benevolently*] Ellie is very naughty, Mr Hushabye. Of course she does not really think that. [*He goes to the bookshelves, and inspects the titles of the volumes*].

Boss Mangan comes in from the hall, followed by the Captain. Mangan, carefully frock-coated as for church or for a directors' meeting, is about fiftyfive, with a careworn, mistrustful expression, standing a little on an entirely imaginary dignity, with a dull complexion, straight, lustreless hair, and features so entirely commonplace that it is impossible to describe them.

CAPTAIN SHOTOVER [*to Mrs Hushabye, introducing the newcomer*] Says his name is Mangan. Not ablebodied.

MRS HUSHABYE [*graciously*] How do you do, Mr Mangan?

MANGAN [*shaking hands*] Very pleased.

CAPTAIN SHOTOVER. Dunn's lost his muscle, but recovered his nerve. Men seldom do after three attacks of delirium tremens. [*He goes into the pantry*].

MRS HUSHABYE. I congratulate you, Mr Dunn.

MAZZINI [*dazed*] I am a lifelong teetotaler.

MRS HUSHABYE. You will find it far less trouble to let papa have his own way than try to explain.

MAZZINI. But three attacks of delirium tremens, really!

MRS HUSHABYE [*to Mangan*] Do you know my husband, Mr Mangan? [*She indicates Hector*].

MANGAN [*going to Hector, who meets him with outstretched*

hand] Very pleased. [*Turning to Ellie*] I hope, Miss Ellie, you have not found the journey down too fatiguing. [*They shake hands*].

MRS HUSHABYE. Hector: shew Mr Dunn his room.

HECTOR. Certainly. Come along, Mr Dunn. [*He takes Mazzini out*].

ELLIE. You havnt shewn me my room yet, Hesione.

MRS HUSHABYE. How stupid of me! Come along. Make yourself quite at home, Mr Mangan. Papa will entertain you. [*She calls to the Captain in the pantry*] Papa: come and explain the house to Mr Mangan.

She goes out with Ellie. The Captain comes from the pantry.

CAPTAIN SHOTOVER. Youre going to marry Dunn's daughter. Dont. Youre too old.

MANGAN [*staggered*] Well! Thats fairly blunt, Captain.

CAPTAIN SHOTOVER. It's true.

MANGAN. She doesnt think so.

CAPTAIN SHOTOVER. She does.

MANGAN. Older men than I have—

CAPTAIN SHOTOVER [*finishing the sentence for him*]—made fools of themselves. That, also, is true.

MANGAN [*asserting himself*] I dont see that this is any business of yours.

CAPTAIN SHOTOVER. It is everybody's business. The stars in their courses are shaken when such things happen.

MANGAN. I'm going to marry her all the same.

CAPTAIN SHOTOVER. How do you know?

MANGAN [*playing the strong man*] I intend to. I mean to. See? I never made up my mind to do a thing yet that I didnt bring it off. Thats the sort of man I am; and there will be a better understanding between us when you make up your mind to that, Captain.

CAPTAIN SHOTOVER. You frequent picture palaces.

MANGAN. Perhaps I do. Who told you?

CAPTAIN SHOTOVER. Talk like a man, not like a movy. You mean that you make a hundred thousand a year.

MANGAN. I dont boast. But when I meet a man that makes a hundred thousand a year, I take off my hat to that man, and stretch out my hand to him and call him brother.

CAPTAIN SHOTOVER. Then you also make a hundred thousand a year, hey?

MANGAN. No. I cant say that. Fifty thousand, perhaps.

CAPTAIN SHOTOVER. His half brother only [*he turns away from Mangan with his usual abruptness, and collects the empty teacups on the Chinese tray*].

MANGAN [*irritated*] See here, Captain Shotover. I dont quite understand my position here. I came here on your daughter's invitation. Am I in her house or in yours?

CAPTAIN SHOTOVER. You are beneath the dome of heaven, in the house of God. What is true within these walls is true outside them. Go out on the seas; climb the mountains; wander through the valleys. She is still too young.

MANGAN [*weakening*] But I'm very little over fifty.

CAPTAIN SHOTOVER. You are still less under sixty. Boss Mangan: you will not marry the pirate's child [*he carries the tray away into the pantry*].

MANGAN [*following him to the half door*] What pirate's child? What are you talking about?

CAPTAIN SHOTOVER [*in the pantry*] Ellie Dunn. You will not marry her.

MANGAN. Who will stop me?

CAPTAIN SHOTOVER [*emerging*] My daughter [*he makes for the door leading to the hall*].

MANGAN [*following him*] Mrs Hushabye! Do you mean to say she brought me down here to break it off?

CAPTAIN SHOTOVER [*stopping and turning on him*] I know nothing more than I have seen in her eye. She w i l l break it off. Take my advice: marry a West Indian negress: they make excellent wives. I was married to one myself for two years.

MANGAN. Well, I a m damned!

CAPTAIN SHOTOVER. I thought so. I was, too, for many years. The negress redeemed me.

MANGAN [*feebly*] This is queer. I ought to walk out of this house.

CAPTAIN SHOTOVER. Why?

MANGAN. Well, many men would be offended by your style of talking.

CAPTAIN SHOTOVER. Nonsense! It's the other sort of talking that makes quarrels. Nobody ever quarrels with me.

A *gentleman, whose firstrate tailoring and frictionless manners proclaim the wellbred West Ender, comes in from the hall. He has an engaging air of being young and unmarried, but on close inspection is found to be at least over forty.*

THE GENTLEMAN. Excuse my intruding in this fashion; but there is no knocker on the door; and the bell does not seem to ring.

CAPTAIN SHOTOVER. Why should there be a knocker? Why should the bell ring? The door is open.

THE GENTLEMAN. Precisely. So I ventured to come in.

CAPTAIN SHOTOVER. Quite right. I will see about a room for you [*he makes for the door*].

THE GENTLEMAN [*stopping him*] But I'm afraid you dont know who I am.

CAPTAIN SHOTOVER. Do you suppose that at my age I make distinctions between one fellowcreature and another? [*He goes out. Mangan and the newcomer stare at one another*].

MANGAN. Strange character, Captain Shotover, sir.

THE GENTLEMAN. Very.

CAPTAIN SHOTOVER [*shouting outside*] Hesione: another person has arrived and wants a room. Man about town, well dressed, fifty.

THE GENTLEMAN. Fancy Hesione's feelings! May I ask are you a member of the family?

MANGAN. No.

THE GENTLEMAN. I am. At least a connexion.

Mrs Hushabye comes back.

MRS HUSHABYE. How do you do? How good of you to come!

THE GENTLEMAN. I am very glad indeed to make your acquaintance, Hesione. [*Instead of taking her hand he kisses her. At the same moment the Captain appears in the doorway*]. You will excuse my kissing your daughter, Captain, when I tell you that—

CAPTAIN SHOTOVER. Stuff! Everyone kisses my daughter. Kiss her as much as you like [*he makes for the pantry*].

THE GENTLEMAN. Thank you. One moment, Captain. [*The Captain halts and turns. The gentleman goes to him affably*]. Do you happen to remember—but probably you dont, as it occurred many years ago—that your younger daughter married a numskull?

CAPTAIN SHOTOVER. Yes. She said she'd marry anybody to get away from this house. I should not have recognized you: your head is no longer like a walnut. Your aspect is softened. You have been boiled in bread and milk for years and years, like other married men. Poor devil! [*He disappears into the pantry*].

MRS HUSHABYE [*going past Mangan to the gentleman and scrutinizing him*] I dont believe you are Hastings Utterword.

THE GENTLEMAN. I am not.

MRS HUSHABYE. Then what business had you to kiss me?

THE GENTLEMAN. I thought I would like to. The fact is, I am Randall Utterword, the unworthy younger brother of Hastings. I was abroad diplomatizing when he was married.

LADY UTTERWORD [*dashing in*] Hesione: where is the key of the wardrobe in my room? My diamonds are in my dressing-bag: I must lock it up—[*recognizing the stranger with a shock*] Randall: how dare you? [*She marches at him past Mrs Hushabye, who retreats and joins Mangan near the sofa*].

RANDALL. How dare I what? I am not doing anything.

LADY UTTERWORD. Who told you I was here?

RANDALL. Hastings. You had just left when I called on you at Claridge's; so I followed you down here. You are looking extremely well.

LADY UTTERWORD. Dont presume to tell me so.

MRS HUSHABYE. What is wrong with Mr Randall, Addy?

LADY UTTERWORD [*recollecting herself*] Oh, nothing. But he has no right to come bothering you and papa without being invited [*she goes to the window-seat and sits down, turning away from them ill-humoredly and looking into the garden, where Hector and Ellie are now seen strolling together*].

MRS HUSHABYE. I think you have not met Mr Mangan, Addy.

LADY UTTERWORD [*turning her head and nodding coldly to*

Mangan] I beg your pardon. Randall: you have flustered me so: I made a perfect fool of myself.

MRS HUSHABYE. Lady Utterword. My sister. My y o u n g e r sister.

MANGAN [*bowing*] Pleased to meet you, Lady Utterword.

LADY UTTERWORD [*with marked interest*] Who is that gentleman walking in the garden with Miss Dunn?

MRS HUSHABYE. I dont know. She quarrelled mortally with my husband only ten minutes ago; and I didnt know anyone else had come. It must be a visitor. [*She goes to the window to look*]. Oh, it i s Hector. Theyve made it up.

LADY UTTERWORD. Your husband! That handsome man?

MRS HUSHABYE. Well, why shouldnt my husband be a handsome man?

RANDALL [*joining them at the window*] One's husband never is, Ariadne [*he sits by Lady Utterword, on her right*].

MRS HUSHABYE. One's sister's husband always is, Mr Randall.

LADY UTTERWORD. Dont be vulgar, Randall. And you, Hesione, are just as bad.

> *Ellie and Hector come in from the garden by the starboard door. Randall rises. Ellie retires into the corner near the pantry. Hector comes forward; and Lady Utterword rises looking her very best.*

MRS HUSHABYE. Hector: this is Addy.

HECTOR [*apparently surprised*] Not this lady.

LADY UTTERWORD [*smiling*] Why not?

HECTOR [*looking at her with a piercing glance of deep but respectful admiration, his moustache bristling*] I thought— [*pulling himself together*] I beg your pardon, Lady Utterword. I am extremely glad to welcome you at last under our roof [*he offers his hand with grave courtesy*].

MRS HUSHABYE. She wants to be kissed, Hector.

LADY UTTERWORD. Hesione! [*but she still smiles*].

MRS HUSHABYE. Call her Addy; and kiss her like a good brother-in-law; and have done with it. [*She leaves them to themselves*].

HECTOR. Behave yourself, Hesione. Lady Utterword is entitled not only to hospitality but to civilization.

LADY UTTERWORD [*gratefully*] Thank you, Hector. [*They shake hands cordially*].

> *Mazzini Dunn is seen crossing the garden from starboard to port.*

CAPTAIN SHOTOVER [*coming from the pantry and addressing Ellie*] Your father has washed himself.

ELLIE [*quite self-possessed*] He often does, Captain Shotover.

CAPTAIN SHOTOVER. A strange conversion! I saw him through the pantry window.

> *Mazzie Dunn enters through the port window door, newly washed and brushed, and stops, smiling benevolently, between Mangan and Mrs Hushabye.*

MRS HUSHABYE [*introducing*] Mr Mazzini Dunn, Lady Ut—oh, I forgot: youve met. [*Indicating Ellie*] Miss Dunn.

MAZZINI [*walking across the room to take Ellie's hand, and beaming at his own naughty irony*] I have met Miss Dunn also. She is my daughter. [*He draws her arm through his caressingly*].

MRS HUSHABYE. Of course: how stupid! Mr Utterword, my sister's-er—

RANDALL [*shaking hands agreeably*] Her brother-in-law, Mr Dunn. How do you do?

MRS HUSHABYE. This is my husband.

HECTOR. We have met, dear. Dont introduce us any more. [*He moves away to the big chair, and adds*] Wont you sit down, Lady Utterword? [*She does so very graciously*].

MRS HUSHABYE. Sorry. I hate it: it's like making people shew their tickets.

MAZZINI [*sententiously*] How little it tells us, after all! The great question is, not who we are, but what we are.

CAPTAIN SHOTOVER. Ha! What are you?

MAZZINI [*taken aback*] What am I?

CAPTAIN SHOTOVER. A thief, a pirate, and a murderer.

MAZZINI. I assure you you are mistaken.

CAPTAIN SHOTOVER. An adventurous life; but what does it end in? Respectability. A ladylike daughter. The language and appearance of a city missionary. Let it be a warning to all of you [*he goes out through the garden*].

DUNN. I hope nobody here believes that I am a thief, a pirate, or a murderer. Mrs Hushabye: will you excuse me a moment? I must really go and explain. [*He follows the Captain*].

MRS HUSHABYE [*as he goes*] It's no use. Youd really better— [*but Dunn has vanished*]. We had better all go out and look for some tea. We never have regular tea; but you can always get some when you want: the servants keep it stewing all day. The kitchen veranda is the best place to ask. May I shew you? [*She goes to the starboard door*].

RANDALL [*going with her*] Thank you, I dont think I'll take any tea this afternoon. But if you will shew me the garden—?

MRS HUSHABYE. Theres nothing to see in the garden except papa's observatory, and a gravel pit with a cave where he keeps dynamite and things of that sort. However, it's pleasanter out of doors; so come along.

RANDALL. Dynamite! Isnt that rather risky?

MRS HUSHABYE. Well, we dont sit in the gravel pit when theres a thunderstorm.

LADY UTTERWORD. Thats something new. What is the dynamite for?

HECTOR. To blow up the human race if it goes too far. He is trying to discover a psychic ray that will explode all the explosives at the will of a Mahatma.

ELLIE. The Captain's tea is delicious, Mr Utterword.

MRS HUSHABYE [*stopping in the doorway*] Do you mean to say that youve had some of my father's tea? that you got round him before you were ten minutes in the house?

ELLIE. I did.

MRS HUSHABYE. You little devil! [*She goes out with Randall*].

MANGAN. Wont you come, Miss Ellie?

ELLIE. I'm too tired. I'll take a book up to my room and rest a little. [*She goes to the bookshelf*].

MANGAN. Right. You cant do better. But I'm disappointed. [*He follows Randall and Mrs Hushabye*].

>   *Ellie, Hector, and Lady Utterword are left. Hector is close to Lady Utterword. They look at Ellie, waiting for her to go.*

ELLIE [*looking at the title of a book*] Do you like stories of adventure, Lady Utterword?

LADY UTTERWORD [*patronizingly*] Of course, dear.

ELLIE. Then I'll leave you to Mr Hushabye. [*She goes out through the hall*].

HECTOR. That girl is mad about tales of adventure. The lies I have to tell her!

LADY UTTERWORD [*not interested in Ellie*] When you saw me what did you mean by saying that you thought, and then stopping short? What did you think?

HECTOR [*folding his arms and looking down at her magnetically*] May I tell you?

LADY UTTERWORD. Of course.

HECTOR. It will not sound very civil. I was on the point of saying "I thought you were a plain woman."

LADY UTTERWORD. Oh for shame, Hector! What right had you to notice whether I am plain or not?

HECTOR. Listen to me, Ariadne. Until today I have seen only photographs of you; and no photograph can give the strange fascination of the daughters of that supernatural old man. There is some damnable quality in them that destroys men's moral sense, and carries them beyond honor and dishonor. You know that, dont you?

LADY UTTERWORD. Perhaps I do, Hector. But let me warn you once for all that I am a rigidly conventional woman. You may think because I'm a Shotover that I'm a Bohemian, because we are all so horribly Bohemian. But I'm not. I hate and loathe Bohemianism. No child brought up in a strict Puritan household ever suffered from Puritanism as I suffered from our Bohemianism.

HECTOR. Our children are like that. They spend their holidays in the houses of their respectable schoolfellows.

LADY UTTERWORD. I shall invite them for Christmas.

HECTOR. Their absence leaves us both without our natural chaperons.

LADY UTTERWORD. Children are certainly very inconvenient sometimes. But intelligent people can always manage, unless they are Bohemians.

HECTOR. You are no Bohemian; but you are no Puritan either: your attraction is alive and powerful. What sort of woman do you count yourself?

LADY UTTERWORD. I am a woman of the world, Hector; and I can assure you that if you will only take the trouble always to do the perfectly correct thing, and to say the perfectly correct thing, you can do just what you like. An ill-conducted, careless woman gets simply no chance. An ill-conducted, careless man is never allowed within arms length of any woman worth knowing.

HECTOR. I see. You are neither a Bohemian woman nor a Puritan woman. You are a dangerous woman.

LADY UTTERWORD. On the contrary, I am a safe woman.

HECTOR. You are a most accursedly attractive woman. Mind: I am not making love to you. I do not like being attracted. But you had better know how I feel if you are going to stay here.

LADY UTTERWORD. You are an exceedingly clever ladykiller, Hector. And terribly handsome. I am quite a good player, myself, at that game. Is it quite understood that we are only playing?

HECTOR. Quite. I am deliberately playing the fool, out of sheer worthlessness.

LADY UTTERWORD [*rising brightly*] Well, you are my brother-in-law. Hesione asked you to kiss me. [*He seizes her in his arms, and kisses her strenuously*]. Oh! that was a little more than play, brother-in-law. [*She pushes him suddenly away*]. You shall not do that again.

HECTOR. In effect, you got your claws deeper into me than I intended.

MRS HUSHABYE [*coming in from the garden*] Dont let me disturb you: I only want a cap to put on daddiest. The sun is setting; and he'll catch cold [*she makes for the door leading to the hall.*]

LADY UTTERWORD. Your husband is quite charming, darling. He has actually condescended to kiss me at last. I shall go into the garden: it's cooler now [*she goes out by the port door*].

MRS HUSHABYE. Take care, dear child. I dont believe any man can kiss Addy without falling in love with her. [*She goes into the hall*].

HECTOR [*striking himself on the chest*] Fool! Goat!

    Mrs Hushabye comes back with the Captain's cap.

HECTOR. Your sister is an extremely enterprising old girl. Wheres Miss Dunn!

MRS HUSHABYE. Mangan says she has gone up to her room for a nap. Addy wont let you talk to Ellie: she has marked you for her own.

HECTOR. She has the diabolical family fascination. I began making love to her automatically. What am I to do? I cant fall in love; and I cant hurt a woman's feelings by telling her so when she falls in love with me. And as women are always falling in love with my moustache I get landed in all sorts of tedious and terrifying flirtations in which I'm not a bit in earnest.

MRS HUSHABYE. Oh, neither is Addy. She has never been in love in her life, though she has always been trying to fall in head over ears. She is worse than you, because you had one real go at least, with me.

HECTOR. That was a confounded madness. I cant believe that such an amazing experience is common. It has left its mark on me. I believe that is why I have never been able to repeat it.

MRS HUSHABYE [*laughing and caressing his arm*] We were frightfully in love with one another, Hector. It was such an enchanting dream that I have never been able to grudge it to you or anyone else since. I have invited all sorts of pretty women to the house on the chance of giving you another turn. But it has never come off.

HECTOR. I dont know that I want it to come off. It was damned dangerous. You fascinated me; but I loved you; so it was heaven. This sister of yours fascinates me; but I hate her; so it is hell. I shall kill her if she persists.

MRS HUSHABYE. Nothing will kill Addy: she is as strong as a horse. [*Releasing him*] Now I am going off to fascinate somebody.

HECTOR. The Foreign Office toff? Randall?

MRS HUSHABYE. Goodness gracious, no! Why should I fascinate him?

HECTOR. I presume you dont mean the bloated capitalist, Mangan?

MRS HUSHABYE. Hm! I think he had better be fascinated by me than by Ellie. [*She is going into the garden when the Captain comes in from it with some sticks in his hand*]. What have you got there, daddiest?

CAPTAIN SHOTOVER. Dynamite.

MRS HUSHABYE. Youve been to the gravel pit. Dont drop it about the house: theres a dear. [*She goes into the garden, where the evening light is now very red*].

HECTOR. Listen, O sage. How long dare you concentrate on a feeling without risking having it fixed in your consciousness all the rest of your life?

CAPTAIN SHOTOVER. Ninety minutes. An hour and a half. [*He goes into the pantry*].

Hector, left alone, contracts his brows, and falls into a daydream. He does not move for some time. Then he folds his arms. Then, throwing his hands behind him, and gripping one with the other, he strides tragically once to and fro. Suddenly he snatches his walking-stick from the teak table, and draws it; for it is a sword-stick. He fights a desperate duel with an imaginary antagonist, and after many vicissitudes runs him through the body up to the hilt. He sheathes his sword and throws it on the sofa, falling into another reverie as he does so. He looks straight into the eyes of an imaginary woman; seizes her by the arms; and says in a deep and thrilling tone "Do you love me!" The Captain comes out of the pantry at this moment; and Hector, caught with his arms stretched out and his fists clenched, has to account for his attitude by going through a series of gymnastic exercises.

CAPTAIN SHOTOVER. That sort of strength is no good. You will never be as strong as a gorilla.

HECTOR. What is the dynamite for?

CAPTAIN SHOTOVER. To kill fellows like Mangan.

HECTOR. No use. They will always be able to buy more dynamite than you.

CAPTAIN SHOTOVER. I will make a dynamite that he cannot explode.

HECTOR. And that you can, eh?

CAPTAIN SHOTOVER. Yes: when I have attained the seventh degree of concentration.

HECTOR. Whats the use of that? You never do attain it.

CAPTAIN SHOTOVER. What then is to be done? Are we to be kept for ever in the mud by these hogs to whom the universe is nothing but a machine for greasing their bristles and filling their snouts?

HECTOR. Are Mangan's bristles worse than Randall's lovelocks?

CAPTAIN SHOTOVER. We must win powers of life and death over them both. I refuse to die until I have invented the means.

HECTOR. Who are we that we should judge them?

CAPTAIN SHOTOVER. What are they that they should judge us? Yet they do, unhesitatingly. There is enmity between our seed and their seed. They know it and act on it, strangling our souls. They believe in themselves. When we believe in ourselves, we shall kill them.

HECTOR. It is the same seed. You forget that your pirate has a very nice daughter. Mangan's son may be a Plato: Randall's a Shelley. What was my father?

CAPTAIN SHOTOVER. The damndest scoundrel I ever met. [*He replaces the drawing-board; sits down at the table; and begins to mix a wash of color*].

HECTOR. Precisely. Well, dare you kill his innocent grandchildren?

CAPTAIN SHOTOVER. They are mine also.

HECTOR. Just so. We are members one of another. [*He throws himself carelessly on the sofa*]. I tell you I have often thought of this killing of human vermin. Many men have thought of it. Decent men are like Daniel in the lion's den: their survival is a miracle; and they do not always survive. We live among the Mangans and Randalls and Billie Dunns as they, poor devils, live among the disease germs and the doctors and the lawyers and the parsons and the restaurant chefs and the tradesmen and the servants and all the rest of the parasites and blackmailers. What are our terrors to theirs? Give me the power to kill them; and I'll spare them in sheer—

CAPTAIN SHOTOVER [*cutting in sharply*] Fellow feeling?

HECTOR. No. I should kill myself if I believed that. I must believe that my spark, small as it is, is divine, and that the red light over their door is hell fire. I should spare them in simple magnanimous pity.

CAPTAIN SHOTOVER. You cant spare them until you have the power to kill them. At present they have the power to kill you. There are millions of blacks over the water for them to train and let loose on us. Theyre going to do it. Theyre doing it already.

HECTOR. They are too stupid to use their power.

CAPTAIN SHOTOVER [*throwing down his brush and coming to the end of the sofa*] Do not deceive yourself: they do use it. We kill the better half of ourselves every day to propitiate them. The knowledge that these people are there to render all our aspirations barren prevents us having the aspirations. And when we are tempted to seek their destruction they bring forth demons to delude us, disguised as pretty daughters, and singers and poets and the like, for whose sake we spare them.

HECTOR [*sitting up and leaning towards him*] May not Hesione be such a demon, brought forth by you lest I should slay you?

CAPTAIN SHOTOVER. That is possible. She has used you up, and left you nothing but dreams, as some women do.

HECTOR. Vampire women, demon women.

CAPTAIN SHOTOVER. Men think the world well lost for them and lose it accordingly. Who are the men that do things? The husbands of the shrew and of the drunkard, the men with the thorn in the flesh. [*Walking distractedly away towards the pantry*] I must think these things out. [*Turning suddenly*] But I go on with the dynamite none the less. I will discover a ray mightier than any X-ray: a mind ray that will explode the ammunition in the belt of my adversary before he can point his gun at me. And I must hurry. I am old: I have no time to waste in talk [*he is about to go into the pantry, and Hector is making for the hall, when Hesione comes back*].

MRS HUSHABYE. Daddiest: you and Hector must come and help me to entertain all these people. What on earth were you shouting about?

HECTOR [*stopping in the act of turning the door handle*] He is madder than usual.

MRS HUSHABYE. We all are.

HECTOR. I must change [*he resumes his door opening*].

MRS HUSHABYE. Stop, stop. Come back, both of you. Come back. [*They return, reluctantly*]. Money is running short.

HECTOR. Money! Where are my April dividends?

MRS HUSHABYE. Where is the snow that fell last year?

CAPTAIN SHOTOVER. Where is all the money you had for that patent lifeboat I invented?

MRS HUSHABYE. Five hundred pounds; and I have made it last since Easter!

CAPTAIN SHOTOVER. Since Easter! Barely four months! Monstrous extravagance! I could live for seven years on £500.

MRS HUSHABYE. Not keeping open house as we do here, daddiest.

CAPTAIN SHOTOVER. Only £500 for that lifeboat! I got twelve thousand for the invention before that.

MRS HUSHABYE. Yes, dear; but that was for the ship with the magnetic keel that sucked up submarines. Living at the rate we do, you cannot afford life-saving inventions. Cant you think of something that will murder half Europe at one bang?

CAPTAIN SHOTOVER. No. I am ageing fast. My mind does not dwell on slaughter as it did when I was a boy. Why doesnt your husband invent something? He does nothing but tell lies to women.

HECTOR. Well, that is a form of invention, is it not? However, you are right: I ought to support my wife.

MRS HUSHABYE. Indeed you shall do nothing of the sort: I should never see you from breakfast to dinner. I want my husband.

HECTOR [*bitterly*] I might as well be your lapdog.

MRS HUSHABYE. Do you want to be my breadwinner, like the other poor husbands?

HECTOR. No, by thunder! What a damned creature a husband is anyhow!

MRS HUSHABYE [*to the Captain*] What about that harpoon cannon?

CAPTAIN SHOTOVER. No use. It kills whales, not men.

MRS HUSHABYE. Why not? You fire the harpoon out of a cannon. It sticks in the enemy's general; you wind him in; and there you are.

HECTOR. You are your father's daughter, Hesione.

CAPTAIN SHOTOVER. There is something in it. Not to wind in generals: they are not dangerous. But one could fire a grapnel and wind in a machine gun or even a tank. I will think it out.

MRS HUSHABYE [*squeezing the Captain's arm affectionately*] Saved! You a r e a darling, daddiest. Now we must go back to these dreadful people and entertain them.

CAPTAIN SHOTOVER. They have had no dinner. Dont forget that.

HECTOR. Neither have I. And it is dark: it must be all hours.

MRS HUSHABYE. Oh, Guinness will produce some sort of dinner for them. The servants always take jolly good care that there is food in the house.

CAPTAIN SHOTOVER [*raising a strange wail in the darkness*] What a house! What a daughter!

MRS HUSHABYE [*raving*] What a father!

HECTOR [*following suit*] What a husband!

CAPTAIN SHOTOVER. Is there no thunder in heaven?

HECTOR. Is there no beauty, no bravery, on earth?

MRS HUSHABYE. What do men want? They have their food, their firesides, their clothes mended, and our love at the end of the day. Why are they not satisfied? Why do they envy us the pain with which we bring them into the world, and make strange dangers and torments for themselves to be even with us?

CAPTAIN SHOTOVER [*weirdly chanting*]

I builded a house for my daughters, and opened the
    doors thereof,
That men might come for their choosing, and their
    betters spring from their love;
But one of them married a numskull;

HECTOR [*taking up the rhythm*]

                                 The other a liar wed;

MRS HUSHABYE [*completing the stanza*]
And now must she lie beside him, even as she made
    her bed.

LADY UTTERWORD [*calling from the garden*] Hesione! Hesione!
Where are you?

HECTOR. The cat is on the tiles.¹

MRS HUSHABYE. Coming, darling, coming [*she goes quickly into
the garden*].

    The Captain goes back to his place at the table.

HECTOR [*going into the hall*] Shall I turn up the lights for you?

CAPTAIN SHOTOVER. No. Give me deeper darkness. Money is not
made in the light.

END OF ACT I

---

1. I.e. she is restless as a cat prowling on the roof.

Act II

The same room, with the lights turned up and the curtains drawn. Ellie comes in, followed by Mangan. Both are dressed for dinner. She strolls to the drawing-table. He comes between the table and the wicker chair.

MANGAN. What a dinner! I dont call it a dinner: I call it a meal.

ELLIE. I am accustomed to meals, Mr Mangan, and very lucky to get them. Besides, the captain cooked some macaroni for me.

MANGAN [*shuddering liverishly*] Too rich: I cant eat such things. I suppose it's because I have to work so much with my brain. Thats the worst of being a man of business: you are always thinking, thinking, thinking. By the way, now that we are alone, may I take the opportunity to come to a little understanding with you?

ELLIE [*settling into the draughtsman's seat*] Certainly. I should like to.

MANGAN [*taken aback*] Should you? That surprises me; for I thought I noticed this afternoon that you avoided me all you could. Not for the first time either.

ELLIE. I was very tired and upset. I wasn't used to the ways of this extraordinary house. Please forgive me.

MANGAN. Oh, thats all right: I dont mind. But Captain Shotover has been talking to me about you. You and me, you know.

ELLIE [*interested*] The Captain! What did he say?

MANGAN. Well, he noticed the difference between our ages.

ELLIE. He notices everything.

MANGAN. You dont mind, then?

ELLIE. Of course I know quite well that our engagement—

MANGAN. Oh! you call it an engagement.

ELLIE. Well, isnt it?

MANGAN. Oh, yes, yes: no doubt it is if you hold to it. This is the first time youve used the word; and I didnt quite know where we stood: thats all. [*He sits down in the wicker chair; and resigns himself to allow her to lead the conversation*]. You were saying—?

ELLIE. Was I? I forget. Tell me. Do you like this part of the country? I heard you ask Mr Hushabye at dinner whether there are any nice houses to let down here.

MANGAN. I like the place. The air suits me. I shouldnt be surprised if I settled down here.

ELLIE. Nothing would please me better. The air suits me too. And I want to be near Hesione.

MANGAN [*with growing uneasiness*] The air may suit us; but the question is, should we suit one another? Have you thought about that?

ELLIE. Mr Mangan: we must be sensible, mustnt we? It's no use

pretending that we are Romeo and Juliet. But we can get on very
well together if we choose to make the best of it. Your kindness
of heart will make it easy for me.

MANGAN [*leaning forward, with the beginning of something like
deliberate unpleasantness in his voice*] Kindness of heart, eh? I
ruined your father, didnt I?

ELLIE. Oh, not intentionally.

MANGAN. Yes I did. Ruined him on purpose.

ELLIE. On purpose!

MANGAN. Not out of ill-nature, you know. And youll admit that I
kept a job for him when I had finished with him. But business is
business; and I ruined him as a matter of business.

ELLIE. I dont understand how that can be. Are you trying to make
me feel that I need not be grateful to you, so that I may choose
freely?

MANGAN [*rising aggressively*] No. I mean what I say.

ELLIE. But how could it possibly do you any good to ruin my
father? The money he lost was yours.

MANGAN [*with a sour laugh*] W a s mine! It i s mine, Miss Ellie,
and all the money the other fellows lost too. [*He shoves his
hands into his pockets and shews his teeth*]. I just smoked them
out like a hive of bees. What do you say to that? A bit of shock,
eh?

ELLIE. It would have been, this morning. N o w! you cant think
how little it matters. But it's quite interesting. Only, you must
explain it to me. I dont understand it. [*Propping her elbows on
the drawing-board and her chin on her hands, she composes herself to listen with a combination of conscious curiosity with
unconscious contempt which provokes him to more and more
unpleasantness, and an attempt at patronage of her ignorance*].

MANGAN. Of course you dont understand: what do you know about
business? You just listen and learn. Your father's business was a
new business; and I dont start new businesses: I let other fellows
start them. They put all their money and their friends' money
into starting them. They wear out their souls and bodies trying
to make a success of them. Theyre what you call enthusiasts. But
the first dead lift of the thing is too much for them; and they
havnt enough financial experience. In a year or so they have
either to let the whole show go bust, or sell out to a new lot of
fellows for a few deferred ordinary shares: that is, if theyre lucky
enough to get anything at all. As likely as not the very same
thing happens to the new lot. They put in more money and a
couple of years more work; and then perhaps t h e y have to sell
out to a third lot. If it's really a big thing the third lot will have
to sell out too, and leave t h e i r work and t h e i r money behind
them. And thats where the real business man comes in: where I
come in. But I'm cleverer than some: I dont mind dropping a
little money to start the process. I took your father's measure. I
saw that he had a sound idea, and that he would work himself
silly for it if he got the chance. I saw that he was a child in busi-

ness, and was dead certain to outrun his expenses and be in too great a hurry to wait for his market. I knew that the surest way to ruin a man who doesnt know how to handle money is to give him some. I explained my idea to some friends in the city, and they found the money; for I take no risks in ideas, even when theyre my own. Your father and the friends that ventured their money with him were no more to me than a heap of squeezed lemons. Youve been wasting your gratitude: my kind heart is all rot. I'm sick of it. When I see your father beaming at me with his moist, grateful eyes, regularly wallowing in gratitude, I sometimes feel I must tell him the truth or burst. What stops me is that I know he wouldnt believe me. He'd think it was my modesty, as you did just now. He'd think anything rather than the truth, which is that he's a blamed fool, and I am a man that knows how to take care of himself. [*He throws himself back into the big chair with large self-approval*]. Now what do you think of me, Miss Ellie?

ELLIE [*dropping her hands*] How strange! that my mother, who knew nothing at all about business, should have been quite right about you! She always said—not before papa, of course, but to us children—that you were just that sort of man.

MANGAN [*sitting up, much hurt*] Oh! did she? And yet she'd have let you marry me.

ELLIE. Well, you see, Mr Mangan, my mother married a very good man—for whatever you may think of my father as a man of business, he is the soul of goodness—and she is not at all keen on my doing the same.

MANGAN. Anyhow, you dont want to marry me now, do you?

ELLIE [*very calmly*] Oh, I think so. Why not?

MANGAN [*rising aghast*] Why not!

ELLIE. I dont see why we shouldnt get on very well together.

MANGAN. Well, but look here, you know— [*he stops, quite at a loss*].

ELLIE [*patiently*] Well?

MANGAN. Well, I thought you were rather particular about people's characters.

ELLIE. If we women were particular about men's characters, we should never get married at all, Mr Mangan.

MANGAN. A child like you talking of "we women"! What next! Youre not in earnest?

ELLIE. Yes I am. Arnt you?

MANGAN. You mean to hold me to it?

ELLIE. Do you wish to back out of it?

MANGAN. Oh no. Not exactly back out of it.

ELLIE. Well?

He has nothing to say. With a long whispered whistle, he drops into the wicker chair and stares before him like a beggared gambler. But a cunning look soon comes into, his face. He leans over towards her on his right elbow, and speaks in a low steady voice.

MANGAN. Suppose I told you I was in love with another woman!

ELLIE [*echoing him*] Suppose I told you I was in love with another man!

MANGAN [*bouncing angrily out of his chair*] I'm not joking.

ELLIE. Who told you I was?

MANGAN. I tell you I'm serious. Youre too young to be serious; but youll have to believe me. I want to be near your friend Mrs Hushabye. I'm in love with her. Now the murder's out.

ELLIE. I want to be near your friend Mr Hushabye. I'm in love with him. [*She rises and adds with a frank air*] Now we are in one another's confidence, we shall be real friends. Thank you for telling me.

MANGAN [*almost beside himself*] Do you think I'll be made a convenience of like this?

ELLIE. Come, Mr Mangan! you made a business convenience of my father. Well, a woman's business is marriage. Why shouldnt I make a domestic convenience of you?

MANGAN. Because I dont choose, see? Because I'm not a silly gull like your father. Thats why.

ELLIE [*with serene contempt*] You are not good enough to clean my father's boots, Mr Mangan; and I am paying you a great compliment in condescending to make a convenience of you, as you call it. Of course you are free to throw over our engagement if you like; but, if you do, youll never enter Hesione's house again: I will take care of that.

MANGAN [*gasping*] You little devil, youve done me. [*On the point of collapsing into the big chair again he recovers himself*] Wait a bit, though: youre not so cute as you think. You cant beat Boss Mangan as easy as that. Suppose I go straight to Mrs Hushabye and tell her that youre in love with her husband.

ELLIE. She knows it.

MANGAN. You told her!!!

ELLIE. She told me.

MANGAN [*clutching at his bursting temples*] Oh, this is a crazy house. Or else I'm going clean off my chump. Is she making a swop with you—she to have your husband and you to have hers?

ELLIE. Well, you dont want us both, do you?

MANGAN [*throwing himself into the chair distractedly*] My brain wont stand it. My head's going to split. Help! Help me to hold it. Quick: hold it: squeeze it. Save me. [*Ellie comes behind his chair; clasps his head hard for a moment; then begins to draw her hands from his forehead back to his ears*]. Thank you. [*Drowsily*] Thats very refreshing. [*Waking a little*] Don't you hypnotize me, though. Ive seen men made fools of by hypnotism.

ELLIE [*steadily*] Be quiet. Ive seen men made fools of without hypnotism.

MANGAN [*humbly*] You dont dislike touching me, I hope. You never touched me before, I noticed.

ELLIE. Not since you fell in love naturally with a grown-up nice woman, who will never expect you to make love to her. And I will never expect him to make love to me.

MANGAN. He may, though.

ELLIE [*making her passes rhythmically*] Hush. Go to sleep. Do you hear? You are to go to sleep, go to sleep, go to sleep; be quiet, deeply deeply quiet; sleep, sleep, sleep, sleep, sleep.

> *He falls asleep. Ellie steals away; turns the light out; and goes into the garden.*
>
> *Nurse Guinness opens the door and is seen in the light which comes in from the hall.*

GUINNESS [*speaking to someone outside*] Mr Mangan's not here, ducky: theres no one here. It's all dark.

MRS HUSHABYE [*without*] Try the garden. Mr Dunn and I will be in my boudoir. Shew him the way.

GUINNESS. Yes, ducky. [*She makes for the garden door in the dark; stumbles over the sleeping Mangan; and screams*]. Ahoo! Oh Lord, sir! I beg your pardon, I'm sure: I didnt see you in the dark. Who is it? [*She goes back to the door and turns on the lights*]. Oh, Mr Mangan, sir, I hope I havnt hurt you plumping into your lap like that. [*Coming to him*] I was looking for you, sir. Mrs. Hushabye says will you please— [*Noticing that he remains quite insensible*] Oh, my good Lord, I hope I havnt killed him. Sir! Mr Mangan! Sir! [*She shakes him; and he is rolling inertly off the chair on the floor when she holds him up and props him against the cushion*]. Miss Hessy! Miss Hessy! Quick, doty darling. Miss Hessy! [*Mrs Hushabye comes in from the hall, followed by Mazzini Dunn*]. Oh, Miss Hessy, Ive been and killed him.

> *Mazzini runs round the back of the chair to Mangan's right hand, and sees that the nurse's words are apparently only too true.*

MAZZINI. What tempted you to commit such a crime, woman?

MRS HUSHABYE [*trying not to laugh*] Do you mean you did it on purpose?

GUINNESS. Now is it likely I'd kill any man on purpose? I fell over him in the dark; and I'm a pretty tidy weight. He never spoke nor moved until I shook him; and then he would have dropped dead on the floor. Isnt it tiresome?

MRS HUSHABYE [*going past the nurse to Mangan's side, and inspecting him less credulously than Mazzini*] Nonsense! he is not dead: he is only asleep. I can see him breathing.

GUINNESS. But why wont he wake?

MAZZINI [*speaking very politely into Mangan's ear*] Mangan! My dear Mangan! [*He blows into Mangan's ear*].

MRS HUSHABYE. Thats no good. [*She shakes him vigorously*]. Mr Mangan: wake up. Do you hear? [*He begins to roll over*]. Oh! Nurse, nurse: he's falling: help me.

> *Nurse Guinness rushes to the rescue. With Mazzini's assistance, Mangan is propped safely up again.*

GUINNESS [*behind the chair; bending over to test the case with her nose*] Would he be drunk, do you think, pet?

MRS HUSHABYE. Had he any of papa's rum?

MAZZINI. It cant be that: he is most abstemious. I am afraid he drank too much formerly, and has to drink too little now. You know, Mrs Hushabye, I really think he has been hypnotized.

GUINNESS. Hip no what, sir?

MAZZINI. One evening at home, after we had seen a hypnotizing performance, the children began playing at it; and Ellie stroked my head. I assure you I went off dead asleep; and they had to send for a professional to wake me up after I had slept eighteen hours. They had to carry me upstairs; and as the poor children were not very strong, they let me slip; and I rolled right down the whole flight and never woke up. [*Mrs Hushabye splutters*]. Oh, you may laugh, Mrs Hushabye; but I might have been killed.

MRS HUSHABYE. I couldnt have helped laughing even if you had been, Mr Dunn. So Ellie has hypnotized him. What fun!

MAZZINI. Oh no, no, no. It was such a terrible lesson to her: nothing would induce her to try such a thing again.

MRS HUSHABYE. Then who did it? *I* didnt.

MAZZINI. I thought perhaps the Captain might have done it unintentionally. He is so fearfully magnetic: I feel vibrations whenever he comes close to me.

GUINNESS. The Captain will get him out of it anyhow, sir: I'll back him for that. I'll go fetch him [*she makes for the pantry*].

MRS HUSHABYE. Wait a bit. [*To Mazzini*] You say he is all right for eighteen hours?

MAZZINI. Well, *I* was asleep for eighteen hours.

MRS HUSHABYE. Were you any the worse for it?

MAZZINI. I dont quite remember. They had poured brandy down my throat, you see: and—

MRS HUSHABYE. Quite. Anyhow, you survived. Nurse, darling: go and ask Miss Dunn to come to us here. Say I want to speak to her particularly. You will find her with Mr Hushabye probably.

GUINNESS. I think not, ducky: Miss Addy is with him. But I'll find her and send her to you. [*She goes out into the garden*].

MRS HUSHABYE [*calling Mazzini's attention to the figure on the chair*] Now, Mr Dunn, look. Just look. Look hard. Do you still intend to sacrifice your daughter to that thing?

MAZZINI [*troubled*] You have completely upset me, Mrs Hushabye, by all you have said to me. That anyone could imagine that I—*I*, a consecrated soldier of freedom, if I may say so—could sacrifice Ellie to anybody or anyone, or that I should ever have dreamed of forcing her inclinations in any way, is a most painful blow to my—well, I suppose you would say to my good opinion of myself.

MRS HUSHABYE [*rather stolidly*] Sorry.

MAZZINI [*looking forlornly at the body*] What is your objection to poor Mangan, Mrs Hushabye? He looks all right to me. But then I am so accustomed to him.

MRS HUSHABYE. Have you no heart? Have you no sense? Look at the brute! Think of poor weak innocent Ellie in the clutches of this slavedriver, who spends his life making thousands of rough violent workmen bend to his will and sweat for him: a man accustomed to have great masses of iron beaten into shape for him by steam-hammers! to fight with women and girls over a halfpenny an hour ruthlessly! a captain of industry, I think you call him, dont you? Are you going to fling your delicate, sweet helpless child into such a beast's claws just because he will keep her in an expensive house and make her wear diamonds to shew how rich he is?

MAZZINI [*staring at her in wide-eyed amazement*] Bless you, dear Mrs Hushabye, what romantic ideas of business you have! Poor dear Mangan isnt a bit like that.

MRS HUSHABYE [*scornfully*] Poor dear Mangan indeed!

MAZZINI. But he doesnt know anything about machinery. He never goes near the men: he couldnt manage them: He is afraid of them. I never can get him to take the least interest in the works: he hardly knows more about them than you do. People are cruelly unjust to Mangan: they think he is all rugged strength just because his manners are bad.

MRS HUSHABYE. Do you mean to tell me he isnt strong enough to crush poor little Ellie?

MAZZINI. Of course it's very hard to say how any marriage will turn out; but speaking for myself, I should say that he wont have a dog's chance against Ellie. You know, Ellie has remarkable strength of character. I think it is because I taught her to like Shakespear when she was very young.

MRS HUSHABYE [*contemptuously*] Shakespear! The next thing you will tell me is that you could have made a great deal more money than Mangan. [*She retires to the sofa, and sits down at the port end of it in the worst of humors*].

MAZZINI [*following her and taking the other end*] No: I'm no good at making money. I dont care enough for it, somehow. I'm not ambitious! that must be it. Mangan is wonderful about money: he thinks of nothing else. He is so dreadfully afraid of being poor. I am always thinking of other things: even at the works I think of the things we are doing and not of what they cost. And the worst of it is, poor Mangan doesnt know what to do with his money when he gets it. He is such a baby that he doesnt know even what to eat and drink: he has ruined his liver eating and drinking the wrong things; and now he can hardly eat at all. Ellie will diet him splendidly. You will be surprised when you come to know him better: he is really the most helpless of mortals. You get quite a protective feeling towards him.

MRS HUSHABYE. Then who manages his business, pray?

MAZZINI. I do. And of course other people like me.

MRS HUSHABYE. Footling people, you mean.

MAZZINI. I suppose youd think us so.

MRS HUSHABYE. And pray why dont you do without him if youre all so much cleverer?

MAZZINI. Oh, we couldnt: we should ruin the business in a year.

I've tried; and I know. We should spend too much on everything. We should improve the quality of the goods and make them too dear. We should be sentimental about the hard cases among the workpeople. But Mangan keeps us in order. He is down on us about every extra halfpenny. We could never do without him. You see, he will sit up all night thinking of how to save sixpence. Wont Ellie make him jump, though, when she takes his house in hand!

MRS HUSHABYE. Then the creature is a fraud even as a captain of industry!

MAZZINI. I am afraid all the captains of industry are what y o u call frauds, Mrs Hushabye. Of course there are some manufacturers who really do understand their own works; but they dont make as high a rate of profit as Mangan does. I assure you Mangan is quite a good fellow in his way. He means well.

MRS HUSHABYE. He doesnt look well. He is not in his first youth, is he?

MAZZINI. After all, no husband is in his first youth for very long, Mrs Hushabye. And men cant afford to marry in their first youth nowadays.

MRS HUSHABYE. Now if *I* said that, it would sound witty. Why cant y o u say it wittily? What on earth is the matter with you? Why dont you inspire everybody with confidence? with respect?

MAZZINI [*humbly*] I think that what is the matter with me is that I am poor. You dont know what that means at home. Mind: I dont say they have ever complained. Theyve all been wonderful: theyve been proud of my poverty. Theyve even joked about it quite often. But my wife has had a very poor time of it. She has been quite resigned—

MRS HUSHABYE [*shuddering involuntarily*]!!

MAZZINI. There! You see, Mrs Hushabye. I dont want Ellie to live on resignation.

MRS HUSHABYE. Do you want her to have to resign herself to living with a man she doesnt love?

MAZZINI [*wistfully*] Are you sure that would be worse than living with a man she did love, if he was a footling person?

MRS HUSHABYE [*relaxing her contemptuous attitude, quite interested in Mazzini now*] You know, I really think you must love Ellie very much; for you become quite clever when you talk about her.

MAZZINI. I didnt know I was so very stupid on other subjects.

MRS HUSHABYE. You are, sometimes.

MAZZINI [*turning his head away; for his eyes are wet*] I have learnt a good deal about myself from you, Mrs Hushabye; and I'm afraid I shall not be the happier for your plain speaking. But if you thought I needed it to make me think of Ellie's happiness you were very much mistaken.

MRS HUSHABYE [*leaning towards him kindly*] Have I been a beast?

MAZZINI [*pulling himself together*] It doesnt matter about me, Mrs Hushabye. I think you like Ellie; and that is enough for me.

MRS HUSHABYE. I'm beginning to like you a little. I perfectly loathed you at first. I thought you the most odious, self-satisfied, boresome elderly prig I ever met.

MAZZINI [*resigned, and now quite cheerful*] I daresay I am all that. I never have been a favorite with gorgeous women like you. They always frighten me.

MRS HUSHABYE [*pleased*] Am I a gorgeous woman, Mazzini? I shall fall in love with you presently.

MAZZINI [*with placid gallantry*] No you wont, Hesione. But you would be quite safe. Would you believe it that quite a lot of women have flirted with me because I am quite safe? But they get tired of me for the same reason.

MRS HUSHABYE [*mischievously*] Take care. You may not be so safe as you think.

MAZZINI. Oh yes, quite safe. You see, I have been in love really: the sort of love that only happens once. [*Softly*] Thats why Ellie is such a lovely girl.

MRS HUSHABYE. Well, really, you a r e coming out. Are you quite sure you wont let me tempt you into a second grand passion?

MAZZINI. Quite. It wouldnt be natural. The fact is, you dont strike on my box, Mrs Hushabye; and I certainly dont strike on yours.

MRS HUSHABYE. I see. Your marriage was a safety match.

MAZZINI. What a very witty application of the expression I used! I should never have thought of it.

> *Ellie comes in from the garden, looking anything but happy.*

MRS HUSHABYE [*rising*] Oh! here is Ellie at last. [*She goes behind the sofa*].

ELLIE [*on the threshold of the starboard door*] Guinness said you wanted me: you and papa.

MRS HUSHABYE. You have kept us waiting so long that it almost came to—well, never mind. Your father is a very wonderful man [*she ruffles his hair affectionately*]: the only one I ever met who could resist me when I made myself really agreeable. [*She comes to the big chair, on Mangan's left*]. Come here. I have something to shew you. [*Ellie strolls listlessly to the other side of the chair*]. Look.

ELLIE [*contemplating Mangan without interest*] I know. He is only asleep. We had a talk after dinner; and he fell asleep in the middle of it.

MRS HUSHABYE. You did it, Ellie. You put him asleep.

MAZZINI [*rising quickly and coming to the back of the chair*] Oh, I hope not. Did you, Ellie?

ELLIE [*wearily*] He asked me to.

MAZZINI. But it's dangerous. You know what happened to me.

ELLIE [*utterly indifferent*] Oh, I daresay I can wake him. If not, somebody else can.

MRS HUSHABYE. It doesnt matter, anyhow, because I have at last persuaded your father that you dont want to marry him.

ELLIE [*suddenly coming out of her listlessness, much vexed*] But why did you do that, Hesione? I do want to marry him. I fully intend to marry him.

MAZZINI. Are you quite sure, Ellie? Mrs Hushabye has made me feel that I may have been thoughtless and selfish about it.

ELLIE [*very clearly and steadily*] Papa. When Mrs Hushabye takes it on herself to explain to you what I think or dont think, shut your ears tight; and shut your eyes too. Hesione knows nothing about me: she hasnt the least notion of the sort of person I am, and never will. I promise you I wont do anything I dont want to do and mean to do for my own sake.

MAZZINI. You are quite, quite sure?

ELLIE. Quite, quite sure. Now you must go away and leave me to talk to Mrs Hushabye.

MAZZINI. But I should like to hear. Shall I be in the way?

ELLIE [*inexorable*] I had rather talk to her alone.

MAZZINI [*affectionately*] Oh, well, I know what a nuisance parents are, dear. I will be good and go. [*He goes to the garden door*]. By the way, do you remember the address of that professional who woke me up? Dont you think I had better telegraph to him?

MRS HUSHABYE [*moving towards the sofa*] It's too late to telegraph tonight.

MAZZINI. I suppose so. I do hope he'll wake up in the course of the night. [*He goes out into the garden*].

ELLIE [*turning vigorously on Hesione the moment her father is out of the room*] Hesione: what the devil do you mean by making mischief with my father about Mangan?

MRS HUSHABYE [*promptly losing her temper*] Dont you dare speak to me like that, you little minx. Remember that you are in my house.

ELLIE. Stuff! Why dont you mind your own business? What is it to you whether I choose to marry Mangan or not?

MRS HUSHABYE. Do you suppose you can bully me, you miserable little matrimonial adventurer?

ELLIE. Every woman who hasnt any money is a matrimonial adventurer. It's easy for you to talk: you have never known what it is to want money; and you can pick up men as if they were daisies. I am poor and respectable—

MRS HUSHABYE [*interrupting*] Ho! respectable! How did you pick up Mangan? How did you pick up my husband? You have the audacity to tell me that I am a—a—a—

ELLIE. A siren. So you are. You were born to lead men by the nose: if you werent, Marcus would have waited for me, perhaps.

MRS HUSHABYE [*suddenly melting and half laughing*] Oh, my poor Ellie, my pettikins, my unhappy darling! I am so sorry about Hector. But what can I do? It's not my fault: I'd give him to you if I could.

ELLIE. I dont blame you for that.

MRS HUSHABYE. What a brute I was to quarrel with you and call you names! Do kiss me and say youre not angry with me.

ELLIE [*fiercely*] Oh, dont slop and gush and be sentimental. Dont you see that unless I can be hard—as hard as nails—I shall go mad? I dont care a damn about your calling me names: do you think a woman in my situation can feel a few hard words?

MRS HUSHABYE. Poor little woman! Poor little situation!

ELLIE. I suppose you think youre being sympathetic. You are just foolish and stupid and selfish. You see me getting a smasher right in the face that kills a whole part of my life: the best part that can never come again; and you think you can help me over it by a little coaxing and kissing. When I want all the strength I can get to lean on: something iron, something stony, I dont care how cruel it is, you go all mushy and want to slobber over me. I'm not angry; I'm not unfriendly; but for God's sake do pull yourself together; and dont think that because youre on velvet and always have been, women who are in hell can take it as easily as you.

MRS HUSHABYE [*shrugging her shoulders*] Very well. [*She sits down on the sofa in her old place*]. But I warn you that when I am neither coaxing and kissing nor laughing, I am just wondering how much longer I can stand living in this cruel, damnable world. You object to the siren: well, I drop the siren. You want to rest your wounded bosom against a grindstone. Well [*folding her arms*], here is the grindstone.

ELLIE [*sitting down beside her, appeased*] Thats better: you really have the trick of falling in with everyone's mood; but you dont understand, because you are not the sort of woman for whom there is only one man and only one chance.

MRS HUSHABYE. I certainly dont understand how your marrying that object [*indicating Mangan*] will console you for not being able to marry Hector.

ELLIE. Perhaps you dont understand why I was quite a nice girl this morning, and am now neither a girl nor particularly nice.

MRS HUSHABYE. Oh yes I do. It's because you have made up your mind to do something despicable and wicked.

ELLIE. I dont think so, Hesione. I must make the best of my ruined house.

MRS HUSHABYE. Pooh! Youll get over it. Your house isnt ruined.

ELLIE. Of course I shall get over it. You dont suppose I'm going to sit down and die of a broken heart, I hope, or be an old maid living on a pittance from the Sick and Indigent Room-keepers' Association. But my heart i s broken, all the same. What I mean by that is that I know that what has happened to me with Marcus will not happen to me ever again. In the world for me there is Marcus and a lot of other men of whom one is just the same as another. Well, if I cant have love, thats no reason why I should have poverty. If Mangan has nothing else, he has money.

MRS HUSHABYE. And are there no y o u n g men with money?

ELLIE. Not within my reach. Besides, a young man would have the right to expect love from me, and would perhaps leave me when he found I could not give it to him. Rich young men can get rid of their wives, you know, pretty cheaply. But this object, as you call him, can expect nothing more from me than I am prepared to give him.

MRS HUSHABYE. He will be your owner, remember. If he buys you, he will make the bargain pay him and not you. Ask your father.

ELLIE [*rising and strolling to the chair to contemplate their subject*] You need not trouble on that score, Hesione. I have more to give Boss Mangan than he has to give me: it is I who am buying him, and at a pretty good price too, I think. Women are better at that sort of bargain than men. I have taken the Boss's measure; and ten Boss Mangans shall not prevent me doing far more as I please as his wife than I have ever been able to do as a poor girl. [*Stooping to the recumbent figure*] Shall they, Boss? I think not. [*She passes on to the drawing-table, and leans against the end of it, facing the windows*]. I shall not have to spend most of my time wondering how long my gloves will last, anyhow.

MRS HUSHABYE [*rising superbly*] Ellie: you are a wicked sordid little beast. And to think that I actually condescended to fascinate that creature there to save you from him! Well, let me tell you this: if you make this disgusting match, you will never see Hector again if I can help it.

ELLIE [*unmoved*] I nailed Mangan by telling him that if he did not marry me he should never see you again [*she lifts herself on her wrists and seats herself on the end of the table*].

MRS HUSHABYE [*recoiling*] Oh!

ELLIE. So you see I am not unprepared for your playing that trump against me. Well, you just try it: thats all. I should have made a man of Marcus, not a household pet.

MRS HUSHABYE [*flaming*] You dare!

ELLIE [*looking almost dangerous*] Set him thinking about me if y o u dare.

MRS HUSHABYE. Well, of all the impudent little fiends I ever met! Hector says there is a certain point at which the only answer you can give to a man who breaks all the rules is to knock him down. What would you say if I were to box your ears?

ELLIE [*calmly*] I should pull your hair.

MRS HUSHABYE [*mischievously*] That wouldnt hurt me. Perhaps it comes off at night.

ELLIE [*so taken aback that she drops off the table and runs to her*] Oh, you dont mean to say, Hesione, that your beautiful black hair is false?

MRS HUSHABYE. [*patting it*] Dont tell Hector. He believes in it.

ELLIE [*groaning*] Oh! Even the hair that ensnared him false! Everything false!

MRS HUSHABYE. Pull it and try. Other women can snare men in their hair; but I can swing a baby on mine. Aha! you cant do that, Goldylocks.

ELLIE [*heartbroken*] No. You have stolen m y babies.

MRS HUSHABYE. Pettikins: dont make me cry. You know, what you said about my making a household pet of him is a little true. Perhaps he ought to have waited for you. Would any other woman on earth forgive you?

ELLIE. Oh, what right had you to take him all for yourself! [*Pulling herself together*] There! You couldnt help it: neither of us could help it. He couldnt help it. No: dont say anything more: I cant bear it. Let us wake the object. [*She begins stroking Mangan's head, reversing the movement with which she put him to sleep*]. Wake up, do you hear? You are to wake up at once. Wake up, wake up, wake—

MANGAN [*bouncing out of the chair in a fury and turning on them*] Wake up! So you think Ive been asleep, do you? [*He kicks the chair violently back out of his way, and gets between them*]. You throw me into a trance so that I cant move hand or foot—I might have been buried alive! it's a mercy I wasnt—and then you think I was only asleep. If youd let me drop the two times you rolled me about, my nose would have been flattened for life against the floor. But Ive found you all out, anyhow. I know the sort of people I'm among now. Ive heard every word youve said, you and your precious father, and [*to Mrs Hushabye*] you too. So I'm an object, am I? I'm a thing, am I? I'm a fool that hasnt sense enough to feed myself properly, am I? I'm afraid of the men that would starve if it werent for the wages I give them, am I? I'm nothing but a disgusting old skinflint to be made a convenience of by designing women and fool managers of my works, am I? I'm—

MRS HUSHABYE [*with the most elegant aplomb*] Sh-sh-sh-sh-sh! Mr Mangan: you are bound in honor to obliterate from your mind all you heard while you were pretending to be asleep. It was not meant for you to hear.

MANGAN. Pretending to be asleep! Do you think if I was only pretending that I'd have sprawled there helpless, and listened to such unfairness, such lies, such injustice and plotting and backbiting and slandering of me, if I could have up and told you what I thought of you! I wonder I didnt burst.

MRS HUSHABYE [*sweetly*] You dreamt it all, Mr Mangan. We were only saying how beautifully peaceful you looked in your sleep. That was all, wasnt it, Ellie? Believe me, Mr Mangan, all those unpleasant things came into your mind in the last half second before you woke. Ellie rubbed your hair the wrong way; and the disagreeable sensation suggested a disagreeable dream.

MANGAN [*doggedly*] I believe in dreams.

MRS HUSHABYE. So do I. But they go by contraries, dont they?

MANGAN [*depths of emotion suddenly welling up in him*] I shant forget, to my dying day, that when you gave me the glad eye that time in the garden, you were making a fool of me. That was a dirty low mean thing to do. You had no right to let me come near you if I disgusted you. It isnt my fault if I'm old and havnt a moustache like a bronze candlestick as your husband has.

There are things no decent woman would do to a man—like a man hitting a woman in the breast.

> *Hesione, utterly shamed, sits down on the sofa and covers her face with her hands. Mangan sits down also on his chair and begins to cry like a child. Ellie stares at them. Mrs Hushabye, at the distressing sound he makes, takes down her hands and looks at him. She rises and runs to him.*

MRS HUSHABYE. Dont cry: I cant bear it. Have I broken your heart? I didnt know you had one. How could I?

MANGAN. I'm a man aint I?

MRS HUSHABYE [*half coaxing, half rallying, altogether tenderly*] Oh no: not what I call a man. Only a Boss: just that and nothing else. What business has a Boss with a heart?

MANGAN. Then youre not a bit sorry for what you did, nor ashamed?

MRS HUSHABYE. I was ashamed for the first time in my life when you said that about hitting a woman in the breast, and I found out what I'd done. My very bones blushed red. Youve had your revenge, Boss. Arnt you satisfied?

MANGAN. Serve you right! Do you hear? Serve you right! Youre just cruel. Cruel.

MRS HUSHABYE. Yes: cruelty would be delicious if one could only find some sort of cruelty that didnt really hurt. By the way [*sitting down beside him on the arm of the chair*], whats your name? It's not really Boss, is it?

MANGAN [*shortly*] If you want to know, my name's Alfred.

MRS HUSHABYE [*springing up*] Alfred!! Ellie: he was christened after Tennyson!!!

MANGAN [*rising*] I was christened after my uncle, and never had a penny from him, damn him! What of it?

MRS HUSHABYE. It comes to me suddenly that you are a real person: that you had a mother, like anyone else. [*Putting her hands on his shoulders and surveying him*] Little Alf!

MANGAN. Well, you have a nerve.

MRS HUSHABYE. And you have a heart, Alfy, a whimpering little heart, but a real one. [*Releasing him suddenly*] Now run and make it up with Ellie. She has had time to think what to say to you, which is more than I had [*she goes out quickly into the garden by the port door*].

MANGAN. That woman has a pair of hands that go right through you.

ELLIE. Still in love with her, in spite of all we said about you?

MANGAN. Are all women like you two? Do they never think of anything about a man except what they can get out of him? Y o u werent even thinking that about me. You were only thinking whether your gloves would last.

ELLIE. I shall not have to think about that when we are married.

MANGAN. And you think I am going to marry you after what I heard there!

ELLIE. You heard nothing from me that I did not tell you before.

MANGAN. Perhaps you think I cant do without you.

ELLIE. I think you would feel lonely without us all now, after coming to know us so well.

MANGAN [*with something like a yell of despair*] Am I never to have the last word?

CAPTAIN SHOTOVER [*appearing at the starboard garden door*] There is a soul in torment here. What is the matter?

MANGAN. This girl doesnt want to spend her life wondering how long her gloves will last.

CAPTAIN SHOTOVER [*passing through*] Dont wear any. I never do [*he goes into the pantry*].

LADY UTTERWORD [*appearing at the port garden door, in a handsome dinner dress*] Is anything the matter?

ELLIE. This gentleman wants to know is he never to have the last word?

LADY UTTERWORD [*coming forward to the sofa*] I should let him have it, my dear. The important thing is not to have the last word, but to have your own way.

MANGAN. She wants both.

LADY UTTERWORD. She wont get them, Mr Mangan. Providence always has the last word.

MANGAN [*desperately*] Now y o u are going to come religion over me. In this house a man's mind might as well be a football. I'm going. [*He makes for the hall, but is stopped by a hail from the Captain, who has just emerged from his pantry*].

CAPTAIN SHOTOVER. Whither away, Boss Mangan?

MANGAN. To hell out of this house: let that be enough for you and all here.

CAPTAIN SHOTOVER. You were welcome to come: you are free to go. The wide earth, the high seas, the spacious skies are waiting for you outside.

LADY UTTERWORD. But your things, Mr Mangan. Your bags, your comb and brushes, your pyjamas—

HECTOR [*who has just appeared in the port doorway in a handsome Arab costume*] Why should the escaping slave take his chains with him?

MANGAN. Thats right, Hushabye. Keep the pyjamas, my lady; and much good may they do you.

HECTOR [*advancing to Lady Utterword's left hand*] Let us all go out into the night and leave everything behind us.

MANGAN. You stay where you are, the lot of you. I want no company, especially female company.

ELLIE. Let him go. He is unhappy here. He is angry with us.

CAPTAIN SHOTOVER. Go, Boss Mangan; and when you have found the land where there is happiness and where there are no women, send me its latitude and longitude; and I will join you there.

LADY UTTERWORD. You will certainly not be comfortable without your luggage, Mr Mangan.

ELLIE [*impatient*] Go, go: why dont you go? It is a heavenly night: you can sleep on the heath. Take my waterproof to lie on: it is hanging up in the hall.

HECTOR. Breakfast at nine, unless you prefer to breakfast with the Captain at six.

ELLIE. Good night, Alfred.

HECTOR. Alfred! [*He runs back to the door and calls into the garden*] Randall: Mangan's Christian name is Alfred.

RANDALL [*appearing in the starboard doorway in evening dress*] Then Hesione wins her bet.

> *Mrs Hushabye appears in the port doorway. She throws her left arm around Hector's neck; draws him with her to the back of the sofa; and throws her right arm round Lady Utterword's neck.*

MRS HUSHABYE. They wouldnt believe me, Alf.

> *They contemplate him.*

MANGAN. Is there any more of you coming in to look at me, as if I was the latest thing in a menagerie?

MRS HUSHABYE. You a r e the latest thing in this menagerie.

> *Before Mangan can retort, a fall of furniture is heard from upstairs; then a pistol shot, and a yell of pain. The staring group breaks up in consternation.*

MAZZINI'S VOICE [*from above*] Help! A burglar! Help!

HECTOR [*his eyes blazing*] A burglar!!!

MRS HUSHABYE. No, Hector: youll be shot [*but it is too late: he has dashed out past Mangan, who hastily moves towards the bookshelves out of his way*].

CAPTAIN SHOTOVER [*blowing his whistle*] All hands aloft! [*He strides out after Hector*].

LADY UTTERWORD. My diamonds! [*She follows the Captain*].

RANDALL [*rushing after her*] No, Ariadne. Let me.

ELLIE. Oh, is papa shot? [*She runs out*].

MRS HUSHABYE. Are you frightened, Alf?

MANGAN. No. It aint my house, thank God.

MRS HUSHABYE. If they catch a burglar, shall we have to go into court as witnesses, and be asked all sorts of questions about our private lives?

MANGAN. You wont be believed if you tell the truth.

> *Mazzini, terribly upset, with a duelling pistol in his hand, comes from the hall, and makes his way to the drawing-table.*

MAZZINI. Oh, my dear Mrs Hushabye, I might have killed him. [*He throws the pistol on the table and staggers round to the chair*]. I hope you wont believe I really intended to.

> *Hector comes in, marching an old and villainous looking man before him by the collar. He plants him in the middle of the room and releases him.*
>
> *Ellie follows, and immediately runs across to the back of her father's chair and pats his shoulders.*

RANDALL [*entering with a poker*] Keep your eye on this door, Mangan. I'll look after the other [*he goes to the starboard door and stands on guard there*].

> *Lady Utterword comes in after Randall, and goes between Mrs. Hushabye and Mangan.*
>
> *Nurse Guinness brings up the rear, and waits near the door, on Mangan's left.*

MRS HUSHABYE. What has happened?

MAZZINI. Your housekeeper told me there was somebody upstairs, and gave me a pistol that Mr Hushabye had been practising with. I thought it would frighten him; but it went off at a touch.

THE BURGLAR. Yes, and took the skin off my ear. Precious near took the top off my head. Why dont you have a proper revolver instead of a thing like that, that goes off if you as much as blow on it?

HECTOR. One of my duelling pistols. Sorry.

MAZZINI. He put his hands up and said it was a fair cop.

THE BURGLAR. So it was. Send for the police.

HECTOR. No, by thunder! It was not a fair cop. We were four to one.

MRS HUSHABYE. What will they do to him?

THE BURGLAR. Ten years. Beginning with solitary. Ten years off my life. I shant serve it all: I'm too old. It will see me out.

LADY UTTERWORD. You should have thought of that before you stole my diamonds.

THE BURGLAR. Well, youve got them back, lady: havnt you? Can you give me back the years of my life you are going to take from me?

MRS HUSHABYE. Oh, we cant bury a man alive for ten years for a few diamonds.

THE BURGLAR. Ten little shining diamonds! Ten long black years!

LADY UTTERWORD. Think of what it is for us to be dragged through the horrors of a criminal court, and have all our family affairs in the papers! If you were a native, and Hastings could order you a good beating and send you away, I shouldnt mind; but here in England there is no real protection for any respectable person.

THE BURGLAR. I'm too old to be giv a hiding, lady. Send for the police and have done with it. It's only just and right you should.

RANDALL [*who has relaxed his vigilance on seeing the burglar so pacifically disposed, and comes forward swinging the poker between his fingers like a well-folded umbrella*] It is neither just nor right that we should be put to a lot of inconvenience to gratify your moral enthusiasm, my friend. You had better get out, while you have the chance.

THE BURGLAR [*inexorably*] No. I must work my sin off my conscience. This has come as a sort of call to me. Let me spend the rest of my life repenting in a cell. I shall have my reward above.

MANGAN [*exasperated*] The very burglars cant behave naturally in this house.

HECTOR. My good sir: you must work out your salvation at some-body else's expense. Nobody here is going to charge you.

THE BURGLAR. Oh, you wont charge me, wont you?

HECTOR. No. I'm sorry to be inhospitable; but will you kindly leave the house?

THE BURGLAR. Right. I'll go to the police station and give myself up. [*He turns resolutely to the door; but Hector stops him*].

HECTOR. ⎫
RANDALL. ⎬
MRS HUSHABYE. ⎭

Oh no. You mustnt do that.
No, no. Clear out, man, cant you; and dont be a fool.
Dont be so silly. Cant you repent at home?

LADY UTTERWORD. You will have to do as you are told.

THE BURGLAR. It's compounding a felony, you know.

MRS HUSHABYE. This is utterly ridiculous. Are we to be forced to prosecute this man when we dont want to?

THE BURGLAR. Am I to be robbed of my salvation to save you the trouble of spending a day at the sessions? Is that justice? Is it right? Is it fair to me?

MAZZINI [*rising and leaning across the table persuasively as if it were a pulpit desk or a shop counter*] Come, come! let me shew you how you can turn your very crimes to account. Why not set up as a locksmith? You must know more about locks than most honest men?

THE BURGLAR. Thats true, sir. But I couldnt set up as a locksmith under twenty pounds.

RANDALL. Well, you can easily steal twenty pounds. You will find it in the nearest bank.

THE BURGLAR [*horrified*] Oh what a thing for a gentleman to put into the head of a poor criminal scrambling out of the bottom-less pit as it were! Oh, shame on you, sir! Oh, God forgive you! [*He throws himself into the big chair and covers his face as if in prayer*].

LADY UTTERWORD. Really, Randall!

HECTOR. It seems to me that we shall have to take up a collection for this inopportunely contrite sinner.

LADY UTTERWORD. But twenty pounds is ridiculous.

THE BURGLAR [*looking up quickly*] I shall have to buy a lot of tools, lady.

LADY UTTERWORD. Nonsense: you have your burgling kit.

THE BURGLAR. Whats a jemmy and a centrebit and an acetylene welding plant and a bunch of skeleton keys? I shall want a forge, and a smithy, and a shop, and fittings. I cant hardly do it for twenty.

HECTOR. My worthy friend, we havnt got twenty pounds.

THE BURGLAR [*now master of the situation*] You can raise it among you, cant you?

MRS HUSHABYE. Give him a sovereign, Hector; and get rid of him.

HECTOR [*giving him a pound*] There! Off with you.

THE BURGLAR [*rising and taking the money very ungratefully*] I wont promise nothing. You have more on you than a quid: all the lot of you, I mean.

LADY UTTERWORD [*vigorously*] Oh, let us prosecute him and have done with it. I have a conscience too, I hope; and I do not feel at all sure that we have any right to let him go, especially if he is going to be greedy and impertinent.

THE BURGLAR [*quickly*] All right, lady, all right. Ive no wish to be anything but agreeable. Good evening, ladies and gentlemen; and thank you kindly.

> He is hurrying out when he is confronted in the doorway by Captain Shotover.

CAPTAIN SHOTOVER [*fixing the burglar with a piercing regard*] Whats this? Are there two of you?

THE BURGLAR [*falling on his knees before the Captain in abject terror*] Oh my good Lord, what have I done? Dont tell me its y o u r house Ive broken into, Captain Shotover.

> The Captain seizes him by the collar; drags him to his feet; and leads him to the middle of the group, Hector falling back beside his wife to make way for them.

CAPTAIN SHOTOVER [*turning him towards Ellie*] Is that your daughter? [*He releases him*].

THE BURGLAR. Well, how do I know, Captain? You know the sort of life you and me has led. Any young lady of that age might be my daughter anywhere in the wide world, as you might say.

CAPTAIN SHOTOVER [*to Mazzini*] You are not Billy Dunn. This is Billy Dunn. Why have you imposed on me?

THE BURGLAR [*indignantly to Mazzini*] Have you been giving yourself out to be me? You, that nigh blew my head off! Shooting y o u r s e l f, in a manner of speaking!

MAZZINI. My dear Captain Shotover, ever since I came into this house I have done hardly anything else but assure you that I am not Mr William Dunn, but Mazzini Dunn, a very different person.

THE BURGLAR. He dont belong to my church, Captain. Theres two sets in the family: the thinking Dunns and the drinking Dunns, each going their own ways. I'm a drinking Dunn: he's a thinking Dunn. But that didnt give him any right to shoot me.

CAPTAIN SHOTOVER. So youve turned burglar, have you?

THE BURGLAR. No, Captain: I wouldnt disgrace our old sea calling by such a thing. I am no burglar.

LADY UTTERWORD. What were you doing with my diamonds?

GUINNESS. What did you break into the house for if youre no burglar?

RANDALL. Mistook the house for your own and came in by the wrong window, eh?

THE BURGLAR. Well, it's no use my telling you a lie: I can take in most captains, but not Captain Shotover, because he sold himself to the devil in Zanzibar, and can divine water, spot gold, explode a cartridge in your pocket with a glance of his eye, and see the truth hidden in the heart of man. But I'm no burglar.

CAPTAIN SHOTOVER. Are you an honest man?

THE BURGLAR. I dont set up to be better than my fellow-creatures, and never did, as you well know, Captain. But what I do is innocent and pious. I enquire about for houses where the right sort of people live. I work it on them same as I worked it here. I break into the house; put a few spoons or diamonds in my pocket; make a noise; get caught; and take up a collection. And you wouldnt believe how hard it is to get caught when youre actually trying to. I have knocked over all the chairs in a room without a soul paying any attention to me. In the end I have had to walk out and leave the job.

RANDALL. When that happens, do you put back the spoons and diamonds?

THE BURGLAR. Well, I dont fly in the face of Providence, if thats what you want to know.

CAPTAIN SHOTOVER. Guinness: you remember this man?

GUINNESS. I should think I do, seeing I was married to him, the blackguard!

HESIONE	*[exclaiming	Married to him!
LADY UTTERWORD	together]*	Guinness!!

THE BURGLAR. It wasnt legal. Ive been married to no end of women. No use coming that over me.

CAPTAIN SHOTOVER. Take him to the forecastle [*he flings him to the door with a strength beyond his years*].

GUINNESS. I suppose you mean the kitchen. They wont have him there. Do you expect servants to keep company with thieves and all sorts?

CAPTAIN SHOTOVER. Land-thieves and water-thieves are the same flesh and blood. I'll have no boatswain on my quarter-deck.[2] Off with you both.

THE BURGLAR. Yes, Captain. [*He goes out humbly*].

MAZZINI. Will it be safe to have him in the house like that?

GUINNESS. Why didnt you shoot him, sir? If I'd known who he was, I'd have shot him myself. [*She goes out*].

MRS HUSHABYE. Do sit down, everybody. [*She sits down on the sofa*].

    They all move except Ellie. Mazzini resumes his seat. Randall sits down in the window seat near the starboard door, again making a pendulum of his poker, and studying it as Galileo might have done. Hector sits on his left, in the middle. Mangan, forgotten, sits in the port corner. Lady Utterword takes the big chair. Captain Shotover goes into the pantry in deep abstraction. They all look after him; and Lady Utterword coughs consciously.

MRS HUSHABYE. So Billy Dunn was poor nurse's little romance. I knew there had been somebody.

---

2. The petty officer is not allowed in the area reserved for the captain and officers of high rank.

RANDALL. They will fight their battles over again and enjoy themselves immensely.

LADY UTTERWORD [*irritably*] You are not married; and you know nothing about it, Randall. Hold your tongue.

RANDALL. Tyrant!

MRS HUSHABYE. Well, we have had a very exciting evening. Everything will be an anticlimax after it. We'd better all go to bed.

RANDALL. Another burglar may turn up.

MAZZINI. Oh, impossible! I hope not.

RANDALL. Why not? There is more than one burglar in England.

MRS HUSHABYE. What do you say, Alf?

MANGAN [*huffily*] Oh, I dont matter. I'm forgotten. The burglar has put my nose out of joint. Shove me into a corner and have done with me.

MRS HUSHABYE [*jumping up mischievously, and going to him*] Would you like a walk on the heath, Alfred? With me?

ELLIE. Go, Mr Mangan. It will do you good. Hesione will soothe you.

MRS HUSHABYE [*slipping her arm under his and pulling him upright*] Come, Alfred. There is a moon: it's like the night in Tristan and Isolde. [*She caresses his arm and draws him to the port garden door*].

MANGAN [*writhing but yielding*] How you can have the face—the heart— [*He breaks down and is heard sobbing as she takes him out*].

LADY UTTERWORD. What an extraordinary way to behave! What is the matter with the man?

ELLIE [*in a strangely calm voice, staring into an imaginary distance*] His heart is breaking: that is all. [*The Captain appears at the pantry door, listening*]. It is a curious sensation: the sort of pain that goes mercifully beyond our powers of feeling. When your heart is broken, your boats are burned: nothing matters any more. It is the end of happiness and the beginning of peace.

LADY UTTERWORD [*suddenly rising in a rage, to the astonishment of the rest*] How dare you?

HECTOR. Good heavens! Whats the matter?

RANDALL [*in a warning whisper*] Tch—tch—tch! Steady.

ELLIE [*surprised and haughty*] I was not addressing you particularly, Lady Utterword. And I am not accustomed to be asked how dare I.

LADY UTTERWORD Of course not. Anyone can see how badly you have been brought up.

MAZZINI. Oh, I hope not, Lady Utterword. Really!

LADY UTTERWORD. I know very well what you meant. The impudence!

ELLIE. What on earth do you mean?

CAPTAIN SHOTOVER [*advancing to the table*] She means that her heart will not break. She has been longing all her life for someone to break it. At last she has become afraid she has none to break.

LADY UTTERWORD [*flinging herself on her knees and throwing her arms around him*] Papa: dont say you think Ive no heart.

CAPTAIN SHOTOVER [*raising her with grim tenderness*] If you had no heart how could you want to have it broken, child?

HECTOR [*rising with a bound*] Lady Utterword: you are not to be trusted. You have made a scene [*he runs out into the garden through the starboard door*].

LADY UTTERWORD. Oh! Hector, Hector! [*she runs out after him*].

RANDALL. Only nerves, I assure you. [*He rises and follows her, waving the poker in his agitation*]. Ariadne! Ariadne! For God's sake be careful. You will— [*he is gone*].

MAZZINI [*rising*] How distressing! Can I do anything, I wonder?

CAPTAIN SHOTOVER [*promptly taking his chair and setting to work at the drawing-board*] No. Go to bed. Goodnight.

MAZZINI [*bewildered*] Oh! Perhaps you are right.

ELLIE. Goodnight, dearest. [*She kisses him*].

MAZZINI. Goodnight, love. [*He makes for the door, but turns aside to the bookshelves*]. I'll just take a book [*he takes one*]. Goodnight. [*He goes out, leaving Ellie alone with the Captain*].

    The Captain is intent on his drawing. Ellie, standing sentry over his chair, contemplates him for a moment.

ELLIE. Does nothing ever disturb you, Captain Shotover?

CAPTAIN SHOTOVER. Ive stood on the bridge for eighteen hours in a typhoon. Life here is stormier; but I can stand it.

ELLIE. Do you think I ought to marry Mr Mangan?

CAPTAIN SHOTOVER [*never looking up*] One rock is as good as another to be wrecked on.

ELLIE. I am not in love with him.

CAPTAIN SHOTOVER. Who said you were?

ELLIE. You are not surprised?

CAPTAIN SHOTOVER. Surprised! At m y age!

ELLIE. It seems to me quite fair. He wants me for one thing: I want him for another.

CAPTAIN SHOTOVER. Money?

ELLIE. Yes.

CAPTAIN SHOTOVER. Well, one turns the cheek: the other kisses it. One provides the cash: the other spends it.

ELLIE. Who will have the best of the bargain, I wonder?

CAPTAIN SHOTOVER. You. These fellows live in an office all day. You will have to put up with him from dinner to breakfast; but you will both be asleep most of that time. All day you will be quit of him; and you will be shopping with his money. If that is too much for you, marry a seafaring man: you will be bothered with him only three weeks in the year, perhaps.

ELLIE. That would be best of all, I suppose.

CAPTAIN SHOTOVER. It's a dangerous thing to be married right up to the hilt, like my daughter's husband. The man is at home all day, like a damned soul in hell.

ELLIE. I never thought of that before.

CAPTAIN SHOTOVER. If youre marrying for business, you cant be too businesslike.

ELLIE. Why do women always want other women's husbands?

CAPTAIN SHOTOVER. Why do horse-thieves prefer a horse that is broken-in to one that is wild?

ELLIE [*with a short laugh*] I suppose so. What a vile world it is!

CAPTAIN SHOTOVER. It doesnt concern me. I'm nearly out of it.

ELLIE. And I'm only just beginning.

CAPTAIN SHOTOVER. Yes; so look ahead.

ELLIE. Well, I think I am being very prudent.

CAPTAIN SHOTOVER. I didnt say prudent. I said look ahead.

ELLIE. Whats the difference?

CAPTAIN SHOTOVER. It's prudent to gain the whole world and lose your own soul. But dont forget that your soul sticks to you if you stick to it; but the world has a way of slipping through your fingers.

ELLIE [*wearily, leaving him and beginning to wander restlessly about the room*] I'm sorry, Captain Shotover; but it's no use talking like that to me. Old-fashioned people are no use to me. Old-fashioned people think you can have a soul without money. They think the less money you have, the more soul you have. Young people nowadays know better. A soul is a very expensive thing to keep: much more so than a motor car.

CAPTAIN SHOTOVER. Is it? How much does your soul eat?

ELLIE. Oh, a lot. It eats music and pictures and books and mountains and lakes and beautiful things to wear and nice people to be with. In this country you cant have them without lots of money: that is why our souls are so horribly starved.

CAPTAIN SHOTOVER. Mangan's soul lives on pigs' food.

ELLIE. Yes: money is thrown away on him. I suppose his soul was starved when he was young. But it will not be thrown away on me. It is just because I want to save my soul that I am marrying for money. All the women who are not fools do.

CAPTAIN SHOTOVER. There are other ways of getting money. Why dont you steal it?

ELLIE. Because I dont want to go to prison.

CAPTAIN SHOTOVER. Is that the only reason? Are you quite sure honesty has nothing to do with it?

ELLIE. Oh, you are very very old-fashioned, Captain. Does any modern girl believe that the legal and illegal ways of getting money are the honest and dishonest ways? Mangan robbed my father and my father's friends. I should rob all the money back from Mangan if the police would let me. As they wont, I must get it back by marrying him.

CAPTAIN SHOTOVER. I cant argue: I'm too old: my mind is made up and finished. All I can tell you is that, old-fashioned or new-fashioned, if you sell yourself, you deal your soul a blow that all the books and pictures and concerts and scenery in the world wont heal [*he gets up suddenly and makes for the pantry*].

ELLIE [*running after him and seizing him by the sleeve*] Then why did you sell yourself to the devil in Zanzibar?

CAPTAIN SHOTOVER [*stopping, startled*] What?

ELLIE. You shall not run away before you answer. I have found out that trick of yours. If you sold yourself, why shouldnt I?

CAPTAIN SHOTOVER. I had to deal with men so degraded that they wouldnt obey me unless I swore at them and kicked them and beat them with my fists. Foolish people took young thieves off the streets; flung them into a training ship where they were taught to fear the cane instead of fearing God; and thought theyd make men and sailors of them by private subscription. I tricked these thieves into believing I'd sold myself to the devil. It saved my soul from the kicking and swearing that was damning me by inches.

ELLIE [*releasing him*] I shall pretend to sell myself to Boss Mangan to save my soul from the poverty that is damning m e by inches.

CAPTAIN SHOTOVER. Riches will damn you ten times deeper. Riches wont save even your body.

ELLIE. Old-fashioned again. We know now that the soul is the body, and the body the soul. They tell us they are different because they want to persuade us that we can keep our souls if we let them make slaves of our bodies. I am afraid you are no use to me, Captain.

CAPTAIN SHOTOVER. What did you expect? A Savior, eh? Are you old-fashioned enough to believe in that?

ELLIE. No. But I thought you were very wise, and might help me. Now I have found you out. You pretend to be busy, and think of fine things to say, and run in and out to surprise people by saying them, and get away before they can answer you.

CAPTAIN SHOTOVER. It confuses me to be answered. It discourages me. I cannot bear men and women. I h a v e to run away. I must run away now [*he tries to*].

ELLIE [*again seizing his arm*] You shall not run away from me. I can hypnotize you. You are the only person in the house I can say what I like to. I know you are fond of me. Sit down. [*She draws him to the sofa*].

CAPTAIN SHOTOVER [*yielding*] Take care: I am in my dotage. Old men are dangerous: it doesnt matter to them what is going to happen to the world.

> They sit side by side on the sofa. She leans affectionately against him with her head on his shoulder and her eyes half closed.

ELLIE [*dreamily*] I should have thought nothing else mattered to old men. They cant be very interested in what is going to happen to themselves.

CAPTAIN SHOTOVER. A man's interest in the world is only the overflow from his interest in himself. When you are a child your vessel is not yet full; so you care for nothing but your own affairs. When you grow up, your vessel overflows; and you are a politician, a philosopher, or an explorer and adventurer. In old age the vessel dries up: there is no overflow: you are a child again. I can give you the memories of my ancient wisdom: mere scraps and leavings; but I no longer really care for anything but my own little wants and hobbies. I sit here working out my old ideas as a means of destroying my fellow-creatures. I see my daughters and their men living foolish lives of romance and sentiment and snobbery. I see you, the younger generation, turning from their romance and sentiment and snobbery to money and comfort and hard common sense. I was ten times happier on the bridge in the typhoon, or frozen into Arctic ice for months in darkness, than you or they have ever been. You are looking for a rich husband. At your age I looked for hardship, danger, horror, and death, that I might feel the life in me more intensely. I did not let the fear of death govern my life; and my reward was, I had my life. You are going to let the fear of poverty govern your life; and your reward will be that you will eat, but you will not live.

ELLIE [*sitting up impatiently*] But what can I do? I am not a sea captain: I cant stand on bridges in typhoons, or go slaughtering seals and whales in Greenland's icy mountains. They wont let women be captains. Do you want me to be a stewardess?

CAPTAIN SHOTOVER. There are worse lives. The stewardesses could come ashore if they liked; but they sail and sail and sail.

ELLIE. What could they do ashore but marry for money? I dont want to be a stewardess: I am too bad a sailor. Think of something else for me.

CAPTAIN SHOTOVER. I cant think so long and continuously. I am too old. I must go in and out. [*He tries to rise*].

ELLIE [*pulling him back*] You shall not. You are happy here, arnt you?

CAPTAIN SHOTOVER. I tell you it's dangerous to keep me. I cant keep awake and alert.

ELLIE. What do you run away for? To sleep?

CAPTAIN SHOTOVER. No. To get a glass of rum.

ELLIE [*frightfully disillusioned*] Is t h a t it? How disgusting! Do you like being drunk?

CAPTAIN SHOTOVER. No: I dread being drunk more than anything in the world. To be drunk means to have dreams; to go soft; to be easily pleased and deceived; to fall into the clutches of women. Drink does that for you when you are young. But when you are old: very very old, like me, the dreams come by themselves. You dont know how terrible that is: you are young: you sleep at night only, and sleep soundly. But later on you will sleep in the afternoon. Later still you will sleep even in the morning; and you will awake tired, tired of life. You will never be free from dozing and dreams: the dreams will steal upon your work every ten minutes unless you can awaken yourself with rum. I drink now to keep sober; but the dreams are conquering: rum is not what it was: I have had ten glasses since you came; and it might be so much water. Go get me another: Guinness knows where it is. You had better see for yourself the horror of an old man drinking.

ELLIE. You shall not drink. Dream. I like you to dream. You must never be in the real world when we talk together.

CAPTAIN SHOTOVER. I am too weary to resist or too weak. I am in my second childhood. I do not see you as you really are. I cant remember what I really am. I feel nothing but the accursed happiness I have dreaded all my life long: the happiness that comes as life goes, the happiness of yielding and dreaming instead of resisting and doing, the sweetness of the fruit that is going rotten.

ELLIE. You dread it almost as much as I used to dread losing my dreams and having to fight and do things. But that is all over for me: m y dreams are dashed to pieces. I should like to marry a very old, very rich man. I should like to marry you. I had much rather marry you than marry Mangan. Are you very rich?

CAPTAIN SHOTOVER. No. Living from hand to mouth. And I have a wife somewhere in Jamaica: a black one. My first wife. Unless she's dead.

ELLIE. What a pity! I feel so happy with you. [*She takes his hand, almost unconsciously, and pats it*]. I thought I should never feel happy again.

CAPTAIN SHOTOVER. Why?

ELLIE. Dont you know?

CAPTAIN SHOTOVER. No.

ELLIE. Heartbreak. I fell in love with Hector, and didnt know he was married.

CAPTAIN SHOTOVER. Heartbreak? Are you one of those who are so sufficient to themselves that they are only happy when they are stripped of everything, even of hope?

ELLIE [*gripping the hand*] It seems so; for I feel now as if there was nothing I could not do, because I want nothing.

CAPTAIN SHOTOVER. Thats the only real strength. Thats genius. Thats better than rum.

ELLIE [*throwing away his hand*] Rum! Why did you spoil it?

 Hector and Randall come in from the garden through the starboard door.

HECTOR. I beg your pardon. We did not know there was anyone here.

ELLIE [*rising*] That means that you want to tell Mr Randall the story about the tiger. Come, Captain: I want to talk to my father; and you had better come with me.

CAPTAIN SHOTOVER [*rising*] Nonsense! the man is in bed.

ELLIE. Aha! Ive caught you. My real father has gone to bed; but the father you gave me is in the kitchen. You knew quite well all along. Come. [*She draws him out into the garden with her through the port door*].

HECTOR. Thats an extraordinary girl. She has the Ancient Mariner on a string like a Pekinese dog.

RANDALL. Now that they have gone, shall we have a friendly chat?

HECTOR. You are in what is supposed to be my house. I am at your disposal.

 Hector sits down in the draughtsman's chair, turning it to face Randall, who remains standing, leaning at his ease against the carpenter's bench.

RANDALL. I take it that we may be quite frank. I mean about Lady Utterword.

HECTOR. Y o u may. I have nothing to be frank about. I never met her until this afternoon.

RANDALL [*straightening up*] What! But you are her sister's husband.

HECTOR. Well, if you come to that, you are her husband's brother.

RANDALL. But you seem to be on intimate terms with her.

HECTOR. So do you.

RANDALL. Yes; but I a m on intimate terms with her. I have known her for years.

HECTOR. It took her years to get to the same point with you that she got to with me in five minutes, it seems.

RANDALL [*vexed*] Really, Ariadne is the limit [*he moves away huffishly towards the windows*].

HECTOR [*coolly*] She is, as I remarked to Hesione, a very enterprising woman.

RANDALL [*returning, much troubled*] You see, Hushabye, you are what women consider a good-looking man.

HECTOR. I cultivated that appearance in the days of my vanity; and Hesione insists on my keeping it up. She makes me wear these ridiculous things [*indicating his Arab costume*] because she thinks me absurd in evening dress.

RANDALL. Still, you d o keep it up, old chap. Now, I assure you I have not an atom of jealousy in my disposition—

HECTOR. The question would seem to be rather whether your brother has any touch of that sort.

RANDALL. What! Hastings! Oh, dont trouble about Hastings. He has the gift of being able to work sixteen hours a day at the dullest detail, and actually likes it. That gets him to the top wherever he goes. As long as Ariadne takes care that he is fed regularly, he is only too thankful to anyone who will keep her in good humour for him.

HECTOR. And as she has all the Shotover fascination, there is plenty of competition for the job, eh?

RANDALL [*angrily*] She encourages them. Her conduct is perfectly scandalous. I assure you, my dear fellow, I havnt an atom of jealousy in my composition; but she makes herself the talk of every place she goes to by her thoughtlessness. It's nothing more: she doesnt really care for the men she keeps hanging about her; but how is the world to know that? It's not fair to Hastings. It's not fair to me.

HECTOR. Her theory is that her conduct is so correct—

RANDALL. Correct! She does nothing but make scenes from morning till night. You be careful, old chap. She will get you into trouble: that is, she would if she really cared for you.

HECTOR. Doesnt she?

RANDALL. Not a scrap. She may want your scalp to add to her collection; but her true affection has been engaged years ago. You had really better be careful.

HECTOR. Do you suffer much from this jealousy?

RANDALL. Jealousy! I jealous! My dear fellow, havnt I told you that there is not an atom of—

HECTOR. Yes. And Lady Utterword told me she never made scenes. Well, dont waste your jealousy on my moustache. Never waste jealousy on a real man: it is the imaginary hero that supplants us all in the long run. Besides, jealousy does not belong to your easy man-of-the world pose, which you carry so well in other respects.

RANDALL. Really, Hushabye, I think a man may be allowed to be a gentleman without being accused of posing.

HECTOR. It is a pose like any other. In this house we know all the poses: our game is to find out the man under the pose. The man under your pose is apparently Ellie's favorite, Othello.

RANDALL. Some of your games in this house are damned annoying, let me tell you.

HECTOR. Yes: I have been their victim for many years. I used to writhe under them at first; but I became accustomed to them. At last I learned to play them.

RANDALL. If it's all the same to you, I had rather you didnt play them on me. You evidently dont quite understand my character, or my notions of good form.

HECTOR. Is it your notion of good form to give away Lady Utterword?

RANDALL [a childishly plaintive note breaking into his huff] I have not said a word against Lady Utterword. This is just the conspiracy over again.

HECTOR. What conspiracy?

RANDALL. You know very well, sir. A conspiracy to make me out to be pettish and jealous and childish and everything I am not. Everyone knows I am just the opposite.

HECTOR [rising] Something in the air of the house has upset you. It often does have that effect. [He goes to the garden door and calls Lady Utterword with commanding emphasis] Ariadne!

LADY UTTERWORD [at some distance] Yes.

RANDALL. What are you calling her for? I want to speak—

LADY UTTERWORD [arriving breathless] Yes. You really are a terribly commanding person. Whats the matter?

HECTOR. I do not know how to manage your friend Randall. No doubt you do.

LADY UTTERWORD. Randall: have you been making yourself ridiculous, as usual? I can see it in your face. Really, you are the most pettish creature.

RANDALL. You know quite well, Ariadne, that I have not an ounce of pettishness in my disposition. I have made myself perfectly pleasant here. I have remained absolutely cool and imperturbable in the face of a burglar. Imperturbability is almost too strong a point of mine. But [puttng his foot down with a stamp, and walking angrily up and down the room] I i n s i s t on being treated with a certain consideration. I will not allow Hushabye to take liberties with me. I will not stand your encouraging people as you do.

HECTOR. The man has a rooted delusion that he is your husband.

LADY UTTERWORD. I know. He is jealous. As if he had any right to be! He compromises me everywhere. He makes scenes all over the place. Randall: I will not allow it. I simply will not allow it. You had no right to discuss me with Hector. I will not be discussed by men.

HECTOR. Be reasonable, Ariadne. Your fatal gift of beauty forces men to discuss you.

LADY UTTERWORD. Oh indeed! what about y o u r fatal gift of beauty?

HECTOR. How can I help it?

LADY UTTERWORD. You could cut off your moustache: I cant cut off my nose. I get my whole life messed up with people falling in love with me. And then Randall says I run after men.

RANDALL. I—

LADY UTTERWORD. Yes you do: you said it just now. Why cant you think of something else than women? Napoleon was quite right when he said that women are the occupation of the idle man. Well, if ever there was an idle man on earth, his name is Randall Utterword.

RANDALL. Ariad—

LADY UTTERWORD [*overwhelming him with a torrent of words*] Oh yes you are: it's no use denying it. What have you ever done? What good are you? You are as much trouble in the house as a child of three. You couldnt live without your valet.

RANDALL. This is—

LADY UTTERWORD. Laziness! You are laziness incarnate. You are selfishness itself. You are the most uninteresting man on earth. You cant even gossip about anything but yourself and your grievances and your ailments and the people who have offended you. [*Turning to Hector*] Do you know what they call him, Hector?

HECTOR ⎱ [*speaking* ⎰ Please dont tell me.
RANDALL ⎰ *together*] ⎱ I'll not stand it—

LADY UTTERWORD. Randall the Rotter: that is his name in good society.

RANDALL [*shouting*] I'll not bear it, I tell you. Will you listen to me, you infernal— [*he chokes*].

LADY UTTERWORD. Well: go on. What were you going to call me? An infernal what? Which unpleasant animal is it to be this time?

RANDALL [*foaming*] There is no animal in the world so hateful as a woman can be. You are a maddening devil. Hushabye: you will not believe me when I tell you that I have loved this demon all my life; but God knows I have paid for it [*he sits down in the draughtsman's chair, weeping*].

LADY UTTERWORD [*standing over him with triumphant contempt*] Cry-baby!

HECTOR [*gravely, coming to him*] My friend: the Shotover sisters have two strange powers over men. They can make them love; and they can make them cry. Thank your stars that you are not married to one of them.

LADY UTTERWORD [*haughtily*] And pray, Hector—

HECTOR [*suddenly catching her round the shoulders; swinging her right round him and away from Randall; and gripping her throat with the other hand*] Ariadne: if you attempt to start on me, I'll choke you: do you hear? The cat-and-mouse game with the other sex is a good game; but I can play your head off at it. [*He throws her, not at all gently, into the big chair, and proceeds, less fiercely but firmly*] It is true that Napoleon said that woman is the occupation of the idle man. But he added that she is the relaxation of the warrior. Well, I am the warrior. So take care.

LADY UTTERWORD [*not in the least put out, and rather pleased by his violence*] My dear Hector: I have only done what you asked me to do.

HECTOR. How do you make that out, pray?

LADY UTTERWORD. You called me in to manage Randall, didnt you? You said you couldnt manage him yourself.

HECTOR. Well, what if I did? I did not ask you to drive the man mad.

LADY UTTERWORD. He isnt mad. Thats the way to manage him. If you were a mother, youd understand.

HECTOR. Mother! What are you up to now?

LADY UTTERWORD. It's quite simple. When the children got nerves and were naughty, I smacked them just enough to give them a good cry and a healthy nervous shock. They went to sleep and were quite good afterwards. Well, I cant smack Randall: he is too big; so when he gets nerves and is naughty, I just rag him till he cries. He will be all right now. Look: he is half asleep already [*which is quite true*].

RANDALL [*waking up indignantly*] I'm not. You are most cruel, Ariadne. [*Sentimentally*] But I suppose I must forgive you, as usual [*he checks himself in the act of yawning*].

LADY UTTERWORD [*to Hector*] Is the explanation satisfactory, dread warrior?

HECTOR. Some day I shall kill you, if you go too far. I thought you were a fool.

LADY UTTERWORD [*laughing*] Everybody does, at first. But I am not such a fool as I look. [*She rises complacently*]. Now, Randall: go to bed. You will be a good boy in the morning.

RANDALL [*only very faintly rebellious*] I'll go to bed when I like. It isnt ten yet.

LADY UTTERWORD. It is long past ten. See that he goes to bed at once, Hector. [*She goes into the garden*].

HECTOR. Is there any slavery on earth viler than this slavery of men to women?

RANDALL [*rising resolutely*] I'll not speak to her tomorrow. I'll not speak to her for another week. I'll give her s u c h a lesson. I'll go straight to bed without bidding her goodnight. [*He makes for the door leading to the hall*].

HECTOR. You are under a spell, man. Old Shotover sold himself to the devil in Zanzibar. The devil gave him a black witch for a wife; and these two demon daughters are their mystical progeny. I am tied to Hesione's apron-string; but I'm her husband; and if I did go stark staring mad about her, at least we became man and wife. But why should y o u let yourself be dragged about and beaten by Ariadne as a toy donkey is dragged about and beaten by a child? What do you get by it? Are you her lover?

RANDALL. You must not misunderstand me. In a higher sense—in a Platonic sense—

HECTOR. Psha! Platonic sense! She makes you her servant; and when pay-day comes round, she bilks you: that is what you mean.

RANDALL [*feebly*] Well, if I dont mind, I dont see what business it is of yours. Besides, I tell you I am going to punish her. You shall see: *I* know how to deal with women. I'm really very sleepy. Say goodnight to Mrs Hushabye for me, will you, like a good chap. Goodnight. [*He hurries out*].

HECTOR. Poor wretch! Oh women! women! women! [*He lifts his fists in invocation to heaven*]. Fall. Fall and crush. [*He goes out into the garden*].

END OF ACT II

Act III

In the garden, Hector, as he comes out through the glass door of the poop, finds Lady Utterword lying voluptuously in the hammock on the east side of the flagstaff, in the circle of light cast by the electric arc, which is like a moon in its opal globe. Beneath the head of the hammock, a campstool. On the other side of the flagstaff, on the long garden seat, Captain Shotover is asleep, with Ellie beside him, leaning affectionately against him on his right hand. On his left is a deck chair. Behind them in the gloom, Hesione is strolling about with Mangan. It is a fine still night, moonless.

LADY UTTERWORD. What a lovely night! It seems made for us.

HECTOR. The night takes no interest in us. What are we to the night? [*He sits down moodily in the deck chair*].

ELLIE [*dreamily, nestling against the Captain*] Its beauty soaks into my nerves. In the night there is peace for the old and hope for the young.

HECTOR. Is that remark your own?

ELLIE. No. Only the last thing the Captain said before he went to sleep.

CAPTAIN SHOTOVER. I'm not asleep.

HECTOR. Randall is. Also Mr Mazzini Dunn. Mangan too, probably.

MANGAN. No.

HECTOR. Oh, you are there. I thought Hesione would have sent you to bed by this time.

MRS HUSHABYE [*coming to the back of the garden seat, into the light, with Mangan*] I think I shall. He keeps telling me he has a presentiment that he is going to die. I never met a man so greedy for sympathy.

MANGAN [*plaintively*] But I have a presentiment. I really have. And you wouldnt listen.

MRS HUSHABYE. I was listening for something else. There was a sort of splendid drumming in the sky. Did none of you hear it? It came from a distance and then died away.

MANGAN. I tell you it was a train.

MRS HUSHABYE. And *I* tell you, Alf, there is no train at this hour. The last is nine fortyfive.

MANGAN. But a goods train.

MRS HUSHBAYE. Not on our little line. They tack a truck on to the passenger train. What can it have been, Hector?

HECTOR. Heaven's threatening growl of disgust at us useless futile creatures. [*Fiercely*] I tell you, one of two things must happen. Either out of that darkness some new creation will come to supplant us as we have supplanted the animals, or the heavens will fall in thunder and destroy us.

LADY UTTERWORD [*in a cool instructive manner, wallowing com-*

fortably in her hammock] We have not supplanted the animals, Hector. Why do you ask heaven to destroy this house, which could be made quite comfortable if Hesione had any notion of how to live? Dont you know what is wrong with it?

HECTOR. We are wrong with it. There is no sense in us. We are useless, dangerous, and ought to be abolished.

LADY UTTERWORD. Nonsense! Hastings told me the very first day he came here, nearly twentyfour years ago, what is wrong with the house.

CAPTAIN SHOTOVER. What! The numskull said there was something wrong with my house!

LADY UTTERWORD. I said Hastings said it; and he is not in the least a numskull.

CAPTAIN SHOTOVER. Whats wrong with my house?

LADY UTTERWORD. Just what is wrong with a ship, papa. Wasnt it clever of Hastings to see that?

CAPTAIN SHOTOVER. The man's a fool. Theres nothing wrong with a ship.

LADY UTTERWORD. Yes there is.

MRS HUSHABYE. But what is it? Dont be aggravating, Addy.

LADY UTTERWORD. Guess.

HECTOR. Demons. Daughters of the witch of Zanzibar. Demons.

LADY UTTERWORD. Not a bit. I assure you, all this house needs to make it a sensible, healthy, pleasant house, with good appetites and sound sleep in it, is horses.

MRS HUSHABYE. Horses! What rubbish!

LADY UTTERWORD. Yes: horses. Why have we never been able to let this house? Because there are no proper stables. Go anywhere in England where there are natural, wholesome, contented, and really nice English people; and what do you always find? That the stables are the real centre of the household; and that if any visitor wants to play the piano the whole room has to be upset before it can be opened, there are so many things piled on it. I never lived until I learned to ride; and I shall never ride really well because I didnt begin as a child. There are only two classes in good society in England: the equestrian classes and the neurotic classes. It isnt mere convention: everybody can see that the people who hunt are the right people and the people who dont are the wrong ones.

CAPTAIN SHOTOVER. There is some truth in this. My ship made a man of me; and a ship is the horse of the sea.

LADY UTTERWORD. Exactly how Hastings explained your being a gentleman.

CAPTAIN SHOTOVER. Not bad for a numskull. Bring the man here with you next time: I must talk to him.

LADY UTTERWORD. Why is Randall such an obvious rotter? He is well bred; he has been at a public school and a university; he has been in the Foreign Office; he knows the best people and has lived all his life among them. Why is he so unsatisfactory, so contemptible? Why cant he get a valet to stay with him longer than a few months? Just because he is too lazy and pleasure-loving to hunt and shoot. He strums the piano, and sketches, and runs after married women, and reads literary books and poems. He actually plays the flute; but I never let him bring it into my house. If he would only— [*she is interrupted by the melancholy strains of a flute coming from an open window above. She raises herself indignantly in the hammock*]. Randall: you have not gone to bed. Have you been listening? [*The flute replies pertly*]:

How vulgar! Go to bed instantly, Randall: how dare you? [*The window is slammed down. She subsides*]. How can anyone care for such a creature!

MRS HUSHABYE. Addy: do you think Ellie ought to marry poor Alfred merely for his money?

MANGAN [*much alarmed*] Whats that? Mrs Hushabye: are my affairs to be discussed like this before everybody?

LADY UTTERWORD. I dont think Randall is listening now.

MANGAN. Everybody is listening. It isnt right.

MRS HUSHABYE. But in the dark, what does it matter? Ellie doesnt mind. Do you, Ellie?

ELLIE. Not in the least. What is your opinion, Lady Utterword? You have so much good sense.

MANGAN. But it isnt right. It— [*Mrs Hushabye puts her hand on his mouth*]. Oh, very well.

LADY UTTERWORD. How much money have you, Mr Mangan?

MANGAN. Really—No: I cant stand this.

LADY UTTERWORD. Nonsense, Mr Mangan! It all turns on your income, doesnt it?

MANGAN. Well, if you come to that, how much money has she?

ELLIE. None.

LADY UTTERWORD. You are answered, Mr Mangan. And now, as you have made Miss Dunn throw her cards on the table, you cannot refuse to shew your own.

MRS HUSHABYE. Come, Alf! out with it! How much?

MANGAN [*baited out of all prudence*] Well, if you want to know, I have no money and never had any.

MRS HUSHABYE. Alfred: you mustnt tell naughty stories.

MANGAN. I'm not telling you stories. I'm telling you the raw truth.

LADY UTTERWORD. Then what do you live on, Mr Mangan?

MANGAN. Travelling expenses. And a trifle of commission.

CAPTAIN SHOTOVER. What more have any of us but travelling expenses for our life's journey?

MRS HUSHABYE. But you have factories and capital and things?

MANGAN. People think I have. People think I'm an industrial Napoleon. Thats why Miss Ellie wants to marry me. But I tell you I have nothing.

ELLIE. Do you mean that the factories are like Marcus's tigers? That they dont exist?

MANGAN. They exist all right enough. But theyre not mine. They belong to syndicates and shareholders and all sorts of lazy good-for-nothing capitalists. I get money from such people to start the factories. I find people like Miss Dunn's father to work them, and keep a tight hand so as to make them pay. Of course I make them keep me going pretty well; but it's a dog's life; and I dont own anything.

MRS HUSHABYE. Alfred, Alfred: you are making a poor mouth of it[3] to get out of marrying Ellie.

MANGAN. I'm telling the truth about my money for the first time in my life; and it's the first time my word has ever been doubted.

LADY UTTERWORD. How sad! Why dont you go in for politics, Mr Mangan?

MANGAN. Go in for politics! Where have you been living? I a m in politics.

LADY UTTERWORD. I'm sure I beg your pardon. I never heard of you.

MANGAN. Let me tell you, Lady Utterword, that the Prime Minister of this country asked me to join the Government without even going through the nonsense of an election, as the dictator of a great public department.

LADY UTTERWORD. As a Conservative or a Liberal?

MANGAN. No such nonsense. As a practical business man. [*They all burst out laughing*]. What are you all laughing at?

MRS HUSHABYE. Oh, Alfred, Alfred!

ELLIE. You! who have to get my father to do everything for you!

MRS HUSHABYE. You! who are afraid of your own workmen!

HECTOR. You! with whom three women have been playing cat and mouse all the evening!

LADY UTTERWORD. You must have given an immense sum to the party funds, Mr Mangan.

MANGAN. Not a penny out of my own pocket. The syndicate found the money: they knew how useful I should be to them in the Government.

LADY UTTERWORD. This is most interesting and unexpected, Mr Mangan. And what have your administrative achievements been, so far?

MANGAN. Achievements? Well, I dont know what you call achievements; but Ive jolly well put a stop to the games of the other fellows in the other departments. Every man of them thought he was going to save the country all by himself, and do me out of the credit and out of my chance of a title. I took good care that if they wouldnt let me do it they shouldnt do it themselves either. I may not know anything about my own machinery; but I

3. That is, you are pleading poverty.

know how to stick a ramrod into the other fellow's. And now they all look the biggest fools going.

HECTOR. And in heaven's name, what do you look like?

MANGAN. I look like the fellow that was too clever for all the others, dont I? If that isnt a triumph of practical business, what is?

HECTOR. Is this England, or is it a madhouse?

LADY UTTERWORD. Do you expect to save the country, Mr Mangan?

MANGAN. Well, who else will? Will your Mr Randall save it?

LADY UTTERWORD. Randall the rotter! Certainly not.

MANGAN. Will your brother-in-law save it with his moustache and his fine talk?

HECTOR. Yes, if they will let me.

MANGAN [*sneering*] Ah! W i l l they let you?

HECTOR. No. They prefer you.

MANGAN. Very well then, as youre in a world where I'm appreciated and youre not, youd best be civil to me, hadnt you? Who else is there but me?

LADY UTTERWORD. There is Hastings. Get rid of your ridiculous sham democracy; and give Hastings the necessary powers, and a good supply of bamboo to bring the British native to his senses: he will save the country with the greatest ease.

CAPTAIN SHOTOVER. It had better be lost. Any fool can govern with a stick in his hand. *I* could govern that way. It is not God's way. The man is a numskull.

LADY UTTERWORD. The man is worth all of you rolled into one. What do y o u say, Miss Dunn?

ELLIE. I think my father would do very well if people did not put upon him and cheat him and despise him because he is so good.

MANGAN [*contemptuously*] I think I see Mazzini Dunn getting into parliament or pushing his way into the Government. Weve not come to that yet, thank God! What do you say, Mrs Hushabye?

MRS HUSHABYE. Oh, *I* say it matters very little which of you governs the country so long as we govern you.

HECTOR. We? Who is we, pray?

MRS HUSHABYE. The devil's granddaughters, dear. The lovely women.

HECTOR [*raising his hands as before*] Fall, I say; and deliver us from the lures of Satan!

ELLIE. There seems to be nothing real in the world except my father and Shakespear. Marcus's tigers are false; Mr Mangan's millions are false; there is nothing really strong and true about Hesione but her beautiful black hair; and Lady Utterword's is too pretty to be real. The one thing that was left to me was the Captain's seventh degree of concentration; and that turns out to be—

CAPTAIN SHOTOVER. Rum.

LADY UTTERWORD [*placidly*] A good deal of my hair is quite genuine. The Duchess of Dithering offered me fifty guineas for this [*touching her forehead*] under the impression that it was a transformation; but it is all natural except the color.

MANGAN [*wildly*] Look here: I'm going to take off all my clothes [*he begins tearing off his coat*].

LADY UTTERWORD.		Mr Mangan!
CAPTAIN SHOTOVER.	[*in consterna-tion*]	Whats that?
HECTOR.		Ha! ha! Do. Do.
ELLIE.		Please dont.

MRS HUSHABYE [*catching his arm and stopping him*] Alfred: for shame! Are you mad?

MANGAN. Shame! What shame is there in this house? Let's all strip stark naked. We may as well do the thing thoroughly when we're about it. Weve stripped ourselves morally naked: well, let us strip ourselves physically naked as well, and see how we like it. I tell you I cant bear this. I was brought up to be respectable. I dont mind the women dyeing their hair and the men drinking: it's human nature. But it's not human nature to tell everybody about it. Every time one of you opens your mouth I go like this [*he cowers as if to avoid a missile*] afraid of what will come next. How are we to have any self-respect if we dont keep it up that we're better than we really are?

LADY UTTERWORD. I quite sympathize with you, Mr Mangan. I have been through it all; and I know by experience that men and women are delicate plants and must be cultivated under glass. Our family habit of throwing stones in all directions and letting the air in is not only unbearably rude, but positively dangerous. Still, there is no use catching physical colds as well as moral ones; so please keep your clothes on.

MANGAN. I'll do as I like: not what you tell me. Am I a child or a grown man? I wont stand this mothering tyranny. I'll go back to the city, where I'm respected and made much of.

MRS HUSHABYE. Goodbye, Alf. Think of us sometimes in the city. Think of Ellie's youth!

ELLIE. Think of Hesione's eyes and hair!

CAPTAIN SHOTOVER. Think of this garden in which you are not a dog barking to keep the truth out!

HECTOR. Think of Lady Utterword's beauty! her good sense! her style!

LADY UTTERWORD. Flatterer. Think, Mr Mangan, whether you can really do any better for yourself elsewhere: that is the essential point, isnt it?

MANGAN [*surrendering*] All right: all right. I'm done. Have it your own way. Only let me alone. I dont know whether I'm on my head or my heels when you all start on me like this. I'll stay. I'll marry her. I'll do anything for a quiet life. Are you satisfied now?

ELLIE. No. I never really intended to make you marry me, Mr Mangan. Never in the depths of my soul. I only wanted to feel my strength: to know that you could not escape if I chose to take you.

MANGAN [*indignantly*] What! Do you mean to say you are going to throw me over after my acting so handsome?

LADY UTTERWORD. I should not be too hasty, Miss Dunn. You can throw Mr Mangan over at any time up to the last moment. Very few men in his position go bankrupt. You can live very comfortably on his reputation for immense wealth.

ELLIE. I cannot commit bigamy, Lady Utterword.

MRS HUSHABYE.		Bigamy! Whatever on earth are you talking about, Ellie?
LADY UTTERWORD.	*[exclaiming all together]*	Bigamy! What do you mean, Miss Dunn?
MANGAN.		Bigamy! Do you mean to say youre married already?
HECTOR.		Bigamy! This is some enigma.

ELLIE. Only half an hour ago I became Captain Shotover's white wife.

MRS HUSHABYE. Ellie! What nonsense! Where?

ELLIE. In heaven, where all true marriages are made.

LADY UTTERWORD. Really, Miss Dunn! Really, papa!

MANGAN. He told me *I* was too old! And him a mummy!

HECTOR [*quoting Shelley*]

> "Their altar the grassy earth outspread,
> And their priest the muttering wind."

ELLIE. Yes: I, Ellie Dunn, give my broken heart and my strong sound soul to its natural captain, my spiritual husband and second father.

> *She draws the Captain's arm through hers, and pats his hand. The Captain remains fast asleep.*

MRS HUSHABYE. Oh, thats very clever of you, pettikins. V e r y clever. Alfred: you could never have lived up to Ellie. You must be content with a little share of me.

MANGAN [*sniffing and wiping his eyes*] It isnt kind— [*his emotion chokes him*].

LADY UTTERWORD. You are well out of it, Mr Mangan. Miss Dunn is the most conceited young woman I have met since I came back to England.

MRS HUSHABYE. Oh, Ellie isnt conceited. Are you, pettikins?

ELLIE. I know my strength now, Hesione.

MANGAN. Brazen, I call you. Brazen.

MRS HUSHABYE. Tut tut, Alfred: dont be rude. Dont you feel how lovely this marriage night is, made in heaven? Arnt you happy, you and Hector? Open your eyes: Addy and Ellie look beautiful enough to please the most fastidious man: we live and love and have not a care in the world. We women have managed all that for you. Why in the name of common sense do you go on as if you were two miserable wretches?

CAPTAIN SHOTOVER. I tell you happiness is no good. You can be happy when you are only half alive. I am happier now I am half dead than ever I was in my prime. But there is no blessing on my happiness.

ELLIE [*her face lighting up*] Life with a blessing! that is what I want. Now I know the real reason why I couldnt marry Mr Mangan: there would be no blessing on our marriage. There is a blessing on my broken heart. There is a blessing on your beauty, Hesione. There is a blessing on your father's spirit. Even on the lies of Marcus there is a blessing; but on Mr Mangan's money there is none.

MANGAN. I dont understand a word of that.

ELLIE. Neither do I. But I know it means something.

MANGAN. Dont say there was any difficulty about the blessing. I was ready to get a bishop to marry us.

MRS HUSHABYE. Isnt he a fool, pettikins?

HECTOR [*fiercely*] Do not scorn the man. We are all fools.

> *Mazzini, in pyjamas and a richly colored silk dressing-gown, comes from the house, on Lady Utterword's side.*

MRS HUSHABYE. Oh! here comes the only man who ever resisted me. Whats the matter, Mr Dunn? Is the house on fire?

MAZZINI. Oh no: nothing's the matter: but really it's impossible to go to sleep with such an interesting conversation going on under one's window, and on such a beautiful night too. I just had to come down and join you all. What has it all been about?

MRS HUSHABYE. Oh, wonderful things, soldier of freedom.

HECTOR. For example, Mangan, as a practical business man, has tried to undress himself and has failed ignominiously; whilst you, as an idealist, have succeeded brilliantly.

MAZZINI. I hope you dont mind my being like this, Mrs Hushabye. [*He sits down on the campstool*].

MRS HUSHABYE. On the contrary, I could wish you always like that.

LADY UTTERWORD. Your daughter's match is off, Mr Dunn. It seems that Mr Mangan, whom we all supposed to be a man of property, owns absolutely nothing.

MAZZINI. Well of course I knew that, Lady Utterword. But if people believe in him and are always giving him money, whereas they dont believe in me and never give me any, how can I ask poor Ellie to depend on what I can do for her?

MANGAN. Dont you run away with this idea that I have nothing. I—

HECTOR. Oh, dont explain. We understand. You have a couple of thousand pounds in exchequer bills, 50,000 shares worth tenpence a dozen, and half a dozen tabloids of cyanide of potassium to poison yourself with when you are found out. Thats the reality of your millions.

MAZZINI. Oh no, no, no. He is quite honest: the businesses are genuine and perfectly legal.

HECTOR [*disgusted*] Yah! Not even a great swindler!

MANGAN. So you think. But Ive been too many for some honest men, for all that.

LADY UTTERWORD. There is no pleasing you, Mr Mangan. You are determined to be neither rich nor poor, honest nor dishonest.

MANGAN. There you go again. Ever since I came into this silly house I have been made to look like a fool, though I'm as good a man in this house as in the city.

ELLIE [*musically*] Yes: this silly house, this strangely happy house, this agonizing house, this house without foundations. I shall call it Heartbreak House.

MRS HUSHABYE. Stop, Ellie; or I shall howl like an animal.

MANGAN [*breaks into a low snivelling*] !!!

MRS HUSHABYE. There! you have set Alfred off.

ELLIE. I like him best when he is howling.

CAPTAIN SHOTOVER. Silence! [*Mangan subsides into silence*]. I say, let the heart break in silence.

HECTOR. Do you accept that name for your house?

CAPTAIN SHOTOVER. It is not my house: it is only my kennel.

HECTOR. We have been too long here. We do not live in this house: we haunt it.

LADY UTTERWORD [*heart torn*] It is dreadful to think how you have been here all these years while I have gone round the world. I escaped young; but it has drawn me back. It wants to break my heart too. But it shant. I have left you and it behind. It was silly of me to come back. I felt sentimental about papa and Hesione and the old place. I felt them calling to me.

MAZZINI. But what a very natural and kindly and charming human feeling, Lady Utterword!

LADY UTTERWORD. So I thought, Mr Dunn. But I know now that it was only the last of my influenza. I found that I was not remembered and not wanted.

CAPTAIN SHOTOVER. You left because you did not want us. Was there no heartbreak in that for your father? You tore yourself up by the roots; and the ground healed up and brought forth fresh plants and forgot you. What right had you to come back and probe old wounds?

MRS HUSHABYE. You were a complete stranger to me at first, Addy; but now I feel as if you had never been away.

LADY UTTERWORD. Thank you, Hesione; but the influenza is quite cured. The place may be Heartbreak House to you, Miss Dunn, and to this gentleman from the city who seems to have so little self-control; but to me it is only a very ill-regulated and rather untidy villa without any stables.

HECTOR. Inhabited by— ?

ELLIE. A crazy old sea captain and a young singer who adores him.

MRS HUSHABYE. A sluttish female, trying to stave off a double chin and an elderly spread, vainly wooing a born soldier of freedom.

MAZZINI. Oh, really, Mrs Hushabye—

MANGAN. A member of His Majesty's Government that everybody sets down as a nincompoop: dont forget him, Lady Utterword.

LADY UTTERWORD. And a very fascinating gentleman whose chief occupation is to be married to my sister.

HECTOR. All heartbroken imbeciles.

MAZZINI. Oh no. Surely, if I may say so, rather a favorable specimen of what is best in our English culture. You are very charming people, most advanced, unprejudiced, frank, humane, unconventional, democratic, free-thinking, and everything that is delightful to thoughtful people.

MRS HUSHABYE. You do us proud, Mazzini.

MAZZINI. I am not flattering, really. Where else could I feel perfectly at ease in my pyjamas? I sometimes dream that I am in very distinguished society, and suddenly I have nothing on but my pyjamas! Sometimes I havnt even pyjamas. And I always feel overwhelmed with confusion. But here, I dont mind in the least: it seems quite natural.

LADY UTTERWORD. An infallible sign that you are not now in really distinguished society, Mr Dunn. If you were in my house, you w o u l d feel embarrassed.

MAZZINI. I shall take particular care to keep out of your house, Lady Utterword.

LADY UTTERWORD. You will be quite wrong, Mr Dunn. I should make you very comfortable; and you would not have the trouble and anxiety of wondering whether you should wear your purple and gold or your green and crimson dressing-gown at dinner. You complicate life instead of simplifying it by doing these ridiculous things.

ELLIE. Y o u r house is not Heartbreak House: is it, Lady Utterword?

HECTOR. Yet she breaks hearts, easy as her house is. That poor devil upstairs with his flute howls when she twists his heart, just as Mangan howls when my wife twists his.

LADY UTTERWORD. That is because Randall has nothing to do but have his heart broken. It is a change from having his head shampooed. Catch anyone breaking Hastings' heart!

CAPTAIN SHOTOVER. The numskull wins, after all.

LADY UTTERWORD. I shall go back to my numskull with the greatest satisfaction when I am tired of you all, clever as you are.

MANGAN [*huffily*] I never set up to be clever.

LADY UTTERWORD. I forgot you, Mr Mangan.

MANGAN. Well, I dont see that quite, either.

LADY UTTERWORD. You may not be clever, Mr Mangan; but you are successful.

MANGAN. But I dont want to be regarded merely as a successful man. I have an imagination like anyone else. I have a presentiment—

MRS HUSHABYE. Oh, you are impossible, Alfred. Here I am devoting myself to you; and you think of nothing but your ridiculous presentiment. You bore me. Come and talk poetry to me under the stars. [*She drags him away into the darkness*].

MANGAN [*tearfully, as he disappears*] Yes: it's all very well to make fun of me; but if you only knew—

HECTOR [*impatiently*] How is all this going to end?

MAZZINI. It wont end, Mr Hushabye. Life doesnt end: it goes on.

ELLIE. Oh, it cant go on for ever. I'm always expecting something. I dont know what it is; but life must come to a point sometime.

LADY UTTERWORD. The point for a young woman of your age is a baby.

HECTOR. Yes, but, damn it, I have the same feeling; and *I* cant have a baby.

LADY UTTERWORD. By deputy, Hector.

HECTOR. But I h a v e children. All that is over and done with for me: and yet I too feel that this cant last. We sit here talking, and leave everything to Mangan and to chance and to the devil. Think of the powers of destruction that Mangan and his mutual admiration gang wield! It's madness: it's like giving a torpedo to a badly brought up child to play at earthquakes with.

MAZZINI. I know. I used often to think about that when I was young.

HECTOR. Think! Whats the good of thinking about it? Why didnt you do something?

MAZZINI. But I did. I joined societies and made speeches and wrote pamphlets. That was all I could do. But, you know, though the people in the societies thought they knew more than Mangan, most of them wouldnt have joined if they had known as much. You see they had never had any money to handle or any men to manage. Every year I expected a revolution, or some frightful smash-up: it seemed impossible that we could blunder and muddle on any longer. But nothing happened, except, of course, the usual poverty and crime and drink that we are used to. Nothing ever does happen. It's amazing how well we get along, all things considered.

LADY UTTERWORD. Perhaps somebody cleverer than you and Mr Mangan was at work all the time.

MAZZINI. Perhaps so. Though I was brought up not to believe in anything, I often feel that there is a great deal to be said for the theory of an overruling Providence, after all.

LADY UTTERWORD. Providence! I meant Hastings.

MAZZINI. Oh, I beg your pardon, Lady Utterword.

CAPTAIN SHOTOVER. Every drunken skipper trusts to Providence. But one of the ways of Providence with drunken skippers is to run them on the rocks.

MAZZINI. Very true, no doubt, at sea. But in politics, I assure you, they only run into jellyfish. Nothing happens.

CAPTAIN SHOTOVER. At sea nothing happens to the sea. Nothing happens to the sky. The sun comes up from the east and goes down to the west. The moon grows from a sickle to an arc lamp, and comes later and later until she is lost in the light as other things are lost in the darkness. After the typhoon, the flying-fish glitter in the sunshine like birds. It's amazing how t h e y get along, all things considered. Nothing happens, except something not worth mentioning.

ELLIE. What is that, O Captain, my captain?

CAPTAIN SHOTOVER [*savagely*] Nothing but the smash of the

drunken skipper's ship on the rocks, the splintering of her rotten timbers, the tearing of her rusty plates, the drowning of the crew like rats in a trap.

ELLIE. Moral: dont take rum.

CAPTAIN SHOTOVER [*vehemently*] That is a lie, child. Let a man drink ten barrels of rum a day, he is not a drunken skipper until he is a drifting skipper. Whilst he can lay his course and stand on his bridge and steer it, he is no drunkard. It is the man who lies drinking in his bunk and trusts to Providence that I call the drunken skipper, though he drank nothing but the waters of the River Jordan.

ELLIE. Splendid! And you havnt had a drop for an hour. You see you dont need it: your own spirit is not dead.

CAPTAIN SHOTOVER. Echoes: nothing but echoes. The last shot was fired years ago.

HECTOR. And this ship that we are all in? This soul's prison we call England?

CAPTAIN SHOTOVER. The captain is in his bunk, drinking bottled ditch-water; and the crew is gambling in the forecastle. She will strike and sink and split. Do you think the laws of God will be suspended in favor of England because you were born in it?

HECTOR. Well, I dont mean to be drowned like a rat in a trap. I still have the will to live. What am I to do?

CAPTAIN SHOTOVER. Do? Nothing simpler. Learn your business as an Englishman.

HECTOR. And what may my business as an Englishman be, pray?

CAPTAIN SHOTOVER. Navigation. Learn it and live; or leave it and be damned.

ELLIE. Quiet, quiet: youll tire yourself.

MAZZINI. I thought all that once, Captain; but I assure you nothing will happen.

A dull distant explosion is heard.

HECTOR [*starting up*] What was that?

CAPTAIN SHOTOVER. Something happening [*he blows his whistle*]. Breakers ahead!

The light goes out.

HECTOR [*furiously*] Who put that light out? Who dared put that light out?

NURSE GUINNESS [*running in from the house to the middle of the esplanade*] I did, sir. The police have telephoned to say we'll be summoned if we dont put that light out: it can be seen for miles.

HECTOR. It shall be seen for a hundred miles [*he dashes into the house*].

NURSE GUINNESS. The rectory is nothing but a heap of bricks, they say. Unless we can give the rector a bed he has nowhere to lay his head this night.

CAPTAIN SHOTOVER. The Church is on the rocks, breaking up. I told him it would unless it headed for God's open sea.

NURSE GUINNESS. And you are all to go down to the cellars.

CAPTAIN SHOTOVER. Go there yourself, you and all the crew. Batten down the hatches.

NURSE GUINNESS. And hide beside the coward I married! I'll go on the roof first. [*The lamp lights up again*]. There! Mr Hushabye's turned it on again.

THE BURGLAR [*hurrying in and appealing to Nurse Guinness*] Here: wheres the way to that gravel pit? The boot-boy says theres a cave in the gravel pit. Them cellars is no use. Wheres the gravel pit, Captain?

NURSE GUINNESS. Go straight on past the flagstaff until you fall into it and break your dirty neck. [*She pushes him contemptuously towards the flagstaff, and herself goes to the foot of the hammock and waits there, as it were by Ariadne's cradle*].

> *Another and louder explosion is heard. The burglar stops and stands trembling.*

ELLIE [*rising*] That was nearer.

CAPTAIN SHOTOVER. The next one will get us. [*He rises*]. Stand by, all hands, for judgment.

THE BURGLAR. Oh my Lordy God! [*He rushes away frantically past the flagstaff into the gloom*].

MRS HUSHABYE [*emerging panting from the darkness*] Who was that running away? [*She comes to Ellie*]. Did you hear the explosions? And the sound in the sky: it's splendid: it's like an orchestra: it's like Beethoven.

ELLIE. By thunder, Hesione: it i s Beethoven.

> *She and Hesione throw themselves into one another's arms in wild excitement. The light increases.*

MAZZINI [*anxiously*] The light is getting brighter.

NURSE GUINNESS [*looking up at the house*] It's Mr Hushabye turning on all the lights in the house and tearing down the curtains.

RANDALL [*rushing in in his pyjamas, distractedly waving a flute*] Ariadne: my soul, my precious, go down to the cellars: I beg and implore you, go down to the cellars!

LADY UTTERWORD [*quite composed in her hammock*] The governor's wife in the cellars with the servants! Really, Randall!

RANDALL. But what shall I do if you are killed?

LADY UTTERWORD. You will probably be killed, too, Randall. Now play your flute to shew that you are not afraid; and be good. Play us Keep the home fires burning.[4]

NURSE GUINNESS [*grimly*] T h e y l l keep the home fires burning for us: them up there.

RANDALL [*having tried to play*] My lips are trembling. I cant get a sound.

MAZZINI. I hope poor Mangan is safe.

MRS HUSHABYE. He is hiding in the cave in the gravel pit.

CAPTAIN SHOTOVER. My dynamite drew him there. It is the hand of God.

HECTOR [*returning from the house and striding across to his former*

---

4. A well-known World War I ballad—the first internal indication of the time of the play.

place] There is not half light enough. We should be blazing to the skies.

ELLIE [*tense with excitement*] Set fire to the house, Marcus.

MRS HUSHABYE. My house! No.

HECTOR. I thought of that; but it would not be ready in time.

CAPTAIN SHOTOVER. The judgment has come. Courage will not save you; but it will shew that your souls are still alive.

MRS HUSHABYE. Sh-sh! Listen: do you hear it now? It's magnificent.

> *They all turn away from the house and look up, listening.*

HECTOR [*gravely*] Miss Dunn: you can do no good here. We of this house are only moths flying into the candle. You had better go down to the cellar.

ELLIE [*scornfully*] I d o n t think.

MAZZINI. Ellie, dear, there is no disgrace in going to the cellar. An officer would order his soldiers to take cover. Mr Hushabye is behaving like an amateur. Mangan and the burglar are acting very sensibly; and it is they who will survive.

ELLIE. Let them. I shall behave like an amateur. But why should you run any risk?

MAZZINI. Think of the risk those poor fellows up there are running!

NURSE GUINNESS. Think of t h e m, indeed, the murdering blackguards! What next?

> *A terrific explosion shakes the earth. They reel back into their seats, or clutch the nearest support. They hear the falling of the shattered glass from the windows.*

MAZZINI. Is anyone hurt?

HECTOR. Where did it fall?

NURSE GUINNESS [*in hideous triumph*] Right in the gravel pit: I seen it. Serve un right! I seen it [*she runs away towards the gravel pit, laughing harshly*].

HECTOR. One husband gone.

CAPTAIN SHOTOVER. Thirty pounds of good dynamite wasted.

MAZZINI. Oh, poor Mangan!

HECTOR. Are you immortal that you need pity him? Our turn next.

> *They wait in silence and intense expectation. Hesione and Ellie hold each other's hand tight.*
>
> *A distant explosion is heard.*

MRS HUSHABYE [*relaxing her grip*] Oh! they have passed us.

LADY UTTERWORD. The danger is over, Randall. Go to bed.

CAPTAIN SHOTOVER. Turn in, all hands. The ship is safe. [*He sits down and goes asleep*].

ELLIE [*disappointedly*] Safe!

HECTOR [*disgustedly*] Yes, safe. And how damnably dull the world has become again suddenly! [*He sits down*].

MAZZINI [*sitting down*] I was quite wrong, after all. It is we who have survived; and Mangan and the burglar—

HECTOR. —the two burglars—

LADY UTTERWORD. —the two practical men of business—

MAZZINI. —both gone. And the poor clergyman will have to get a new house.

MRS HUSHABYE. But what a glorious experience! I hope theyll come again tomorrow night.

ELLIE [*radiant at the prospect*] Oh, I hope so.

> *Randall at last succeeds in keeping the home fires burning on his flute.*

CURTAIN

Saint Joan

Scene I

A fine spring morning on the river Meuse, between Lorraine and Champagne, in the year 1429 A.D., in the castle of Vaucouleurs.

Captain Robert de Baudricourt, a military squire, handsome and physically energetic, but with no will of his own, is disguising that defect in his usual fashion by storming terribly at his steward, a trodden worm, scanty of flesh, scanty of hair, who might be any age from 18 to 55, being the sort of man whom age cannot wither because he has never bloomed.

The two are in a sunny stone chamber on the first floor of the castle. At a plain strong oak table, seated in chair to match, the captain presents his left profile. The steward stands facing him at the other side of the table, if so deprecatory a stance as his can be called standing. The mullioned thirteenth-century window is open behind him. Near it in the corner is a turret with a narrow arched doorway leading to a winding stair which descends to the courtyard. There is a stout fourlegged stool under the table, and a wooden chest under the window.

ROBERT. No eggs! No eggs!! Thousand thunders, man, what do you mean by no eggs?

STEWARD. Sir: it is not my fault. It is the act of God.

ROBERT. Blasphemy. You tell me there are no eggs; and you blame your Maker for it.

STEWARD. Sir: what can I do? I cannot lay eggs.

ROBERT [*sarcastic*] Ha! You jest about it.

STEWARD. No, sir, God knows. We all have to go without eggs just as you have, sir. The hens will not lay.

ROBERT. Indeed! [*Rising*] Now listen to me, you.

STEWARD [*humbly*] Yes, sir.

ROBERT. What am I?

STEWARD. What are you, sir?

ROBERT [*coming at him*] Yes: what am I? Am I Robert, squire of Baudricourt and captain of this castle of Vaucouleurs; or am I a cowboy?

STEWARD. Oh, sir, you know you are a greater man here than the king himself.

ROBERT. Precisely. And now, do you know what you are?

STEWARD. I am nobody, sir, except that I have the honor to be your steward.

ROBERT [*driving him to the wall, adjective by adjective*] You have not only the honor of being my steward, but the privilege of being the worst, most incompetent, drivelling snivelling jibbering jabbering idiot of a steward in France. [*He strides back to the table*].

STEWARD [*cowering on the chest*] Yes, sir: to a great man like you I must seem like that.

ROBERT [*turning*] My fault, I suppose. Eh?

STEWARD [*coming to him deprecatingly*] Oh, sir: you always give my most innocent words such a turn!

ROBERT. I will give your neck a turn if you dare tell me, when I ask you how many eggs there are, that you cannot lay any.

STEWARD [*protesting*] Oh sir, oh sir—

ROBERT. No: not oh sir, oh sir, but no sir, no sir. My three Barbary hens and the black are the best layers in Champagne. And you come and tell me that there are no eggs! Who stole them? Tell me that, before I kick you out through the castle gate for a liar and a seller of my goods to thieves. The milk was short yesterday, too: do not forget that.

STEWARD [*desperate*] I know, sir. I know only too well. There is no milk: there are no eggs: tomorrow there will be nothing.

ROBERT. Nothing! You will steal the lot: eh?

STEWARD. No, sir: nobody will steal anything. But there is a spell on us: we are bewitched.

ROBERT. That story is not good enough for me. Robert de Baudricourt burns witches and hangs thieves. Go. Bring me four dozen eggs and two gallons of milk here in this room before noon, or Heaven have mercy on your bones! I will teach you to make a fool of me. [*He resumes his seat with an air of finality*].

STEWARD. Sir: I tell you there are no eggs. There will be none—not if you were to kill me for it—as long as The Maid is at the door.

ROBERT. The Maid! What maid? What are you talking about?

STEWARD. The girl from Lorraine, sir. From Domrémy.

ROBERT [*rising in fearful wrath*] Thirty thousand thunders! Fifty thousand devils! Do you mean to say that that girl, who had the impudence to ask to see me two days ago, and whom I told you to send back to her father with my orders that he was to give her a good hiding, is here still?

STEWARD. I have told her to go, sir. She wont.

ROBERT. I did not tell you to tell her to go: I told you to throw her out. You have fifty men-at-arms and a dozen lumps of ablebodied servants to carry out my orders. Are they afraid of her?

STEWARD. She is so positive, sir.

ROBERT [*seizing him by the scruff of the neck*] Positive! Now see here. I am going to throw you downstairs.

STEWARD. No, sir. Please.

ROBERT. Well, stop me by being positive. It's quite easy: any slut of a girl can do it.

STEWARD [*hanging limp in his hands*] Sir, sir: you cannot get rid of her by throwing me out. [*Robert has to let him drop. He squats on his knees on the floor, contemplating his master resignedly*]. You see, sir, you are much more positive than I am. But so is she.

ROBERT. I am stronger than you are, you fool.

STEWARD. No, sir: it isnt that: it's your strong character, sir. She is weaker than we are: she is only a slip of a girl; but we cannot make her go.

ROBERT. You parcel of curs: you are afraid of her.

STEWARD [*rising cautiously*] No, sir: we are afraid of you; but she puts courage into us. She really doesnt seem to be afraid of anything. Perhaps you could frighten her, sir.

ROBERT [*grimly*] Perhaps. Where is she now?

STEWARD. Down in the courtyard, sir, talking to the soldiers as usual. She is always talking to the soldiers except when she is praying.

ROBERT. Praying! Ha! You believe she prays, you idiot. I know the sort of girl that is always talking to soldiers. She shall talk to me a bit. [*He goes to the window and shouts fiercely through it*] Hallo, you there!

A GIRL'S VOICE [*bright, strong and rough*] Is it me, sir?

ROBERT. Yes, you.

THE VOICE. Be you captain?

ROBERT. Yes, damn your impudence, I be captain. Come up here. [*To the soldiers in the yard*] Shew her the way, you. And shove her along quick. [*He leaves the window, and returns to his place at the table, where he sits magisterially*].

STEWARD [*whispering*] She wants to go and be a soldier herself. She wants you to give her soldier's clothes. Armor, sir! And a sword! Actually! [*He steals behind Robert*].

Joan appears in the turret doorway. She is an ablebodied country girl of 17 or 18, respectably dressed in red, with an uncommon face: eyes very wide apart and bulging as they often do in very imaginative people, a long well-shaped nose with wide nostrils, a short upper lip, resolute but full-lipped mouth, and handsome fighting chin. She comes eagerly to the table, delighted at having penetrated to Baudricourt's presence at last, and full of hope as to the result. His scowl does not check or frighten her in the least. Her voice is normally a hearty coaxing voice, very confident, very appealing, very hard to resist.

JOAN [*bobbing a curtsey*] Good morning, captain squire. Captain: you are to give me a horse and armor and some soldiers, and send me to the Dauphin. Those are your orders from my Lord.

ROBERT [*outraged*] Orders from your lord! And who the devil may your lord be? Go back to him, and tell him that I am neither duke nor peer at his orders: I am squire of Baudricourt; and I take no orders except from the king.

JOAN [*reassuringly*] Yes, squire: that is all right. My Lord is the King of Heaven.

ROBERT. Why, the girl's mad. [*To the steward*] Why didnt you tell me so, you blockhead?

STEWARD. Sir: do not anger her: give her what she wants.

JOAN [*impatient, but friendly*] They all say I am mad until I talk to them, squire. But you see that it is the will of God that you are to do what He has put into my mind.

ROBERT. It is the will of God that I shall send you back to your father with orders to put you under lock and key and thrash the madness out of you. What have you to say to that?

JOAN. You think you will, squire; but you will find it all coming quite different. You said you would not see me; but here I am.

STEWARD [*appealing*] Yes, sir. You see, sir.

ROBERT. Hold your tongue, you.

STEWARD [*abjectly*] Yes, sir.

ROBERT [*to Joan, with a sour loss of confidence*] So you are presuming on my seeing you, are you?

JOAN [*sweetly*] Yes, squire.

ROBERT [*feeling that he has lost ground, brings down his two fists squarely on the table, and inflates his chest imposingly to cure the unwelcome and only too familiar sensation*] Now listen to me. I am going to assert myself.

JOAN [*busily*] Please do, squire. The horse will cost sixteen francs. It is a good deal of money; but I can save it on the armor. I can find a soldier's armor that will fit me well enough: I am very hardy; and I do not need beautiful armor made to my measure like you wear. I shall not want many soldiers: the Dauphin will give me all I need to raise the siege of Orleans.

ROBERT [*flabbergasted*] To raise the siege of Orleans!

JOAN [*simply*] Yes, squire: that is what God is sending me to do. Three men will be enough for you to send with me if they are good men and gentle to me. They have promised to come with me. Polly and Jack and—

ROBERT. Polly!! You impudent baggage, do you dare call squire Bertrand de Poulengey Polly to my face?

JOAN. His friends call him so, squire: I did not know he had any other name. Jack—

ROBERT. That is Monsieur John of Metz, I suppose?

JOAN. Yes, squire. Jack will come willingly: he is a very kind gentleman, and gives me money to give to the poor. I think John Godsave will come, and Dick the Archer, and their servants John of Honecourt and Julian. There will be no trouble for you, squire: I have arranged it all: you have only to give the order.

ROBERT [*contemplating her in a stupor of amazement*] Well, I am damned!

JOAN [*with unruffled sweetness*] No, squire: God is very merciful; and the blessed saints Catherine and Margaret, who speak to me every day [*he gapes*], will intercede for you. You will go to paradise; and your name will be remembered for ever as my first helper.

ROBERT [*to the steward, still much bothered, but changing his tone as he pursues a new clue*] Is this true about Monsieur de Poulengey?

STEWARD [*eagerly*] Yes, sir, and about Monsieur de Metz too. They both want to go with her.

ROBERT [*thoughtful*] Mf! [*He goes to the window, and shouts into the courtyard*] Hallo! You there: send Monsieur de Poulengey to me, will you? [*He turns to Joan*] Get out; and wait in the yard.

JOAN [*smiling brightly at him*] Right, squire. [*She goes out*].

ROBERT [*to the steward*] Go with her, you, you dithering imbecile. Stay within call; and keep your eye on her. I shall have her up here again.

STEWARD. Do so in God's name, sir. Think of those hens, the best layers in Champagne; and—

ROBERT. Think of my boot; and take your backside out of reach of it.

> *The steward retreats hastily and finds himself confronted in the doorway by Bertrand de Poulengey, a lymphatic French gentleman-at-arms, aged 36 or thereabout, employed in the department of the provost-marshal, dreamily absent-minded, seldom speaking unless spoken to, and then slow and obstinate in reply: altogether in contrast to the self-assertive, loud-mouthed, superficially energetic, funda-mentally will-less Robert. The steward makes way for him, and vanishes.*

> *Poulengey salutes, and stands awaiting orders.*

ROBERT [*genially*] It isnt service, Polly. A friendly talk. Sit down. [*He hooks the stool from under the table with his instep*].

> *Poulengey, relaxing, comes into the room; places the stool between the table and the window; and sits down rumina-tively. Robert, half sitting on the end of the table, begins the friendly talk.*

ROBERT. Now listen to me, Polly. I must talk to you like a father.

> *Poulengey looks up at him gravely for a moment, but says nothing.*

ROBERT. It's about this girl you are interested in. Now, I have seen her. I have talked to her. First, she's mad. That doesnt matter. Second, she's not a farm wench. She's a bourgeoise. That matters a good deal. I know her class exactly. Her father came here last year to represent his village in a lawsuit: he is one of their nota-bles. A farmer. Not a gentleman farmer: he makes money by it, and lives by it. Still, not a laborer. Not a mechanic. He might have a cousin a lawyer, or in the Church. People of this sort may be of no account socially; but they can give a lot of bother to the authorities. That is to say, to me. Now no doubt it seems to you a very simple thing to take this girl away, humbugging her into the belief that you are taking her to the Dauphin. But if you get her into trouble, you may get me into no end of a mess, as I am her father's lord, and responsible for her protection. So friends or no friends, Polly, hands off her.

POULENGEY [*with deliberate impressiveness*] I should as soon think of the Blessed Virgin herself in that way, as of this girl.

ROBERT [*coming off the table*] But she says you and Jack and Dick have offered to go with her. What for? You are not going to tell me that you take her crazy notion of going to the Dau-phin seriously, are you?

POULENGEY [*slowly*] There is something about her. They are pretty foulmouthed and foulminded down there in the guard room, some of them. But there hasnt been a word that has anything to do with her being a woman. They have stopped swearing before her. There is something. Something. It may be worth trying.

ROBERT. Oh, come, Polly! pull yourself together. Commonsense was never your strong point; but this is a little too much. [*He retreats disgustedly*].

POULENGEY [*unmoved*] What is the good of commonsense? If we had any commonsense we should join the Duke of Burgundy and the English king. They hold half the country, right down to the Loire. They have Paris. They have this castle: you know very well that we had to surrender it to the Duke of Bedford, and that you are only holding it on parole. The Dauphin is in Chinon, like a rat in a corner, except that he wont fight. We dont even know that he is the Dauphin: his mother says he isnt; and she ought to know. Think of that! the queen denying the legitimacy of her own son!

ROBERT. Well, she married her daughter to the English king. Can you blame the woman?

POULENGEY. I blame nobody. But thanks to her, the Dauphin is down and out; and we may as well face it. The English will take Orleans: the Bastard will not be able to stop them.

ROBERT. He beat the English the year before last at Montargis. I was with him.

POULENGEY. No matter: his men are cowed now; and he cant work miracles. And I tell you that nothing can save our side now but a miracle.

ROBERT. Miracles are all right, Polly. The only difficulty about them is that they dont happen nowadays.

POULENGEY. I used to think so. I am not so sure now. [*Rising, and moving ruminatively towards the window*] At all events this is not a time to leave any stone unturned. There is something about the girl.

ROBERT. Oh! You think the girl can work miracles, do you?

POULENGEY. I think the girl herself is a bit of a miracle. Anyhow, she is the last card left in our hand. Better play her than throw up the game. [*He wanders to the turret*].

ROBERT [*wavering*] You really think that?

POULENGEY [*turning*] Is there anything else left for us to think?

ROBERT [*going to him*] Look here, Polly. If you were in my place would you let a girl like that do you out of sixteen francs for a horse?

POULENGEY. I will pay for the horse.

ROBERT. You will!

POULENGEY. Yes: I will back my opinion.

ROBERT. You will really gamble on a forlorn hope to the tune of sixteen francs?

POULENGEY. It is not a gamble.

ROBERT. What else is it?

POULENGEY. It is a certainty. Her words and her ardent faith in God have put fire into me.

ROBERT [*giving him up*] Whew! You are as mad as she is.

POULENGEY [*obstinately*] We want a few mad people now. See where the sane ones have landed us!

ROBERT [*his irresoluteness now openly swamping his affected decisiveness*] I shall feel like a precious fool. Still, if you feel sure—

POULENGEY. I feel sure enough to take her to Chinon—unless you stop me.

ROBERT. This is not fair. You are putting the responsibility on me.

POULENGEY. It is on you whichever way you decide.

ROBERT. Yes: thats just it. Which way am I to decide? You dont see how awkward this is for me. [*Snatching at a dilatory step with an unconscious hope that Joan will make up his mind for him*] Do you think I ought to have another talk to her?

POULENGEY [*rising*] Yes. [*He goes to the window and calls*] Joan!

JOAN'S VOICE. Will he let us go, Polly?

POULENGEY. Come up. Come in. [*Turning to Robert*] Shall I leave you with her?

ROBERT. No: stay here; and back me up.

> *Poulengey sits down on the chest. Robert goes back to his magisterial chair, but remains standing to inflate himself more imposingly. Joan comes in, full of good news.*

JOAN. Jack will go halves for the horse.

ROBERT. Well!! [*He sits, deflated.*]

POULENGEY [*gravely*] Sit down, Joan.

JOAN [*checked a little, and looking to Robert*] May I?

ROBERT. Do what you are told.

> *Joan curtsies and sits down on the stool between them. Robert outfaces his perplexity with his most peremptory air.*

ROBERT. What is your name?

JOAN [*chattily*] They always call me Jenny in Lorraine. Here in France I am Joan. The soldiers call me The Maid.

ROBERT. What is your surname?

JOAN. Surname? What is that? My father sometimes calls himself d'Arc; but I know nothing about it. You met my father. He—

ROBERT. Yes, yes: I remember. You come from Domrémy in Lorraine, I think.

JOAN. Yes; but what does it matter? we all speak French.

ROBERT. Dont ask questions: answer them. How old are you?

JOAN. Seventeen: so they tell me. It might be nineteen. I dont remember.

ROBERT. What did you mean when you said that St Catherine and St Margaret talked to you every day?

JOAN. They do.

ROBERT. What are they like?

JOAN [*suddenly obstinate*] I will tell you nothing about that: they have not given me leave.

ROBERT. But you actually see them; and they talk to you just as I am talking to you?

JOAN. No: it is quite different. I cannot tell you: you must not talk to me about my voices.

ROBERT. How do you mean? voices?

JOAN. I hear voices telling me what to do. They come from God.

ROBERT. They come from your imagination.

JOAN. Of course. That is how the messages of God come to us.

POULENGEY. Checkmate.

ROBERT. No fear! [*To Joan*] So God says you are to raise the siege of Orleans?

JOAN. And to crown the Dauphin in Rheims Cathedral.

ROBERT [*gasping*] Crown the D——! Gosh!

JOAN. And to make the English leave France.

ROBERT [*sarcastic*] Anything else?

JOAN [*charming*] Not just at present, thank you, squire.

ROBERT. I suppose you think raising a siege is as easy as chasing a cow out of a meadow. You think soldiering is anybody's job?

JOAN. I do not think it can be very difficult if God is on your side, and you are willing to put your life in His hand. But many soldiers are very simple.

ROBERT [*grimly*] Simple! Did you ever see English soldiers fighting?

JOAN. They are only men. God made them just like us; but He gave them their own country and their own language; and it is not His will that they should come into our country and try to speak our language.

ROBERT. Who has been putting such nonsense into your head? Dont you know that soldiers are subject to their feudal lord, and that it is nothing to them or to you whether he is the duke of Burgundy or the king of England or the king of France? What has their language to do with it?

JOAN. I do not understand that a bit. We are all subject to the King of Heaven; and He gave us our countries and our languages, and meant us to keep to them. If it were not so it would be murder to kill an Englishman in battle; and you, squire, would be in great danger of hell fire. You must not think about your duty to your feudal lord, but about your duty to God.

POULENGEY. It's no use, Robert: she can choke you like that every time.

ROBERT. Can she, by Saint Dennis! We shall see. [*To Joan*] We are not talking about God: we are talking about practical affairs. I ask you again, girl, have you ever seen English soldiers fighting? Have you ever seen them plundering, burning, turning the countryside into a desert? Have you heard no tales of their Black Prince who was blacker than the devil himself, or of the English king's father?

JOAN. You must not be afraid, Robert—

ROBERT. Damn you, I am not afraid. And who gave you leave to call me Robert?

JOAN. You were called so in church in the name of our Lord. All the other names are your father's or your brother's or anybody's.

ROBERT. Tcha!

JOAN. Listen to me, squire. At Domrémy we had to fly to the next village to escape from the English soldiers. Three of them were left behind, wounded. I came to know these three poor goddams quite well. They had not half my strength.

ROBERT. Do you know why they are called goddams?

JOAN. No. Everyone calls them goddams.

ROBERT. It is because they are always calling on their God to condemn their souls to perdition. That is what goddam means in their language. How do you like it?

JOAN. God will be merciful to them; and they will act like His good children when they go back to the country He made for them, and made them for. I have heard the tales of the Black Prince. The moment he touched the soil of our country the devil entered into him and made him a black fiend. But at home, in the place made for him by God, he was good. It is always so. If I went into England against the will of God to conquer England, and tried to live there and speak its language, the devil would enter into me; and when I was old I should shudder to remember the wickednesses I did.

ROBERT. Perhaps. But the more devil you were the better you might fight. That is why the goddams will take Orleans. And you cannot stop them, nor ten thousand like you.

JOAN. One thousand like me can stop them. Ten like me can stop them with God on our side. [*She rises impetuously, and goes at him, unable to sit quiet any longer*]. You do not understand, squire. Our soldiers are always beaten because they are fighting only to save their skins; and the shortest way to save your skin is to run away. Our knights are thinking only of the money they will make in ransoms: it is not kill or be killed with them, but pay or be paid. But I will teach them all to fight that the will of God may be done in France; and then they will drive the poor goddams before them like sheep. You and Polly will live to see the day when there will not be an English soldier on the soil of France; and there will be but one king there: not the feudal English king, but God's French one.

ROBERT [*to Poulengey*] This may be all rot, Polly; but the troops might swallow it, though nothing that we can say seems able to put any fight into them. Even the Dauphin might swallow it. And if she can put fight into him, she can put it into anybody.

POULENGEY. I can see no harm in trying. Can you? And there is something about the girl—

ROBERT [*turning to Joan*] Now listen you to me; and [*desperately*] dont cut in before I have time to think.

JOAN [*plumping down on the stool again, like an obedient school-girl*] Yes, squire.

ROBERT. Your orders are, that you are go to to Chinon under the escort of this gentleman and three of his friends.

JOAN [*radiant, clasping her hands*] Oh, squire! Your head is all circled with light, like a saint's.

POULENGEY. How is she to get into the royal presence?

ROBERT [*who has looked up for his halo rather apprehensively*] I dont know: how did she get into my presence? If the Dauphin can keep her out he is a better man than I take him for. [*Rising*] I will send her to Chinon; and she can say I sent her. Then let come what may: I can do no more.

JOAN. And the dress? I may have a soldier's dress, maynt I, squire?

ROBERT. Have what you please. I wash my hands of it.

JOAN [*wildly excited by her success*] Come, Polly. [*She dashes out*].

ROBERT [*shaking Poulengey's hand*] Goodbye, old man, I am taking a big chance. Few other men would have done it. But as you say, there is something about her.

POULENGEY. Yes: there is something about her. Goodbye. [*He goes out*].

> *Robert, still very doubtful whether he has not been made a fool of by a crazy female, and a social inferior to boot, scratches his head and slowly comes back from the door. The steward runs in with a basket.*

STEWARD. Sir, sir—

ROBERT. What now?

STEWARD. The hens are laying like mad, sir. Five dozen eggs!

ROBERT [*stiffens convulsively; crosses himself; and forms with his pale lips the words*] Christ in heaven! [*Aloud but breathless*] She d i d come from God.

Scene II

Chinon, in Touraine. An end of the throne room in the castle, curtained off to make an antechamber. The Archbishop of Rheims, close on 50, a full-fed political prelate with nothing of the ecclesiastic about him except his imposing bearing, and the Lord Chamberlain, Monseigneur de la Trémouille, a monstrous arrogant wineskin of a man, are waiting for the Dauphin. There is a door in the wall to the right of the two men. It is late in the afternoon on the 8th of March, 1429. The Archbishop stands with dignity whilst the Chamberlain, on his left, fumes about in the worst of tempers.

LA TRÉMOUILLE. What the devil does the Dauphin mean by keeping us waiting like this? I dont know how you have the patience to stand there like a stone idol.

THE ARCHBISHOP. You see, I am an archbishop; and an archbishop is a sort of idol. At any rate he has to learn to keep still and suffer fools patiently. Besides, my dear Lord Chamberlain, it is the Dauphin's royal privilege to keep you waiting, is it not?

LA TRÉMOUILLE. Dauphin be damned! saving your reverence. Do you know how much money he owes me?

THE ARCHBISHOP. Much more than he owes me, I have no doubt, because you are a much richer man. But I take it he owes you all you could afford to lend him. That is what he owes me.

LA TRÉMOUILLE. Twenty-seven thousand: that was his last haul. A cool twenty-seven thousand!

THE ARCHBISHOP. What becomes of it all? He never has a suit of clothes that I would throw to a curate.

LA TRÉMOUILLE. He dines on a chicken or a scrap of mutton. He borrows my last penny; and there is nothing to shew for it. [*A page appears in the doorway*]. At last!

THE PAGE. No, my lord: it is not His Majesty. Monsieur de Rais is approaching.

LA TRÉMOUILLE. Young Bluebeard! Why announce h i m?

THE PAGE. Captain La Hire is with him. Something has happened, I think.

Gilles de Rais, a young man of 25, very smart and self-possessed, and sporting the extravagance of a little curled beard dyed blue at a clean-shaven court, comes in. He is determined to make himself agreeable, but lacks natural joyousness, and is not really pleasant. In fact when he defies the Church some eleven years later he is accused of trying to extract pleasure from horrible cruelties, and hanged. So far, however, there is no shadow of the gallows on him. He advances gaily to the Archbishop. The page withdraws.

BLUEBEARD. Your faithful lamb, Archbishop. Good day, my lord. Do you know what has happened to La Hire?

LA TRÉMOUILLE. He has sworn himself into a fit, perhaps.

BLUEBEARD. No: just the opposite. Foul Mouthed Frank, the only

man in Touraine who could beat him at swearing, was told by a
soldier that he shouldnt use such language when he was at the
point of death.

THE ARCHBISHOP. Nor at any other point. But was Foul Mouthed
Frank on the point of death?

BLUEBEARD. Yes: he has just fallen into a well and been drowned.
La Hire is frightened out of his wits.

> *Captain La Hire comes in: a war dog with no court man-
> ners and pronounced camp ones.*

BLUEBEARD. I have just been telling the Chamberlain and the
Archbishop. The Archbishop says you are a lost man.

LA HIRE [*striding past Bluebeard, and planting himself between
the Archbishop and La Trémouille*] This is nothing to joke
about. It is worse than we thought. It was not a soldier, but an
angel dressed as a soldier.

THE ARCHBISHOP ⎫
THE CHAMBERLAIN ⎬ [*exclaiming all together*] An angel!
BLUEBEARD ⎭

LA HIRE. Yes, an angel. She has made her way from Champagne
with half a dozen men through the thick of everything: Burgundians, Goddams, deserters, robbers, and Lord knows who; and
they never met a soul except the country folk. I know one of
them: de Poulengey. He says she's an angel. If ever I utter an
oath again may my soul be blasted to eternal damnation!

THE ARCHBISHOP. A very pious beginning, Captain.

> *Bluebeard and La Trémouille laugh at him. The page
> returns.*

THE PAGE. His Majesty.

*They stand perfunctorily at court attention. The Dauphin, age
26, really King Charles the Seventh since the death of his father,
but as yet uncrowned, comes in through the curtains with a paper
in his hands. He is a poor creature physically; and the current fashion of shaving closely, and hiding every scrap of hair under the
head-covering or headdress, both by women and men, makes the
worst of his appearance. He has little narrow eyes, near together, a
long pendulous nose that droops over his thick short upper lip, and
the expression of a young dog accustomed to be kicked, yet incorrigible and irrepressible. But he is neither vulgar nor stupid; and he
has a cheeky humor which enables him to hold his own in conversation. Just at present he is excited, like a child with a new toy. He
comes to the Archbishop's left hand. Bluebeard and La Hire retire
towards the curtains.*

CHARLES. Oh, Archbishop, do you know what Robert de Baudricourt is sending me from Vaucouleurs?

THE ARCHBISHOP [*contemptuously*] I am not interested in the
newest toys.

CHARLES [*indignantly*] It isnt a toy. [*Sulkily*] However, I can
get on very well without your interest.

THE ARCHBISHOP. Your Highness is taking offence very unnecessar-
ily.

CHARLES. Thank you. You are always ready with a lecture, arnt you?

LA TRÉMOUILLE [*roughly*] Enough grumbling. What have you got there?

CHARLES. What is that to you?

LA TRÉMOUILLE. It is my business to know what is passing between you and the garrison at Vaucouleurs. [*He snatches the paper from the Dauphin's hand, and begins reading it with some difficulty, following the words with his finger and spelling them out syllable by syllable.*]

CHARLES [*mortified*] You all think you can treat me as you please because I owe you money, and because I am no good at fighting. But I have the blood royal in my veins.

THE ARCHBISHOP. Even that has been questioned, your Highness. One hardly recognizes in you the grandson of Charles the Wise.

CHARLES. I want to hear no more of my grandfather. He was so wise that he used up the whole family stock of wisdom for five generations, and left me the poor fool I am, bullied and insulted by all of you.

THE ARCHBISHOP. Control yourself, sir. These outbursts of petulance are not seemly.

CHARLES. Another lecture! Thank you. What a pity it is that though you are an archbishop saints and angels dont come to see y o u!

THE ARCHBISHOP. What do you mean?

CHARLES. Aha! Ask that bully there [*pointing to La Trémouille*].

LA TREMOUILLE [*furious*] Hold your tongue. Do you hear?

CHARLES. Oh, I hear. You neednt shout. The whole castle can hear. Why dont you go and shout at the English, and beat them for me?

LA TRÉMOUILLE [*raising his fist*] You young—

CHARLES [*running behind the Archbishop*] Dont you raise your hand to me. It's high treason.

LA HIRE. Steady, Duke! Steady!

THE ARCHBISHOP [*resolutely*] Come, come! this will not do. My Lord Chamberlain: please! please! we must keep some sort of order. [*To the Dauphin*] And you, sir: if you cannot rule your kingdom, at least try to rule yourself.

CHARLES. Another lecture! Thank you.

LA TRÉMOUILLE [*handing the paper to the Archbishop*] Here: read the accursed thing for me. He has sent the blood boiling into my head: I cant distinguish the letters.

CHARLES [*coming back and peering round La Trémouille's left shoulder*] I will read it for you if you like. I c a n read, you know.

LA TRÉMOUILLE [*with intense contempt, not at all stung by the taunt*] Yes: reading is about all you are fit for. Can you make it out, Archbishop?

THE ARCHBISHOP. I should have expected more commonsense from De Baudricourt. He is sending some cracked country lass here—

CHARLES [*interrupting*] No: he is sending a saint: an angel. And she is coming to me: to m e, the king, and not to you, Archbishop, holy as you are. She knows the blood royal if you dont. [*He struts up to the curtains between Bluebeard and La Hire*].

THE ARCHBISHOP. You cannot be allowed to see this crazy wench.

CHARLES [*turning*] But I am the king; and I will.

LA TRÉMOUILLE [*brutally*] Then she cannot be allowed to see y o u. Now!

CHARLES. I tell you I will. I am going to put my foot down—

BLUEBEARD [*laughing at him*] Naughty! What would your wise grandfather say?

CHARLES. That just shews your ignorance, Bluebeard. My grandfather had a saint who used to float in the air when she was praying, and told him everything he wanted to know. My poor father had two saints, Marie de Maillé and the Gasque of Avignon. It is in our family; and I dont care what you say: I will have my saint too.

THE ARCHBISHOP. This creature is not a saint. She is not even a respectable woman. She does not wear women's clothes. She is dressed like a soldier, and rides round the country with soldiers. Do you suppose such a person can be admitted to your Highness's court?

LA HIRE. Stop. [*Going to the Archbishop*] Did you say a girl in armor, like a soldier?

THE ARCHBISHOP. So De Baudricourt describes her.

LA HIRE. But by all the devils in hell—Oh, God forgive me, what am I saying?—by Our Lady and all the saints, this must be the angel that struck Foul Mouthed Frank dead for swearing.

CHARLES [*triumphant*] You see! A miracle!

LA HIRE. She may strike the lot of us dead if we cross her. For Heaven's sake, Archbishop, be careful what you are doing.

THE ARCHBISHOP [*severely*] Rubbish! Nobody has been struck dead. A drunken blackguard who has been rebuked a hundred times for swearing has fallen into a well, and been drowned. A mere coincidence.

LA HIRE. I do not know what a coincidence is. I do know that the man is dead, and that she told him he was going to die.

THE ARCHBISHOP. We are all going to die, Captain.

LA HIRE [*crossing himself*] I hope not. [*He backs out of the conversation*].

BLUEBEARD. We can easily find out whether she is an angel or not. Let us arrange when she comes that I shall be the Dauphin, and see whether she will find me out.

CHARLES. Yes: I agree to that. If she cannot find the blood royal I will have nothing to do with her.

THE ARCHBISHOP. It is for the Church to make saints: let De Baudricourt mind his own business, and not dare usurp the function of his priest. I say the girl shall not be admitted.

BLUEBEARD. But, Archbishop—

THE ARCHBISHOP [*sternly*] I speak in the Church's name. [*To the Dauphin*] Do you dare say she shall?

CHARLES. [*intimidated but sulky*] Oh, if you make it an excommunication matter, I have nothing more to say, of course. But you havnt read the end of the letter. De Baudricourt says she will raise the siege of Orleans, and beat the English for us.

LA TRÉMOUILLE. Rot!

CHARLES. Well, will you save Orleans for us, with all your bullying?

LA TRÉMOUILLE [*savagely*] Do not throw that in my face again: do you hear? I have done more fighting than you ever did or ever will. But I cannot be everywhere.

THE DAUPHIN. Well, thats something.

BLUEBEARD [*coming between the Archbishop and Charles*] You have Jack Dunois at the head of your troops in Orleans: the brave Dunois, the handsome Dunois, the wonderful invincible Dunois, the darling of all the ladies, the beautiful bastard. Is it likely that the country lass can do what he cannot do?

CHARLES. Why doesnt he raise the siege, then?

LA HIRE. The wind is against him.

BLUEBEARD. How can the wind hurt him at Orleans? It is not on the Channel.

LA HIRE. It is on the river Loire; and the English hold the bridgehead. He must ship his men across the river and upstream, if he is to take them in the rear. Well, he cannot, because there is a devil of a wind blowing the other way. He is tired of paying the priests to pray for a west wind. What he needs is a miracle. You tell me that what the girl did to Foul Mouthed Frank was no miracle. No matter: it finished Frank. If she changes the wind for Dunois, that may not be a miracle either; but it may finish the English. What harm is there in trying?

THE ARCHBISHOP [*who has read the end of the letter and become more thoughtful*] It is true that De Baudricourt seems extraordinarily impressed.

LA HIRE. De Baudricourt is a blazing ass; but he is a soldier; and if he thinks she can beat the English, all the rest of the army will think so too.

LA TRÉMOUILLE [*to the Archbishop, who is hesitating*] Oh, let them have their way. Dunois' men will give up the town in spite of him if somebody does not put some fresh spunk into them.

THE ARCHBISHOP. The Church must examine the girl before anything decisive is done about her. However, since his Highness desires it, let her attend the Court.

LA HIRE. I will find her and tell her. [*He goes out*].

CHARLES. Come with me, Bluebeard; and let us arrange so that she will not know who I am. You will pretend to be me. [*He goes out through the curtains*].

BLUEBEARD. Pretend to be that thing! Holy Michael! [*He follows the Dauphin*].

LA TRÉMOUILLE. I wonder will she pick him out!

THE ARCHBISHOP. Of course she will.

LA TRÉMOUILLE. Why? How is she to know?

THE ARCHBISHOP. She will know what everybody in Chinon knows:

that the Dauphin is the meanest-looking and worst-dressed figure in the Court, and that the man with the blue beard is Gilles de Rais.

LA TRÉMOUILLE. I never thought of that.

THE ARCHBISHOP. You are not so accustomed to miracles as I am. It is part of my profession.

LA TRÉMOUILLE [*puzzled and a little scandalized*] But that would not be a miracle at all.

THE ARCHBISHOP [*calmly*] Why not?

LA TRÉMOUILLE. Well, come! what is a miracle?

THE ARCHBISHOP. A miracle, my friend, is an event which creates faith. That is the purpose and nature of miracles. They may seem very wonderful to the people who witness them, and very simple to those who perform them. That does not matter: if they confirm or create faith they are true miracles.

LA TRÉMOUILLE. Even when they are frauds, do you mean?

THE ARCHBISHOP. Frauds deceive. An event which creates faith does not deceive: therefore it is not a fraud, but a miracle.

LA TRÉMOUILLE [*scratching his neck in his perplexity*] Well, I suppose as you are an archbishop you must be right. It seems a bit fishy to me. But I am no churchman, and dont understand these matters.

THE ARCHBISHOP. You are not a churchman; but you are a diplomatist and a soldier. Could you make our citizens pay war taxes, or our soldiers sacrifice their lives, if they knew what is really happening instead of what seems to them to be happening?

LA TRÉMOUILLE. No, by Saint Dennis: the fat would be in the fire before sundown.

THE ARCHBISHOP. Would it not be quite easy to tell them the truth?

LA TRÉMOUILLE. Man alive, they wouldnt believe it.

THE ARCHBISHOP. Just so. Well, the Church has to rule men for the good of their souls as you have to rule them for the good of their bodies. To do that, the Church must do as you do: nourish their faith by poetry.

LA TRÉMOUILLE. Poetry! I should call it humbug.

THE ARCHBISHOP. You would be wrong, my friend. Parables are not lies because they describe events that have never happened. Miracles are not frauds because they are often—I do not say always—very simple and innocent contrivances by which the priest fortifies the faith of his flock. When this girl picks out the Dauphin among his courtiers, it will not be a miracle for me, because I shall know how it has been done, and my faith will not be increased. But as for the others, if they feel the thrill of the supernatural, and forget their sinful clay in a sudden sense of the glory of God, it will be a miracle and a blessed one. And you will find that the girl herself will be more affected than anyone else. She will forget how she really picked him out. So, perhaps, will you.

LA TRÉMOUILLE. I wish I were clever enough to know how

much of you is God's archbishop and how much the most artful
fox in Touraine. Come on, or we shall be late for the fun; and I
want to see it, miracle or no miracle.

THE ARCHBISHOP [*detaining him a moment*] Do not think that I
am a lover of crooked ways. There is a new spirit rising in men:
we are at the dawning of a wider epoch. If I were a simple
monk, and had not to rule men, I should seek peace for my spirit
with Aristotle and Pythagoras rather than with the saints and
their miracles.

LA TRÉMOUILLE. And who the deuce was Pythagoras?

THE ARCHBISHOP. A sage who held that the earth is round, and
that it moves round the sun.

LA TRÉMOUILLE. What an utter fool! Couldnt he use his eyes?

> *They go out together through the curtains, which are pres-
> ently withdrawn, revealing the full depth of the throne
> room with the Court assembled. On the right are two
> Chairs of State on a dais. Bluebeard is standing theatrically
> on the dais, playing the king, and, like the courtiers, enjoy-
> ing the joke rather obviously. There is a curtained arch in
> the wall behind the dais; but the main door, guarded by
> men-at-arms, is at the other side of the room; and a clear
> path across is kept and lined by the courtiers. Charles is in
> this path in the middle of the room. La Hire is on his right.
> The Archbishop, on his left, has taken his place by the dais:
> La Trémouille at the other side of it. The Duchess de la
> Trémouille, pretending to be the Queen, sits in the Con-
> sort's chair, with a group of ladies in waiting close by,
> behind the Archbishop.*
>
> *The chatter of the courtiers makes such a noise that no-
> body notices the appearance of the page at the door.*

THE PAGE. The Duke of— [*Nobody listens*]. The Duke of—
[*The chatter continues. Indignant at his failure to command a
hearing, he snatches the halberd of the nearest man-at-arms, and
thumps the floor with it. The chatter ceases; and everybody
looks at him in silence*]. Attention! [*He restores the halberd to
the man-at-arms*]. The Duke of Vendôme presents Joan the
Maid to his Majesty.

CHARLES [*putting his finger on his lip*] Ssh! [*He hides behind
the nearest courtier, peering out to see what happens*].

BLUEBEARD [*majestically*] Let her approach the throne.

> *Joan, dressed as a soldier, with her hair bobbed and hang-
> ing thickly round her face, is led in by a bashful and speech-
> less nobleman, from whom she detaches herself to stop and
> look round eagerly for the Dauphin.*

THE DUCHESS [*to the nearest lady in waiting*] My dear! Her hair!

> *All the ladies explode in uncontrollable laughter.*

BLUEBEARD [*trying not to laugh, and waving his hand in depreca-
tion of their merriment*] Ssh—ssh! Ladies! Ladies!!

JOAN [*not at all embarrassed*] I wear it like this because I am a
soldier. Where be Dauphin?

A titter runs through the Court as she walks to the dais.

BLUEBEARD [*condescendingly*] You are in the presence of the Dauphin.

> *Joan looks at him sceptically for a moment, scanning him hard up and down to make sure. Dead silence, all watching her. Fun dawns in her face.*

JOAN. Coom, Bluebeard! Thou canst not fool me. Where be Dauphin?

> *A roar of laughter breaks out as Gilles, with a gesture of surrender, joins in the laugh, and jumps down from the dais beside La Trémouille. Joan, also on the broad grin, turns back, searching along the row of courtiers, and presently makes a dive, and drags out Charles by the arm.*

JOAN [*releasing him and bobbing him a little curtsey*] Gentle little Dauphin, I am sent to you to drive the English away from Orleans and from France, and to crown you king in the cathedral at Rheims, where all true kings of France are crowned.

CHARLES [*triumphant, to the Court*] You see, all of you: she knew the blood royal. Who dare say now that I am not my father's son [*To Joan*] But if you want me to be crowned at Rheims you must talk to the Archbishop, not to me. There he is [*he is standing behind her*]!

JOAN [*turning quickly, overwhelmed with emotion*] Oh, my lord! [*She falls on both knees before him, with bowed head, not daring to look up*] My lord: I am only a poor country girl; and you are filled with the blessedness and glory of God Himself; but you will touch me with your hands, and give me your blessing, wont you?

BLUEBEARD [*whispering to La Trémouille*] The old fox blushes.

LA TRÉMOUILLE. Another miracle!

THE ARCHBISHOP [*touched, putting his hand on her head*] Child: you are in love with religion.

JOAN [*startled: looking up at him*] Am I? I never thought of that. Is there any harm in it?

THE ARCHBISHOP. There is no harm in it, my child. But there is danger.

JOAN [*rising, with a sunflush of reckless happiness irradiating her face*] There is always danger, except in heaven. Oh, my lord, you have given me such strength, such courage. It must be a most wonderful thing to be Archbishop.

> *The Court smiles broadly: even titters a little.*

THE ARCHBISHOP [*drawing himself up sensitively*] Gentlemen: your levity is rebuked by this maid's faith. I am, God help me, all unworthy; but your mirth is a deadly sin.

> *Their faces fall. Dead silence.*

BLUEBEARD. My lord: we were laughing at her, not at you.

THE ARCHBISHOP. What? Not at my unworthiness but at her faith! Gilles de Rais: this maid prophesied that the blasphemer should be drowned in his sin—

JOAN [*distressed*] No!

THE ARCHBISHOP [*silencing her by a gesture*] I prophesy now
that you will be hanged in yours if you do not learn when to
laugh and when to pray.

BLUEBEARD. My lord: I stand rebuked. I am sorry: I can say no
more. But if you prophesy that I shall be hanged, I shall never
be able to resist temptation, because I shall always be telling
myself that I may as well be hanged for a sheep as a lamb.

The courtiers take heart at this. There is more tittering.

JOAN [*scandalized*] You are an idle fellow, Bluebeard; and you
have great impudence to answer the Archbishop.

LA HIRE [*with a huge chuckle*] Well said, lass! Well said!

JOAN [*impatiently to the Archbishop*] Oh, my lord, will you send
all these silly folks away so that I may speak to the Dauphin
alone?

LA HIRE [*goodhumoredly*] I can take a hint. [*He salutes; turns
on his heel; and goes out*].

THE ARCHBISHOP. Come, gentlemen. The Maid comes with God's
blessing, and must be obeyed.

*The courtiers withdraw, some through the arch, others at
the opposite side. The Archbishop marches across to the
door, followed by the Duchess and La Trémouille. As the
Archbishop passes Joan, she falls on her knees, and kisses
the hem of his robe fervently. He shakes his head in instinc-
tive remonstrance; gathers the robe from her; and goes out.
She is left kneeling directly in the Duchess's way.*

THE DUCHESS [*coldly*] Will you allow me to pass, please?

JOAN [*hastily rising, and standing back*] Beg pardon, maam, I am
sure.

*The Duchess passes on. Joan stares after her; then whis-
pers to the Dauphin.*

JOAN. Be that Queen?

CHARLES. No. She thinks she is.

JOAN [*again staring after the Duchess*] Oo-oo-oooh! [*Her awe-
struck amazement at the figure cut by the magnificently dressed
lady is not wholly complimentary*].

LA TRÉMOUILLE [*very surly*] I'll trouble your Highness not to
gibe at my wife. [*He goes out. The others have already gone*].

JOAN [*to the Dauphin*] Who be old Gruff-and-Grum?

CHARLES. He is the Duke de la Trémouille.

JOAN. What be his job?

CHARLES. He pretends to command the army. And whenever I find
a friend I can care for, he kills him.

JOAN. Why dost let him?

CHARLES [*petulantly moving to the throne side of the room to
escape from her magnetic field*] How can I prevent him? He
bullies me. They all bully me.

JOAN. Art afraid?

CHARLES. Yes: I am afraid. It's no use preaching to me about it.
It's all very well for these big men with their armor that is too
heavy for me, and their swords that I can hardly lift, and their

muscle and their shouting and their bad tempers. They like fighting: most of them are making fools of themselves all the time they are not fighting; but I am quiet and sensible; and I dont want to kill people: I only want to be left alone to enjoy myself in my own way. I never asked to be a king: it was pushed on me. So if you are going to say "Son of St Louis: gird on the sword of your ancestors, and lead us to victory" you may spare your breath to cool your porridge; for I cannot do it. I am not built that way; and there is an end of it.

JOAN [*trenchant and masterful*] Blethers! We are all like that to begin with. I shall put courage into thee.

CHARLES. But I dont want to have courage put into me. I want to sleep in a comfortable bed, and not live in continual terror of being killed or wounded. Put courage into the others, and let them have their bellyful of fighting; but let me alone.

JOAN. It's no use, Charlie: thou must face what God puts on thee. If thou fail to make thyself king, thoult be a beggar: what else art fit for! Come! Let me see thee sitting on the throne. I have looked forward to that.

CHARLES. What is the good of sitting on the throne when the other fellows give all the orders? However! [*he sits enthroned, a piteous figure*] here is the king for you! Look your fill at the poor devil.

JOAN. Thourt not king yet, lad: thourt but Dauphin. Be not led away by them around thee. Dressing up dont fill empty noddle. I know the people: the real people that make thy bread for thee; and I tell thee they count no man king of France until the holy oil has been poured on his hair, and himself consecrated and crowned in Rheims Cathedral. And thou needs new clothes, Charlie. Why does not Queen look after thee properly?

CHARLES. We're too poor. She wants all the money we can spare to put on her own back. Besides, I like to see her beautifully dressed; and I dont care what I wear myself: I should look ugly anyhow.

JOAN. There is some good in thee, Charlie; but it is not yet a king's good.

CHARLES. We shall see. I am not such a fool as I look. I have my eyes open; and I can tell you that one good treaty is worth ten good fights. These fighting fellows lose all on the treaties that they gain on the fights. If we can only have a treaty, the English are sure to have the worst of it, because they are better at fighting than at thinking.

JOAN. If the English win, it is they that will make the treaty; and then God help poor France! Thou must fight, Charlie, whether thou will or no. I will go first to hearten thee. We must take our courage in both hands: aye, and pray for it with both hands too.

CHARLES [*descending from his throne and again crossing the room to escape from her dominating urgency*] Oh do stop talking about God and praying. I cant bear people who are always praying. Isnt it bad enough to have to do it at the proper times?

JOAN [*pitying him*] Thou poor child, thou hast never prayed in thy life. I must teach thee from the beginning.

CHARLES. I am not a child: I am a grown man and a father; and I will not be taught any more.

JOAN. Aye, you have a little son. He that will be Louis the Eleventh when you die. Would you not fight for him?

CHARLES. No: a horrid boy. He hates me. He hates everybody, selfish little beast! I dont want to be bothered with children. I dont want to be a father; and I dont want to be a son: especially a son of St Louis. I dont want to be any of these fine things you all have your heads full of: I want to be just what I am. Why cant you mind your own business, and let me mind mine?

JOAN [*again contemptuous*] Minding your own business is like minding your own body: it's the shortest way to make yourself sick. What is my business? Helping mother at home. What is thine? Petting lapdogs and sucking sugar-sticks. I call that muck. I tell thee it is God's business we are here to do: not our own. I have a message to thee from God; and thou must listen to it, though thy heart break with the terror of it.

CHARLES. I dont want a message; but can you tell me any secrets? Can you do any cures? Can you turn lead into gold, or anything of that sort?

JOAN. I can turn thee into a king, in Rheims Cathedral; and that is a miracle that will take some doing, it seems.

CHARLES. If we go to Rheims, and have a coronation, Anne will want new dresses. We cant afford them. I am all right as I am.

JOAN. As you are! And what is that? Less than my father's poorest shepherd. Thourt not lawful owner of thy own land of France till thou be consecrated.

CHARLES. But I shall not be lawful owner of my own land anyhow. Will the consecration pay off my mortgages? I have pledged my last acre to the Archbishop and that fat bully. I owe money even to Bluebeard.

JOAN [*earnestly*] Charlie: I come from the land, and have gotten my strength working on the land; and I tell thee that the land is thine to rule righteously and keep God's peace in, and not to pledge at the pawnshop as a drunken woman pledges her children's clothes. And I come from God to tell thee to kneel in the cathedral and solemnly give thy kingdom to him for ever and ever, and become the greatest king in the world as His steward and His bailiff, His soldier and His servant. The very clay of France will become holy: her soldiers will be the soldiers of God: the rebel dukes will be rebels against God: the English will fall on their knees and beg thee let them return to their lawful homes in peace. Wilt be a poor little Judas, and betray me and Him that sent me?

CHARLES [*tempted at last*] Oh, if I only dare!

JOAN. I shall dare, dare, and dare again, in God's name! Art for or against me?

CHARLES [*excited*] I'll risk it, I warn you I shant be able to keep it up; but I'll risk it. You shall see. [*Running to the main door and shouting*] Hallo! Come back, everybody. [*To Joan, as he runs back to the arch opposite*] Mind you stand by and dont let me be bullied. [*Through the arch*] Come along, will you: the whole Court. [*He sits down in the royal chair as they all hurry in to their former places, chattering and wondering*]. Now I'm in for it; but no matter: here goes! [*To the page*] Call for silence, you little beast, will you?

THE PAGE [*snatching a halberd as before and thumping with it repeatedly*] Silence for His Majesty the King. The King speaks. [*Peremptorily*] Will you be silent there? [*Silence*].

CHARLES [*rising*] I have given the command of the army to The Maid. The Maid is to do as she likes with it. [*He descends from the dais*].

> General amazement. La Hire, delighted, slaps his steel thigh-piece with his gauntlet.

LA TRÉMOUILLE [*turning threateningly towards Charles*] What is this? I command the army.

> Joan quickly puts her hand on Charles's shoulder as he instinctively recoils. Charles, with a grotesque effort culminating in an extravagant gesture, snaps his fingers in the Chamberlain's face.

JOAN. Thourt answered, old Gruff-and-Grum. [*Suddenly flashing out her sword as she divines that her moment has come*] Who is for God and His Maid? Who is for Orleans with me?

LA HIRE [*carried away, drawing also*] For God and His Maid! To Orleans!

ALL THE KNIGHTS [*following his lead with enthusiasm*] To Orleans!

> Joan, radiant, falls on her knees in thanksgiving to God. They all kneel, except the Archbishop, who gives his benediction with a sign, and La Trémouille, who collapses, cursing.

Scene III

Orleans, April 29th, 1429. Dunois, aged 26, is pacing up and down a patch of ground on the south bank of the silver Loire, commanding a long view of the river in both directions. He has had his lance stuck up with a pennon, which streams in a strong east wind. His shield with its bend sinister[1] lies beside it. He has his commander's baton in his hand. He is well built, carrying his armor easily. His broad brow and pointed chin give him an equilaterally triangular face, already marked by active service and responsibility, with the expression of a goodnatured and capable man who has no affectations and no foolish illusions. His page is sitting on the ground, elbows on knees, cheeks on fists, idly watching the water. It is evening; and both man and boy are affected by the loveliness of the Loire.

DUNOIS [*halting for a moment to glance up at the streaming pennon and shake his head wearily before he resumes his pacing*] West wind, west wind, west wind. Strumpet: steadfast when you should be wanton, wanton when you should be steadfast. West wind on the silver Loire: what rhymes to Loire? [*He looks again at the pennon, and shakes his fist at it*] Change, curse you, change, English harlot of a wind, change. West, west, I tell you. [*With a growl he resumes his march in silence, but soon begins again*] West wind, wanton wind, wilful wind, womanish wind, false wind from over the water, will you never blow again?

THE PAGE [*bounding to his feet*] See! There! There she goes!

DUNOIS [*startled from his reverie: eagerly*] Where? Who? The Maid?

THE PAGE. No: the kingfisher. Like blue lightning. She went into that bush.

DUNOIS [*furiously disappointed*] Is that all? You infernal young idiot: I have a mind to pitch you into the river.

THE PAGE [*not afraid, knowing his man*] It looked frightfully jolly, that flash of blue. Look! There goes the other!

DUNOIS [*running eagerly to the river brim*] Where? Where?

THE PAGE [*pointing*] Passing the reeds.

DUNOIS [*delighted*] I see.

They follow the flight till the bird takes cover.

THE PAGE. You blew me up because you were not in time to see them yesterday.

DUNOIS. You knew I was expecting The Maid when you set up your yelping. I will give you something to yelp for next time.

THE PAGE. Arnt they lovely? I wish I could catch them.

DUNOIS. Let me catch you trying to trap them, and I will put you in the iron cage for a month to teach you what a cage feels like. You are an abominable boy.

1. A band from top left to bottom right, indicating, in heraldry, illegitimacy.

THE PAGE [*laughs, and squats down as before*]!

DUNOIS [*pacing*] Blue bird, blue bird, since I am friend to thee, change thou the wind for me. No: it does not rhyme. He who has sinned for thee: thats better. No sense in it, though. [*He finds himself close to the page*] You abominable boy! [*He turns away from him*] Mary in the blue snood[2], kingfisher color: will you grudge me a west wind?

A SENTRY'S VOICE WESTWARD. Halt! Who goes there?

JOAN'S VOICE. The Maid.

DUNOIS. Let her pass. Hither, Maid! To me!

> Joan, in splendid armor, rushes in in a blazing rage. The
> wind drops; and the pennon flaps idly down the lance; but
> Dunois is too much occupied with Joan to notice it.

JOAN [*bluntly*] Be you Bastard of Orleans?

DUNOIS [*cool and stern, pointing to his shield*] You see the bend sinister. Are you Joan the Maid?

JOAN. Sure.

DUNOIS. Where are your troops?

JOAN. Miles behind. They have cheated me. They have brought me to the wrong side of the river.

DUNOIS. I told them to.

JOAN. Why did you? The English are on the other side!

DUNOIS. The English are on both sides.

JOAN. But Orleans is on the other side. We must fight the English there. How can we cross the river?

DUNOIS [*grimly*] There is a bridge.

JOAN. In God's name, then, let us cross the bridge, and fall on them.

DUNOIS. It seems simple; but it cannot be done.

JOAN. Who says so?

DUNOIS. I say so; and older and wiser heads than mine are of the same opinion.

JOAN [*roundly*] Then your older and wiser heads are fat-heads: they have made a fool of you; and now they want to make a fool of me too, bringing me to the wrong side of the river. Do you not know that I bring you better help than ever came to any general or any town?

DUNOIS [*smiling patiently*] Your own?

JOAN. No: the help and counsel of the King of Heaven. Which is the way to the bridge?

DUNOIS. You are impatient, Maid.

JOAN. Is this a time for patience? Our enemy is at our gates; and here we stand doing nothing. Oh, why are you not fighting? Listen to me: I will deliver you from fear. I—

DUNOIS [*laughing heartily, and waving her off*] No, no, my girl: if you delivered me from fear I should be a good knight for a story book, but a very bad commander of the army. Come! let me begin to make a soldier of you. [*He takes her to the water's edge*]. Do you see those two forts at this end of the bridge? the big ones?

2. Poetically addressing the kingfisher as the Virgin in a blue cap.

JOAN. Yes. Are they ours or the goddams'?

DUNOIS. Be quiet, and listen to me. If I were in either of those forts with only ten men I could hold it against an army. The English have more than ten times ten goddams in those forts to hold them against us.

JOAN. They cannot hold them against God. God did not give them the land under those forts: they stole it from Him. He gave it to us. I will take those forts.

DUNOIS. Single-handed?

JOAN. Our men will take them. I will lead them.

DUNOIS. Not a man will follow you.

JOAN. I will not look back to see whether anyone is following me.

DUNOIS [*recognizing her mettle, and clapping her heartily on the shoulder*] Good. You have the makings of a soldier in you. You are in love with war.

JOAN [*startled*] Oh! And the Archbishop said I was in love with religion.

DUNOIS. I, God forgive me, am a little in love with war myself, the ugly devil! I am like a man with two wives. Do you want to be like a woman with two husbands?

JOAN [*matter-of-fact*] I will never take a husband. A man in Toul took an action against me for breach of promise; but I never promised him. I am a soldier: I do not want to be thought of as a woman. I will not dress as a woman. I do not care for the things women care for. They dream of lovers, and of money. I dream of leading a charge, and of placing the big guns. You soldiers do not know how to use the big guns: you think you can win battles with a great noise and smoke.

DUNOIS [*with a shrug*] True. Half the time the artillery is more trouble than it is worth.

JOAN. Aye, lad; but you cannot fight stone walls with horses: you must have guns, and much bigger guns too.

DUNOIS [*grinning at her familiarity, and echoing it*] Aye, lass; but a good heart and a stout ladder will get over the stoniest wall.

JOAN. I will be first up the ladder when we reach the fort, Bastard. I dare you to follow me.

DUNOIS. You must not dare a staff officer, Joan: only company officers are allowed to indulge in displays of personal courage. Besides, you must know that I welcome you as a saint, not as a soldier. I have daredevils enough at my call, if they could help me.

JOAN. I am not a daredevil: I am a servant of God. My sword is sacred: I found it behind the altar in the church of St Catherine, where God hid it for me; and I may not strike a blow with it. My heart is full of courage, not of anger. I will lead; and your men will follow: that is all I can do. But I must do it: you shall not stop me.

DUNOIS. All in good time. Our men cannot take those forts by a sally across the bridge. They must come by water, and take the English in the rear on this side.

JOAN [*her military sense asserting itself*] Then make rafts and put big guns on them; and let your men cross to us.

DUNOIS. The rafts are ready; and the men are embarked. But they must wait for God.

JOAN. What do you mean? God is waiting for them.

DUNOIS. Let Him send us a wind then. My boats are downstream: they cannot come up against both wind and current. We must wait until God changes the wind. Come: let me take you to the church.

JOAN. No. I love church; but the English will not yield to prayers: they understand nothing but hard knocks and slashes. I will not go to church until we have beaten them.

DUNOIS. You must: I have business for you there.

JOAN. What business?

DUNOIS. To pray for a west wind. I have prayed; and I have given two silver candlesticks; but my prayers are not answered. Yours may be: you are young and innocent.

JOAN. Oh yes: you are right. I will pray: I will tell St Catherine: she will make God give me a west wind. Quick: shew me the way to the church.

THE PAGE [*sneezes violently*] At-cha!!!

JOAN. God bless you, child! Coom, Bastard.

> *They go out. The page rises to follow. He picks up the shield, and is taking the spear as well when he notices the pennon, which is now streaming eastward.*

THE PAGE [*dropping the shield and calling excitedly after them*] Seigneur! Seigneur! Mademoiselle!

DUNOIS [*running back*] What is it? The kingfisher? [*He looks eagerly for it up the river*].

JOAN [*joining them*] Oh, a kingfisher! Where?

THE PAGE. No: the wind, the wind, the wind [*pointing to the pennon*]: that is what made me sneeze.

DUNOIS [*looking at the pennon*] The wind has changed. [*He crosses himself*] God has spoken. [*Kneeling and handing his baton to Joan*] You command the king's army. I am your soldier.

THE PAGE [*looking down the river*] The boats have put off. They are ripping upstream like anything.

DUNOIS [*rising*] Now for the forts. You dared me to follow. Dare you lead?

JOAN [*bursting into tears and flinging her arms round Dunois, kissing him on both cheeks*] Dunois, dear comrade in arms, help me. My eyes are blinded with tears. Set my foot on the ladder, and say "Up, Joan."

DUNOIS [*dragging her out*] Never mind the tears: make for the flash of the guns.

JOAN [*in a blaze of courage*] Ah!

DUNOIS. [*dragging her along with him*] For God and Saint Dennis!

THE PAGE [*shrilly*] The Maid! The Maid! God and The Maid! Hurray-ay-ay! [*He snatches up the shield and lance, and capers out after them, mad with excitement*].

Scene IV

A tent in the English camp. A bullnecked English chaplain of 50 is sitting on a stool at a table, hard at work writing. At the other side of the table an imposing nobleman, aged 46, is seated in a handsome chair turning over the leaves of an illuminated Book of Hours. The nobleman is enjoying himself: the chaplain is struggling with suppressed wrath. There is an unoccupied leather stool on the nobleman's left. The table is on his right.

THE NOBLEMAN. Now this is what I call workmanship. There is nothing on earth more exquisite than a bonny book, with well-placed columns of rich black writing in beautiful borders, and illuminated pictures cunningly inset. But nowadays, instead of looking at books, people read them. A book might as well be one of those orders for bacon and bran that you are scribbling.

THE CHAPLAIN. I must say, my lord, you take our situation very coolly. Very coolly indeed.

THE NOBLEMAN [*supercilious*] What is the matter?

THE CHAPLAIN. The matter, my lord, is that we English have been defeated.

THE NOBLEMAN. That happens, you know. It is only in history books and ballads that the enemy is always defeated.

THE CHAPLAIN. But we are being defeated over and over again. First, Orleans—

THE NOBLEMAN [*poohpoohing*] Oh, Orleans!

THE CHAPLAIN. I know what you are going to say, my lord: that was a clear case of witchcraft and sorcery. But we are still being defeated. Jargeau, Meung, Beaugency, just like Orleans. And now we have been butchered at Patay, and Sir John Talbot taken prisoner. [*He throws down his pen, almost in tears*] I feel it, my lord: I feel it very deeply. I cannot bear to see my countrymen defeated by a parcel of foreigners.

THE NOBLEMAN. Oh! you are an Englishman, are you?

THE CHAPLAIN. Certainly not, my lord: I am a gentleman. Still, like your lordship, I was born in England; and it makes a difference.

THE NOBLEMAN. You are attached to the soil, eh?

THE CHAPLAIN. It pleases your lordship to be satirical at my expense: your greatness privileges you to be so with impunity. But your lordship knows very well that I am not attached to the soil in a vulgar manner, like a serf. Still, I have a feeling about it; [*with growing agitation*] and I am not ashamed of it; and [*rising wildly*] by God, if this goes on any longer I will fling my cassock to the devil, and take arms myself, and strangle the accursed witch with my own hands.

THE NOBLEMAN [*laughing at him goodnaturedly*] So you shall, chaplain: so you shall, if we can do nothing better. But not yet, not quite yet.

The Chaplain resumes his seat very sulkily.

THE NOBLEMAN [*airily*] I should not care very much about the witch—you see, I have made my pilgrimage to the Holy Land; and the Heavenly Powers, for their own credit, can hardly allow me to be worsted by a village sorceress—but the Bastard of Orleans is a harder nut to crack; and as he has been to the Holy Land too, honors are easy between us as far as that goes.

THE CHAPLAIN. He is only a Frenchman, my lord.

THE NOBLEMAN. A Frenchman! Where did you pick up that expression? Are these Burgundians and Bretons and Picards and Gascons beginning to call themselves Frenchmen, just as our fellows are beginning to call themselves Englishmen? They actually talk of France and England as their countries. Theirs, if you please! What is to become of me and you if that way of thinking comes into fashion?

THE CHAPLAIN. Why, my lord? Can it hurt us?

THE NOBLEMAN. Men cannot serve two masters. If this cant of serving their country once takes hold of them, goodbye to the authority of their feudal lords, and goodbye to the authority of the Church. That is, goodbye to you and me.

THE CHAPLAIN. I hope I am a faithful servant of the Church; and there are only six cousins between me and the barony of Stogumber, which was created by the Conqueror. But is that any reason why I should stand by and see Englishmen beaten by a French bastard and a witch from Lousy Champagne?

THE NOBLEMAN. Easy, man, easy: we shall burn the witch and beat the bastard all in good time. Indeed I am waiting at present for the Bishop of Beauvais, to arrange the burning with him. He has been turned out of his diocese by her faction.

THE CHAPLAIN. You have first to catch her, my lord.

THE NOBLEMAN. Or buy her. I will offer a king's ransom.

THE CHAPLAIN. A king's ransom! For that slut!

THE NOBLEMAN. One has to leave a margin. Some of Charles's people will sell her to the Burgundians; the Burgundians will sell her to us; and there will probably be three or four middlemen who will expect their little commissions.

THE CHAPLAIN. Monstrous. It is all those scoundrels of Jews: they get in every time money changes hands. I would not leave a Jew alive in Christendom if I had my way.

THE NOBLEMAN. Why not? The Jews generally give value. They make you pay; but they deliver the goods. In my experience the men who want something for nothing are invariably Christians.

A page appears.

THE PAGE. The Right Reverend the Bishop of Beauvais: Monseigneur Cauchon.

Cauchon, aged about 60, comes in. The page withdraws. The two Englishmen rise.

THE NOBLEMAN [*with effusive courtesy*] My dear Bishop, how good of you to come! Allow me to introduce myself: Richard de Beauchamp, Earl of Warwick, at your service.

CAUCHON. Your lordship's fame is well known to me.

WARWICK. This reverend cleric is Master John de Stogumber.

THE CHAPLAIN [*glibly*] John Bowyer Spenser Neville de Stogumber, at your service, my lord: Bachelor of Theology, and Keeper of the Private Seal to His Eminence the Cardinal of Winchester.

WARWICK [*to Cauchon*] You call him the Cardinal of England, I believe. Our king's uncle.

CAUCHON. Messire John de Stogumber: I am always the very good friend of His Eminence. [*He extends his hand to the chaplain, who kisses his ring*].

WARWICK. Do me the honor to be seated. [*He gives Cauchon his chair, placing it at the head of the table*].

Cauchon accepts the place of honor with a grave inclination. Warwick fetches the leather stool carelessly, and sits in his former place. The chaplain goes back to his chair.

Though Warwick has taken second place in calculated deference to the Bishop, he assumes the lead in opening the proceedings as a matter of course. He is still cordial and expansive; but there is a new note in his voice which means that he is coming to business.

WARWICK. Well, my Lord Bishop, you find us in one of our unlucky moments. Charles is to be crowned at Rheims, practically by the young woman from Lorraine; and—I must not deceive you, nor flatter your hopes—we cannot prevent it. I suppose it will make a great difference to Charles's position.

CAUCHON. Undoubtedly. It is a masterstroke of The Maid's.

THE CHAPLAIN [*again agitated*] We were not fairly beaten, my lord. No Englishman is ever fairly beaten.

Cauchon raises his eyebrow slightly, then quickly composes his face.

WARWICK. Our friend here takes the view that the young woman is a sorceress. It would, I presume, be the duty of your reverend lordship to denounce her to the Inquisition, and have her burnt for that offence.

CAUCHON. If she were captured in my diocese: yes.

WARWICK [*feeling that they are getting on capitally*] Just so. Now I suppose there can be no reasonable doubt that she is a sorceress.

THE CHAPLAIN. Not the least. An arrant witch.

WARWICK [*gently reproving the interruption*] We are asking for the Bishop's opinion, Messire John.

CAUCHON. We shall have to consider not merely our own opinions here, but the opinions—the prejudices, if you like—of a French court.

WARWICK [*correcting*] A Catholic court, my lord.

CAUCHON. Catholic courts are composed of mortal men, like other courts, however sacred their function and inspiration may be. And if the men are Frenchmen, as the modern fashion calls them, I am afraid the bare fact that an English army has been defeated by a French one will not convince them that there is any sorcery in the matter.

THE CHAPLAIN. What! Not when the famous Sir John Talbot himself has been defeated and actually taken prisoner by a drab from the ditches of Lorraine!

CAUCHON. Sir John Talbot, we all know, is a fierce and formidable soldier, Messire; but I have yet to learn that he is an able general. And though it pleases you to say that he has been defeated by this girl, some of us may be disposed to give a little of the credit to Dunois.

THE CHAPLAIN [*contemptuously*] The Bastard of Orleans!

CAUCHON. Let me remind—

WARWICK [*interposing*] I know what you are going to say, my lord. Dunois defeated me at Montargis.

CAUCHON [*bowing*] I take that as evidence that the Seigneur Dunois is a very able commander indeed.

WARWICK. Your lordship is the flower of courtesy. I admit, on our side, that Talbot is a mere fighting animal, and that it probably served him right to be taken at Patay.

THE CHAPLAIN [*chafing*] My lord: at Orleans this woman had her throat pierced by an English arrow, and was seen to cry like a child from the pain of it. It was a death wound; yet she fought all day; and when our men had repulsed all her attacks like true Englishmen, she walked alone to the wall of our fort with a white banner in her hand; and our men were paralyzed, and could neither shoot nor strike whilst the French fell on them and drove them on to the bridge, which immediately burst into flames and crumbled under them, letting them down into the river, where they were drowned in heaps. Was this your bastard's generalship? or were those flames the flames of hell, conjured up by witchcraft?

WARWICK. You will forgive Messire John's vehemence, my lord; but he has put our case. Dunois is a great captain, we admit; but why could he do nothing until the witch came?

CAUCHON. I do not say that there were no supernatural powers on her side. But the names on that white banner were not the names of Satan and Beelzebub, but the blessed names of our Lord and His holy mother. And your commander who was drowned—Clahz-da I think you call him—

WARWICK. Glasdale. Sir William Glasdale.

CAUCHON. Glass-dell, thank you. He was no saint; and many of our people think that he was drowned for his blasphemies against The Maid.

WARWICK [*beginning to look very dubious*] Well, what are we to infer from all this, my lord? Has The Maid converted you?

CAUCHON. If she had, my lord, I should have known better than to have trusted myself here within your grasp.

WARWICK [*blandly deprecating*] Oh! oh! My lord!

CAUCHON. If the devil is making use of this girl—and I believe he is—

WARWICK [*reassured*] Ah! You hear, Messire John? I knew your lordship would not fail us. Pardon my interruption. Proceed.

CAUCHON. If it be so, the devil has longer views than you give him credit for.

WARWICK. Indeed? In what way? Listen to this, Messire John.

CAUCHON. If the devil wanted to damn a country girl, do you think so easy a task would cost him the winning of half a dozen battles? No, my lord: any trumpery imp could do that much if the girl could be damned at all. The Prince of Darkness does not condescend to such cheap drudgery. When he strikes, he strikes at the Catholic Church, whose realm is the whole spiritual world. When he damns, he damns the souls of the entire human race. Against that dreadful design The Church stands ever on guard. And it is as one of the instruments of that design that I see this girl. She is inspired, but diabolically inspired.

THE CHAPLAIN. I told you she was a witch.

CAUCHON [*fiercely*] She is not a witch. She is a heretic.

THE CHAPLIAN. What difference does that make?

CAUCHON. You, a priest, ask me that! You English are strangely blunt in the mind. All these things that you call witchcraft are capable of a natural explanation. The woman's miracles would not impose on a rabbit: she does not claim them as miracles herself. What do her victories prove but that she has a better head on her shoulders than your swearing Glass-dells and mad bull Talbots, and that the courage of faith, even though it be a false faith, will always outstay the courage of wrath?

THE CHAPLAIN [*hardly able to, believe his ears*] Does your lordship compare Sir John Talbot, three times Governor of Ireland, to a mad bull?!!!

WARWICK. It would not be seemly for you to do so, Messire John, as you are still six removes from a barony. But as I am an earl, and Talbot is only a knight, I may make bold to accept the comparison. [*To the Bishop*] My lord: I wipe the slate as far as the witchcraft goes. None the less, we must burn the woman.

CAUCHON. I cannot burn her. The Church cannot take life. And my first duty is to seek this girl's salvation.

WARWICK. No doubt. But you do burn people occasionally.

CAUCHON. No. When The Church cuts off an obstinate heretic as a dead branch from the tree of life, the heretic is handed over to the secular arm. The Church has no part in what the secular arm may see fit to do.

WARWICK. Precisely. And I shall be the secular arm in this case. Well, my lord, hand over your dead branch; and I will see that the fire is ready for it. If you will answer for The Church's part, I will answer for the secular part.

CAUCHON [*with smouldering anger*] I can answer for nothing. You great lords are too prone to treat The Church as a mere political convenience.

WARWICK [*smiling and propitiatory*] Not in England, I assure you.

CAUCHON. In England more than anywhere else. No, my lord: the soul of this village girl is of equal value with yours or your king's before the throne of God; and my first duty is to save it. I will not suffer your lordship to smile at me as if I were repeating a meaningless form of words, and it were well understood between us that I should betray the girl to you. I am no mere political bishop: my faith is to me what your honor is to you; and if there be a loophole through which this baptized child of God can creep to her salvation, I shall guide her to it.

THE CHAPLAIN [*rising in a fury*] You are a traitor.

CAUCHON [*springing up*] You lie, priest. [*Trembling with rage*] If you dare do what this woman has done—set your country above the holy Catholic Church—you shall go to the fire with her.

THE CHAPLAIN. My lord: I—I went too far. I—[*he sits down with a submissive gesture*].

WARWICK [*who has risen apprehensively*] My lord: I apologize to you for the word used by Messire John de Stogumber. It does not mean in England what it does in France. In your language traitor means betrayer: one who is perfidious, treacherous, unfaithful, disloyal. In our country it means simply one who is not wholly devoted to our English interests.

CAUCHON. I am sorry: I did not understand. [*He subsides into his chair with dignity*].

WARWICK [*resuming his seat, much relieved*] I must apologize on my own account if I have seemed to take the burning of this poor girl too lightly. When one has seen whole countrysides burnt over and over again as mere items in military routine, one has to grow a very thick skin. Otherwise one might go mad: at all events, I should. May I venture to assume that your lordship also, having to see so many heretics burned from time to time, is compelled to take—shall I say a professional view of what would otherwise be a very horrible incident?

CAUCHON. Yes: it is a painful duty: even, as you say, a horrible one. But in comparison with the horror of heresy it is less than nothing. I am not thinking of this girl's body, which will suffer for a few moments only, and which must in any event die in some more or less painful manner, but of her soul, which may suffer to all eternity.

WARWICK. Just so; and God grant that her soul may be saved! But the practical problem would seem to be how to save her soul without saving her body. For we must face it, my lord: if this cult of The Maid goes on, our cause is lost.

THE CHAPLAIN [*his voice broken like that of a man who has been crying*] May I speak, my lord?

WARWICK. Really, Messire John, I had rather you did not, unless you can keep your temper.

THE CHAPLAIN. It is only this. I speak under correction; but The Maid is full of deceit: she pretends to be devout. Her prayers and confessions are endless. How can she be accused of heresy when she neglects no observance of a faithful daughter of The Church?

CAUCHON [*flaming up*] A faithful daughter of The Church! The Pope himself at his proudest dare not presume as this woman presumes. She acts as if she herself were The Church. She brings the message of God to Charles; and The Church must stand aside. She will crown him in the cathedral of Rheims: she, not The Church! She sends letters to the king of England giving him God's command through her to return to his island on pain of God's vengeance, which she will execute. Let me tell you that the writing of such letters was the practice of the accursed Mahomet, the anti-Christ. Has she ever in all her utterances said one word of The Church? Never. It is always God and herself.

WARWICK. What can you expect? A beggar on horseback! Her head is turned.

CHUCHON. Who has turned it? The devil. And for a mighty purpose. He is spreading this heresy everywhere. The man Hus, burnt only thirteen years ago at Constance, infected all Bohemia with it. A man named WcLeef, himself an anointed priest, spread the pestilence in England; and to your shame you let him die in his bed. We have such people here in France too: I know the breed. It is cancerous: if it be not cut out, stamped out, burnt out, it will not stop until is has brought the whole body of human society into sin and corruption, into waste and ruin. By it an Arab camel driver drove Christ and His Church out of Jerusalem, and ravaged his way west like a wild beast until at last there stood only the Pyrenees and God's mercy between France and damnation. Yet what did the camel driver do at the beginning more than this shepherd girl is doing? He had his voices from the angel Gabriel: she has her voices from St Catherine and St Margaret and the Blessed Michael. He declared himself the messenger of God, and wrote in God's name to the kings of the earth. Her letters to them are going forth daily. It is not the Mother of God now to whom we must look for intercession, but to Joan the Maid. What will the world be like when The Church's accumulated wisdom and knowledge and experience, its councils of learned, venerable pious men, are thrust into the kennel by every ignorant laborer or dairymaid whom the devil can puff up with the monstrous self-conceit of being directly inspired from heaven? It will be a world of blood, of fury, of devastation, of each man striving for his own hand: in the end a world wrecked back into barbarism. For now you have only Mahomet and his dupes, and the Maid and her dupes; but what will it be when every girl thinks herself a Joan and every man a Mahomet? I shudder to the very marrow of my bones when I think of it. I have fought it all my life; and I will fight it to the end. Let all this woman's sins be forgiven her except only this sin; for it is the sin against the Holy Ghost; and if she does not recant in the dust before the world, and submit herself to the last inch of her soul to her Church, to the fire she shall go if she once falls into my hand.

WARWICK [*unimpressed*] You feel strongly about it, naturally.

CAUCHON. Do not you?

WARWICK. I am a soldier, not a churchman. As a pilgrim I saw something of the Mahometans. They were not so ill-bred as I had been led to believe. In some respects their conduct compared favorably with ours.

CAUCHON [*displeased*] I have noticed this before. Men go to the East to convert the infidels. And the infidels pervert them. The Crusader comes back more than half a Saracen. Not to mention that all Englishmen are born heretics.

THE CHAPLAIN. Englishmen heretics!!! [*Appealing to Warwick*] My lord: must we endure this? His lordship is beside himself. How can what an Englishman believes be heresy? It is a contradiction in terms.

CAUCHON. I absolve you, Messire de Stogumber, on the ground of invincible ignorance. The thick air of your country does not breed theologians.

WARWICK. You would not say so if you heard us quarrelling about religion, my lord! I am sorry you think I must be either a heretic or a blockhead because, as a travelled man, I know that the followers of Mahomet profess great respect for our Lord, and are more ready to forgive St Peter for being a fisherman than your lordship is to forgive Mahomet for being a camel driver. But at least we can proceed in this matter without bigotry.

CAUCHON. When men call the zeal of the Christian Church bigotry I know what to think.

WARWICK. They are only east and west views of the same thing.

CAUCHON [*bitterly ironical*] O n l y east and west! Only!!

WARWICK. Oh, my Lord Bishop, I am not gainsaying you. You will carry The Church with you; but you have to carry the nobles also. To my mind there is a stronger case against The Maid than the one you have so forcibly put. Frankly, I am not afraid of this girl becoming another Mahomet, and superseding The Church by a great heresy. I think you exaggerate that risk. But have you noticed that in these letters of hers, she proposes to all the kings of Europe, as she has already pressed on Charles, a transaction which would wreck the whole social structure of Christendom?

CAUCHON. Wreck The Church. I tell you so.

WARWICK [*whose patience is wearing out*] My lord: pray get The Church out of your head for a moment; and remember that there are temporal institutions in the world as well as spiritual ones. I and my peers represent the feudal aristocracy as you represent The Church. We are the temporal power. Well, do you not see how this girl's idea strikes at us?

CAUCHON. How does her idea strike at you, except as it strikes at all of us, through The Church?

WARWICK. Her idea is that the kings should give their realms to God, and then reign as God's bailiffs.

CAUCHON [*not interested*] Quite sound, theologically, my lord. But the king will hardly care, provided he reign. It is an abstract idea: a mere form of words.

WARWICK. By no means. It is a cunning device to supersede the aristocracy, and make the king sole and absolute autocrat.

Instead of the king being merely the first among his peers, he becomes their master. That we cannot suffer: we call no man master. Nominally we hold our lands and dignities from the king, because there must be a keystone to the arch of human society; but we hold our lands in our own hands, and defend them with our own swords and those of our own tenants. Now by The Maid's doctrine the king will take our lands—o u r lands!—and make them a present to God; and God will then vest them wholly in the king.

CAUCHON. Need you fear that? You are the makers of kings after all. York or Lancaster in England, Lancaster or Valois in France: they reign according to your pleasure.

WARWICK. Yes; but only as long as the people follow their feudal lords, and know the king only as a travelling show, owning nothing but the highway that belongs to everybody. If the people's thoughts and hearts were turned to the king, and their lords became only the king's servants in their eyes, the king could break us across his knee one by one; and then what should we be but liveried courtiers in his halls?

CAUCHON. Still you need not fear, my lord. Some men are born kings; and some are born statesmen. The two are seldom the same. Where would the king find counsellors to plan and carry out such a policy for him?

WARWICK [*with a not too friendly smile*] Perhaps in the Church, my lord.

> *Cauchon, with an equally sour smile, shrugs his shoulders, and does not contradict him.*

WARWICK. Strike down the barons; and the cardinals will have it all their own way.

CAUCHON [*conciliatory, dropping his polemical tone*] My lord: we shall not defeat The Maid if we strive against one another. I know well that there is a Will to Power in the world. I know that while it lasts there will be a struggle between the Emperor and the Pope, between the dukes and the political cardinals, between the barons and the kings. The devil divides us and governs. I see you are no friend to The Church: you are an earl first and last, as I am a churchman first and last. But can we not sink our differences in the face of a common enemy? I see now that what is in your mind is not that this girl has never once mentioned The Church, and thinks only of God and herself, but that she has never once mentioned the peerage, and thinks only of the king and herself.

WARWICK. Quite so. These two ideas of hers are the same idea at bottom. It goes deep, my lord. It is the protest of the individual soul against the interference of priest or peer between the private man and his God. I should call it Protestantism if I had to find a name for it.

CAUCHON [*looking hard at him*] You understand it wonderfully well, my lord. Scratch an Englishman, and find a Protestant.

WARWICK [*playing the pink of courtesy*] I think you are not entirely void of sympathy with The Maid's secular heresy, my lord. I leave you to find a name for it.

CAUCHON. You mistake me, my lord. I have no sympathy with her political presumptions. But as a priest I have gained a knowledge of the minds of the common people; and there you will find yet another most dangerous idea. I can express it only by such phrases as France for the French, England for the English, Italy for the Italians, Spain for the Spanish, and so forth. It is sometimes so narrow and bitter in country folk that it surprises me that this country girl can rise above the idea of her village for its villagers. But she can. She does. When she threatens to drive the English from the soil of France she is undoubtedly thinking of the whole extent of country in which French is spoken. To her the French-speaking people are what the Holy Scriptures describe as a nation. Call this side of her heresy Nationalism if you will: I can find you no better name for it. I can only tell you that it is essentially anti-Catholic and anti-Christian; for the Catholic Church knows only one realm, and that is the realm of Christ's kingdom. Divide that kingdom into nations, and you dethrone Christ. Dethrone Christ, and who will stand between our throats and the sword? The world will perish in a welter of war.

WARWICK. Well, if you will burn the Protestant, I will burn the Nationalist, though perhaps I shall not carry Messire John with me there. England for the English will appeal to him.

THE CHAPLAIN. Certainly England for the English goes without saying: it is the simple law of nature. But this woman denies to England her legitimate conquests, given her by God because of her peculiar fitness to rule over less civilized races for their own good. I do not understand what your lordships mean by Protestant and Nationalist: you are too learned and subtle for a poor clerk like myself. But I know as a matter of plain commonsense that the woman is a rebel; and that is enough for me. She rebels against Nature by wearing man's clothes, and fighting. She rebels against The Church by usurping the divine authority of the Pope. She rebels against God by her damnable league with Satan and his evil spirits against our army. And all these rebellions are only excuses for her great rebellion against England. That is not to be endured. Let her perish. Let her burn. Let her not infect the whole flock. It is expedient that one woman die for the people.

WARWICK [*rising*] My lord: we seem to be agreed.

CAUCHON [*rising also, but in protest*] I will not imperil my soul. I will uphold the justice of the Church. I will strive to the utmost for this woman's salvation.

WARWICK. I am sorry for the poor girl. I hate these severities. I will spare her if I can.

THE CHAPLAIN [*implacably*] I would burn her with my own hands.

CAUCHON [*blessing him*] Sancta simplicitas!

Scene V

The ambulatory in the cathedral of Rheims, near the door of the vestry. A pillar bears one of the stations of the cross. The organ is playing the people out of the nave after the coronation. Joan is kneeling in prayer before the station. She is beautifully dressed, but still in male attire. The organ ceases as Dunois, also splendidly arrayed, comes into the ambulatory from the vestry.

DUNOIS. Come, Joan! you have had enough praying. After that fit of crying you will catch a chill if you stay here any longer. It is all over: the cathedral is empty; and the streets are full. They are calling for The Maid. We have told them you are staying here alone to pray; but they want to see you again.

JOAN. No: let the king have all the glory.

DUNOIS. He only spoils the show, poor devil. No, Joan: you have crowned him; and you must go through with it.

JOAN [*shakes her head reluctantly*].

DUNOIS [*raising her*] Come come! it will be over in a couple of hours. It's better than the bridge at Orleans: eh?

JOAN. Oh, dear Dunois, how I wish it were the bridge at Orleans again! We lived at that bridge.

DUNOIS. Yes, faith, and died too: some of us.

JOAN. Isnt it strange, Jack? I am such a coward: I am frightened beyond words before a battle; but it is so dull afterwards when there is no danger: oh, so dull! dull! dull!

DUNOIS. You must learn to be abstemious in war, just as you are in your food and drink, my little saint.

JOAN. Dear Jack: I think you like me as a soldier likes his comrade.

DUNOIS. You need it, poor innocent child of God. You have not many friends at court.

JOAN. Why do all these courtiers and knights and churchmen hate me? What have I done to them? I have asked nothing for myself except that my village shall not be taxed; for we cannot afford war taxes. I have brought them luck and victory: I have set them right when they were doing all sorts of stupid things: I have crowned Charles and made him a real king; and all the honors he is handing out have gone to them. Then why do they not love me?

DUNOIS [*rallying her*] Sim-ple-ton! Do you expect stupid people to love you for shewing them up? Do blundering old military dug-outs love the successful young captains who supersede them? Do ambitious politicians love the climbers who take the front seats from them? Do archbishops enjoy being played off their own altars, even by saints? Why, I should be jealous of you myself if I were ambitious enough.

JOAN. You are the pick of the basket here, Jack: the only friend I have among all these nobles. I'll wager your mother was from the country. I will go back to the farm when I have taken Paris.

DUNOIS. I am not so sure that they will let you take Paris.

JOAN [*startled*] What!

DUNOIS. I should have taken it myself before this if they had all been sound about it. Some of them would rather Paris took you, I think. So take care.

JOAN. Jack: the world is too wicked for me. If the goddams and the Burgundians do not make an end of me, the French will. Only for my voices I should lose all heart. That is why I had to steal away to pray here alone after the coronation. I'll tell you something, Jack. It is in the bells I hear my voices. Not to-day, when they all rang: that was nothing but jangling. But here in this corner, where the bells come down from heaven, and the echoes linger, or in the fields, where they come from a distance through the quiet of the countryside, my voices are in them. [*The cathedral clock chimes the quarter*] Hark! [*She becomes rapt*] Do you hear? "Dear-child-of-God": just what you said. At the half-hour they will say "Be-brave-go-on." At the three-quarters they will say "I-am-thy-Help." But it is at the hour, when the great bell goes after "God-will-save-France": it is then that St Margaret and St Catherine and sometimes even the blessed Michael will say things that I cannot tell beforehand. Then, oh then—

DUNOIS [*interrupting her kindly but not sympathetically*] Then, Joan, we shall hear whatever we fancy in the booming of the bell. You make me uneasy when you talk about your voices: I should think you were a bit cracked if I hadnt noticed that you give me very sensible reasons for what you do, though I hear you telling others you are only obeying Madame Saint Catherine.

JOAN [*crossly*] Well, I have to find reasons for you, because you do not believe in my voices. But the voices come first; and I find the reasons after: whatever you may choose to believe.

DUNOIS. Are you angry, Joan?

JOAN. Yes. [*Smiling*] No: not with you. I wish you were one of the village babies.

DUNOIS. Why?

JOAN. I could nurse you for awhile.

DUNOIS. You are a bit of a woman after all.

JOAN. No: not a bit: I am a soldier and nothing else. Soldiers always nurse children when they get a chance.

DUNOIS. That is true. [*He laughs*].

> *King Charles, with Bluebeard on his left and La Hire on his right, comes from the vestry, where he has been disrobing. Joan shrinks away behind the pillar. Dunois is left between Charles and La Hire.*

DUNOIS. Well, your Majesty is an anointed king at last. How do you like it?

CHARLES. I would not go through it again to be emperor of the sun and moon. The weight of those robes! I thought I should have dropped when they loaded that crown on to me. And the famous holy oil they talked so much about was rancid: phew! The Archbishop must be nearly dead: his robes must have weighed a ton: they are stripping him still in the vestry.

DUNOIS [*drily*] Your majesty should wear armor oftener. That would accustom you to heavy dressing.

CHARLES. Yes: the old jibe! Well, I am not going to wear armor: fighting is not my job. Where is The Maid?

JOAN [*coming forward between Charles and Bluebeard, and falling on her knee*] Sire: I have made you king: my work is done. I am going back to my father's farm.

CHARLES [*surprised, but relieved*] Oh, are you? Well, that will be very nice.

    Joan rises, deeply discouraged.

CHARLES [*continuing heedlessly*] A healthy life, you know.

DUNOIS. But a dull one.

BLUEBEARD. You will find the petticoats tripping you up after leaving them off for so long.

LA HIRE. You will miss the fighting. It's a bad habit, but a grand one, and the hardest of all to break yourself of.

CHARLES [*anxiously*] Still, we dont want you to stay if you would really rather go home.

JOAN [*bitterly*] I know well that none of you will be sorry to see me go. [*She turns her shoulder to Charles and walks past him to the more congenial neighborhood of Dunois and La Hire*].

LA HIRE. Well, I shall be able to swear when I want to. But I shall miss you at times.

JOAN. La Hire: in spite of all your sins and swears we shall meet in heaven; for I love you as I love Pitou, my old sheep dog. Pitou could kill a wolf. You will kill the English wolves until they go back to their country and become good dogs of God, will you not?

LA HIRE. You and I together: yes.

JOAN. No: I shall last only a year from the beginning.

ALL THE OTHERS. What!

JOAN. I know it somehow.

DUNOIS. Nonsense!

JOAN. Jack: do you think you will be able to drive them out?

DUNOIS [*with quiet conviction*] Yes: I shall drive them out. They beat us because we thought battles were tournaments and ransom markets. We played the fool while the goddams took war seriously. But I have learnt my lesson, and taken their measure. They have no roots here. I have beaten them before; and I shall beat them again.

JOAN. You will not be cruel to them, Jack?

DUNOIS. The goddams will not yield to tender handling. We did not begin it.

JOAN [*suddenly*] Jack: before I go home, let us take Paris.

CHARLES [*terrified*] Oh no no. We shall lose everything we have gained. Oh dont let us have any more fighting. We can make a very good treaty with the Duke of Burgundy.

JOAN. Treaty! [*She stamps with impatience*].

CHARLES. Well, why not, now that I am crowned and anointed?

Oh, that oil!

> *The Archbishop comes from the vestry, and joins the group between Charles and Bluebeard.*

CHARLES. Archbishop: The Maid wants to start fighting again.

THE ARCHBISHOP. Have we ceased fighting, then? Are we at peace?

CHARLES. No: I suppose not; but let us be content with what we have done. Let us make a treaty. Our luck is too good to last; and now is our chance to stop before it turns.

JOAN. Luck! God has fought for us; and you call it luck! And you would stop while there are still Englishmen on this holy earth of dear France!

THE ARCHBISHOP [*sternly*] Maid: the king addressed himself to me, not to you. You forget yourself. You very often forget yourself.

JOAN [*unabashed, and rather roughly*] Then speak, you; and tell him that it is not God's will that he should take his hand from the plough.

THE ARCHBISHOP. If I am not so glib with the name of God as you are, it is because I interpret His will with the authority of the Church and of my sacred office. When you first came you respected it, and would not have dared to speak as you are now speaking. You came clothed with the virtue of humility; and because God blessed your enterprises accordingly, you have stained yourself with the sin of pride. The old Greek tragedy is rising among us. It is the chastisement of hubris.[3]

CHARLES. Yes: she thinks she knows better than everyone else.

JOAN [*distressed, but naïvely incapable of seeing the effect she is producing*] But I do know better than any of you seem to. And I am not proud: I never speak unless I know I am right.

BLUEBEARD ⎱ [*exclaiming* ⎰ Ha ha!
CHARLES   ⎰ *together*]   ⎱ Just so.

THE ARCHBISHOP. How do you know you are right?

JOAN. I always know. My voices—

CHARLES. Oh, your voices, your voices. Why dont the voices come to me? I am king, not you.

JOAN. They do come to you; but you do not hear them. You have not sat in the field in the evening listening for them. When the angelus rings you cross yourself and have done with it; but if you prayed from your heart, and listened to the thrilling of the bells in the air after they stop ringing, you would hear the voices as well as I do. [*Turning brusquely from him*] But what voices do you need to tell you what the blacksmith can tell you: that you must strike while the iron is hot? I tell you we must make a dash at Compiègne and relieve it as we relieved Orleans. Then Paris will open its gates; or if not, we will break through them. What is your crown worth without your capital?

LA HIRE. That is what I say too. We shall go through them like a red hot shot through a pound of butter. What do you say, Bastard?

---

3. Man's arrogance towards the gods: the classic sin of the Greek heroes.

DUNOIS. If our cannon balls were all as hot as your head, and we had enough of them, we should conquer the earth, no doubt. Pluck and impetuosity are good servants in war, but bad masters: they have delivered us into the hands of the English every time we have trusted to them. We never know when we are beaten: that is our great fault.

JOAN. You never know when you are victorious: that is a worse fault. I shall have to make you carry looking-glasses in battle to convince you that the English have not cut off all your noses. You would have been besieged in Orleans still, you and your councils of war, if I had not made you attack. You should always attack; and if you only hold on long enough the enemy will stop first. You dont know how to begin a battle; and you dont know how to use your cannons. And I do.

She squats down on the flags with crossed ankles, pouting.

DUNOIS. I know what you think of us, General Joan.

JOAN. Never mind that, Jack. Tell them what you think of me.

DUNOIS. I think that God was on your side; for I have not forgotten how the wind changed, and how our hearts changed when you came; and by my faith I shall never deny that it was in your sign that we conquered. But I tell you as a soldier that God is no man's daily drudge, and no maid's either. If you are worthy of it He will sometimes snatch you out of the jaws of death and set you on your feet again; but that is all: once on your feet you must fight with all your might and all your craft. For He has to be fair to your enemy too: dont forget that. Well, He set us on our feet through you at Orleans; and the glory of it has carried us through a few good battles here to the coronation. But if we presume on it further, and trust to God to do the work we should do ourselves, we shall be defeated; and serve us right!

JOAN. But—

DUNOIS. Sh! I have not finished. Do not think, any of you, that these victories of ours were won without generalship. King Charles: you have said no word in your proclamations of my part in this campaign; and I make no complaint of that; for the people will run after The Maid and her miracles and not after the Bastard's hard work finding troops for her and feeding them. But I know exactly how much God did for us through The Maid, and how much He left me to do by my own wits; and I tell you that your little hour of miracles is over, and that from this time on he who plays the war game best will win—if the luck is on his side.

JOAN. Ah! if, if, if, if! If ifs and ans were pots and pans there'd be no need of tinkers. [*Rising impetuously*] I tell you, Bastard, your art of war is no use, because your knights are no good for real fighting. War is only a game to them, like tennis and all their other games: they make rules as to what is fair and what is not fair, and heap armor on themselves and on their poor horses to keep out the arrows; and when they fall they cant get up, and have to wait for their squires to come and lift them to arrange about the ransom with the man that has poked them off their horse. Cant you see that all the like of that is gone by and done with? What use is armor against gunpowder? And if it was, do you think men that are fighting for France and for God will stop to bargain about ransoms, as half your knights live by doing? No: they will fight to win; and they will give up their lives out of their own hand into the hand of God when they go into battle, as I do. Common folks understand this. They cannot afford armor and cannot pay ransoms; but they followed me half naked into the moat and up the ladder and over the wall. With them it is my life or thine, and God defend the right! You may shake your head, Jack; and Bluebeard may twirl his billygoat's beard and cock his nose at me; but remember the day your knights and captains refused to follow me to attack the English at Orleans! You locked the gates to keep me in; and it was the townsfolk and the common people that followed me, and forced the gate, and shewed you the way to fight in earnest.

BLUEBEARD [*offended*] Not content with being Pope Joan, you must be Caesar and Alexander as well.

THE ARCHBISHOP. Pride will have a fall, Joan.

JOAN. Oh, never mind whether it is pride or not: is it true? is it commonsense?

LA HIRE. It is true. Half of us are afraid of having our handsome noses broken; and the other half are out for paying off their mortgages. Let her have her way, Dunois; she does not know everything; but she has got hold of the right end of the stick. Fighting is not what it was; and those who know least about it often make the best job of it.

DUNOIS. I know all that. I do not fight in the old way: I have learnt the lesson of Agincourt, of Poitiers and Crecy. I know how many lives any move of mine will cost; and if the move is worth the cost I make it and pay the cost. But Joan never counts the cost at all: she goes ahead and trusts to God: she thinks she has God in her pocket. Up to now she has had the numbers on her side; and she has won. But I know Joan; and I see that some day she will go ahead when she has only ten men to do the work of a hundred. And then she will find that God is on the side of the big battalions. She will be taken by the enemy. And the lucky man that makes the capture will receive sixteen thousand pounds from the Earl of Ouareek.

JOAN [*flattered*] Sixteen thousand pounds! Eh, laddie, have they offered that for me? There cannot be so much money in the world.

DUNOIS. There is, in England. And now tell me, all of you, which of you will lift a finger to save Joan once the English have got her? I speak first, for the army. The day after she has been dragged from her horse by a goddam or a Burgundian, and he is not struck dead: the day after she is locked in a dungeon, and the bars and bolts do not fly open at the touch of St Peter's angel: the day when the enemy finds out that she is as vulnerable as I am and not a bit more invincible, she will not be worth the life of a single soldier to us; and I will not risk that life, much as I cherish her as a companion-in-arms.

JOAN. I dont blame you, Jack: you are right. I am not worth one soldier's life if God lets me be beaten; but France may think me worth my ransom after what God has done for her through me.

CHARLES. I tell you I have no money; and this coronation, which is all your fault, has cost me the last farthing I can borrow.

JOAN. The Church is richer than you. I put my trust in the Church.

THE ARCHBISHOP. Woman: they will drag you through the streets, and burn you as a witch.

JOAN [*running to him*] Oh, my lord, do not say that. It is impossible. I a witch!

THE ARCHBISHOP. Peter Cauchon knows his business. The University of Paris has burnt a woman for saying that what you have done was well done, and according to God!

JOAN [*bewildered*] But why? What sense is there in it? What I have done is according to God. They could not burn a woman for speaking the truth.

THE ARCHBISHOP. They did.

JOAN. But you know that she was speaking the truth. You would not let them burn me.

THE ARCHBISHOP. How could I prevent them?

JOAN. You would speak in the name of the Church. You are a great prince of the Church. I would go anywhere with your blessing to protect me.

THE ARCHBISHOP. I have no blessing for you while you are proud and disobedient.

JOAN. Oh, why will you go on saying things like that? I am not proud and disobedient. I am a poor girl, and so ignorant that I do not know A from B. How could I be proud? And how can you say that I am disobedient when I always obey my voices, because they come from God.

THE ARCHBISHOP. The voice of God on earth is the voice of the Church Militant; and all the voices that come to you are the echoes of your own wilfulness.

JOAN. It is not true.

THE ARCHBISHOP [*flushing angrily*] You tell the Archbishop in his cathedral that he lies; and yet you say you are not proud and disobedient.

JOAN. I never said you lied. It was you that as good as said my voices lied. When have they ever lied? If you will not believe in them: even if they are only the echoes of my own commonsense, are they not always right? and are not your earthly counsels always wrong?

THE ARCHBISHOP [*indignantly*] It is waste of time admonishing you.

CHARLES. It always comes back to the same thing. She is right; and everyone else is wrong.

THE ARCHBISHOP. Take this as your last warning. If you perish through setting your private judgment above the instructions of your spiritual directors, the Church disowns you, and leaves you to whatever fate your presumption may bring upon you. The Bastard has told you that if you persist in setting up your military conceit above the counsels of your commanders—

DUNOIS [interposing] To put it quite exactly, if you attempt to relieve the garrison in Compiègne without the same superiority in numbers you had at Orleans—

THE ARCHBISHOP. The army will disown you, and will not rescue you. And His Majesty the King has told you that the throne has not the means of ransoming you.

CHARLES. Not a penny.

THE ARCHBISHOP. You stand alone: absolutely alone, trusting to your own conceit, your own ignorance, your own headstrong presumption, your own impiety in hiding all these sins under the cloak of a trust in God. When you pass through these doors into the sunlight, the crowd will cheer you. They will bring you their little children and their invalids to heal: they will kiss your hands and feet, and do what they can, poor simple souls, to turn your head, and madden you with the self-confidence that is leading you to your destruction. But you will be none the less alone: they cannot save you. We and we only can stand between you and the stake at which our enemies have burnt that wretched woman in Paris.

JOAN [her eyes skyward] I have better friends and better counsel than yours.

THE ARCHBISHOP. I see that I am speaking in vain to a hardened heart. You reject our protection, and are determined to turn us all against you. In future, then, fend for yourself; and if you fail, God have mercy on your soul.

DUNOIS. That is the truth, Joan. Heed it.

JOAN. Where would you all have been now if I had heeded that sort of truth? There is no help, no counsel, in any of you. Yes: I am alone on earth: I have always been alone. My father told my brothers to drown me if I would not stay to mind his sheep while France was bleeding to death: France might perish if only our lambs were safe. I thought France would have friends at the court of the king of France; and I find only wolves fighting for pieces of her poor torn body. I thought God would have friends everywhere, because He is the friend of everyone; and in my innocence I believed that you who now cast me out would be like strong towers to keep harm from me. But I am wiser now; and nobody is any the worse for being wiser. Do not think you can frighten me by telling me that I am alone. France is alone; and God is alone; and what is my loneliness before the loneliness of my country and my God? I see now that the loneliness of God is His strength: what would He be if He listened to your jealous little counsels? Well, my loneliness shall be my strength too; it is better to be alone with God: His friendship will not fail me, nor His counsel, nor His love. In His strength I will dare, and dare, and dare, until I die. I will go out now to the common people, and let the love in their eyes comfort me for the hate in yours. You will all be glad to see me burnt; but if I go through the fire I shall go through it to their hearts for ever and ever. And so, God be with me!

> *She goes from them. They stare after her in glum silence for a moment. Then Gilles de Rais twirls his beard.*

BLUEBEARD. You know, the woman is quite impossible. I dont dislike her, really; but what are you to do with such a character?

DUNOIS. As God is my judge, if she fell into the Loire I would jump in in full armor to fish her out. But if she plays the fool at Compiègne, and gets caught, I must leave her to her doom.

LA HIRE. Then you had better chain me up; for I could follow her to hell when the spirit rises in her like that.

THE ARCHBISHOP. She disturbs my judgment too: there is a dangerous power in her outbursts. But the pit is open at her feet; and for good or evil we cannot turn her from it.

CHARLES. If only she would keep quiet, or go home!

> *They follow her dispiritedly.*

Scene VI

Rouen, 30th May 1431. A great stone hall in the castle, arranged for a trial-at-law, but not a trial-by-jury, the court being the Bishop's court with the Inquisition participating: hence there are two raised chairs side by side for the Bishop and the Inquisitor as judges. Rows of chairs radiating from them at an obtuse angle are for the canons, the doctors of law and theology, and the Dominican monks, who act as assessors. In the angle is a table for the scribes, with stools. There is also a heavy rough wooden stool for the prisoner. All these are at the inner end of the hall. The further end is open to the courtyard through a row of arches. The court is shielded from the weather by screens and curtains.

Looking down the great hall from the middle of the inner end, the judicial chairs and scribes' table are to the right. The prisoner's stool is to the left. There are arched doors right and left. It is a fine sunshiny May morning.

Warwick comes in through the arched doorway on the judges' side, followed by his page.

THE PAGE [*pertly*] I suppose your lordship is aware that we have no business here. This is an ecclesiastical court; and we are only the secular arm.

WARWICK. I am aware of that fact. Will it please your impudence to find the Bishop of Beauvais for me, and give him a hint that he can have a word with me here before the trial, if he wishes?

THE PAGE [*going*] Yes, my lord.

WARWICK. And mind you behave yourself. Do not address him as Pious Peter.

THE PAGE. No, my lord. I shall be kind to him, because, when The Maid is brought in, Pious Peter will have to pick a peck of pickled pepper.
Cauchon enters through the same door with a Dominican monk and a canon, the latter carrying a brief.

THE PAGE. The Right Reverend his lordship the Bishop of Beauvais. And two other reverend gentlemen.

WARWICK. Get out; and see that we are not interrupted.

THE PAGE. Right, my lord [*he vanishes airily*].

CAUCHON. I wish your lordship good-morrow.

WARWICK. Good-morrow to your lordship. Have I had the pleasure of meeting your friends before? I think not.

CAUCHON [*introducing the monk, who is on his right*] This, my lord, is Brother John Lemaître, of the order of St Dominic. He is acting as deputy for the Chief Inquisitor into the evil of heresy in France. Brother John: the Earl of Warwick.

WARWICK. Your Reverence is most welcome. We have no Inquisitor in England, unfortunately; though we miss him greatly, especially on occasions like the present.

The Inquisitor smiles patiently, and bows. He is a mild elderly gentleman, but has evident reserves of authority and firmness.

CAUCHON [*introducing the Canon, who is on his left*] This gentleman is Canon John D'Estivet, of the Chapter of Bayeux. He is acting as Promoter.

WARWICK. Promoter?

CAUCHON. Prosecutor, you would call him in civil law.

WARWICK. Ah! prosecutor. Quite, quite. I am very glad to make your acquaintance, Canon D'Estivet.

D'Estivet bows. [*He is on the young side of middle age, well mannered, but vulpine beneath his veneer*].

WARWICK. May I ask what stage the proceedings have reached? It is now more than nine months since The Maid was captured at Compiègne by the Burgundians. It is fully four months since I bought her from the Burgundians for a very handsome sum, solely that she might be brought to justice. It is very nearly three months since I delivered her up to you, my Lord Bishop, as a person suspected of heresy. May I suggest that you are taking a rather unconscionable time to make up your minds about a very plain case? Is this trial never going to end?

THE INQUISITOR [*smiling*] It has not yet begun, my lord.

WARWICK. Not yet begun! Why, you have been at it eleven weeks!

CAUCHON. We have not been idle, my lord. We have held fifteen examinations of The Maid: six public and nine private.

THE INQUISTOR [*always patiently smiling*] You see, my lord, I have been present at only two of these examinations. They were proceedings of the Bishop's court solely, and not of the Holy Office. I have only just decided to associate myself—that is, to associate the Holy Inquisition—with the Bishop's court. I did not at first think that this was a case of heresy at all. I regarded it as a political case, and The Maid as a prisoner of war. But having now been present at two of the examinations, I must admit that this seems to be one of the gravest cases of heresy within my experience. Therefore everything is now in order, and we proceed to trial this morning. [*He moves towards the judicial chairs*].

CAUCHON. This moment, if your lordship's convenience allows.

WARWICK [*graciously*] Well, that is good news, gentlemen. I will not attempt to conceal from you that our patience was becoming strained.

CAUCHON. So I gathered from the threats of your soldiers to drown those of our people who favor The Maid.

WARWICK. Dear me! At all events their intentions were friendly to you, my lord.

CAUCHON [*sternly*] I hope not. I am determined that the woman shall have a fair hearing. The justice of the Church is not a mockery, my lord.

THE INQUISITOR [*returning*] Never has there been a fairer examination within my experience, my lord. The Maid needs no lawyers to take her part: she will be tried by her most faithful friends, all ardently desirous to save her soul from perdition.

D'ESTIVET. Sir: I am the Promoter; and it has been my painful duty to present the case against the girl; but believe me, I would throw up my case today and hasten to her defence if I did not know that men far my superiors in learning and piety, in eloquence and persuasiveness, have been sent to reason with her, to explain to her the danger she is running, and the ease with which she may avoid it. [*Suddenly bursting into forensic eloquence, to the disgust of Cauchon and the Inquisitor, who have listened to him so far with patronizing approval*] Men have dared to say that we are acting from hate; but God is our witness that they lie. Have we tortured her? No. Have we ceased to exhort her; to implore her to have pity on herself; to come to the bosom of her Church as an erring but beloved child? Have we—

CAUCHON [*interrupting drily*] Take care, Canon. All that you say is true; but if you make his lordship believe it I will not answer for your life, and hardly for my own.

WARWICK [*deprecating, but by no means denying*] Oh, my lord, you are very hard on us poor English. But we certainly do not share your pious desire to save The Maid: in fact I tell you now plainly that her death is a political necessity which I regret but cannot help. If the Church lets her go—

CAUCHON [*with fierce and menacing pride*] If the Church lets her go, woe to the man, were he the Emperor himself, who dares lay a finger on her! The Church is not subject to political necessity, my lord.

THE INQUISITOR [*interposing smoothly*] You need have no anxiety about the result, my lord. You have an invincible ally in the matter: one who is far more determined than you that she shall burn.

WARWICK. And who is this very convenient partisan, may I ask?

THE INQUISITOR. The Maid herself. Unless you put a gag in her mouth you cannot prevent her from convicting herself ten times over every time she opens it.

D'ESTIVET. That is perfectly true, my lord. My hair bristles on my head when I hear so young a creature utter such blasphemies.

WARWICK. Well, by all means do your best for her if you are quite sure it will be of no avail. [*Looking hard at Cauchon*] I should be sorry to have to act without the blessing of the Church.

CAUCHON [*with a mixture of cynical admiration and contempt*] And yet they say Englishmen are hypocrites! You play for your side, my lord, even at the peril of your soul. I cannot but admire such devotion; but I dare not go so far myself. I fear damnation.

WARWICK. If we feared anything we could never govern England, my lord. Shall I send your people in to you?

CAUCHON. Yes: it will be very good of your lordship to withdraw and allow the court to assemble.

Warwick turns on his heel, and goes out through the courtyard. Cauchon takes one of the judicial seats; and

D'Estivet sits at the scribes' table, studying his brief.

CAUCHON [*casually, as he makes himself comfortable*] What scoundrels these English nobles are!

THE INQUISITOR [*taking the other judicial chair on Cauchon's left*] All secular power makes men scoundrels. They are not trained for the work; and they have not the Apostolic Succession. Our own nobles are just as bad.

The Bishop's assessors hurry into the hall, headed by Chaplain de Stogumber and Canon de Courcelles, a young priest of 30. The scribes sit at the table, leaving a chair vacant opposite D'Estivet. Some of the assessors take their seats: others stand chatting, waiting for the proceedings to begin formally. De Stogumber, aggrieved and obstinate, will not take his seat: neither will the Canon, who stands on his right.

CAUCHON. Good morning, Master de Stogumber. [*To the Inquisitor*] Chaplain to the Cardinal of England.

THE CHAPLAIN [*correcting him*] Of Winchester, my lord. I have to make a protest, my lord.

CAUCHON. You make a great many.

THE CHAPLAIN. I am not without support, my lord. Here is Master de Courcelles, Canon of Paris, who associates himself with me in my protest.

CAUCHON. Well, what is the matter?

THE CHAPLAIN [*sulkily*] Speak you, Master de Courcelles, since I do not seem to enjoy his lordship's confidence. [*He sits down in dudgeon next to Cauchon, on his right*].

COURCELLES. My lord: we have been at great pains to draw up an indictment of The Maid on sixty-four counts. We are now told that they have been reduced, without consulting us.

THE INQUISITOR. Master de Courcelles: I am the culprit. I am overwhelmed with admiration for the zeal displayed in your sixty-four counts; but in accusing a heretic, as in other things, enough is enough. Also you must remember that all the members of the court are not so subtle and profound as you, and that some of your very great learning might appear to them to be very great nonsense. Therefore I have thought it well to have your sixty-four articles cut down to twelve—

COURCELLES [*thunderstruck*] Twelve!!!

THE INQUISITOR. Twelve will, believe me, be quite enough for your purpose.

THE CHAPLAIN. But some of the most important points have been reduced almost to nothing. For instance, The Maid has actually declared that the blessed saints Margaret and Catherine, and the holy Archangel Michael, spoke to her in French. That is a vital point.

THE INQUISITOR. You think, doubtless, that they should have spoken in Latin?

CAUCHON. No: he thinks they should have spoken in English.

THE CHAPLAIN. Naturally, my lord.

THE INQUISITOR. Well, as we are all here agreed, I think, that these voices of The Maid are the voices of evil spirits tempting her to her damnation, it would not be very courteous to you, Master de Stogumber, or to the King of England, to assume that English is the devil's native language. So let it pass. The matter is not wholly omitted from the twelve articles. Pray take your places, gentlemen; and let us proceed to business.

All who have not taken their seats, do so.

THE CHAPLAIN. Well, I protest. That is all.

COURCELLES. I think it hard that all our work should go for nothing. It is only another example of the diabolical influence which this woman exercises over the court. [*He takes his chair, which is on the Chaplain's right*].

CAUCHON. Do you suggest that I am under diabolical influence?

COURCELLES. I suggest nothing, my lord. But it seems to me that there is a conspiracy here to hush up the fact that The Maid stole the Bishop of Senlis's horse.

CAUCHON [*keeping his temper with difficulty*] This is not a police court. Are we to waste our time on such rubbish?

COURCELLES [*rising, shocked*] My lord: do you call the Bishop's horse rubbish?

THE INQUISITOR [*blandly*] Master de Courcelles: The Maid alleges that she paid handsomely for the Bishop's horse, and that if he did not get the money the fault was not hers. As that may be true, the point is one on which The Maid may well be acquitted.

COURCELLES. Yes, if it were an ordinary horse. But the Bishop's horse! how can she be acquitted for that? [*He sits down again, bewildered and discouraged*].

THE INQUISITOR. I submit to you, with great respect, that if we persist in trying The Maid on trumpery issues on which we may have to declare her innocent, she may escape us on the great main issue of heresy, on which she seems so far to insist on her own guilt. I will ask you, therefore, to say nothing, when The Maid is brought before us, of these stealings of horses, and dancings round fairy trees with the village children, and prayings at haunted wells, and a dozen other things which you were diligently inquiring into until my arrival. There is not a village girl in France against whom you could not prove such things: they all dance round haunted trees, and pray at magic wells. Some of them would steal the Pope's horse if they got the chance. Heresy, gentlemen, heresy is the charge we have to try. The detection and suppression of heresy is my peculiar business: I am here as an inquisitor, not as an ordinary magistrate. Stick to the heresy, gentlemen; and leave the other matters alone.

CAUCHON. I may say that we have sent to the girl's village to make inquiries about her? and there is practically nothing serious against her.

THE CHAPLAIN ⎱ [*rising and* ⎰ Nothing serious, my lord—
COURCELLES ⎰ *clamoring* ⎱ What! The fairy tree not—
          ⎰ *together*] ⎱

CAUCHON [*out of patience*] Be silent, gentlemen; or speak one at a time.

Courcelles collapses into his chair, intimidated.

THE CHAPLAIN [*sulkily resuming his seat*] That is what The Maid said to us last Friday.

CAUCHON. I wish you had followed her counsel, sir. When I say nothing serious, I mean nothing that men of sufficiently large mind to conduct an inquiry like this would consider serious. I agree with my colleague the Inquisitor that it is on the count of heresy that we must proceed.

LADVENU [*a young but ascetically fine-drawn Dominican who is sitting next Courcelles, on his right*] But is there any great harm in the girl's heresy? Is it not merely her simplicity? Many saints have said as much as Joan.

THE INQUISITOR [*dropping his blandness and speaking very gravely*] Brother Martin: if you had seen what I have seen of heresy, you would not think it a light thing even in its most apparently harmless and even lovable and pious origins. Heresy begins with people who are to all appearance better than their neighbors. A gentle and pious girl, or a young man who has obeyed the command of our Lord by giving all his riches to the poor, and putting on the garb of poverty, the life of austerity, and the rule of humility and charity, may be the founder of a heresy that will wreck both Church and Empire if not ruthlessly stamped out in time. The records of the holy Inquisition are full of histories we dare not give to the world, because they are beyond the belief of honest men and innocent women; yet they all began with saintly simpletons. I have seen this again and again. Mark what I say: the woman who quarrels with her clothes, and puts on the dress of a man, is like the man who throws off his fur gown and dresses like John the Baptist: they are followed, as surely as the night follows the day, by bands of wild women and men who refuse to wear any clothes at all. When maids will neither marry nor take regular vows, and men reject marriage and exalt their lusts into divine inspirations, then, as surely as the summer follows the spring, they begin with polygamy, and end by incest. Heresy at first seems innocent and even laudable; but it ends in such a monstrous horror of unnatural wickedness that the most tender-hearted among you, if you saw it at work as I have seen it, would clamor against the mercy of the Church in dealing with it. For two hundred years the Holy Office has striven with these diabolical madnesses; and it knows that they begin always by vain and ignorant persons setting up their own judgment against the Church, and taking it upon themselves to be the interpreters of God's will. You must not fall into the common error of mistaking these simpletons for liars and hypocrites. They believe honestly and sincerely that their diabolical inspiration is divine. Therefore you must be on your guard against your natural compassion. You are all, I hope, merciful men: how else could you have devoted your lives to the service of our gentle Savior? You are going to see before you a young girl, pious and chaste; for I must tell you, gentlemen, that the things said of her by our English friends are supported by no evidence, whilst there is abundant testimony that her excesses have been excesses of religion and charity and not of worldliness and wantonness. This girl is not one of those whose hard features are the sign of hard hearts, and whose brazen looks and lewd demeanor condemn them before they are accused. The devilish pride that has led her into her present peril has left no mark on her countenance. Strange as it may seem to you, it has even left no mark on her character outside those special matters in which she is proud; so that you will see a diabolical pride and a natural humility seated side by side in the selfsame soul. Therefore be on your guard. God forbid that I should tell you to harden your hearts; for her punishment if we condemn her will be so cruel that we should forfeit our own hope of divine mercy were there one grain of malice against her in our hearts. But if you hate cruelty—and if any man here does not hate it I command him on his soul's salvation to quit this holy court—I say, if you hate cruelty, remember that nothing is so cruel in its consequences as the toleration of heresy. Remember also that no court of law can be so cruel as the common people are to those whom they suspect of heresy. The heretic in the hands of the Holy Office is safe from violence, is assured of a fair trial, and cannot suffer death, even when guilty, if repentance follows sin. Innumerable lives of heretics have been saved because the Holy Office has taken them out of the hands of the people, and because the people have yielded them up, knowing that the Holy Office would deal with them. Before the Holy Inquisition existed, and even now when its officers are not within reach, the unfortunate wretch suspected of heresy, perhaps quit ignorantly and unjustly, is stoned, torn in pieces, drowned, burned in his house with all his innocent children, without a trial, unshriven, unburied save as a dog is buried: all of them deeds hateful to God and most cruel to man. Gentlemen: I am compassionate by nature as well as by my profession; and though the work I have to do may seem cruel to those who do not know how much more cruel it would be to leave it undone, I would go to the stake myself sooner than do it if I did not know its righteousness, its necessity, its essential mercy. I ask you to address yourself to this trial in that conviction. Anger is a bad counsellor: cast out anger. Pity is sometimes worse: cast out pity. But do not cast out mercy. Remember only that justice comes first. Have you anything to say, my lord, before we proceed to trial?

CAUCHON. You have spoken for me, and spoken better than I could. I do not see how any sane man could disagree with a word that has fallen from you. But this I will add. The crude heresies of which you have told us are horrible; but their horror is like that of the black death: they rage for a while and then die out, because sound and sensible men will not under any incitement be reconciled to nakedness and incest and polygamy and the like.

But we are confronted today throughout Europe with a heresy
that is spreading among men not weak in mind nor diseased in
brain: nay, the stronger the mind, the more obstinate the heretic. It is neither discredited by fantastic extremes nor corrupted
by the common lusts of the flesh; but it, too, sets up the private
judgment of the single erring mortal against the considered
wisdom and experience of the Church. The mighty structure of
Catholic Christendom will never be shaken by naked madmen or
by the sins of Moab and Ammon.[4] But it may be betrayed from
within, and brought to barbarous ruin and desolation, by this
arch heresy which the English Commander calls Protestantism.

THE ASSESSORS [*whispering*] Protestantism! What was that?
What does the Bishop mean? Is it a new heresy? The English
Commander, he said. Did you ever hear of Protestantism? etc.,
etc.

CAUCHON [*continuing*] And that reminds me. What provision
has the Earl of Warwick made for the defence of the secular arm
should The Maid prove obdurate, and the people be moved to
pity her?

THE CHAPLAIN. Have no fear on that score, my lord. The noble earl
has eight hundred men-at-arms at the gates. She will not slip
through our English fingers even if the whole city be on her side.

CAUCHON [*revolted*] Will you not add, God grant that she repent
and purge her sin?

THE CHAPLAIN. That does not seem to me to be consistent; but of
course I agree with your lordship.

CAUCHON [*giving him up with a shrug of contempt*] The court
sits.

THE INQUISITOR. Let the accused be brought in.

LADVENU [*calling*] The accused. Let her be brought in.

> *Joan, chained by the ankles, is brought in through the
> arched door behind the prisoner's stool by a guard of Eng-
> lish soldiers. With them is the Executioner and his assist-
> ants. They lead her to the prisoner's stool, and place them-
> selves behind it after taking off her chain. She wears a
> page's black suit. Her long imprisonment and the strain of
> the examinations which have preceded the trial have left
> their mark on her; but her vitality still holds: She con-
> fronts the court unabashed, without a trace of the awe
> which their formal solemnity seems to require for the com-
> plete success of its impressiveness.*

THE INQUISITOR [*kindly*] Sit down, Joan. [*She sits on the prisoner's stool*]. You look very pale today. Are you not well?

JOAN. Thank you kindly: I am well enough. But the Bishop sent
me some carp; and it made me ill.

CAUCHON. I am sorry. I told them to see that it was fresh.

JOAN. You meant to be good to me, I know; but it is a fish that
does not agree with me. The English thought you were trying to
poison me—

4. Incest. These are the sons of Lot by his own daughters. (Genesis 19:30–38).

CAUCHON   } [*together*] {What!
THE CHAPLAIN }   {No, my lord.

JOAN [*continuing*] They are determined that I shall be burnt as
a witch; and they sent their doctor to cure me; but he was forbidden to bleed me because the silly people believe that a witch's
witchery leaves her if she is bled; so he only called me filthy
names. Why do you leave me in the hands of the English? I
should be in the hands of the Church. And why must I be
chained by the feet to a log of wood? Are you afraid I will fly
away?

D'ESTIVET [*harshly*] Woman: it is not for you to question the
court: it is for us to question you.

COURCELLES. When you were left unchained, did you not try to
escape by jumping from a tower sixty feet high? If you cannot fly
like a witch, how is it that you are still alive?

JOAN. I suppose because the tower was not so high then. It has
grown higher every day since you began asking me questions
about it.

D'ESTIVET. Why did you jump from the tower?

JOAN. How do you know that I jumped?

D'ESTIVET. You were found lying in the moat. Why did you leave
the tower?

JOAN. Why would anybody leave a prison if they could get out?

D'ESTIVET. You tried to escape?

JOAN. Of course I did; and not for the first time either. If you
leave the door of the cage open the bird will fly out.

D'ESTIVET [*rising*] That is a confession of heresy. I call the attention of the court to it.

JOAN. Heresy, he calls it! Am I a heretic because I try to escape
from prison?

D'ESTIVET. Assuredly, if you are in the hands of the Church, and
you wilfully take yourself out of its hands, you are deserting the
Church; and that is heresy.

JOAN. It is great nonsense. Nobody could be such a fool as to think
that.

D'ESTIVET. You hear, my lord, how I am reviled in the execution of
my duty by this woman. [*He sits down indignantly*].

CAUCHON. I have warned you before, Joan, that you are doing yourself no good by these pert answers.

JOAN. But you will not talk sense to me. I am reasonable if you
will be reasonable.

THE INQUISITOR [*interposing*] This is not yet in order. You
forget, Master Promoter, that the proceedings have not been formally opened. The time for questions is after she has sworn on
the Gospels to tell us the whole truth.

JOAN. You say this to me every time. I have said again and again
that I will tell you all that concerns this trial. But I cannot tell
you the whole truth: God does not allow the whole truth to be
told. You do not understand it when I tell it. It is an old saying
that he who tells too much truth is sure to be hanged. I am

weary of this argument: we have been over it nine times already. I have sworn as much as I will swear; and I will swear no more.

COURCELLES. My lord: she should be put to the torture.

THE INQUISITOR. You hear, Joan? That is what happens to the obdurate. Think before you answer. Has she been shewn the instruments?

THE EXECUTIONER. They are ready, my lord. She has seen them.

JOAN. If you tear me limb from limb until you separate my soul from my body you will get nothing out of me beyond what I have told you. What more is there to tell that you could understand? Besides, I cannot bear to be hurt; and if you hurt me I will say anything you like to stop the pain. But I will take it all back afterwards; so what is the use of it?

LADVENU. There is much in that. We should proceed mercifully.

COURCELLES. But the torture is customary.

THE INQUISITOR. It must not be applied wantonly. If the accused will confess voluntarily, then its use cannot be justified.

COURCELLES. But this is unusual and irregular. She refuses to take the oath.

LADVENU [*disgusted*] Do you want to torture the girl for the mere pleasure of it?

COURCELLES [*bewildered*] But it is not a pleasure. It is the law. It is customary. It is always done.

THE INQUISITOR. That is not so, Master, except when the inquiries are carried on by people who do not know their legal business.

COURCELLES. But the woman is a heretic. I assure you it is always done.

CAUCHON [*decisively*] It will not be done today if it is not necessary. Let there be an end of this. I will not have it said that we proceeded on forced confessions. We have sent our best preachers and doctors to this woman to exhort and implore her to save her soul and body from the fire: we shall not now send the executioner to thrust her into it.

COURCELLES. Your lordship is merciful, of course. But it is a great responsibility to depart from the usual practice.

JOAN. Thou art a rare noodle, Master. Do what was done last time is thy rule, eh?

COURCELLES [*rising*] Thou wanton: dost thou dare call me noodle?

THE INQUISITOR. Patience, Master, patience: I fear you will soon be only too terribly avenged.

COURCELLES [*mutters*] Noodle indeed! [*He sits down, much discontented*].

THE INQUISITOR. Meanwhile, let us not be moved by the rough side of a shepherd lass's tongue.

JOAN. Nay: I am no shepherd lass, though I have helped with the sheep like anyone else. I will do a lady's work in the house—spin or weave—against any woman in Rouen.

THE INQUISITOR. This is not a time for vanity, Joan. You stand in great peril.

JOAN. I know it: have I not been punished for my vanity? If I had not worn my cloth of gold surcoat in battle like a fool, that Burgundian soldier would never have pulled me backwards off my horse; and I should not have been here.

THE CHAPLAIN. If you are so clever at woman's work why do you not stay at home and do it?

JOAN. There are plenty of other women to do it; but there is nobody to do my work.

CAUCHON. Come! we are wasting time on trifles. Joan: I am going to put a most solemn question to you. Take care how you answer; for your life and salvation are at stake on it. Will you for all you have said and done, be it good or bad, accept the judgment of God's Church on earth? More especially as to the acts and words that are imputed to you in this trial by the Promoter here, will you submit your case to the inspired interpretation of the Church Militant?

JOAN. I am a faithful child of the Church. I will obey the Church—

CAUCHON [*hopefully leaning forward*] You will?

JOAN. —provided it does not command anything impossible.
> *Cauchon sinks back in his chair with a heavy sigh. The Inquisitor purses his lips and frowns. Ladvenu shakes his head pitifully.*

D'ESTIVET. She imputes to the Church the error and folly of commanding the impossible.

JOAN. If you command me to declare that all that I have done and said, and all the visions and revelations I have had, were not from God, then that is impossible: I will not declare it for anything in the world. What God made me do I will never go back on; and what He has commanded or shall command I will not fail to do in spite of any man alive. That is what I mean by impossible. And in case the Church should bid me do anything contrary to the command I have from God, I will not consent to it, no matter what it may be.

THE ASSESSORS [*shocked and indignant*] Oh! The Church contrary to God! What do you say now? Flat heresy. This is beyond everything, etc., etc.

D'ESTIVET [*throwing down his brief*] My lord: do you need anything more than this?

CAUCHON. Woman: you have said enough to burn ten heretics. Will you not be warned? Will you not understand?

THE INQUISITOR. If the Church Militant tells you that your revelations and visions are sent by the devil to tempt you to your damnation, will you not believe that the Church is wiser than you?

JOAN. I believe that God is wiser than I; and it is His commands that I will do. All the things that you call my crimes have come to me by the command of God. I say that I have done them by the order of God: it is impossible for me to say anything else. If any Churchman says the contrary I shall not mind him: I shall mind God alone, whose command I always follow.

LADVENU [*pleading with her urgently*] You do not know what you are saying, child. Do you want to kill yourself? Listen. Do you not believe that you are subject to the Church of God on earth?

JOAN. Yes. When have I ever denied it?

LADVENU. Good. That means, does it not, that you are subject to our Lord the Pope, to the cardinals, the archbishops, and the bishops for whom his lordship stands here today?

JOAN. God must be served first.

D'ESTIVET. Then your voices command you not to submit yourself to the Church Militant?

JOAN. My voices do not tell me to disobey the Church; but God must be served first.

CAUCHON. And you, and not the Church, are to be the judge?

JOAN. What other judgment can I judge by but my own?

THE ASSESSORS [*scandalized*] Oh! [*They cannot find words*].

CAUCHON. Out of your own mouth you have condemned yourself. We have striven for your salvation to the verge of sinning ourselves: we have opened the door to you again and again; and you have shut it in our faces and in the face of God. Dare you pretend, after what you have said, that you are in a state of grace?

JOAN. If I am not, may God bring me to it: if I am, may God keep me in it!

LADVENU. That is a very good reply, my lord.

COURCELLES. Were you in a state of grace when you stole the Bishop's horse?

CAUCHON [*rising in a fury*] Oh, devil take the Bishop's horse and you too! We are here to try a case of heresy; and no sooner do we come to the root of the matter than we are thrown back by idiots who understand nothing but horses. [*Trembling with rage, he forces himself to sit down*].

THE INQUISITOR. Gentlemen, gentlemen: in clinging to these small issues you are The Maid's best advocates. I am not surprised that his lordship has lost patience with you. What does the Promoter say? Does he press these trumpery matters?

D'ESTIVET. I am bound by my office to press everything; but when the woman confesses a heresy that must bring upon her the doom of excommunication, of what consequence is it that she has been guilty also of offences which expose her to minor penances? I share the impatience of his lordship as to these minor charges. Only, with great respect, I must emphasize the gravity of two very horrible and blasphemous crimes which she does not deny. First, she has intercourse with evil spirits, and is therefore a sorceress. Second, she wears men's clothes, which is indecent, unnatural, and abominable; and in spite of our most earnest remonstrances and entreaties, she will not change them even to receive the sacrament.

JOAN. Is the blessed St Catherine an evil spirit? Is St Margaret? Is Michael the Archangel?

COURCELLES. How do you know that the spirit which appears to you is an archangel? Does he not appear to you as a naked man?

JOAN. Do you think God cannot afford clothes for him?

The assessors cannot help smiling, especially as the joke is against Courcelles.

LADVENU. Well answered, Joan.

THE INQUISITOR. It is, in effect, well answered. But no evil spirit would be so simple as to appear to a young girl in a guise that would scandalize her when he meant her to take him for a messenger from the Most High? Joan: the Church instructs you that these apparitions are demons seeking your soul's perdition. Do you accept the instruction of the Church?

JOAN. I accept the messenger of God. How could any faithful believer in the Church refuse him?

CAUCHON. Wretched woman: again I ask you, do you know what you are saying?

THE INQUISITOR. You wrestle in vain with the devil for her soul, my lord: she will not be saved. Now as to this matter of the man's dress. For the last time, will you put off that impudent attire, and dress as becomes your sex?

JOAN. I will not.

D'ESTIVET [*pouncing*] The sin of disobedience, my lord.

JOAN [*distressed*] But my voices tell me I must dress as a soldier.

LADVENU. Joan, Joan: does not that prove to you that the voices are the voices of evil spirits? Can you suggest to us one good reason why an angel of God should give you such shameless advice?

JOAN. Why, yes: what can be plainer commonsense? I was a soldier living among soldiers. I am a prisoner guarded by soldiers. If I were to dress as a woman they would think of me as a woman; and then what would become of me? If I dress as a soldier they think of me as a soldier, and I can live with them as I do at home with my brothers. That is why St Catherine tells me I must not dress as a woman until she gives me leave.

COURCELLES. When will she give you leave?

JOAN. When you take me out of the hands of the English soldiers. I have told you that I should be in the hands of the Church, and not left night and day with four soldiers of the Earl of Warwick. Do you want me to live with them in petticoats?

LADVENU. My lord: what she says is, God knows, very wrong and shocking; but there is a grain of worldly sense in it such as might impose on a simple village maiden.

JOAN. If we were as simple in the village as you are in your courts and palaces, there would soon be no wheat to make bread for you.

CAUCHON. That is the thanks you get for trying to save her, Brother Martin.

LADVENU. Joan: we are all trying to save you. His lordship is trying to save you. The Inquisitor could not be more just to you if you were his own daughter. But you are blinded by a terrible pride and self-sufficiency.

JOAN. Why do you say that? I have said nothing wrong. I cannot understand.

THE INQUISITOR. The blessed St Athanasius[5] has laid it down in his creed that those who cannot understand are damned. It is not enough to be simple. It is not enough even to be what simple people call good. The simplicity of a darkened mind is no better than the simplicity of a beast.

JOAN. There is great wisdom in the simplicity of a beast, let me tell you; and sometimes great foolishness in the wisdom of scholars.

LADVENU. We know that, Joan: we are not so foolish as you think us. Try to resist the temptation to make pert replies to us. Do you see that man who stands behind you [*he indicates the Executioner*]?

JOAN [*turning and looking at the man*] Your torturer? But the Bishop said I was not to be tortured.

LADVENU. You are not to be tortured because you have confessed everything that is necessary to your condemnation. That man is not only the torturer: he is also the Executioner. Executioner: let The Maid hear your answers to my questions. Are you prepared for the burning of a heretic this day?

THE EXECUTIONER. Yes, Master.

LADVENU. Is the stake ready?

THE EXECUTIONER. It is. In the market-place. The English have built it too high for me to get near her and make the death easier. It will be a cruel death.

JOAN [*horrified*] But you are not going to burn me now?

THE INQUISITOR. You realize it at last.

LADVENU. There are eight hundred English soldiers waiting to take you to the market-place the moment the sentence of excommunication has passed the lips of your judges. You are within a few short moments of that doom.

JOAN [*looking round desperately for rescue*] Oh God!

LADVENU. Do not despair, Joan. The Church is merciful. You can save yourself.

JOAN [*hopefully*] Yes: my voices promised me I should not be burnt. St Catherine bade me be bold.

CAUCHON. Woman: are you quite mad? Do you not yet see that your voices have deceived you?

JOAN. Oh no: that is impossible.

CAUCHON. Impossible! They have led you straight to your excommunication, and to the stake which is there waiting for you.

LADVENU [*pressing the point hard*] Have they kept a single promise to you since you were taken at Compiègne? The devil has betrayed you. The Church holds out its arms to you.

JOAN [*despairing*] Oh, it is true: it is true: my voices have deceived me. I have been mocked by devils: my faith is broken. I

5. In the translation of J. D. N. Kelly, D.D., the Athanasian Creed begins: "Whoever desires to be saved must above all things hold the Catholic faith. Unless a man keeps it in its entirety inviolate, he will assuredly perish eternally."

have dared and dared; but only a fool will walk into a fire: God, who gave me my commonsense, cannot will me to do that.

LADVENU. Now God be praised that He has saved you at the eleventh hour! [*He hurries to the vacant seat at the scribes' table, and snatches a sheet of paper, on which he sets to work writing eagerly*].

CAUCHON. Amen!

JOAN. What must I do?

CAUCHON. You must sign a solemn recantation of your heresy.

JOAN. Sign? That means to write my name. I cannot write.

CAUCHON. You have signed many letters before.

JOAN. Yes; but someone held my hand and guided the pen. I can make my mark.

THE CHAPLAIN [*who has been listening with growing alarm and indignation*] My lord: do you mean that you are going to allow this woman to escape us?

THE INQUISITOR. The law must take its course, Master de Stogumber. And you know the law.

THE CHAPLAIN [*rising, purple with fury*] I know that there is no faith in a Frenchman. [*Tumult, which he shouts down*]. I know what my lord the Cardinal of Winchester will say when he hears of this. I know what the Earl of Warwick will do when he learns that you intend to betray him. There are eight hundred men at the gate who will see that this abominable witch is burnt in spite of your teeth.

THE ASSESSORS [*meanwhile*] What is this? What did he say? He accuses us of treachery! This is past bearing. No faith in a Frenchman! Did you hear that? This is an intolerable fellow. Who is he? Is this what English Churchmen are like? He must be mad or drunk, etc., etc.

THE INQUISITOR [*rising*] Silence, pray! Gentlemen: pray silence! Master Chaplain: bethink you a moment of your holy office: of what you are, and where you are. I direct you to sit down.

THE CHAPLAIN [*folding his arms doggedly, his face working convulsively*] I will NOT sit down.

CAUCHON. Master Inquisitor: this man has called me a traitor to my face before now.

THE CHAPLAIN. So you are a traitor. You are all traitors. You have been doing nothing but begging this damnable witch on your knees to recant all through this trial.

THE INQUISITOR [*placidly resuming his seat*] If you will not sit, you must stand: that is all.

THE CHAPLAIN. I will NOT stand [*he flings himself back into his chair*].

LADVENU [*rising with the paper in his hand*] My lord: here is the form of recantation for The Maid to sign.

CAUCHON. Read it to her.

JOAN. Do not trouble. I will sign it.

THE INQUISITOR. Woman: you must know what you are putting your hand to. Read it to her, Brother Martin. And let all be silent.

LADVENU [*reading quietly*] "I, Joan, commonly called The Maid, a miserable sinner, do confess that I have most grievously sinned in the following articles. I have pretended to have revelations from God and the angels and the blessed saints, and perversely rejected the Church's warnings that these were temptations by demons. I have blasphemed abominably by wearing an immodest dress, contrary to the Holy Scripture and the canons of the Church. Also I have clipped my hair in the style of a man, and, against all the duties which have made my sex specially acceptable in heaven, have taken up the sword, even to the shedding of human blood, inciting men to slay each other, invoking evil spirits to delude them, and stubbornly and most blasphemously imputing these sins to Almighty God. I confess to the sin of sedition, to the sin of idolatry, to the sin of disobedience, to the sin of pride, and to the sin of heresy. All of which sins I now renounce and abjure and depart from, humbly thanking you Doctors and Masters who have brought me back to the truth and into the grace of our Lord. And I will never return to my errors, but will remain in communion with our Holy Church and in obedience to our Holy Father the Pope of Rome. All this I swear by God Almighty and the Holy Gospels, in witness whereto I sign my name to this recantation."

THE INQUISITOR. You understand this, Joan?

JOAN [*listless*] It is plain enough, sir.

THE INQUISITOR. And it is true?

JOAN. It may be true. If it were not true, the fire would not be ready for me in the market-place.

LADVENUE [*taking up his pen and a book, and going to her quickly lest she should compromise herself again*] Come, child: let me guide your hand. Take the pen. [*She does so; and they begin to write, using the book as a desk*] J.E.H.A.N.E. So. Now make your mark by yourself.

JOAN [*makes her mark, and gives him back the pen, tormented by the rebellion of her soul against her mind and body*] There!

LADVENU [*replacing the pen on the table, and handing the recantation to Cauchon with a reverence*] Praise be to God, my brothers, the lamb has returned to the flock; and the shepherd rejoices in her more than in ninety and nine just persons. [*He returns to his seat*].

THE INQUISITOR [*taking the paper from Cauchon*] We declare thee by this act set free from the danger of excommunication in which thou stoodest. [*He throws the paper down to the table*].

JOAN. I thank you.

THE INQUISITOR. But because thou hast sinned most presumptuously against God and the Holy Church, and that thou mayst repent thy errors in solitary contemplation, and be shielded from all temptation to return to them, we, for the good of thy soul, and for a penance that may wipe out thy sins and bring thee finally unspotted to the throne of grace, do condemn thee to eat the bread of sorrow and drink the water of affliction to the end of thy earthly days in perpetual imprisonment.

JOAN [*rising in consternation and terrible anger*] Perpetual imprisonment! Am I not then to be set free?

LADVENU [*mildly shocked*] Set free, child, after such wickedness as yours! What are you dreaming of?

JOAN. Give me that writing. [*She rushes to the table; snatches up the paper; and tears it into fragments*] Light your fire: do you think I dread it as much as he life of a rat in a hole? My voices were right.

LADVENU. Joan! Joan!

JOAN. Yes: they told me you were fools [*the word gives great offence*], and that I was not to listen to your fine words nor trust to your charity. You promised me my life; but you lied [*indignant exclamations*]. You think that life is nothing but not being stone dead. It is not the bread and water I fear: I can live on bread: when have I asked for more? It is no hardship to drink water if the water be clean. Bread has no sorrow for me, and water no affliction. But to shut me from the light of the sky and the sight of the fields and flowers; to chain my feet so that I can never again ride with the soldiers nor climb the hills; to make me breathe foul damp darkness, and keep from me everything that brings me back to the love of God when your wickedness and foolishness tempt me to hate Him: all this is worse than the furnace in the Bible that was heated seven times. I could do without my warhorse; I could drag about in a skirt; I could let the banners and the trumpets and the knights and soldiers pass me and leave me behind as they leave the other women, if only I could still hear the wind in the trees, the larks in the sunshine, the young lambs crying through the healthy frost, and the blessed blessed church bells that send my angel voices floating to me on the wind. But without these things I cannot live; and by your wanting to take them away from me, or from any human creature, I know that your counsel is of the devil, and that mine is of God.

THE ASSESSORS [*in great commotion*] Blasphemy! blasphemy! She is possessed. She said our counsel was of the devil. And hers of God. Monstrous! The devil is in our midst, etc., etc.

D'ESTIVET [*shouting above the din*] She is a relapsed heretic, obstinate, incorrigible, and altogether unworthy of the mercy we have shewn her. I call for her excommunication.

THE CHAPLAIN [*to the Executioner*] Light your fire, man. To the stake with her.

> *The Executioner and his assistants hurry out through the courtyard.*

LADVENU. You wicked girl: if your counsel were of God would He not deliver you?

JOAN. His ways are not your ways. He wills that I go through the fire to His bosom; for I am His child, and you are not fit that I should live among you. This is my last word to you.

> *The soldiers seize her.*

CAUCHON [*rising*] Not yet.

They wait. There is a dead silence. Cauchon turns to the Inquisitor with an inquiring look. The Inquisitor nods affirmatively. They rise solemnly, and intone the sentence antiphonally.

CAUCHON. We decree that thou art a relapsed heretic.

THE INQUISITOR. Cast out from the unity of the Church.

CAUCHON. Sundered from her body.

THE INQUISITOR. Infected with the leprosy of heresy.

CAUCHON. A member of Satan.

THE INQUISITOR. We declare that thou must be excommunicate.

CAUCHON. And now we do cast thee out, segregate thee, and abandon thee to the secular power.

THE INQUISITOR. Admonishing the same secular power that it moderate its judgment of thee in respect of death and division of the limbs. [*He resumes his seat*].

CAUCHON. And if any true sign of penitence appear in thee, to permit our Brother Martin to administer to thee the sacrament of penance.

THE CHAPLAIN. Into the fire with the witch [*he rushes at her, and helps the soldiers to push her out*].

    Joan is taken away from the courtyard. The assessors rise in disorder, and follow the soldiers, except Ladvenu, who has hidden his face in his hands.

CAUCHON [*rising again in the act of sitting down*] No, no: this is irregular. The representative of the secular arm should be here to receive her from us.

THE INQUISITOR [*also on his feet again*] That man is an incorrigible fool.

CAUCHON. Brother Martin: see that everything is done in order.

LADVENU. My place is at her side, my lord. You must exercise your own authority. [*He hurries out*].

CAUCHON. These English are impossible: they will thrust her straight into the fire. Look!

    He points to the courtyard, in which the glow and flicker of fire can now be seen reddening the May daylight. Only the Bishop and the Inquisitor are left in the court.

CAUCHON [*turning to go*] We must stop that.

THE INQUISITOR [*calmly*] Yes; but not too fast, my lord.

CAUCHON [*halting*] But there is not a moment to lose.

THE INQUISITOR. We have proceeded in perfect order. If the English choose to put themselves in the wrong, it is not our business to put them in the right. A flaw in the procedure may be useful later on: one never knows. And the sooner it is over, the better for that poor girl.

CAUCHON [*relaxing*] That is true. But I suppose we must see this dreadful thing through.

THE INQUISITOR. One gets used to it. Habit is everything. I am accustomed to the fire: it is soon over. But it is a terrible thing to see a young and innocent creature crushed between these mighty forces, the Church and the Law.

CAUCHON. You call her innocent!

THE INQUISITOR. Oh, quite innocent. What does she know of the Church and the Law? She did not understand a word we were saying. It is the ignorant who suffer. Come, or we shall be late for the end.

CAUCHON [*going with him*] I shall not be sorry if we are: I am not so accustomed as you.

> *They are going out when Warwick comes in, meeting them.*

WARWICK. Oh, I am intruding. I thought it was all over. [*He makes a feint of retiring*].

CAUCHON. Do not go, my lord. It is all over.

THE INQUISITOR. The execution is not in our hands, my lord; but it is desirable that we should witness the end. So by your leave— [*He bows, and goes out through the courtyard*].

CAUCHON. There is some doubt whether your people have observed the forms of law, my lord.

WARWICK. I am told that there is some doubt whether your authority runs in this city, my lord. It is not in your diocese. However, if you will answer for that I will answer for the rest.

CAUCHON. It is to God that we both must answer. Good morning, my lord.

WARWICK. My lord: good morning.

> *They look at one another for a moment with unconcealed hostility. Then Cauchon follows the Inquisitor out. Warwick looks round. Finding himself alone, he calls for attendance.*

WARWICK. Hallo: some attendance here! [*Silence*]. Hallo, there! [*Silence*]. Hallo! Brian, you young blackguard, where are you? [*Silence*]. Guard! [*Silence*]. They have all gone to see the burning: even that child.

> *The silence is broken by someone frantically howling and sobbing.*

WARWICK. What in the devil's name—?

> *The Chaplain staggers in from the courtyard like a demented creature, his face streaming with tears, making the piteous sounds that Warwick has heard. He stumbles to the prisoner's stool, and throws himself upon it with heart-rending sobs.*

WARWICK [*going to him and patting him on the shoulder*] What is it, Master John? What is the matter?

THE CHAPLAIN [*clutching at his hands*] My lord, my lord: for Christ's sake pray for my wretched guilty soul.

WARWICK [*soothing him*] Yes, yes: of course I will. Calmly, gently—

THE CHAPLAIN [*blubbering miserably*] I am not a bad man, my lord.

WARWICK. No, no: not at all.

THE CHAPLAIN I meant no harm. I did not know what it would be like.

WARWICK [*hardening*] Oh! You saw it, then?

THE CHAPLAIN. I did not know what I was doing. I am a hot-headed fool; and I shall be damned to all eternity for it.

WARWICK. Nonsense! Very distressing, no doubt; but it was not your doing.

THE CHAPLAIN [*lamentably*] I let them do it. If I had known, I would have torn her from their hands. You dont know: you havnt seen: it is so easy to talk when you dont know. You madden yourself with words: you damn yourself because it feels grand to throw oil on the flaming hell of your own temper. But when it is brought home to you; when you see the thing you have done; when it is blinding your eyes, stifling your nostrils, tearing your heart, then—then— [*Falling on his knees*] O God, take away this sight from me! O Christ, deliver me from this fire that is consuming me! She cried to Thee in the midst of it: Jesus! Jesus! Jesus! She is in Thy bosom; and I am in hell for evermore.

WARWICK [*summarily hauling him to his feet*] Come come, man! you must pull yourself together. We shall have the whole town talking of this. [*He throws him not too gently into a chair at the table*] If you have not the nerve to see these things, why do you not do as I do, and stay away?

THE CHAPLAIN [*bewildered and submissive*] She asked for a cross. A soldier gave her two sticks tied together. Thank God he was an Englishman! I might have done it; but I did not: I am a coward, a mad dog, a fool. But he was an Englishman too.

WARWICK. The fool! they will burn him too if the priests get hold of him.

THE CHAPLAIN [*shaken with a convulsion*] Some of the people laughed at her. They would have laughed at Christ. They were French people, my lord: I know they were French.

WARWICK. Hush! someone is coming. Control yourself.

> *Ladvenu comes back through the courtyard to Warwick's right hand, carrying a bishop's cross which he has taken from a church. He is very grave and composed.*

WARWICK. I am informed that it is all over, Brother Martin.

LADVENU [*enigmatically*] We do not know, my lord. It may have only just begun.

WARWICK. What does that mean, exactly?

LADVENU. I took this cross from the church for her that she might see it to the last: she had only two sticks that she put into her bosom. When the fire crept round us, and she saw that if I held the cross before her I should be burnt myself, she warned me to get down and save myself. My lord: a girl who could think of another's danger in such a moment was not inspired by the devil. When I had to snatch the cross from her sight, she looked up to heaven. And I do not believe that the heavens were empty. I firmly believe that her Savior appeared to her then in His tenderest glory. She called to Him and died. This is not the end for her, but the beginning.

WARWICK. I am afraid it will have a bad effect on the people.

LADVENU. It had, my lord, on some of them. I heard laughter. Forgive me for saying that I hope and believe it was English laughter.

THE CHAPLAIN [*rising frantically*] No: it was not. There was only one Englishman there that disgraced his country; and that was the mad dog, de Stogumber. [*He rushes wildly out, shrieking*] Let them torture him. Let them burn him. I will go pray among her ashes. I am no better than Judas: I will hang myself.

WARWICK. Quick, Brother Martin: follow him: he will do himself some mischief. After him, quick.

> *Ladvenu hurries out, Warwick urging him. The Executioner comes in by the door behind the judges' chairs; and Warwick, returning, finds himself face to face with him.*

WARWICK. Well, fellow: who are you?

THE EXECUTIONER [*with dignity*] I am not addressed as fellow, my lord. I am the Master Executioner of Rouen: it is a highly skilled mystery. I am come to tell your lordship that your orders have been obeyed.

WARWICK. I crave your pardon, Master Executioner; and I will see that you lose nothing by having no relics to sell. I have your word, have I, that nothing remains, not a bone, not a nail, not a hair?

THE EXECUTIONER. Her heart would not burn, my lord; but everything that was left is at the bottom of the river. You have heard the last of her.

WARWICK [*with a wry smile, thinking of what Ladvenu said*] The last of her? Hm! I wonder!

Epilogue

A restless fitfully windy night in June, 1456, full of summer lightning after many days of heat. King Charles the Seventh of France, formerly Joan's Dauphin, now Charles the Victorious, aged 51, is in bed in one of his royal chateaux. The bed, raised on a dais of two steps, is towards the side of the room so as to avoid blocking a tall lancet window in the middle. Its canopy bears the royal arms in embroidery. Except for the canopy and the huge down pillows there is nothing to distinguish it from a broad settee with bedclothes and a valance. Thus its occupant is in full view from the foot.

Charles is not asleep: he is reading in bed, or rather looking at the pictures in Fouquet's Boccaccio with his knees doubled up to make a reading desk. Beside the bed on his left is a little table with a picture of the Virgin, lighted by candles of painted wax. The walls are hung from ceiling to floor with painted curtains which stir at times in the draughts. At first glance the prevailing yellow and red in these hanging pictures is somewhat flamelike when the folds breathe in the wind.

The door is on Charles's left, but in front of him close to the corner farthest from him. A large watchman's rattle, handsomely designed and gaily painted, is in the bed under his hand.

Charles turns a leaf. A distant clock strikes the half-hour softly. Charles shuts the book with a clap; throws it aside; snatches up the rattle; and whirls it energetically, making a deafening clatter. Ladvenu enters, 25 years older, strange and stark in bearing, and still carrying the cross from Rouen. Charles evidently does not expect him; for he springs out of bed on the farther side from the door.

CHARLES. Who are you? Where is my gentleman of the bedchamber? What do you want?

LADVENU [*solemnly*] I bring you glad tidings of great joy. Rejoice, O king; for the taint is removed from your blood, and the stain from your crown. Justice, long delayed, is at last triumphant.

CHARLES. What are you talking about? Who are you?

LADVENU. I am brother Martin.

CHARLES. And who, saving your reverence, may Brother Martin be?

LADVENU. I held this cross when The Maid perished in the fire. Twenty-five years have passed since then: nearly ten thousand days. And on every one of those days I have prayed God to justify His daughter on earth as she is justified in heaven.

CHARLES [*reassured, sitting down on the foot of the bed*] Oh, I remember now. I have heard of you. You have a bee in your bonnet about The Maid. Have you been at the inquiry?

LADVENU. I have given my testimony.

CHARLES. Is it over?

LADVENU. It is over.

CHARLES. Satisfactorily?

LADVENU. The ways of God are very strange.

CHARLES. How so?

LADVENU. At the trial which sent a saint to the stake as a heretic and a sorceress, the truth was told; the law was upheld; mercy was shewn beyond all custom; no wrong was done but the final and dreadful wrong of the lying sentence and the pitiless fire. At this inquiry from which I have just come, there was shameless perjury, courtly corruption, calumny of the dead who did their duty according to their lights, cowardly evasion of the issue, testimony made of idle tales that could not impose on a ploughboy. Yet out of this insult to justice, this defamation of the Church, this orgy of lying and foolishness, the truth is set in the noonday sun on the hilltop; the white robe of innocence is cleansed from the smirch of the burning faggots; the holy life is sanctified; the true heart that lived through the flame is consecrated; a great lie is silenced for ever; and a great wrong is set right before all men.

CHARLES. My friend: provided they can no longer say that I was crowned by a witch and a heretic, I shall not fuss about how the trick has been done. Joan would not have fussed about it if it came all right in the end: she was not that sort: I knew her. Is her rehabilitation complete? I made it pretty clear that there was to be no nonsense about it.

LADVENU. It is solemnly declared that her judges were full of corruption, cozenage, fraud, and malice. Four falsehoods.

CHARLES. Never mind the falsehoods: her judges are dead.

LADVENU. The sentence on her is broken, annulled, annihilated, set aside as non-existent, without value or effect.

CHARLES. Good. Nobody can challenge my consecration now, can they?

LADVENU. Not Charlemagne nor King David himself was more sacredly crowned.

CHARLES [*rising*] Excellent. Think of what that means to me!

LADVENU. I think of what it means to her!

CHARLES. You cannot. None of us ever knew what anything meant to her. She was like nobody else; and she must take care of herself wherever she is; for *I* cannot take care of her; and neither can you, whatever you may think: you are not big enough. But I will tell you this about her. If you could bring her back to life, they would burn her again within six months, for all their present adoration of her. And you would hold up the cross, too, just the same. So [*crossing himself*] let her rest; and let you and I mind our own business, and not meddle with hers.

LADVENU. God forbid that I should have no share in her, nor she in me! [*He turns and strides out as he came, saying*] Henceforth my path will not lie through palaces, nor my conversation be with kings.

CHARLES [*following him towards the door, and shouting after him*] Much good may it do you, holy man! [*He returns to the middle of the chamber, where he halts, and says quizzically to*

himself] That was a funny chap. How did he get in? Where
are my people? [*He goes impatiently to the bed, and swings the
rattle. A rush of wind through the open door sets the walls sway-
ing agitatedly. The candles go out. He calls in the darkness*]
Hallo! Someone come and shut the windows: everything is being
blown all over the place. [*A flash of summer lightning shews up
the lancet window. A figure is seen in silhouette against it*]
Who is there? Who is that? Help! Murder! [*Thunder. He
jumps into bed, and hides under the clothes*].

JOAN'S VOICE. Easy, Charlie, easy. What art making all that noise
for? No one can hear thee. Thourt asleep. [*She is dimly seen in
a pallid greenish light by the bedside*].

CHARLES [*peeping out*] Joan! Are you a ghost, Joan?

JOAN. Hardly even that, lad. Can a poor burnt-up lass have a
ghost? I am but a dream that thourt dreaming. [*The light
increases: they become plainly visible as he sits up*] Thou looks
older, lad.

CHARLES. I a m older. Am I really asleep?

JOAN. Fallen asleep over thy silly book.

CHARLES. That's funny.

JOAN. Not so funny as that I am dead, is it?

CHARLES. Are you really dead?

JOAN. As dead as anybody ever is, laddie. I am out of the body.

CHARLES. Just fancy! Did it hurt much?

JOAN. Did what hurt much?

CHARLES. Being burnt.

JOAN. Oh, that! I cannot remember very well. I think it did at
first; but then it all got mixed up; and I was not in my right
mind until I was free of the body. But do not thou go handling
fire and thinking it will not hurt thee. How hast been ever since?

CHARLES. Oh, not so bad. Do you know, I actually lead my army
out and win battles? Down into the moat up to my waist in mud
and blood. Up the ladders with the stones and hot pitch raining
down. Like you.

JOAN. No! Did I make a man of thee after all, Charlie?

CHARLES. I am Charles the Victorious now. I had to be brave
because you were. Agnes put a little pluck into me too.

JOAN. Agnes! Who was Agnes?

CHARLES. Agnes Sorel. A woman I fell in love with. I dream of her
often. I never dreamed of you before.

JOAN. Is she dead, like me?

CHARLES. Yes. But she was not like you. She was very beautiful.

JOAN [*laughing heartily*] Ha ha! I was no beauty: I was always a
rough one: a regular soldier. I might almost as well have been a
man. Pity I wasnt: I should not have bothered you all so much
then. But my head was in the skies; and the glory of God was
upon me; and, man or woman, I should have bothered you as
long as your noses were in the mud. Now tell me what has happened since you wise men knew no better than to make a heap
of cinders of me?

CHARLES. Your mother and brothers have sued the courts to have your case tried over again. And the courts have declared that your judges were full of corruption and cozenage, fraud and malice.

JOAN. Not they. They were as honest a lot of poor fools as ever burned their betters.

CHARLES. The sentence on you is broken, annihilated, annulled: null, non-existent, without value or effect.

JOAN. I was burned, all the same. Can they unburn me?

CHARLES. If they could, they would think twice before they did it. But they have decreed that a beautiful cross be placed where the stake stood, for your perpetual memory and for your salvation.

JOAN. It is the memory and the salvation that sanctify the cross, not the cross that sanctifies the memory and the salvation. [*She turns away, forgetting him*] I shall outlast that cross. I shall be remembered when men will have forgotten where Rouen stood.

CHARLES. There you go with your self-conceit, the same as ever! I think you might say a word of thanks to me for having had justice done at last.

CAUCHON [*appearing at the window between them*] Liar!

CHARLES. Thank you.

JOAN. Why, if it isnt Peter Cauchon! How are you, Peter? What luck have you had since you burned me?

CAUCHON. None. I arraign the justice of Man. It is not the justice of God.

JOAN. Still dreaming of justice, Peter? See what justice came to with me! But what has happened to thee? Art dead or alive?

CAUCHON. Dead. Dishonored. They pursued me beyond the grave. They excommunicated my dead body: they dug it up and flung it into the common sewer.

JOAN. Your dead body did not feel the spade and the sewer as my live body felt the fire.

CAUCHON. But this thing that they have done against me hurts justice; destroys faith; saps the foundation of the Church. The solid earth sways like the treacherous sea beneath the feet of men and spirits alike when the innocent are slain in the name of law, and their wrongs are undone by slandering the pure of heart.

JOAN. Well, well, Peter, I hope men will be the better for remembering me; and they would not remember me so well if you had not burned me.

CAUCHON. They will be the worse for remembering me: they will see in me evil triumphing over good, falsehood over truth, cruelty over mercy, hell over heaven. Their courage will rise as they think of you, only to faint as they think of me. Yet God is my witness I was just: I was merciful: I was faithful to my light: I could do no other than I did.

CHARLES [*scrambling out of the sheets and enthroning himself on the side of the bed*] Yes: it is always you good men that do the big mischiefs. Look at me! I am not Charles the Good, nor Charles the Wise, nor Charles the Bold. Joan's worshippers may even call me Charles the Coward because I did not pull her out of the fire. But I have done less harm than any of you. You people with your heads in the sky spend all your time trying to turn the world upside down; but I take the world as it is, and say that top-side-up is right-side-up; and I keep my nose pretty close to the ground. And I ask you, what king of France has done better, or been a better fellow in his little way?

JOAN. Art really king of France, Charlie? Be the English gone?

DUNOIS [*coming through the tapestry on Joan's left, the candles relighting themselves at the same moment, and illuminating his armor and surcoat cheerfully*] I have kept my word: the English are gone.

JOAN. Praised be God! now is fair France a province in heaven. Tell me all about the fighting, Jack. Was it thou that led them? Wert thou God's captain to thy death?

DUNOIS. I am not dead. My body is very comfortably asleep in my bed at Chateaudun; but my spirit is called here by yours.

JOAN. And you fought them my way, Jack: eh? Not the old way, chaffering for ransoms; but The Maid's way: staking life against death, with the heart high and humble and void of malice, and nothing counting under God but France free and French. Was it my way, Jack?

DUNOIS. Faith, it was any way that would win. But the way that won was always your way. I give you best, lassie. I wrote a fine letter to set you right at the new trial. Perhaps I should never have let the priests burn you; but I was busy fighting; and it was the Church's business, not mine. There was no use in both of us being burned, was there?

CAUCHON. Ay! put the blame on the priests. But I, who am beyond praise and blame, tell you that the world is saved neither by its priests nor its soldiers, but by God and His Saints. The Church Militant sent this woman to the fire; but even as she burned, the flames whitened into the radiance of the Church Triumphant.

The clock strikes the third quarter. A rough male voice is heard trolling an improvised tune.

Rum tum trumpledum,
Bacon fat and rumpledum,
Old Saint mumpledum,
Pull his tail and stumpledum
O my Ma—ry Ann!

A *ruffianly English soldier comes through the curtains and marches between Dunois and Joan.*

DUNOIS. What villainous troubadour taught you that doggrel?

THE SOLDIER. No troubadour. We made it up ourselves as we marched. We were not gentlefolks and troubadours. Music straight out of the heart of the people, as you might say. Rum tum trumpledum, Bacon fat and rumpledum, Old Saint mumpledum, Pull his tail and stumpledum: that dont mean anything, you know; but it keeps you marching. Your servant, ladies and gentlemen. Who asked for a saint?

JOAN. Be you a saint?

THE SOLDIER. Yes, lady, straight from hell.

DUNOIS. A saint, and from hell!

THE SOLDIER. Yes, noble captain: I have a day off. Every year, you know. Thats my allowance for my one good action.

CAUCHON. Wretch! In all the years of your life did you do only one good action?

THE SOLDIER. I never thought about it: it came natural like. But they scored it up for me.

CHARLES. What was it?

THE SOLDIER. Why, the silliest thing you ever heard of. I—

JOAN [*interrupting him by strolling across to the bed, where she sits beside Charles*] He tied two sticks together, and gave them to a poor lass that was going to be burned.

THE SOLDIER. Right. Who told you that?

JOAN.ˋNever mind. Would you know her if you saw her again?

THE SOLDIER. Not I. There are so many girls! and they all expect you to remember them as if there was only one in the world. This one must have been a prime sort; for I have a day off every year for her; and so, until twelve o'clock punctually, I am a saint, at your service, noble lords and lovely ladies.

CHARLES. And after twelve.

THE SOLDIER. After twelve, back to the only place fit for the likes of me.

JOAN [*rising*] Back there! You! that gave the lass the cross!

THE SOLDIER [*excusing his unsoldierly conduct*] Well, she asked for it; and they were going to burn her. She had as good a right to a cross as they had; and they had dozens of them. It was her funeral, not theirs. Where was the harm in it?

JOAN. Man: I am not reproaching you. But I cannot bear to think of you in torment.

THE SOLDIER [*cheerfully*] No great torment, lady. You see I was used to worse.

CHARLES. What! worse than hell?

THE SOLDIER. Fifteen years' service in the French wars. Hell was a treat after that.

> *Joan throws up her arms, and takes refuge from despair of humanity before the picture of the Virgin.*

THE SOLDIER [*continuing*]—Suits me somehow. The day off was dull at first, like a wet Sunday. I dont mind it so much now. They tell me I can have as many as I like as soon as I want them.

CHARLES. What is hell like?

THE SOLDIER. You wont find it so bad, sir. Jolly. Like as if you were always drunk without the trouble and expense of drinking. Tip top company too: emperors and popes and kings and all sorts.

They chip me about giving that young judy the cross; but I dont care: I stand up to them proper, and tell them that if she hadnt a better right to it than they, she'd be where they are. That dumbfounds them, that does. All they can do is gnash their teeth, hell fashion; and I just laugh, and go off singing the old chanty: Rum tum trumple—Hullo! Who's that knocking at the door?

They listen. A long gentle knocking is heard.

CHARLES. Come in.

The door opens; and an old priest, white-haired, bent, with a silly but benevolent smile, comes in and trots over to Joan.

THE NEWCOMER. Excuse me, gentle lords and ladies. Do not let me disturb you. Only a poor old harmless English rector. Formerly chaplain to the cardinal: to my lord of Winchester. John de Stogumber, at your service. [*He looks at them inquiringly*] Did you say anything? I am a little deaf, unfortunately. Also a little—well, not always in my right mind, perhaps; but still, it is a small village with a few simple people. I suffice: I suffice: they love me there; and I am able to do a little good. I am well connected, you see; and they indulge me.

JOAN. Poor old John! What brought thee to this state?

DE STOGUMBER. I tell my folks they must be very careful. I say to them, "If you only saw what you think about you would think quite differently about it. It would give you a great shock. Oh, a great shock." And they all say "Yes, parson: we all know you are a kind man, and would not harm a fly." That is a great comfort to me. For I am not cruel by nature, you know.

THE SOLDIER. Who said you were?

DE STOGUMBER. Well, you see, I did a very cruel thing once because I did not know what cruelty was like. I had not seen it, you know. That is the great thing: you must see it. And then you are redeemed and saved.

CAUCHON. Were not the sufferings of our Lord Christ enough for you?

DE STOGUMBER. No. Oh no: not at all. I had seen them in pictures, and read of them in books, and been greatly moved by them, as I thought. But it was no use: it was not our Lord that redeemed me, but a young woman whom I saw actually burned to death. It was dreadful: oh, most dreadful. But it saved me. I have been a different man ever since, though a little astray in my wits sometimes.

CAUCHON. Must then a Christ perish in torment in every age to save those that have no imagination?

JOAN. Well, if I saved all those he would have been cruel to if he had not been cruel to me, I was not burnt for nothing, was I?

DE STOGUMBER. Oh no; it was not you. My sight is bad: I cannot distinguish your features: but you are not she: oh no: she was burned to a cinder: dead and gone, dead and gone.

THE EXECUTIONER [*stepping from behind the bed curtains on*

Charles's right, the bed being between them] She is more alive than you, old man. Her heart would not burn; and it would not drown. I was a master at my craft: better than the master of Paris, better than the master of Toulouse; but I could not kill The Maid. She is up and alive everywhere.

THE EARL OF WARWICK [*sallying from the bed curtains on the other side, and coming to Joan's left hand*] Madam: my congratulations on your rehabilitation. I feel that I owe you an apology.

JOAN. Oh, please dont mention it.

WARWICK [*pleasantly*] The burning was purely political. There was no personal feeling against you, I assure you.

JOAN. I bear no malice, my lord.

WARWICK. Just so. Very kind of you to meet me in that way: a touch of true breeding. But I must insist on apologizing very amply. The truth is, these political necessities sometimes turn out to be political mistakes; and this one was a veritable howler; for your spirit conquered us, madam, in spite of our faggots. History will remember me for your sake, though the incidents of the connection were perhaps a little unfortunate.

JOAN. Ay, perhaps just a little, you funny man.

WARWICK. Still, when they make you a saint, you will .owe your halo to me, just as this lucky monarch owes his crown to you.

JOAN [*turning from him*] I shall owe nothing to any man: I owe everything to the spirit of God that was within me. But fancy me a saint! What would St Catherine and St Margaret say if the farm girl was cocked up beside them!

A *clerical-looking gentleman in black frockcoat and trousers, and tall hat, in the fashion of the year 1920, suddenly appears before them in the corner on their right. They all stare at him. Then they burst into uncontrollable laughter.*

THE GENTLEMAN. Why this mirth, gentlemen?

WARWICK. I congratulate you on having invented a most extraordinarily comic dress.

THE GENTLEMAN. I do not understand. You are all in fancy dress: I am properly dressed.

DUNOIS. All dress is fancy dress, is it not, except our natural skins?

THE GENTLEMAN. Pardon me: I am here on serious business, and cannot engage in frivolous discussions. [*He takes out a paper, and assumes a dry official manner*]. I am sent to announce to you that Joan of Arc, formerly known as The Maid, having been the subject of an inquiry instituted by the Bishop of Orleans—

JOAN [*interrupting*] Ah! They remember me still in Orleans.

THE GENTLEMAN [*emphatically, to mark his indignation at the interruption*]—by the Bishop of Orleans into the claim of the said Joan of Arc to be canonized as a saint—

JOAN [*again interrupting*] But I never made any such claim.

THE GENTLEMAN [*as before*]—the Church has examined the claim exhaustively in the usual course, and, having admitted the said Joan successively to the ranks of Venerable and Blessed,—

JOAN [*chuckling*] Me venerable!

THE GENTLEMAN. —has finally declared her to have been endowed with heroic virtues and favored with private revelations, and calls the said Venerable and Blessed Joan to the communion of the Church Triumphant as Saint Joan.

JOAN [*rapt*] Saint Joan!

THE GENTLEMAN. On every thirtieth day of May, being the anniversary of the death of the said most blessed daughter of God, there shall in every Catholic church to the end of time be celebrated a special office in commemoration of her; and it shall be lawful to dedicate a special chapel to her, and to place her image on its altar in every such church. And it shall be lawful and laudable for the faithful to kneel and address their prayers through her to the Mercy Seat.

JOAN. Oh no. It is for the saint to kneel. [*She falls on her knees, still rapt*].

THE GENTLEMAN [*putting up his paper, and retiring beside the Executioner*] In Basilica Vaticana, the sixteenth day of May, nineteen hundred and twenty.

DUNOIS [*raising Joan*] Half an hour to burn you, dear Saint: and four centuries to find out the truth about you!

DE STOGUMBER. Sir: I was chaplain to the Cardinal of Winchester once. They always would call him the Cardinal of England. It would be a great comfort to me and to my master to see a fair statue to The Maid in Winchester Cathedral. Will they put one there, do you think?

THE GENTLEMAN. As the building is temporarily in the hands of the Anglican heresy, I cannot answer for that.

A vision of the statue in Winchester Cathedral is seen through the window.

DE STOGUMBER. Oh look! look! that is Winchester.

JOAN. Is that meant to be me? I was stiffer on my feet.

The vision fades.

THE GENTLEMAN. I have been requested by the temporal authorities of France to mention that the multiplication of public statues to The Maid threatens to become an obstruction to traffic. I do so as a matter of courtesy to the said authorities, but must point out on behalf of the Church that The Maid's horse is no greater obstruction to traffic than any other horse.

JOAN. Eh! I am glad they have not forgotten my horse.

A vision of the statue before Rheims Cathedral appears.

JOAN. Is that funny little thing me too?

CHARLES. That is Rheims Cathedral where you had me crowned. It must be you.

JOAN. Who has broken my sword? My sword was never broken. It is the sword of France.

DUNOIS. Never mind. Swords can be mended. Your soul is unbroken; and you are the soul of France.

The vision fades. The Archbishop and the Inquisitor are now seen on the right and left of Cauchon.

JOAN. My sword shall conquer yet: the sword that never struck a blow. Though men destroyed my body, yet in my soul I have seen God.

CAUCHON [*kneeling to her*] The girls in the field praise thee; for thou hast raised their eyes; and they see that there is nothing between them and heaven.

DUNOIS [*kneeling to her*] The dying soldiers praise thee, because thou art a shield of glory between them and the judgment.

THE ARCHBISHOP [*kneeling to her*] The princes of the Church praise thee, because thou hast redeemed the faith their worldlinesses have dragged through the mire.

WARWICK [*kneeling to her*] The cunning counsellors praise thee, because thou hast cut the knots in which they have tied their own souls.

DE STOGUMBER [*kneeling to her*] The foolish old men on their deathbeds praise thee, because their sins against thee are turned into blessings.

THE INQUISITOR [*kneeling to her*] The judges in the blindness and bondage of the law praise thee, because thou hast vindicated the vision and the freedom of the living soul.

THE SOLDIER [*kneeling to her*] The wicked out of hell praise thee, because thou hast shewn them that the fire that is not quenched is a holy fire.

THE EXECUTIONER [*kneeling to her*] The tormentors and executioners praise thee, because thou hast shewn that their hands are guiltless of the death of the soul.

CHARLES [*kneeling to her*] The unpretending praise thee, because thou hast taken upon thyself the heroic burdens that are too heavy for them.

JOAN. Woe unto me when all men praise me! I bid you remember that I am a saint, and that saints can work miracles. And now tell me: shall I rise from the dead, and come back to you a living woman?

A *sudden darkness blots out the walls of the room as they all spring to their feet in consternation. Only the figures and the bed remain visible.*

JOAN. What! Must I burn again? Are none of you ready to receive me?

CAUCHON. The heretic is always better dead. And mortal eyes cannot distinguish the saint from the heretic. Spare them. [*He goes out as he came*].

DUNOIS. Forgive us, Joan: we are not yet good enough for you. I shall go back to my bed. [*He also goes*].

WARWICK. We sincerely regret our little mistake; but political necessities, though occasionally erroneous, are still imperative; so if you will be good enough to excuse me— [*He steals discreetly away*].

THE ARCHBISHOP. Your return would not make me the man you once thought me. The utmost I can say is that though I dare not bless you, I hope I may one day enter into your blessedness. Meanwhile, however— [*He goes*].

THE INQUISITOR. I who am of the dead, testified that day that you
were innocent. But I do not see how The Inquisition could possibly be dispensed with under existing circumstances. Therefore—
[*He goes*].

DE STOGUMBER. Oh, do not come back: you must not come back. I
must die in peace. Give us peace in our time, O Lord! [*He
goes*].

THE GENTLEMAN. The possibility of your resurrection was not contemplated in the recent proceedings for your canonization. I
must return to Rome for fresh instructions. [*He bows formally,
and withdraws*].

THE EXECUTIONER. As a master in my profession I have to consider
its interests. And, after all, my first duty is to my wife and children. I must have time to think over this. [*He goes*].

CHARLES. Poor old Joan! They have all run away from you except
this blackguard who has to go back to hell at twelve o'clock. And
what can I do but follow Jack Dunois' example, and go back to
bed too? [*He does so*].

JOAN [*sadly*] Goodnight, Charlie.

CHARLES [*mumbling in his pillows*] Goo ni. [*He sleeps. The
darkness envelops the bed*].

JOAN [*to the soldier*] And you, my one faithful? What comfort
have you for Saint Joan?

THE SOLDIER. Well, what do they all amount to, these kings and
captains and bishops and lawyers and such like? They just leave
you in the ditch to bleed to death; and the next thing is, you
meet them down there, for all the airs they give themselves.
What I say is, you have as good a right to your notions as they
have to theirs, and perhaps better. [*Settling himself for a lecture
on the subject*] You see, it's like this. If— [*the first stroke of
midnight is heard softly from a distant bell*]. Excuse me: a
pressing appointment— [*He goes on tiptoe*].

> The last remaining rays of light gather into a white radi-
> ance descending on Joan. The hour continues to strike.

JOAN. O God that madest this beautiful earth, when will it be
ready to receive T h y saints? How long, O Lord, how long?

Too True to Be Good

Act I

Night. One of the best bedrooms in one of the best suburban villas in one of the richest cities in England. A young lady with an unhealthy complexion is asleep in the bed. A small table at the head of the bed, convenient to her right hand, and crowded with a medicine bottle, a measuring glass, a pill box, a clinical thermometer in a glass of water, a half read book with the place marked by a handkerchief, a powder puff and handmirror, and an electric bell handle on a flex, shews that the bed is a sick bed and the young lady an invalid.

The furniture includes a very handsome dressing table with silver-backed hairbrushes and toilet articles, a dainty pincushion, a stand of rings, a jewel box of black steel with the lid open and a rope of pearls heaped carelessly half in and half out, a Louis Quinze writing table and chair with inkstand, blotter, and cabinet of stationery, a magnificent wardrobe, a luxurious couch, and a tall screen of Chinese workmanship which, like the expensive carpet and everything else in the room, proclaims that the owner has money enough to buy the best things at the best shops in the best purchaseable taste.

The bed is nearly in the middle of the room, so that the patient's nurses can pass freely between the wall and the head of it. If we contemplate the room from the foot of the bed, with the patient's toes pointing straight at us, we have the door (carefully sandbagged lest a draught of fresh air should creep underneath) level with us in the righthand wall, the couch against the same wall farther away, the window (every ray of moonlight excluded by closed curtains and a dark green spring blind) in the middle of the left wall with the wardrobe on its right and the writing table on its left, the screen at right angles to the wardrobe, and the dressing table against the wall facing us half way between the bed and the couch.

Besides the chair at the writing table there is an easy chair at the medicine table, and a chair at each side of the dressing table.

The room is lighted by invisible cornice lights, and by two mirror lights on the dressing table and a portable one on the writing table; but these are now switched off; and the only light in action is another portable one on the medicine table, very carefully subdued by a green shade.

The patient is sleeping heavily. Near her, in the easy chair, sits a Monster. In shape and size it resembles a human being; but in substance it seems to be made of a luminous jelly with a visible skeleton of short black rods. It droops forward in the chair with its head in its hands, and seems in the last degree wretched.

THE MONSTER. Oh! Oh!! Oh!!! I am so ill! so miserable! Oh, I wish I were dead. Why doesnt she die and release me from my sufferings? What right has she to get ill and make me ill like this? Measles: thats what she's got. Measles! German measles! And she's given them to me, a poor innocent microbe that never did her any harm. And she says that I gave them to her. Oh, is this justice? Oh, I feel so rotten. I wonder what my temperature is: they took it from under her tongue half an hour ago. [*Scrutinizing the table and discovering the thermometer in the glass*]. Here's the thermometer: theyve left it for the doctor to see instead of shaking it down. If it's over a hundred I'm done for: I darent look. Oh, can it be that I'm dying? I must look. [*It looks, and drops the thermometer back into the glass with a gasping scream*]. A hundred and three! It's all over. [*It collapses.*]

The door opens; and an elderly lady and a young doctor come in. The lady steals along on tiptoe, full of the deepest concern for the invalid. The doctor is indifferent, but keeps up his bedside manner carefully, though he evidently does not think the case so serious as the lady does. She comes to the bedside on the invalid's left. He comes to the other side of the bed and looks attentively at his patient.

THE ELDERLY LADY [*in a whisper sibillant enough to wake the dead*] She is asleep.

THE MONSTER. I should think so. This fool here, the doctor, has given her a dose of the latest fashionable opiate that would keep a cock asleep til half past eleven on a May morning.

THE ELDERLY LADY. Oh doctor, do you think there is any chance? Can she possibly survive this last terrible complication.

THE MONSTER. Measles! He mistook it for influenza.

THE ELDERLY LADY. It was so unexpected! such a crushing blow! And I have taken such care of her. She is my only surviving child: my pet: my precious one. Why do they all die? I have never neglected the smallest symptom of illness. She has had doctors in attendance on her almost constantly since she was born.

THE MONSTER. She has the constitution of a horse or she'd have died like the others.

THE ELDERLY LADY. Oh, dont you think, dear doctor—of course you know best; but I am so terribly anxious—dont you think you ought to change the prescription? I had such hopes of that last bottle; but you know it was after that that she developed measles.

THE DOCTOR. My dear Mrs Mopply, you may rest assured that the bottle had nothing to do with the measles. It was merely a gentle tonic—

THE MONSTER. Strychnine!

THE DOCTOR. —to brace her up.

THE ELDERLY LADY. But she got measles after it.

THE DOCTOR. That was a specific infection: a germ, a microbe.

THE MONSTER. Me! Put it all on me.

THE ELDERLY LADY. But how did it get in? I keep the windows closed so carefully. And there is a sheet steeped in carbolic acid always hung over the door.

THE MONSTER [*in tears*] Not a breath of fresh air for me!

THE DOCTOR. Who knows? It may have lurked here since the house was built. You never can tell. But you must not worry. It is not serious: a light rubeola: you can hardly call it measles. We shall pull her through, believe me.

THE ELDERLY LADY. It is such a comfort to hear you say so, doctor. I am sure I shall never be able to express my gratitude for all you have done for us.

THE DOCTOR. Oh, that is my profession. We do what we can.

THE ELDERLY LADY. Yes; but some doctors are dreadful. There was that man at Folkestone: he was impossible. He tore aside the curtain and let the blazing sunlight into the room, though she cannot bear it without green spectacles. He opened the windows and let in all the cold morning air. I told him he was a murderer; and he only said "One guinea, please". I am sure he let in that microbe.

THE DOCTOR. Oh, three months ago! No: it was not that.

THE ELDERLY LADY. Then what was it? Oh, are you quite q u i t e sure that it would not be better to change the prescription?

THE DOCTOR. Well, I have already changed it.

THE MONSTER. Three times!

THE ELDERLY LADY. Oh, I know you have, doctor: nobody could have been kinder. But it really did not do her any good. She got worse.

THE DOCTOR. But, my dear lady, she was sickening for measles. That was not the fault of my prescription.

THE ELDERLY LADY. Oh, of course not. You mustnt think that I ever doubted for a moment that everything you did was for the best. Still—

THE DOCTOR. Oh, very well, very well: I will write another prescription.

THE ELDERLY LADY. Oh, thank you, thank you: I felt sure you would. I have so often known a change of medicine work wonders.

THE DOCTOR. When we have pulled her through this attack I think a change of air—

THE ELDERLY LADY. Oh no: dont say that. She must be near a doctor who knows her constitution. Dear old Dr Newland knew it so well from her very birth.

THE DOCTOR. Unfortunately, Newland is dead.

THE ELDERLY LADY. Yes; but you bought his practice. I should never be easy in my mind if you were not within call. You persuaded me to take her to Folkestone; and see what happened! No: never again.

THE DOCTOR. Oh, well! [*He shrugs his shoulders resignedly, and goes to the bedside table*]. What about the temperature?

THE ELDERLY LADY. The day nurse took it. I havnt dared to look.

THE DOCTOR [*looking at the thermometer*] Hm!

THE ELDERLY LADY [*trembling*] Has it gone up? Oh, doctor!

THE DOCTOR [*hastily shaking the mercury down*] No. Nothing. Nearly normal.

THE MONSTER. Liar!

THE ELDERLY LADY. What a relief!

THE DOCTOR. You must be careful, though. Dont fancy she's well yet: she isnt. She must not get out of bed for a moment. The slightest chill might be serious.

THE ELDERLY LADY. Doctor: are you sure you are not concealing something from me? Why does she n e v e r get well in spite of the fortune I have spent on her illnesses? There must be some deep-rooted cause. Tell me the worst: I have dreaded it all my life. Perhaps I should have told you the whole truth; but I was afraid. Her uncle's stepfather died of an enlarged heart. Is that what it is?

THE DOCTOR. Good gracious, NO! What put that into your head?

THE ELDERLY LADY. But even before this rash broke out there were pimples.

THE MONSTER. Boils! Too many chocolate creams.

THE DOCTOR. Oh, that! Nothing. Her blood is not quite what it should be. But we shall get that right.

THE ELDERLY LADY. You are sure it is not her lungs?

THE DOCTOR. My good lady, her lungs are as sound as a seagull's.

THE ELDERLY LADY. Then it must be her heart. Dont deceive me. She has palpitations. She told me the other day that it stopped for five minutes when that horrid nurse was rude to her.

THE DOCTOR. Nonsense! She wouldnt be alive now if her heart had stopped for five seconds. There is nothing constitutionally wrong. A little below par: that is all. We shall feed her up scientifically. Plenty of good fresh meat. A half bottle of champagne at lunch and a glass of port after dinner will make another woman of her. A chop at breakfast, rather underdone, is sometimes very helpful.

THE MONSTER. I shall die of overfeeding. So will she too: thats one consolation.

THE DOCTOR. Dont worry about the measles. It's really quite a light case.

THE ELDERLY LADY. Oh, you can depend on me for that. Nobody can say that I am a worrier. You wont forget the new prescription?

THE DOCTOR. I will write it here and now [*he takes out his pen and book, and sits down at the writing table.*]

THE ELDERLY LADY. Oh, thank you. And I will go and see what the new night nurse is doing. They take so long with their cup sof tea [*she goes to the door and is about to go out when she hesitates and comes back*]. Doctor: I know you dont believe in inoculations; but I cant help thinking she ought to have one. They do so much good.

THE DOCTOR [*almost at the end of his patience*] My dear Mrs Mopply: I never said that I dont believe in inoculations. But it is no use inoculating when the patient is already fully infected.

THE ELDERLY LADY. But I have found it so necessary myself. I was inoculated against influenza three years ago; and I have had it only four times since. My sister has it every February. Do, to please me, give her an inoculation. I feel such a responsibility if anything is left undone to cure her.

THE DOCTOR. Oh very well, very well: I will see what can be done. She shall have both an inoculation and a new prescription. Will that set your mind at rest?

THE ELDERLY LADY. Oh, thank you. You have lifted such a weight from my conscience. I feel sure they will do her the greatest good. And now excuse me a moment while I fetch the nurse. [*She goes out*].

THE DOCTOR. What a perfectly maddening woman!

THE MONSTER [*rising and coming behind him*] Yes: aint she?

THE DOCTOR [*starting*] What! Who is that?

THE MONSTER. Nobody but me and the patient. And you have dosed her so that she wont speak again for ten hours. You will overdo that some day.

THE DOCTOR. Rubbish! She thought it was an opiate; but it was only an aspirin dissolved in ether. But who am I talking to? I must be drunk.

THE MONSTER. Not a bit of it.

THE DOCTOR. Then who are you? What are you? Where are you? Is this a trick?

THE MONSTER. I'm only an unfortunate sick bacillus.

THE DOCTOR. A sick bacillus!

THE MONSTER. Yes. I suppose it never occurs to you that a bacillus can be sick like anyone else.

THE DOCTOR. Whats the matter with you?

THE MONSTER. Measles.

THE DOCTOR. Rot! The microbe of measles has never been discovered. If there is a microbe it cannot be measles: it must be parameasles.

THE MONSTER. Great Heavens! what are parameasles?

THE DOCTOR. Something so like measles that nobody can see any difference.

THE MONSTER. If there is no measles microbe why did you tell the old girl that her daughter caught measles from a microbe?

THE DOCTOR. Patients insist on having microbes nowadays. If I told her there is no measles microbe she wouldnt believe me; and I should lose my patient. When there is no microbe I invent one.

Am I to understand that you are the missing microbe of measles, and that you have given them to this patient here?

THE MONSTER. No: she gave them to me. These humans are full of horrid diseases: they infect us poor microbes with them; and you doctors pretend that it is we that infect them. You ought all to be struck off the register.

THE DOCTOR. We should be, if we talked like that.

THE MONSTER. Oh, I feel so wretched! Please cure my measles.

THE DOCTOR. I cant. I cant cure any disease. But I get the credit when the patients cure themselves. When she cures herself she will cure you too.

THE MONSTER. But she cant cure herself because you and her mother wont give her a dog's chance. You wont let her have even a breath of fresh air. I tell you she's naturally as strong as a rhinoceros. Curse your silly bottles and inoculations! Why dont you chuck them and turn faith healer?

THE DOCTOR. I a m a faith healer. You dont suppose I believe the bottles cure people? But the patient's faith in the bottle does.

THE MONSTER. Youre a humbug: thats what you are.

THE DOCTOR. Faith is humbug. But it works.

THE MONSTER. Then why do you call it science?

THE DOCTOR. Because people believe in science. The Christian Scientists call their fudge science for the same reason.

THE MONSTER. The Christian Scientists let their patients cure themselves. Why dont you?

THE DOCTOR. I do. But I help them. You see, it's easier to believe in bottles and inoculations than in oneself and in that mysterious power that gives us our life and that none of us knows anything about. Lots of people believe in the bottles and wouldnt know what you were talking about if you suggested the real thing. And the bottles do the trick. My patients get well as often as not. That is, unless their number's up. Then we all have to go.

THE MONSTER. No girl's number is up until she's worn out. I tell you this girl could cure herself and cure me if youd let her.

THE DOCTOR. And I tell you that it would be very hard work for her. Well, why should she work hard when she can afford to pay other people to work for her? She doesnt black her own boots or scrub her own floors. She pays somebody else to do it. Why should she cure herself, which is harder work than blacking boots or scrubbling floors, when she can afford to pay the doctor to cure her? It pays her and it pays me. That's logic, my friend. And now, if you will excuse me, I shall take myself off before the old woman comes back and provokes me to wring her neck. [*Rising*] Mark my words: someday somebody will fetch her a clout over the head. Somebody who can afford to. Not the doctor. She has driven me mad already: the proof is that I hear voices and talk to them. [*He goes out*].

THE MONSTER. Youre saner than most of them, you fool. They think I have the keys of life and death in my pocket; but I have nothing but a horrid headache. Oh dear! oh dear!

The Monster wanders away behind the screen. The

patient, left alone, begins to stir in her bed. She turns over and calls querulously for somebody to attend to her.

THE PATIENT. Nurse! Mother! Oh, is anyone there? [*Crying*] Selfish beasts! to leave me like this. [*She snatches angrily at the electric bell which hangs within her reach and presses the button repeatedly*].

> *The Elderly Lady and the night nurse come running in. The nurse is young, quick, active, resolute, and decidedly pretty. Mrs Mopply goes to the bedside table, the nurse going to the patient's left.*

THE ELDERLY LADY. What is it, darling? Are you awake? Was the sleeping draught no good? Are you worse? What has happened? What has become of the doctor?

THE PATIENT. I am in the most frightful agony. I have been lying here ringing for ages and ages, and no one has come to attend to me. Nobody cares whether I am alive or dead.

THE ELDERLY LADY. Oh, how can you say such things, darling? I left the doctor here. I was away only for a minute. I had to receive the new night nurse and give her her instructions. Here she is. And oh, do cover up your arm, darling. You will get a chill; and then it will be all over. Nurse: see that she is never uncovered for a moment. Do you think it would be well to have another hot water bottle against her arm until it is quite warm again? Do you feel it cold, darling?

THE PATIENT [*angrily*] Yes, deadly cold.

THE ELDERLY LADY. Oh dont say that. And there is so much pneumonia about. I wish the doctor had not gone. He could sound your lungs—

NIGHT NURSE [*feeling the patient's arm*] She is quite warm enough.

THE PATIENT [*bursting into tears*] Mother: take this hateful woman away. She wants to kill me.

THE ELDERLY LADY. Oh no, dear: she has been so highly recommended. I cant get a new nurse at this hour. Wont you try, for my sake, to put up with her until the day nurse comes in the morning?

THE NURSE. Come! Let me arrange your pillows and make you comfortable. You are smothered with all this bedding. Four thick blankets and an eiderdown! No wonder you feel irritable.

THE PATIENT [*screaming*] Dont touch me. Go away. You want to murder me. Nobody cares whether I am alive or dead.

THE ELDERLY LADY. Oh, darling, dont keep on saying that. You know it's not true; and it does hurt me so.

THE NURSE. You must not mind what a sick person says, madam. You had better go to bed and leave the patient to me. You are quite worn out. [*She comes to Mrs Mopply and takes her arm coaxingly but firmly*].

THE ELDERLY LADY. I know I am: I am ready to drop. How sympathetic of you to notice it! But how can I leave her at such a moment?

THE NURSE. She ought not to have more than one person in the room at a time. You see how it excites and worries her.

THE ELDERLY LADY. Oh, thats very true. The doctor said she was to be kept as quiet as possible.

THE NURSE [*leading her to the door*] You need a good night's sleep. You may trust me to do what is right and necessary.

THE ELDERLY LADY [*whispering*] I will indeed. How kind of you! You will let me know if anything—

THE NURSE. Yes, yes. I promise to come for you and wake you if anything happens. Good night, madam.

THE ELDERLY LADY [*sotto voce*] Good night. [*She steals out*].
> *The nurse, left alone with her patient, pays no attention to her, but goes to the window. She opens the curtains and raises the blind, admitting a flood of moonlight. She unfastens the sash and throws it right up. She then makes for the door, where the electric switch is.*

THE PATIENT [*huddling herself up in the bedclothes*] What are you doing? Shut that window and pull down that blind and close those curtains at once. Do you want to kill me?
> *The nurse turns all the lights full on.*

THE PATIENT [*hiding her eyes*] Oh! Oh! I cant bear it: turn it off.
> *The nurse switches the lights off.*

THE PATIENT. So inconsiderate of you!
> *The nurse switches the lights on again.*

THE PATIENT. Oh, please, please. Not all that light.
> *The nurse switches off.*

THE PATIENT. No, no. Leave me something to read by. My bedside lamp is not enough, you stupid idiot.
> *The nurse switches on again, and calmly returns to the bedside.*

THE PATIENT. I cant imagine how anyone can be so thoughtless and clumsy when I am so ill. I am suffering horribly. Shut that window and switch off half those lights at once: do you hear?
> *The nurse snatches the eiderdown and one of the pillows rudely from the bed, letting the patient down with a jerk, and arranges them comfortably in the bedside chair.*

THE PATIENT. How dare you touch my pillow? The audacity!
> *The nurse sits down; takes out a leaf cut from an illustrated journal; and proceeds to study it attentively.*

THE PATIENT. Well! How much longer are you going to sit there neglecting me? Shut that window instantly.

THE NURSE [*insolently, in her commonest dialect*] Oh go to—to sleep [*she resumes her study of the document*].

THE PATIENT. Dont dare address me like that. I dont believe you are a properly qualified nurse.

THE NURSE [*calmly*] I should think not. I wouldnt take five thousand a year to be a nurse. But I know how to deal with you and your like, because I was once a patient in a hospital where the women patients were a rough lot, and the nurses had to treat them accordingly. I kept my eyes open there, and learnt a little of the game. [*She takes a paper packet from her pocket and opens it on the bedside table. It contains about half a pound of kitchen salt*]. Do you know what that is and what it's for?

THE PATIENT. Is it medicine?

THE NURSE. Yes. It's a cure for screaming and hysterics and tantrums. When a woman starts making a row, the first thing she does is to open her mouth. A nurse who knows her business just shoves a handful of this into it. Common kitchen salt. No more screaming. Understand?

THE PATIENT [*hardily*] No I dont [*she reaches for the bell*].

THE NURSE [*intercepting her quickly*] No you dont. [*She throws the bell cord with its button away on the floor behind the bed*]. Now we shant be disturbed. No bell. And if you open your mouth too wide, youll get the salt. See?

THE PATIENT. And do you think I am a poor woman in a hospital whom you can illtreat as you please? Do you know what will happen to you when my mother comes in the morning?

THE NURSE. In the morning, darling, I shall be over the hills and far away.

THE PATIENT. And you expect me, sick as I am, to stay here alone with you!

THE NURSE. We shant be alone. I'm expecting a friend.

THE PATIENT. A friend!

THE NURSE. A gentleman friend. I told him he might drop in when he saw the lights switched off twice.

THE PATIENT. So that was why—

THE NURSE. That was why.

THE PATIENT. And you calmly propose to have your young man here in my room to amuse yourself all night before my face.

THE NURSE. You can go to sleep.

THE PATIENT. I shall do nothing of the sort. You will have to behave yourself decently before me.

THE NURSE. Oh, dont worry about that. He's coming on business. He's my business partner, in fact: not my best boy.

THE PATIENT. And can you not find some more suitable place for your business than in my room at night?

THE NURSE. You see, you dont know the nature of the business yet. It's got to be done here and at night. Here he is, I think.

> *A burglar, well dressed, wearing rubber gloves and a small white mask over his nose, clambers in. He is still in his early thirties and quite goodlooking. His voice is disarmingly pleasant.*

THE BURGLAR. All right, Sweetie?

THE NURSE. All right, Popsy.

> *The burglar closes the window softly; draws the curtains; and comes past the nurse to the bedside.*

THE BURGLAR. Damn it, she's awake. Didnt you give her a sleeping draught?

THE PATIENT. Do you expect me to sleep with you in the room? Who are you? and what are you wearing that mask for?

THE BURGLAR. Only so that you will not recognize me if we should happen to meet again.

THE PATIENT. I have no intention of meeting you again. So you may just as well take it off.

THE NURSE. I havnt broken to her what we are here for, Popsy.

THE PATIENT. I neither know nor care what you are here for. All I can tell you is that if you dont leave the room at once and send my mother to me, I will give you both measles.

THE BURGLAR. We have both had them, dear invalid. I am afraid we must intrude a little longer. [*To the nurse*] Have you found out where it is?

THE NURSE. No: I havnt had time. The dressing table's over there. Try that.

> *The burglar crosses to the other side of the bed, coming round by the foot of it, and is making for the dressing table when—*

THE PATIENT. What do you want at my dressing table?

THE BURGLAR. Obviously, your celebrated pearl necklace.

THE PATIENT [*escaping from her bed with a formidable bound and planting herself with her back to the dressing table as a bulwark for the jewel case*] Not if I know it, you shant.

THE BURGLAR [*approaching her*] You really must allow me.

THE PATIENT. Take that.

> *Holding on to the table edge behind her, she lifts her foot vigorously waist high, and shoots it hard into his solar plexus. He curls up on the bed with an agonized groan and rolls off on to the carpet at the other side. The nurse rushes across behind the head of the bed and tackles the patient. The patient swoops at her knees; lifts her; and sends her flying. She comes down with a thump flat on her back on the couch. The patient pants hard; sways giddily; staggers to the bed and falls on it, exhausted. The nurse, dazed by the patient's very unexpected athleticism, but not hurt, springs up.*

THE NURSE. Quick, Popsy: tie her feet. She's fainted.

THE BURGLAR [*utters a lamentable groan and rolls over on his face*]!!

THE NURSE. Be quick, will you?

THE BURGLAR [*trying to rise*] Ugh! Ugh!

THE NURSE [*running to him and shaking him*] My God, you are a fool, Popsy. Come and help me before she comes to. She's too strong for me.

THE BURGLAR. Ugh! Let me die.

THE NURSE. Are you going to lie there for ever? Has she killed you?

THE BURGLAR [*rising slowly to his knees*] As nearly as doesnt matter. Oh, Sweetest, why did you tell me that this heavyweight champion was a helpless invalid?

THE NURSE. Shut up. Get the pearls.

THE BURGLAR [*rising with difficulty*] I dont seem to want any pearls. She got me just in the wind. I am sorry to have been of so little assistance; but oh, my Sweetie-Weetie, Nature never intended us to be burglars. Our first attempt has been a hopeless failure. Let us apologize and withdraw.

THE NURSE. Fathead! Dont be such a coward. [*Looking closely at the patient*] I say, Popsy: I believe she's asleep.

THE BURGLAR. Let her sleep. Wake not the lioness's wrath.

THE NURSE. You maddening fool, dont you see that we can tie her feet and gag her before she wakes, and get away with the pearls. It's quite easy if we do it quick together. Come along.

THE BURGLAR. Do not deceive yourself, my pet: we should have about as much chance as if we tried to take a female gorilla to the Zoo. No: I am not going to steal those jewels. Honesty is the best policy. I have another idea, and a much better one. You leave this to me. [*He goes to the dressing table. She follows him*].

THE NURSE. Whatever have you got into your silly head now?

THE BURGLAR. You shall see. [*Handling the jewel case*] One of these safes that open by a secret arrangement of letters. As they are as troublesome as an automatic telephone nobody ever locks them. Here is the necklace. By Jove! If they are all real, it must be worth about twenty thousand pounds. Gosh! here's a ring with a big blue diamond in it. Worth four thousand pounds if it's worth a penny. Sweetie: we are on velvet for the rest of our lives.

THE NURSE. What good are blue diamonds to us if we dont steal them?

THE BURGLAR. Wait. Wait and see. Go and sit down in that chair and look as like a nice gentle nurse as you can.

THE NURSE. But—

THE BURGLAR. Do as you are told. Have faith—faith in your Popsy.

THE NURSE [*obeying*] Well, I give it up. Youre mad.

THE BURGLAR. I was never saner in my life. Stop. How does she call people? Hasnt she an electric bell? Where is it?

THE NURSE [*picking it up*] Here. I chucked it out of her reach when she was grabbing at it.

THE BURGLAR. Put it on the bed close to her hand.

THE NURSE. Popsy: youre off your chump. She—

THE BURGLAR. Sweetie: in our firm I am the brains: you are the hand. This is going to be our most glorious achievement. Obey me instantly.

THE NURSE [*resignedly*] Oh, very well. [*She places the handle of the bell as desired*]. I wash my hands of this job. [*She sits down doggedly*].

THE BURGLAR [*coming to the bedside*] By the way, she is hardly a success as The Sleeping Beauty. She has a wretched complexion; and her breath is not precisely ambrosial. But if we can turn her out to grass she may put up some good looks. And if her punch is anything like her kick she will be an invaluable body-guard for us two weaklings—if I can persuade her to join us.

THE NURSE. Join us! What do you mean?

THE BURGLAR. Shshshshsh. Not too much noise: we must wake her gently. [*He stoops to the patient's ear and whispers*] Miss Mopply.

THE PATIENT [*in a murmur of protest*] Mmmmmmmmmmmm-mmmmm.

THE NURSE. What does she say?

THE BURGLAR. She says, in effect, "You have waked me too soon: I must slumber again." [*To the patient, more distinctly*] It is not your dear mother, Miss Mopply: it is the burglar. [*The patient springs half up, threateningly. He falls on his knees and throws up his hands*]. Kamerad,[1] Miss Mopply: Kamerad! I am utterly at your mercy. The bell is on your bed, close to your hand: look at it. You have only to press the button to bring your mother and the police in upon me [*she seizes the handle of the bell*] and be a miserable invalid again for the rest of your life. [*She drops the bell thoughtfully*]. Not an attractive prospect, is it? Now listen. I have something to propose to you of the greatest importance: something that may make another woman of you and change your entire destiny. You can listen to me in perfect security: at any moment you can ring your bell, or throw us out of the window if you prefer it. I ask you for five minutes only.

THE PATIENT [*still dangerously on guard*] Well?

THE BURGLAR [*rising*] Let me give you one more proof of my confidence. [*He takes off his mask*]. Look. Can you be afraid of such a face? Do I look like a burglar?

THE PATIENT [*relaxing, and even shewing signs of goodhumor*] No: you look like a curate.

THE BURGLAR [*a little hurt*] Oh, not a curate. I hope I look at least like a beneficed clergyman. But it is very clever of you to have found me out. The fact is, I a m a clergyman. But I must ask you to keep it a dead secret; for my father, who is an atheist, would disinherit me if he knew. I was secretly ordained when I was up at Oxford.

THE PATIENT. Oh, this is ridiculous. I'm dreaming. It must be that new sleeping draught the doctor gave me. But it's delicious, because I'm dreaming that I'm perfectly well. Ive never been so happy in my life. Go on with the dream, Pops: the nicest part of it is that I am in love with you. My beautiful Pops, my own, my darling, you are a perfect film hero, only more like an English gentleman. [*She waves him a kiss*].

THE NURSE. Well I'll be da—

THE BURGLAR. Shshshshsh. Break not the spell.

THE PATIENT [*with a deep sigh of contentment*] Let nobody wake me. I'm in heaven. [*She sinks back blissfully on her pillows*]. Go on, Pops. Tell me another.

THE BURGLAR. Splendid. [*He takes a chair from beside the dressing table and seats himself comfortably at the bedside*]. We are

---

1. Supposedly the cry of German soldiers who wanted to surrender in World War I.

going to have an ideal night. Now listen. Picture to yourself a heavenly afternoon in July: a Scottish loch surrounded by mirrored mountains, and a boat—may I call it a shallop?—

THE PATIENT [*ecstatically*] A shallop! Oh, Popsy!

THE BURGLAR. —with Sweetie sitting in the stern, and I stretched out at full length with my head pillowed on Sweetie's knees.

THE PATIENT. You can leave Sweetie out, Pops. Her amorous emotions do not interest me.

THE BURGLAR. You misunderstand. Sweetie's thoughts were far from me. She was thinking about you.

THE PATIENT. Just like her impudence! How did she know about me?

THE BURGLAR. Simply enough. In her lily hand was a copy of The Lady's Pictorial. It contained an illustrated account of your jewels. Can you guess what Sweetie said to me as she gazed at the soft majesty of the mountains and bathed her soul in the beauty of the sunset?

THE PATIENT. Yes. She said "Popsy: we must pinch that necklace."

THE BURGLAR. Exactly. Word for word. But now can you guess what *I* said?

THE PATIENT. I suppose you said "Right you are, Sweetie" or something vulgar like that.

THE BURGLAR. Wrong. I said, "If that girl had any sense she'd steal the necklace herself."

THE PATIENT. Oh! This is getting interesting. How could I steal my own necklace?

THE BURGLAR. Sell it; and have a glorious spree with the price. See life. Live. You dont call being an invalid living, do you?

THE PATIENT. Why shouldnt I call it living? I am not dead. Of course when I am awake I am terribly delicate—

THE BURGLAR. Delicate! It's not five minutes since you knocked me out, and threw Sweetie all over the room. If you can fight like that for a string of pearls that you never have a chance of wearing, why not fight for freedom to do what you like, with your pocket full of money and all the fun in the wide world at your command? Hang it all, dont you want to be young and goodlooking and have a sweet breath and be a lawn tennis champion and enjoy everything that is to be enjoyed instead of frowsting here and being messed about by your silly mother and all the doctors that live on her folly? Have you no conscience, that you waste God's gifts so shamefully? You think you are in a state of illness. Youre not: youre in a state of sin. Sell the necklace and buy your salvation with the proceeds.

THE PATIENT. Youre a clergyman all right, Pops. But I dont know how to sell the necklace.

THE BURGLAR. I do. Let me sell it for you. You will of course give us a fairly handsome commission on the transaction.

THE PATIENT. Theres some catch in this. If I trust you with it how do I know that you will not keep the whole price for yourself?

THE BURGLAR. Sweetie: Miss Mopply has the makings of a good

business woman in her. [*To the patient*] Just reflect, Mops
(Let us call one another Mops and Pops for short). If I steal
that necklace, I shall have to sell it as a burglar to a man who
will know perfectly well that I have stolen it. I shall be lucky if I
get a fiftieth of its value. But if I sell it on the square, as the
agent of its lawful owner, I shall be able to get its full market
value. The payment will be made to you; and I will trust you to
pay me the commission. Sweetie and I will be more than satisfied with fifty per cent.

THE PATIENT. Fifty! Oh!

THE BURGLAR [*firmly*] I think you will admit that we deserve it
for our enterprise, our risk, and the priceless boon of your eman-
cipation from this wretched home. Is it a bargain, Mops?

THE PATIENT. It's a monstrous overcharge; but in dreamland generosity costs nothing. You shall have your fifty. Lucky for you that
I'm asleep. If I wake up I shall never get loose from my people
and my social position. It's all very well for you two criminals:
you can do what you like. If you were ladies and gentlemen,
youd know how hard it is not to do what everybody else does.

THE BURGLAR. Pardon me; but I think you will feel more at ease
with us if I inform you that we are ladies and gentlemen. My
own rank—not that I would presume on it for a moment—is, if
you ask Burke or Debrett,[2] higher than your own. Your people's
money was made in trade: my people have always lived by
owning property or governing Crown Colonies. Sweetie would be
a woman of the highest position but for the unfortunate fact
that her parents, though united in the sight of Heaven, were not
legally married. At least so she tells me.

THE NURSE [*hotly*] I tell you what is true. [*To the patient*]
Popsy and I are as good company as ever y o u kept.

THE PATIENT. No, Sweetie: you are a common little devil and a
liar. But you amuse me. If you were a real lady you wouldnt
amuse me. Youd be afraid to be so unladylike.

THE BURGLAR. Just so. Come! confess! we are better fun than your
dear anxious mother and the curate and all the sympathizing relatives, arnt we? Of course we are.

THE PATIENT. I think it perfectly scandalous that you two, who
ought to be in prison, are having all the fun while I, because I
am respectable and a lady, might just as well be in prison.

THE BURGLAR. Don't you wish you could come with us?

THE PATIENT [*calmly*] I fully intend to come with you. I'm going
to make the most of this dream. Do you forget that I love you,
Pops. The world is before us. You and Sweetie have had a week
in the land of the mountain and the flood for seven guineas, tips
included. Now you shall have an eternity with your Mops in the
loveliest earthly paradise we can find, for nothing.

THE NURSE. And where do I come in?

THE PATIENT. You will be our chaperone.

2. That is, if you will consult "Burke's Peerage" or "Debrett's Peerage of
England, Scotland and Ireland."

THE NURSE. Chaperone! Well, you have a nerve, you have.

THE PATIENT. Listen. You will be a Countess. We shall go abroad, where nobody will know the difference. You shall have a splendid foreign title. The Countess Valbrioni: doesnt that tempt you?

THE NURSE. Tempt me hell! I'll see you further first.

THE BURGLAR. Stop. Sweetie: I have another idea. A regular dazzler. Lets stage a kidnap.

THE NURSE. What do you mean? stage a kidnap.

THE BURGLAR. It's quite simple. We kidnap Mops: that is, we shall hide her in the mountains of Corsica or Istria or Dalmatia or Greece or in the Atlas or where you please that is out of reach of Scotland Yard. We shall pretend to be brigands. Her devoted mother will cough up five thousand to ransom her. We shall share the ransom fifty-fifty: fifty for Mops, twentyfive for you, twentyfive for me. Mops: you will realize not only the value of the pearls, but of yourself. What a stroke of finance!

THE PATIENT [*excited*] Greece! Dalmatia! Kidnapped! Brigands! Ransomed! [*Collapsing a little*] Oh, dont tantalize me, you two fools: you have forgotten the measles.

The Monster suddenly reappears from behind the screen. It is transfigured. The bloated moribund Caliban has become a dainty Ariel.

THE MONSTER [*picking up the last remark of the patient*] So have you. No more measles: that scrap for the jewels cured you and cured me. Ha ha! I am well, I am well, I am well. [*It bounds about ecstatically, and finally perches on the pillows and gets into bed beside the patient*].

THE NURSE. If you could jump out of bed to knock out Popsy and me you can jump out to dress yourself and hop it from here. Wrap yourself up well: we have a car waiting.

THE BURGLAR. It's no worse than being taken to a nursing home, Mops. Strike for freedom. Up with you!

They pull her out of bed.

THE PATIENT. But I cant dress myself without a maid.

THE NURSE. Have you ever tried?

THE BURGLAR. We will give you five minutes. If you are not ready we go without you [*he looks at his watch*].

The patient dashes at the wardrobe and tears out a fur cloak, a hat, a walking dress, a combination, a pair of stockings, black silk breeches, and shoes, all of which she flings on the floor. The nurse picks up most of them; the patient snatches up the rest; the two retire behind the screen. Meanwhile the burglar comes forward to the foot of the bed and comments oratorically, half auctioneer, half clergyman.

THE BURGLAR. Fur cloak. Seal. Old fashioned but worth forty-five guineas. Hat. Quiet and ladylike. Tailor made frock. Combination: silk and wool. Real silk stockings without ladders. Knickers: how daringly modern! Shoes: heels only two inches but no use for the mountains. What a theme for a sermon! The well brought up maiden revolts against her respectable life. The aspiring soul escapes from home, sweet home, which, as a wellknown author has said, is the girl's prison and the woman's workhouse.[3] The intrusive care of her anxious parents, the officious concern of the family clergyman for her salvation and of the family doctor for her health, the imposed affection of uninteresting brothers and sisters, the outrage of being called by her Christian name by distant cousins who will not keep their distance, the invasion of her privacy and independence at every turn by questions as to where she has been and what she has been doing, the whispering behind her back about her chances of marriage, the continual violation of that sacred aura which surrounds every living soul like the halo surrounding the heads of saints in religious pictures: against all these devices for worrying her to death the innermost uppermost life in her rises like milk in a boiling saucepan and cries "Down with you! away with you! henceforth my gates are open to real life, bring what it may. For what sense is there in this world of hazards, disasters, elations and victories, except as a field for the adventures of the life everlasting? In vain do we disfigure our streets with scrawls of Safety First: in vain do the nations clamor for Security, security, security. They who cry Safety First never cross the street: the empires which sacrifice life to security find it in the grave. For me Safety Last; and Forward, Forward, always For—"

THE NURSE [*coming from behind the screen*] Dry up, Popsy: she's ready.

> *The patient, cloaked, hatted, and shoed, follows her breathless, and comes to the burglar, on his left.*

THE PATIENT. Here I am, Pops. One kiss; and then—Lead on.

THE BURGLAR. Good. Your complexion still leaves something to be desired; but [*kissing her*] your breath is sweet: you breathe the air of freedom.

THE MONSTER. Never mind her complexion: look at mine!

THE BURGLAR [*releasing the patient and turning to the nurse*] Did you speak?

THE NURSE. No. Hurry up, will you.

THE BURGLAR. It must have been your mother snoring, Mops. It will be long before you hear that music again. Drop a tear.

THE PATIENT. Not one. A woman's future is not with her mother.

THE NURSE. If you are going to start preaching like Popsy, the milkman will be here before we get away. Remember, I have to take off this uniform and put on my walking things downstairs. Popsy: there may be a copper on his beat outside. Spy out and see. Safety First [*she hurries out*].

THE BURGLAR. Well, for just this once, safety first [*he makes for the window*].

THE PATIENT [*stopping him*] Idiot: the police cant touch you if I back you up. It's I who run the risk of being caught by my mother.

---

3. The "wellknown author" is, of course, Shaw, writing as John Tanner in *The Revolutionist's Handbook*, appended to *Man and Superman*.

THE BURGLAR. True. You have an unexpectedly powerful mind. Pray Heaven that in kidnapping you I am not biting off more than I can chew. Come along. [*He runs out*].

THE PATIENT. He's forgotten the pearls!!! Thank Heaven he's a fool, a lovely fool: I shall be able to do as I like with him. [*She rushes to the dressing table; bundles the jewels into their case; and carries it out*].

THE MONSTER [*sitting up*] The play is now virtually over; but the characters will discuss it at great length for two acts more. The exit doors are all in order. Goodnight. [*It draws up the bedclothes round its neck and goes to sleep*].

Act II

A sea beach in a mountainous country. Sand dunes rise to a brow which cuts off the view of the plain beyond, only the summits of the distant mountain range which bounds it being visible. An army hut on the hither side, with a klaxon electric horn projecting from a board on the wall, shews that we are in a military cantoonment. Opposite the hut is a particolored canvas bathing pavilion with a folding stool beside the entrance. As seen from the sand dunes the hut is on the right and the pavilion on the left. From the neighborhood of the hut a date palm throws a long shadow; for it is early morning.

In this shadow sits a British colonel in a deck chair, peacefully reading the weekly edition of The Times, but with a revolver in his equipment. A light cane chair for use by his visitors is at hand by the hut. Though well over fifty, he is still slender, handsome, well set up, and every inch a commanding officer. His full style and title is Colonel Tallboys V.C., D.S.O.[4] He won his cross as a company-officer, and has never looked back since then.

He is disturbed by a shattering series of explosions announcing the approach of a powerful and very imperfectly silenced motor bicycle from the side opposite to the huts.

TALLBOYS. Damn that noise!

> *The unseen rider dismounts and races his engine with a hideous clatter.*

TALLBOYS [*angrily*] Stop that motorbike, will you?

> *The noise stops; and the bicyclist, having hoiked his machine up on to its stand, taken off his goggles and gloves, and extracted a letter from his carrier, comes past the pavilion into the colonel's view with the letter in his hand.*

> *He is an insignificant looking private soldier, dusty as to his clothes and a bit gritty as to his windbeaten face. Otherwise there is nothing to find fault with: his tunic and puttees are smart and correct, and his speech ready and rapid. Yet the colonel, already irritated by the racket of the bicycle and the interruption to his newspaper, contemplates him with stern disfavor; for there is something exasperatingly and inexplicably wrong about him. He wears a pith helmet with a pagri; and in profile this pagri suggests a shirt which he has forgotten to tuck in behind, whilst its front view as it falls on his shoulders gives him a feminine air of having ringlets and a veil which is in the last degree unsoldierly. His figure is that of a boy of seventeen; but he seems to have borrowed a long head and Wellingtonian nose and chin from somebody else for the express purpose of annoying the colonel. Fortunately for him these are offences which cannot be stated on a charge sheet and dealt with by the provo-marshal; and of this the colonel is angrily aware.*

4. The Victoria Cross and the Distinguished Service Order, military honors.

The dispatch rider seems conscious of his incongruities; for, though very prompt, concise, and soldierly in his replies, he somehow suggests that there is an imprescriptible joke somewhere by an invisible smile which unhappily produces at times an impression of irony.[5]

He salutes; hands the letter to the colonel; and stands at attention.

TALLBOYS [*taking the letter*] Whats this?

THE RIDER. I was sent with a letter to the headman of the native village in the mountains, sir. That is his answer, sir.

TALLBOYS. I know nothing about it. Who sent you?

THE RIDER. Colonel Saxby, sir.

TALLBOYS. Colonel Saxby has just returned to the base, seriously ill. I have taken over from him. I am Colonel Tallboys.

THE RIDER. So I understand, sir.

TALLBOYS. Well, is this a personal letter to be sent on to him, or is it a dispatch?

THE RIDER. Dispatch, sir. Service document, sir. You may open it.

TALLBOYS [*turning in his chair and concentrating on him with fierce sarcasm*] Thank you. [*He surveys him from his instep to his nose*]. What is your name?

THE RIDER. Meek, sir.

TALLBOYS [*with disgust*] What!

THE RIDER. Meek, sir. M, double e, k.

The Colonel looks at him with loathing, and tears open the letter. There is a painful silence whilst he puzzles over it.

TALLBOYS. In dialect. Send the interpreter to me.

MEEK. It's of no consequence, sir. It was only to impress the headman.

TALLBOYS. INNdeed. Who picked you for this duty?

MEEK. Sergeant, sir.

TALLBOYS. He should have selected a capable responsible person, with sufficient style to impress the native headman to whom Colonel Saxby's letter was addressed. How did he come to select you?

MEEK. I volunteered, sir.

TALLBOYS. Did you indeed? You consider yourself an impressive person, eh? You think you carry about with you the atmosphere of the British Empire, do you?

MEEK. No, sir. I know the country. I can speak the dialects a little.

TALLBOYS. Marvellous! And why, with all these accomplishments, are you not at least a corporal?

MEEK. Not educationally qualified, sir.

TALLBOYS. Illiterate! Are you not ashamed?

MEEK. No, sir.

TALLBOYS. Proud of it, eh?

MEEK. Cant help it, sir.

5. By Shaw's admission Meek is drawn directly from T. E. Lawrence. Stanley Weintraub has made the more interesting suggestion that the Burglar (Aubrey) is on a more profound level, also suggested by Lawrence. See p. 472.

TALLBOYS. Where did you pick up your knowledge of the country?

MEEK. I was mostly a sort of tramp before I enlisted, sir.

TALLBOYS. Well, if I could get hold of the recruiting sergeant who enlisted you, I'd have his stripes off. Youre a disgrace to the army.

MEEK. Yessir.

TALLBOYS. Go and send the interpreter to me. And dont come back with him. Keep out of my sight.

MEEK [*hesitates*] Er—

TALLBOYS [*peremptorily*] Now then! Did you hear me give you an order? Send me the interpreter.

MEET. The fact is, Colonel—

TALLBOYS [*outraged*] How dare you say Colonel and tell me that the fact is? Obey your order and hold your tongue.

MEEK. Yessir. Sorry, sir. *I* am the interpreter.

> *Tallboys bounds to his feet; towers over Meek, who looks smaller than ever; and folds his arms to give emphasis to a terrible rejoinder. On the point of delivering it, he suddenly unfolds them again and sits down resignedly.*

TALLBOYS [*wearily and quite gently*] Very well. If you are the interpreter you had better interpret this for me. [*He proffers the letter*].

MEEK [*not accepting it*] No need, thank you, sir. The headman couldnt compose a letter, sir. I had to do it for him.

TALLBOYS. How did you know what was in Colonel Saxby's letter?

MEEK. I read it to him, sir.

TALLBOYS. Did he ask you to?

MEEK. Yessir.

TALLBOYS. He had no right to communicate the contents of such a letter to a private soldier. He cannot have known what he was doing. You must have represented yourself as being a responsible officer. Did you?

MEEK. It would be all the same to him, sir. He addressed me as Lord of the Western Isles.

TALLBOYS. You! You worm! If my letter was sent by the hands of an irresponsible messenger it should have contained a statement to that effect. Who drafted it?

MEEK. Quartermaster's clerk, sir.

TALLBOYS. Send him to me. Tell him to bring his note of Colonel Saxby's instructions. Do you hear? Stop making idiotic faces; and get a move on. Send me the quartermaster's clerk.

MEEK. The fact is—

TALLBOYS [*thundering*] Again!!

MEEK. Sorry, sir. *I* am the quartermaster's clerk.

TALLBOYS. What! You wrote both the letter and the headman's answer?

MEEK. Yessir.

TALLBOYS. Then either you are lying now or you were lying when you said you were illiterate. Which is it?

MEEK. I dont seem to be able to pass the examination when they want to promote me. It's my nerves, sir, I suppose.

TALLBOYS. Your nerves! What business has a soldier with nerves? You mean that you are no use for fighting, and have to be put to do anything that can be done without it.

MEEK. Yessir.

TALLBOYS. Well, next time you are sent with a letter I hope the brigands will catch you and keep you.

MEEK. There are no brigands, sir.

TALLBOYS. No brigands! Did you say no brigands?

MEEK. Yessir.

TALLBOYS. You are acquainted with the Articles of War, are you not?

MEEK. I have heard them read out, sir.

TALLBOYS. Do you understand them?

MEEK. I think so, sir.

TALLBOYS. You think so! Well, do a little more thinking. You are serving on an expeditionary force sent out to suppress brigandage in this district and to rescue a British lady who is being held for ransom. You know that. You dont think it: you know it, eh?

MEEK. So they say, sir.

TALLBOYS. You know also that under the Articles of War any soldier who knowingly does when on active service any act calculated to imperil the success of his Majesty's forces or any part thereof shall be liable to suffer death. Do you understand? Death!

MEEK. Yessir. Army Act, Part One, Section Four, Number Six. I think you mean Section Five, Number Five, sir.

TALLBOYS. Do I? Perhaps you will be good enough to quote Section Five, Number Five.

MEEK. Yessir. "By word of mouth spreads reports calculated to create unnecessary alarm or despondency."

TALLBOYS. It is fortunate for you, Private Meek, that the Act says nothing about private soldiers who create despondency by their personal appearance. Had it done so your life would not be worth half an hour's purchase.

MEEK. No, sir. Am I to file the letter and the reply with a translation, sir?

TALLBOYS [*tearing the letter to pieces and throwing them away*] Your folly has made a mockery of both. What did the headman say?

MEEK. Only that the country has very good roads now, sir. Motor coaches ply every day all the year around. The last active brigand retired fifteen years ago, and is ninety years old.

TALLBOYS. The usual tissue of lies. That headman is in league with the brigands. He takes a turn himself occasionally, I should say.

MEEK. I think not, sir. The fact is—

TALLBOYS. Did I hear you say "The fact is"?

MEEK. Sorry, sir. That old brigand was the headman himself. He is sending you a present of a sheep and six turkeys.

TALLBOYS. Send them back instantly. Take them back on your damned bicycle. Inform him that British officers are not orientals, and do not accept bribes from officials in whose districts they have to restore order.

MEEK. He wont understand, sir. He wont believe you have any authority unless you take presents. Besides, they havnt arrived yet.

TALLBOYS. Well, when his messengers arrive pack them back with their sheep and their turkeys and a note to say that my favor can be earned by honesty and diligence, but not purchased.

MEEK. They wont dare take back either the presents or the note, sir. Theyll steal the sheep and turkeys and report gracious messages from you. Better keep the meat and the birds, sir: they will be welcome after a long stretch of regulation food.

TALLBOYS. Private Meek.

MEEK. Yessir.

TALLBOYS. If you should be at any future time entrusted with the command of this expedition you will no doubt give effect to your own views and moral standards. For the present will you be good enough to obey my orders without comment?

MEEK. Yessir. Sorry, sir.

> *As Meek salutes and turns to go, he is confronted by the nurse, who, brilliantly undressed for bathing under a variegated silk wrap, comes from the pavilion, followed by the patient in the character of a native servant. All traces of the patient's illness have disappeared: she is sunburnt to the color of terra cotta; and her muscles are hard and glistening with unguent. She is disguised* en belle sauvage *by headdress, wig, ornaments, and girdle proper to no locality on earth except perhaps the Russian ballet. She carries a sun umbrella and a rug.*

TALLBOYS [*rising gallantly*] Ah, my dear Countess, delighted to see you. How good of you to come!

THE COUNTESS [*giving him her finger tips*] How do, Colonel? Hot, isnt it? [*Her dialect is now a spirited amalgamation of the foreign accents of all the waiters she has known*].

TALLBOYS. Take my chair. [*He goes behind it and moves it nearer to her*].

THE COUNTESS. Thanks. [*She throws off her wrap, which the patient takes, and flings herself with careless elegance into the chair, calling*] Mr Meek. Mr Mee-e-e-eek!

> *Meek returns smartly, and touches the front of his cap.*

THE COUNTESS. My new things from Paris have arrived at last. If you would be so very sweet as to get them to my bungalow somehow. Of course I will pay anything necessary. And could you get a letter of credit cashed for me. I'd better have three hundred pounds to go on with.

MEEK [*quite at ease: unconsciously dropping the soldier and assuming the gentleman*] How many boxes, Countess?

THE COUNTESS. Six, I am afraid. Will it be a lot of trouble?

MEEK. It will involve a camel.

THE COUNTESS. Oh, strings of camels if necessary. Expense is no object. And the letter of credit?

MEEK. Sorry, Countess: I have only two hundred on me. You shall have the other hundred tomorrow. [*He hands her a roll of notes; and she gives him the letter of credit*].

THE COUNTESS. You are never at a loss. Thanks. So good of you.

TALLBOYS. Chut! Dismiss.

> *Meek comes to attention, salutes, left-turns, and goes out at the double.*

TALLBOYS [*who has listened to this colloquy in renewed stupefaction*] Countess: that was very naughty of you.

THE COUNTESS. What have I done?

TALLBOYS. In camp you must never forget discipline. We keep it in the background; but it is always there and always necessary. That man is a private soldier. Any sort of social relation—any hint of familiarity with him—is impossible for you.

THE COUNTESS. But surely I may treat him as a human being.

TALLBOYS. Most certainly not. Your intention is natural and kindly; but if you treat a private soldier as a human being the result is disastrous to himself. He presumes. He takes liberties. And the consequence of that is that he gets into trouble and has a very bad time of it until he is taught his proper place by appropriate disciplinary measures. I must ask you to be particularly careful with this man Meek. He is only half-witted: he carries all his money about with him. If you have occasion to speak to him, make him feel by your tone that the relation between you is one of a superior addressing a very distant inferior. Never let him address you on his own initiative, or call you anything but "my lady." If there is anything we can do for you we shall be delighted to do it; but you must always ask me.

> *The patient, greatly pleased with the colonel for snubbing Sweetie, deposits her rug and umbrella on the sand, and places a chair for him on the lady's right with grinning courtesy. She then seats herself on the rug, and listens to them, hugging her knees and her umbrella, and trying to look as indigenous as possible.*

TALLBOYS. Thank you. [*He sits down*].

THE COUNTESS. I am so sorry. But if I ask anyone else they only look helpless and say "You had better see Meek about it."

TALLBOYS. No doubt they put everything on the poor fellow because he is not quite all there. Is it understood that in future you come to me, and not to Meek?

THE COUNTESS. I will indeed, Colonel. I am so sorry, and I thoroughly understand. I am scolded and forgiven, arnt I?

TALLBOYS [*smiling graciously*] Admonished, we call it. But of course it is not your fault: I have no right to scold you. It is I who must ask your forgiveness.

THE COUNTESS. Granted.

THE PATIENT [*in waiting behind them, coughs significantly*]!!

THE COUNTESS [*hastily*] A vulgar expression, Colonel, isnt it? But so simple and direct. I like it.

TALLBOYS. I didnt know it was vulgar. It is concise.

THE COUNTESS. Of course it isnt really vulgar. But a little lower middle class, if you follow me.

THE PATIENT [*pokes the chair with the sun umbrella*]!

THE COUNTESS [*as before*] Any news of the brigands, Colonel?

TALLBOYS. No; but Miss Mopply's mother, who is in a distracted condition—very naturally of course, poor woman!—has actually sent me the ransom. She implores me to pay it and release her child. She is afraid that if I make the slightest hostile demonstration the brigands will cut off the girl's fingers and send them in one by one until the ransom is paid. She thinks they may even begin with her ears, and disfigure her for life. Of course that is a possibility: such things have been done; and the poor lady points out very justly that I cannot replace her daughter's ears by exterminating the brigands afterwards, as I shall most certainly do if they dare lay a hand on a British lady. But I cannot countenance such a concession to deliberate criminality as the payment of a ransom. [*The two conspirators exchange dismayed glances*]. I have sent a message to the old lady by wireless to say that payment of a ransom is out of the question, but that the British Government is offering a substantial reward for information.

THE COUNTESS [*jumping up excitedly*] Wotjesoy? A reward on top of the ransom?

THE PATIENT [*pokes her savagely with the umbrella*]!!!

TALLBOYS [*surprised*] No. Instead of the ransom.

THE COUNTESS [*recollecting herself*] Of course. How silly of me! [*She sits down and adds, reflectively*] If this native girl could find out anything would she get the reward?

TALLBOYS. Certainly she would. Good idea that: what?

THE COUNTESS. Yes, Colonel, isnt it?

TALLBOYS. By the way, Countess, I met three people yesterday who know you very well.

THE PATIENT [*forgetting herself and scrambling forward to her knees*] But you—

THE COUNTESS [*stopping her with a backhanded slap on the mouth*] Silence, girl. How dare you interrupt the colonel? Go back to your place and hold your tongue.

> The Patient obeys humbly until the Colonel delicately turns his head away, when she shakes her fist threateningly at the smiter.

TALLBOYS. One of them was a lady. I happened to mention your brother's name; and she lit up at once and said "Dear Aubrey Bagot! I know his sister intimately. We were all three children together."

THE COUNTESS. It must have been dear Florence Dorchester. I hope she wont come here. I want to have an absolute holiday. I dont want to see anybody—except you, Colonel.

TALLBOYS. Haw! Very good of you to say so.

The Burglar comes from the bathing tent, very elegant in black and white bathing costume and black silken wrap with white silk lapels: a clerical touch.

TALLBOYS [*continuing*] Ah, Bagot! Ready for your dip? I was just telling the Countess that I met some friends of yours yesterday. Fancy coming on them out here of all places! Shews how small the world is, after all. [*Rising*] And now I am off to inspect stores. There is a shortage of maroons that I dont understand.

THE COUNTESS. What a pity! I love maroons. They have such nice ones at that confectioner's near the Place Vendôme.

TALLBOYS. Oh, youre thinking of marrons glacés. No: maroons are fireworks: things that go off with a bang. For signalling.

THE COUNTESS. Oh! the things they used to have in the war to warn us of an air raid?

TALLBOYS. Just so. Well, au revoir.

THE COUNTESS. Au revoir. Au revoir.

The Colonel touches his cap gallantly and bustles off past the hut to his inspection.

THE PATIENT [*rising vengefully*] You dare smack me in the face again, my girl, and I'll lay you out flat, even if I have to give away the whole show.

THE COUNTESS. Well, you keep that umbrella to yourself next time. What do you suppose I'm made of? Leather?

AUBREY [*coming between them*] Now! now! now! Children! children! Whats wrong?

THE PATIENT. This silly bitch—

AUBREY. Oh no, no, no, Mops. Damn it, be a lady. Whats the matter, Sweetie?

THE COUNTESS. You shouldnt talk like that, dearie. A low girl might say a thing like that; but youre expected to know better.

AUBREY. Mops: youve shocked Sweetie.

THE PATIENT. Well: do you think she never shocks me? She's a walking earthquake. And now what are we to do if these people the colonel has met turn up? There must be a real Countess Valbrioni.

THE COUNTESS. Not much there isnt. Do you suppose we three are the only liars in the world? All you have to do is give yourself a swell title, and all the snobs within fifty miles will swear that you are their dearest friend.

AUBREY. The first lesson a crook has to learn, darling, is that nothing succeeds like lying. Make any statement that is so true that it has been staring us in the face all our lives, and the whole world will rise up and passionately contradict you. If you dont withdraw and apologize, it will be the worse for you. But just tell a thundering silly lie that everyone knows is a lie, and a murmur of pleased assent will hum up from every quarter of the globe. If Sweetie had introduced herself as what she obviously is: that is, an ex-hotel chambermaid who became a criminal on principle through the preaching of an ex-army chaplain—me!—with whom she fell in love deeply but transitorily, nobody would have believed her. But she has no sooner made the impossible statement that she is a countess, and that the ex-chaplain is her half stepbrother the Honorable Aubrey Bagot, than clouds of witnesses spring up to assure Colonel Tallboys that it is all gospel truth. So have no fear of exposure, darling; and do you, my Sweetie, lie and lie and lie until your imagination bursts.

THE PATIENT [*throwing herself moodily into the deck chair*] I wonder are all crooks as fond of preaching as you are.

AUBREY [*bending affectionately over her*] Not all, dearest. I dont preach because I am a crook, but because I have a gift—a divine gift—that way.

THE PATIENT. Where did you get it? Is your father a bishop?

AUBREY [*straightening himself up to declaim*] Have I not told you that he is an atheist, and, like all atheists, an inflexible moralist? He said I might become a preacher if I believed what I preached. That, of course, was nonsense: my gift of preaching is not confined to what I believe: I can preach anything, true or false. I am like a violin, on which you can play all sorts of music, from jazz to Mozart. [*Relaxing*] But the old man never could be brought to see it. He said the proper profession for me was the bar. [*He snatches up the rug; replaces it on the patient's left; and throws himself down lazily on it*].

THE COUNTESS. Aint we going to bathe?

AUBREY. Oh, dash it, dont lets go into the water. Lets sunbathe.

THE COUNTESS. Lazy devil! [*She takes the folding stool from the pavilion, and sits down discontentedly*].

THE PATIENT. Your father was right. If you have no conscience about what you preach, your proper job is at the bar. But as you have no conscience about what you do, you will probably end in the dock.

AUBREY. Most likely. But I am a born preacher, not a pleader. The theory of legal procedure is that if you set two liars to expose one another, the truth will emerge. That would not suit me. I greatly dislike being contradicted; and the only place where a man is safe from contradiction is in the pulpit. I detest argument: it is unmannerly, and obscures the preacher's message. Besides, the law is too much concerned with crude facts and too little with spiritual things; and it is in spiritual things that I am interested: they alone call my gift into full play.

THE PATIENT. You call preaching things you dont believe spiritual, do you?

AUBREY. Put a sock in it, Mops. My gift is divine: it is not limited by my petty personal convictions. It is a gift of lucidity as well as of eloquence. Lucidity is one of the most precious of gifts: the gift of the teacher: the gift of explanation. I can explain anything to anybody; and I love doing it. I feel I must do it if only the doctrine is beautiful and subtle and exquisitely put together. I may feel instinctively that it is the rottenest nonsense. Still, if I can get a moving dramatic effect out of it, and preach a really splendid sermon about it, my gift takes possession of me and obliges me to sail in and do it. Sweetie: go and get me a cushion for my head: there's a dear.

THE PATIENT. Do nothing of the kind, Sweetie. Let him wait on himself.

THE COUNTESS [*rising*] He'd only mess everything about looking for it. I like to have my rooms left tidy. [*She goes into the pavilion*].

THE PATIENT. Isnt that funny, Pops? She has a conscience as a chambermaid and none as a woman.

AUBREY. Very few people have more than one point of honor, Mops. And lots of them havnt even one.

THE COUNTESS [*returning with a silk cushion, which she hurls hard at Aubrey's head*] There! And now I give you both notice. I'm getting bored with this place.

AUBREY [*making himself comfortable with his cushion*] Oh, you are always getting bored.

THE PATIENT. I suppose that means that you are tired of Tallboys.

THE COUNTESS [*moving restlessly about*] I am fed up with him to that degree that I sometimes feel I could almost marry him, just to put him on the list of the inevitables that I must put up with willynilly, like getting up in the morning, and washing and dressing and eating and drinking: things you darent let yourself get tired of because if you did theyd drive you mad. Lets go and have a bit of real life somewhere.

THE PATIENT. Real life! I wonder where thats to be found! Weve spent nearly six thousand pounds in two months looking for it. The money we got for the necklace wont last for ever.

AUBREY. Sweetie: you will have to stick it in this spot until we touch that ransom; and that's all about it.

THE COUNTESS. I'll do as I like, not what you tell me. And I tell you again—the two of you—you can take a week's notice. I'm bored with this business. I need a change.

AUBREY. What are we to do with her, Mops? Always change! change! change!

THE COUNTESS. Well, I like to see new faces.

AUBREY. I could be happy as a Buddha in a temple, eternally contemplating my own middle and having the same old priest to polish me up every day. But Sweetie wants a new face every fortnight. I have known her fall in love with a new face twice in the same week. [*Turning to her*] Woman: have you any sense of the greatness of constancy?

COUNTESS. I might be constant if I were a real countess. But I'm only a hotel chambermaid; and a hotel chambermaid gets so used to new faces that at last they become a necessity. [*She sits down on the stool*].

AUBREY. And the oftener the faces change the more the tips come to, eh?

COUNTESS. Oh, it's not that, though of course that counts. The real secret of it is that though men are awfully nice for the first few days, it doesnt last. You get the best out of men by having them always new. What I say is that a love affair should always be a honeymoon. And the only way to make sure of that is to keep changing the man; for the same man can never keep it up. In all my life I have known only one man that kept it up til he died.

THE PATIENT [*interested*] Ah! Then the thing is possible?

COUNTESS. Yes: it was a man that married my sister: that was how I came to know about it.

AUBREY. And his ardor never palled? Day in and day out, until death did them part, he was the same as on the wedding day? Is that really true, Sweetie?

THE COUNTESS. It is. But then he beat her on their wedding day; and he beat her just as hard every day afterwards. I made her get a separation order; but she went back to him because nobody else paid her any attention.

AUBREY. Why didnt you tell me that before? I'd have beaten you black and blue sooner than lose you. [*Sitting up*] Would you believe it, Mops, I was in love with this woman: madly in love with her. She was not my intellectual equal; and I had to teach her table manners. But there was an extraordinary sympathy between our lower centres; and when after ten days she threw me over for another man I was restrained from murder and suicide only by the most resolute exercise of my reasoning powers, my determination to be a civilized man, and fear of the police.

THE COUNTESS. Well, I gave you a good time for the ten days, didnt I? Lots of people dont get that much to look back on. Besides, you know it was for your own good, Popsy. We werent really suited, were we?

AUBREY. You had acquired an insatiable taste for commercial travellers. You could sample them at the rate of three a week. I could not help admiring such amazing mobility of the affections. I had heard operatic tenors bawling Woman Is Fickle; but it always seemed to me that what was to be dreaded in women was their implacable constancy. But you! Fickle! I should think so.

THE COUNTESS. Well, the travellers were just as bad, you know.

AUBREY. Just as bad! Say just as good. Fickleness means simply mobility, and mobility is a mark of civilization. You should pride yourself on it. If you dont you will lose your self-respect; and I cannot endure a woman who has no self-respect.

THE COUNTESS. Oh, whats the use of us talking about self-respect? You are a thief and so am I. I go a little further than that, myself; and so would you if you were a woman. Dont you be a hypocrite, Popsy: at least not with me.

AUBREY. At least not with you! Sweetie: that touch of concern for my spiritual welfare almost convinces me that you still love me.

THE COUNTESS. Not me. Not much. I'm through with you, my lad. And I cant quite fancy the colonel: he's too old, and too much the gentleman.

AUBREY. He's better than nobody. Who else is there?

THE COUNTESS. Well, there's the sergeant. I daresay I have low tastes; but he's my sort, and the colonel isnt.

THE PATIENT. Have you fallen in love with Sergeant Fielding, Sweetie?

THE COUNTESS. Well, yes; if you like to call it that.

AUBREY. May I ask have you sounded him on the subject?

THE COUNTESS. How can I? I'm a countess; and he's only a sergeant. If I as much as let on that I'm conscious of his existence I give away the show to the colonel. I can only look at him. And I cant do even that when anyone else is looking. And all the time I want to hug him [*she breaks down in tears*].

AUBREY. Oh for Heaven's sake dont start crying.

THE PATIENT. For all you know, Sweetie, the sergeant may be a happily married man.

THE COUNTESS. What difference does that make to my feelings? I am so lonely. The place is so dull. No pictures. No dances. Nothing to do but be ladylike. And the one really lovable man going to waste! I'd rather be dead.

THE PATIENT. Well, it's just as bad for me.

THE COUNTESS. No it isnt. Youre a real lady: youre broken in to be dull. Besides, you have Popsy. And youre supposed to be our servant. That gives you the run of the whole camp when youre tired of him. You can pick up a private when you like. Whats to prevent you?

THE PATIENT. My ladylike morals, I suppose.

THE COUNTESS. Morals your grandmother! I thought youd left all that flapdoodle behind you when you came away with us.

THE PATIENT. I meant to. Ive tried to. But you shock me in spite of myself every second time you open your mouth.

THE COUNTESS. Dont you set up to be a more moral woman than I am, because youre not.

THE PATIENT. I dont pretend to be. But I may tell you that my infatuation for Popsy, which I now see was what really nerved me to this astonishing breakaway, has been, so far, quite innocent. Can you believe that, you clod?

THE COUNTESS. Oh yes I can: Popsy's satisfied as long as you let him talk. What I mean is—and I tell it to you straight—that with all my faults I'm content with one man at a time.

THE PATIENT. Do you suggest that I am carrying on with two men?

THE COUNTESS. I dont suggest anything. I say what I mean straight out; and if you dont like it you can lump it. You may be in love with Popsy; but youre interested in Private Meek, though what you see in that dry little worm beats me.

THE PATIENT. Have you noticed, my Sweetie, that your big strapping splendid sergeant is completely under the thumb of that dry little worm?

THE COUNTESS. He wont be when I get him under m y thumb. But you just be careful. Take this tip from me: one man at a time. I am advising you for your good, because youre only a beginner; and what you think is love, and interest, and all that, is not real love at all: three quarters of it is only unsatisfied curiosity. Ive lived at that address myself; and I know. When I love a man now it's all love and nothing else. It's the real thing while it lasts. I havnt the least curiosity about my lovely sergeant: I know just what he'll say and what he'll do. I just want him to do it.

THE PATIENT [*rising, revolted*] Sweetie: I really cannot bear any more of this. No doubt it's perfectly true. It's quite right that you should say it frankly and plainly. I envy and admire the frightful coolness with which you plump it all out. Perhaps I shall get used to it in time. But at present it knocks me to pieces. I shall simply have to go away if you pursue the subject. [*She sits down in the cane chair with her back to them*].

AUBREY. Thats the worst of Sweetie. We all have—to put it as nicely as I can—our lower centres and our higher centres. Our lower centres act: they act with a terrible power that sometimes destroys us; but they dont talk. Speech belongs to the higher centres. In all the great poetry and literature of the world the higher centres speak. In all respectable conversation the higher centres speak, even when they are saying nothing or telling lies. But the lower centres are there all the time: a sort of guilty secret with every one of us, though they are dumb. I remember asking my tutor at college whether, if anyone's lower centres began to talk, the shock would not be worse than the one Balaam got when his donkey began talking to him. He only told me half a dozen improper stories to shew how openminded he was. I never mentioned the subject again until I met Sweetie. Sweetie is Balaam's ass.

THE COUNTESS. Keep a civil tongue in your head, Popsy. I—

AUBREY [*springing to his feet*] Woman: I am paying you a compliment: Balaam's ass was wiser than Balaam. You should read your Bible. That is what makes Sweetie almost superhuman. Her lower centres speak. Since the war the lower centres have become vocal. And the effect is that of an earthquake. For they speak truths that have never been spoken before—truths that the makers of our domestic institutions have tried to ignore. And now that Sweetie goes shouting them all over the place, the institutions are rocking and splitting and sundering. They leave us no place to live, no certainties, no workable morality, no heaven, no hell, no commandments, and no God.

THE PATIENT. What about the light in our own souls that you were so eloquent about the day before yesterday at lunch when you drank a pint of champagne?

AUBREY. Most of us seem to have no souls. Or if we have them, they have nothing to hang on to. Meanwhile, Sweetie goes on shouting. [*He takes refuge in the deck chair*].

THE COUNTESS [*rising*] Oh, what are you gassing about? I am not shouting. I should be a good woman if it wasnt so dull. If youre goodnatured, you just get put upon. Who are the good women? Those that enjoy being dull and like being put upon. Theyve no appetites. Life's thrown away on them: they get nothing out of it.

THE PATIENT. Well, come, Sweetie! What do you get out of it?

THE COUNTESS. Excitement: thats what I get out of it. Look at Popsy and me! We're always planning robberies. Of course I know it's mostly imagination; but the fun is in the planning and the expectation. Even if we did them and were caught, there would be the excitement of being tried and being in all the papers. Look at poor Harry Smiler that murdered the cop in Croydon! When he came and told us what he'd done Popsy offered to go out and get him some cyanide to poison himself; for it was a dead sure thing that he'd be caught and bumped off. "What!" says Harry; "and lose the excitement of being tried for my life! I'd rather be hanged" he says; and hanged he was. And I say it must have been almost worth it. After all, he'd have died anyhow: perhaps of something really painful. Harry wasnt a bad man really; but he couldnt bear dullness. He had a wonderful collection of pistols that he had begun as a boy: he picked up a lot in the war. Just for the romance of it, you know: he meant no harm. But he'd never shot anyone with them; and at last the temptation was too great and he went out and shot the cop. Just for nothing but the feeling that he'd fired the thing off and done somebody in with it. When Popsy asked him why he'd done it, all he could say was that it was a sort of fulfilment. But it gives you an idea, doesnt it, of what I mean? [*She sits down again, relieved by her outburst*].

AUBREY. All it means is a low vitality. Here is a man with all the miracles of the universe to stagger his imagination and all the problems of human destiny to employ his mind, and he goes out and shoots an innocent policeman because he can think of nothing more interesting to do. Quite right to hang him. And all the people who can find nothing more exciting to do than to crowd into the court to watch him being sentenced to death should have been hanged too. You will be hanged someday, Sweetie, because you have not what people call a richly stored mind. I have tried to educate you—

THE COUNTESS. Yes: you gave me books to read. But I couldnt read them: they were as dull as ditchwater. Ive tried crossword puzzles to occupy my mind and keep me off planning robberies; but what crossword puzzle is half the fun and excitement of picking somebody's pocket, let alone that you cant live by it? You wanted me to take to drink to keep me quiet. But I dont like being drunk; and what would become of my good looks if I did? Ten bottles of champagne couldnt make you feel as you do when you walk past a policeman who has only to stop you and search you to put you away for three years.

THE PATIENT. Pops: did you really try to set her drinking? What a thoroughpaced blackguard you are!

AUBREY. She is much better company when she's half drunk. Listen to her now, when she is sober!

THE PATIENT. Sweetie: are you really having such a jolly time after all? You began by threatening to give up our exciting enterprise because it is so dull.

AUBREY. She is free. There is the sergeant. And there is always the hope of something turning up and the sense of being ready for it without having to break all the shackles and throw down all the walls that imprison a respectable woman.

THE PATIENT. Well, what about me?

AUBREY [*puzzled*] Well, what about you? You are free, arnt you?

THE PATIENT [*rising very deliberately, and going behind him to his left hand, which she picks up and fondles as she sermonizes, seated on the arm of his chair*] My angel love, you have rescued me from respectability so completely that I have for a month past been living the life of a mountain goat. I have got rid of my anxious worrying mother as completely as a weaned kid, and I no longer hate her. My slavery to cooks stuffing me with long meals of fish, flesh, and fowl is a thing of the miserable past: I eat dates and bread and water and raw onions when I can get them; and when I cant get them I fast, with the result that I have forgotten what illness means; and if I ran away from you two neither of you could catch me; and if you did I could fight the pair of you with one hand tied behind me. I revel in all your miracles of the universe: the delicious dawns, the lovely sunsets, the changing winds, the cloud pictures, the flowers, the animals and their ways, the birds and insects and reptiles. Every day is a day of adventure with its cold and heat, its light and darkness, its cycles of exultant vigor and exhaustion, hunger and satiety, its longings for action that change into a longing for sleep, its thoughts of heavenly things that change so suddenly into a need for food.

AUBREY. What more could any mortal desire?

THE PATIENT [*seizing him by the ears*] Liar.

AUBREY. Thank you. You mean, I presume, that these things do not satisfy you: you want me as well.

THE PATIENT. You!! You!!! you selfish lazy sugary tongued blackguard. [*Releasing him*] No: I included you with the animals and their ways, just as I included Sweetie and the sergeant.

THE COUNTESS. You let Sweetie and her sergeant alone: d'y'hear? I have had enough of that joke on me.

THE PATIENT [*rising and taking her by the chin to turn her face up*] It is no joke, Sweetiest: it is the dead solemn earnest. I called Pops a liar, Sweetie, because all this is not enough. The glories of nature dont last any decently active person a week, unless theyre professional naturalists or mathematicians or a painter or something. I want something sensible to do. A beaver has a jolly time because it has to build its dam and bring up its family. I want my little job like the beaver. If I do nothing but contemplate the universe there is so much in it that is cruel and terrible and wantonly evil, and so much more that is oppressively astronomical and endless and inconceivable and impossible, that I shall just go stark raving mad and be taken back to my mother with straws in my hair. The truth is, I am free; I am healthy; I am happy; and I am utterly miserable. [*Turning on Aubrey*] Do you hear? Utterly miserable.

AUBREY [*losing his temper*] And what do you suppose I am? Here with nothing to do but drag about two damn' silly women and talk to them.

THE COUNTESS. It's worse for them. They have to listen to you.

THE PATIENT. I despise you. I hate you. You—you—you—you gentleman thief. What right has a thief to be a gentleman? Sweetie is bad enough, heaven knows, with her vulgarity and her low cunning: always trying to get the better of somebody or to get hold of a man; but at least she's a woman; and she's real. Men are not real: theyre all talk, talk, talk—

THE COUNTESS [*half rising*] You keep a civil tongue in your head: do you hear?

THE PATIENT. Another syllable of your cheek, Sweetie; and I'll give you a hiding that will keep you screaming for half an hour. [*Sweetie subsides*]. I want to beat somebody: I want to kill somebody. I shall end by killing the two of you. What are we, we three glorious adventurers? Just three inefficient fertilizers.

AUBREY. What on earth do you mean by that?

THE PATIENT. Yes: inefficient fertilizers. We do nothing but convert good food into bad manure. We are walking factories of bad manure: thats what we are.

THE COUNTESS [*rising*] Well, I am not going to sit here and listen to that sort of talk. You ought to be ashamed of yourself.

AUBREY [*rising also, shocked*] Miss Mopply: there are certain disgusting truths that no lady would throw in the teeth of her fellow creatures—

THE PATIENT. I am not a lady: I am free now to say what I please. How do you like it?

THE COUNTESS [*relenting*] Look here, dearie. You mustnt go off at the deep end like this. You— [*The patient turns fiercely on her: she screams*]. Ah-a-a-ah! Popsy: she's mad. Save me. [*She runs away, out past the pavilion*].

AUBREY. What is the matter with you? Are you out of your senses? [*He tries to hold her; but she sends him sprawling*].

THE PATIENT. No. I am exercising my freedom. The freedom you preached. The freedom you made possible for me. You dont like to hear Sweetie's lower centres shouting. Well, now you hear my higher centres shouting. You dont seem to like it any better.

AUBREY. Mops: youre hysterical. You felt splendid an hour ago; and you will feel splendid again an hour from now. You will always feel splendid if you keep yourself fit.

THE PATIENT. Fit for what? A lost dog feels fit: thats what makes him stray; but he's the unhappiest thing alive. I am a lost dog: a tramp, a vagabond. Ive got nothing to do. Ive got nowhere to go. Sweetie's miserable; and youre miserable; and I'm miserable; and I shall just kick you and beat you to a jelly.

> *She rushes at him. He dodges her and runs off past the hut. At that moment Tallboys returns with Meek past the other side of the hut; and the patient, unable to check herself, crashes into his arms.*

TALLBOYS [*sternly*] Whats this? What are you doing here? Why are you making this noise? Dont clench your fists in my presence. [*She droops obsequiously*]. Whats the matter?

THE PATIENT [*salaaming and chanting*] Bmal elttil a dah yram, Tuan.

TALLBOYS. Can you speak English?

THE PATIENT. No Engliss.

TALLBOYS. Or French?

THE PATIENT. No Frennss, Tuan. Wons sa etihw saw eceelf sti.

TALLBOYS. Very well: dont do it again. Now off with you.

> *She goes out backward into the pavilion, salaaming. Tallboys sits down in the deck chair.*

TALLBOYS [*to Meek*] Here, you. You say youre the interpreter. Did you understand what that girl said to me?

MEEK. Yessir.

TALLBOYS. What dialect was it? It didnt sound like what the natives speak here.

MEEK. No sir. I used to speak it at school. English back slang, sir.

TALLBOYS. Back slang? What do you mean?

MEEK. English spelt backwards. She reversed the order of the words too, sir. That shews that she has those two little speeches off by heart.

TALLBOYS. But how could a native girl do such a thing? I couldnt do it myself.

MEEK. That shews that she's not a native girl, sir.

TALLBOYS. But this must be looked into. Were you able to pick up what she said?

MEEK. Only bmal elttil, sir. That was quite easy. It put me on to the rest.

TALLBOYS. But what does bmal elttil mean?

MEEK. Little lamb, sir.

TALLBOYS. She called me a little lamb!

MEEK. No sir. All she said was "Mary had a little lamb." And when you asked her could she speak French she said, of course, "Its fleece was white as snow."

TALLBOYS. But that was insolence.

MEEK. It got her out of her difficulty, sir.

TALLBOYS. This is very serious. The woman is passing herself off on the Countess as a native servant.

MEEK. Do you think so, sir?

TALLBOYS. I dont think so: I know so. Dont be a fool, man. Pull yourself together, and dont make silly answers.

MEEK. Yessir. No sir.

TALLBOYS [*angrily bawling at him*] "Ba Ba black sheep: have you any wool? Yes sir, no sir, three bags full." Dont say yessir no sir to me.

MEEK. No sir.

TALLBOYS. Go and fetch that girl back. Not a word to her about my finding her out, mind. When I have finished with her you will explain to me about those maroons.

MEEK. Yessir. [*He goes into the pavilion*].

TALLBOYS. Hurry up. [*He settles himself comfortably and takes out his cigaret case*].

> The Countess peers round the corner of the pavilion to see whether she may safely return. Aubrey makes a similar reconnaissance round the corner of the hut.

THE COUNTESS. Here I am again, you see. [*She smiles fascinatingly at the Colonel and sits down on her stool*].

AUBREY. Moi aussi. May I— [*he stretches himself on the rug*].

TALLBOYS [*sitting up and putting the cigaret case back in his pocket*] Just in the nick of time. I was about to send for you. I have made a very grave discovery. That native servant of yours is not a native. Her lingo is a ridiculous fraud. She is an English-woman.

AUBREY. You dont say so!

THE COUNTESS. Oh, impossible.

TALLBOYS. Not a doubt of it. She's a fraud: take care of your jewels. Or else—and this is what I suspect—she's a spy.

AUBREY. A spy! But we are not at war.

TALLBOYS. The League of Nations has spies everywhere. [*To the Countess*] You must allow me to search her luggage at once, before she knows that I have found her out.

THE COUNTESS. But I have missed nothing. I am sure she hasnt stolen anything. What do you want to search her luggage for?

TALLBOYS. For maroons.

THE COUNTESS ⎱ [*together*] ⎰ Maroons!
AUBREY   ⎰   ⎱ Maroons!

TALLBOYS. Yes, maroons. I inspected the stores this morning; and the maroons are missing. I particularly wanted them to recall me at lunch time when I go sketching. I am rather a dab at water co-lors. And there is not a single maroon left. There should be fifteen.

AUBREY. Oh, I can clear that up. It's one of your men: Meek. He goes about on a motor bicycle with a sack full of maroons and a lot of wire. He said he was surveying. He was evidently very anxious to get rid of me; so I did not press my inquiries. But that accounts for the maroons.

TALLBOYS. Not at all. This is very serious. Meek is a half witted creature who should never have been enlisted. He is like a child: this woman could do anything she pleases with him.

THE COUNTESS. But what could she possibly want with maroons?

TALLBOYS. I dont know. This expedition has been sent out without the sanction of the League of Nations. We always forget to con-sult it when there is anything serious in hand. The woman may be an emissary of the League. She may be working against us.

THE COUNTESS. But even so, what harm can she do us?

TALLBOYS [*tapping his revolver*] My dear lady, do you suppose I am carrying this for fun? Dont you realize that the hills here are full of hostile tribes who may try to raid us at any moment? Look at that electric horn there. If it starts honking, look out;

for it will mean that a body of tribesmen has been spotted advancing on us.

THE COUNTESS [*alarmed*] If I'd known that, you wouldnt have got me here. Is that so, Popsy?

AUBREY. Well, yes; but it doesnt matter: theyre afraid of us.

TALLBOYS. Yes, because they dont know that we are a mere handful of men. But if this woman is in communication with them and has got hold of that idiot Meek, we may have them down on us like a swarm of hornets. I dont like this at all. I must get to the bottom of it at once. Ah! here she comes.

> *Meek appears at the entrance to the pavilion. He stands politely aside to let the patient pass him, and remains there.*

MEEK. The colonel would like a word with you, Miss.

AUBREY. Go easy with her, Colonel. She can run like a deer. And she has muscles of iron. You had better turn out the guard before you tackle her.

TALLBOYS. Pooh! Here, you!

> *The patient comes to him past the Countess with an air of disarming innocence; falls on her knees; lifts her palms; and smites the ground with her forehead.*

TALLBOYS. They tell me you can run fast. Well, a bullet can run faster. [*He taps his revolver*]. Do you understand that?

THE PATIENT [*salaaming*] Bmal elttil a dah yram snow sa etihw saw eceelf tsi—

TALLBOYS [*tonitruant*[6]] And everywhere that Mary went—

THE PATIENT [*adroitly cutting in*] That lamb was sure to go. Got me, Colonel. How clever of you! Well, what of it?

TALLBOYS. That is what I intend to find out. You are not a native.

THE PATIENT. Yes, of Somerset.

TALLBOYS. Precisely. Well, why are you disguised? Why did you try to make me believe that you dont understand English?

THE PATIENT. For a lark, Colonel.

TALLBOYS. That's not good enough. Why have you passed yourself off on this lady as a native servant? Being a servant is no lark. Answer me. Dont stand there trying to invent a lie. Why did you pretend to be a servant?

THE PATIENT. One has so much more control of the house as a servant than as a mistress nowadays, Colonel.

TALLBOYS. Very smart, that. You will tell me next that one controls a regiment much more effectively as a private than as a colonel, eh?

> *The klaxon sounds stridently. The Colonel draws his revolver and makes a dash for the top of the sandhill, but is outraced by Meek, who gets there first and takes the word of command with irresistible authority, leaving him stupent. Aubrey, who has scrambled to his feet, moves towards the sand dunes to see what is happening. Sweetie clutches the patient's arm in terror and drags her towards the pavilion.*

6. Thundering.

*She is fiercely shaken off; and Mops stands her ground
defiantly and runs towards the sound of the guns when they
begin.*

MEEK. Stand to. Charge your magazines. Stand by the maroons.
How many do you make them, sergeant? How far off?

SERGEANT FIELDING [*invisible*] Forty horse. Nine hundred yards,
about, I make it.

MEEK. Rifles at the ready. Cut-offs open. Sights up to eighteen
hundred, right over their heads: no hitting. Ten rounds rapid:
fire. [*Fusillade of rifles*]. How is that?

SERGEANT'S VOICE. Theyre coming on, sir.

MEEK. Number one maroons: ready. Contact. [*Formidable explosions on the right*]. How is that?

SERGEANT'S VOICE. Theyve stopped.

MEEK. Number two maroons ready. Contact. [*Explosions on the
left*]. How is that?

SERGEANT'S VOICE. Bolted, sir, every man of them.

*Meek returns from the hill in the character of an insignifi-
cant private, followed by Aubrey, to the Colonel's left and
right respectively.*

MEEK. Thats all right, sir. Excuse interruption.

TALLBOYS. Oh! You call this an interruption?

MEEK. Yessir: theres nothing in it to trouble you about. Shall I
draw up the report, sir? Important engagement: enemy routed:
no British casualties. D.S.O. for you, perhaps, sir.

TALLBOYS. Private Meek: may I ask—if you will pardon my presumption—who is in command of this expedition, you or I?

MEEK. You, sir.

TALLBOYS [*repouching the revolver*] You flatter me. Thank you.
May I ask, further, who the devil gave you leave to plant the entire regimental stock of maroons all over the hills and explode
them in the face of the enemy?

MEEK. It was the duty of the intelligence orderly, sir. I'm the intelligence orderly. I had to make the enemy believe that the hills
are bristling with British cannon. They think that now, sir. No
more trouble from them.

TALLBOYS. Indeed! Quartermaster's clerk, interpreter, intelligence
orderly. Any further rank of which I have not been informed?

MEEK. No sir.

TALLBOYS. Quite sure youre not a fieldmarshal, eh?

MEEK. Quite sure, sir. I never was anything higher than a colonel.

TALLBOYS. You a colonel? What do you mean?

MEEK. Not a real colonel, sir. Mostly a brevet,[7] sir, to save appearances when I had to take command.

TALLBOYS. And how do you come to be a private now?

MEEK. I prefer the ranks, sir. I have a freer hand. And the conversation in the officers' mess doesnt suit me. I always resign a commission and enlist again.

TALLBOYS. Always! How many commissions have you held?

7. In the military, a temporary or emergency rank.

MEEK. I dont quite remember, sir. Three, I think.

TALLBOYS. Well, I am dashed!

THE PATIENT. Oh, Colonel! And you mistook this great military genius for a half wit!!!

TALLBOYS [*with aplomb*] Naturally. The symptoms are precisely the same. [*To Meek*] Dismiss.

    Meek salutes and trots smartly out past the hut.

AUBREY. By Jove!!

THE COUNTESS. Well I ne— [*Correcting herself*] Tiens, tiens, tiens, tiens!

THE PATIENT. What are you going to do about him, Colonel?

TALLBOYS. Madam: the secret of command, in the army and elsewhere, is never to waste a moment doing anything that can be delegated to a subordinate. I have a passion for sketching in watercolors. Hitherto the work of commanding my regiment has interfered very seriously with its gratification. Henceforth I shall devote myself almost entirely to sketching, and leave the command of the expedition to Private Meek. And since you all seem to be on more intimate terms with him that I can claim, will you be good enough to convey to him—casually, you understand—that I already possess the D.S.O. and that what I am out for at present is a K.C.B.[8] Or rather, to be strictly accurate, that is what my wife is out for. For myself, my sole concern for the moment is whether I should paint that sky with Prussian blue or with cobalt.

THE COUNTESS. Fancy you wasting your time on painting pictures!

TALLBOYS. Countess: I paint pictures to make me feel sane. Dealing with men and women makes me feel mad. Humanity always fails me: Nature never.

8. Knight Commander of the Bath.

Act III

A narrow gap leading down to the beach through masses of soft brown sandstone, pitted with natural grottoes. Sand and big stones in the foreground. Two of the grottoes are accessible from the beach by mounting from the stones, which make rough platforms in front of them. The soldiers have amused themselves by hewing them into a rude architecture and giving them fancy names. The one on your right as you descend the rough path through the gap is taller than it is broad, and has a natural pillar and a stone like an altar in it, giving a Gothic suggestion which has been assisted by knocking the top of the opening into something like a pointed arch, and surmounting it with the inscription SN PAULS. The grotto to the left is much wider. It contains a bench long enough to accommodate two persons; its recesses are illuminated rosily by bulbs wrapped in pink paper; and some scholarly soldier has carved above it in Greek characters the word Αγαπεμονε, beneath which is written in red chalk THE ABODE OF LOVE, under which again some ribald has added in white chalk, NO NEED TO WASTE THE ELECTRIC LIGHT.

For the moment The Abode of Love has been taken possession of by the sergeant, a wellbuilt handsome man, getting on for forty. He is sitting on the bench, and is completely absorbed in two books, comparing them with rapt attention.

St Pauls is also occupied. A very tall gaunt elder, by his dress and bearing a well-to-do English gentleman, sits on a stone at the altar, resting his elbows on it with his chin in his hands. He is in the deepest mourning; and his attitude is one of hopeless dejection.

Sweetie, now fully and brilliantly dressed, comes slowly down the path through the gap, moody and bored. On the beach she finds nothing to interest her until the sergeant unconsciously attracts her notice by finding some remarkable confirmation or contradiction between his two books, and smiting one of them appreciatively with his fist. She instantly brightens up; climbs to the mouth of the grotto eagerly; and posts herself beside him, on his right. But he is so rapt in his books that she waits in vain to be noticed.

SWEETIE [contemplating him ardently] Ahem!
> The Sergeant looks up. Seeing who it is, he springs to his feet and stands to attention.

SWEETIE [giving herself no airs] You neednt stand up for me, you know.

THE SERGEANT [stiffly] Beg pardon, your ladyship. I was not aware of your ladyship's presence.

SWEETIE. Can all that stuff, Sergeant. [She sits on the bench on his right]. Dont lets waste time. This place is as dull for me as it is for you. Dont you think we two could amuse ourselves a bit if we were friends?

THE SERGEANT [*with stern contempt*] No, my lady, I dont. I saw
a lot of that in the war: pretty ladies brightening up the hospitals and losing their silly heads, let alone upsetting the men; and
I dont hold with it. Keep to your class: I'll keep to mine.

SWEETIE. My class! Garn! I'm no countess; and I'm fed up with
pretending to be one. Didnt you guess?

THE SERGEANT [*resuming his seat and treating her as one of his
own class*] Why should I trouble to start guessing about you?
Any girl can be a countess nowadays if she's goodlooking enough
to pick up a count.

SWEETIE. Oh! You think I'm goodlooking, do you?

THE SERGEANT. Come! If youre not a countess what are you?
Whats the game, eh?

SWEETIE. The game, darling, is that youre my fancy. I love you.

THE SERGEANT. Whats that to me? A man of my figure can have
his pick.

SWEETIE. Not here, dear. Theres only one other white woman
within fifty miles; and she's a real lady. She wouldnt look at you.

THE SERGEANT. Well, thats a point. Thats a point, certainly.

SWEETIE [*snuggling to him*] Yes, isnt it?

THE SERGEANT [*suffering the advance but not responding*] This
climate plays the devil with a man, no matter how serious
minded he is.

SWEETIE [*slipping her arm through his*] Well, isnt it natural?
Whats the use of pretending?

THE SERGEANT. Still, I'm not a man to treat a woman as a mere necessity. Many soldiers do: to them a woman is no more than a
jar of marmalade, to be consumed and put away. I dont take
that view. I admit that there is that side to it, and that for people incapable of anything better—mere animals as you might
say—thats the beginning and the end of it. But to me thats only
the smallest part of it. I like getting a woman's opinions. I like
to explore her mind as well as her body. See these two little
books I was deep in when you accosted me? I carry them with
me wherever I go. I put the problems they raise for me to every
woman I meet.

SWEETIE [*with growing misgiving*] What are they?

THE SERGEANT [*pointing to them successively*] The Bible. The
Pilgrim's Progress from this world to that which is to come.

SWEETIE [*dismayed, trying to rise*] Oh, my God!

SERGEANT [*holding her ruthlessly in the crook of his elbow*] No
you dont. Sit quiet; and dont take the name of the Lord your
God in vain. If you believe in him, it's blasphemy: if you dont,
it's nonsense. You must learn to exercise your mind: what is a
woman without an active mind to a man but a mere convenience?

SWEETIE. I have plenty to exercise my mind looking after my own
affairs. What I look to you for, my lad, is a bit of fun.

THE SERGEANT. Quite. But when men and women pick one another
up just for a bit of fun, they find theyve picked up more than

they bargained for, because men and women have a top storey as
well as a ground floor; and you cant have the one without the
other. Theyre always trying to; but it doesnt work. Youve picked
up my mind as well as my body; and youve got to explore it. You
thought you could have a face and a figure like mine with the
limitations of a gorilla. Youre finding out your mistake: thats all.

SWEETIE. Oh, let me go: I have had enough of this. If I'd thought
you were religious I'd have given you a wide berth, I tell you. Let
me go, will you?

THE SERGEANT. Wait a bit. Nature may be using me as a sort of
bait to draw you to take an interest in things of the mind. Nature may be using your pleasant animal warmth to stimulate my
mind. I want your advice. I dont say I'll take it; but it may suggest something to me. You see, I'm in a mess.

SWEETIE. Well, of course. Youre in the sergeants' mess.

THE SERGEANT. Thats not the mess I mean. My mind's in a
mess—a muddle. I used to be a religious man; but I'm not so
clear about it as I was.

SWEETIE. Thank goodness for that, anyhow.

THE SERGEANT. Look at these two books. I used to believe every
word of them because they seemed to have nothing to do with
real life. But war brought those old stories home quite real; and
then one starts asking questions. Look at this bit here [*he points
to a page of The Pilgrim's Progress*]. It's on the very first page
of it. "I am for certain informed that this our city will be burned
with fire from heaven, in which fearful overthrow both myself,
with thee my wife, and you my sweet babes, shall miserably
come to ruin, except some way of escape can be found whereby
we may be delivered." Well, London and Paris and Berlin and
Rome and the rest of them will be burned with fire from heaven
all right in the next war: thats certain. Theyre all Cities of Destruction. And our Government chaps are running about with a
great burden of corpses and debts on their backs, crying "What
must we do to be saved?" There it is: not a story in a book as it
used to be, but God's truth in the real actual world. And all the
comfort they get is "Flee from the wrath to come." But where
are they to flee to? There they are, meeting at Geneva or hob-
nobbing at Chequers over the weekend, asking one another, like
the man in the book, "Whither must we flee?" And nobody can
tell them. The man in the book says "Do you see yonder shining
light?" Well, today the place is blazing with shining lights: shining lights in parliament, in the papers, in the churches, and in
the books that they call Outlines—Outlines of History and Science and what not—and in spite of all their ballyhoo here we are
waiting in the City of Destruction like so many sheep for the
wrath to come. This uneducated tinker tells me the way is
straight before us and so narrow that we cant miss it. But he
starts by calling the place the wilderness of this world. Well,
theres no road in a wilderness: you have to make one. All the
straight roads are made by soldiers; and the soldiers didnt get to

heaven along them. A lot of them landed up in the other place. No, John: you could tell a story well; and they say you were a soldier; but soldiers that try to make storytelling do for service end in the clink; and thats where they put you. Twelve years in Bedford Gaol, he got. He used to read the Bible in gaol; and—

SWEETIE. Well, what else was there to read there? It's all they give you in some gaols.

THE SERGEANT. How do you know that?

SWEETIE. Never you mind how I know it. It's nothing to do with you.

THE SERGEANT. Nothing to do with me! You dont know me, my lass. Some men would just order you off; but to me the most interesting thing in the world is the experience of a woman thats been shut up in a cell for years at a time with nothing but a Bible to read.

SWEETIE. Years! What are you talking about? The longest I ever did was nine months; and if anyone says I ever did a day longer she's a liar.

THE SERGEANT [*laying his hand on the bible*] You could read that book from cover to cover in nine months.

SWEETIE. Some of it would drive you melancholy mad. It only got me into trouble: it did. The chaplain asked me what I was in for. Spoiling the Egyptians,[9] I says; and heres chapter and verse for it. He went and reported me, the swine; and I lost seven days remission for it.

THE SERGEANT. Serve you right! I dont hold with spoiling the Egyptians. Before the war, spoiling the Egyptians was something holy. Now I see plainly it's nothing but thieving.

SWEETIE [*shocked*] Oh, you shouldnt say that. But what I say is, if Moses might do it why maynt I?

THE SERGEANT. If thats the effect it had on your mind, it's a bad effect. Some of this scripture is all right. Do justice; love mercy; and walk humbly before your God.[1] That appeals to a man if only it could be set out in plain army regulations. But all this thieving, and slaughtering your enemies without giving quarter, and offering up human sacrifices, and thinking you can do what you like to other people because youre the chosen people of God, and you are in the right and everyone else is in the wrong: how does that look when you have had four years of the real thing instead of merely reading about it. No: damn it, we're civilized men; and though it may have gone down with those old Jews it isnt religion. And, if it isnt, where are we? Thats what I want to know.

SWEETIE. And is this all you care about? Sitting here and thinking of things like that?

THE SERGEANT. Well, somebody must think about them, or whats going to become of us all? The officers wont think about them.

9. When the Children of Israel left Egypt they took some of the Egyptians' treasure with them, as Jehovah had told them to do. (Exodus 12:35). 1. Micah 6:8.

The colonel goes out sketching: the lootnants go out and kill the birds and animals, or play polo. They wont flee from the wrath to come, not they. When they wont do their military duties I have to do them. It's the same with our religious duties. It's the chaplain's job, not mine; but when you get a real religious chaplain you find he doesnt believe any of the old stuff; and if you get a gentleman, all he cares about is to shew you that he's a real sport and not a mealy mouthed parson. So I have to puzzle it out for myself.

SWEETIE. Well, God help the woman that marries you: thats all I have to say to you. I dont call you a man. [*She rises quickly to escape from him*].

THE SERGEANT [*also rising, and seizing her in a very hearty embrace*] Not a man, eh? [*He kisses her*] How does that feel, Judy?

SWEETIE [*struggling, but not very resolutely*] You let me go, will you. I dont want you now.

THE SERGEANT. You will if I kiss you half a dozen times, more than you ever wanted anything in your life before. Thats a hard fact of human nature; and its one of the facts that religion has to make room for.

SWEETIE. Oh, well, kiss me and have done with it. You cant kiss and talk about religion at the same time.

THE ELDER [*springing from his cell to the platform in front of it*] Forbear this fooling, both of you. You, sir, are not an ignorant man: you know that the universe is wrecked.

SWEETIE [*clinging to the sergeant*] He's mad.

THE ELDER. I am sane in a world of lunatics.

THE SERGEANT [*putting Sweetie away*] It's a queer thing, isnt it, that though there is a point at which I'd rather kiss a woman than do anything else in the world, yet I'd rather be shot than let anyone see me doing it?

THE ELDER. Sir: women are not, as they suppose, more interesting than the universe. When the universe is crumbling let women be silent; and let men rise to something nobler than kissing them.

The Sergeant, interested and overawed, sits down quietly and makes Sweetie sit beside him as before. The Elder continues to declaim with fanatical intensity.

THE ELDER. Yes, sir: the universe of Isaac Newton, which has been an impregnable citadel of modern civilization for three hundred years, has crumbled like the walls of Jericho before the criticism of Einstein. Newton's universe was the stronghold of rational Determinism: the stars in their orbits obeyed immutably fixed laws; and when we turned from surveying their vastness to study the infinite littleness of the atoms, there too we found the electrons in their orbits obeying the same universal laws. Every moment of time dictated and determined the following moment, and was itself dictated and determined by the moment that came before it. Everything was c a l c u l a b l e : everything happened because it must: the commandments were erased from the tables of the law; and in their place came the cosmic algebra: the equations of the mathematicians. Here was my faith: here I found my dogma of infallibility: I, who scorned alike the Catholic with his vain dream of responsible Free Will, and the Protestant with his pretence of private judgment. And now—now—what is left of it? The orbit of the electron obeys no law: it chooses one path and rejects another: it is as capricious as the planet Mercury, who wanders from his road to warm his hands at the sun. All is caprice: the calculable world has become incalculable: Purpose and Design, the pretexts for all the vilest superstitions, have risen from the dead to cast down the mighty from their seats and put paper crowns on presumptuous fools. Formerly, when differences with my wife, or business worries, tried me too hard, I sought consolation and reassurance in our natural history museums, where I could forget all common cares in wondering at the diversity of forms and colors in the birds and fishes and animals, all produced without the agency of any designer by the operation of Natural Selection. Today I dare not enter an aquarium, because I can see nothing in those grotesque monsters of the deep but the caricatures of some freakish demon artist: some Zeus-Mephistopheles with paintbox and plasticine, trying to surpass himself in the production of fantastic and laughable creatures to people a Noah's ark for his baby. I have to rush from the building lest I go mad, crying, like the man in your book, "What must I do to be saved?" Nothing can save us from a perpetual headlong fall into a bottomless abyss but a solid footing of dogma; and we no sooner agree to that than we find that the only trustworthy dogma is that there is no dogma. As I stand here I am falling into that abyss, down, down, down. We are all falling into it; and our dizzy brains can utter nothing but madness. My wife has died cursing me. I do not know how to live without her: we were unhappy together for forty years. My son, whom I brought up to be an incorruptible Godfearing atheist, has become a thief and a scoundrel; and I can say nothing to him but "Go, boy: perish in your villainy; for neither your father nor anyone else can now give you a good reason for being a man of honor."

> *He turns from them and is rushing distractedly away when Aubrey, in white tropicals, comes strolling along the beach from the St. Pauls side, and hails him nonchalantly.*

AUBREY. Hullo, father, is it really you? I thought I heard the old trombone: I couldnt mistake it. How the dickens did you turn up here?

THE ELDER [*to the sergeant*] This is my prodigal son.

AUBREY. I am not a prodigal son. The prodigal son was a spendthrift and neer-do-weel who was reduced to eating the husks that the swine did eat. I am not ruined: I am rolling in money. I have never owed a farthing to any man. I am a model son; but I regret to say that you are very far from being a model father.

THE ELDER. What right have you to say that, sir? In what way have I fallen short?

AUBREY. You tried to thwart my manifest destiny. Nature meant me for the Church. I had to get ordained secretly.

THE ELDER. Ordained! You dared to get ordained without my knowledge!

AUBREY. Of course. You objected. How could I have done it with your knowledge? You would have stopped my allowance.

THE ELDER [*sitting down on the nearest stone, overwhelmed*] My son a clergyman! This will kill me.

AUBREY [*coolly taking another stone, on his father's right*] Not a bit of it: fathers are not so easily killed. It was at the university that I became what was then called a sky pilot. When the war took me it seemed natural that I should pursue that avocation as a member of the air force. As a flying ace I won a very poorly designed silver medal for committing atrocities which were irreconcilable with the profession of a Christian clergyman. When I was wounded and lost my nerve for flying, I became an army chaplain. I then found myself obliged to tell mortally wounded men that they were dying in a state of grace and were going straight to heaven when as a matter of fact they were dying in mortal sin and going elsewhere. To expiate this blasphemy I kept as much under fire as possible; but my nerve failed again: I·had to take three months leave and go into a nursing home. In that home I met my doom.

THE ELDER. What do you mean by your doom? You are alive and well, to my sorrow and shame.

AUBREY. To be precise, I met Sweetie. Thats Sweetie.

SWEETIE. Very pleased to meet Popsy's father, I'm sure.

THE ELDER. My son was called Popsy in his infancy. I put a stop to it, on principle, when he entered on his sixth year. It is strange to hear the name from your lips after so long an interval.

SWEETIE. I always ask a man what his mother called him, and call him that. It takes the starch out of him, somehow.

AUBREY [*resuming his narrative*] Sweetie was quite the rottenest nurse that ever raised the mortality of a hospital by ten per cent. But—

SWEETIE. Oh, what a lie! It was the other nurses that killed the men: waking them up at six in the morning and washing them! Half of them died of chills.

AUBREY. Well, you will not deny that you were the prettiest woman in the place.

SWEETIE. You thought so, anyhow.

THE ELDER. Oh, cease—cease this trifling. I cannot endure this unending sex appeal.

AUBREY. During the war it was found that sex appeal was as necessary for wounded or shellshocked soldiers as skilled nursing; so pretty girls were allowed to pose as nurses because they could sit about on beds and prevent the men from going mad. Sweetie did not prevent me going mad: on the contrary, she drove me mad. I saw in Sweetie not only every charm, but every virtue. And she returned my love. When I left that nursing home, she left it too.

I was discharged as cured on the third of the month: she had been kicked out on the first. The trained staff could stand a good deal; but they could not stand Sweetie.

SWEETIE. They were jealous; and you know it.

AUBREY. I daresay they were. Anyhow, Sweetie and I took the same lodgings; and she was faithful to me for ten days. It was a record for her.

SWEETIE. Popsy: are you going to give the whole show away, or only part of it? The Countess Valbrioni would like to know.

AUBREY. We may as well be frank up to the point at which we should lose money by it. But perhaps I am boring the company.

THE ELDER. Complete your confession, sir. You have just said that you and this lady took the same lodging. Am I to understand that you are husband and wife.

SWEETIE. We might have been if we could have depended on you for a good time. But how could I marry an army chaplain with nothing but his pay and an atheist for his father?

AUBREY. So that was the calculation, Sweetie, was it? I never dreamt that the idea of marriage had occurred to either of us. It certainly never occurred to me. I went to live with you quite simply because I felt I could not live without you. The improbability of that statement is the measure of my infatuation.

SWEETIE. Dont you be so spiteful. Did I give you a good time or did I not?

AUBREY. Heavenly. That also seems improbable; but it is gospel truth.

THE ELDER. Wretched boy: do not dare to trifle with me. You said just now that you owe no man anything, and that you are rolling in money. Where did you get that money?

AUBREY. I stole a very valuable pearl necklace and restored it to the owner. She rewarded me munificently. Hence my present opulence. Honesty is the best policy—sometimes.

THE ELDER. Worse even than a clergyman! A thief!

AUBREY. Why make such a fuss about nothing?

THE ELDER. Do you call the theft of a pearl necklace nothing?

AUBREY. Less than nothing, compared to the things I have done with your approval. I was hardly more than a boy when I first dropped a bomb on a sleeping village. I cried all night after doing that. Later on I swooped into a street and sent machine gun bullets into a crowd of civilians: women, children, and all. I was past crying by that time. And now you preach to me about stealing a pearl necklace! Doesnt that seem a little ridiculous?

THE SERGEANT. That was war, sir.

AUBREY. It was m e, sergeant: ME. You cannot divide my conscience into a war department and a peace department. Do you suppose that a man who will commit murder for political ends will hesitate to commit theft for personal ends? Do you suppose you can make a man the mortal enemy of sixty millions of his fellow creatures without making him a little less scrupulous about his next door neighbor?

THE ELDER. I did not approve. Had I been of military age I should have been a conscientious objector.

AUBREY. Oh, you were a conscientious objector to everything, even to God. But my mother was an enthusiast for everything: that was why you never could get on with her. She would have shoved me into the war if I had needed any shoving. She shoved my brother into it, though he did not believe a word of all the lies we were stuffed with, and didnt want to go. He was killed; and when it came out afterwards that he was right, and that we were all a parcel of fools killing one another for nothing, she lost the courage to face life, and died of it.

THE SERGEANT. Well, sir, I'd never let a son of mine talk to me like that. Let him have a bit of your Determinism, sir.

THE FATHER [*rising impulsively*] Determinism is gone, shattered, buried with a thousand dead religions, evaporated with the clouds of a million forgotten winters. The science I pinned my faith to is bankrupt: its tales were more foolish than all the miracles of the priests, its cruelties more horrible than all the atrocities of the Inquisition. Its spread of enlightenment has been a spread of cancer: its counsels that were to have established the millennium have led straight to European suicide. And I—I who believed in it as no religious fanatic has ever believed in his superstition! For its sake I helped to destroy the faith of millions of worshippers in the temples of a thousand creeds. And now look at me and behold the supreme tragedy of the atheist who has lost his faith—his faith in atheism, for which more martyrs have perished than for all the creeds put together. Here I stand, dumb before my scoundrel of a son; for that is what you are, boy, a common scoundrel and nothing else.

AUBREY. Well, why not? If I become an honest man I shall become a poor man; and then nobody will respect me: nobody will admire me: nobody will say thank you to me. If on the contrary I am bold, unscrupulous, acquisitive, successful and rich, everyone will respect me, admire me, court me, grovel before me. Then no doubt I shall be able to afford the luxury of honesty. I learnt that from my religious education.

THE ELDER. How dare you say that you had a religious education. I shielded you from that, at least.

AUBREY. You thought you did, old man; but you reckoned without my mother.

THE ELDER. What!

AUBREY. You forbad me to read the Bible; but my mother made me learn three verses of it every day, and whacked me if I could not repeat them without misplacing a word. She threatened to whack me still worse if I told you.

THE ELDER [*thunderstruck*] Your mother!!!

AUBREY. So I learnt my lesson. Six days on the make, and on the seventh shalt thou rest. I shall spend another six years on the make, and then I shall retire and be a saint.

THE ELDER. A saint! Say rather the ruined son of an incorrigibly superstitious mother. Retire n o w—from the life you have dishonored. There is the sea. Go. Drown yourself. In that graveyard there are no lying epitaphs. [*He mounts to his chapel and again gives way to utter dejection*].

AUDREY [*unconcerned*] I shall do better as a saint. A few thousands to the hospitals and the political party funds will buy me a halo as large as Sweetie's sun hat. That is my program. What have any of you to say against it?

THE SERGEANT. Not the program of a gentleman, as I understand the word, sir.

AUBREY. You cannot be a gentleman on less than fifty thousand a year nowadays, sergeant.

THE SERGEANT. You can in the army, by God.

AUBREY. Yes: because you drop bombs on sleeping villages. And even then you have to be an officer. Are you a gentleman?

THE SERGEANT. No, sir: it wouldnt pay me. I couldnt afford it.

> *Disturbance. A voice is heard in complaint and lamentation. It is that of the Elderly Lady, Mrs Mopply. She is pursuing Colonel Tallboys down the path through the gap, the lady distracted and insistent, the colonel almost equally distracted: she clutching him and stopping him: he breaking loose and trying to get away from her. She is dressed in black precisely as if she were in Cheltenham, except that she wears a sun helmet. He is equipped with a box of sketching materials slung over his shoulder, an easel, which he has tucked under his left arm, and a sun umbrella, a substantial affair of fawn lined with red, podgily rolled up, which he carries in his right hand.*

MRS MOPPLY. I wont be patient. I wont be quiet. My child is being murdered.

TALLBOYS. I tell you she is not being murdered. Will you be good enough to excuse me whilst I attend to my business.

MRS MOPPLY. Your business is to save my child. She is starving.

TALLBOYS. Nonsense. Nobody starves in this country. There are plenty of dates. Will you be good enough—

MRS MOPPLY. Do you think my child can live on dates? She has to have a sole for breakfast, a cup of nourishing soup at eleven, a nice chop and a sweetbread for lunch, a pint of beef-tea with her ordinary afternoon tea, and a chicken and some lamb or veal—

TALLBOYS. Will you be good enough—

MRS MOPPLY. My poor delicate child with nothing to eat but dates! And she is the only one I have left: they were all delicate—

TALLBOYS. I really must— [*He breaks away and hurries off along the beach past the Abode of Love*].

MRS MOPPLY [*running after him*] Colonel, Colonel: you might have the decency to listen to a distracted mother for a moment. Colonel: my child is dying. She may be dead for all I know. And nobody is doing anything: nobody cares. Oh dear, wont you listen— [*Her voice is lost in the distance*].

Whilst they are staring mutely after the retreating pair, the patient, still in her slave girl attire, but with some brilliant variations, comes down the path.

THE PATIENT. My dream has become a nightmare. My mother has pursued me to these shores. I cannot shake her off. No woman can shake off her mother. There should be no mothers: there should be only women, strong women able to stand by themselves, not clingers. I would kill all the clingers. Mothers cling: daughters cling: we are all like drunken women clinging to lamp posts: none of us stands upright.

THE ELDER. There is great comfort in clinging, and great loneliness in standing alone.

THE PATIENT. Hallo! [*She climbs to the St Pauls platform and peers into the cell*]. A sententious anchorite! [*To Aubrey*]. Who is he?

AUBREY. The next worst thing to a mother: a father.

THE ELDER. A most unhappy father.

AUBREY. M y father, in fact.

THE PATIENT. If only I had had a father to stand between me and my mother's care. Oh, that I had been an orphan!

THE SERGEANT. You will be, miss, if the old lady drives the colonel too hard. She has been at him all the morning, ever since she arrived; and I know the colonel. He has a temper; and when it gives way, it's a bit of high explosive. He'll kill her if she pushes him too far.

THE PATIENT. Let him kill her. I am young and strong: I want a world without parents: there is no room for them in my dream. I shall found a sisterhood.

AUBREY. All right, Mops. Get thee to a nunnery.

THE PATIENT. It need not be a nunnery if men will come in without spoiling everything. But all the women must be rich. There must be no chill of poverty. There are plenty of rich women like me who hate being devoured by parasites.

AUBREY. Stop. You have the most disgusting mental pictures. I really cannot stand intellectual coarseness. Sweetie's vulgarity I can forgive and even enjoy. But you say perfectly filthy things that stick in my mind, and break my spirit. I can bear no more of it. [*He rises angrily and tries to escape by the beach past the Abode of Love*].

SWEETIE. Youre dainty, arnt you? If chambermaids were as dainty as you, youd have to empty your own slops.

AUBREY [*recoiling from her with a yell of disgust*] You need not throw them in my teeth, you beast. [*He sits in his former place, sulking*].

THE ELDER. Silence, boy. These are home truths. They are good for you. [*To the patient*] May I ask, young woman, what are the relations between you and my son, whom you seem to know.

THE PATIENT. Popsy stole my necklace, and got me to run away with him by a wonderful speech he made about freedom and sunshine and lovely scenery. Sweetie made me write it all down and sell it to a tourist agency as an advertisement. And then I was devoured by parasites: by tourist agencies, steamboat companies, railways, motor car people, hotel keepers, dressmakers, servants, all trying to get my money by selling me things I dont really want; shoving me all over the globe to look at what they call new skies, though they know as well as I do that it is only the same old sky everywhere; and disabling me by doing all the things for me that I ought to do for myself to keep myself in health. They preyed on me to keep themselves alive: they pretended they were making me happy when it was only by drinking and drugging—cocktails and cocaine—that I could endure my life.

AUBREY. I regret to have to say it, Mops; but you have not the instincts of a lady. [*He sits down moodily on a stone a little way up the path*].

THE PATIENT. You fool, there is no such thing as a lady. I have the instincts of a good housekeeper: I want to clean up this filthy world and keep it clean. There must be other women who want it too. Florence Nightingale had the same instinct when she went to clean up the Crimean war. She wanted a sisterhood; but there wasnt one.

THE ELDER. There were several. But steeped in superstition, unfortunately.

THE PATIENT. Yes, all mixed up with things that I dont believe. Women have to set themselves apart to join them. I dont want to set myself apart. I want to have every woman in my sisterhood, and to have all the others strangled.

THE ELDER. Down! down! down! Even the young, the strong, the rich, the beautiful, feel that they are plunging into a bottomless pit.

THE SERGEANT. Your set, miss, if you will excuse me saying so, is only a small bit of the world. If you dont like the officers' mess, the ranks are open to you. Look at Meek! That man could be an emperor if he laid his mind to it: but he'd rather be a private. He's happier so.

THE PATIENT. I dont belong to the poor, and dont want to. I always knew that there were thousands of poor people; and I was taught to believe that they were poor because God arranged it that way to punish them for being dirty and drunken and dishonest, and not knowing how to read and write. But I didnt know that the rich were miserable. I didnt know that I was miserable. I didnt know that our respectability was uppish snobbery and our religion gluttonous selfishness, and that my soul was starving on them. I know now. I have found myself out thoroughly—in my dream.

THE ELDER. You are young. Some good man may cure you of this for a few happy years. When you fall in love, life will seem worth living.

THE PATIENT. I did fall in love. With that thing. And though I was never a hotel chambermaid I got tired of him sooner than Sweetie did. Love gets people into difficulties, not out of them.

No more lovers for me: I want a sisterhood. Since I came here I have been wanting to join the army, like Joan of Arc. It's a brotherhood, of a sort.

THE SERGEANT. Yes, miss: that is so; and there used to be a peace of mind in the army that you could find nowhere else. But the war made an end of that. You see, miss, the great principle of soldering, I take it, is that the world is kept going by the people who want the right thing killing the people who want the wrong thing. When the soldier is doing that, he is doing the work of God, which my mother brought me up to do. But thats a very different thing from killing a man because he's a German and he killing you because youre an Englishman. We were not killing the right people in 1915. We werent even killing the wrong people. It was innocent men killing one another.

THE PATIENT. Just for the fun of it.

THE SERGEANT. No, miss: it was no fun. For the misery of it.

THE PATIENT. For the devilment of it, then.

THE SERGEANT. For the devilment of the godless rulers of this world. Those that did the killing hadnt even the devilment to comfort them: what comfort is there in screwing on a fuse or pulling a string when the devilment it makes is from three to forty miles off, and you dont know whether you have only made a harmless hole in the ground or blown up a baby in its cradle that might have been your own? That wasnt devilment: it was damnation. No, miss: the bottom has come out of soldiering. What the gentleman here said about our all falling into a bottomless pit came home to me. I feel like that too.

THE ELDER. Lost souls, all of us.

THE PATIENT. No: only lost dogs. Cheer up, old man: the lost dogs always find their way home. [*The voice of the Elderly Lady is heard returning*]. Oh! here she comes again!

> *Mrs Mopply is still pursuing the colonel, who is walking doggedly and steadily away from her, with closed lips and a dangerous expression on his set features.*

MRS MOPPLY. You wont even speak to me. It's a disgrace. I will send a cable message home to the Government about it. You were sent out here to rescue my daughter from these dreadful brigands. Why is nothing being done? What are the relations between yourself and that disgraceful countess who ought to have her coronet stripped off her back? You are all in a conspiracy to murder my poor lost darling child. You are in league with the brigands. You are—

> *The Colonel turns at bay, and brings down his umbrella whack on poor Mrs Mopply's helmet.*

MRS MOPPLY. Oh! Oh! Oh! Oh! [*With a series of short, dry, detached screams she totters and flutters back along the beach out of sight like a wounded bird*].

> *General stupefaction. All stare at the Colonel aghast. The Sergeant rises in amazement, and remains standing afterwards as a matter of military etiquette.*

THE PATIENT. Oh, if only someone had done that to her twenty years ago, how different my childhood would have been! But I must see to the poor old dear. [*She runs after her mother*].

AUBREY. Colonel: you have our full, complete, unreserved sympathy. We thank you from the bottom of our hearts. But that does not alter the fact that the man who would raise his hand to a woman, save in the way of kindness, is unworthy the name of Briton.

TALLBOYS. I am perfectly aware of that, sir. I need no reminder. The lady is entitled to an apology. She shall have it.

THE ELDER. But have you considered the possibility of a serious injury—

TALLBOYS [*cutting him short*] My umbrella is quite uninjured, thank you. The subject is now closed. [*He sits down on the stone below St Pauls recently vacated by Aubrey. His manner is so decisive that nobody dares carry the matter further*].

As they sit uneasily seeking one another's eyes and avoiding them again, dumbfounded by the violence of the catastrophe, a noise like that of a machine gun in action reaches their ears from afar. It increases to shattering intensity as it approaches. They all put their fingers to their ears. It diminishes slightly, then suddenly rises to a climax of speed and uproar, and stops.

TALLBOYS. Meek.

AUBREY. Meek.

SWEETIE. Meek.

THE ELDER. What is this? Why do you all say Meek?

Meek, dusty and gritty, but very alert, comes down the path through the gap with a satchel of papers.

TALLBOYS. My dear Meek, can you not be content with a motor cycle of ordinary horse power? Must you always travel at eighty miles an hour?

MEEK. I have good news for you, Colonel; and good news should travel fast.

TALLBOYS. For me?

MEEK. Your K.C.B., sir. [*Presenting a paper*] Honors list by wireless.

TALLBOYS [*rising joyously to take the paper*] Ah! Congratulate me, my friends. My dear Sarah is Lady Tallboys at last. [*He resumes his seat and pores over the paper*].

AUBREY		Splendid!
THE SERGEANT	[*together*]	You deserve it, sir, if I may say so.
SWEETIE		Delighted, I am sure.

THE ELDER. May I crave to know the nature of the distinguished service which has won this official recognition, sir?

TALLBOYS. I have won the battle of the maroons. I have suppressed brigandage here. I have rescued a British lady from the clutches of the brigands. The Government is preparing for a general election, and has had to make the most of these modest achievements.

THE ELDER. Brigands! Are there any here?

TALLBOYS. None.

THE ELDER. But— The British lady? In their clutches?

TALLBOYS. She has been in my clutches, and perfectly safe, all the time.

THE ELDER [*more and more puzzled*] Oh! Then the battle of the—

TALLBOYS. Won by Private Meek. I had nothing whatever to do with it.

AUBREY. I invented the brigands and the British lady. [*To Tallboys*] By the way, Colonel, the impressive old party in the shrine is my father.

TALLBOYS. Indeed! Happy to meet you, sir, though I cannot congratulate you on your son, except in so far as you have brought into the world the most abandoned liar I have ever met.

THE ELDER. And may I ask, sir, is it your intention not only to condone my son's frauds, but to take advantage of them to accept a distinction which you have in no way earned?

TALLBOYS. I have earned it, sir, ten times over. Do you suppose, because the brigandage which I am honored for suppressing has no existence, that I have never suppressed real brigands? Do you forget that though this battle of which I am crowned victor was won by a subordinate, I, too, have won real battles, and seen all the honors go to a brigadier who did not even know what was happening? In the army these things average themselves out: merit is rewarded in the long run. Justice is none the less justice though it is always delayed, and finally done by mistake. My turn today: Private Meek's tomorrow.

THE FATHER. And meanwhile Mr Meek—this humble and worthy soldier—is to remain in obscurity and poverty whilst you are strutting as a K.C.B.

TALLBOYS. How I envy him! Look at me and look at him! I, loaded with responsibilities whilst my hands are tied, my body disabled, my mind crippled because a colonel must not do anything but give orders and look significant and profound when his mind is entirely vacant! he, free to turn his hand to everything and to look like an idiot when he feels like one! I have been driven to sketching in watercolors because I may not use my hands in life's daily useful business. A commanding officer must not do this, must not do that, must not do the other, must not do anything but tell other men to do it. He may not even converse with them. I see this man Meek doing everything that is natural to a complete man: carpentering, painting, digging, pulling and hauling, fetching and carrying, helping himself and everybody else, whilst I, with a bigger body to exercise and quite as much energy, must loaf and loll, allowed to do nothing but read the papers and drink brandy and water to prevent myself going mad. I should have become a drunkard had it not been for the colors.

THE SERGEANT. Ah yes, sir, the colors. The fear of disgracing them has kept me off the drink many a time.

TALLBOYS. Man: I do not mean the regimental colors, but the watercolors. How willingly would I exchange my pay, my rank, my K.C.B., for Meek's poverty, his obscurity!

MEEK. But, my dear Colonel—sorry, sir: what I mean to say is that you can become a private if you wish. Nothing easier: I have done it again and again. You resign your commission; take a new and a very common name by deed poll; dye your hair and give your age to the recruiting sergeant as twenty-two; and there you are! You can select your own regiment.

TALLBOYS. Meek: you should not tantalize your commanding officer. No doubt you are an extraordinary soldier. But have you ever passed the extreme and final test of manly courage?

MEEK. Which one is that, sir?

TALLBOYS. Have you ever married?

MEEK. No, sir.

TALLBOYS. Then do not ask me why I do not resign my commission and become a free and happy private. My wife would not let me.

THE COUNTESS. Why dont you hit her on the head with your umbrella?

TALLBOYS. I dare not. There are moments when I wish some other man would. But not in my presence. I should kill him.

THE ELDER. We are all slaves. But at least your son is an honest man.

TALLBOYS. Is he? I am glad to hear it. I have not spoken to him since he shirked military service at the beginning of the war and went into trade as a contractor. He is now so enormously rich that I cannot afford to keep up his acquaintance. Neither need you keep up that of your son. By the way, he passes here as the half step-brother of this lady, the Countess Valbrioni.

SWEETIE. Valbrioni be blowed! My name is Susan Simpkins. Being a countess isnt worth a damn. There's no variety in it: no excitement. What I want is a month's leave for the sergeant. Wont you give it to him, Colonel?

TALLBOYS. What for?

SWEETIE. Never mind what for. A fortnight might do; but I dont know for certain yet. There's something steadying about him; and I suppose I will have to settle down some day.

TALLBOYS. Nonsense! The sergeant is a pious man, not your sort. Eh, Sergeant?

SERGEANT. Well, sir, a man should have one woman to prevent him from thinking too much about women in general. You cannot read your Bible undisturbed if visions and wandering thoughts keep coming between you and it. And a pious man should not marry a pious woman: two of a trade never agree. Besides, it would give the children a onesided view of life. Life is very mixed, sir: it is not all piety and it is not all gaiety. This young woman has no conscience; but I have enough for two. I have no money; but she seems to have enough for two. Mind: I am not committing myself; but I will go so far as to say that I

am not dead set against it. On the plane of this world and its
vanities—and weve got to live in it, you know, sir—she appeals
to me.

AUBREY. Take care, sergeant. Constancy is not Sweetie's strong
point.

THE SERGEANT. Neither is it mine. As a single man and a wandering soldier I am fair game for every woman. But if I settle down
with this girl she will keep the others off. I'm a bit tired of
adventures.

SWEETIE. Well, if the truth must be told, so am I. We were made
for one another, Sergeant. What do you say?

THE SERGEANT. Well, I dont mind keeping company for a while,
Susan, just to see how we get along together.

> The voice of Mrs Mopply is again heard. Its tone is hardy
> and even threatening; and its sound is approaching
> rapidly.

MRS MOPPLY'S VOICE. You just let me alone, will you? Nobody
asked you to interfere. Get away with you.

> General awe and dismay. Mrs Mopply appears striding
> resolutely along the beach. She walks straight up to the
> Colonel, and is about to address him when he rises firmly to,
> the occasion and takes the word out of her mouth.

TALLBOYS. Mrs Mopply: I have a duty to you which I must discharge at once. At our last meeting, I struck you.

MRS MOPPLY. Struck me! You bashed me. Is that what you mean?

TALLBOYS. If you consider my expression inadequate I am willing
to amend it. Let us put it that I bashed you. Well, I apologize
without reserve, fully and amply. If you wish, I will give it to you
in writing.

MRS MOPPLY. Very well. Since you express your regret, I suppose
there is nothing more to be said.

TALLBOYS [*darkening ominously*] Pardon me. I apologized. I did
not express my regret.

AUBREY. Oh, for heaven's sake, Colonel, dont start her again. Dont
qualify your apology in any way.

MRS MOPPLY. You shut up, whoever you are.

TALLBOYS. I do not qualify my apology in the least. My apology is
complete. The lady has a right to it. My action was inexcusable.
But no lady—no human being—has a right to impose a falsehood on me. I do not regret my action. I have never done anything which gave me more thorough and hearty satisfaction.
When I was a company officer I once cut down an enemy in the
field. Had I not done so he would have cut me down. It gave
me no satisfaction: I was half ashamed of it: I have never before
spoken of it. But this time I struck with unmixed enjoyment. In
fact I am grateful to Mrs Mopply. I owe her one of the very few
delightfully satisfactory moments of my life.

MRS MOPPLY. Well, thats a pretty sort of apology, isnt it?

TALLBOYS [*firmly*] I have nothing to add, madam.

MRS MOPPLY. Well, I forgive you, you peppery old blighter.

Sensation. They catch their breaths, and stare at one another in consternation. The patient arrives.

THE PATIENT. I am sorry to say, Colonel Tallboys, that you have unsettled my mother's reason. She wont believe that I am her daughter. She's not a bit like herself.

MRS MOPPLY. Isnt she? What do you know about myself? my real self? They told me lies; and I had to pretend to be somebody quite different.

TALLBOYS. Who told you lies, madam? It was not with my authority.

MRS MOPPLY. I wasnt thinking of you. My mother told me lies. My nurse told me lies. My governess told me lies. Everybody told me lies. The world is not a bit like what they said it was. I wasnt a bit like what they said I ought to be. I thought I had to pretend. And I neednt have pretended at all.

THE ELDER. Another victim! She, too, is falling through the bottomless abyss.

MRS MOPPLY. I dont know who you are or what you think you mean; but you have just hit it: I dont know my head from my heels. Why did they tell me that children couldnt live without medicine and three meat meals a day? Do you know that I have killed two of my children because they told me that? My own children! Murdered them, just!

THE ELDER. Medea! Medea!

MRS MOPPLY. It isnt an idea: it's the truth. I will never believe anything again as long as I live. I'd have killed the only one I had left if she hadnt run away from me. I was told to sacrifice myself—to live for others; and I did it if ever a woman did. They told me that everyone would love me for it; and I thought they would; but my daughter ran away when I had sacrificed myself to her until I found myself wishing she would die like the others and leave me a little to myself. And now I find it was not only my daughter that hated me but that all my friends, all the time they were pretending to sympathize, were just longing to bash me over the head with their umbrellas. This poor man only did what all the rest would have done if theyd dared. When I said I forgave you I meant it: I am greatly obliged to you. [*She kisses him*]. But now what am I to do? How am I to behave in a world thats just the opposite of everything I was told about it?

THE PATIENT. Steady, mother! steady! steady! Sit down. [*She picks up a heavy stone and places it near the Abode of Love for Mrs Mopply to sit on*].

MRS MOPPLY [*seating herself*] Dont you call me mother. Do you think my daughter could carry rocks about like that? she that had to call the nurse to pick up her Pekingese dog when she wanted to pet it! You think you can get round me by pretending to be my daughter; but that just shews what a fool you are; for I hate my daughter and my daughter hates me, because I sacrificed myself to her. She was a horrid selfish girl, always ill and complaining, and never satisfied, no matter how much you did for her. The only sensible thing she ever did was to steal her own necklace and sell it and run away to spend the money on herself. I expect she's in bed somewhere with a dozen nurses and six doctors all dancing attendance on her. Youre not a bit like her, thank goodness: thats why Ive taken a fancy to you. You come with me, darling. I have lots of money, and sixty years of a misspent life to make up for; so you will have a good time with me. Come with me as my companion; and lets forget that there are such miserable things in the world as mothers and daughters.

THE PATIENT. What use shall we be to one another?

MRS MOPPLY. None, thank God. We can do without one another if we dont hit it off.

THE PATIENT. Righto! I'll take you on trial until Ive had time to look about me and see what I'm going to do. But only on trial, mind.

MRS MOPPLY. Just so, darling. We'll both be on trial. So thats settled.

THE PATIENT. And now, Mr Meek, what about the little commission you promised to do for me? Have you brought back my passport?

THE COUNTESS. Your passport! Whatever for?

AUBREY. What have you been up to, Mops? Are you going to desert me?

> *Meek advances and empties a heap of passports from his satchel on the sand, kneeling down to sort out the patient's.*

TALLBOYS. What is the meaning of this? Whose passports are these? What are you doing with them? Where did you get them?

MEEK. Everybody within fifty miles is asking me to get a passport visa'd.

TALLBOYS. Visa'd! For what country?

MEEK. For Beotia, sir.

TALLBOYS. Beotia?

MEEK. Yessir. The Union of Federated Sensible Societies, sir. The U.F.S.S. Everybody wants to go there now, sir.

THE COUNTESS. Well I never!

THE ELDER. And what is to become of our unhappy country if all its inhabitants desert it for an outlandish place in which even property is not respected?

MEEK. No fear, sir: they wont have us. They wont admit any more English, sir: they say their lunatic asylums are too full already. I couldnt get a single visa, except [*to the Colonel*] for you, sir.

TALLBOYS. For me! Damn their impudence! I never asked for one.

MEEK. No, sir; but their people have so much leisure that they are at their wits' end for some occupation to keep them out of mischief. They want to introduce the only institution of ours that they admire.

THE ELDER. And pray which one is that?

MEEK. The English school of watercolor painting, sir. Theyve seen some of the Colonel's work; and theyll make him head of their centres of repose and culture if he'll settle there.

TALLBOYS. This cannot be true, Meek. It indicates a degree of intelligence of which no Government is capable.

MEEK. It's true, sir, I assure you.

TALLBOYS. But my wife—

MEEK. Yessir: I told them. [*He repacks his satchel*].

TALLBOYS. Well, well: there is nothing for it but to return to our own country.

THE ELDER. Can our own country return to its senses, sir? that is the question.

TALLBOYS. Ask Meek.

MEEK. No use, sir: all the English privates want to be colonels: there's no salvation for snobs. [*To Tallboys*] Shall I see about getting the expedition back to England, sir?

TALLBOYS. Yes. And get me two tubes of rose madder and a big one of Chinese White, will you?

MEEK [*about to go*] Yessir.

THE ELDER. Stop. There are police in England. What is to become of my son there?

SWEETIE [*rising*] Make Popsy a preacher, old man. But dont start him until weve gone.

THE ELDER. Preach, my son, preach to your heart's content. Do anything rather than steal and make your military crimes an excuse for your civil ones. Let men call you the reverend. Let them call you anything rather than thief.

AUBREY [*rising*] If I may be allowed to improve the occasion for a moment—

> *General consternation. All who are seated rise in alarm, except the patient, who jumps up and claps her hands in mischievous encouragement to the orator.*

MRS MOPPLY		You hold your tongue, young man.
SWEETIE		Oh Lord! we're in for it now.
THE ELDER	[*together*]	Shame and silence would better become you, sir.
THE PATIENT		Go on, Pops. It's the only thing you do well.

AUBREY [*continuing*]—it is clear to me that though we seem to be dispersing quietly to do very ordinary things: Sweetie and the Sergeant to get married [*the Sergeant hastily steals down from his grotto, beckoning to Sweetie to follow him. They both escape along the beach*] the colonel to his wife, his watercolors, and his K.C.B. [*the colonel hurries away noiselessly in the opposite direction*] Napoleon Alexander Trotsky Meek to his job of repatriating the expedition [*Meek takes to flight up the path through the gap*] Mops, like Saint Teresa, to found an unlady-like sisterhood with her mother as cook-housekeeper [*Mrs Mopply hastily follows the sergeant, dragging with her the patient, who is listening to Aubrey with signs of becoming rapt in his discourse*] yet they are all, like my father here, falling, falling, falling endlessly and hopelessly through a void in which they can find no footing. [*The Elder vanishes into the recesses of St Pauls, leaving his son to preach in solitude*]. There is something fantastic about them, something unreal and perverse, something profoundly unsatisfactory. They are too absurd to be believed in; yet they are not fictions: the newspapers are full of them: what storyteller, however reckless a liar, would dare to invent figures so improbable as men and women with their minds stripped naked? Naked bodies no longer shock us: our sunbathers, grinning at us from every illustrated summer number of our magazines, are nuder than shorn lambs. But the horror of the naked mind is still more than we can bear. Throw off the last rag of your bathing costume; and I shall not blench nor expect you to blush. You may even throw away the outer garments of your souls: the manners, the morals, the decencies. Swear; use dirty words; drink cocktails; kiss and caress and cuddle until girls who are like roses at eighteen are like battered demireps at twenty-two: in all these ways the bright young things of the victory have scandalized their dull prewar elders and left nobody but their bright young selves a penny the worse. But how are we to bear this dreadful new nakedness: the nakedness of the souls who until now have always disguised themselves from one another in beautiful impossible idealisms to enable them to bear one another's company. The iron lightning of war has burnt great rents in these angelic veils, just as it has smashed great holes in our cathedral roofs and torn great gashes in our hillsides. Our souls go in rags now; and the young are spying through the holes and getting glimpses of the reality that was hidden. And they are not horrified: they exult in having found us out: they expose their own souls; and when we their elders desperately try to patch our torn clothes with scraps of old material, the young lay violent hands on us and tear from us even the rags that were left to us. But when they have stripped themselves and us utterly naked, will they be able to bear the spectacle? You have seen me try to strip my soul before my father; but when these two young women stripped themselves more boldly than I—when the old woman had the mask struck from her soul and revelled in it instead of dying of it—I shrank from the revelation as from a wind bringing from the unknown regions of the future a breath which may be a breath of life, but of a life too keen for me to bear, and therefore for me a blast of death. I stand midway between youth and age like a man who has missed his train: too late for the last and too early for the next. What am I to do? What am I? A soldier who has lost his nerve, a thief who at his first great theft has found honesty the best policy and restored his booty to its owner. Nature never intended me for soldiering or thieving: I am by nature and destiny a preacher. I am the new Ecclesiastes. But I have no Bible, no creed: the war has shot both out of my hands. The war has been a fiery forcing house in which we have grown with a rush like flowers in a late spring following a terrible winter. And with what result? This: that we have outgrown our religion, outgrown our political system, out-

grown our own strength of mind and character. The fatal word
NOT has been miraculously inserted into all our creeds: in the
desecrated temples where we knelt murmuring "I believe" we
stand with stiff knees and stiffer necks shouting "Up, all! the
erect posture is the mark of the man: let lesser creatures kneel
and crawl: we will not kneel and we do not believe." But what
next? Is NO enough? For a boy, yes: for a man, never. Are we any
the less obsessed with a belief when we are denying it than when
we were affirming it? No: I must have affirmations to preach.
Without them the young will not listen to me; for even the
young grow tired of denials. The negative-monger falls before the
soldiers, the men of action, the fighters, strong in the old uncompromising affirmations which give them status, duties, certainty
of consequences; so that the pugnacious spirit of man in them
can reach out and strike deathblows with steadfastly closed
minds. Their way is straight and sure; but it is the way of death;
and the preacher must preach the way of life. Oh, if I could only
find it! [*A white sea fog swirls up from the beach to his feet,
rising and thickening round him*]. I am ignorant: I have lost
my nerve and am intimidated: all I know is that I must find the
way of life, for myself and all of us, or we shall surely perish.
And meanwhile my gift has possession of me: I must preach and
preach and preach no matter how late the hour and how short
the day, no matter whether I have nothing to say—

> *The fog has enveloped him; the gap with its grottoes is
> lost to sight; the ponderous stones are wisps of shifting
> white cloud; there is left only fog: impenetrable fog; but
> the incorrigible preacher will not be denied his peroration,
> which, could we only hear it distinctly, would probably
> run—*

—or whether in some pentecostal flame of revelation the Spirit
will descend on me and inspire me with a message the sound
whereof shall go out unto all lands and realize for us at last the
Kingdom and the Power and the Glory for ever and ever. Amen.

*The audience disperses (or the reader puts down the book)
impressed in the English manner with the Pentecostal flame and
the echo from the Lord's Prayer. But fine words butter no parsnips.
A few of the choicer spirits will know that the Pentecostal flame is
always alight at the service of those strong enough to bear its terrible intensity. They will not forget that it is accompanied by a rushing mighty wind, and that any rascal who happens to be also a
windbag can get a prodigious volume of talk out of it without ever
going near enough to be shrivelled up. The author, though himself
a professional talk maker, does not believe that the world can be
saved by talk alone. He has given the rascal the last word; but his
own favorite is the woman of action, who begins by knocking the
wind out of the rascal, and ends with a cheerful conviction that the
lost dogs always find their way home. So they will, perhaps, if the
women go out and look for them.*

Backgrounds
and Criticism

Note

In the following commentaries the footnotes of the originals have been retained, with an occasional addition by the present editor, marked [*Editor*].

An exception is made in the case of direct references to the plays included in this volume, where page references to some other edition would seem irrelevant.

On Shaw

JOHN GASSNER

Bernard Shaw and the Making of the Modern Mind†

Shaw *knew* he was one of the creators of modern consciousness and modern conscience. He told us so himself many times, and with perfect seriousness. An apt summary of both Shaw's historical position and self-appreciation is contained in a Max Beerbohm cartoon in which the jaunty young nineteenth-century Shaw offers some old clothes for sale to the great European critic Georg Brandes standing behind the counter as "a merchant of ideas."

"What'll you take for the lot?" asks Brandes.

"Immortality," says Shaw.

Brandes protests: "Come, I've handled those goods before! Coat, Mr. Schopenhauer's; waistcoat, Mr. Ibsen's; Mr. Nietzsche's trousers—"

To which Shaw blandly replies, "Ah, but look at the patches."

It is perfectly apparent that Shaw would not have been non-plussed either if Brandes had also referred to some other articles of clothing such as, shirt belonging to Samuel Butler, shoes borrowed from Karl Marx, and gloves and hat from Lamarck and Bergson. It is my suspicion that Shaw would have resented only an attribution of "cummerbund from Freud," since Shaw preferred moral passion to any other kind (his plays were once called "as unemotional as a mushroom"), and since he placed Economics above Eros as the source of good and evil, happiness and misery. And this reflection reminds me that he would have winced at some such phrase as "collar worn by Darwin" unless assured that the collar symbolized strangulation and was being rightly discarded, for Shaw was the sworn enemy of "Social Darwinism." The Darwinian struggle for existence was anathema to the intensely combative Shaw, who once

† Since Shaw's death in 1950 there have been many attempts to discover his lasting place in history. The following is the estimate of the late Sterling Professor of Playwriting and Dramatic Literature at Yale University. The paper is based on a lecture given at Brown University on October 19, 1961, one of a series on the "Makers of the Modern Mind." It is reprinted from *College English*, Vol. 23 (April, 1962), pp. 517–525.

proposed to revise the rules of tennis and penalize players who hit the ball too hard to be successfully returned by their opponents. The Darwinian doctrine of the "survival of the fittest," so sacred to old-line Victorian Liberals that they frowned on social legislation, was altogether abhorrent to this "fittest of the fit" who was in danger, indeed, of carrying survival to excess until he died of a fall in his 94th year.

Considering his virtuosity as a writer of comedies, which he appreciated even more than his audiences did at the time, Shaw declared in an early volume (*Three Plays for Puritans*), "I am a natural-born mountebank;" and Shaw was undoubtedly a born showman and devotee of pyrotechnical displays. But he was also a born preacher, and he was not in the least exaggerating when he declared as early as his 1893 Preface to *Mrs. Warren's Profession*, "I have spared no pains to make known that my plays are built to induce not voluptuous reverie but intellectual interest. . . ." Shaw, however, found it possible to reconcile his pedagogical and histrionic inclinations in the same person and the same works. In this achievement, more perhaps than in any other, lay his power as a literary and dramatic genius. And he did not truly do justice to it when he proclaimed, as he was wont to do, that he merely made Mountebank Shaw serve the sermonizing Preacher Shaw. He could advance this estimate of himself well enough, and sometimes brilliantly, for no one writing English could sustain a half-truth with more verbal skill.

Thirty years later, with the world floundering in the economic depression of the 1930's, we find him insisting, in the Preface to his aptly titled political drama *On the Rocks*, that "All great Art and Literature is propaganda." I say that Shaw did not do justice to himself in representing his art as the handmaiden of preachment, because it was often in his preachment that he found his art, as in *Major Barbara*, *Heartbreak House*, and *Man and Superman*. It is certainly impossible to say with respect to his plays that one side of him was the reformer and the other side the comedian; or that one side of him was the thinker and the other side the artist. Many of his most memorable lines and effective conceits, on the contrary, were inseparable from his social convictions or hopes, his will to teach and his will to create being often the same thing. What Shaw's "Serpent" says in *Back to Methuselah* applies to his best writing and explains why his work has dated so much less than the plays of his contemporaries from Pinero to John Galsworthy: ". . . imagination," says the Serpent, "is the beginning of creation. You imagine what you desire; you will what you imagine; and at last you create what you will."

It is a valid conclusion that Shaw the thinker and Shaw the artist are one and the same person. His tracts, of course, deserve a historian's consideration and can stand examination; and in their turn of phrase they too reflect his lively intelligence and talent for language. But he was not at all unique in grinding out programs of social legislation, denunciations of capitalistic laissez-faire, and unorthodox views on church, state, and economics. In retrospect, the content of the purely sociological and political writings may even seem quite outmoded if for no other reason than that the moderate social program of Shaw and his late Victorian associates was in large part adopted and made the law of the land. Besides, the program was tame from the start, even if Shaw's rhetoric was often, fortunately, unbridled. At the height of his political career as a stump speaker, London vestryman, and spokesman for the Fabian Society, founded in 1884, Shaw was committed to practical policies distinctly more evolutionary than revolutionary. With Sidney Webb, the tireless civil servant and statistician, Sidney Olivier, later the English Governor of Jamaica and Secretary of State for India, Graham Wallas, and (later) H. G. Wells, Shaw was the representative of a reformist group that picked the right label when it called itself the Fabian Society.[1] Its program for socialization and social reform was growlingly gradualist.

At the height of its prestige the Fabian Society scarcely reached a membership of 1,500, and its policy was wisely one of permeation of established political parties. Bluster as he might, the Shaw who engaged in politics proposed the manna of reform in the middle of the road while thundering Marxism on the left. In old age he once declared, "Karl Marx made a man of me," but in the course of his life he repudiated virtually all of Marx's economics and sociology. The young Shaw, moreover, concurred at least officially with his fellow-Fabians when they called for patience with the historical process. Their slogan was "For the right moment you must wait, as Fabius did, most patiently," earning the ironic retort of a member of the Socialist Party who once said to them, "Comrades, we must not allow ourselves to be carried away by patience!"

Now this account of the Fabian Society hardly accords with our impression of Shaw, who lived on until 1950 and retained a reputation to the end of his days that was anything but suggestive of the temperament and mentality of civil servants, statisticians, and reliable sociologists. The Fabian picture is one thing; the Shaw who upset the applecart of middle-class society and recommended all sorts of public upheavals is another. What to make of Shaw became a problem as early as the 1890's when he distinguished

1. Named for Fabius Cuncator ("the Delayer"), who, by his patient but vig- orous tactics, recaptured Tarentum from Hannibal in 209 B.C. [*Editor*].

himself as a dynamitard among music and drama critics and as a volatile and incalculable heretic among playwrights. He acquired a formidable reputation for irresponsibility while actually leading an exemplary life as the late-blooming husband of an Irish millionairess and as a hard-driving businessman in his dealings with publishers and stage producers. It was plainly his manner, more than his matter, that brought him both his notoriety and fame.

We may return then to the old clothes-and-patches theory of the Max Beerbohm cartoon, and we may end by endorsing its subject's insistence that the patches make a difference. Very much of a difference, indeed, which is tantamount to saying, as I have already done, that Shaw the thinker or maker of the modern mind is actually Shaw the *artist*. He is Shaw the essayist whose imaginative and satirical prose is the best in English after the prose of Jonathan Swift, and Shaw the playwright, for whom no peer can be found in English unless we return to the spacious stage of Queen Elizabeth and James I.

To the great variety of his interests Shaw added an impressive variety of insights and provocative presentations—the presentations of a master stylist, debater, orator, farceur, comedian, fantasist and even poet. It is safe to say that he brought more zest to debate than any of his contemporaries in England, more eloquence to oratory, more vitality to farce (with the possible exception of Oscar Wilde), more wit to comedy and more poetry to the "play of ideas" than any of his contemporaries. Moreover, in Shaw's case the manner was the man himself, so that behind all his postures and poses there was a remarkable unity of passion, energy, and levity.

This is my contention, and there is no other way to substantiate it than to examine the works themselves. A modest start can be made by reviewing in summary form Shaw's treatment of some of the tendencies, problems and challenges he encountered at the turn of the century. We can set his treatment beside that normally accorded to some particular matter by Shaw's contemporaries and so observe the singularity of his temper.

We may start with Shaw's work as a critic of the drama and theatre, since this brings us to his main form of expression. It is important to observe, in the first place, that unlike many advanced drama critics of the late nineteenth century in Europe, Shaw was not impressed by realistic dialogue, realistic play construction, and realistic theatre convention. He certainly did not write for the Stanislavskian[2] actor and director. The only realism he had any use

2. Constantin Stanislavsky, director of the Moscow Art Theatre, champion of the new naturalism, especially in connection with the plays of Anton Chekhov: See the discussions on *Heartbreak House* [Editor].

for was neither structural nor scenic, but intellectual and psychological. He had the astuteness to observe how easy it was to make a show of superficial reality and yet *evade* reality, to make accuracy of detail a substitute for essential truth, to feign boldness by presenting an unconventional subject but scrupulously refrain from examining it. While virtually everyone in England was crowning Arthur Wing Pinero the laureate of dramatic realism on the strength of such so-called problem plays as *The Second Mrs. Tanqueray* and *The Notorious Mrs. Ebbsmith*, Shaw was firing away at Pinero's pretensions to realism.

Shaw accused Pinero of presenting modern characters or problems and then employing shameless contrivances to reduce the action to banality and the meaning to commonplaceness. A case in point is *The Second Mrs. Tanqueray*, in which Pinero was modern enough to start with the marriage of a Victorian gentleman to a woman with a past, and conventional enough to conclude with the failure of that marriage. In order to provide a conclusion so comforting to Victorian audiences, moreover, Pinero drew upon the same contrived plot-making that discredited the so-called well-made, but actually ill-made, plays of the century. No wonder Shaw declared that Pinero's formula for popular success consisted of presenting a situation and then running away from it. This policy was the pseudo-Ibsenism that had such vogue in the English-speaking theatre. Shaw, who would have none of it and was clever enough to detect it behind all masquerades of verisimilitude, insisted that for a modern sensibility "an interesting play cannot in the nature of things mean anything but a play in which problems of conduct and character of personal importance to the audience are raised and suggestively discussed."

In attacking Pinero's realism at a time when even William Archer considered it a model of "playmaking," Shaw stood in the forefront of modern criticism. Pinero, to whom constant reference is made in Archer's classic manual on playwriting,[3] is virtually forgotten today except for a few farces such as *The Magistrate* that possess theatrical liveliness.

It was plain that while the majority of Shaw's contemporaries were interested in "well-made" plays, Shaw was interested only in alive ones. And for him they could not really be alive unless they were provocative and constituted drama of ideas. This is important to our understanding of Shaw's own plays, too. If they belong to the genre of realism it is by virtue of their engagement to reality, chiefly by comprising a conflict of ideas, principles, ways of thinking, and ways of living. For the sake of reality, Shaw was always

3. William Archer, *Play-Making, a Manual of Craftsmanship* (Boston, 1923) [*Editor*].

prepared to violate realistic structure and verisimilitude, to turn somersaults of the most farcical or fantastic kind, and to be arbitrary with his plot or to discard plot altogether.

He was ever ready to stop the overt action for a good discussion or good lecture, or even step out of the proscenium frame to harangue the audience in behalf of a relevant philosophy or sociology which is beyond, if not indeed antithetical to, the illusion achieved by plodding realists and the designers who provided scenic realism. And to serve the "reality principle" of social criticism Shaw also had no hesitation to curtail characterization, to color situations, and to invent a fantasy such as that of a Last Judgment in *The Simpleton of the Unexpected Isles* in which God removes all useless individuals, or of *Back to Methuselah*, in which the world is ruled by men who have willed themselves in some Lamarckian way into living many centuries, since little sense could be expected from the mere infants of 60, 70, or 80 who determine the fate of societies.

Shaw also availed himself of every freedom of comic invention or extravagance to overcome public indifference with provocative reversals of viewpoint, as in *Man and Superman*, in which Don Juan is turned into a paragon of virtue for whom the only passion worth having is "moral passion," and *Major Barbara*, in which Shaw maintained the cold-sober argument that all moral problems had their source in economics. In *Major Barbara*, the real benefactor of mankind, it is bizarrely argued, is none other than the munitions magnate Andrew Undershaft who builds the good society with the well paid, well housed, and well entertained employees of his factory; moreover, Undershaft is perfectly willing to sell his dynamite for peaceful purposes or for the eradication of injustice if humanity should ever have sense enough to make proper use of his product.

Shaw, to sum up, took a view of dramatic art that was essentially theatrical rather than anti-theatrical, provided true realism—that is, realism of content or idea—was well served. Mind and spirit carried him far beyond the provinciality of realism, which was already, by 1880, little more than the tired avant-gardism of the nineteenth-century European bourgeoisie. So it happened that Shaw, who greatly enriched the realistic substance of the drama by bringing economics and sociological realities into the theatre and by turning the British drawing room into a forum, actually liberated the stage from the limitations of realism. He recalled the theatre to its classic and Elizabethan heritage of freedom from picayune illusionism; in other words, he drew close to the freedom of presentational as against the stringencies of representational art. In his own work, he turned to "musical form" in discussion drama, composing plays in the manner of a theme and variations; and he exercised his flair for opera in never hesitating to stop the action in favor of a verbal aria on some subject, which is a mode of drama, too, when competently managed, as old as Euripides and Aristophanes. Granville-Barker in staging some of Shaw's early plays in London was wont to remind the actors indeed that they *were* in an opera.

Shaw was surely in the vanguard of dramatic expression whether he championed a species of dialectical realism in becoming Ibsen's most fervid advocate in the 'eighties or anticipated the imaginative styles of twentieth-century dramatic art that favor theatricalism. (It is noteworthy that he made himself an ardent champion of O'Casey's expressionist anti-war drama *The Silver Tassie*.) We move backward with him to the theatricalist art of earlier ages and forward with him to the dramatic art of Pirandello, Giraudoux, and Brecht. And lest we be misled by his championship of Ibsen, let us observe that in many pieces on Ibsen and most notably in his Fabian Society Lectures, *The Quintessence of Ibsenism*, Shaw paid little attention to the outward and rather provincial realism of the Scandinavian pioneer. Shaw analyzed each play as early as 1891, when he delivered his lectures, in terms of its challenge and reversal of accepted beliefs, its paradoxes and contradiction of commonplace attitudes. Shaw's Ibsen is a fascinating dialectician and a veritable Robin Goodfellow of the realm of comedy who plays havoc with humdrum opinion and custom. And when Shaw ultimately arrived at a view of Ibsen's real achievement he made him not the father of external realism but of discussion drama or the "play of ideas." Beginning with *A Doll's House*, Ibsen, according to Shaw, created a new form of drama by introducing a new movement into it. "Formerly," Shaw explained, "You had in what was called a well-made play an exposition in the first act, a situation in the second, and unraveling in the third. Now you have exposition, situation, and discussion; and the discussion is the best of the playwright." For Shaw modern drama and true realism started in 1879 when Ibsen's *Doll House* heroine Nora made her husband sit down and discuss the nature of her marriage to him.

Estheticism was one of the recognized ways of revolting against nineteenth-century laissez-faire industrialism and materialism. The Pre-Raphaelite movement, the agitation of Ruskin and William Morris, and the Yellow Book estheticism of Oscar Wilde, Aubrey Beardsley and others in England, the movement of the "decadents" and "symbolists" across the English channel—these and other art-for-art's sake phenomena of the turn-of-the-century could not but be noticed and in some way or other reflected by Shaw, who was equally conscious of art and sociology. And for William Morris especially Shaw always expressed the highest regard. Against Philistine attacks on art and artists Shaw was indeed ever watchful. He was one of the few Englishmen to remain well disposed toward Wilde after his prison sentence. He wrote a vigorous defense of art against the allegations of Max Nordau that modern art was decadent and tended to be manifestation of disease. Shaw's defense was the brilliant essay *The Sanity of Art*.[4]

Yet Shaw's estheticism was radically different from that of most of his contemporaries or successors, and here too his originality and force are apparent. In the first place, he emphatically rejected the doctrine of art for art's sake. He rejected just as categorically the nihilistic or negativistic tendencies that have characterized estheticism from the 1890's to our own times, from the poet-drunkards and suicides of the turn of the century to the beatniks of the mid-century, from the works of Huysmans to the works of Samuel Beckett. In the very depths of Shaw's disillusionment in 1932, in his play *Too True to Be Good*, in which his clergyman hero mouthpiece Aubrey declared that the Western world was "damned beyond Salvation," Shaw made Aubrey conclude with a ringing disavowal of negativism. "Is No enough?" asks Shaw's desperate clergyman, and replies, "For a boy, yes; for a man never. . . . I must preach and preach no matter how late the hour and how short the day . . ."; to which Shaw the chronic activist added a postscript reading, "The author, though himself a professional talk maker, does not believe that the world can be saved by talk alone."

For Shaw art was an act of liberation from materialistic interests, a release of the spirit, and, at the turn of the century, a weapon against Victorian Philistinism in general. He defended the right of free expression fiercely and fought British censorship. He drew that censorship down on himself indeed, most notably in the case of *Mrs. Warren's Profession*. He championed Wagner in England, especially with his pamphlet *The Perfect Wagnerite*, published in 1898. But it was as Wagner the social revolutionist, reconstituted into a semi-Marxist and Shavian artist, that Shaw championed him, interpreting *The Ring of the Nibelung* as a drama of the overthrow of the old order and the triumph of the heroic human spirit. It was possible then for Shaw to give his allegiance almost equally to Mozart, his favorite composer, and to Wagner, his favorite musical cause. And particularly bracing was Shaw's view of the true artist as an unusually strong and independent, supremely *healthy*, individual even behind a mask of frailty and a cloud of alienation and loneliness. Nothing contrasts more sharply with the romantic idealization of the artist as an easily wilted "blue" flower in vogue during the 1890's and Shaw's portrait of Marchbanks, the boy-artist in *Candida*, written in 1893. Marchbanks may delude others and

4. This, along with *The Quintessence of Ibsenism* and *The Perfect Wagnerite*, comprise Shaw's *Major Critical Essays* in the Standard Edition (1931) [*Editor*].

even himself, for a time, that he is a weakling, but to a perceptive "womanly woman" such as Candida he is compact of strength precisely because he is a poet at heart; he remains unimpressed by domestic felicity, refuses to submit to family authority, and is willing to learn to live without happiness.

Shaw put the matter beautifully in a letter he sent at the turn of the century to the Ibsenite actress Janet Achurch. He wrote her: "I realize the full significance of the singular fate which led me to play with all the serious things of life and to deal seriously with all its plays." To be *oneself* and at the same time labor in full knowledge of the fact that we are all members of each other was Shaw's most insistent thought on the privilege of being an artist in society. I believe that the visionary Mrs. George speaking in a trance in Shaw's discussion play *Getting Married* speaks for Shaw himself when she declares: "I've been myself, I've not been afraid of myself. And at last I have *escaped from myself*, and am become a voice for them that are afraid to speak, and a cry for the hearts that break in silence."

Inevitably with Shaw we end up—or nearly end up—with his involvement with the social conflicts and expectations and with the views on numerous specific issues such as feminism and social reform that agitated the world of his youth in the 1880's (Shaw, it may be hard to realize, was born in 1856), of his maturity before World War I, and of his old age. Characteristically, he embraced the fashion in ideas with a difference, and gave these the stamp of his individuality while employing them in some provocative synthesis of contradictions and paradoxes. For Shaw, who was one of the least ambiguous of modern authors, was also one of the most ambivalent, and we have owed much of his provocativeness and artistry to his ambivalences.

For one thing, we have owed to them his capacity for writing comedy that is serious and serious drama that is comic. And the duality of his temperament gave us both his magnificent anger and superb geniality, his zeal for reform and genuine aversion to physical aggression, well expressed in his late revision of Shakespeare's *Cymbeline*, in which Imogen says in, alas, bad verse,

> Oh, do not make me laugh.
> Laughter dissolves too many resentments,
> Pardons too many sins.

To this Iachimo replies,

> And saves the world
> A many thousand murders.[5]

5. Unhappy with the last act of Shakespeare's *Cymbeline*, Shaw contributed a *Cymbeline Refinished* in 1945 [*Editor*].

The He-Ancient in *Back to Methuselah* also recognizes the potency of laughter when he declares concerning the will to longevity that "Like all revolutionary truths, it began as a joke." One of the physicians in *The Doctor's Dilemma* also scores well for Shaw in saying, "Life does not cease to be funny when people die any more than it ceases to be serious when people laugh."

In specific cases, moreover, we find Shaw gloriously at work in the fine, and difficult, art of reconciling contradictions. We find him, for example, an ardent feminist, yet a blithe satirist of turn-of-the-century feminist fads and extravagances in so early a piece as *The Philanderer*. We find him urging war on the Victorian ideal of femininity or feminine dependency in the 1890's; and right up to the plays written after 1920, from *Saint Joan* to *The Millionairess*, he persists in glorifying the *unfeminine* woman. Yet how warmly he writes of Joan, and how constantly he creates characters who are marvelous mother-surrogates while also flourishing as clever and sophisticated women of the world. We need only glance at the marvellous portrait Shaw gave us in Candida, who is both mother-image and minx, loyal wife and flirt, housekeeper and sockmender and yet a supremely intelligent person as well. And how neatly and perceptively he reverses norms and yet rights them in the long run, so that Candida remains a loyal wife equally for unconventional and natural (or, if you will, conventional) reasons. Shaw, we may say, was progressive in his espousal of feminism in the 1880's and progressive, too, in going *beyond* feminism in the 1800's.

Shaw's variations on the themes of love and sex are too many to consider here. It is especially noteworthy, however, that he protested equally against the Victorian repressive attitude and the post-Victorian permissive one. Both seemed to him mere obsessiveness with sex when the real problem was to avoid all forms of enslavement, including enslavement to sex, and all excuses for the evasion of social reality. Unlike the run-of-the-mill opponent of Victorian prudery, Shaw endorsed progress in the relations between the sexes as a means toward achieving freedom from voluptuousness for the sake of progress in *all* relations. And with this in mind he undertook to modify evolutionary theory itself. He could not be satisfied with the established disbelief in the inheritance of acquired traits any more than he could believe that evolution had come to an end. Annexing nineteenth-century evolutionary theory to his social idealism and adopting pseudoscientific vitalism as a credo, Shaw endorsed the Lamarckian theory of the inheritance of acquired characteristics as a necessary assurance that man could progress as a species; and with that other philosophical evolutionist Nietzsche, though without the latter's advocacy of "the will to power" as a dynamic factor, Shaw reposed hope in the coming of the superman.

Humanity, as he came to know it, was a race made up largely of duffers, and what was especially distressing to him was man's failure as a political animal. But Shaw consoled himself with the reflection that "We have no reason to believe that we are the Creator's last word."

Shaw, noting the unreliability of social progress, the failures of parliamentary democracy to which he devoted two plays after World War I (*The Apple Cart* and *On the Rocks*) and concluding that "every technical qualification for doing good is a technical qualification for doing evil as well"—Shaw, growing impatient with the inertia of the masses and the flabbiness of their elected representatives and misleaders, tended to pin his hopes more and more on self-propelled leaders in whom he saw the superior beings who had thus far appeared among men only as sports of nature. Around this faith he was apt to spin some of his most provocative plays and vivid characterizations before and after World War I. The Caesar of *Caesar and Cleopatra* is the superman as political leader; Undershaft is the superman as industrialist; Joan of Arc is the superman (or "superwoman") as saint. The eagerness with which Shaw believed or *wanted to believe* in savior-heroes who overleap the barriers of moral sloth and general mediocrity ultimately deceived him. It betrayed him into a kinder view of Mussolini, Hitler, and Stalin than his intelligence should have permitted. In this respect he was almost pathetically a man of the divided and self-betrayed modern mind. Shaw was touchingly aware in the famous epilogue to *Saint Joan* that simple humanity was not yet ready for its saints. He could not but become aware that simple humanity was not yet ready for any other species of superman. He was less inclined to realize that the supermen who arose in the shape of the Caesars, Napoleons, and Undershafts of the world were not necessarily ready for simple humanity.

Shaw, like so many other intellectuals of his time, was also tripped up in the long run by his faith in collectivism. Apparently, it did not occur to him sufficiently that society might manifest a unified effort at a frightful sacrifice of life and liberty. He also evinced an exaggerated trust in economics as the basis of human happiness and advancement. But we can never be fair to Shaw's creative intelligence by measuring his genius by the errors of the amateur sociologist, errors he shared with many other makers of the modern mind. In speaking of Shaw we must ultimately conclude with a proper acknowledgment of Shaw the "poet"—the visionary who refused to accept limits for the human race, the believer in the possibility of a creative will ideally capable of producing perfect men in a perfected society irradiated by right reason and good will. In this faith there could be no antinomies or conflicts of reason and instinct, rationalism and religiousness, individualism and collectivism, truth and poetry.

Shaw speaks best perhaps through one of his most attractive masks, that of the unfrocked Irish priest Father Keegan of *John Bull's Other Island*. Asked by the pragmatical Englishman Broadbent "What is it [heaven] like in your dreams?", Father Keegan declares that he dreams of "a country where the State is the Church and the Church the people; three in one and one in three." This ideal state is "a commonwealth in which work is play and play is life; three in one and one in three. It is a godhead in which all life is human and all humanity divine; three in one and one in three." And Shaw's heretical mystic reminds the sceptical materialist that "Every dream is a promise in the womb of time."[6] In nothing more is Shaw so notably a man of the twentieth century as in this trust in the desirability and inevitability of progress as well as in his perilous impatience with delay after his initial faith in gradualist reform. For all his brilliant show of hard-headedness, Shaw was also at one with the post-Renaissance Western spirit in sharing its dominantly Rousseauist romanticism, its perfectibility-worship, its "Faustian" restlessness. In virtually all his work he also gave us a distinctively nineteenth- and twentieth-century translation, into by now perhaps overfamiliar, social and political terms of the words of Leonardo da Vinci, who, standing brilliantly poised between the modern and the medieval world, concluded that "Every artist has two subjects: Man and the hopes of his soul."

MARTIN MEISEL

Opera and Drama†

"My method, my system, my tradition, is founded upon music. It is not founded upon literature at all. I was brought up on music. I did not read plays very much because I could not get hold of them, except, of course, Shakespear, who was mother's milk to me. What I was really interested in was musical development. If you study operas and symphonies, you will find a useful clue to my particular type of writing."—Shaw at Malvern, 1939.[1]

In the theater of Barry Sullivan,[2] opera and drama were much closer to each other than they are today. The two forms supplied

6. Actually Peter Keegan says (near the end of Act IV, *John Bull's Other Island*): "Every dream is a prophecy: every jest is an earnest in the womb of Time" [*Editor*].

† There is no simple explanation of Shaw's dramaturgy, but Martin Meisel's treatment of the plays as opera is a most helpful view. This is a chapter from his book, *Shaw and the Nine-*teenth-Century Theater* (Princeton: Princeton University Press, 1963), pp. 38–61.

1. In Robert F. Rattray, *Bernard Shaw: A Chronicle* (London, 1951), p. 20.

2. Barry Sullivan (1821–1891) was a leading Shakespearean actor who frequently played in Dublin during Shaw's boyhood [*Editor*].

each other with conventions and materials, and the playhouse was the opera house. The attitude of the audience for both forms was very like that of a modern opera audience; for in a day of permanent companies, great touring stars, and a familiar grand repertory, the audience judged not the play but the performance. They expressed instant approval and disapproval, waited expectantly for the virtuoso bits, and, when particularly pleased, stopped the performance and demanded the same aria or the same bravura passage over again. The actors also moved more freely between opera and drama. Barry Sullivan, Shaw's favorite among all actors, sang in opera at the beginning of his career, and Shaw classed his kind of acting with Chaliapin's.[3] On the London stage, the gap between opera and drama widened more rapidly than in the provinces. Consequently Shaw's experience in Dublin of a more intimately related opera and drama had great importance for his later critical thinking, and ultimately for his playwriting.

More than any other form of music or drama, opera in Dublin was fashionable and distinguished. Dublin saw grand opera with the great singers of the age, usually at the Theatre Royal, three to six weeks each year. The stars of the visiting company included the legendary Mario, Zelia Trebelli, Thérèse Titiens, Ilma de Murska, and Charles Santley. From 1864 to 1876 these singers presented some three dozen different operas, mostly in Italian; but the schedules were heavily weighted with the dozen or so favorites in the repertory.[4] In addition to the regular season, there were visiting "English Opera" companies singing nearly the same repertory in English, Offenbach companies, comic opera companies, and occasional nights of amateur opera, at the Theatre Royal and later at the Gaiety, under the direction of George John Vandeleur Lee.

Lee was one of the leading musical personages in Dublin, and Shaw has described at length, in various autobiographical reminiscences, the remarkable intimacy between Lee and the Shaw family. Shaw's mother became Lee's leading mezzo-soprano, disciple, and factotum, and took leading roles in various productions which were rehearsed in the joint Shaw-Lee household. She sang Azucena in *Il Trovatore*, Donna Anna in *Don Giovanni*, Margaret in Gounod's *Faust*, and the title role in *Lucrezia Borgia*.[5] Meanwhile Shaw's

---

3. A Russian opera singer, highly theatrical [*Editor*].

4. See *Annals of the Theatre Royal*, esp. pp. 224–58. Except for one year, during Shaw's residence in Dublin the company was brought by the notable London impresario, James Henry Mapleson. (See Shaw's critical comments on Mapleson and the opera of the seventies in *London Music* in 1888–1889, pp. 39–40.) For Shaw's recollection of the astonishment and delight of his first trip to the opera, see Preface to *Heartbreak House*, pp. 29–30.

5. Letter to Archibald Henderson, reprinted in *Shaw, Man of the Century*, pp. 36–37. A review of Lee's *Il Trovatore*, presented at the Theatre Royal on 31 March 1868, is of particular interest for the notice it gives to Mrs. Shaw: "Mrs Shaw made much of the part of Azucena. She does not possess the rich contralto voice we are accustomed to associate with the character, but she sings with great care and accuracy, and her acting for a non-professional is exceptionally good" ("Amateur Italian Opera," D.E.M., 1 April 1868).

sister Lucy became Lee's star pupil, and later went on to a modest career as a singer.

Shaw took no direct part in all this musical activity; he taught himself the piano, he declared, only after Lee and his mother and Lucy had gone to London and he found the dearth of music intolerable. But all through his childhood Shaw had been surrounded by music, especially great choral music and the music of Italian Opera. "At the end of my schooling I knew nothing of what the school professed to teach; but I was a highly educated boy all the same. I could sing and whistle from end to end leading works by Handel, Haydn, Mozart, Beethoven, Rossini, Bellini, Donizetti and Verdi" (*London Music*, p. 15).[6] Shaw claimed that music, and particularly vocal and operatic music, was the only power in the parochial Ireland of his boyhood "religious enough to redeem me from the abomination of desolation" (*Sixteen Self Sketches*, p. 46). What he believed had saved his soul remained a power throughout his life. "From my earliest recorded sign of an interest in music when as a small child I encored my mother's singing of the page's song from the first act of Les Huguenots . . . music has been an indispensable part of my life. Harley Granville-Barker was not far out when, at a rehearsal of one of my plays, he cried out 'Ladies and gentlemen: will you please remember that this is Italian opera' " (*London Music*, p. 28).

As a critic of all the arts in turn, Shaw recognized no fixed invisible bar between opera and drama such as, in some quarters, made the opera house respectable and the theater immoral. Shaw persisted in considering opera as a specialization of drama, and drama as a broad spectrum which terminates at one end in opera. Many of his most acute comments on the drama depend upon his clear perception of this continuity.

Opera was, for Shaw, above all other forms of theatrical expression, the drama of the passions. Music could carry the passions alive into the heart as mere words could never hope to do. In a significant article urging "The Religion of the Pianoforte" on an unmusical generation, Shaw asks, "how if you could find a sort of book that would give you not merely a description of these thrilling sensations, but the sensations themselves—the stirring of the blood, the bristling of the fibres, the transcendent, fearless fury which makes romance so delightful, and realizes that ideal which Mr. Gilbert has aptly summed up in the phrase, 'heroism without risk'?" Just take an operatic vocal score to the piano, Shaw urges, and pound away. "In the music you will find the body and reality of

6. Parenthetical references are to Shaw's works in the Standard Edition [*Editor*].

that feeling which the mere novelist could only describe to you."[7]
And just as an opera score is superior to a romantic novel, an opera
presenting a tale of passions will be far more real to a spectator
than a play presenting the very same story, because of the greater
intensity of musical expression.

"The fact is, there is a great deal of feeling, highly poetic and
highly dramatic, which cannot be expressed by mere words—
because words are the counters of thinking, not of feeling—but
which can be supremely expressed by music. The poet tries to make
words serve his purpose by arranging them musically, but is ham-
pered by the certainty of becoming absurd if he does not make his
musically arranged words mean something to the intellect as well as
to the feeling.

"For example, the unfortunate Shakespear could not make Juliet
say:

O Romeo, Romeo, Romeo, Romeo, Romeo;

and so on for twenty lines. He had to make her, in an extremity of
unnaturalness, begin to argue the case in a sort of amatory legal
fashion . . .

"Now these difficulties do not exist for the tone poet. He can
make Isolde say nothing but 'Tristan, Tristan, Tristan, Tristan,
Tristan,' and Tristan nothing but 'Isolde, Isolde, Isolde, Isolde,
Isolde,' to their hearts' content without creating the smallest
demand for more definite explanations; and as for the number if
times a tenor and soprano can repeaet 'Addio, addio, addio,' there is
no limit to it. . . . Nay, you may not only reduce the words to pure
ejaculation, you may substitute mere roulade vocalization, or even
balderdash, for them, provided the music sustains the feeling which
is the real subject of the drama. . . ." (*Music in London*, III, 228;
133–34).

With opera possessed of the overwhelming advantage of being
the drama of passions *par excellence*, it was evident to Shaw that
verbal drama had to develop its own specializations, according to its
own qualities. Yet, the nineteenth-century drama was intensely
operatic. It was above all a drama of passions. Even if we ignore
the ordinary theatrical burlesque of opera, there was scarcely an
opera libretto which lacked a serious version in the spoken drama.
And if opera drew upon the drama for its libretti, the play was

7. *Fortnightly Review*, 61 (1894), 257.

sometimes written to exploit the success of the opera.[8] The kinship was close; and in Melodrama, the most popular and characteristic form of the century, a drama of passions was acted out to music. The aspiring actor was advised that:

"In melo-drame, and serious pantomime, a slight knowledge of music is indispensable, where a certain number of things are to be done upon the stage during the execution of so many bars of music; the cues too for entrances and exits are frequently only the changes of the air, and unless the ear is cultivated (if naturally bad) the performer will be led into error. . . . when, as continually occurs, a certain act is to be done to a single note, nothing but learning the music, or counting the time, can insure correctness."[9]

At the end of the dramatic spectrum occupied by the pure drama of passions, Shaw saw opera and play losing all distinctions. When Verdi died, Shaw wrote of him: "Verdi's genius, like Victor Hugo's, was hyperbolical and grandiose: he expressed all the common passions with an impetuosity and intensity which produced an effect of sublimity. If you ask What is it all about? the answer must be that it is mostly about the police intelligence melodramatized" (*London Music*, p. 390). On the other hand, Shaw declares that, uniquely among Shakespeare's works, "Othello is a play written by Shakespear in the style of Italian opera." It has a "prima donna, with handerkerchief, confidante, and vocal solo all complete." Iago, as Stage Villain, is scarcely more lifelike than the Count di Luna. And "Othello's transports are conveyed by a magnificent but senseless music which rages from the Propontick to the Hellespont in an orgy of thundering sound and bounding rhythm. . . ." (*London Music*, p. 394).

But Shaw would have it that what Shakespeare had leave to do, by virtue of his supreme musicianship and the undeveloped state of an operatic rival, the modern playwright mistakenly imitates. It is on these grounds that Shaw scolds the audiences for crowding to see Sarah Bernhardt in Sardou's *Gismonda*. "It seems a strange thing to me that we should still be so little awake to the fact that in these plays which depend wholly on poignant intensity of

8. For example, Tom Taylor's *The Fool's Revenge* (1859). "In the 'Fool's Revenge,' Mr. Tom Taylor has transformed the nightmare story, best known to Londoners in association with the opera of 'Rigoletto,' into a wholesome English-natured plot."— Henry Morley, *The Journal of a London Playgoer, From 1851 to 1866* (London, 1866), p. 236. The opera in turn was based on Victor Hugo's play *Le Roi s'amuse*.
9. *Road to the Stage* (1827), p. 62.

The same advice is still offered as useful in French's edition of 1872 (p. 5): "In melo-drama and serious pantomime a little knowledge of music is quite indispensable. A great many of the *cues* are given in some of our melo-drama merely by a change of the tune, and exits, entrances, and deaths are often regulated simply by a change of the air." Compare "melodrame," or speech, against a musical background, in opera.

expression for the simple emotions the sceptre has passed to the operatic artist" (*Our Theatres in the Nineties*, I, p. 138). On another occasion, he writes:

"The drama of pure feeling is no longer in the hands of the playwright: it has been conquered by the musician, after whose enchantments all the verbal arts seem cold and tame. . . . there is, flatly, no future now for any drama without music except the drama of thought. The attempt to produce a genus of opera without music (and this absurdity is what our fashionable theatres have been driving at for a long time past without knowing it) is far less hopeful than my own determination to accept problem as the normal material of the drama" (*Mrs. Warren's Profession* pp. 161–62).

Yet, to banish from grace the drama of pure feeling was by no means to banish all feeling from the non-operatic play. And to condemn " a genus of opera without music" was to condemn neither a play with music, verbal or instrumental, nor a genus of opera with thought. There was room in Heaven for Wagner, from whom Shaw borrowed many of his categories, and for the allegorical music-drama of ideas, as Shaw understood *The Ring*. There was room for Shaw's own drama, with its musically conceived overtures, arias, and ensembles, thematic development, and tonal relations. There was room for a drama in which ideas are charged with emotion, "and for the drama in which emotion exists only to make thought live and move us" (*OTN*, I, 138.)

Shaw's thinking as a critic, like his earlier experiences as a spectator, bore ultimate fruit in his playwriting. However, it is by no means easy to define the practical significance in his art of his musical heritage, "which is so important in my development that nobody can really understand my art without being soaked in symphonies and operas, in Mozart, Verdi and Meyerbeer, to say nothing of Handel, Beethoven and Wagner, far more completely than in the literary drama and its poets and playwrights."[1] Numerous similar statements by Shaw, general but positive, have led his critics into numerous reiterations, general but uncertain, because what Shaw means changes with the occasion and context.[2] When he says, "My own practice varies, as far as the mechanical conditions allow me, from the ultra-classic to the ultra-operatic,"[3] he is talking, in context, about *mise en scène*, and the classical observance or

1. Letter to Nora Ervine, 12 May 1934, in St. John Ervine, *Bernard Shaw; His Life, Work, and Friends* (London, 1956), p. 555.
2. Two exceptions are Edmond Wilson in "Bernard Shaw at Eighty," *Eight Essays* (New York, 1950), where Mr. Wilson presents a symphonic analysis of *The Apple Cart* with ideas treated as musical themes, and Terrence J. Spencer in *The Dramatic Principles of George Bernard Shaw*, unpub. diss. (Stanford, 1957), pp. 116–22, where Mr. Spencer makes a similar analysis of *Caesar*.
3. "Playhouses and Plays," *New York Tribune*, 14 Nov. 1926, reprinted in *Shaw on Theatre*, p. 182.

baroque neglect of the unities. When he asserts that Herman de Lange, "though an excellent comedian and intelligent enough to have a foible for omniscience, was in complete reaction against the rhetorical, declamatory, Italian operatic tradition of acting; and neither he nor anyone else could imagine that Shaw, nursed on Italian Opera, was bent on reviving it as the classical stage method," he is talking, plainly, about acting.[4] When he writes, "the fact that I was brought up on Italian and German opera must have influenced me a good deal: there is *much more* of 'Il Trovatore' and 'Don Giovanni' in my style than of 'The Mourning Bride' and 'The School for Scandal'; but it would take me too far to pursue this,"[5] it is not at all certain what he is talking about.

It appears eventually that the relevance of Shaw's operatic background to his spoken drama is at least fourfold: He uses direct operatic allusion, because of the arch-romantic associations of opera, as part of his attack on romantic sentiment. He uses operatic conceptions in combining the *dramatis personae* of each play. He uses operatic conceptions in creating scene and dialogue, shaping them as overtures, arias, ensembles, and duets. He brings operatic ideas to acting, and seeks a rhetorical notation based on musical pitch and dynamics.

The first of these four reflections of Shaw's operatic background appears in *Arms and the Man* ("An Anti-Romantic Comedy"), where opera is put on a level with Byron and Pushkin as a source of romantic ideals. Bluntschli declares of Sergius in the charge, "He did it like an operatic tenor" (p. 15). Raina announces "We go to Bucharest every year for the opera season," and asks Bluntschli if he knows *Ernani*.

> RAINA. I thought you might have remembered the great scene where Ernani, flying from his foes just as you were tonight, takes refuge in the castle of his bitterest enemy, an old Castilian noble. The noble refuses to give him up. His guest is sacred to him.
> THE MAN (*quickly waking up a little*) Have your people got that notion? (*Arms*, p. 19)

Needless to say, Shaw draws a double benefit from *Ernani*. First of all, it plays its part in the ridicule of romance; and secondly, since Raina acts on her operatic inspiration, the motif of the

4. From the foreword to Michael Orme's *J. T. Grein: The Story of a Pioneer 1862–1935* (London, 1936), p. 12. "Written by Conal O'Riordan and Censored and Revised by George Bernard Shaw." O'Riordan makes plain in an introductory note that most of the personal reminiscences are his, and most of the objective criticism is Shaw's.

5. "Mr. Shaw on Mr. Shaw," *New York Times*, 12 June 1927.

hunted quarry (Bluntschli) who takes shelter in the bosom of his enemies actually enters the plot.

Ernani appears again, in *Man and Superman,* in a less obvious invocation of operatic high romance for anti-romantic purposes. The opening scene of the opera presents Ernani, a brigand chief of noble blood, on a summit in the mountains of Aragon. He gazes sadly down the valley at a castle in the distance where Elvira, his true love, is about to be married unhappily. Nearby his followers, in conventional brigand style, make merry around the campfire with a drinking song.

The third-act opening of *Man and Superman* is a precise visual allusion to this scene. But the solitary man on the summit is only a lookout, and the men around the smouldering fire, with "an air of being conscious of themselves as picturesque scoundrels honoring the Sierra by using it as an effective pictorial background," are engaged in a political meeting with their chief in the chair, and in place of the chorus of "beviam, beviam," we hear that they have spent three evenings in discussing the question, "Have Anarchists or Social-Democrats the most personal courage?" Most of the brigands are dressed in bowler, coat, and muffler; and their leader, in boots, cloak, and sombrero, "with a striking cockatoo nose, glossy black hair, pointed beard, upturned moustache, and a Mephistophelean affectation," seems scarcely to belong among them (pp. 71–72.)

Like Ernani, Mendoza, the brigand chief, is pining for a love that is denied him. (Elvira in the opera is about to be married, reluctantly, to her guardian. It is worth noting Shaw's reversal of this convention with Ann and Jack Tanner, where it is the designing ward who pursues the reluctant guardian. But Shaw's point about the consciously picturesque and sentimental Mendoza is that his romantic love-affliction is driving him to waste, absurdly, his remarkable gifts of energy, intelligence, and imagination in the mountains of the Sierra Nevada. Here, as in *Arms and the Man,* the arch-romantic associations of opera are being used for anti-romantic purposes. The comedy is in the irreverence.

The second influence of Shaw's operatic background on his art was in the forming of his casts of characters. In opera, range of character and character balance were not, as in drama, chiefly a matter of age, station, and comic-pathetic quality; they were a matter of voice. When Shaw contrived his casts of characters, it was with an eye to vocal balance in addition to everything else. As advice to directors of any play, not just his own, Shaw wrote:

"In selecting the cast no regard should be given to whether the actors understand the play or not (players are not walking encyclopedias); but their ages and personalities should be suitable, and their voices should not be alike. The four principals should be soprano, alto, tenor, and bass. Vocal contrast is of the greatest importance, and is indispensable for broadcasting. . . .

"The director must accordingly take care that every speech contrasts as strongly as possible in speed, tone, manner, and pitch with the one which provokes it, as if coming unexpected as a shock, surprise, stimulant, offence, amusement, or what not. It is for the author to make this possible; for in it lies the difference between dramatic dialogue and epic narrative."[6]

In his author's task, Shaw was immensely assisted by the unmistakable coincidence of dramatic line and operatic voice which further underlines the operatic quality of so much of nineteenth-century drama. In the drama itself certain voice qualities were associated with certain types. Heavy Villains, for example, were expected to speak in deep, reverberating tones.[7] In opera, where vocal qualities were paramount and where vocal balance had to be attained, there was a much more thorough-going identification of particular plot functions with particular kinds of voice. Since the operatic and dramatic stages shared stories and materials, a list of correspondences may be drawn between dramatic and operatic lines of work. For example, corresponding to the male Heavy parts in the written drama were the bass or baritone parts in opera (as, drawing on opera available in Dublin, Pizarro in *Fidelio*, Kaspar in *Der Freischütz*, Rigoletto and Sparafucile in *Rigoletto*, the Count di Luna in *Trovatore*, Mephistopheles in *Faust*, Telramund in *Lohengrin*). Corresponding to the female Heavy parts were the contralto or mezzo-soprano parts (as Azucena in *Trovatore*, Amneris in *Aïda*, Ulrica in *Un Ballo in Maschera*, Ortrud in *Lohengrin*). Corresponding to the Juvenile Leads or leading lovers were the tenor and soprano parts (as Florestan and Lenore in *Fidelio*, Manrico and Leonora in *Trovatore*, Ernani and Elvira in *Ernani*, Faust and Marguerite in *Faust*, Edgardo and Lucia in *Lucia*, Radames and Aïda in *Aïda*, Alfredo and Violetta in *Traviata*). "The operatic artist of today," wrote Shaw in a scathing criticism of operatic acting, "is a 'stock company' artist. He calls himself a *primo tenore* or a *basso cantante* instead of a juvenile lead or a first old man; but the difference is only technical."[8]

6. "Shaw's Rules for Directors," *Theatre Arts*, 33 (Aug. 1949) 7, 9.
7. See Thomas W. Erle, *Letters from a Theatrical Scene Painter* (London, 1880), pp. 48-49. Of the "strong-minded and bold villain" (as distinguished from the "cowardly or white-livered villain"), Erle notes: "His voice is a basso profundo, or rather profundissimo. . . . It is as gruff as the sound of a Christmas wait's trombone . . ."
8. "The Opera Season" (1889), reprinted in *How to Become a Musical Critic*, ed. Dan H. Laurence (New York, 1961), p. 152.

In providing his casts of characters, Shaw did not obviously equip each play with a leading quartet of soprano, alto, tenor, and bass, though a number of his plays are precisely so equipped, and scarcely one strays further from this ideal than the ordinary opera. Among those plays with an obvious operatic quartet are *Major Barbara* (Barbara, Lady Britomart, Cusins, and Undershaft), *Heartbreak House* (Ellie, Hesione, Hector, and Shotover) and *The Dark Lady of the Sonnets* (the Dark Lady, Queen Elizabeth, Shakespeare, the Warder). However, in all his plays, in each cast, and in each scene, Shaw takes care to contrive the best possible vocal range and balance in the interests of liveliness and harmony. The operatic translation of dramatic line into voice quality usually provides him with a proper variety, but occasionally these vocal associations are not sufficient. For example, in the "Don Juan in Hell" episode of *Man and Superman*, to achieve a proper balance and contrast Shaw must excuse himself and make the Statue a tenor—indeed, a counter-tenor—in spite of Mozart, decorum, and the convention of the *père noble* who in opera was always baritone or bass. By tuning Doña Ana, the Statue, Don Juan, and the Devil like a family of viols, Shaw provides a quartet better capable of sustaining a concert-length scene of difficult and highly developed intellectual substance. Similarly, in *The Apple Cart*, where Act I is largely a discursive meeting between King and Cabinet, Shaw takes care to make two of the ministers women: Amanda, a music-hall soprano who wins elections with comic songs, and Lysistrata, *"a grave lady in academic robes"* who speaks *"in a sepulchral contralto"* (pp. 210, 218).

The third aspect of musical and operatic conceptions in Shaw's dramatic art was in the composition, instrumentation, and succession of scenes. Scenic composition and instrumentation was the immediate practical consideration which required a vocally balanced and distributed cast. Sybil Thorndike said of Shaw's reading of *Saint Joan*, "It was like listening to a great executant who knows intuitively how every note should be played. The lines came like music; each character was a different instrument in the orchestra, and he could play them all. Listening to that symphony was the greatest experience of my life."[9] Shaw read like an orchestra because he had conceived each scene musically and operatically. "Opera taught me to shape my plays into recitatives, arias, duets, trios, ensemble finales, and bravura pieces to display the technical accomplishments of the executants. . . ."[1] The "verbal music" of

9. Quoted by Hesketh Pearson in *Bernard Shaw: His Life and Personality* (London, 1942), p. 377.

1. Shaw, "The Play of Ideas," *New Statesman and Nation*, n.s., 39 (1950), 511.

Shakespeare, the verbal texture which Shaw cried up vigorously and consistently while crying down Shakespeare's philosophical attitudes, he conceived as taking musical and operatic forms. "To Shaw," he wrote of himself, "the wonderful storm trio [in *Lear*] in which the king, the fool, and the sham madman have their parts 'concerted,' as musicians say, like the statue, the hero, and the comic valet in Shaw's favorite *Don Giovanni*, is the summit of Shakespeare's achievement as poet and playwright."[2]

Shaw's own equivalent in a "concerted" trio is perhaps what Sybil Thorndike calls "that marvellous three-handed scene between Cauchon, Warwick and de Stogumber" in *Saint Joan*, "the pith and essence of what the play means." In reading the play to her, Shaw said: "That's all flapdoodle up to there—just 'theatre' to get you interested—now the play begins."[3] Up to this point of the play we have had considerable stage action, some melodrama, and even some farce; but Scene IV, which follows, unmasks the drama of ideas. It is "concerted," as in *Don Giovanni*, between a comic buffo, a worldly baritone, and an other-worldly bass. In the storm scene and the supper scene in *Lear* and *Don Giovanni*, the total effect depends upon a counterpoint of three distinct melodic lines carried by three distinct voices playing against each other: for example, terror in the servant, bravado in the Don, awesome stern-ness in the statue. In Shaw's concerted trio, it is the ideas as well as the tones and emotions which play against each other: de Stog-umber's simple chauvinism, Warwick's feudalism, the Bishop's Catholicism. The final blending of the three voices comes not so much from connection in their discourse—the Bishop, the Earl, and the Chauvinist are rather impervious to each other's point of view and seem to talk past each other—as from parallelism in their situation with respect to Joan. The three vocal and intellectual lines finally join in the resolve to destroy Joan. This is not unity, but a temporary harmony emerging from the counterpoint. The counterpoint of ideas and points of view in "concerted" scenes was not restricted to *Saint Joan*; rather it was an intrinsic part of Shaw's dramatic art. As early as 1895 he wrote to the actor Charles Char-rington, "when you see a man like me, trying to do in counterpoint in even so few as three real parts, as in *Candida*, or in seven, as in the finale of *The Philanderer*, never tell him he ought to go and write choruses instead."[4]

Though many of Shaw's characters are, like Warwick and Cau-

2. Part of a comparison, by Shaw, of Moliére and himself in Henderson. *Man of the Century*, p. 741.
3. Dame Sybil Thorndike, "Thanks to Bernard Shaw" in Raymond Mander and Joe Mitchenson, *Theatrical Companion to Shaw* (London, 1954), p. 14.
4. Letter of 1 March 1895 in St. John Ervine, *Bernard Shaw*, p. 257.

chon, intended as equals in ideological significance and personal
force, a developed scene involving these characters rarely takes the
form of a witty tennis match. Shaw's technique is not to shift the
lead with each stroke, but rather to allow a character to retain the
lead through a repeated pattern of speeches before losing the lead
to someone else. Each part dominates the others in turn. The shifts
are crucial, of course, and the character emerging with final dominance has usually won something substantial. An illustration is the
beginning of the second act of *Mrs. Warren.* Mrs. Warren enters
with Frank Gardner in attendance, Mrs. Warren very much in the
lead, even flirting with Frank, until Frank unabashedly declares he
had made love to her daughter Vivie. Mrs. Warren is taken aback
and positions are briefly reversed, until the entrance of Crofts and
the Reverend Samuel Gardner. Frank subsides, and Mrs. Warren
leads all four voices, until the question of Frank and Vivie is once
more raised. The voices of the quartet are the clergyman's hollow
bass, Crofts' nasal baritone, *"reedier than might be expected from
his strong frame,"* Frank's tenor, and Mrs. Warren's alto.

The Reverend Samuel Gardner, Frank's father and Mrs. Warren's former lover, is shocked and startled at the thought of a
match between the children. As he takes the lead (p. 197,) the
conversation assumes a characteristic pattern (each line below
represents a speech):

BASS *rising startled . . . into real force and sincerity*
    Baritone [*assenting*]
    Tenor *with enchanting placidity*
    Alto *reflectively*
BASS *astounded*
    Baritone [*assenting*]
    Alto *nettled*
    Bass [*plaintively—losing the lead*]
ALTO *defiantly*
    Bass *collapsing helplessly into his chair*
    Tenor [*continuing unperturbed*]
    Baritone *gets up . . . frowning determinedly*
ALTO *turning on him sharply*
    Tenor *with his prettiest lyrical cadence*
    Baritone [*defending his challenge for the lead*]
    Bass [*supporting Baritone*]—*Mrs Warren's face falls*

Up to this point there has been a four-part counterpoint with a
leading part defined, passing from Bass to Alto. Instead of supporting Gardner in declaring a marriage between their children
"out of the question," Mrs. Warren has taken the stand "Why

not?" and Frank's father dares not give the reasons. Crofts, however, who has his own designs on Vivie, raises the question of money.
Gardner declares Frank will get no money, and "*Mrs. Warren's face
falls.*" Then Crofts utters a triumphant "There! I told you" and
sits down "*as if the matter were finally disposed of,*" to crown his
displacement of the Alto theme and as transitional punctuation; for
the rhythm speeds up, the four voices become two, and Frank, who
has heretofore taken an unobstrusive part, starts his own melody:

TENOR *plaintively*
  Alto [*firmly*]
TENOR *much amused* [*to Bass*]
  Bass [*weakly*]
TENOR [*patronizingly, to Baritone*]
  Baritone *turning angrily on his elbow*
TENOR *pointedly*
  baritone *contemptuously* . . . *he turns away again*
TENOR *rising* [*to Alto*]
  Alto *muttering*
TENOR *continuing* [*he is metaphorically still rising*] *They stare
  at him and he begins to declaim gracefully*

Frank announces he shall place his case before Vivie. While the
others stand stupefied, he actually rises into verse, a short aria
signaling his temporary triumph. Then the cottage door opens
and all relations change.

The quality of the scene, in its energy and vivacity, is typically
Shaw's. It is operatic in a number of ways (character balance, vocal
quality); but is musical chiefly in that much of the pleasure, conscious or unconscious, comes from the repetitions, variations, and
transformations of a pattern. The clarity and handling of the pattern are what seem to justify Shaw's frequent remark that "I still
call myself a pupil of Mozart in comedy much more than of any of
the English literary dramatists."[5]

Shaw imagined, not only voice, cast, and scene in the conceptual
framework of music and opera, but also the succession of scenes,
and the play as a whole. Fretting over Max Reinhardt's German
production of *The Apple Cart*, Shaw complains to his translator
that Reinhardt has attempted to transform Shaw's original Mozart
into vulgarized Offenbach. He objects to Maria Bard's making

5. MS letter to Siegfried Trebitsch, 1
July 1902. See also *Music in London*,
I, 296: "In my small-boyhood I by
good luck had an opportunity of learning the Don thoroughly, and if it were
only for the sense of the value of fine
workmanship which I gained from it, I
should still esteem that lesson the most
important part of my education. Indeed, it educated me artistically in all
sorts of ways, and disqualified me only
in one—that of criticizing Mozart
fairly. Everyone appears a sentimental,
hysterical bungler in comparison when
anything brings his finest work vividly
back to me."

Orinthia a whore and Magnus a libertine. "Naturally, when the play is transposed into that amusing and popular but utterly vulgar key, everything that establishes my own higher key has to come out." He gives as an example "my little overture for Sempronius & Pamphilius," whose tone of quiet refinement gives relief and effect to the violent entrance of Boanerges; "so Max has to cut it out and begin with a vulgarized Boanerges waiting for a vieux marcheur[6] king, a male Duchess of Gerolstein.[7] Both in its debased and "higher" version, everything in the play seems operatically conceived; Mozart or Offenbach.

Shaw habitually referred to questions of tone and style as a matter of "key." Writing about the drama of sex in the preface to *Overruled*, he declares, "Now if all this can be done in the key of tragedy and philosophic comedy, it can, I have always contended, be done in the key of farcical comedy; and Overruled is a trifling experiment in that manner" (pp. 164–165). In a note to Lillah McCarthy concerning *Man and Superman*, Shaw makes certain corrective suggestions on a transition from a scene of bustle: "Otherwise you will not get the new key and the slow movement."[8] He writes to Siegfried Trebitsch of Trebitsch's own play, *Die Letzte Wille*, "let the people in your next play have a little will and a little victory [Sieg], and then you will begin to enjoy yourself and write your plays in the Shavian Key—D flat major, vivacissimo."[9] The irrepressible tempo is strictly Shavian; but the tonality, a good key for brass instruments, Shaw would associate with *The Ring*.

The fourth influence of Shaw's musical and operatic experience on his dramatic art was the effect on his notions of acting, or "performance." Up to 1920, Shaw was his own director. The extensive descriptions of character and the parenthetical characterizations of almost every speech in his printed texts were attempts to reproduce for the reader all that Shaw as director would bring out of the play. Shaw genuinely lamented the lack of a musical-rhetorical notation which could send his plays to posterity as he conceived them:

"But I must repeat that the notation at my disposal cannot convey the play as it should really exist: that is, in its oral delivery. I have to write melodies without bars, without indications of pitch, pace, or timbre, and without modulation, leaving the actor or producer to divine the proper treatment of what is essentially word-music. I turn over a score by Richard Strauss, and envy him his bar divisions, his assurance that his trombone passages will not be

6. An old soldier [*Editor*].
7. MS letter to Siegfried Trebitsch, 23 April 1930.
8. Lillah McCarthy, *Myself and My*

Friends (London, 1934) p. 70.
9. MS letter to Trebitsch, 28 March 1906.

played on the triangle, his power of giving directions without making his music unreadable. What would we not give for a copy of *Lear* marked by Shakespear 'somewhat broader,' 'always quieter and quieter,' 'amiably,' or, less translatably, 'mit grossem Schwung und Begeisterung,' 'mit Steigerung,' much less Meyerbeer's 'con esplosione,' or Verdi's *fffff* or *pppppp*, or *cantando* or *parlando*, or any of the things that I say at rehearsal, and that in my absence must be left to the intuitions of some kindred spirit?"[1]

Though Shaw had no hope of developing an adequate rhetorical notation, he made shift with the language of music in directing his actors. Winifred Loraine, in the biography of her actor-husband, writes, "Shaw annotated *Don Juan*, the dream in the third act of *Superman*, like a symphony for Robert. The margin in the book twinkled with crotchets, crescendoes and minims; with G clefs, F clefs, and pianissimos; and Robert, who did not know how to read music, learned how to do so by this."[2] G. W. Bishop, writing on Shaw as a rehearsalist, declares:

"It would not be a misstatement to say that he orchestrates the parts for the actors, and in one instance he actually annotated a copy of the play in musical terms. This was for Scott Sunderland who appeared as Cain in Act 2 of the first part of *Back to Methuselah*, and as the Elderly Gentleman in Part 4.

·   ·   ·   ·   ·   ·

"The actor is told to pitch his first long speech—'Whose fault was it that I killed Abel . . .'— 'say, in C Major.' 'He is to be happy and condescending.' When he gets down to the line, 'I envied his happiness, his freedom . . .' he is told to 'drop without modulation to A flat, and abandon all affectation. He is now *talking about himself*, and much more serious than when he was talking about Abel.'

"[In the speech following Cain's protest 'I do not want to kill women,'] 'begin at a low pitch and drag the time a little; then take the whole speech as a *crescendo—p.* to *ff*.' Against the words 'fighting, fighting, killing, killing!' there is a note: '*martellato*,' and after 'burning, overwhelming life,' Mr. Shaw has written '*meno mosso*.'

·   ·   ·   ·   ·

"With the line, 'I revolt against the clay,' he is to reach 'his top note; it is the climax—and indeed the end—of this part. His style in this speech is large and grand and harmonious, in longer bars, a little restrained in speed, but otherwise all out.' "

1. "Shakespeare: A Standard Text," *Times Literary Supplement*, 17 March 1921, p. 178; in *Shaw on Theatre*, p. 144.
2. Winifred Loraine, *Head Wind* (New York, 1939), p. 90.

Most significant is Bishop's final statement: "I have quoted a few of the more important notes—leaving out most of the technical musical terms that are scattered through the part. . . ."[3]

Further traces of Shaw's musical-rhetorical notation may be found among the scrawled rehearsal notes in his hand which survive in the Enthoven Collection of the Victoria & Albert Museum. For *Arms and the Man* (produced April, 1894) Shaw noted:

Raina   Chocolate cream soldier—much longer ⌢;

for *Getting Married* (produced May, 1908):

[Collins] No maam: it didnt come natural⎫
         Oh yes, maam, yes; very often   ⎬ same song;
                                   ⎭

for *Fanny's First Play* (produced April, 1911):

Gilby   The solo on a lower note
Mrs K   Revenlations [*sic*]—But I do say—*sf*
Mrs K   But dont *you* think—a third lower.

Though sharps and flats, clefs and key signatures, are almost entirely barred from Shaw's printed texts, occasionally the musical conception of an actor's part in a scene shows through, as for example in the brief "Recruiting Pamphlet" *O'Flaherty* V. C.

> MRS O'FLAHERTY (*solo*): You impudent young heifer, how dar [sic] you say such a thing to me? (*Teresa retorts furiously; the men interfere; and the solo becomes a quartet, fortissimo*). (p. 216)

Other examples occur in the bravura sections of the waiter's part in *You Never Can Tell*. As the waiter greets Valentine and Crampton, he begins a line of chatter designed to soothe and at the same time to reveal to Crampton, as delicately as possible, that Crampton is the father of the family that has asked him to lunch (pp. 230–31). In the course of the revelation, the waiter bustles professionally, helps Crampton with his coat, takes a stick from Valentine. The directions for all this are musical directions. The waiter begins "*smoothly melodious*" [*legato cantabile*]; then speaks "*Quickly, to Crampton, who has risen to get the overcoat off.*" Rid of his overcoat, Crampton sits down, "*and the waiter resumes the broken melody.*" He drops a hint which startles Crampton, and continues "*With gentle archness;*" then turns to Valentine,

3. G. W. Bishop, *Barry Jackson and the London Theatre* (London, 1933), pp. 28, 29.

"(*Again changing his tempo to say to Valentine, who is putting his stick down against the corner of the garden seat*) If youll allow me, sir?" Capturing the stick, "*The waiter turns to Crampton and continues his lay*," to the point of the catastrophic revelation.

It was such bravura acting that Shaw had in mind when he wrote to one of his critics, "You are right in saying that my plays require a special technique of acting, and, in particular, great virtuosity in sudden transistions of mood that seem to the ordinary actor to be transitions from one 'line' of character to another. But, after all, this is only fully accomplished acting; for there is no other sort of acting except bad acting, acting that is the indulgence of imagination instead of the exercise of skill."[4] And it was to secure such acting for a drama which came to depend more and more for its interest on the rapid fire of its words and ideas that Shaw wished for something like a musical-rhetorical dramatic notation.

In revolting against "a genus of opera without music," the drama of pure emotion, Shaw committed himself to a species of drama much more musical in its fundamental nature: the drama of ideas. For "If you want to produce anything in the way of great poetic drama," he declared, "you have to take a theme, as Beethoven did in his symphonies, and keep hammering at the one theme."[5] As Shaw developed from his first exploitations of popular genres to the full-fledged Discussion Play, he became more and more adept at the development and counterpointing of ideas as if they were musical themes. At the same time, he became less and less patient with the requirement of first-night comprehensibility. He wrote, at about the time of *Misalliance* and *Getting Married*,

"Even when the author raises no hostility or misunderstanding by breaking new ground, as Beethoven did, yet it is not in the nature of things possible for a person to take in a play fully until he is in complete possession of its themes; or, to put it in another way, nobody can understand the beginning of a play until he knows the end of it: a condition which cannot be fulfilled at first hearing ... In music this goes without saying: no one pretends to be able to follow the Ninth Symphony until he knows all the themes as well as he knows God Save the King. Now probably there are many more people who can pick up and remember a new tune at one hearing than can master a new idea at its first utterance."[6]

4. "Mr. Shaw on Mr. Shaw," *New York Times*, 12 June 1927.
5. Rattray, *Bernard Shaw: A Chronicle*, p. 20, quoting a statement by Shaw at Malvern in 1939.

6. "Mr. Trench's Dramatic Values," a letter to *The Saturday Review*, 110 (2 July 1910), reprinted in West, *Shaw on Theatre*, p. 114.

The play, in this passage, is conceived as a musical composition, built from the progression, development, and counterpointing of themes. Theme as melody and theme as idea are equated. The playwright is regarded as a composer, and the spectator is required to adopt the concert-goer's frame of mind.

Shaw's conception of *Back to Methuselah* was similar. He conceived of it, on the analogy of Wagner's *Ring* cycle, as an allegorical music-drama in which ideas were made flesh.[7] After an unsatisfactory reading of the work in progress, he wrote to Granville-Barker, "To the end I may have to disregard the boredom of the spectator who has not mastered all the motifs, as Wagner had to do; but I daresay I shall manage to make the people more amusing, some of them more poetic, and all of them more intelligible than they now are in this first draft."[8]

When Shaw defined opera as the extreme and supreme drama of the passions, he was careful to distinguish opera from Wagnerian music-drama. Thereafter, he campaigned against those dramatists who still attempted to beat opera at its own game, but he nevertheless exploited aspects of opera in writing his own plays. He used its arch-romantic associations in attacking the romantic view of the world; he imported its vocal and structural concepts for forming his casts, and for constructing scenes and creating dialogue; he borrowed its fundamentally musical idea of performance and infused it into the acting his scenes and dialogue require. All this he took largely from a form whose purest expression, Shaw declared, was a tenor and soprano infinitely repeating "Addio, addio, addio.'

But in Wagner's music-drama Shaw believed he had found the possibility of conveying impassioned thought to an audience, thought interpenetrated with intense feeling. "It is only when a thought interpenetrated with intense feeling has to be expressed," he wrote, "as in the Ode to Joy in the Ninth Symphony, that coherent words must come with the music."[9] The converse seemed to follow: if thought was to be conveyed with all possible passion, music would have to come with the coherent words; to infuse thought with the life and passion he had found in opera as a boy, Shaw would have to bring the world of music to his playwriting. The consistent aesthetic direction of Shaw's entire playwriting career was toward the creation of a drama of impassioned thought, a heroic drama of ideas.

7. See MS letters to Siegfried Trebitsch, 20 July 1919 and 15 Sept. 1920.
8. 18 Dec. 1918, *Bernard Shaw's Letters to Granville Barker,* ed. C. B. Purdom (New York, 1957), p. 198.
9. *Music in London, III,* 134. (Compare Wagner on the Ninth Symphony in *Opera and Drama.)*

JULIAN B. KAYE

Shaw and Nineteenth-Century Political Economists†

Shaw is a Victorian socialist. Aside from the Webbs his political teachers
were Henry George, Karl Marx, Stanley Jevons, and Edward Bellamy.
—Eric Bentley, *Bernard Shaw*, 32–33

In all my plays my economic studies have played as important a part as
a knowledge of anatomy does in the works of Michael Angelo.
—Letter from Bernard Shaw to Archibald Henderson[1]

A new life began for Bernard Shaw on the evening when he
heard Henry George lecture on the single tax and land nationalization.[2] Although his conversion to George was quickly followed by a
conversion to Marx,[3] George not only aroused Shaw's interest in
economic problems, but also prepared the way for his abandonment
of Marx's and espousal of Jevons' economics; moreover, Shaw's re-
iterated assertion that the law of economic rent is the pons asino-
rum of economics[4] indicates the importance of George to Shavian
economics.

George's thesis is that the owners of land are the principal bene-
ficiaries of the enormous increase in productivity and population
that followed the industrialization of western Europe and the
United States. Labor and capital, both scarce and therefore valuable in the sparsely populated, predominantly agricultural nations
of the preindustrial era, were, by the end of the nineetnth century,
a glut on the market; at the same time, productivity was greater
than ever. The only possible beneficiary of the increase in wealth,
George concluded, must be the landlord.[5] The remedy George proposed is the substitution of a single tax on land for all other sources
of government revenue. The landlord would retain only enough of
his rent to induce him to act as an agent for the government by
maintaining and managing his property.

† Political economy was never a dry
subject for Shaw, but rather the basis
for a deeply humanistic philosophy.
His attitude toward Socialism infuses
everything he wrote. In an attempt to
understand his plays it is therefore useful to focus on him not only in the
company of his fellow artists, but also
in the company of his fellow political
economists. The chapter following is
from Julian B. Kaye's study, *Bernard
Shaw and the Nineteenth-Century Tradition* (Norman, Okla.: University of
Oklahoma Press, 1958), pp. 132–152.
1. Dated June 30, 1904. It is quoted in
Archibald Henderson, *George Bernard
Shaw: His Life and Works*, 291.
2. See Henderson, *Bernard Shaw: Play-
boy and Prophet*, 148. The lecture was

delivered on September 5, 1882. On p.
149, Henderson prints a letter from
Shaw to Hamlin Garland in which
Shaw gives an account of his lecture,
which was delivered in Memorial Hall,
Farringdon Street.
3. *Ibid.*, 153.
4. See, for example, *The Intelligent
Woman's Guide*, 108–109, and "The
Impossibilities of Anarchism," in *Fabian Essays*. [The "asses' bridge" in
Euclidean geometry was the fundamental thesis on which everything else
rested—*Editor*.]
5. See Henry George, *Progress and
Poverty*, in *The Complete Works of
Henry George*, I, xii–xiii, 247,
280–81, *et passim*.

Incomplete though this economic theorem and the corollary panacea proposed may seem to us who live in an economy characterized by huge oligopolistic industries, it seemed quite plausible during the eighties to Shaw and many of his contemporaries. At that time, both in England and America, the great fortunes were principally real-estate fortunes. In England the situation was aggravated by the fact that a few aristocratic families owned a large proportion of all urban real estate. Cities like Liverpool, Birmingham, and Manchester had grown, in the early part of the nineteenth century, from market towns or villages into great metropolises, and the estates of a few landlords had consequently become urban centers. In America the first multimillionaires—e.g., the Astors and the Goelets—almost all derived their wealth principally from the ownership of urban land. The cities of Chicago and San Francisco, among the most prosperous in the United States, had been villages within the memory of middle-aged men. Within the memory of these same men, the rise in the standard of living of the average workingman had been so slow and so subject to periodic reversals by depressions that it was almost imperceptible.[6] No wonder Shaw was immediately converted to Georgeism!

When Shaw tried to propagate his new faith at a meeting of Hyndman's Democratic Federation, he was told to read Karl Marx. Shaw did read *Das Kapital*, and as a result, he became an enthusiastic Marxist. (His brief adherence to George, followed by a conversion to Marx, is symptomatic of the rapid rise and fall of Henry George's reputation and the absorption of most of the Georgeites by various socialist groups.)

Shaw found that George's law of rent has as its corollary a law of economic rent which makes Georgeism untenable.[7] This same law of economic rent, however, invalidates Marx's abstract economics, and Shaw was too intelligent and fair minded not to admit this when it was pointed out to him.

The record of Shaw's abandonment of Marxian economics and his advocacy of the "marginal utility" school, associated in Anglo-Saxon countries with Jevons, is found in *Bernard Shaw and Karl Marx: A Symposium*, which is a collection of articles written during the mid-eighties for now obscure English magazines. The attack on Marx's economics was initiated by Philip H. Wicksteed,[8] who challenges Marx's theory of value and, consequently, his

6. The enormous increase in the percentage of urban workers probably also masked the increase in the standard of living. The rural workers seemed more prosperous—and may have been more comfortable—because they did not live in crowded urban slums. Thus the increase in real wages may not have been, for most workers, an increase in comfort.

7. See *Everybody's Political What's What*, 16.

8. Philip H. Wicksteed, "*Das Kapital*, a Criticism," in Bernard Shaw, *Bernard Shaw and Karl Marx: A symposium*, 11–65.

theory of surplus value. Wicksteed denies that the value of a commodity is the labor expended in its production. Goods have value because people want them.[9] Practically speaking, the value of almost all commodities is determined by their labor cost, but labor is expended on raw materials only because the product of labor will be "desirable" to men. Wicksteed then points out that it was Jevons who formulated the laws by which desirability determines value. According to his law of indifference, no one will pay more for one part of the supply of a commodity than for another. Therefore, "it is the force of demand *at the margin of supply* which determines the exchange value of the whole."[1] This force of demand is called the final utility of a commodity. Since the capitalist will seek to apply labor as profitably as possible, the final utility of a commodity will determine the amount of labor applied to the manufacture of that commodity; therefore, it is usually possible to measure the value of a commodity by the labor cost of its production. However, there are questions concerning the value of commodities to which the labor theory of value is completely inapplicable: e.g., the value of paintings and sculptures of deceased artists, the supply of which is obviously constant; the value of two articles produced at equal labor cost, one of which is damaged in transportation or packaging.

What parts of Marx's economics are invalidated by his inexact definition of value? Most important, his definition of the value of labor as its subsistence wage, and consequently his whole theory of surplus value, collapses.[2] The value of labor (instead of being its cost of production—i.e., a subsistence wage) depends upon the margin of supply, which, in free countries, is only partially dependent on economic conditions. Therefore, the whole conception of surplus value becomes meaningless.

Shaw replied to this attack on Marx by what he frankly admitted to be "a counterblast to Mr. Wicksteed rather than a thorough analysis and discussion of his interesting contribution."[3] The counterblast was easily rebutted by Wicksteed.[4]

Shaw did not pursue the controversy during the next two years; he then published, in the fall of 1887, a series of three articles on *Das Kapital* in *The National Reformer* in which he admitted that Wicksteed had been right and Shaw had been wrong. Although in these articles Shaw is an ardent Jevonian, he remains a socialist and

9. *Ibid.*, 34–35.
1. *Ibid.*, 51. Cf. W. Stanley Jevons, *The Theory of Political Economy*, 95.
2. Wicksteed, "*Das Kapital*, a Criticism," in *Bernard Shaw and Karl Marx*, 64.
3. Bernard Shaw, "The Jevonian Criticism of Marx: A Comment on the Rev. P. H. Wicksteed's Article," in *Bernard Shaw and Karl Marx*, 86.
4. Philip H. Wicksteed, "The Jevonian Criticism of Marx: A Rejoinder," in *Bernard Shaw and Karl Marx*, 91–99.

points out that Jevons' economics are not at all inconsistent with socialism. Although, according to Jevons, the value of labor is not necessarily its subsistence wage, the value of unskilled labor in nineteenth-century England can be demonstrated by his law of indifference[5] to be zero, since there is always unemployment.

In an article written two years later (1889), Shaw points out that Jevons, applied to George and Ricardo, supplies a far more powerful economic weapon for socialism than Marx's surplus-value theory—namely, the law of economic rent. If the price of a commodity at the margin of supply is the value of the commodity, the consumer will have to pay as much for the most easily—and therefore most cheaply—obtained raw materials as for those obtained with the greatest difficulty and expense. The revenue that goes to the fortunate possessor of fertile farmland and rich mineral deposits is economic rent.[6]

After demolishing Marx's abstract economics, Shaw asserts that the only reason he can find for their continued popularity among socialists is that they are easy to understand and to explain to large masses of men, whereas Jevons' theories are complex and difficult.[7] Shaw felt obliged to attack Marx because he believed that it is very dangerous for socialism to be based on theories which can be easily refuted.[8]

Although Shaw does not consider Marx a great economist, he again and again praises Marx as a great social thinker and as a great denouncer of the infamies of capitalism. Shaw was not a Marxist; but neither, said Shaw, was Marx:[9] "I do not accuse Karl Marx of Marxism, and ... I think he deserves something worthier from his pupils than idolatry."[1] Shaw had no more patience with the orthodox Marxists and with "Scientific Socialism" than he had with Neo-Darwinism. Marx's theories are hypotheses which must be verified, like anyone else's, by their accurate prediction of social phenomena before they are accepted as scientific truths.[2]

Shaw discarded many of Marx's most important hypotheses

5. Jevons, *The Theory of Political Economy*, 91: ". . . in the same open market, at any one moment, there cannot be two prices for the same kind of article."
6. Bernard Shaw, "Bluffing the Value Theory," in *Bernard Shaw and Karl Marx*, 195–96.
7. Bernard Shaw, "Karl Marx and *Das Kapital*," in *Bernard Shaw and Karl Marx*, 146; cf. Shaw's "The Illusions of Socialism," in *Forecasts of the Coming Century*, ed. by Edward Carpenter (Manchester, 1897).
8. "Bluffing the Value Theory," in *Bernard Shaw and Karl Marx*, 195-96.

9. See Sidney Hook, *Towards the Understanding of Karl Marx*, 3: "He himself [Marx] lived to say, 'Je ne suis pas un Marxiste.'"
1. "Bluffing the Value Theory," in *Bernard Shaw and Karl Marx*, 200.
2. "Karl Marx and *Das Kapital*," in *Bernard Shaw and Karl Marx*, 118; cf. Hook, *Towards the Understanding of Karl Marx*, 103, 181, 248. Hook asserts that Marx regarded his theories as prophecies that would have to be validated by the future; moreover, these prophecies would help to validate themselves in that they would change the course of the future.

during the course of his career. His most devastating attack on the social science of the orthodox Marxists is found in "The Illusions of Socialism," where he describes the class struggle as

> the dramatic illusion of struggle ... which presents the working-class as a virtuous hero and heroine in the toils of a villain called the capitalist; suffering terribly and struggling nobly, but with a happy ending for them, and a fearful retribution for the villain, in full view before the curtain on a future of undisturbed bliss.

The culmination of the class struggle in the seizure of power by the working class is described as

> the religious illusion ... [which] presents Socialism as consummating itself by a great day of wrath called "The Revolution," in which capitalism, commercialism, and all the lust of the Exchange, shall be brought to judgment and cast out, leaving the earth free for the kingdom of heaven on earth, all of which is revealed in an infallible book by a great prophet and leader. In this illusion the capitalist is not a stage villain, but the devil; Socialism is not the happy ending of a drama, but heaven; and Karl Marx's "Das Kapital" is "the Bible of the workingclasses."[3]

Shaw next attacks the Marxists' inconsistent practice of praising the workingman as being more virtuous than the capitalist and denouncing, at the same time, the system which produces him because it degrades and brutalizes him:

> ... it is perverse stupidity to declare in one breath that the working-classes are starved, degraded, and left in ignorance by a system which heaps victuals, education, and refinements on the capitalist, and to assume in the next that the capitalist is a narrow, sordid scoundrel, and the working-man a high-minded, enlightened, magnanimous philanthropist.[4]

Moreover, the socialist is

> in conflict, not with the wicked machinations of the capitalist, but with the stupidity, the narrowness ... the idiocy[5] ... of all classes, and especially of the class which suffers most by the existing system.[6]

In *On the Rocks* (Act II), Sir Arthur Chavender presents still another Shavian objection to Marx's theory of class struggle: "half

3. "The Illusions of Socialism," in *Forecasts of the Coming Century,* 156–57.
4. *Ibid.,* 161.
5. Shaw adds in parenthese: "using the word in its precise and original meaning." In that sense, the word means lack of concern for public affairs, just as an idiot, in classical Greek, is a person who does not hold public office. When the word was introduced into English, that was its sole meaning.
6. "The Illusions of Socialsm," in *Forecasts of the Coming Century,* 161.

the working class is slaving away to pile up riches, only to be smoked out like a hive of bees and plundered of everything but a bare living by our class. But what is the other half doing? Living on the plunder at second hand. Plundering the plunderers . . . these parasites will fight for the rights of property as they would fight for their own skins."

Shaw denies Marx credit for originating the theory of historical materialism: "His theory of civilization had been promulgated in Buckle's History of Civilization, a book as epoch-making in the minds of its readers as Das Kapital."[7] Moreover, Shaw finds that economic determinism, as interpreted by orthodox Marxists, cannot be logically reconciled with socialist political activity. Speaking, in his *Intelligent Woman's Guide*, of the members of the Third International as "missionaries of Church Socialism," he points out that

> Two of their tenets contradict one another as flatly as the first two paragraphs of Article 28 of the Church of England. One is that the evolution of Capitalism into Socialism is predestined, implying that we have nothing to do but sit down and wait for it to occur. This is their version of Salvation by Faith. The other is that it must be effected by a revolution establishing a dictatorship of the proletariat. This is their version of Salvation by Works.[8]

In spite of this attack on economic determinism, Shaw unquestionably considers economics the most important factor in the making of history; moreover, some of his greatest blunders in the interpretation of historical events stem from attempts to explain them completely in economic terms. In *What I Really Wrote About the War*, he categorically rejects the notion that "wars are caused by the Capitalist struggle for markets."[9] Nevertheless, in *Everybody's Political What's What*, written during World War II, he asserts that the South African War and World War I and II were caused by the necessity to raise the rate of interest by destroying capital.[1] One cannot reconcile the two statements. One can only say that Shaw adhered to his formal disclaimer of economic determinism in his analysis of historical events, but that often, when he was determined to find a stick with which to beat the capitalist dog, he made judgments that can be validated only by a theory of economic determinism.

Shaw would probably have justified his inconsistency by adopting a position close to that of Sidney Hook in *Towards the Understanding of Karl Marx*: namely, that Marx's theories are weapons in

7. "Darwin and Karl Marx," in the preface to *Back to Methuselah*.
8. *Intelligent Woman's Guide*, 441.
9. "Before the War," in *What I Really Wrote About the War*.
1. *Everybody's Political What's What*, 143–44.

the battle for socialism.² Indeed, to Shaw, Marx's greatness consists in the veritable arsenal of weapons he provides for that battle. As an economist and social scientist Marx is, in Shaw's opinion, second rate:

> ... his economics, half borrowed, and half home-made by a literary amateur, were not, when strictly followed up, even favorable to Socialism. ... There was nothing about Socialism in the widely read first volume of Das Kapital: every reference it made to workers and capitalists showed that Marx had never breathed industrial air, and had dug his case out of bluebooks in the British Museum. Compared with Darwin, he seemed to have no power of observation: there was not a fact in Das Kapital that had not been taken out of a book, nor a discussion that had not been opened by somebody else's pamphlet.³

Marx cannot compete as an economist with Mill and Cairnes and Sidgwick, who also realized that radical economic change was both necessary and inevitable, but, says Shaw, "the fact is that the average pupil of Mill and the rest never learns it."⁴ To Shaw, Marx's greatness is his tremendous power as a writer, his "fine Jewish literary gift, with terrible powers of hatred, invective, irony."⁵ With that gift "he exposed the bourgeoisie and made an end of its moral prestige. That was enough: like Darwin he had for the moment the World Will by the ear."⁶

Marx, according to this estimate, is fundamentally the socialist Carlyle. His importance lies in the fact that his fervent denunciations of a nineteenth-century society captured the imagination of the late Victorian and Edwardian intellectuals, just as Carlyle had captured the imagination of their fathers.

Significantly, both writers provided Shaw with basic social metaphors. In "The Communist Manifesto," Marx and Engels assert that one of the greatest gains that will follow the abolition of capitalism will be the abolition of "prostitution both public and private."⁷ In one of Shaw's earliest plays, Mrs Warren's Profession, Mrs. Warren becomes a prostitute because it is the only way she can avoid the greater indignities of poverty. She points out that success in prostitution, just like success in any other business, demands business ability and all the other traditional capitalist virtues. "Liz and I had to work and save and calculate just like other people; elseways we should be as poor as any good-for-nothing

2. See *Towards the Understanding of Karl Marx*, 105, 222–24. Shaw, however, admits that Marx's abstract economics are faulty and should therefore be abandoned, since it is easy for opponents of socialism to damage the socialist cause by refuting them. See "Bluffing the Value Theory," in *Bernard Shaw and Karl Marx*, 182.
3. "Darwin and Karl Marx" in the

preface to *Back to Methuselah*.
4. "Karl Marx and *Das Kapital*," in *Bernard Shaw and Karl Marx*, 116.
5. "Darwin and Karl Marx," in the preface to *Back to Methuselah*.
6. *Ibid*.
7. Karl Marx and Friedrich Engels, "The Communist Manifesto," in *Essentials of Marxism* (N.Y., 1926), p. 50.

waster of a woman that thinks her luck will last forever."[8] Mrs. Warren is also quick to point out to her daughter that in capitalist society marriage is merely a legal and respectable form of prostitution.

> What is any respectable girl brought up to do but to catch some rich man's fancy and get the benefit of his money by marrying him?—as if a marriage ceremony could make any difference in the right or wrong of the thing! Oh, the hypocrisy of the world makes me sick![9]

When Sir George Crofts, Mrs. Warren's business partner, proposes to her daughter, Vivie, the latter indignantly refuses him because of his part in her mother's business. "My mother was a very poor woman who had no reasonable choice but to do as she did. You were a rich gentleman; and you did the same for the sake of 35 per cent."[1] Sir George answers by maintaining that most of the wealth in England is accumulated by subjecting human beings to conditions as brutalizing and degrading as those of Mrs. Warren's brothels.

> Do you remember your Crofts scholarship at Newnham? Well, that was founded by my brother the M. P. He gets his 22 per cent out of a factory with 600 girls in it, and not one of them getting wages enough to live on. How d'ye suppose they manage when they have no family to fall back on? Ask your mother.[2]

Vivie, like Harry Trench in *Widowers' Houses*, comes to the conclusion that Shaw wants his cultivated and humanitarian reader—who would not dream of operating a brothel or a sweatshop—to come to: "You might go on to point out that I never asked where the money I spent came from. I believe that I am just as bad as you."[3] It is impossible to be virtuous in capitalist society in which every one prostitutes either himself or others; therefore, the system must be changed.

It is significant that when Shaw, in the plays beginning with *Man and Superman* in 1903, abandoned a merely institutional view of social problems, he also rejected, quite deliberately, the metaphor of prostitution. In "The Revolutionist's Handbook," Jack Tanner, who is the leading character as well as the mouthpiece for Shaw's ideas in *Man and Superman*, asserts that only a fundamental improvement in the human race can make for genuine progress. Socialism alone will not solve the problem, but it will make the improvement of the race more feasible; moreover, the converse of this proposition is also true. From this point of view, any activities in capitalist society which seem likely to improve the human breed

8. Act II.
9. *Ibid*.
1. Act III.

2. *Ibid*.
3. *Ibid*.

should be encouraged, since such activities will inevitably produce socialism.

E. Strauss, in *Bernard Shaw: Art and Socialism*, astutely observes that Ann Whitefield, the "heroine" of *Man and Superman*, is acquisitive capitalist society as well as an incarnation of the Life-Force.[4] The terms that Tanner uses to describe marriage— "apostasy, profanation of the sanctuary of my soul, violation of my manhood, sale of my birthright, shameful surrender, ignominious capitulation, acceptance of defeat"—seem exaggerated unless we understand that by marriage he means acceptance of the prostitution of capitalism. In *Major Barbara*, which, according to Eric Bentley, "was to have been called *Andrew Undershaft's Profession*,"[5] Barbara rejects the Salvation Army for Undershaft: "Turning our backs on Bodger and Undershaft [prostitution] is turning our backs on life."[6] What Strauss does not understand is that Shaw is not deserting socialism, but abandoning a view of society which is too simple to explain the complexity of a capitalism of big business, with its multimillionaire philanthropists, research laboratories, and garden cities for workers.[7] It is significant that in *Major Barbara*, Shaw, while he repudiates the prostitution metaphor of *Mrs Warren's Profession*, which he identifies with Marx, uses Marx's dialectic to justify this repudiation.

Andrew Undershaft, a multimillionaire munitions manufacturer, is the archcapitalist. Supremely self-conscious, he believes in money and gunpowder as the "two things necessary to salvation."[8] He also agrees with Marx that "force is the midwife of progress."[9] His activities set loose forces which may destroy mankind, but they also create a prosperous class of workers who, because of the very prosperity he provides for them, are "saved."

BARBARA: And their souls?
UNDERSHAFT: I save their souls just as I saved yours.
BARBARA (*revolted*): You saved my soul! What do you mean?
UNDERSHAFT: I fed you and clothed you and housed you. I took care that you should have enough money to live handsomely—more than enough; so that you could be wasteful, careless, generous.[1]

Thus Undershaft's wealth (the productive power of capitalism) is the thesis which initiates a dialectical process. It creates, as an

4. See pp. 44–46.
5. Bentley, *Bernard Shaw*, 167.
6. Act III.
7. It is ironical that Shaw, who almost always misunderstood and belittled the United States, gave so sympathetic an account, in *Major Barbara*, of what are virtually American capitalism and American capitalist ideals. Nevertheless, it is a tribute to Shaw's extraordinary powers as a social thinker that he was able to envision, in pre-World War

I England, the kind of capitalism described in *Major Barbara*.
8. See Act II, the dialogue between Cusins and Undershaft beginning: Cusins: By the way, have you any religion?
9. Karl Marx, *Capital: A Critique of Political Economy*, 824. There are several passages in *Major Barbara* in which Undershaft praises the use of force.
1. *Major Barbara*, Act III.

antithesis, an intelligent, prosperous working class "whose souls are hungry because their bodies are full";[2] therefore, they see the necessity for the destruction of the evils of capitalism, of which Bodger and Undershaft are representative. From an interaction of these forces there results a synthesis of capitalism's great productive power and the utilization of that power for social ends which is achieved by socialism.

I have said that *Major Barbara* is a critique of Comtianism.[3] It is also a critique of Marxism as a way of understanding historical change. Shaw accepts the dialectical method of Marx as *one* method of understanding history. He rejects as inconsistent with that method what he calls, in "The Illusions of Socialism," the religious and dramatic illusions, the refusal to work within the framework of capitalist society, and the consequent irresponsibility and "impossibilism" of most Marxists. He does not, however, reject in principle the use of force to gain power.[4] Nevertheless, feeling as he does that the proletariat is the most backward class in the community, he almost always views the change to socialism as orderly and legal. Revolution is not feasible; moreover, violence would be more likely to defer than to hasten the transformation of capitalism into socialism, since it would probably retard the development of the economy of the nation. A socialist society, in order to function efficiently,[5] must inherit the wealth that capitalism has created. Therefore the transition to socialism must be gradual as well as constitutional.

Although Shaw was too much of a pragmatist and relativist to attempt to plan the course of such a transition or to describe in detail the socialist state, he did make many suggestions concerning its policy and goals. In his suggestions, he was very strongly influenced by *Looking Backward* and its sequel, *Equality*, two Utopian novels of the American social reformer Edward Bellamy. Like Shaw and Marx, Bellamy viewed capitalism as a huge prostitution.[6] Unlike Marx, Bellamy, along with Shaw, rejected class struggle and revolution. Both Bellamy and Shaw agree that although property rights have no moral value, they should be respected during the transition from capitalism to socialism for reasons of economic efficiency and humanity. Shaw suggests that the owners of national-

2. *Ibid.*
3. Kaye makes this point in an earlier chapter. Comtianism, or the Positivism of Auguste Comte, sets up a highly regulated form of state capitalism, and assumes the capitalist-industrialist to be a beneficent moral force [*Editor*].
4. Shaw, in his preface to the 1908 edition of *Fabian Essays,* speaks of Marx as "certainly a bit of a liberal fatalist (did he not say that force is the midwife of progress without reminding us that force is equally the midwife of

chaos, and chaos the midwife of martial law?)." Note, however, that this is not a repudiation *in principle* of force. Shaw felt, in 1908, that the use of force was not feasible (p. 304).
5. See *The Intelligent Woman's Guide,* 274–75.
6. Edward Bellamy, *Equality,* 101: "Your whole industrial system seems ... best and most fitly described by a word which you oddly enough reserved to designate a particular phase of self-selling practiced by women."

ized industries be fully compensated for their property and that a steeply graduated income tax be enacted to raise funds to pay them.[7] In that way capital and land would be expropriated gradually and equitably.[8] Bellamy, writing in an era when a tax on income was unconstitutional in the United States, suggested that the government compensate stockholders of nationalized corporations by paying them a reasonable return on their investments.[9] The nationalization of large corporations would have two immediate advantages: the country would be rid of the corrupt managers of big business, who cheated both stockholders and workers;[1] large groups of workers would become employees of the government and would therefore acquire socialist values by working for an organization whose goal is service rather than profits.

When the process of nationalization has been completed, all will receive an equal income in the form of a dividend on the united national industries.[2] Equality of income as the foundation of society is Bellamy's most important contribution to Shavian economics. Under Bellamy's influence, Shaw rejected Marx's formula of distribution according to social contribution in the transitional or socialist stage of proletarian society and distribution according to need in the final or communist stage.[3] In *The Intelligent Woman's Guide*, he advocates complete equality of income; in *Everybody's Political What's What*, he qualifies his opinion by pointing out that incomes cannot be equalized immediately. They must first be leveled up to the standard of living of the average professional man. This "and not a mathematical abstraction like equality of income is its [socialism's] real goal."[4]

Shaw also adopted Bellamy's solution of the problem of who, under this system, is to perform the unpleasant tasks that are socially necessary. According to *Looking Backward*, this problem may be solved simply:

> It is the business of the administration to seek constantly to equalize the attractions of the trades, so far as the conditions of labor in them are concerned, so that all trades shall be equally attractive to persons having natural tastes for them. This is done by making the hours of labor in different trades to differ according to their arduousness. The lighter trades prosecuted under the most agreeable circumstances, have in this way the longest hours, while an arduous trade, such as mining, has very short hours. There is no theory, no *a priori* rule, by which the respective at-

7. *The Intelligent Woman's Guide*, 268–74.
8. *Ibid.*
9. *Equality*, 377.
1. *Ibid.* See Gustavus Myers, *History of the Great American Fortunes, passim*, for a very thorough and copious account of the methods by which, during the late nineteenth century, the directors of many large corporations swindled the owners, that is, the stockholders, of the corporations they managed.
2. Bellamy, *Equality*, 377.
3. See Shaw's discussion of equality of income in the preface to *Androcles and the Lion*.
4. *Everybody's Political What's What*, 57.

tractiveness of industries is determined. The administration, in taking burdens off one class of workers and adding them to other classes, simply follows the fluctuations of opinion among the workers as indicated by the rate of volunteering.[5]

In *The Intelligent Woman's Guide*, Shaw echoes this passage from Bellamy.[6] Moreover, both Shaw and Bellamy point out that many occupations seem unpleasant, not so much because they are actually disgusting, but because there is a strong social prejudice against them. On the other hand, many occupations which involve "messy" work, such as medicine, are very popular because they are highly valued by society. Bellamy therefore concludes that in a society which, because it is socialist and equalitarian, will be without social snobbishness, many occupations which now seem repellent will no longer be so.[7]

Not only is equality of income feasible, but it is the most efficient as well as the most equitable mode of distributing the wealth of the community. Unlike Marx, who was primarily concerned with the mode of production of wealth, Bellamy and Shaw were "distributists."

In *Equality*, we visit a classroom in which it is rather tiresomely demonstrated that equal distribution creates the greatest demand for goods and therefore affords the greatest stimulus to production.[8] Shaw's explanation of the "depression" as an economic phenomenon is based on this premise. Inequality of income causes more goods to be produced than can be consumed by those who can pay for them (in economic terms, the supply exceeds the effective demand). This artificial overproduction causes a fall in prices, unemployment, less effective demand, more unemployment, and so forth;[9] the cycle continues until production is lowered to the level of effective demand.

The damage done to the English economy by these periodic crises is increased, according to Shaw, by the sending abroad of capital by English investors because the effective demand for goods in England is low as a result of inequality of income. As a consequence of this practice, English prosperity came to depend, by the end of the nineteenth century, on foreign investments. Shaw prophetically warned his countrymen, before World War I, when England seemed to be at the height of its prosperity, of the precariousness of such a position in the event of war.[1]

Another consequence of the constant export of money was that England's competitors, financed by English capital, built plants and machinery that made England's obsolete. Eventually, England re-

5. Edward Bellamy, *Looking Backward*, 51.
6. *The Intelligent Woman's Guide*, 78.
7. Bellamy, *Looking Backward*, chap. XI.

8. Bellamy, *Equality*, 193–94.
9. Shaw, *The Intelligent Woman's Guide*, 144.
1. See, for example, the preface to *Man and Superman*, written in 1903.

stricted itself almost completely to supplying a few luxury goods and services. The prosperity of late Victorian and Edwardian England was therefore artificial and unstable. Thus Shaw was able to say, in 1903[2] in the preface to *Man and Superman*:

> The city papers prate of the competition of Bombay with Manchester and the like. The real competition is the competition of Regent Street with the Rue de Rivoli, of Brighton and the south coast with the Riviera, for the spending money of the American Trusts.

The religious argument for equality of income, like the economic, is derived by Shaw principally from Bellamy.[3] In *Equality*, Bellamy points out that equality of income is one of Jesus' essential tenets and that only in a society in which equality makes men brothers will the mass of men be able to accept Jesus' vision of God.[4] Shaw takes exactly the same position in the preface to *Androcles and the Lion*.[5] He even uses the arguments by which Bellamy supports his contention: for example, only in a society based on equality of income will men be able to follow Jesus' injunction to "take no care for the morrow."[6]

Surprisingly, the eugenic argument for equality of income in "The Revolutionist's Handbook" is also found in *Looking Backward*.[7] In a society in which incomes are equal, not only will there be no mercenary marriages, but men and women will not be limited by class habits and education in choosing a mate; therefore better sexual selection will bring about a more rapid improvement in the race.[8]

> To cut humanity up into small cliques, and effectively limit the selection of the individual to his own clique, is to postpone the Superman for eons, if not for ever. Not only should every person be nourished and trained as a possible parent, but there thould be no possibility of such an obstacle to natural selection as the objection of a countess to a navvy or of a duke to a charwoman. Equality is essential to good breeding.[9]

2. The accuracy of Shaw's prophecy constitutes very good evidence for the validity of his analysis of England's economy of the late nineteenth century.
3. Bellamy's conception of God as "the Greater Self" is close to Shaw's conception of the Life-Force and James's conception of the Finite God. See Dr. Barton's sermon, in *Equality*, 153.
4. *Equality*, 268.
5. See, in this preface, "Why Not Give Christianity a Trial?", "Vital Distribution," "Jesus as Economist," *et al.*
6. Bellamy, *Looking Backward*, 70: "No man any more has any care for the morrow, either for himself or his children, for the nation guarantees the nurture, education, and comfortable maintenance of every citizen from the cradle to the grave." Cf. the preface to

Androcles and the Lion, "Vital Distribution"; in "Jesus as Economist," we have the same theme.
7. It has generally been taken for granted that the eugenic argument for equality is a Shavian variation on the Nietzschean theme of breeding the race. Nevertheless, it is Bellamy who advances, as an argument for equality, the hypothesis that a classless society will result in more marriages of love and therefore not only in more happiness, but also in better sexual selection.
8. See *Looking Backward*, 218.
9. "The Revolutionist's Handbook" chap. II, "Property and Marriage." In "The Political and Biological Objections to Inequality," in the preface to *Androcles and the Lion*, we find the same comment.

In Bellamy's Utopia, the importance of eugenics is acknowledged, and therefore women are paid for their services as mothers. Dr. Leete, the *raisonneur* of *Looking Backwards*, observes: "Can you think of any service constituting a stronger claim to the nation's gratitude than bearing and nursing the nation's children?"[1] Shaw agrees with this statement frequently and vehemently. In the preface to *Getting Married*, he affirms, much more passionately than Bellamy, the necessity for women to be economically independent of men:

> The truth is that family life will never be decent, much less ennobling, until this central horror of the dependence of women on men is done away with. At present it reduces the difference between marriage and prostitution to the difference between Trade Unionism and unorganized casual labor: a huge difference, no doubt, as to order and comfort, but not a difference in kind.[2]

Shaw also follows Bellamy in demanding that the state protect the rights of children from the tyranny of their parents. This, both believe, will be easier to accomplish in a society of men and women with equal incomes.[3]

It may seem strange that such topics are these should be discussed in a chapter devoted to economics, but for Shaw and his nineteenth-century teachers, economics was inextricably bound up with politics, sociology, women's rights, eugenics, evolution, and religion. To consider Shaw's economic theories apart from their context would be to falsify and denigrate them.

WARREN SYLVESTER SMITH

[Shaw as a Religious Heretic]†

Shaw once wrote in the third person, pretending to be Frank Harris: "Shaw is almost a hopeless subject, because there is nothing interesting to be said about him that he has not already said about himself."[1] If this was true when he wrote it in 1919, it has been verified a thousand times posthumously. The mountain of corres-

---

1. *Looking Backward*, 213.
2. "The Economic Slavery of Women"; cf. *Man and Superman*, Act III, in which Don Juan says: "What is virtue but the Trade Unionism of the married?" The comparison between marriage and trade-unionism appears in an essay by Ernest Belfort Bax, "From Phallism to Purism," in *Outspoken Essays on Social Subjects*, 6. Shaw acknowledges his indebtedness to Bax in the preface to *Major Barbara*, "First Aid to Critics."
3. Bellamy, *Equality*, 373; cf. "The

Parents' Intolerable Burden," *passim*, in the preface to *Misalliance*.
† Shaw was a self-proclaimed mystic who believed that Creative Evolution was the religion of the twentieth century. He is treated as a religious figure in this essay, adapted from a chapter in *The London Heretics*, by Warren Sylvester Smith (New York: Dodd, Mead, 1968), pp. 270–279.
1. "How Frank Ought to Have Done It," in *Sixteen Self Sketches* (London, 1949), p. 133.

pondence, speeches, and critical writings from his own pen grows higher every year, and 20 years after his death the end is not yet in sight. For a man who refused to write his own autobiography on the grounds that all written reminiscences are conscious lies, he made abundantly sure that others who were to tackle the job should have sufficient first-hand material.

During his first decade in London the diffident young Dubliner George B. Shaw went through the crucible of London art galleries, music halls, lecture halls, editorial rooms, libraries, committee rooms, outdoor meetings, and ladies' boudoirs to emerge as the delicately adjusted schizophrenic prophet-jokester, Bernard Shaw-GBS. The stormy debates were the practicum of his belated education. They were, for the most part, his night school. He spent most of his days in the reading room of the British Museum. A more effective curriculum can hardly be imagined.

The secular-religious heretical societies, with which the city abounded, were made to order for him for two reasons. First, he needed desperately forums in which to develop his skills as a speaker and a committee man. Second, he needed to resolve his own deeply motivated concerns about religion and society. In 1909, in what is still the best all-round critical work on Shaw, G. K. Chesterton made an illuminating observation about him as a prophet: the more ancient variety, Jesus or Socrates, for example, knew what they wanted to say before they said it. For Shaw the act of communication *was* the thought-process itself. Shaw could store up information from the British Museum, store up images from galleries and concerts and the view from Dalkey Hill. Before he could make them into a proper pattern for himself, he needed, so to speak, to "try them on," to rub them against other people, to stimulate and to respond, to discard and retain.

When he first came to London at the age of twenty in 1876 to join his mother and his surviving sister, Lucy, he spent a good deal of his time writing novels. He wrote five of them in seven years with hardly any success at all. In the meantime he began to search out the lecture halls, and the story of his finding Henry George and Sidney Webb, and finally the Fabians, is so well known it will hardly need attention here. The truth is he joined all sorts of societies. In addition to the Dialectical and the Zetetical, which were vigorous debating groups, he was taken with the literary societies of F. J. Furnivall: the New Shakespeare Society, the Browning Society, and the Shelley Society. He mentions also the Bedford Debating Society of Stopford Brooke at Bedford Chapel. It was at the Nonconformist Memorial Hall in Farringdon Street that he first heard Henry George, in 1882.[2]

2. See "How I Became a Public Speaker," in *Sixteen Self Sketches*. Shaw's recollection of the date as 1884 is at variance with Henderson's documentation. See footnote 2, page 320 [*Editor*].

Shaw became a joiner, but he was careful not to align himself with any organization that committed him to a religious or political point of view to which he could not wholeheartedly subscribe. It was in the end only the Fabian Society that earned his devotion over the years. But he asked questions or made replies wherever he went, and was inevitably called upon to serve on committees. Shaw actually enjoyed committee work, and learned a great deal about human nature in the process. He also learned how to get his own way. Often he sat through stormy sessions, patiently waiting for the proper moment to submit the plan he had devised long in advance. Shaw said, only half facetiously, that the only people who saw much of him were those who served on committees with him.[3] It is unlikely that anyone in London had at least passing acquaintance with so many different shades of heretics. Shaw took it for granted that the various circles which he inhabited did not themselves intersect. "As my friends lived in different worlds and I rarely introduced one to the other they did not necessarily know one another."[4]

Once at the Hall of Science, when he was still a novice, Shaw, sitting far back in the Hall, rose to make a comment after a lecture by the eminent secularist and popular orator Charles Bradlaugh. He had hardly uttered two sentences, when Bradlaugh rose and said, "The gentleman is a speaker. Come to the platform." Shaw reports that he did so and that Bradlaugh devoted considerable time to a reply. But he never formally debated with Bradlaugh. He was once scheduled to do so but the debate was called off—Shaw admits to his relief at the time, though later he regretted the lost opportunity. History regrets it too. "It pleased me to imagine," Shaw mused, "that he refused a set debate with me much as Edmund Kean refused to act with Macready." But this was wishful thinking. Bradlaugh, in those days, was taking on all comers.[5]

The time came when his life became too full for constant public speaking. He had not time to prepare new presentations and was afraid of becoming "a windbag with only one speech." About 1895 he began to limit his public appearances to special occasions. The special occasions included not only Socialist gatherings, but instances where he was specifically requested to speak on religious themes. He made appearances at the City Temple and before the Guild of St. Matthew; he delivered religious speeches at Kensington Town Hall, the New Reform Club, Cambridge University, and elsewhere before World War I, and thereafter less frequently until the end of his life.[6] At seventy-seven he made his single public appearance in America, giving a long political lecture to a crowded

3. *Sixteen Self Sketches*, p. 130.
4. Stephen Winsten, Preface to *Salt and his Circle* (London and New York, 1951), p. 13.
5. *Sixteen Self Sketches*, pp. 61–62.

6. See W. S. Smith, ed., *Religious Speeches of George Bernard Shaw*, for a collection of eleven of these addresses.

audience in the Metropolitan Opera House. He confessed that he had to rest for two days afterwards. More and more he made use of radio broadcasting.

Among the many London heretics, Shaw was unique in that he had developed his own substitute religion, really his own theology. Although his reputation steadily grew as the great idol-smasher, he made it a point always to have replacements for the broken crockery. Too often, with the help of the GBS-jokester, the smashing ceremony was such fun, and provided such welcome release, that no one really investigated the worth of the new article. As recently as 1960, to mark the tenth anniversary of Shaw's death, the *New York Times Magazine* presented a page of Shavian paradoxes completely out of context, simply as jokes, with no overtones of the prophetic voice. Eric Bentley, in 1947, was among the first to point out in so many words that the comic puppet which Shaw so skilfully constructed to win him an audience turned on the old sage and almost overcame him.[7] In vain Peter Keegan (in *John Bull's Other Island*) cried out, "Every dream is a prophecy: every jest is an earnest in the womb of Time."

There was for Shaw none of the early suffering that so many of his contemporaries experienced in breaking from the old faith. He was born and baptized in the Established Church of Ireland, but his mother, he tells us, had been brought up so strictly that, in reaction, churchgoing was dropped in his family before he was ten years old. He considered himself a sceptic from early childhood. He did feel, for a time, disposed to say prayers.

> I cannot recall the final form I adopted; but I remember that it was in three movements, like a sonata, and in the best Church of Ireland style. It ended with the Lord's prayer; and I repeated it every night in bed. I had been warned by my nurse that warm prayers were no use, and that only by kneeling by my bedside in the cold could I hope for a hearing; but I criticized this admonition unfavourably on various grounds, the real one being my preference for warmth and comfort. I did not disparage my nurse's authority in these matters because she was a Roman Catholic: I even tolerated her practice of sprinkling me with holy water occasionally. But her asceticism did not fit the essentially artistic and luxurious character of my devotional exploits. Besides, the penalty did not apply to my prayer; for it was not a petition. I had too much sense to risk my faith by begging for things I knew very well I should not get; so I did not care whether my prayers were answered or not: they were a literary performance for the entertainment and propitiation of the Almighty; and though I should not have dreamt of daring to say that if He did not like them He might lump them (perhaps I

7. *Bernard Shaw* (New York, 1957). See especially Part IV, "The Fool in Christ."

was too confident of their quality to apprehend such a rebuff), I certainly behaved as if my comfort were an indispensable condition of the performance taking place at all.[8]

He was never confirmed. He did not think his parents were either. Irish Protestantism was for him not a religion at all, but a social convention. His few exposures to it were not for the sake of his own salvation, but for his father's respectability. When they went to live at Torca Cottage on Dalkey Hill in 1866, all religious practice was discontinued.

> Imagine being taught that there is one God, a Protestant and perfect gentleman, keeping Heaven select for the gentry against an idolatrous imposter called the Pope! Imagine the pretensions of the English peerage on the incomes of the English middle class! I remember Stopford Brooke one day telling me that he discerned in my books an intense and contemptuous hatred for society. No wonder![9]

His revolt against the Church was of a piece with his revolt against society. When he was too young to be allowed out by himself, a nurse was dispatched to take him for a walk in some nicer neighborhood. Instead, the servant would meet a male acquaintance and the three of them would go into a public house bar where he was treated with lemonade or ginger beer. But young Shaw knew that his own father's life had been made miserable by drink, and looked upon the public house as a wicked place.

> Thus were laid the foundations of my lifelong hatred of poverty, and the devotion of all my public life to the task of exterminating the poor and rendering their resurrection for ever impossible.[1]

Shaw's humor never concealed the bitterness he felt about his early years. He would have been more decently brought up, he maintains, if his parents had been too poor to afford servants.[2]

It is not surprising, then, to find the adult Shaw in London proclaiming himself an Atheist. But, as he later pointed out, there are several kinds of Atheism. "There is the youthful Atheism with which every able modern mind begins: an Atheism that clears the soul of superstitions and terrors and servilities and base compliances and hypocrisies, and lets in the light of heaven. And then there is the Atheism of despair and pessimism."[3] It was the former kind Shaw subscribed to when he shocked some of the ladies of the

8. G. B. Shaw, Preface to *Immaturity*, Standard Edition (London, 1931), pp. xviii–xix.
9. *Sixteen Self Sketches*, p. 46.
1. Preface to *London Music in 1888–89*, Standard Edition (London, 1937), p. 13.

2. The most detailed treatment of Shaw's early years, some of it speculative, is in B. C. Rosset, *Shaw of Dublin* (University Park, Pa., 1964).
3. *What I Really Wrote About the War* (New York, 1932), p. 84.

Shelley Society by proclaiming that he was, like Shelley, a Socialist, an Atheist, and a Vegetarian. Besides, this was in the days when the opposition to Bradlaugh and his successor G. W. Foote had achieved such proportions that Shaw preferred to be counted among their supporters rather than their attackers. "I preferred to call myself an Atheist because belief in God then meant belief in the old tribal idol called Jehovah; and I would not, by calling myself an Agnostic, pretend that I did not know whether it existed or not."[4]

But Socialism alone was not enough. This was precisely the limitation of H. M. Hyndman, the Marxist leader of the Social Democratic Federation—he never went beyond Marx and internationalism. "He never went on from the industrial revolution to the next things—to the revolution in morals, and to the formulation and establishment of a credible and effective indigenous Western religion."[5] Shaw found Bradlaugh's survivors in the National Secular Society to be, in this regard, "Freethought Fundamentalists," unable to accept even the poetic imagery of mysticism. Their position remained essentially one of denial, Shaw felt; and although this position had been forced upon Bradlaugh by the nature of his pioneering campaigns against the Establishment, the time had come for affirmation.

Since there was no affirmative religion in the Western world in which a reasonably intelligent man could believe, Shaw proceeded to devise one for himself. He enjoyed using old words in fresh ways, and one can find him calling himself a Catholic at one point and a Protestant at another. He used the word "Catholic" to mean "universal" (it meant the same as "communist," he said). When he called himself Protestant, he thought of himself as a Separatist from the Establishment. "Now of separation there is no end until every human being is a Separate Church, for which there is much to be said."[6] His aim, therefore, was a belief that could be at the same time individual and universal. Scattered statements of this sort have led the unwary to suppose that Shaw's religious beliefs kept fluctuating in order to produce the best paradox at any given moment. Instead his religion, as it matured, formed a steadying and consistent strain in one of the most complex minds of the twentieth century. That complexity involved such unexplored wells of despair and such extremes of what is presently called "existential pain" that even now the Shavian playgoer, still watched over and protected by the GBS-jokester, has never had more than a glimpse within. But that is a matter for another time.

It goes without saying that any religion devised by Shaw would

4. *Sixteen Self Sketches*, p. 74.
5. *Pen Portraits and Reviews*, In Shaw's review of Hyndman's memoirs, in Standard Edition (London, 1932), p. 128.
6. "How William Archer Impressed Bernard Shaw," in *Pen Portraits and Reviews*, p. 4.

have to complement his Socialism. It would have to be, therefore, concerned with justice and the social order and the improvement of life on this planet. Yet a purely Pragmatist approach did not appeal to him. Pragmatism tended to maintain that whatever works is good, and he perceived that many systems which produced some good results were inherently evil. Napoleon, for instance, brought many beneficent changes to Europe, yet it would have been better for the world if he had never been born. Shaw preferred a mystical revelation to a Rationalist one. He says he abandoned Rationalism after his second novel—which would have been in 1880.

Neither could he accept the whole cult of Science, nor the Scientist as the new priest. He was forced to accept the fact of evolution, but he rebelled, with Samuel Butler, against the idea of "the survival of the fittest," if by that was meant a cosmos governed by mere accident. He preferred the earlier revolutionary theory of Chevalier de Lamarck, which permitted the presence of mind or will in the evolutionary process. Whereas Darwinians might assume that the giraffe had a long neck because, in an area where the only available food was ever higher in the trees, only those lucky enough to have a "neck-advantage" could survive and breed, Shaw and Butler would have argued that only those animals with sufficient *will* to stretch their necks a little farther would survive. The results in both instances would be the same, but the conception of the nature of life wholly different.

What, then, was the source of this will that ran through all living things? Shaw preferred the term and the conception of Henri Bergson—the *Elan Vital*, the Life Force. He sometimes called it the Evolutionary Appetite. He did not like to call it God, though occasionally, for City Temple audiences, he did so with careful stipulations. It was more proper, perhaps, to call it the Holy Spirit ("the only surviving member of the Trinity"). Near the end of his life he consented to refer to it as Divine Providence.

The familiar terminology may be initially disarming, but his readers and listeners soon discovered (and in some cases were all the more shocked) to find that the Life Force, by whatever name, had few of the attributes usually associated with Godhead. It had no "personality." It was not omnipotent. It was not necessarily beneficent. But it was persistent. It had a direction. It was moving towards Godhead and would continue so to move indefinitely. At first this may seem to have been a kind of unjustifiable optimism on Shaw's part, but if so it was optimism only on a cosmic plane. For there was no guarantee that the human race as we know it, or even that this planet as we know it, would succeed in being a proper instrument of the Life Force. Indeed as Shaw grew older, there seemed to be more and more evidence that we would be "scrapped." When Lawrence Langner of the Theatre Guild brought Shaw greetings from Eugene O'Neill (whom he had never met), Shaw politely inquired about O'Neill's health and state of mind. Langner reported that O'Neill was pessimistic about the state of the world and was of the opinion that our present civilization was on its way downhill and headed for ultimate disaster.

> "Tell him not to worry about that," said Shaw cheerily. "If mankind turns out, as I suspect, to be a failure, it will destroy itself and be replaced by some other creature."[7]

Shaw's oft-vaunted optimism turns out to be, on closer examination, a combination of good health, cheerfulness, and a remarkable kind of detachment. Furthermore he was constitutionally opposed to cynicism. He could see no point in continually addressing a dying civilization. Unlike a later Irish expatriate, Samuel Beckett, he made the assumption that there were those in his audiences and among his readers who could be stirred to action by his message and might rescue our tottering civilization from the abyss. "We live," he said in one of those remarkably Shavian images, "as in a villa on Vesuvius."[8]

Hence the tone of the schoolmaster and the preacher. We must set our house in order, eliminate poverty, and learn government, so we may have at least an off-chance for survival. But this is rudimentary. Our real aim must be to become more sentient beings, longer lived, and more abundantly alive, so that we can carry out the will of the Life Force. The Life Force has no hands or mind of its own. When he spoke of these matters in public, the familiar GBS-jokester vanished, and audiences described as "consternated" or even "terrified" heard him say:

> If you don't do his work it won't be done; if you turn away from it, if you sit down and say, "Thy will be done," you might as well be the most irreligious person on the face of the earth. But if you will stand by your God, if you will say, "My business is to do your will, my hands are your hands, my tongue is your tongue, my brain is your brain, I am here to do thy work, and I will do it," you will get rid of otherworldiness, you will get rid of all that religion which is made an excuse and a cloak for doing nothing, and you will learn not only to worship your God, but also to have a fellow feeling with him.[9]

After that, it is not too difficult to accept his repeated claim to affinity with the Society of Friends. "If I had to be fitted into any

7. L. Langner, *G. B. S. and the Lunatic* (New York, 1963) p. 5.
8. *The Intelligent Woman's Guide to Socialism and Capitalism*, Standard Edition (London, 1932), p. 302.
9. W. S. Smith, ed., *Religious Speeches*, pp. 6–7.
1. Blanche Patch, *Thirty Years with Bernard Shaw* (New York, 1951), p. 227. See my article, "Bernard Shaw and the Quakers," *Bulletin of Friends Historical Association*, 45, 2, 105.

religious denomination, the Society of Friends ... would have the best chance," he once explained to newspaper questioning.[1] But he goes on to say at once that in the face of his very explicit writings on the subject there is no excuse for regarding him as a member of any Church or sect "unless the believers in Creative Evolution can be described as a sect." I know of no instance where Shaw ever attended a Quaker Meeting for worship or in any way identified himself with the Society of Friends as an organization. He was attracted to their method of silent worship, their dependence on "the inner light" (a phrase he occasionally borrowed), and their courageous pacifism at the time of World War I. In later years he became particularly interested in the life of the Quaker founder, George Fox, and included him in the cast of characters of *In Good King Charles's Golden Days*.

The essay, "What Is My Religious Faith?" in *Sixteen Self Sketches* is capsule size. His most complete exposition is the sixty-page preface to *Back to Methuselah*. But the theme is unmistakable in all his works, especially from *Man and Superman* (1903) onwards. His most perceptive critics—Chesterton, J. S. Collis, C. E. M. Joad, Eric Bentley—have dealt seriously with his religion. And it is encouraging to note that a younger commentator, Anthony S. Abbott, has published a study of *Shaw and Christianity*.[2]

Bernard Shaw proclaimed himself an actor who was destined to play many parts—author, journalist, orator, politician, committee man, man of the world, and so forth—as he himself enumerated them. These roles were held together into a single personality by his twin beliefs in Socialism and the Life Force. First one, then the other, grew from the spiritual turmoil of the London into which he consciously threw himself during his first decade there. Both served to sustain him through the longest and most productive of the many careers that emerged from that same crucible.

STANLEY WEINTRAUB

The Avant-Garde Shaw†

To most people—even most theatregoers—Bernard Shaw is much closer to seeming old hat than *avant-garde*. Yet much that has been associated with the most advanced theatre in our generation can be

2. New York: The Seabury Press, 1965.
† Stanley Weintraub's estimate of Shaw as a contemporary in today's theatre is from Brock University's *Shaw Seminar Papers of 1965* (Toronto: Copp Clark, 1966) pp. 33–52.

found in GBS's plays or his writings about the drama. As far back as 1896, for example, Shaw, commenting as a working drama critic, rather than playwright, suggested that

> any play performed on a platform amidst the audience gets closer home to its hearers than when it is presented as a picture framed by a proscenium. Also, that we are less conscious of the artificiality of the stage when a few well-understood conventions, adroitly handled, are substituted for attempts at an impossible scenic verisimilitude. All the old-fashioned tale-of-adventure plays, with their frequent changes of scene, and all the new problem plays, with their intense intimacies, should be done in this way.[1]

Today we might consider Shaw's remarks as an *avant-garde* anticipation of theatre-in-the-round techniques. And his plays, when performed on the arena stage for which he never wrote, exhibit a high level of adaptability to the "new" method. What he thought the playhouse should look like is still largely an ideal, for (as he wrote in 1926) the "sort of theatre" his newer plays needed was one which had to "combine the optics and acoustics of a first-rate lecture theatre and a first-rate circus."[2]

Those of Shaw's plays written in the Neanderthal era of films even have anticipated the possibilities of that medium. A Shaw critic once observed that the treatment of the stage directions in *Caesar and Cleopatra*

> anticipates the technique of the movies with uncanny accuracy. It will be remembered that the play was written in 1898. The . . . film production in which Claude Rains and Vivien Leigh appeared followed precisely the 1898 stage direction:

> 'The moonlight wanes: the horizon again shows black against the sky, broken only by the fantastic silhouette of the Sphinx. The sky itself vanishes in darkness, from which there is no relief until the gleam of a distant torch falls on great Egyptian pillars supporting the roof of a majestic corridor. At the further end of the corridor a Nubian slave appears carrying a torch. Caesar, still led by Cleopatra, follows him. They come down the corridor, Caesar peering keenly about at the strange architecture and at the pillar shadows, between which, as the passing torch makes them hurry noiselessly backwards, figures of men with wings and hawks' heads, and vast black marble cats, seem to flit in and out of ambush. Further along, the wall turns a corner and makes a transept in which Caesar sees, on his right, a throne, and behind the throne, a door.'[3]

1. *Our Theatres in the Nineties*, II, p. 184.
2. E. J. West, ed., *Shaw on Theatre*, New York, 1958, p. 181.
3. Homer Woodbridge, *G. B. Shaw: Creative Artist* (Carbondale, Ill., 1963), p. 52.

In 1898, of course, this could be done only with words, for readers.

Perhaps because GBS was often ahead of his time, possibly because he regularly probed for universals to underline the particulars of his plays, the Shavian canon has remained remarkably alive—even advanced—while theatre fashions come and go and yesterday's *avant-garde* becomes today's fashion or fades from view. Nearly half of Shaw's fifty-odd plays are staged somewhere in the world each year, and the results are often remarkable. A useful example is the 1965 London revival of *Widowers Houses*, Shaw's first, and far from his most "modern", play. As the critic for *Plays and Players* wrote:

> *Widowers' Houses* is not just early Shaviana, but [it] is a good, well-constructed and intensely theatrical play which, due to cunning timing by the management, has the genuinely contemporary theme of slum landlordism. The jokes and satirical writings are fantastically up to date, so much so they would not be out of place in the BBC's "*Not So Much a Programme*". . . .[4]

Strangely enough, much of Shaw's modernism consists of his adapting to the modern stage, and his bringing back to life, theatrical conventions which had been discarded when naturalism and realism took hold in the theatre. In order to make ideas behave dramatically, for example, he wanted his characters to be able to step out of their roles now and then to become bigger than life. Thus he made use of the pre-naturalistic stage convention that characters may have written into their roles an artificial amount of self-consciousness. The device not only permitted the use of certain kinds of ironic wit Shaw loved, but permitted a clarity of expression in dialogue unavailable to a doctrinaire realist. Thus, of his characters in *Saint Joan*, Shaw wrote that

> . . . it is the business of the stage to make the figures more intelligible to themselves than they would be in real life; for by no other means can they be made intelligible to the audience. . . . All I claim is that by this inevitable sacrifice of verisimilitude . . . the things I represent these three exponents of drama [in *Joan*] as saying are the things they actually would have said if they had known what they were really doing.[5]

Shaw was never, he insisted, "a representation[al]ist or realist." Rather, he said, he

> . . . was always in the classic tradition, recognizing that stage characters must be endowed by the author with a conscious

4. Alan Simpson, review of *Widowers' Houses, Plays and Players*, May, 1965, pp. 38–39.
5. Preface, *Saint Joan*, p. 51.

self-knowledge and power of expression, and . . . a freedom of in-
hibitions, which in real life would make them monsters. . . . It is
the power to do this that differentiates me (or Shakespear)
from a gramophone and a camera. The representational part of
the business is mere costume and scenery; and I would not give
tuppence for any play that could not be acted in curtains and
togas as effectively as in elaborately built stage drawing rooms and
first-rate modern tailoring.[6]

Shavian characterization permitted non-realistic eloquence in
places in the dialogue where it becomes necessary. This was not
only justifiable on the grounds of psychological validity but because
of its consistency with the self-consciousness of the role. Ibsen and
others modified downward the level of dramatic language, Ibsen
even commenting in a letter that writing "the genuine, plain language spoken in real life" was a "very much more difficult art"
than writing poetic or pseudopoetic lines for a character to speak.
"My desire," Ibsen added, "was to depict human beings, and
therefore I would not make them speak the language of the gods."
Realist writers who attempted to represent life as it was, accepted at
first the limits of normal expression. If they were concerned with
surface emotions these limitations presented no difficulty: conversational resources for the discussion of meals or money or other basic
needs remained adequate. But a dramatist could not express the
whole range of human experience while committed to the language
of probable conversation. To overcome this limitation Shaw
employed the player whose speech had a vitality beyond what
would be normal for his role, using normal conversational speech
throughout the play, but shifting into intensified rhetoric (possibly
poetic prose, or even verse) at the points of crisis. The technique is
psychologically valid, for at times of crisis or peaks of emotion we
all reach for another, and more metaphorical, level of language (at
its lowest, that of the formerly unprintable variety). In some of the
earlier plays the rhetorical heightening is formal, as in Caesar's
apostrophe to the Sphinx, or the great, impassioned speeches of
Don Juan and the Devil. In some later plays the technique is still
traditional. Joan, for example, has a great outburst which narrowly
"realistic" critics condemn as out of keeping with Joan's earthy,
peasant intellect—her passionate, biblical-cadenced renunciation of
her recantation, beginning,

Light your fire. . . . You think that life is nothing but not being
stone dead. It is not the bread and water I fear: I can live on
bread: when have I asked for more? It is no hardship to drink
water if the water be clean. Bread has no sorrow for me, and
water no affliction. But to shut me from the light of the sky and
the sight of the fields and flowers; to chain my feet so that I can

6. *Shaw on Theatre*, p. 185.

never again ride with the soldiers nor climb the hills; to make me breathe foul damp darkness, and keep from me everything that brings me back to the love of God ..., without these things I cannot live. . . .

In some of the earlier plays there is the foreshadowing of a Shavian technique to come, particularly in "mad" Father Keegan's chat with the grasshopper (*John Bull's Other Island*) and the Mayoress's great speech from the depth of a trance (in *Getting Married*). In the latter plays there is sometimes "a sudden shift to a patterned, semi-poetic, ritualistic speech [which] indicates a passionate intensity of perception or revelation which transcends the ordinary levels of the play." We see it in the darkness of the close of the first act of *Heartbreak House*, in the trio of Captain Shotover, Hector and Hesione. We see it in the quintet of Adam, Eve, Cain, the Serpent and Lilith, as they vanish one by one to end the last scene of *Back to Methuselah*. We see it in the chanting praise, and agonized rejection, of Joan in the Epilogue to *Saint Joan*. We see it again in such allegorical and extravagant plays of the thirties as *Too True to Be Good* and *The Simpleton of the Unexpected Isles*. Scenes and speeches such as these do not escape from a commitment to reality—they provide for Shaw and later dramatists who use the device opportunities for creating a reality of ideas and emotions which goes beyond a commitment to external details.

A logical step beyond is Shaw's player who is both actor and character in the same person—the self-conscious character, or actor directly aware of his audience. This was a Shavian anti-illusionary device used as early as the turn of the century, yet still considered in current playwrights the epitome of modernity. Shaw had combined two of the most primitive, yet most basic, elements of the self-conscious theatre in his work—the platform of the philosopher with the stage of the clown. Perhaps he was only as *avant-garde* as Aristophanes. "Theatre technique," Shaw observed, "begins with the circus clown and ringmaster and the Greek tribune, which is a glorified development of the pitch from which the poet of the market place declaims his verses. . . . " He might have added that Shavian theatre techniques include the amusement park's distorting mirrors held up to human nature, the old-fashioned yet timeless routines of burlesque and the music hall, and the exhortations of "the roofless pavement orator." In other refinements these are the techniques of *Waiting for Godot*, Ionesco's *The Chairs*, or Genet's *The Balcony*. And the techniques, too, of Bertolt Brecht.

Martin Esslin sees Brecht's "innovations" in a threatre which rejects illusion—like the earlier Shaw, from whom Brecht learned—and abandons "the pretense that the audience is eavesdropping on actual events." It openly admits "that the theatre is a theatre and not the world itself," and "approximates the lecture hall, to which audiences come in the expectation that they will be informed, and also the circus arena, where an audience, without identification or illusion, watches performers exhibit their special skills."[7] By destroying stage illusion and by inhibiting the possibilities of empathic identification between audience and characters, the playwright, theoretically, at least, creates a distance which forces the spectator to look at the action onstage in a detached and critical spirit.

In this manner Shaw begins *Caesar and Cleopatra* with an old-fashioned, pre-naturalistic prologue spoken by the Egyptian god Ra, who makes the audience well aware that it *is* an audience, and that the play is a play:

> (. . . *He surveys the modern audience with great contempt; and finally speaks the following words to them.*) Peace! Be silent and hearken to me, ye quaint little islanders.
> . . . I ask you not for worship but for silence. Let not your men speak, or your women cough; for I am come to draw you back over the graves of sixty generations. . . . Are ye impatient with me? Do ye crave for a story of an unchaste woman? Hath the name of Cleopatra tempted ye hither? . . .

In similar spirit, after the improbable incidents of the first act of Shaw's *Too True to Be Good*, the act ends with the announcement by one of the cast: "The play is now virtually over; but the characters will discuss it at great length for two acts more. The exit doors are all in order. Goodnight." And the play ends with the impassioned but interminable oration of a young man which goes on while the other characters exit, leaving him to preach in solitude; while at last he is enveloped in fog and darkness. In the opening words of Shaw's last stage direction, "The audience disperses. . . ."

Shaw was always, after his first few plays satisfied his commitment to Ibsen,

> . . . ready to stop the overt action for a good discussion or good lecture, or even step out of the proscenium frame to harangue the audience in behalf of a relevant philosophy or sociology which is beyond, if not indeed antithetical to, the illusion achieved by plodding realists and the designers who provided scenic realism.[8]

As early as his *Quintessence of Ibsenism*, parts of which were written before he had even completed his first full-length play, Shaw had written about the future of the theatre in a way that made clear that he wanted to see realistic subject matter presented in a

7. Martin Esslin, *Brecht* (New York, 1961), p. 126.
8. John Gassner, *Bernard Shaw and the Making of the Modern Mind.* See above.

way which involved the audience both intellectually and emotionally, but not empathically. Spectators were not to identify themselves with roles in the drama, but were to be instead "guilty creatures sitting at a play." Concerning the subject matter of modern
drama Shaw wrote:

> Now an interesting play cannot in the nature of things mean
> anything but a play in which problems of conduct and character
> of personal importance to the audience are raised and sugges-
> tively discussed. . . . the drama arises through a conflict of unset-
> tled ideals rather than through vulgar attachments, rapacities, gen-
> erosities, ambitions, misunderstandings, oddities and so forth as
> to which moral question is raised. The conflict is not between
> clear right and wrong. . . .[9]

The modern play, Shaw insisted, would make ideas themselves
dramatic, and increase the importance of discussion. In *The
Quintessence of Ibsenism* he summarized the "technical novelties"
of the new drama as

> . . . first, the introduction of the discussion and its development
> until it so overspreads and interpenetrates the action that it
> finally assimilates it, making play and discussion practically iden-
> tical; and second, as a consequence of making the spectators
> themselves the persons of the drama and the incidents of their
> own lives its incidents, the disuse of the old stage tricks by which
> audiences had to be induced to take an interest in unreal people
> and improbable circumstances, and in the substitution [for these
> unreal people and improbable circumstances] of a forensic tech-
> nique of recrimination, disillusion, and penetration through the
> [false] ideals to the truth, with a free use on the part of the
> playwright of all the rehtorical and lyrical arts of the orator, the
> preacher, the pleader, and the rhapsodist.[1]

A later critic, writing about the "new" drama of Camus and
Brecht, concluded that its major feature was

> . . . an engagement of the audience as well as the actor and the
> playwright. The removed observation of the naturalist's theatre is
> completely abandoned. . . . The play is a dialogue in which the
> audience must participate. . . . To Brecht, the audience must not
> be a group of "people to whom something is being done." The
> audience must change, so that the world may be changed.[2]

Since the 1890's this had been Shaw's principle as well as his practice.

Like some more "modern" saints of the contemporary

9. *Major Critical Essays*, p. 139.
1. p. 146.
2. James H. Clancy, "Beyond Despair:
A New Drama of Ideas," reprinted
from *Educational Theatre Journal* in
Morris Friedman, ed., *Essays in the
Modern Drama*, Boston, 1964, p. 170.

theatre—Artaud or Genet, for example—Shaw looked to the theatre as a force to remedy the ills of civilization, and as a replacement
for the waning influence of the church, from whence theatre first
sprang. It "would be a very good thing," Shaw wrote in 1906, "if
the theatre took itself seriously as a factory of thought, prompter of
conscience, an elucidator of social conduct, an armory against
despair and dullness, and a temple of the Ascent of Man." Like his
most advanced twentieth-century successors, Shaw believed that
indifference in audience or playwright was a major sin, and that the
playwright's clear duty was to shock audiences out of that state
whenever necessary—and, in fact, more than necessary. The
means—and specific aims—of a Genet or an Artaud might have
repelled Shaw, but not the general concept, for when Shaw was setting the theoretical foundations of modern drama in *The Quintessence of Ibsenism*, he had written of the necessity of the playwright's devoting himself to showing that "the spirit or will of Man
is constantly outgrowing the ideals, and that thoughtless conformity to them is constantly producing results no less tragic than those
which follow thoughtless violation of them." Thus it was crucial
for the playwright "to keep before the public the importance of
being always prepared to act immorally." This meant theatrical
shock treatment, Shaw realized, and concluded: "The plain working truth is that it is not only good for people to be shocked occasionally, but absolutely necessary to the progress of society that
they should be shocked pretty often."

It is only now, more a result of court action than a real change
of public attitudes, that another aspect of Shaw's *avant-gardism*
appears less shocking than it once did. Shaw deliberately and early
met the prudish spirit head-on in his Ibsenite *Mrs Warren's
Profession*, evoking outcries still echoing around the world. Not
very many years ago the play—paradoxically by then accepted in
Dublin—was banned in Paris! And a play of the same period as
Mrs Warren, Shaw's *The Philanderer*, evokes in at least one scene
as much sensual sex as the ordinary language of the stage can
convey. William Archer once complained that Shaw's plays "reek
of sex," yet complained further that Shaw's characters lacked flesh
and blood. A later critic called Shaw's plays "as unemotional as a
mushroom." Yet the plays remain as full-blooded as their direction
is resourceful. Exaggeratedly, Shaw once claimed to have gone so
far in mentioning the unmentionable and dramatizing the undra-
matizable as to have "put the physical act of sexual intercourse on
the stage" (in *Overruled*). And the heterosexual wrestling match is
a feature of several later plays (especially *The Apple Cart* and *The
Millionairess*.)

Although Shaw praised Ibsen's social realism all his life, his own plays as well as his concluding chapters of *The Quintessence of Ibsenism* show that he rapidly outgrew the confines of realism and, as John Gassner has written, if Shaw's later plays belong at all

> ... to the genre of realism it is by virtue of their engagement to reality, chiefly by comprising a conflict of ideas, principles, ways of thinking, and ways of living. For the sake of reality, Shaw was always prepared to violate realistic structure and verisimilitude, to turn somersaults of the most farcical or fantastic kind, and to be arbitrary with his plot or discard plot altogether.[3]

In *Caesar and Cleopatra* the sense of fantasy that Shaw developed more fully later emerged for the first time. Yet at the same time the play is firmly set in history, and follows the usual Shavian formula of the testing and discarding of illusion. As one critic recently has put it: "At odds with the tenets of naturalism—for which he professed to stand—Shaw is never in doubt that drama is a matter of illusion and that, far from mirroring nature, reality and life were outside the theatre, with the audience and not on the stage." *Caesar and Cleopatra*, with its irreverent and anachronistic approach to history, a generation before Lytton Strachey, has spawned hundreds of modern plays utilizing its techniques. Since few of them have approached Shaw's history plays in quality, the inheritance may have been a dangerous one. But the play helped inspire the theatre of Giraudoux, Anouilh and Brecht, and on its own has enjoyed consistent success on the stage for sixty years.

Shaw's twentieth-century approach to the historical drama was that the theory had to be discredited that

> ... the only way to write a play which shall convey to the general public an impression of antiquity is to make the characters speak blank verse and abstain from reference to steam, telegraphy, and any of the material conditions of their existence.

What the purposeful use of anachronism shows in a play about history, Shaw insisted, is that

> ... the period of time covered by history is far too short to allow any perceptible progress in the popular sense of Evolution of the Human Species. The notion that there has been any such progress since Caesar's time (twenty centuries) is too absurd for discussion. All the savagery, barbarism, dark ages and the rest of it of which we have record as existing in the past, exists at the present moment.

Thus anachronism gives us better perspective in understanding the relativity of time. Further, writes Shaw:

3. Gassner, see above.

Nobody knows whether Shakespear thought that ancient Athenian joiners, weavers, or bellows menders were any different from Elizabethan ones; but it is quite certain that he could not have made them so.[4]

A playwright who often directed and cast his own plays, Shaw was as much interested in the problems of staging as he was in the intellectual and emotional climate he was writing into his plays. Because they became for him aspects of the same problem, he experimented not only with new theoretical wine in familiar bottles, and finely aged wine in new and unfamiliar bottles, but with the indivisibility of technique and theme. The result was often a play which by orthodox, contemporary standards only baffled orthodox contemporary critics. Max Beerbohm (in 1903) was convinced that *Man and Superman*, particularly the *Don Juan in Hell* interlude, was a "peculiar article," and "of course, not a play at all." Paradoxically, Max added, "It is 'as good as a play'—infinitely better, to my peculiar taste, than any play I have ever read or seen enacted. But a play it is not." Within two years Max had recanted, admitting that the failure had been his own—his own narrowness of theatrical imagination.

Sometimes the complaints about Shaw's playcrafting were really expressions of frustration at not finding a conventional plot and predictable characters moving within it. When Shaw was ninety-four he observed that this was an old story:

Now it is quite true that my plays are all talk, just as Raphael's pictures are all paint, Michael Angelo's statues all marble, Beethoven's symphonies all noise.[5]

In 1908, when an interviewer from the *Daily Telegraph* had prodded GBS for "some notion of the plot" of *Getting Married*, which proved to be one of Shaw's most disquisitory dramas, the author, with jesting truthfulness, responded:

MR. SHAW: The play has no plot. Surely nobody expects a play by me to have a plot. I am a dramatic poet, not a plot-monger.
INTERVIEWER: But at least there is a story.
MR. SHAW: Not at all. If you look at any of the old editions of our classical plays, you will see that the description of the play is not called a plot or story but an argument—an argument lasting three hours, and carried on with unflagging cerebration by twelve people and a beadle.[6]

4. *Three Plays for Puritains*, pp. 195, 197.
5. *Shaw on Theatre*, p. 290.
6. Quoted in Archibald Henderson,

George Bernard Shaw: Man of the Century, New York, 1956, pp. 609–10, footnote.

Unprepared by conventional drama for this genre of theatre, a later critic wrote of *The Apple Cart*:

Here is the final exaggeration of all of Shaw's tendencies as a dramatist. Action has totally disappeared and all the characters sit on chairs, hour in and hour out. And in the place of human emotion is the brain of Shaw, bulging larger and larger, filling the stage, hard and brilliant, glittering like a jewel.[7]

The cerebral fantasies and dramatic debates—Shavian plays of passionate ideas—were to come to life in a variety of symbolic or naturalistic settings. When Shaw's plays after the First World War were inaugurated by *Heartbreak House*, one unsung Shaw commentator noted that Shaw's "was a grave message: it would issue gravely if it were not for the instinct for absurdity which has never deserted him." But it caused his public, unready for this approach to drama, to desert him when *Heartbreak House* was first staged in 1920. It played to nearly empty houses, and even a return look arranged for the London reviewers failed to convince any of them that they had been wrong the first time. After sixty-three performances, it had to close. Forty years later, a reviewer of the London revival of the play observed:

If, as is so often claimed, public appreciation and approval is always half a century behind the times, then this great work is just about to receive the seal of public favour. ... And, heartbreakingly enough, Shaw's tragic vision of England in the first world war as a captainless ship drifting towards the world's final calamity has an even greater urgency today than it possessed in the twenties. At that time, and indeed ever since, it has been fashionable to dismiss the whole of Shaw's drama as a polemical exchange of mouthpieces lacking real human substance and feeling. Those who still doubt that Shaw had any heart to break should not fail to see this revival.[8]

"Without its solid basis in social polemic ever being obscured," a critic has observed, "*Heartbreak House* simultaneously achieves the quality of dream." It is just possible, in fact, that the play is largely the dream of Ellie Dunn, who falls asleep in the Hushabye (Heartbreak) House before the play is two pages old. Similarly, a later Shavian play in which the *Heartbreak House* techniques and themes are extended, *Too True to Be Good*, may also be largely the dream fantasy of a woman, ill and delirious, who fantasizes her recovery and escape from the sickbed.

A number of twentieth century critics have pointed out that

7. F. R. Bellamy, review of *The Apple Cart*, *Outlook*, March 12, 1930, p. 429.
8. Peter Roberts, review of *Heartbreak House*, *Plays and Players*, December, 1961, p. 13.

although medieval and renaissance drama sometimes used the device of a dream, it is only modern drama that uses dream-structure and dream imagery significantly. Here again Shaw's contribution is significant. One of the earliest twentieth century plays to combine both approaches was Shaw's *Man and Superman*, which combines what is apparently a conventional play with a dream-vision, where grand, representative figures of myth parallel characters in the play. Martin Esslin, in *The Theatre of the Absurd*, suggests that "the first to put on the stage a dream world in the spirit of modern psychological thinking was August Strindberg. The three parts of *To Damascus* (1898–1904), *A Dream Play* (1902), and *The Ghost Sonata* (1907) are masterly transcriptions of dreams and obsessions, and direct sources of the theatre of the Absurd." Strindberg himself wrote of his aims in his introductory note to *A Dream Play*:

> In this dream play, . . . the author has sought to reproduce the disconnected but apparently logical form of a dream. Anything can happen; everything is possible and probable. Time and space do not exist. On a slight groundwork of reality, imagination spins and weaves new patterns made up of memories, experiences, unfettered fancies, absurdities, and improvisations. The characters are split, double and multiply; they evaporate, crystallize, scatter and converge. But a single consciousness holds sway over them all—that of the dreamer. . . .

Concurrently, and differently, Shaw was using the concept of the dream-vision, uninfluenced by Strindberg. The concepts with which they were working were part of the then-current intellectual climate, and each, according to his nature, had put these ideas into his playwriting. Shaw, in the "Don Juan In Hell" episode in *Man and Superman*, had projected into his art a momentary vision of how man and the cosmos might be transfigured:

> As the bandit Mendoza falls asleep upon the Sierra desert in the third act of the play, the camp fire grows dim, the mountains and starlit sky blur; all of the physical world swims before one's consciousness, transforming into a timeless, omnipresent void. This is the great change, instantaneous evolution of the real world of politics, war, destitution, and ignorance into the future realm of Shaw's thought whirlpool. For one discovers that the void is inhabited by bodiless intelligences, who manifest themselves by willing ghostly forms, and engage in what Don Juan calls the song of the philosophic man and what also might be called a Shavio-Mozartian quartet. The uncanny world of the Hell scene is the nearest approach that Shaw ever made to his own inner vision of the real. Using words as if they were music, the four intelligences sing a song of ideas in a sphere without

time, space or dimension . . . an objectification of Shaw's deepest spiritual desires, a fusion of form and content into an astonishingly original and personal artistic creation.[9]

Continuing to use elements of dream and of myth, Shaw often combined the two, as in *Androcles and the Lion, Pygmalion, Back to Methuselah,* and *Saint Joan.* As one critic (Lionel Abel) recently remarked, Shaw

> . . . would have furiously protested against our ascribing to him any such notion as that life is a dream. But when we look at some of his finest works this is what they say. Take such a masterpiece as *Pygmalion,* for example. Here we have the complete transformation of a vulgar, dirty and illiterate girl into a dazzling lady, brought about by cleansing her, dressing her, and altering her diction. The play is incidentally a Cinderella story.[1]

The critic might have added that Shaw, in a realistic setting, had utilized the myths of both Pygmalion and Cinderella, and, as dreams do, inverted elements of them.

Saint Joan—as we have seen, one of Shaw's most influential plays, as far as its impact upon dramatists is concerned—also uses a figure about which an entire mythos has grown up. Shaw presents her story as a realistic chronicle, then concludes with a dream-fantasy apparently no less real than the earlier reality, yet which wrenches the audience, moved by Joan's death, back into a more objective frame of mind, its humor leaving the audience nonetheless "guilty creatures sitting at a play." An alert audience, watching the epilogue, would realize that the appearance of the clerical gentleman in 1920 costume breaks the illusion of the dream, just as when the "Dream in Hell" interlude in *Man and Superman* closes, we have the following lines in the transitional scene:

MENDOZA: Did you dream?
TANNER: Damnably. Did you?
MENDOZA: Yes. I forget what. You were in it.
TANNER: So were you. Amazing.

Shattering illusions, even the illusion of the dream, was always as basic to Shaw's techniques as it was to his themes.

Philosophically, Shaw's plays have lost little of their relevance, and may have actually gained some. One critic sees the "most distilled expression" of the *Zeitgeist* "in the theatre of Beckett and Genet, Shaw and Brecht, where heroic forms for the individual in the democratic and industrialized society are explored." Another

9. John G. Demaray, "Bernard Shaw and C. E. M. Joad: The Adventures of Two Puritans in Their Search for God," *PMLA* 78 (June, 1963), 269–70.

1. Lionel Abel, *Metatheatre: A New View of Dramatic Form* (New York, 1963), p. 106.

sees Shaw as precursor of the "existentialist drama represented by Sartre's *No Exit* and *The Flies.*" Still another, writing of Shaw's existentialism, includes Shaw under that much misused term because such a play as *Don Juan in Hell* or *Major Barbara* "contains all the *germs* of the twentieth—and the twenty-first—century, just as Goethe's *Faust* contains all the germs of the nineteenth." In particular the critic (Colin Wilson) citing *Heartbreak House* as well, sees Shaw as recognizing the modern world as a "maelstrom of neurosis and futility" in need of "direction and purpose." Shaw's Don Juan asks: "Does this colossal mechanism have no purpose?" And his response—and Shaw's—remains that whether or not the mechanism has purpose, man must go beyond disillusion to at least act out his life as if purpose existed. As Shaw, a generation before Sartre, proclaimed in "The Religion of the Future," speaking in his own person and not through a character creation: "We must drive into the heads of men the full consciousness of moral responsibility that comes with the knowledge that there will never be a God unless we make him."

From the religious standpoint Shaw's plays and other writings have retained more currency than it might seem, for the issue is clouded by the immense success and acceptance of *Saint Joan*, with its surface orthodoxy. But as Warren S. Smith points out,

> A selection from almost any of his religious speeches could be placed in a sermon in almost any church without violating the sermon's context; yet there is no doubt that his utterances are truly heretical. They were when he made them, and they still are.[2]

Shaw's heresies in the religious plays, according to yet another recent critic, have still a further parallel in the theological *avant-garde;* for according to Daniel Leary, who has made a thorough study of Shaw's philosophy, its

> ... abiding significance—both as an explanation of the present and as a vision of the future—is underscored by its striking parallels to the writings of the scientist-priest, Pierre Teilhard de Chardin, [and] the emotional experiences of Shaw's dramas are essentially the expression in character and structure of this philosophy.[3]

That Shaw will remain in tune with the *avant-garde* in thought and theatrical theory and practice is clearly impossible. Although men will continue to debate man's role in the universe and con-

2. Warren S. Smith, *The Religious Speeches of Bernard Shaw* (University Park, Pa., 1963), p. xxiii.
3. Daniel J. Leary, "The Evolutionary Dialectic of Shaw and Teilhard: A Perennial Philosophy," *The Shaw Review*, IX (January; 1966), 15.

tinue as well to mime or play roles which take them beyond themselves, the ideas and the practices will undergo change. Yesterday's
avant-garde at its most advanced demonstrates its validity as today's
orthodoxy and tomorrow's discards. That many of Shaw's ideas
have held on so long is remarkable; but GBS would have been the
first to see no value in their fixity. Although the ironic blend of the
comic and the serious labeled "dark comedy" today owes much to
Shaw, he might have answered, as he once wrote, that "Every jest
is an earnest in the womb of Time," or that "The jests do not
become poorer as they mature into earnest." GBS never intended
to found schools of thought or of playwriting, although he did
intend to influence the thought and the drama which came after
him. He wrote and published his plays because, he said, the worst
attitude concerning the theatre current at the time he began his
writing career was

> . . . that intellectual seriousness is out of place on the stage; that
> the theatre is a place of shallow amusement; that people go there
> to be soothed after the enormous intellectual strain of a day in
> the city; in short, that a playwright is a person whose business it
> is to make unwholesome confectionery out of cheap emotions.
> My answer to this was to put all my intellectual goods in the
> shop window under the sign of *Man and Superman.* That part of
> my design succeeded. By good luck and [good] acting, the com-
> edy triumphed on the stage; and the book was a good deal dis-
> cussed. Since then the sweet-shop view of the theatre has been
> out of countenance. . . . And the younger playwrights are not
> only taking their art seriously, but being taken seriously
> themselves.[4]

That was all he wanted, he wrote in 1921. The important thing
was not for future dramatists to imitate him but to surpass him.
Not realizing, in his mid-sixties, that he still had a *Saint Joan* in
him, and nearly three more decades of playwriting as well, he
closed his preface to *Back To Methuselah* by confessing that he
felt that his powers were waning. Nevertheless, he concluded with
the hope that the future of the theater lay in remaining modern
through ceaseless change:

> It is my hope that a hundred apter and more elegant parables by
> younger hands will soon leave mine as far behind as the religious
> pictures of the fifteenth century left behind the first attempts of
> the early Christians at iconography. In that hope, I withdraw
> and ring up the curtain.

4. *Back to Methuselah,* Preface, p. lxxxv.

On Major Barbara

G. K. CHESTERTON

[A 1909 View of *Major Barbara*]†

Major Barbara * * * contains a strong religious element; but, when all is said, the whole point of the play is that the religious element is defeated. Moreover, the actual expressions of religion in the play are somewhat unsatisfactory as expressions of religion—or even of reason. I must frankly say that Bernard Shaw always seems to me to use the word God not only without any idea of what it means, but without one moment's thought about what it could possibly mean. He said to some atheist, "Never believe in a God that you cannot improve on." The atheist (being a sound theologian) naturally replied that one should not believe in a God whom one could improve on; as that would show that he was not God. In the same style in *Major Barbara* the heroine ends by suggesting that she will serve God without personal hope, so that she may owe nothing to God and He owe everything to her. It does not seem to strike her that if God owes everything to her He is not God. These things affect me merely as tedious perversions of a phrase. It is as if you said, 'I will never have a father unless I have begotten him."

But the real sting and substance of *Major Barbara* is much more practical and to the point. It expresses not the new spirituality but the old materialism of Bernard Shaw. Almost every one of Shaw's plays is an expanded epigram. But the epigram is not expanded (as with most people) into a hundred commonplaces. Rather the epigram is expanded into a hundred other epigrams; the work is at least as brilliant in detail as it is in design. But it is generally possible to discover the original and pivotal epigram which is the centre and purpose of the play. It is generally possible, even amid that blinding jewellery of a million jokes, to discover the grave, solemn and sacred joke for which the play itself was written.

† In 1909 G. K. Chesterton made a full-length study of his friend and some-time adversary in *George Bernard Shaw* (New York: Hill and Wang, 1960). The book took Shaw far more seriously than most of his contemporaries did, and it remains a standard piece of literary criticism. Chesterton, who later became a notable convert to Roman Catholicism, recognized Shaw's essential religiosity while strongly disagreeing with what he regarded as its basis in secular rationalism. His view of *Major Barbara* was penned four years after the first production.

⌐ne ultimate epigram of *Major Barbara* can be put thus. People say that poverty is no crime; Shaw says that poverty is a crime; that it is a crime to endure it, a crime to be content with it, that it is the mother of all crimes of brutality, corruption, and fear. If a man says to Shaw that he is born of poor but honest parents, Shaw tells him that the very word "but" shows that his parents were probably dishonest. In short, he maintains here what he had maintained elsewhere: that what the people at this moment require is not more patriotism or more art or more religion or more morality or more sociology, but simply more money. The evil is not ignorance or decadence or sin or pessimism; the evil is poverty. The point of this particular drama is that even the noblest enthusiasm of the girl who becomes a Salvation Army officer fails under the brute money power of her father who is a modern capitalist. When I have said this it will be clear why this play, fine and full of bitter sincerity as it is, must in a manner be cleared out of the way before we come to talk of Shaw's final and serious faith. For this serious faith is in the sanctity of human will, in the divine capacity for creation and choice rising higher than environment and doom; and so far as that goes, *Major Barbara* is not only apart from his faith but against his faith. *Major Barbara* is an account of environment victorious over heroic will. There are a thousand answers to the ethic in *Major Barbara* which I should be inclined to offer. I might point out that the rich do not so much buy honesty as curtains to cover dishonesty: that they do not so much buy health as cushions to comfort disease. And I might suggest that the doctrine that poverty degrades the poor is much more likely to be used as an argument for keeping them powerless than as an argument for making them rich. But there is no need to find such answers to the materialistic pessimism of *Major Barbara*. The best answer to it is in Shaw's own best and crowning philosophy. * * *

BARBARA BELLOW WATSON

[Sainthood for Millionaires]†

The major difficulty of *Major Barbara* lies in its simple and necessary irony, which is only the irony of life itself. Shaw, in his preface to the play, gives copious "First Aid to Critics," but the confusion remains, partly because, as he himself points out, if you tell the truth nobody will believe you, and partly because this pref-

† A quite recent scholarly view of the same play uses Chesterton as a point of departure. Barbara Bellow Watson's article is from *Modern Drama*, Vol. 11 (December, 1968), pp. 227–244.

ace deals with ideas rather than with dramatic method. That method is, as Chesterton calls it, "the grave, solemn and sacred joke for which the play itself was written,"[1] an irony designed to show that we may not accept the least of capitalism's benefits without accepting the last of its depredations: also that the damage it does and the audacity of its excuses beggar invective and so thoroughly satirize themselves that no response is left but irony, a weapon Shaw wields as superbly as Swift. There is even a modest echo of "A Modest Proposal" in the preface:

> Suppose we were to abolish all penalties for such activities as burglary, arson, rape and murder, and decide that poverty is the one thing we will not tolerate—that every adult with less than, say, £365 a year, shall be painlessly but inexorably killed, and every hungry half naked child forcibly fattened and clothed, would not that be an enormous improvement on our existing system, which has already destroyed so many civilizations, and is visibly destroying ours in the same way?[2]

But the philosophy of the play is far from being a "materialistic pessimism" as Chesterton claims.[3] Chesterton, a Christian, was poignantly aware that Barbara's belief in her work for the Salvation Army comes down in ruins, although the nobility and the sincerity of that belief remain standing. Money and power rise triumphant. But, as the play shows once its irony is understood, neither the Christian thesis nor the capitalist anti-thesis carries the ultimate day. That belongs to the third religion in the play, Shaw's secular religion of Creative Evolution, which is closely related to his socialism. It is the Life Force that wants the marriage of Cusins and Barbara. It is also the Life Force that has led Undershaft to adopt his religion and his success—one and the same—for in the vital genius the Life Force runs powerfully towards its objects—and attracts others irresistibly.

The central conflict of the play is between the ideas of Andrew Undershaft on the one hand, and the ideas of the whole society, represented by his whole family, on the other. St. Andrew (canonized in Shaw's preface, not in the play) lives by money and gunpowder; nothing remarkable in that, except that he is not ashamed to admit it. Opposed to him stand his daughter, a major in the Salvation Army, who believes intensely in the Christian virtues and not at all in money; his estranged wife, Lady Britomart, an aristocrat with no nonsense about her; his lesser children, Stephen, a worldly weakling, and Sarah, a nonentity; and Barbara's fiancé, a

1. G. K. Chesterton, *George Bernard Shaw* (New York, 1956), p. 146. [See above—*Editor*.]
2. *John Bull's Other Island with How He Lied to Her Husband and Major Barbara* (London, 1931), p. 211. All later references to this volume are listed as *Major Barbara*.
3. Chesterton, p. 148.

professor of Greek and something of a poet. Given the fact that Barbara, the central force in this opposition, is a realist like her father, in spite of being a missionary, the outcome of the drama is inevitable. Undershaft has (sometimes silently) the last word in every argument. And he has something better than the last word: he has the last act. He has, in other words, not only convincing arguments, which would always be countered by other convincing arguments (Chesterton offers a few, cogent in themselves, but dramatically false[4]), but also the reversal of all the stubbornly held opinions of his opponents. In a clean sweep of the board, Undershaft converts to his own view the representatives of Christian spirituality, of academic classicism, of the old aristocracy, and even the limp indifference of the idle rich. All are forced to recognize the unity of body and soul, the fusion of money with morality. In the model town that so persuades them, the aristocrat sees power and order, the professor of Greek sees lucidity, and the Salvation Army lass sees liberation of the spirit. Not that this conversion is made easy for them. Undershaft displays no redeeming sentimentalities, but insists on all his infamies, following the logic of the capitalist structure to its last iron law, its last starving innocent, its last bath of blood and fire.

Now all this is paradoxical only if we expect a socialist author to render simplistic fantasies in which virtue (poverty) triumphs over vice (money and power), or suffers in the right way, without exercising the intellect at all. Although it is perfectly true that all his plays are polemical in the strictest sense, the essential difference between Shaw and the ordinary writer of didactic plays is that the message is not mouthed by the actors or moralized by artificial rewards and punishments, but embodied in the living movement of the drama. Hence the theme of *Major Barbara* is not by any means the beneficence of capitalism (the products of capitalism being miserably on display in Act II), not even the necessity of cannons. Instead the theme is an ironic egg within a visible shell. The shell, an inclusive idea that pervades Shaw's work early and late, is the necessity of realism. Here a distinction must be drawn. The supposed realism of those who accept the *status quo* out of indifference abetted by stupidity, like Sarah and Charles, or out of moral cowardice of the intellect, like Mrs. Baines, is at the opposite pole from the genuine realism of the Undershaft mind that accepts no catchwords and pretends no unfelt feelings. Cynical realists like Charles Lomax are in truth of the Devil's party without knowing it. Chesterton says:

> The truth is that the ordinary anti-humanitarian only manages to harden his heart by having already softened his head. It is the re-

4. Chesterton, P. 147. [See above—*Editor*.]

verse of sentimental to insist that a colonial is being burned alive; for sentimentalism must be the clinging to pleasant thoughts. And no one, not even a Higher Evolutionist, can think a colonial burned alive a pleasant thought. The sentimental thing is to warm your hands at the fire while denying the existence of the colonial, and that is the ruling habit in England, as it has been the chief business of Bernard Shaw to show. And in this the brutalitarians hate him not because he is soft, but because he is hard, because he is not softened by conventional excuses; because he looks hard at a thing—and hits harder.[5]

This liberation from cant leads quite inevitably to Major Barbara's discovery of the yolk in the ironic egg: the idea that capitalism as a system is so pervasive and so corrupting that it makes even charity into an evil force. The Salvation Army prevents riots, fends off revolution:

> CUSINS. I dont think you quite know what the Army does for the poor.
> UNDERSHAFT. Oh yes I do. It draws their teeth: that is enough for me as a man of business.
> CUSINS. Nonsense! It makes them sober—
> UNDERSHAFT. I prefer sober workmen. The profits are larger.
> CUSINS. —honest—
> UNDERSHAFT. Honest workmen are the most economical.
> CUSINS. —attached to their homes—
> UNDERSHAFT. So much the better: they will put up anything rather than change their shop.
> CUSINS. —happy—
> UNDERSHAFT. An invaluable safeguard against revolution.
> CUSINS. —unselfish—
> UNDERSHAFT. Indifferent to their own interest, which suits me exactly.
> CUSINS. —with their thoughts on heavenly things—
> UNDERSHAFT. And not on Trade Unionism nor Socialism. Excellent.
> CUSINS. You really are an infernal old rascal.[6]

Furthermore, this Army feeds and shelters the body in return for dishonesty of the spirit, a rotten bargain wherever it is made. Mrs. Baines is as blind to this, and Barbara early in the play as naïve, as the missionaries in *A Passage to India*:

> Old Mr. Graysford and young Mr. Sorley made converts during a famine, because they distributed food; but when times improved they were naturally left alone again, and though surprised and aggrieved each time this happened, they never learnt wisdom.[7]

It is a mockery to attempt religion in a soul whose body is sore

5. Chesterton, P. 60.
6. *Major Barbara*, Act II.

7. E. M. Forster, *A Passage to India* (New York, 1924) p. 101.

beset by the seven deadly sins: "Food, clothing, firing, rent, taxes, respectability and children."[8] But religion is not a mockery at Perivale St. Andrews, where Undershaft has, as a moment's thought will show, set up a little island of private enterprise socialism, an examplar of all that socialism might be. In this earthly paradise, created by a man who is labelled throughout the play with tags that suggest the devil, capitalism has been only a means to an end. In the last scene there is even an indication that the guns may be also a means to the same utopian end.[9] This is hardly a plea for capitalism.

And behind the polemical structure of the play stands the polemical explanation of the Preface. But Shaw's "First Aid to Critics" does less to explain his attitude toward Undershaft than certain remarks in the *Preface to Mrs Warren's Profession*. In both cases a vital character has to choose between poverty (practical) and "infamy" (spiritual) and both are extreme cases chosen to strip the principle mercilessly. Both Undershaft and Mrs. Warren choose prostitution. The whole mystery of *Major Barbara* vanishes when we see Undershaft's dilemma in Mrs. Warren's:

> Though it is quite natural and *right* for Mrs. Warren to choose what is, according to her lights, the least immoral alternative, it is none the less infamous of society to offer such alternatives. For the alternatives offered are not morality and immorality, but two sorts of immorality.[1]

Seen in these terms, the choice between honest poverty and unscrupulous riches is an outmoded melodramatic cliché completely superseded by the choice between an immoral society and a moral society. The significance of millionaires changes radically. Balanced by Peter Shirley, his counterpart at the other end of the economic scale, our millionaire is an eloquent hyperbole, another example of that figure of speech so dear to Shaw's prose and so pitifully inadequate to the expression of our wars, our cruelties, our hypocrisies. This millionaire is, in other words, an attempt to open desperate darkness by a desperate illumination. For only the greatest munitions maker in England can, by a calm insistence on the Undershaft motto, "Unashamed," convey the shame that attaches to every one of us for our complicity in the crimes of capitalism. "The notion that you can earmark certain coins as tainted is an unpractical individualist superstition."[2] This much Shaw had already established in *Widowers' Houses* and *Mrs Warren's Profession*. In *Major Barbara*, he goes further, putting a more insistent pressure

8. *Major Barbara*, Act III.
9. Act III.
1. *Plays: Pleasant and Unpleasant*

(London, 1931), I, p. 166.
2. *Major Barbara*, Preface, p. 219.

on the limits of our complacency, and going one step beyond the guilt to the responsibility. The

> . . . enthusiastic young clergyman of the Established Church . . . cannot help himself by refusing to accept money from anybody except sweet old ladies with independent incomes and gentle and lovely ways of life. He has only to follow up the income of the sweet ladies to its industrial source, and there he will find Mrs. Warren's profession and the poisonous canned meat and all the rest of it. His own stipend has the same root. He must either share the world's guilt or go to another planet. He must save the world's honor if he is to save his own.[3]

Undershaft does just this. He at least is without self-deception. And he has also taken a step in the direction of saving the world's honor. As poor-but-honest teachers, mothers, writers, professional reformers and such, we are all too quick to excuse complicity by ranking its degrees, or to mask it under some disguise that conceals guilt but cures nothing. Speaking of an assassination attempt in Madrid, Shaw reminds us of a truth that applies equally well to terrorism of any kind:

> . . . he launches his sixpennorth of fulminate, missing his mark, but scattering the bowels of as many horses as any bull in the arena, and slaying twentythree persons, besides wounding ninety-nine. And of all these, the horses alone are innocent of the guilt he is avenging: had he blown all Madrid to atoms with every adult person in it, not one could have escaped the charge of being an accessory, before, at, and after the fact, to poverty and prostitution, to such wholesale massacre of infants as Herod never dreamt of, to plague, pestilence and famine, battle, murder and lingering death—perhaps not one who had not helped, through example, precept, connivance, and even clamor, to teach the dynamiter his well-learnt gospel of hatred and vengeance, by approving every day of sentences of years of imprisonment so infernal in their unnatural stupidity and panic-stricken cruelty, that their advocates can disavow neither the dagger nor the bomb without stripping the mask of justice and humanity from themselves also.[4]

Besides denying us the moral superiority to millionaires that we all clutch to our Pharisaic bosoms, Undershaft serves a second purpose. He is a reminder that, in any such world as ours, even as an individual, the man who accepts poverty is a social liability, both an active and a passive force for evil. Here is Shaw speaking *ex cathedra*:

Now what does this Let Him Be Poor mean? It means let him

3. *Major Barbara*, Preface, p. 219.   4. *Major Barbara*, Preface, pp. 232-33.

be weak. Let him be ignorant. Let him become a nucleus of disease. Let him be a standing exhibition and example of ugliness and dirt. Let him have rickety children. Let him be cheap, and drag his fellows down to his own price by selling himself to do their work. Let his habitations turn our cities into poisonous congeries of slums. Let his daughters infect our young men with the diseases of the streets, and his sons revenge him by turning the nation's manhood into scrofula, cowardice, cruelty, hypocrisy, political imbecility, and all the other fruits of oppression and malnutrition. Let the undeserving become still less deserving; and let the deserving lay up for himself, not treasures in heaven, but horrors in hell upon earth. This being so, is it really wise to let him be poor? Would he not do ten times less harm as a prosperous burglar, incendiary, ravisher or murderer, to the utmost limits of humanity's comparatively negligible impulses in these directions?[5]

A hundred learned commissions have sat since those words were written and have told us no more about the active dangers of poverty.

As to the passive dangers, in the Shavian theater early and late, the vital genius refuses martyrdom of this kind. All very well for Dick Dudgeon in *The Devil's Disciple* to put his neck into the noose out of a sense of honor (*l'acte gratuit* in an unfamiliar flavor), but the martyrdom of poverty produces the opposite result, loss of self-respect (not to mention teeth and other desirable attributes), and is rejcted by Mrs. Warren, who knows what the white lead factory does to a woman, by Violet, in *Man and Superman*, who knows that a husband with no money is no use as a husband, by Eliza Doolittle, who labors up out of the gutter in *Pygmalion*, by Ellie Dunn, daughter of an idealist, who is ready to sell herself to a repulsive millionaire in *Heartbreak House* because a soul is more expensive than a body, and most spectacularly in *The Millionairess*, by a lady who outdoes Undershaft in ruthlessness, which she loves for its own sake as few love milder virtues.

And Shaw reminds us again and again that any man or woman who sees how capitalism works, must either replace it or use it for his own survival. He is not one of those who believe that individual acts of anarchistic protest will gradually inspire some incalculable degree of rebellion in "the people" and lead to the revolution that will sweep all this away. And surely the increasing political conservatism of the labor unions in the last quarter century indicates that the working class is more inclined to reason like Andrew Undershaft than to reason like Karl Marx. But Shaw does more than justify the munitions millionaire as a private person. (One thundering

5. *Major Barbara*, Preface, p. 211.

denunciation in the Shavian vocabulary is powerfully cadenced up to the phrase, "a hopelessly Private Person.")[6] The insistent lesson of the play is that Undershaft (as even that chief of denigrators, the ex-wife, must finally admit) is socially as well as personally sound. The demonstration is logical to a wonder, but only if we take note of the missing term supplied in the second act. In Act One the major and the millionaire assert their opposed values: the soul and the pound sterling, or the Christian-social and the pagan-selfish points of view. In Act Three these resolve into a harmony so large that it sweeps into it the intellect of the ivory tower—Cusins—and the energy of the old aristocracy—Lady Brito-mart—in a joyful inclusiveness like the finale of Beethoven's Ninth, but returned at the last moment to a poignantly small comic diapason that reminds us we still live in this world as men have made it. The great sound, of which I have more to say later, the synthesis that does not yet exist in this world, is off stage, but it controls the ultimate meaning of the play. And only the vital genius, the man who has both brains and fight, and puts them to use on the side of life, can move society. But it is quite significant that in the Shavian theater the vital genius is so often a woman, which brings us back from Undershaft to his daughter.

Most certainly Barbara is her father's daughter. *Major Barbara* is also a family drama, as social as it is socialist. In fact, the public and private questions are no less interwoven than in *Oedipus Rex* or *Hamlet*. Besides her father, the heroine has a strong mother, a brother and sister, both nonentities, a prospective brother-in-law more null than all the rest, and a remarkable fiancé of her own. Among all these, Shaw schematizes and dramatizes the interplay of moral forces in society. In fact, since Undershaft's money and munitions are the real power behind the government of England, the drama may be said to expand to the same heroic magnitude as Greek or Elizabethan tragedy, but transposed into a key so different that we fail to recognize the old theme.

The strong bond between father and daughter is treated early and late in his career by Shaw, who did not wait for Freud to point it out to him. This theme interests him far more than mother-son relationships, largely because the mother's influence on the son seems to transmit weakness, while the fathers in question are usually unconventional and strong-willed men who (quite plausibly, as ordinary fathers will not think of training a *daughter* up to be a great man) consciously create strength and independence in their daughters. The necessary condition is, of course, that these fathers

6. "The man who cannot see that star-vation, overwork, dirt, and disease are as anti-social as prostitution—that they are the vices and virtues of a na-tion and not merely misfortunes—is (to put it as politely as possible) a hopelessly Private Person." *Plays: Pleasant and Unpleasant*, I, p. 166.

leave enough money to support an independent spirit, otherwise an intolerable luxury for a woman, since Shaw never fails to take into account that fact that female slavery (inside marriage or out) is firmly based on economic dependence and not, as presumably in the Stone Age, on biological factors. In *Cashel Byron's Profession*, his novel of 1886, the heroine horrifies all her Victorian acquaintances by talking unconventional common sense taught to her by her father, and by falling in love with an athlete for the sake of his physical beauty. In *The Millionairess* (1936), another daughter in love with the memory of a strong father triumphs over convention in every conceivable department. In *Major Barbara*, father and daughter interest each other at once when they meet as adults. This relationship is subtler and more dramatic. Since the Undershaft children do not know their father and have been brought up to deplore him (rather like the Clandon-Crampton clan, children of another strong mother and discarded father, in *You Never Can Tell*), there is both recognition and reversal in the return of Barbara from the blood-and-fire banner of her father in heaven to the blood-and-fire business of her father on earth. These two recognize each other at the end of Act I by an affinity of spirit more unmistakable than the strawberry marks in the old stories. Cusins acknowledges the bond when he says teasingly:

> A father's love for a grown-up daughter is the most dangerous of all infatuations. I apologize for mentioning my own pale, coy, mistrustful fancy in the same breath with it.[7]

And the Grecian overtones of mysterious intervention of fate (consonant with the subject Cusins professes) are strengthened indirectly when the long-lost daughter is found to have provided her foundling father with the very foundling son-in-law he needs. The Undershaft tradition requires that the business be handed down to an adopted son, and Barbara has unconsciously provided this quasi-incestuous heir. For the square knot of this family's relationship is tied even tighter when the reconciliation of father and daughter draws with it his former wife and her future husband into a community of sympathetic equals.

The schematic relation of Barbara with her mother is quite different. While the father functions psychologically and symbolically, the mother, Lady Britomart, is most interesting seen historically. She is unique among Shavian mothers, who, when they appear at all in Shaw's drama, neglect, pet and bully their sons, hamper and mislead their daughters. Some, like Mrs. Whitefield in *Man and Superman* and Mrs. Collins in *Getting Married*, are so thoroughly subjugated by Victorian womanism that they are merely

7. *Major Barbara*, Act II.

ineffectual, bewildered burdens on their competent children. The genuine crabby tyrant of the puritan fireside, like Mrs. Dudgeon in *The Devil's Disciple*, appears very seldom. But caricatures are not needed. Even the most enlightened mother, Mrs. Clandon in *You Never Can Tell*, is quite impossible. She is an Advanced Woman, theory-ridden and self-conscious in the extreme, and she fails precisely because of her determination to succeed, to form her children into models of future humanity.[8] She and Lady Britomart make the same mistakes, in both theory and practice, by assuming that life can be ladylike, and by cutting their children off from an imperfect father.

But Lady Britomart contains woman's unrealized potential, which shows itself best (as Shaw makes clear in *Misalliance*) in the aristocracy, whose women are neither hobbled by middle-class respectability nor crushed by the weight of poverty. True, this overpowering dowager is a stock figure of comedy, and Lady Britomart is introduced at the beginning of Act I in just this way. Superficially, she is like Lady Bracknell in Wilde's *The Importance of Being Earnest*, a woman whose husband must either abjectly submit, like Lord Bracknell, or leave home, like Undershaft. Nevertheless, the opening scene shows her son as a natural object for bullying. And, unlike Lady Bracknell, a pure comic figure, Lady Britomart moves her whole monolithic presence into the new world, and in moving shows us how much more she potentially is than the elegant bully of comedy. For though Wilde's dowager (and her daughter) are portrayed with all the accuracy of caricature, they are frozen in their entrancing poses, but Lady Britomart, her daughter, and all Shavian heroines are able to move and breathe, simply because Shaw likes women and understands what makes them tick, viz:

> I am a dramatic author, and people wonder what is the secret of my extraordinary knowledge of women which enchants the whole world. Women come to me and ask: "Where did you get this amazing knowledge of women?" Very often I am suspected of having in the course of my life been a most abandoned character, and that is how I acquired this knowledge. But I never acquired it at all. I always assumed that a woman was a person exactly like myself, and that is how the trick is done.[9]

The comment applies most fully to the fully realized character of Major Barbara, but behind her stands Lady Britomart, who contains in herself the qualities that, in the next generation, emanci-

8. "The vilest abortionist is he who attempts to mould a child's character." *Man and Superman* (London, 1903), p. 213.

9. "As Bernard Shaw Sees Woman," *The New York Times Magazine* (June 19, 1927), 1–2.

pated from the fierce corsetry of Victorian rules, must resolve themselves either into the freedom and energy of her daughter Barbara or into the nullity of Sarah. The difference between the two daughters is reinforced by the difference between their fiancés. The imbecilic Lomax "likes Sarah and thinks it will be rather a lark to marry her."[1] Cusins, the character derived from Gilbert Murray, Regius Professor of Greek at Oxford during the early part of this century, is a man of intellect, poise and passion, whose state of mind is accurately characterized by Lady Britomart when she says he "went to the Salvation Army to worship Barbara and nothing else."[2] The word "worship" combines colloquialism with the religious overtone that Shaw intends. For not two but three religions are present in this play: the Salvation Army's, Undershaft's, and Shaw's—Creative Evolution. It is the last of these that triumphs, even though it is not understood, scarcely mentioned, by any character in the play. It is the Life Force that leads many a Shavian hero into the arms of a vital genius, although he should—and does—know better. On the other hand, the Life Force does not depend on mystical apprehensions. Like all the attractive women in Shaw's works, Barbara Undershaft has the energy that is the eternal delight of Shavian suitors. And Cusins, like other Shavian heroes, makes the not entirely foolish assumption that a girl who is good at one sort of thing will be good at another. He puts the classic Shavian case with the calm of a desperate lucidity when he says:

> Mr. Undershaft: I am in many ways a weak, timid, ineffectual person; and my health is far from satisfactory. But whenever I feel that I must have anything, I get it, sooner or later. I feel that way about Barbara. I dont like marriage; I feel intensely afraid of it; and I dont know what I shall do with Barbara or what she will do with me. But I feel that I and nobody else must marry her. Please regard that as settled.—Not that I wish to be arbitrary; but why should I waste your time discussing what is inevitable?[3]

Or, as Shaw puts it in his stage direction for Cusins' entrance: "By the operation of some instinct which is not merciful enough to blind him with the illusions of love, he is obstinately bent on marrying Barbara."[4] His enslavement goes further than this. In Act II Cusins makes a confession:

> Yes, a confession. Listen, all. Until I met Barbara I thought myself in the main an honorable, truthful man, b~cause I wanted the approval of my conscience more than I wanted anything else. But the moment I saw Barbara, I wanted her far more than the approval of my conscience.[5]

1. *Major Barbara*, Act I.
2. Act I.
3. Act II.
4. Act I.
5. Act III.

And here again Shaw insists on the extreme case in order to sharpen the edge of his argument. Such abjectness is normally portrayed only as an example of the horrible dominance of the female, which leads some men to say things like:

> You may add that in the hive and the anthill we see fully realized the two things that some of us must dread for our own species—the dominance of the female and the dominance of the collective.[6]

But Shaw, as I have already pointed out, sees women as people like himself, a compliment we should be quick to accept. And in the dramatic working-out of his relationship it is quite clear that Cusins, though he may think himself enslaved to a woman, is in fact enslaved to the Life Force that makes itself felt through her, no less in her social crusading than in her sexual charm. Tanner, in *Man and Superman*, is pursued and entrapped by Ann Whitefield, and, as one realist comments: "I dunno about the bee and the spider. But the marked down victim, that's what you are and no mistake; and a jolly good job for you, too, I should say."[7] We are not allowed to doubt for one moment that Tanner's resistance and capitulation are anything but a delightful dance of the mating season. Even more so in the case of Cusins, whose beloved has other things on her mind than husband-hunting. The effect would be quite different if Barbara were really her mother all over again. It is amusing enough that one of Oscar Wilde's young men should remark: "All women become like their mothers; that is their tragedy. No man does; that is his."[8] But the truth, as Wilde points out elsewhere, is never pure and very seldom simple. Between mother and daughter, in this case, two factors intervene to create a considerable change. First, the difference of a generation puts Barbara into the period of the liberated woman, though she is an early example. Second, she is a vital genius, one of a long line of such women in Shaw's plays, and of them all Barbara is most like Saint Joan, a character who needs none of the hampering protection of Wilton Circle or the circling camouflage of petticoats. Both heroines work in uniform—or, to be exact, out of the normal uniform for women. In the same way, their relations with men are outside all ordinary patterns. Saint Joan is not the camp follower conventional gossips assume her to be. Neither does Barbara fit the expected patterns in her dealings with Cusins. In fact, she reverses even the established Shavian pattern, the pursuit of the man by the woman, for her magnetism is so powerful that Cusins, a man of unusual personal dignity, literally joins the parade that follows after her. This is not

6. C. S. Lewis, *Surprised by Joy* (New York, 1956), p. 9.
7. *Man and Superman*, p. 67.

8. *The Plays of Oscar Wilde* (New York, n.d.), p. 70.

bullying, unless we accuse the cosmos of bullying. The test of the relationship comes at the moment when Cusins must make his final choice, knowing that if he chooses wrong he may lose the woman about whom he holds such extreme views. But he does make his choice, saying, ". . . I had to decide without consulting you."[9] Later, with "evident dread," he asks, "And now, is it all over between us?"[1] But the man's soul is his own, although he does not call it his own. He says of his business proposition:

> It is not the sale of my soul that troubles me: I have sold it too often to care about that. I have sold it for a professorship. I have sold it for an income. I have sold it to escape being imprisoned for refusing to pay taxes for hangmen's ropes and unjust wars and things that I abhor.[2]

Considering all this, it is a remarkable tribute that he should not have sold his soul for Barbara. Clearly, he is not a man to be tyrannized, for all his infatuation, nor is she any kind of a tyrant. Here, and elsewhere in Shaw, the implication is that the more freedom and strength a woman has, the less domineering she will be.

Here the two thematic elements in the play merge. Socialism and feminism move to the same kind of social dynamic. Pernicious alternatives can lead only to a pernicious choice. Women in a state of slavery and men in a state of poverty must make a private choice that saves the self, and any critic must morally approve that choice, whatever pieties it may seem to contravene. Our horror at selling the body or selling the soul must be translated into social terms, remembering always that Shaw deplores the individual gesture of protest or, at least in theory, the individual gesture of charity. The whole basis of society must be revolutionized to make the world fit for humanity. The foundling then need not choose between becoming the next Undershaft and becoming another Peter Shirley, worthless to society and himself except as an interchangeable unit, and often, as here, a pure liability to both. A woman would not have to choose between death in the white lead factory and being, as Shaw politely puts it, "a jewelled vamp" or, in the upper classes, between being an unpleasantly overbearing mammoth and an even more unpleasantly submissive mite. In any case, capitalism and inequality are condemned as much by the loathesomeness of their successes as by the pathos of their failures.

The successes of Andrew Undershaft may seem to deny all this and do confuse the interpretation of the play unless they are sorted out from other ideas of Shaw's, chiefly the idea that some people are natural bosses and will achieve power in any setting, whether

9. *Major Barbara*, Act III.   2. Act III.
1. Act III.

the factory, the government, the sweatshop or the brothel. These views are expatiated upon in the prefaces to *The Millionairess* and *The Apple Cart* and elsewhere. In these plays the heiress in one and the king in the other are stripped of the advantages with which they begin, after which they go on to demonstrate Shaw's thesis by rising to power again through their own executive abilities. The Shavian boss is not entirely distinct from the vital genius, except that she (or he, as the case may be) adds managing ability to natural vitality. Rare, but never quite clear, cases like Eliza Doolittle in *Pygmalion* may have vital genius without being natural bosses. But the bosses run through Shaw's work in a long comforting line that includes Caesar, Saint Joan, Mrs. Warren, Lina Szczepanowska, Epifania Ognisanti di Parerga, King Magnus,[3] and our own man Undershaft. They can save humanity from the perils of democracy, the perils of chaos and ineffectuality. But, even though Undershaft is one of this perhaps saving remnant, and even though the author's admiration for such men colors the portrait, that does not change the meaning of capitalism in the play. When Shaw condemned democracy, he was far from condoning oligarchy. The two go together in his polemics as they have in fact. Shaw's attacks on "freedom" or in his terms, anarchy, are in essence attacks on free enterprise or, in his terms, economic anarchy. And the apologists for laissez-faire capitalism prove the correctness of this approach by making the same combination in reverse, treating limitations on free enterprise as limitations on personal freedom. So the success of Undershaft, as a man and as a character, prove exactly nothing about the value of millionaires. Dominators will rise to dominate under any system, and "Communism is the fairy godmother who can transform Bosses into 'servants to all the rest'; but only a creed of Creative Evolution can set the souls of the people free."[4] As is usual in Shaw, all ideas work together, but in a work of art there must be a center. In his 'Preface on Bosses," Shaw says, "But private property is not the subject of my demonstration in The Millionairess."[5] The reverse is true of *Major Barbara. Private property is the subject of his demonstration; bosses are not: they are merely one instrument in the service of the idea that private property must go, and with it all the sham and all the cant disguising its hideous realities.*

These changes in emphasis may be confusing, but we know that Shaw did not write for schools or schoolteachers and dreaded the day (now fully dawned) when he would be forced on students as

3. From the plays (in order) *Caesar and Cleopatra, Saint Joan, Mrs. Warren's Profession, Misalliance, The Millionairess,* and *The Apple Cart* [Editor.]

4. *The Simpleton, The Six, and The Millionairess* (London, 1936), p. 129.
5. *Ibid.*

required reading. He conceived each play as a piece of dramatic art, a piece for the theater, although powerfully aware of drama as "demonstration." He did not forget the function of bosses in writing *Major Barbara* or deny his socialism in *The Millionairess*, but each has its emphasis. There is a special emphasis also in Undershaft's remarks on warfare. Although he is as plausible as the devil who represents worldly wisdom in *Man and Superman*, he is not merely a devil's advocate. The content of the two speeches that follow is very much the same, but the context is so different that in one instance a truth is being used to defeat the human spirit, and in the other that same truth is one of its triumphs. In the third act of *Man and Superman*, the Devil says:

> In a battle two bodies of men shoot at one another with bullets and explosive shells until one body runs away, when the others chase the fugitives on horseback and cut them to pieces as they fly. And this, the chronicle concludes, shews the greatness and majesty of empires, and the littleness of the vanquished. Over such battles the people run about the streets yelling with delight, and egg their Governments on to spend hundreds of millions of money in the slaughter, whilst the strongest Ministers dare not spend an extra penny in the pound against the poverty and pestilence through which they themselves daily walk. I could give you a thousand instances; but they all come to the same thing: the power that governs the earth is not the power of Life but of Death; and the inner need that has nerved Life to the effort of organizing itself into the human being is not the need for higher life but for a more efficient engine of destruction.[6]

These lines, which resound with appalling relevance in the nuclear age, are answered in their own context by Don Juan, representative of the Life Force, who does not deny their truth, but does recognize their devilishness and their partiality. Certainly their cynicism, like all cynicism ultimately, is devilish, but the same does not hold true for Undershaft's similar remarks in *Major Barbara*. It will not do to forget that the subject of the colloquy in hell is, naturally, the nature of man, whereas Undershaft's subject, as we shall see, is the nature of war. And in complaining about the nature of man, it is only reasonable to note his unreasonable expenditures on death. But the Devil is by implication taunting mankind for engaging in warfare at all, while Undershaft is getting a somewhat different question, central to the ideas of the play: the illusions with which society drapes the obscene limbs of war, illusions expressed in our own time by such euphemisms as "clean bomb" and "tactical nuclear weapons," and "pacification." A fool like Lomax assumes that conversation with a maker of cannons calls for a mealy mouth:

6. *Man and Superman*, pp. 103–104.

"Well, the more destructive war becomes, the sooner it will be abolished, eh?" Undershaft answers:

> Not at all. The more destructive war becomes the more fascinating we find it. No, Mr. Lomax: I am obliged to you for making the usual excuse for my trade; but I am not ashamed of it. I am not one of those men who keep their morals and their business in watertight compartments. All the spare money my trade rivals spend on hospitals, cathedrals, and other receptacles for conscience money, I devote to experiments and researches in improved methods of destroying life and property. I have always done so; and I always shall.[7]

But Undershaft, though diabolonian in one sense, is not excluding, as the Devil does, all other human values. He says a moment later: "For me there is only one true morality; but it might not fit you, as you do not manufacture aerial battleships. There is only one true morality for every man; but every man has not the same true morality."[8] This is not a man who celebrates murder, merely a realist who calls it by its true name. If his realism makes us shudder, that is intended to make us shudder at the size of the "defense" budget, at the work going forward daily on ABC Warfare, at the truth itself, not at Undershaft. That he should be the form in which the Life Force triumphs under our present system is in fact our tragedy.

And even if there were any doubt about the meaning of the great final triumph which sweeps along every member of the family in a degree of commitment and comprehension exactly tailored to his dramatic figure, there could be no mistake about the meaning of the failures. Poverty *is* a crime: one that fits, with only a little Machiavellianism in the logic, any working definition of the terms. If crime is an action that harms other people or the state, then the crime of poverty is enunciated in the Jeremiad already quoted on the subject of 'Let Him Be Poor." If crime is that which society punishes, then poverty is a crime. (Logicians are asked to sympathize *pro tem* with Shaw's preference for strict truth over strict logic.) It would take no particular ingenuity to show that the poor are daily and hourly punished as no enlightened state would punish any criminal. Shaw's debt to Butler and Bellamy in this matter is no secret. The pitch of persuasiveness to which he raises the idea is his own.

Besides being based on the same kind of social dynamic, Shaw's socialism and his feminism merge in another and more significant way in *Major Barbara*. As I said earlier, there are three religions in this play. Just as in *Saint Joan*, two religions grapple for the her-

---

7. *Major Barbara*, Act I.   8. Act I.

oine's soul. Catholicism and Protestantism are so mighty, with all the secular issues weighting them both, that Joan is crushed between them. The religions that fight for Barbara's soul are quite another matter. The Salvation Army, in spite of Shaw's faint praise in the preface, is no match for St. Andrew Undershaft. His creed is simple: "My religion? Well, my dear. I am a millionaire. That is my religion."[9] This is to say: I am a materialist and a realist. He has seen and understood the realist. He has seen and understood the reality that Barbara at last understands when she says:

> Undershaft and Bodger; their hands stretch everywhere: when we feed a starving fellow creature, it is with their bread, because there is no other bread; when we tend the sick, it is in the hospitals they endow; if we turn from the churches they build, we must kneel on the stones of the streets they pave. As long as that lasts. there is no getting away from them. Turning our backs on Bodger and Undershaft is turning our backs on life.[1]

When she has seen the benefits of millionairism as well as the bitterness of the bread of charity, she grows even more dithyrambic:

> ... it was really all the human souls to be saved; not weak souls in starved bodies, sobbing with gratitude for a scrap of bread and treacle, but fullfed, quarrelsome, snobbish, uppish creatures, all standing on their little rights and dignities, and thinking that my father ought to be greatly obliged to them for making so much money for him—and so he ought. That is where salvation is really wanted. My father shall never throw it in my teeth again that my converts were bribed with bread. . . . I have got rid of the bribe of bread. I have got rid of the bribe of heaven. Let God's work be done for its own sake; the work he had to create us to do because it cannot be done except by living men and women. When I die, let him be in my debt, not I in his; and let me forgive him as becomes a woman of my rank.[2]

In a play that ends (almost) on this note, Christianity may be vanquished, but materialism has not triumphed, except in the sense that a millionaire has been needed—and a millionaire who makes that his religion is clearly a vital genius—to create a model of socialism. Instead of being crushed between the two forces, Barbara steps from the shaken foundation to the solid one, but the rhythm of the comedy implies that she will go on upward. As the curtain falls she is babbling about a house in the village to live in with her Dolly. The contrast with the ending of *Saint Joan* is instructive. That play ends in bitter sadness, with the question: "Oh God that madest this beautiful earth, when will it be ready to receive Thy saints?" And the implied answer is: Not now; perhaps never. Even taking into account the passage of two decades and a world war,

9. Act II.
1. Act III.

2. Act III.

this is more than a historical difference, for Major Ba... one of God's saints but one of the saints of this worl... possible to infer that the world must be saved by work... that innocence cannot carry us through, but intellect... power may. And will power must be backed up by fir... ower. Therefore this play needs no epilogue. Its last lines explode forward into an essentially new future. Barbara drags her mother off to pick out a house in the village, and Undershaft orders his new son-in-law to report for work: "Six o'clock tomorrow morning, Euripides." Two things are certain. Babies are certain, babies blessed with a mother who cares about human souls. This is not a guess. The Life Force means business, not pleasure. And guns for the revolution are almost a certainty. If we read them as standing for all the power that "can destroy the higher powers just as a tiger can destroy a man," then it becomes certain that guns are the tool of revolution no less than the tool of oppression. Disinterested intellect dare not leave the world to the vested interests. This was sometime a platitude, but now the time gives it teeth. The hope is classic, then. Bigger and better babies, and power on the side of life instead of death.

> Plato says, my friend, that society cannot be saved until either the Professors of Greek take to making gunpowder, or else the makers of gunpowder become Professors of Greek.[3]

Major Barbara is Shaw's Republic of saints.

SIDNEY P. ALBERT

"In More Ways Than One": *Major Barbara's* Debt to Gilbert Murray†

N.B. The Euripidean verses in the second act of Major Barbara are not by me, nor even directly by Euripides. They are by Professor Gilbert Murray, whose English version of The Bacchae came into our dramatic literature with all the impulsive power of an original work shortly before Major Barbara was begun. The play, indeed, stands indebted to him in more ways than one.

G.B.S.

The published text of *Major Barbara* bears this introductory note by the author, set off as conspicuously as possible from both play

3. Act III.
† It is always one of the games of scholarship to trace down sources—an exercise that presumably leads to a deeper understanding of the work. Certainly Sidney P. Albert's use of the correspondence between Shaw and Gil-

bert Murray throws fresh light on an old subject. Dr. Albert is a philosopher as well as a Shavian; his examination of Shaw's "debt" appeared in the *Educational Theatre Journal*, Vol. 20 (May, 1968), pp. 123–140.

and Preface. When, some forty years after composing the stage play, Bernard Shaw published the screen version in 1945, he revised this note extensively, but still left unspecified the ways of indebtedness: "My play stands indebted to Gilbert Murray in more ways than the way from Athens."[1] In both versions the note acknowledges explicitly only the borrowing from Murray's translation of the *Bacchae*. Later on Shaw disclosed a second way in which he drew upon his friend, namely, as a model for one of the play's *dramatis personae*. But are there even more ways in which *Major Barbara* "stands indebted" to Gilbert Murray?

Murray has left in print two reminiscences about his involvement in Shaw's drama. The first appears in a brief article, "The Early G.B.S.," published in the *New Statesman and Nation*, August 16, 1947. The second account, which varies in minor details, appeared several years later, in an essay titled "A Few Memories," written for the Shaw memorial issue of *Drama* (Spring, 1951). In these reminiscences Murray reports that Shaw once informed him that he was writing a play called *Murray's Mother in Law*, and asked whether he minded being represented in the play as a foundling. Murray replied, "Not in the least." A year later Shaw came to Oxford to read the play, now called *Major Barbara*, to the Murrays. Since Murray's wife, Lady Mary Murray, and his mother-in-law, the Countess of Carlisle, evidently were models for Barbara and Lady Britomart respectively, Shaw wanted to make sure that nothing in the play would offend the family. In the later article Murray questions his own likeness to 'Cusens,' the misspelling of whose name became chronic with him. In the earlier account Murray gives a telling, albeit passing, glimpse of the reception the Murrays accorded Shaw's new play: "At the end of Act 2 my wife and I were thrilled with enthusiasm, especially at the Salvation Army scenes. Act 3, in which the idealists surrender to the armament industries, was a terrible disappointment to us and, I think, unsatisfying to Shaw himself. He tried to justify his general line of solution, but muttered: 'I don't know how to end the thing.' He did to some extent alter it." This muted report, it will be seen, hardly does justice to the impact on the play of Murray's "terrible disappointment" with its final act.

On July 6, 1905, Shaw had retired to Derry in County Cork, Ireland, in order to escape the pressures of his many other commitments and complete the composition of his play. At that time only about one act and a half had been written. He finished the whole work September 8, 1905. On the 29th of September he left Ireland, reaching London the following afternoon. It was the day after

1. *Major Barbara*, London: Penguin Books, 1945, p. v.

his return, Sunday, October 1st, that he went to Oxford to read his play to the Murrays. The effect of this reading he imparted to J. E. Vedrenne (Granville Barker's partner in management of the Royal Court Theatre, where the play was to be produced) in the post-script of a letter on October 2nd: "I now doubt whether Major B will be ready. I read it yesterday to Barker & Murray. The last act is a total failure: I must sit down and write it absolutely afresh."[2] Since it is extremely unlikely that Shaw would have undertaken to read a play of *Major Barbara's* length twice in the same day, Barker must have been another interested member of the audience at the Oxford reading.

The first notable revision resulting from that reading, and a re-luctant one at that, was made in the final line of the first scene of the third act. Years later Lillah McCarthy related that Shaw told the following story to Robert Bridges: "When I wrote 'Major Bar-bara,' the characters were modelled on people I knew. The like-nesses were unmistakable, and therefore I was anxious to make sure that no words used in the play could hurt the originals. I read the play to an old, dear friend of the family. All went well till I came to the lines: 'Never call me Mother again.' 'Oh,' said she, 'you must not say that for those are the very words used by ... (the character copied in the play), and used in tragic circumstances.' "[3]

The "dear friend of the family" very likely was Lady Mary Mur-ray, and the occasion the October 1st reading. The actual manu-script line was "And dont call me mother," spoken by Lady Brito-mart to her son, Stephen. Since Lady Carlisle had serious rifts with virtually every one of her six sons it is impossible to identify with certainty the particular son in question, but it was in all probability the eldest son, Charles James Stanley Howard, Lord Morpeth.[4]

Shaw changed the line, "And dont call me mother," to the less concise "And dont forget that you have outgrown your mother."[5] But on the very same day of his visit to Oxford (October 1st) he sent a post card to Murray from London:

10. Adelphi Terrace. W.C.

I find that the result of our conference is a most appallingly strong temptation *not* to delete "And dont call me mother" but to develop it to full tragic proportions with the utmost Euripid-ity. Fortunately there is not room in the play for this; so I hand

2. Quoted by permission of the present holder of the manuscript letter, the Ac-ademic Center Library, University of Texas.

3. *Myself and My Friends*, London: Thornton Butterworth, 1933, p. 166. Ellipsis is Lillah McCarthy's.

4. See Dorothy Henley, *Rosalind How-ard: Countess of Carlisle*, London: Ho-

garth Press, 1958, Ch. 3, "Six Broth-ers," for details of Lady Carlisle's strained relations with her sons, includ-ing her break with the eldest son.

5. British Museum, MS 50616D, folio 52. Manuscripts and other materials from the Shaw Papers are quoted with the kind permission of The Trustees of the British Museum.

the temptation on to you. Clearly there is a great dramatic theme here—a Woman Lear with three sons—just the sort of Æschylean subject in modern life you want.

I am quite desperate about my last act: I think I must simply rewrite it. Merely cutting the cackle—and cackle is just what it is—will be no use.

G.B.S.[6]

So Shaw undertook to rewrite the ending of the play, after drawing emotional sustenance from a rousing Salvation Army memorial service at the Royal Albert Hall on Monday, October 2nd. He repaired to Edstaston, home of his sister-in-law and her husband, Colonel Cholmondeley, in Shropshire, and began writing once more on October 4th. The following day he wrote to Beatrice Webb in the same vein as he had written to Vedrenne two days before. But this time he went on to tell how unusual was the necessity to rewrite: "Charlotte & her sister enjoyed Derry so extraordinarily that I got a sort of secondhand enjoyment—largely mixed with resignation—out of it; but it is significant of the worthlessness of the climate that though I thought I had finished my play, the result of my reading it to Gilbert Murray in Oxford on Sunday is that I am now writing the last scene over again—the first time I have ever had to do such a thing."[7] He remained at Edstaston rewriting until October 13, and, according to the notation at the end of the revised version, completed the revision in London on October 15.

Because of Murray's close association with *Major Barbara* there has been speculation that he was to some extent involved in the writing of the play. Dame Sybil Thorndike, for one, has drawn this inference from a letter (reprinted below) Shaw wrote to Murray on October 5, 1905. Lacking access to Murray's side of the correspondence, she concludes that the letter "makes it clear that Murray had a hand in its composition."[8] Since the claim rests on a letter written after Shaw had read a completed version of the play to Murray, any question of collaboration reduces to one about the nature and extent of Murray's assistance in the rewriting his criticism occasioned. The answer is to be sought, not in a single letter, but in the whole correspondence between the two friends during the period from October to December, 1905. Happily both sides of that correspondence have survived, although in widely separated repositories. They are now brought together for the first time for examination in relation to the manuscript changes upon which they bear.

6. All of the Shaw communications to Murray are used by permission of the British Drama League.
7. Passfield Trust Papers, British Library of Political and Economic Science. By permission of the Passfield Trust.
8. *Gilbert Murray: An Unfinished Autobiography*, ed. Jean Smith and Arnold Toynbee, London: George Allen & Unwin, 1960, p. 155.

Here then, in chronological order, are the letters, quoted in full, beginning with that of Murray on October 2nd:[9]

131, Banbury Road, Oxford

Oct. 2 1905

My dear Shaw,

In brooding over Act iii, the accompanying thoughts came to me. I put them down in the form of a dialogue merely for clearness' sake, on the chance of your finding them some use. What I am driving at, is to get the real dénouement of the play, after Act ii. And I think that something like what I suggest *is* the real dénouement. It makes Cusens come out much stronger, but I think that rather an advantage. Otherwise you get a simple defeat of the Barbara principles by the Undershaft principles, which is neither what one wants, nor so interesting as the (as it seems to me) right way out: viz. that the Barbara principles should, after their first crushing defeat, turn upon the U. principles, and embrace them with a view of destroying or subduing them for the B.P.'s own ends. It is a gamble, and the issue uncertain.

Excuse the cheek of this interference. It is indeed "a bit thick." And it may be only a nuisance; but it seemed to me that this was your real meaning, and that you had not brought it out clearly. And I am so tremendously interested and moved by Act ii that the problem keeps working in my mind.

I expect that one error—perhaps the only one in the bones of the thing—is that you have made Undershaft too strong and both Barbara and Cusens too weak. You cant get any but an unhappy solution if they are really overpowered. (This looks as if it were all a plot to induce you not to represent me drunk like Prossie [in *Candida*]. And I am not sure that the incident is right. But it is perhaps the sin of all others which I least mind being associated with; and my motives are pure.) Also I rather think, though I cant be sure, that there are a few lines here and there which definitely blur the right impression and give a false one . . . I mean, as the "meaning" of the last Act.

I must post this at once, lest I repent of rushing in between the author and his play.

Yours very sincerely,

G M.

Accompanying Murray's letter is the following dialogue:

9. The correspondence about *Major Barbara* began, of course, with Shaw's post card of October 1st already quoted. The three Murray letters to Shaw, including the dialogue passages, are published by permission of the copyright owners, George Allen & Unwin Ltd. and of their present holder, the Academic Center Library, The University of Texas, to whose Librarian, Mrs. Mary M. Hirth, I am particularly indebted. The Shaw-Murray correspondence, as well as the passages from the *Major Barbara* manuscripts, are reproduced with a bare minimum of editorial emendation. Ellipses are those of the writers unless otherwise indicated, and line outs indicate pertinent cancelled wording.

Somewhere late in Act II, when it has become clear that the Army and society in g[e]neral is run by Bodgers [sic] and Undershaft: that they hold the lever that works society.

Und. Wouldnt you like to get your hand on the lever?

Cusens. If I did, I would work it very differently from what you think.

Und. You would work it very differently from what y o u think![1]

In Act iii, before and after the Armourer's Faith.

Someone, perhaps Lady Brit. "I have no patience with all these fads. You can use your arms for philanthropy if you like!

Und.   No, none of [t]hat. You must swear to the Armourer's Faith &c &c. (*Gives it, as at present.*) You must swear to that.

This depends, of course, on how far B is with him, or is keeping aloof

Cus.   Not a bit of it. I am not going to swear to anything. I want (or Barbara and I want) to get the lever in ~~our~~ my hands, and then I shall see what I want to do—or what Barbara wants to do. It may be all sorts of things.

Und.   All right. Dont swear. You're all right, and in a year's time you'll be just like me! (*Gasp from Barbara.*) You'll love the business, and run it for all it is worth, and come at six in the morning &c &c.

Cus.   I shall probably love the business, because I always do like any work I am doing; and I shall come at six in the morning, because that sort of [t]hing is ~~a habit~~ a second nature with me! But whether I shall be like you . . .

Und.   You will; that's a[l]l right.

Cus.   I venture to think I have got more will power than you.

Und.   More will power than m e!

This c^d be developed

Cus.   Yes; you're entirely in the power of the business. You dont work it, it works you. You say you're a lever to move society; but who works the lever? Society itself and all the rascality of society. You simply drift . . . I wonder whether I should drift too.
(*Remark from Lomax or the like?*)

CUS. Plato says that society cannot be saved until either the Professors of Greek take to making whiskey and gunpowder, or else the makers of whiskey and gunpowder become professors of Greek.

Lady B. Nonsense. There werent any professors of Greek in Plato's time. ~~I suppose that is why he wrote it so well.~~

1. Here and elsewhere in the dialogue Murray employs Shaw's own technical devices of spacing the letters of a word for emphasis.

CUS. There was a Salvation Army, though . . . .It is a frightful gamble but I'ld [sic] like to try it.

Lomax. There you're unjust. It [is] a sound business affair, no gambling. I'll say that for the old man.

CUS. Barbara's a born gambler, too.

Barb. Yes! (*This point could be explained, if necessary.*)

CUS. ~~So am I.~~ Then here goes.—Mephistophiles, give me the power, and I'll take it. But I'll make no pledge. I may use it for &c &c

UND. That's all right, my boy. You'll use it just as I use it; You love power, with all your delicacy of intellect. You'll want more of it. It'll grow under your hand; and you'll live for it . . . for power and for ~~the firm of~~ "Andrew Undershaft"!

CUS. Well, all the powerful men in Euripides are bad. I have often wondered whether . . . .

BARB. Dolly, have you no faith in anything? I know you hadnt in the Army?

CUS. Well, I have a kind of strong belief that if you and I really want to do a thing, we can do it.

BARB. (Some Salvation Army religious phrase? Something she said in Ac[t] ii, about God helping them, or faith in God.)

The letter Shaw wrote in reply has already appeared, by itself, in *Gilbert Murray: An Unfinished Autobiography* (pp. 155-7). As here reprinted it contains some minor emendations, based upon the original.

Edstaston, Wem, Shropshire.
7th October 1905

Dear Murray

Thanks for the Barbara stuff. If anything further occurs to you, send it along.

I want to get Cusins beyond the point of wanting power. I shall use your passage to bring out the point that Undershaft is a fly on the wheel; but Cusins would not make the mistake of imagining that he could be anything else. The fascination that draws him in is the fascination of reality, or rather—for it is hardly a fascination—the impossibility of refusing to put his hand to Undershaft's plough, which is at all events doing something, when the alternative is to hold aloof in a superior attitude and beat the air with words. To use your metaphor of getting his hand on the lever, his choice lies, not between going with Undershaft or not going with him, but between standing on the footplate at work, and merely sitting in a first class carriage reading Ruskin & explaining what a low dog the driver is and how steam is ruining the country.

I am writing the whole scene over again. The moisture which serves for air in Ireland spoiled it hopelessly. I will send the new version to you when it is in shape.

I have taken rather special care to make Cusins the reverse in every point of the theatrical strong man. I want him to go on his quality wholly, and not to make the smallest show of physical robustness or brute determination. His selection by Undershaft should be a puzzle to the people who believe in the strong-silent-still-waters-run-deep hero of melodrama. The very name Adolphus Cusins is selected to that end.

As to the triumph of Undershaft, that is inevitable because I am in the mind that Undershaft is in the right, and that Barbara and Adolphus, with a great deal of his natural insight and clever-ness, are very young, very romantic, very academic, very ignorant of the world. I think it would be unnatural if they were able to cope with him. Cusins averts discomfiture & scores off him by wit & humorous dexterity; but the facts are too much for him; and his strength lies in the fact that he, like Barbara, refuses the Impossibilist position (which their circumstances make particu-larly easy for them) even when the alternative is the most sensa-tionally anti-moral department of commerce. The moral is drawn by Lomax "There is a certain amount of tosh about this notion of wickedness."

I have been writing this letter in scraps for three days—impossible to write letters here. I shall be back in London on Friday at latest.

Handsome of me not to make you a Rhodes scholar, by the way.

GBS

At the top of his next letter Murray wrote out in Greek. πυκινὸν δόμον ἐλθεῖν. This letter bears the same date as Shaw's, evidently crossing the latter in the post:

Oct. 7 1905.   131, Banbury Road, Oxford.

My dear Shaw,

About "a bit thick:" Homer, speaking of Autolycus, the prince and archetype of robbers, uses the phrase "pŭkĭnŏn dŏmŏn ĕlthĕῐn" meaning "to come into a thick—i.e. a strong or fortified—house" but it would also construe "It was thick (a bit thick) to come to the house." Which fairly suits the Undershaft circumstances. Autolycus simply came as a burglar.

On thinking it over, it seems to me that the *labelling* of Cusens as me is a flaw in the play! (I hesitated to say this, lest it should seem as if my feelings were hurt. They are not in the least hurt, there is nothing whatever to hurt them: but my judg-ment remains pretty firm.) I think you fall between two stools a little. If you made a study, or caricature, of me, it would no doubt be edifying and interesting and "legitimate." If you got Barker up like me, with spectacles and a mustache and a bald wig, & had all the Euripides business, as now, it would have a kind of music-hall funniness for the few people who knew about me, though I dont think it would be high art. But I feel now a sort of swear in it, something that leads one on a wrong scent. . . . As if, for instance, you ga[ve] Undershaft an orchid and an eyeglass, and said he made screws in Birmingham, without otherwise changing his character. It would seem pointless; a joke, but a joke not worth making.

Do not bother about this—I mean, dont treat this as a personal request. It is only a piece of advice. Has W A seen it, and, if so, what does he say? Of course I am [r]ather in the habit of thinking that you dont know how good your best work is, and that consequently you allow the Devil to come and sow tares in it. But I think these labels—Australian, Greek Professor, translator of Euripides—are rather in the nature of tares.

My blessings on Act iii. I do hope it is shaping well.

> Yours ever
> G M.

In a week or so Shaw completed the rewriting, although he later made additional modifications in the script. Soon thereafter he was caught up in rehearsals, so that he did not write to Murray again until just after the play's opening. But before turning to that phase of the correspondence, it will be well to pause and consider what bearing the October letters have on the composition of Shaw's drama.

Fortunately, it is possible to compare the contents of these letters with the *Major Barbara* manuscripts in order to trace their influence on the rewriting of the play. It will be useful to begin with the Greek phrase in Murray's October 7th letter, since this appears in the first act of *Major Barbara*. There is a puzzling aspect to the correspondence insofar as it deals with this phrase. In the second paragraph of his October 2nd letter Murray describes his interference as "a bit thick." Then, without intervening comment from Shaw, he begins his next letter, "About 'a bit thick' . . ." The first impression is of the loss of a bridging communication from Shaw. But there is a simpler hypothesis, based on evidence in the play's manuscript notebooks.

Shaw wrote his first draft consecutively on the recto pages of a notebook, leaving the adjoining verso pages blank and available for lengthy intercalary or substituted passages. In all likelihood these extra page modifications were added in the course of the revisory process. Murray's phrase from Homer appears on the verso page across from where it fits into the continuous text. This is the corrected speech:

> Cusins (gently) If I may say so, Lady Brit., I think Charles has expressed what we all feel. Homer, speaking of Autolycus, uses the same phrase. πυκινὸν δομον ἐλθεῖν. [sic] (pŭkĭnŏn dŏmŏn ĕltheîn) means a bit thick.

The supplanted original speech, although lined through, is decipherable. It reads (with the words in parentheses denoting an early revision, the lined out words and the substitution of "Homer" a later one, made in darker ink):

> Cusins (gently) If I may say so, Lady Brit, I think Charles has ex-
> Homer
> pressed what we all feel, ~~rather~~ ~~happily~~. ^ ~~Euripides~~ uses (puts) the same phrase (into the mouth of Zeus) when Heracles proposes to bring Prometheus to Olympus. τον θεκηον means literally a bit thick.[2]

The first version of the speech, with its apocryphal Euripidean allusion and fabricated Greek word, in all probability served as a stopgap for Shaw, pending the borrowing of more satisfactory language from Murray. Shaw had called upon his friend's classical knowledge before (for example, when writing *Caesar and Cleopatra*) and very likely did so here again. A request for such scholarly assistance at the time he read the play to Murray would fully account for Murray's abrupt linking of "a bit thick" with Homer at the very beginning of his October 7th letter. That Murray recollected the phrase from Shaw's drama is obvious from his having quoted it previously in his October 2nd letter.

In *Major Barbara* the words are uttered by Lomax when he learns of Undershaft's impending visit to his estranged wife's home: "Well, you must admit that this is a bit thick." Murray's explanation of the passage from Homer is a helpful clue to what Shaw sought from him at this point—an apt classical allusion that would serve to illuminate the character of Cusins on stage, exhibit-

---

2. British Museum, MS 50616 B, folio 33.

Shaw's Greek is imprecise, and the second Greek word is partially reconstructed, its second and third letters being slightly obscured by a thickening of the line drawn through the bottom of the word. Professor Arnold Toynbee has suggested to me that the word could be a try at a pun for "thick." τον θεκηον (ton thekeon), the most likely reading of Shaw's Greek, I believe is an attempt at something sounding like "thick" in Greek, with a Greek ending added on. In support of his hypothesis is the fact that Cusins says that the word means *literally* a bit thick, and the word "literally" disappears in the revised version. It may very well be that this "Greek" phrasing also came originally from Murray.

ing simultaneously his qualifications as a professor of Greek and as a ready wit. Evidently Shaw wanted to show Cusins equal to the comic demand of offering both a suitable Greek rendering of Lomax's slang outburst and a fitting Greek precedent for the dramatic occasion that prompted it. Although it is Murray who connects Undershaft with the line from Homer, the idea of tying an appropriate Greek phrase to Undershaft is plainly implicit in Shaw's original line about bringing Prometheus to Olympus. It is also apparent that Shaw would have preferred the Greek phrase to have come from Euripides, with whom he repeatedly identified Murray (and Cusins).

Murray's explanation also clears up what is otherwise a puzzling bit of Greek translation in Shaw's play. The second and peculiar construction Murray put on Homer's phrase is plainly offered in jest, depending as it does on reading the Greek word πυκινὸν to mean "thick" in the British slang sense of "disagreeably excessive." Shaw might have contributed to the intelligibility of Cusins' artful translation had he at least made him say " πυκινὸν δόμον ἐλθεῖν means it was a bit thick to come to the house." As it is, the passage has remained an obscure joke between Murray and Shaw. Even so, it is not the only line in the play whose full significance has been known only to these two men.

But if the Murray letter eliminates one puzzle, it introduces another. For Murray's quotation from Homer is not quite accurate. The cited passage is in the *Iliad*, X, 267, where the Greek phrase is πυκινὸν δόμον αντιτορήσας describing Autolycus as having "broken into" the thick-walled house or palace of Amyntor. The original Greek verb in the *Iliad* would have been less applicable to Undershaft's situation, for he was not, strictly speaking, breaking into the home of his family, but merely coming to it, as the verb ἐλθεῖν would indicate. It may be that Murray recalled the Greek words incorrectly, but if so, it is surprising that, given the circumstances of seeking out an apposite passage, he would not have checked the text in the interests of accuracy. Whatever the explanation, his alteration of the Homeric phrase shows that even the worthy Murray could nod. An ironical consequence was to render vulnerable part of the very evidence being adduced in support of Cusins' claim to classical Greek scholarship. As for the mistake thus perpetuated in *Major Barbara*, no evidence has yet appeared to suggest that Shaw ever became aware of it or that Murray undertook to correct it.

Murray's October 7th letter also displays more openly his equivocal attitude toward being portrayed in *Major Barbara*. His objections are not personal, but esthetic, or so he insists. The Birmingham screw manufacturer with orchid and eyeglass, with whom Murray connects Undershaft, is clearly Joseph Chamberlain, whose political career embraced radical social reform at home and imperialism abroad. The highly conditional and illustrative character of Murray's allusion to him as a prototype for Undershaft renders it frustratingly ambiguous as evidence. Was Murray merely presenting Shaw with a provocative analogue to his own portrait in the play? Or does this lead one on the same kind of "wrong scent" that traces Cusins' origins to Murray? At the least Chamberlain is an intriguing possibility to add to all the other conjectural models for Shaw's millionaire business man. The "WA" mentioned in Murray's letter is, of course, William Archer, the dramatic critic.

Turning to the dialogue Murray submitted to Shaw with his October 2nd letter, it is not too difficult to determine where and to what extent Shaw made use of it. Despite the importance the dramatist seemed to attach to Murray's figure of the lever, he made scant use of it in the play. Murray proposed his lines about the lever for the second act, where they could hardly have been added conveniently. Shaw disregarded them. The only reference to a lever occurs in the second scene of the third act. It appears first in the earlier Derry manuscript as a modification of a line of Undershaft's in the midst of an extensive verso revision. Interpolated at the end of his reply to Barbara's question about killing—"It is the final test of conviction"—is the additional clause: "the sole lever strong enough to lift a whole people." Appended to a revised passage, this clause may very well have stemmed from Murray's suggestion. In any event the author rephrased it in the October rewriting: "It is the final test of conviction—the only lever strong enough to overturn a social system— . . ."[3] In Shaw's hands the lever thus came to acquire a much more precise and drastic function than Murray had contemplated.

The section of the revised Edstaston manuscript to which Murray's suggested third act dialogue pertains is readily discoverable. But comparison with the earlier Derry manuscript is more difficult, since a major feature of Shaw's rewriting was a radical rearrangement of much of the previously written dialogue. Originally the raising of "the moral question" by Cusins had no direct connection with Undershaft's exposition of "the true faith of an Armorer." In keeping with Murray's advice, Shaw uses a speech by Lady Britomart to bridge them, and accepts the proposed transitional line for Undershaft. At the same time he enormously improves on the draft speech Murray submitted for Lady Britomart:

—Lady B—
There is no moral question in the matter at all, Adolphus.

---

3. British Museum, MS 50616 E, folio 18, and MS 50616 A, folio 45. Subsequent citations are to the latter manuscript, with the folios given parenthetically in the text.

You must simply sell cannons and weapons to people whose cause is right and just, and refuse them to foreigners and criminals.

—Undershaft—

No: none of that. You must keep the true faith of an Armourer, or you dont come in here. (fol. 28.)

In the Edstaston manuscript, the armorer's faith, which Undershaft delivers in his next speech, ends at the top of a page, the remainder of which is left blank. The dialogue resumes on the succeeding page. This may indicate that Shaw left open the possibility of adding the lines that come after the armorer's faith speech in the first version, finally deciding not to do so. What follows is the principal passages in which the changes reflect the influence both of Murray's criticisms and of the bulk of his dialogue recommendations. It is an instructive stretch of script to consider in relation to the Murray draft dialogue:

—Cusins—

My good Machiavelli, I shall certainly write something up on the wall; only, as I shall write it in Greek, you wont be able to read it. But as to your Armourer's faith, if I take my neck out of the noose of my own morality I am not going to put it into the noose of yours. I shall sell cannons to whom I please and refuse them to whom I please. So there!

—Undershaft—

From the moment you become Andrew Undershaft, you will never do as you please again: Do not come here lusting for power, young man I have no power.

—Cusins—

If power were my aim I should not come here for it. *You* have no power.

—Undershaft—

None of my own, certainly.

—Cusins—

~~You have no will, I think~~. I have more power than you, more will. You do not drive this place, it drives you. And what drives the place?

—Undershaft—(*enigmatically*)

A will of which I am a part.

—Barbara—(*startled & coming down to Undershaft's left*)

Father! Do you know what you are saying; or are you laying a snare for my soul?

—Cusins—

Don't listen to his metaphysics, Barbara. The place is driven by the most rascally part of society, the money hunters, the pleasure hunters, the military promotion hunters; and you are their slave. (foll. 31–32.)[4]

Barbara's "snare for my soul" line had appeared elsewhere in the Derry manuscript. It is now relocated. But all the other lines are new. Moreover, the speeches coming after the first two quoted here are written on the verso page, the adjoining page displaying Shaw's preliminary reworking of the lines as he shifted from Murray's version to his own. The Murray thesis that Cusins has more "will power" than Undershaft becomes Cusins' contention that he has more power *and* will. Murray's diagnosis that Undershaft's business works him and that the business is itself worked by society and all its "rascality" emerges as a disagreement about whether the millionaire industrialist's "place," which "drives" him, is driven by a mystical "will," as Undershaft claims, or by the most "rascally part" of society, as Cusins insists.

As underpinning for this exchange Shaw interposes an earlier short new speech by Undershaft. Almost immediately after her arrival on the scene Lady Britomart exclaims, "To think of all that (*indicating the town*) being yours! and that you have kept it to yourself all these years!" To which Undershaft replies, "It does not belong to me. I belong to it. It is the Undershaft inheritance" (fol. 14). In the earlier manuscript, the munitions manufacturer told his wife that the whole town was "part" of the Undershaft inheritance, but the first two sentences in the rewritten speech are fresh additions.

The burden of these changes, as of Murray's dialogue, is to strengthen Cusins, and what he represents, in opposition to Undershaft. This is accomplished by having the young scholar-poet stress limitations on the millionaire's power—limitations that need not operate on him in the same way—and by having him voice greater independence of spirit in confronting the man he is eventually to succeed. At the same time Undershaft, if not directly weakened, is given a contextual framework in which he becomes more an accessory of ambiguous social and cosmic forces than a free and autonomous agent. Likened by Shaw to the fly of Aesop's fable, who thought he was raising the coach wheel's dust, the capitalist is shown to be riding, not turning, the wheels moving civilized society. The effect of this shift in support is a better balance between the exponents of the contending outlooks, and a surer groundwork for the eventual liaison between them.

Still, Murray's most important single dialogue contribution to the drama is his paraphrase of the famous paradox about philoso-

4. In the original production typescript (Houghton Library, Harvard University, and Academic Center Library, University of Texas) "he is" replaces the more ambiguous "you are" at the end of this speech of Cusins'.

pher-kings in Plato's *Republic*. Evidently Shaw rejected it initially, for it appears nowhere in his manuscript. When it does turn up for the first time, in the production typescript, it has undergone a Shaw change. Sharpened by the omission of whiskey making, it is given, not to Cusins as Murray indicated, but to Undershaft. In this way it has greater dramatic effect, benefiting from the impact it makes on Cusins at a critical juncture in the contest between the munitions maker and the Greek scholar. Shaw also followed it with the exact speech that Murray submitted for Lady Britomart, including the lined out sentence, but withdrew this additional speech from the text of the published version of the play in 1907.

In terms of the total number of his actual words and lines that were incorporated in *Major Barbara*, Murray's contribution is minor indeed: the obscure Homeric phrase with its factitious translation in the first act and, in the third act, a short transitional sentence ("No: none of that."); the phraseology of lever, will, power, and rascality; and the Platonic paraphrase. In addition, there is the acknowledged borrowing from Murray's translation of the *Bacchae* in the second act. But even these lines underwent modification as Shaw substituted "money and guns" for "gold and power," and, more radically, "Fate" for "Hate," to which he appended Cusins' playful use of "Barbara" for "loveliness." In all of this Murray was helpful, but he was far from being a collaborator. The drama is entirely Shaw's: whatever came from Murray or elsewhere he substantially transformed into distinctively Shavian dramatic terms. But then, Murray had not really tried to do more than modify the course of a play already written. Hence even some of his dialogue proposals were but minor variations of ideas originating with the author, such as that about Cusins coming to work at six in the morning.

Nonetheless Murray's contribution to this play transcends in significance the recommended changes in language that found their way into the play. For one thing, the unprecedented rewriting of the third act, which immeasurably improved the whole work, was undertaken as a consequence of Murray's criticisms. It was therefore as critic (the only role he really essayed) that Murray exerted his greatest influence on this drama. Viewed in this light, the changes he effected in the lines of the play were substantial. Thus, although Murray's dialogue suggestions, excepting the *Republic* paraphrase, lack the dramatic incisiveness of the lines they eventually elicited from the play's author, they do signalize the direction toward which Shaw turned in much of his rewriting.

Very perceptively Murray recognized that a stronger Cusins could fortify the "Barbara principles" in their encounter with the "Undershaft principles" and supply firmer grounds for resolving the conflict between them on some basis other than the simple over-powering of the young people by Undershaft. Murray also proposed leaving the eventual outcome in doubt. To a considerable degree Shaw accepted these recommendations. The issue between them seems to develop from Murray's further contention that the end in view for the Barbara principles is the ultimate destruction or sub-duing of the Undershaft principles. This more conventional solu-tion could hardly have served Shaw's dramatic purposes.

Because of the disagreement on this issue Shaw asserts so deter-minedly in his October 7th letter, it is necessary to detail the less apparent points where he accedes to Murray's criticism. The open-ing words of that very letter show him not only welcoming the "Barbara stuff," but inviting more. He goes on to affirm unequivo-cally that he will use Murray's passage to establish Undershaft as "a fly on the wheel." As we have seen, he did adopt the bent and adapt the content of Murray's dialogue to his own purposes. It should also be kept in mind that this letter was written during the period when he was still rewriting: it does not necessarily reflect a fixed or final position on every point discussed. For Shaw eventually did even more with Cusins, and with Barbara too, than Murray specifically recommended. In particular, he so expanded and devel-oped their conversation at the end of the play as to create a vir-tually new consummation to his drama. This new content is un-questionably an outgrowth of the "Murray passage." Coming after Cusins' speech about the sale of his soul, now shifted to this new location, the added dialogue returns at once to the theme of power introduced in the earlier Murray-inspired lines:

—Cusins—

... What I am now selling it for is neither money nor position nor comfort, but for reality and for power.

—Barbara—

You know that you will have no power, and that he has none.

—Cusins—

I know. It is not for myself alone. I want to make power for the world.

—Barbara—

I want to make power for the world too; but it must be spiritual power.

—Cusins—

I think all power is spiritual: these cannons will not go off by themselves. I have tried to make spiritual power by teaching Greek. But the world can never be really touched by a dead lan-guage and a dead civilization. The people must have power; and the people cannot have Greek. Now the power that is made here can be wielded by all men.

—Barbara—

Power to burn women's houses down and kill their sons and tear their husbands to pieces.

—Cusins—

You cannot have power for good without having power for evil too. You cannot even grow wheat without nourishing murderers. This power which only tears men's bodies to pieces, has never been so horribly abused as the intellectual power, the imaginative power, the poetic, religious power that can destroy men's souls. As a teacher of Greek I gave the intellectual man weapons against the common man. I now want to give the common man weapons against the intellectual man. I love the common people. I want to arm them against the lawyer, the doctor, the priest, the literary man, professor, the artist, and the politician, who, once in authority, are the most dangerous, disastrous and tyrannical of all the fools, rascals and impostors. I want a democratic power strong enough to force the intellectual oligarchy to use its genius for the general good or else perish. (foll. 66–69.)

This remarkable passage, revised slightly when first published, and again years later for the Ayot St. Lawrence Edition of Shaw's works, certainly goes beyond what Murray, or anyone else for that matter, might have expected in view of Shaw's October 7th letter. Nothing like this discussion of power is to be found in the earlier version. Cusins' next speech, which completes his defense of the decision to succeed to Undershaft's position, introduces another new element, as we shall soon see.

This entire apologia of Cusins precedes lines Shaw had already written to indicate Barbara's converted outlook. But then the dramatist goes on—perhaps taking up in his own way the vague suggestion at the end of Murray's dialogue about having Barbara utter a religious phrase—to incorporate the following new language in her final declarations to Cusins:

—Barbara—

. . . My father shall never throw it in my teeth again that my converts were bribed with bread. (*She is transfigured*) I have got rid of the bribe of bread. I have got rid of the . . .[5] bribe of heaven. Let God's work be done for its own sake—the work He created us to do because it cannot be done except by living men and women. When I die, let Him be in my debt, not I in His; and let me forgive Him as becomes a woman of my rank.

The first two sentences that follow are modifications of the language in the earlier Derry version of the act—that of Cusins under-

5. Ellipsis mine. Omitted is a superfluous "with bread" Shaw neglected to delete. By the time this passage appeared in the first published edition of the play in 1907 the capital "H's" in the divine personal pronouns were reduced to lower case.

going minor, Barbara's more radical alteration. The remainder of her speech is completely new:

—*Cusins*—
The way of life through the factory of death!

—*Barbara*—
The raising of earth to heaven and of man to God, the unveiling of an eternal light in the Valley of The Shadow (*Turning on him & seizing him by the shoulders*) Oh, did you think my courage would never come back? did you believe that I had left the Army? that I, who have stood in the streets, and taken my people to my heart, and talked of the holiest and greatest things with them, could ever turn back and chatter foolishly to fashionable people about nothing in a drawing room? Never, never, never, never: Major Barbara will die with the colors ... (foll. 75–77)

The upshot of these later revisions again is a considerable enlargement of the roles of Barbara and Cusins, especially of the latter. At the same time we learn how they view their decision to accept the succession to the Undershaft firm. If this contributes in part to Undershaft's success in his conversion venture, it also brings out how the aims of Barbara and Cusins differ from his. In particular, Cusins' intent to make power for the common people is hardly in line with Undershaft's designs. It makes for the kind of uncertainty in the issue that Murray wanted. In sum, the net result of all these changes is a decided move toward Murray's stated desire to have the defenders of the Barbara principles strengthened in the drama.

The point is therefore moot whether Shaw fully adhered in the end to the position he argued so insistently in his October 7th letter. For the correspondence between the two friends reveals them engaged in a fascinating polemic about the dénouement of *Major Barbara*—a polemic which had a profound effect on the last act of Shaw's drama. Shaw obviously took full dramatic advantage of a situation in which Cusins' original was championing the cause his stage counterpart shared with Barbara. An inevitable dramatic consequence was to cast the author all the more forcefully in the role of an unremitting Undershaft undertaking to convince a recalcitrant Cusins in the flesh concerning the wisdom of assuming power in the Undershaft firm. But in the long run the resultant changes in the text must weigh more heavily in judging the eventual thrust of the drama than any disputative points made by the author before he had completed his rewriting.

As it turned out, Shaw reserved a crucial riposte to Murray's critical objections for delivery within the play itself. Indeed, included in the expanded Barbara-Cusins scene at the end were some lines intended to have special meaning for this particular member of the play's audience. And these lines, designed to settle the debate in Shaw's favor, were to be hurled at Murray from the stage not by Undershaft, but by his own dramatic alter ego, Cusins. Shaw prepares his critic for this experience in his next letter, written the day after the play's opening:

> 10. Adelphi Terrace. W.C.
> 29th Nov. 1905.

My dear Murray

I have to congratulate you on a remarkable success. Your lines went immensely; and Barker surpassed himself in your spectacles.

I intended to send you the script of the last act; but I refrained, partly because I hadnt time to write, and partly because your reluctance to accept the Undershaft inheritance finally drove me to clinch the matter by a surpassingly mean reference to Brailsford, which I thought had better be exploded on you from the stage. I do not see how you can get out of it now. Barker suggested that if Stephen (the pious son) were to talk Murray-Margolouth the effect would be irresistible; but we resisted the temptation as a breach of good taste.

Barker was at his best, even as a drum virtuoso: he came out magnificently after being sticklike beyond all belief at rehearsals. Calvert suddenly realized that his part was blasphemous, and that Balfour, glaring from a box, might order him to the stake at any moment. He collapsed hopelessly and said, in the last act, "They have to find their own drains; but I look after their dreams." The last act was consequently a hideous failure.

I hear you are all coming to next Friday's performance. For your presence I do not give a damn; but the prospect of Lady Carlisle, filled with idle rumors, contemplating Miss Filippi and drawing conclusions as to my conception of her, terrifies me. Miss Filippi, though genial and artistic, has not the grand manner. Her nose is seriously enlarged by a bad cold; and she doesnt know her part. She also thinks the play wicked. She is on the whole, about as like the alleged original as I am like Gladstone.

Barker has been cultivating the closest resemblance to you in private life for a fortnight past. Everybody recognized it—Charlotte, Mrs. Pat Campbell &c &c—instantly & spontaneously the moment the spectacles went on. On the stage he obliterated it by a careful make-up. Calvert, on the other hand, made up so exactly like a photograph of the Turkish ambassador I supplied him with, that he could get his dinner any day at the Embassy & give the real Turk to the police as an impostor. Yet nobody will find out Calvert; and everybody will find out Euripides.

I am urging Barker to take a music hall engagement for a turn entitled "Bad Taste: or My Gallery of Eminent Men."

Yrs ever
G. Bernard Shaw.

"The surpassingly mean reference to Brailsford" emerges as the climactic point in Cusins' justification of his decision to accept Undershaft's offer of partnership and succession. After he proclaims his dedication to the cause of giving power to the common people in the passage already quoted, Barbara asks, "And is there no higher a power than this?" Then comes Cusins' final answer:

—*Cusins*—

Yes; but this power can destroy the higher powers just as a tiger can destroy a man: therefore man must master this power first. I admitted this when the Turks and Greeks were last at war. My best pupil went out to fight for Hellas. My parting gift to him was not a copy of Plato's Republic, but a revolver and a hundred Undershaft cartridges. The blood of every Turk he shot—if he shot any—is on my head as well as on Undershaft's. That act committed me to this place for ever. And now, is it all over between us? (foll. 69–70.)

In this manner Shaw sought to convince Murray that by a previous act of his own he was already implicated in whatever social guilt attaches to the making of armaments. Murray has left an independent account of the incident to which Cusins refers: "Another very brilliant student who had just taken his degree told me he proposed to go and fight for the Greeks in the Greco-Turkish war of 1899. We had a long talk, and I have him my blessing and a revolver which I had taken with me in travels in the East. His name was H. N. Brailsford."[6] Thus another prominent writer found his way into Shaw's drama. The manuscript (fol. 69) discloses that Shaw had considered using the name "Ropesford" for Cusins' pupil, but then decided against it. It would have been an apt *nom de guerre*, "brails" having the nautical signification of ropes used to truss up sails or fish nets.

Shaw's answer to Murray's critical reservations about being "labelled" in the play is, characteristically, to chide him with the information that he had considered putting still another associate of Murray into the play. He is intimating that, with Barker as accomplice, he could have added to the "Gallery of Eminent Men" Murray's friend and colleague at Oxford, D. S. Margoliouth, whose name Shaw misspells as Margolouth. Margoliouth was a scholar in Hebrew, Arabic, and Greek, whom Murray had consulted on other occasions in connection with Shaw requests for scholarly data and

6. *An Unfinished Autobiography*, p. 97. Louis Crompton has previously noted the connection between Cusins' comment and this passage. "Shaw's Challenge to Liberalism," *Prairie Schooner*, XXXVII, 3 (Fall, 1963), p. 243, reprinted in *G. B. Shaw: A Collection of Critical Essays*, ed. R. J. Kaufmann, Englewood Cliffs, N. J.: Prentice-Hall (Spectrum), 1965, p. 99.

opinion.[7] Professor Arnold Toynbee informs me that these close friends were very different from one another, especially since Margoliouth did not expose himself to the outside world as Murray did. Murray, he says, had no lecturing manner; there was nothing donnish about him. Since Murray was already amply represented in the play by Cusins, it seems reasonable to conjecture that it was Margoliouth's professorial speech and manner Barker had suggested that Stephen imitate. The pairing of Murray with his colleague as joint model would then constitute one more waggish thrust in the Shavian counterattack on his friend's demurers against being identifiable in the play.

Shaw's letter also suggests that Murray had loaned his spectacles to Barker to assist that actor in his portrayal of Cusins. It could hardly have been a great surprise to Murray to learn of Barker's imitative efforts. For, in the course of a letter in September discussing plans for their Greek drama productions, Barker asked Murray when he would be in town, adding, "Also I want to 'study' you."[8]

Barker's obliteration by make-up of his cultivated resemblance to Murray could have been prompted by Murray's protestations in his October 7th letter. Similarly, the modeling of Louis Calvert's make-up as Undershaft on the Turkish ambassador may have been a Shavian ruse to avoid the kind of identification with a particular industrialist that Murray had criticized in the same letter. As it was, one of the newspaper reviewers reported that Calvert, as a "steel king," was "made up in every way to resemble Mr. Carnegie," and another echoed this description.[9] For the record, the Turkish ambassador to England at the time was Stephen Musurus Pasha, whose photograph displays a beard closer in appearance to that adorning Calvert than the one in pictures of Andrew Carnegie. But no report has come down to us to indicate whether or not Balfour, the "glaring" (or laughing, as the *Clarion* review described him) Prime Minister, recognized in the apprehensive actor the stage double of a member of the diplomatic corps.

Shaw's trepidation about the reaction of the Countess of Carlisle may well have been genuine. As epigraph for her biography of her redoubtable mother, *Rosalind Howard: Countess of Carlisle*, Lady Dorothy Henley chose the lines from *Hamlet*: "An eye like Mars, to threaten and command," a characterization concurred in by the Countess's nephew, Bertrand Russell, in his introduction to the book.[1] Lady Carlisle was fully capable of displaying her displeasure on the spot, and actually did so on another such occasion. Lady Henley recalls that "once in another Shaw play Mrs. Patrick Camp-

7. On Margoliouth see *An Unfinished Autobiography*, pp. 90–1, and Arnold J. Toynbee, *Acquaintances*, London: Oxford Univ. Press, 1967, pp. 44–48.
8. C B. Purdom, *Harley Granville-Barker*, London: Rockliff, 1955, p. 52.

9. *Daily Chronicle*, November 29, 1905, 5:3, and Alex M. Thompson in the *Clarion*, December 8, 1905, 3:1.
1. "Lady Carlisle's Ancestry" in Henley, p. 13.

bell complained bitterly that my mother, from the stalls, had made very audibly disapproving commentaries as the play progressed!"[2]

Fortunately, the dread prospects Shaw feared failed to materialize. Murray reported Lady Carlisle's reactions, as well as his own, in a letter written after they had witnessed the fourth performance of *Major Barbara* on December 1st. Once again he takes exception to the presence of "personalities" in the play, connecting Shaw's practice with that of Mrs. Humphry Ward, who had used T. H. Green, Professor of Moral Philosophy at Oxford as one character, and—so the Oxford community believed—the Balliol tutor, R. L. Nettleship, as another, in her *Robert Elsemere*.[3] This letter gives Murray's own critique of the revised drama as performed, and rounds out the correspondence with Shaw about the play, *Major Barbara*:

Dec 3 1905.   131, Branbury Road, Oxford.

My dear Shaw,

I dont think that Lady Carlisle minded a bit, though she was rather severe on Miss Filippi's acting. For my own part, though I do not think the personalities added to the value of the play, and on general grounds I rather regret to see you imitating Mrs Humphrey [sic] Ward, it strikes me as really remarkable that you can manage to be so exceedingly personal without being in the faintest degree disagreeable or offensive. When your Great Exemplar put Nettleship into a book, she made my blood boil by her unintentional offensiveness. Stupidity, I suppose it was.

As to the play, the criticism that I most agree with is that of Desmond Macarthey [sic] in the Speaker. The whole thing strikes me as 1. a prologue, quite good but slight, and damaged by Miss F's bad acting: 2. a really magnificent religious tragedy, leading to an almost desperate situation: 3. a courageous and ingenious, but not successful, attempt to get out of that desperate situation by casuistry. I admit [t]hat Miss Russell gave you away at the end by not understanding or perhaps remembering her lines. But, even with a great deal of good will, I was not able to feel her speeches satisfactory. I suggest some thoughts that cross my mind as causes of this unsatisfactoriness . . . though perhaps you, like Barker, deny that there is any unsatisfactoriness.

1. The emotional effect of Act 2 is so great, that mere intellect, without emotion, is not enough to set against it. Could you have got some *emotional* statement, so to speak, of the Nietzschian position, as well as the dialectical statement?

2. The rapidity of the change is too much for one. Barbara takes the shattering of her religion too lightly. She could scarcely have acted so promptly if it had merely been a question of transferring her affections from me to Lomax.

2. In a letter to the present writer. December 25, 1966. Quoted by permission of Lady Henley.

3. See Stephen Gwynn, *Mrs. Humphry Ward*, New York: Henry Holt, n.d., p. 30.

3. I suspect that you really wanted four acts, and some more "story." The audience tended to feel the end as merely a giving up of all religion, and morality, too, for that matter, instead of realising that it was a change from one system to another— equally strenuous and earnest. Hence the rage of the Heathen in the Morning Post and elsewhere.

It would, of course, be against your principles to re-write the end (again!) making it into four acts, and you are so dogmatically attached to your principles. I dont think I have seen anything on the stage so deeply . . . I cannot get the word; so moving to emotions and intellect at once, as the second Act.

Yours ever
G M.

I see that, don like, I have written entirely about what I disapproved. I c^d write—& have written—pages of admiration for the other parts.

This letter makes fairly clear Murray's judgments about the work, especially when supplemented by Desmond McCarthy's criticism, preserved in his book, *Shaw*.[4] The "Heathen in the Morning Post," mentioned by Murray, were the readers who followed the lead of that paper's critic in attacking *Major Barbara* as blasphemous. They kept Shaw busy writing letters to the paper defending his play. The "pages of admiration" have not yet turned up; in the absence of a published review of the drama one may guess that they were written in letters to other friends. If so, they would have had to be composed between the December 1st performance Murray witnessed and December 3rd, the date of this letter.

Sufficient evidence has now been given, it would seem, to permit a summary appraisal of the extent of *Major Barbara's* indebtedness to Gilbert Murray. The case for considering him a collaborator in the writing of the drama has very little to sustain it. Although some of the play's lines can be traced back to him, these are few in number, and in but only one or two cases are they of any critical importance. More significantly, he was the constructive critic of a completed version of the play, whose helpful counsel persuaded Shaw to rewrite part of it and improve it greatly. The play and its composition remain indisputably Shaw's, but the dramatist availed himself fully of the provocative material provided so generously by the mind and very person of his gifted friend, and by the personalities of members of the family into which Murray had married. It was this modest but active and valuable behind-the-scenes assistance that left *Major Barbara* indebted to Murray "in more ways than one."

4. London: Macgibbon & Kee, pp. 44–56.

On *Heartbreak House*

MICHAEL J. MENDELSOHN

The Heartbreak Houses of Shaw and Chekhov†

"Youll get used to it, miss; this house is full of surprises for them that dont know our ways." With this word of encouragement, Nurse Guinness initiates young Ellie Dunn into the baffling house of surprise and disillusion that Shaw calls, in his Preface to *Heartbreak House*, "cultured, leisured Europe before the war." And of course Nurse Guinness is correct; Ellie does make her adjustment to Heartbreak House—even though a reader may have more of a problem. Undoubtedly many readers or viewers of Shaw's play have turned away from it uneasily, feeling perhaps that they have not yet achieved the seventh degree of concentration, or whatever it is that Shaw demands for complete insight. Here is Shaw at his most challenging and, I believe, at his most serious. But to a reader accustomed to following the action of a play easily, *Heartbreak House* is indeed full of surprises. It appears at times that it is not a play at all, but a dreamy Ellie-in-Wonderland or a genial rendition of the importance of being Darnley.

Shaw's answer to the question of meaning in *Heartbreak House* was direct: " 'How should *I* know! I am only the author.' "[1] Nevertheless, there is certainly a purpose underlying the play which makes it more than a Shavian parlor game; one needs to look no farther than the first part of the preface to realize that the playwright is in earnest. Profoundly disturbed by England's apathy and sluggishness, by its totally lucky ability to "muddle through," Shaw attempts to portray an entire society—European rather than just English—muddling through, heedless of the fact that its days are numbered. The dramatist's most brilliant description of his subject comes through the eyes of Lady Utterword early in Act I: ". . . the

† From the beginning, *Heartbreak House* provoked the most contrasting judgments of any of the Shaw plays. Though the original press was largely negative, Shaw himself regarded it as one of his best plays, and time has, on the whole, tended to underscore its importance.

Undoubtedly Shaw was influenced by Chekhov, though there is an argument as to how far below the surface of the play the Chekhovian mood penetrates. Michael J. Mendelsohn makes the case for a rather deep affinity with Chekhov, particularly with *The Cherry Orchard*. The article is from *The Shaw Review*, Vol. 6 (September, 1963), pp. 89–95.

1. Quoted by Hesketh Pearson, *G. B. S.* (New York, 1950), p. 336.

luggage lying on the steps, the servants spoilt and impossible, no-body at home to receive anybody, no regular meals, nobody ever hungry because they are always gnawing bread and butter or munching apples, and, what is worse, the same disorder in ideas, in talk, in feeling." In my opinion Shaw's basic premises are indis-putable: both a Heartbreak House and a Horseback Hall did in fact exist. Since Shaw was Shaw, he employed the methods of com-edy to state his case. But the result of all his playfulness in this work is not comic at all, is not actually much different from the ac-cumulation of spiritually dead things in "The Wasteland" or the resignation to *nada* in Hemingway. *Heartbreak House* almost reeks with decay, pessimism, and futility.

Since Shaw himself calls attention to his debt to Chekhov, one way to approach the play is to consider its points of comparison to Chekhov's best known play, *The Cherry Orchard*. I suspect that it was in the speech of Trofimov that Shaw first began to feel the kin-ship between Chekhov's play and his own thinking:

> The vast majority of the intellectual people I know seek nothing, do nothing, are not fit as yet for work of any kind. They call themselves intellectual, but they treat their servants as inferiors, behave to the peasants as though they were animals, learn little, read nothing seriously, do practically nothing, only talk about sci-ence and know very little about art. (II)

The speech is almost a direct restatement of Shaw's preface. And of course when Shaw extends his play to all Europe, he is only enlarg-ing and echoing Trofimov's statement, "All Russia is our garden" (II). I shall consider five general areas of comparison: the apparent plotlessness; dialogue peculiarities; tone; characters; theme. I would add at the outset that there are probably as many dissimilarities as there are likenesses; some careful analysts of the drama have gone to great lengths to point these out. And Desmond MacCarthy speaks for several critics when he writes:

> The great difference [between Chekhov and Shaw] is due to the temperament of the author. Mr. Shaw does not know what heart-break is. He conceives it as a sudden disillusionment . . . cauteris-ing like a flash of lightning; as a sharp pain, but not as a maim-ing misery. Compared with the vital and restless inmates of *Heartbreak House* Chekhov's characters are like dying flies in a glue-pot.[2]

However, Shaw is not attempting a translation of Chekhov, nor a slavish imitation of his technique. He offers us *Heartbreak House* as "a fantasia in the Russian manner on English themes," and

2. *Shaw* (London, 1951), p. 144.

there is an inescapable feeling of kinship between the Shotover ship and the Ranevsky manor house.

There is an apparent similarity between *The Cherry Orchard* and *Heartbreak House* in the method of plotting. If the writer of tragedy asks himself what *must* my characters do, and the writer of melodrama asks himself what *can* my characters do for the most exciting effect, Shaw's question often seems to be what is the least likely, the most surprising thing my characters can do or say. There is in some ways a feeling of plotlessness; certainly Aristotle would be reluctant to call the events that occur on stage in either *The Cherry Orchard* or *Heartbreak House* a plot, a point underscored by John Gassner:

> Ever since Chekhov became a successful playwright, the plotless play, which is usually little more than a string of little occurrences forming a story . . . has won the greatest degree of respect and affection. Modern drama has been the result of fundamentally anti-Aristotelian playwriting—largely plotless, meandering, semi-comic, and semi-tragic.[3]

In a place of an Aristotelian arrangement of incidents, there is almost a non-arrangement, leading another critic to use such terms as "drama of inaction" and "negative plot" to describe what doesn't happen in a Chekhov play.[4] Chekhov is dealing with basic nineteenth century melodramatic plot material—the foreclosure of the mortgage on the old homestead; yet no reader seriously gives much attention to this aspect of the play. Talk dominates and anticlimaxes are the order of the day. Shaw falls into the pattern with ease. In *Man and Superman*, for example, a reader gets a definite impression that the playwright pauses in the drama for one act of generally enjoyable chit-chat; in *Heartbreak House* he wastes no time on the drama at all and gets directly to the talk.

Such an idea, however, can become oversimplified. Although both playwrights avoid climax and emphatic curtains, and although they refuse to lean heavily on plot as the most important element of the play, there is at least enough plot to keep the action progressing. The technique is deceptive. Both forward movement and conflict are present, if not always shown on the stage. The auction and the axes are quite real in Chekhov's play, just as the high finance, the dynamite, and the husband-switching are real in Shaw's. Offstage maneuvering and presences are essential in both plays; a British civil servant working his sixteen-hour day actually becomes an important character even though he never appears. Immediately focusing on Ellie, as Chekhov focuses on Mme. Ranevsky, Shaw widens his camera gradually until the entire en-

3. *The Theatre in Our Times* (New York, 1954), p. 79.

4. Stark Young, *The Theatre* (New York, 1959), p. 5.

semble comes into view. Thus plot becomes firmly enmeshed in theme, and the entire group or society becomes protagonist.

Talk surpasses action in order of importance in these plays, and it is necessary to examine what sort of talk. The characters in *Heartbreak House* and *The Cherry Orchard* employ some rather unusual ground rules. Rule number one is talk, but avoid listening whenever possible. An exchange between Lopahin and Mme. Ranevsky suggests the principle:

> LOPAHIN. One tells you in plain Russian that your estate is going to be sold, and you seem not to understand it.
> LYUBOV. What are we to do? Tell us what to do?
> LOPAHIN. I do tell you every day. Every day I say the same thing. (II)

The characters are all exemplified by Firs, who is actually deaf; when he replies "The day before yesterday" to Mme. Ranevsky's congratulations on his health (I), he is acting no differently from any of the other characters—all of whom presumably are equipped with normal ears. Although Shaw does not carry this policy to the extreme that Chekhov does, there is a parallel in Captain Shotover, who loves to speak but hates to listen: "I cant think so long and continuously. I am too old. I must go in and out" (II). It is part of the same malady that he will not believe either Ellie or his own daughter when they attempt to tell him who they really are.

Rule number two is avoid answering a direct question under any circumstances. The impatient Lopahin, attempting to get an answer from Mme. Ranevsky, finds only frustration:

> LOPAHIN. Will you consent to letting land for building or not? One word in answer: Yes or no? Only one word!
> LYUBOV. Who is smoking such horrible cigars here? (II)

Shotover is a master at this game, avoiding the answers to every question until Ellie finally corners him late in Act II. The Chekhovian technique through which each character is so wrapped up in his own thoughts that he responds only partially to the preceding statement is best employed in the final act of *Heartbreak House*, in the lines preceding Mangan's wild attempt to tear off his clothes. This scene presents a tremendously facile picture of modern, self-centered mind processes. And Ariadne specifically calls attention to this facet of *Heartbreak House* when, in the speech already noted, she speaks of "the same disorder in ideas, in talk, in feeling" (I).

There is a distinctive tone to both *The Cherry Orchard* and *Heartbreak House* which lends them something of a dreamlike quality. Both plays are ostensibly comedies, although the net result of each is probably more disturbing than we normally expect from

a comedy. Gassner's term, "drama of attrition,"[5] might be the best
description of these plays: a society is visibly withering away before
us in both. A desire to escape from reality, to withdraw into an iso-
lated protective shell, motivates many of the characters. And both
plays, while undeniably funny, are permeated by an otherworld-
liness suggested by the type of conversations noted earlier, Charlot-
ta's magic tricks, the melancholy sounds of Randall's flute and
Epihodov's guitar, and concerns for the reality of Marcus's tigers or
Lady Utterword's hair. Mme. Ranevsky herself, obsessed like Mr.
Micawber with the futile notion that "something will turn up" to
save the estate, contributes greatly to the feeling that all life is a
bad dream from which we will certainly awake. *Heartbreak House*
may well be more nightmare than dream. But the tone is not that
of complete distortion like a hall of mirrors in an amusement park;
rather it is slightly askew, slightly misty—much as a room would
appear through three empty martini glasses.

At first reading there appears to be a marked similarity between
The Cherry Orchard and *Heartbreak House* in the employment of
the characters. Certainly both use a large cast, and to an extent
both introduce people from various levels of society. Closer examination reveals, however, that Shaw presents only two obvious representatives of a decadent aristocracy (Lady Utterword and Randall
the Rotter), and only two members of the non-privileged classes
(Nurse Guinness and her pirate husband). All the others are less
characters than symbols of various aspects of "cultured, leisured
Europe." Chekhov's people fall much more easily into sharply-
defined groups representative of Russian society: the descending
aristocrat, the rising worker, and the still-groping intellectual. With
one exception, Chekhov's characters are merely comic or pitiable;
the one despicable exception is Yasha, an insensitive, ruthless self-
seeker. Gaev and Firs live completely in the past, Trofimov in the
future. The others attempt a compromise with today that Chekhov
suggests is impossible. At best the fate of *fin-de-siecle* Russia can be
bought off for a few more years, as the preposterous Pishtchik displays with his incredible sale of clay to some Englishmen.

Shaw's characters in *Heartbreak House* point up an odd weakness
in the playwright. If he intends to put complacent leisure-class
England on trial, the indictment breaks down from too much sheer
kindness. For, as Kenneth Tynan has pointed out, Shaw may see
his group as "a bunch of feckless loafers, drifting blindfold to perdition," but "despite their shiftlessness and stupidity, we cannot dislike them."[6] The result of his treatment is that we tend to consider
no one in Shotover's little ship as an overt criminal—not even

5. *The Theatre in Our Times*, p. 71.
6. "Ireland Unvanquished," *New Yorker*, XXXV (Oct. 31, 1959), 131.

Mangan, and certainly not Billy Dunn. All are guilty of crimes of omission or the kind of failures Shaw discusses in the Preface when he suggests that war was allowed to come even though it was preventable.

If we accept Shaw's characters as allegorical, they are not too difficult to fathom. Ellie becomes a sort of Everywoman who is "thrice disillusioned—once in each Act, by Hector, by Mangan, by Shotover."[7] Rebounding from the romantic to the mercenary, she eventually approaches that desirable stage of wanting nothing— "Thats the only real strength" (II). Professor McDowell has suggested further that "as a result of the insight and tolerance gained from heartbreak and experience, she can now accommodate the illusion to the reality."[8] Though the play begins and ends with Ellie and the old Captain, Shaw seems more interested in his other characters, so that eventually the two sisters Shotover and Hector emerge as the most vital personalities in Shaw's scheme. Ariadne persists in her snobbishness, unaware that the white man's burden is going out of fashion; Hesione is the cool, unruffled *femme fatale*—a most entrancing if somewhat useless fixture in English society; Hector thrives on a self-inflated reputation for bravery, but can really rise to the occasion when necessary.

The Skipper calls for a bit more attention. Of all the characters in Shaw's plays, Captain Shotover seems most often to speak for the author. But here again Shaw is playing a perverse game with the reader: Shotover's frankness masks a mind that often only *seems* clever. The Captain's profundities are frequently not very profound, and his habit of firing only one volley and then disappearing may well be caused by the fact that he is incapable of sustaining a longer idea. Ellie's discovery that the Captain is almost as hollow as Cusins' Salvation Army drum leads to her final disillusionment. His wisdom rests on the foundation of rum. Perhaps such a basis is desirable. More likely a whimsical Shaw is suggesting that he sees himself, in the mirror of Captain Shotover, in the same way that Chekhov views the aged retainer, Firs: held together only by sealing wax.

Eric Bentley's statement of the theme of *Heartbreak House* comes closest to describing what I feel was on Shaw's mind: "Heartbreak House might be called the Nightmare of a Fabian ... It is a picture of failure. The world belongs to the Mangans, the Utterwords, and the Hushabyes."[9] Similarly, Chekhov's world has also failed and is in the midst of a great cataclysm, with Lopahin, Yasha, and the far-seeing Trofimov coming to the fore to supplant

7. Eric Bentley, *Bernard Shaw* (Norfolk, Conn., 1947) p. 137. This observation is slightly inaccurate; her third disillusionment occurs near the end of Act II.

8. F. P. W. McDowell, "Technique, Symbol and Theme in *Heartbreak House*," *PMLA*, LXVIII (June 1953), 337.

9. *Bernard Shaw*, p. 140.

the delicate but frivolous entourage surrounding Mme. Ranevsky. "There's no turning back, the path is overgrown," says Trofimov (III). The fantastic orchestra plays a grotesque death dance for the aristocracy, while the axes are poised to fall upon the lovely cherry trees.

If heartbreak is essential to both *The Cherry Orchard* and *Heartbreak House*, there is, nevertheless, a difference in involvement. Because Shaw becomes more emotionally involved in his theme, the end result is a more serious one. Chekhov remains an objective observer of the heartbreak; Shaw enters into the scene through Captain Shotover. Thus, paradoxically, the play which appears to be more ludicrous is actually more serious in intent and in outcome. It is difficult to agree with one critic's assertion that *Heartbreak House* is optimistic, that rebirth is still possible. Much more logical is the opposite belief in an "enveloping despair and hopelessness."[1] While Ellie moves from one disillusionment to another, observing the stupidity around her, her process of education becomes a whirl of disenchantment and increasing cynicism. As Robert Corrigan wrote, "It is in *Heartbreak House* that Shaw first came to grips without equivocation with those questions that haunted Ibsen, Strindberg, and Chekhov before him. How is one to live in an irrational world? How is one to give meaning to life in a world where you don't know the rules? How are human relationships to be meaningfully maintained when you can't be sure of your feelings and when your feelings can change without your knowing it? How can man live without being destroyed when irreconcilable conflict is the central fact of all life?"[2]

That sacrosanct bible of English graduate students, *A Literary History of England*, devotes a total of one sentence to an appraisal of Shaw's play: "*Heartbreak House*, attacking the ruling classes held responsible for the crash of civilization, is an inartistic amalgam of discussion and farce, making use of parable and symbol and anticipating the mood of disillusioned futility which was to prevail in the literature of the nineteen-twenties."[3] Much of the criticism of various productions of the play is no kinder. Arnold Bennett, describing the first production, complained of nearly four hours "of the most intense tedium."[4] Highly literate reviewers like Joseph Wood Krutch and Stark Young are among those contributing unfavorable articles in 1938, with Young revising an earlier enthusiasm for the play into a new opinion that the work is "garrulous, unfelt and tiresome."[5]

1. McDowell, pp. 34 ff.
2. Robert W. Corrigan, *"Heartbreak House*: Shaw's Elegy for Europe," *The Shaw Review*, II, no. ix (September 1959), p. 2.
3. p. 1523.
4. Quoted by Pearson, p. 336.

5. *Immortal Shadows* (New York, 1948), p. 207. Young also re-read the play in order to determine whether it was only the Orson Welles production that had bothered him, but found the play full of "wilted opinion, half point and half patter."

But in spite of critical barbs, there remains something powerful, something compelling about Shaw's blend of the fatuous and the ominous. The world eventually catches up with its far-sighted prophets. Mary McCarthy led the way toward our growing understanding of the play with her perceptive essay on the 1938 production, in which she discerned "the terror of the play's lost author, who could not, in conscience, make his story come out right, or, indeed, come out at all."[6] And insights such as Miss McCarthy's— in addition to bigger and better world neuroses—have increased the acceptance of *Heartbreak House*. Such a new climate aided the reviewer in *The New Republic* when *Heartbreak House* had its most recent American production:

> In a time when our own middle classes are obsessed with the cultivation of their pleasures, when our own government is in the hands of the practical businessmen, and when our own ingenuity has led us to the doors of destruction, even a glossy version of the play is enough to make us shift uneasily in our chairs.[7]

A 1961 English revival continued to spur a reassessment of the play, with what *Plays and Players* called "its dark Chekhovian undertones":

> To the perpetual shame of the theatregoing public in 1921, *Heartbreak House* was a failure when it was given its first London performance 40 years ago. If, as is so often claimed, public appreciation and approval is always half a century behind the times, then this great work is just about due to receive the seal of public favour.
>
> Miscasting, that is supposed to have brought ruin to the original London production, certainly does not apply to Frank Hauser's revival. And, heartbreakingly enough, Shaw's tragic vision of England in the first world war as a captainless ship drifting towards the world's final calamity has an even greater urgency today than it possessed in the twenties. At that time, and indeed ever since, it has been fashionable to dismiss the whole of Shaw's drama as a polemical exchange of mouthpieces lacking real human substance and feeling. Those who still doubt that Shaw had any heart to break should not fail to see this revival.[8]

It would seem, then, that Shaw once again outfoxed his detractors. He planned to write a play for 1910 and was really half a century ahead of schedule. We of the western world have continued to muddle through, continued to draw upon the "very long credit"

6. *Sights and Spectacles* (New York, 1956), p. 40.
7. Robert Brustein, "The Man is Dangerous," *The New Republic*, CXLI (November 2, 1959), 21.
8. Peter Roberts, review of *Heartbreak House*, *Plays and Players*, IX (December, 1961), 13.

which Nature provided. Meanwhile, evidence mounts that just possibly our credit is nearing its end. Have we not, with Ellie, groped toward various panaceas and illusions? Have we not engaged in ulcer-stimulating quests for wealth? Have we not flirted with sham ideals, all the while neatly balancing a keg of rum and a keg of dynamite? And finally have we not almost resigned ourselves to accepting the advice of Pishtchik and jumping off a roof? Our recent behavior occasionally suggests that we may be preparing to turn on all the lights and to shout, "Bring on the bomb!"

HAROLD CLURMAN

Notes for a Production of *Heartbreak House*†

FIRST NOTES

This *crazy* house is a truth house—for adults.

There is a certain "childishness" in this play.

The play of a bunch of brilliant kids not as old as the people they impersonate—much wiser and gayer and more crackingly articulate than such people would "normally" (naturalistically!) be.

A charming, surprising *harlequinade*. (An intellectual vaudeville.)

Make them funnier—"nuttier"—than Shavian "realism" (or literalism) usually permits.

"The house is full of surprises" the Nurse says. The Captain's whistle, the sudden entrances and exits are Shaw's clues to this.

Another character says "something odd about this house."

The style tends toward a bright-minded whackiness. A puppet show! (Shaw jokes about bowings, introductions, greetings, etc.)

"We are under the dome of heaven."—The garden outside should be very much part of the first act "interior." (Variable nonrealistic lighting.)

Sound—"a sort of splendid drumming in the air." Later the air raid is compared to Beethoven. Ideally the air raid should be orchestrated—use musical instruments—on a Beethoven annunciatory theme—but not the motto of the 5th!

† Harold Clurman's insight comes not from scholarship in the usual sense, but from dealing with the play in rehearsal and production. His production of *Heartbreak House* was one of the highlights of the 1959–60 New York season. It starred Maurice Evans, Pamela Brown, Sam Levene, Diana Wynyard, Diane Cilento, and Dennis Price. The notes of a thoughtful and experienced director may be a way of getting close to the language of theater for which Shaw wrote.

In any case, under the surface, Clurman finds a quite un-Chekhovian play. These notes were published in the *Tulane Drama Review*, Vol. 5, (March, 1961) pp. 58–67.

SECOND NOTES (on further reading).

Shaw's characters are ideas—conceptions of people, theatrically and comically colored. The adverse criticism of certain critics who say that Shaw's characters are merely puppets spouting ideas should be made a positive element of the production style.

They may be made as puppet-like as the nature of the play's dramatic structure and the audience's taste will allow.

Mangan says he wants to get "to hell out of this house." Everyone in the play wants somehow to escape his or her condition. All are dissatisfied with it . . . it's a crazy house, driving them crazy!

All in a sense are "crazy," not true to themselves, not what he or she seems or pretends to be. So that everyone is somehow odd, a *clown*—disguised, masked. Outside is "the wide earth, the high seas, the spacious skies"—waiting.

"In this house," says Hector, "everybody poses." "The Trick is to find the man under the pose."

This is the director's job as well:
  a) What is the pose?
  b) What is the man or woman under the pose?

MORE RANDOM NOTES (after still further readings).

These English in *Heartbreak House* do not behave as English people do: an Irishman has rendered them! They are more impish, more extrovert, more devilish, devilishly *comic*.

Hesione is a "serpent"—she has mischief in her—not a "proper" lady. She's the cat who swallowed the canary, an intelligent minx. Mentally speaking she *winks*.

An element of "ballet-extravaganza" throughout—as if everyone were "high."

The audience is to enjoy: ideas as color, comedy, and "show," or intelligence as clowning.

They are all aware that they are living in a looney world, which they are expected to take seriously—but can't. As they progress they become aware of the need to act mad in order to approximate reality. To achieve their liberation—their world must be destroyed.

Some of the madness demands that they hide it—which is the greatest madness. Thus they speak of "form," of not making scenes—while they are always making scenes. (Lady Utterword.)

They want to burst the bonds of the old times—convention—"to get the hell out." Thus the comic outbursts. (Prelude to England's "angry young men.")

RANDOM NOTES CONTINUED.

Shotover roars.
The world's askew (the set to begin with).

They are all flying off the handle: the "handle" being the old steady values, the desire to get the hell out of a situation which no longer supports anybody. The "handle" supplies the form—which these people no longer can grip. Lady Utterword still wants to hold on with her unseen husband Hastings Utterword. (A "wooden" handle!)

The movement of the play is not placid, polite (or Chekhovian!). It is rapid, hectic, almost "wild." (The actors are asked by Shaw to sit on tables, etc.)

Mangan "not able-bodied." Has aches and pains—presses his liver when he is irritated.

Randall—curly hair ("lovelocks"—like the fop in the film of *Kipps*).

SPINE (or Main Action).

To get the hell out of this place.

This "hell" suggests some of the explosive quality desired in the playing—the element of *opera-bouffe* involved.

THE CHARACTERS.

Shotover: The Sage of Heartbreak House.

This "sage" has fed himself on rum, worked hard with his body, his fists, and his wits. The rugged person on whose hard work and tough life the house was built. But this sage has a mask—a Pose—as important for the actor as his wisdom—indeed more important. It is the mask of the Drinking Devil—almost the "debauchee" with his West Indian Black wife.

Bluff, gruff, hardy—also shut off from anything but his own thoughts and "ways." (Modern England was built by such men: born 1818 ... in their prime in 1865.)

His dismissal of everything secondary comes from his urge to get at fundamental reality—to run the ship—to find the means to set the boat on its due course. This requires the "seventh degree of concentration."

To drive toward *that* goal (the seventh degree, etc.) is his spine—his prime motive or action. (To scare people into doing what he wants, or to be free of their nonsense, their blather.)

He wants to go on with his quest; his energy is great enough to do so, but at 88 he knows it's late. Therefore he's wistful too. Despite himself he has to relax into a resignation which is a sort of "happiness." This is his pathetic side.

(The clearing and cleaning up necessary to achieve the "seventh degree" will entail a certain amount of destruction—dynamite. He is prepared for that too.)

He moves with nervous energy, sudden shifts of pace, to absolute quiet or concentrated energy—as when he sits down to work on his drawing board.

I'd rather he looked like old Walt Whitman than Shaw!

Ellie: The new life or youth in Heartbreak House.

She wants to find Port. (A goal for her life.)

The Pose is the Sweet Young Thing: the well-bred ingenue.

The real person is eager, intelligent, with a strong will and capacity to fight.

The House is bewildering, heartbreaking: all the facts she learns are upsetting. . . . She encounters hidden or masked wisdom in the Devil—the ogre Shotover. So she ends bravely in a sort of exaltation—"greater than happiness."

In the transition between these two aspects of her character she is miserable, hard, calculating.

Then she "falls in love"—differently—with life itself, in all its danger in the person or symbol of Shotover.

This is the Education of Ellie.

Shotover's dreams and ravings—his wisdom and idealism—are the most real things in the world to her—new blood.

She knows her strength (the last curtain), so she *looks forward* to another air raid . . . as toward the prospect of a new world, a fresh start!

Hesione: Heartbreak House is *her* house.

The Eternal Womanly! (And an "actress" by nature.) She wants to make life beautiful, to keep it romantically beautiful.

She wants to get out of the house too (they all do) because she knows its madness . . . yet she likes it here—the adventure, the uncertainty, the fun . . . like an actress who understands the theatre's absurdity and deception but at the same time enjoys its warm charm.

She is loving but so intelligent that she occasionally is sharp—in the face of hypocrisy, or stuffiness.

Hushabye (the Soother!). She loves company, the "menagerie." She sees through her husband, admires and laughs at him. . . .

She is active . . . yet "lazy" . . . likes to fall asleep when unoccupied because she enjoys all agreeable sensations and experiences. She is not a particularly good housekeeper . . . not thrifty . . . not very neat (show this through "business" at the very outset) . . . the maid takes care of "all that."

She likes to gossip . . . so she's socially endearing. Frank, open, *Enthusiastic*, likes to tease affectionately.

She's a flirt—for fun. It is also gracious, it keeps things "interesting."

Something of the improvident Bohemian—with very little care for money.

"You are your father's daughter, Hesione." (She's got the Devil in her too.)

She has temperament and temper too—like an actress!

She is changeable—with swift alternations of mood.

Lady Utterword (Addy): The Fine Lady of Horseback Hall.

Conventionality is her mask and protection—the sense of "form" in the "Colonel's lady" manner.

Her reality beneath the mask is a hunger for experience . . . her desire to escape the prison of her class convention. This expresses itself secretly, stealthily, unobserved . . . except in unguarded moments of hysteria.

"The first impression is one of comic silliness." She has the English "twitter."

Her "form" makes her appear more stagey than Hesione (who is real theatre!). Addy is what we call theatrical theatre of the old *very* English school (1910).

She swishes quite a bit.

Her way out of Heartbreak House is to run off to India, to the garden, to tea, to fashionable behavior.

She wants to cultivate, hold on to the "manner" which "saves" her and perhaps gives her the best of both worlds—that of feeling and that of decorum: the one utterly private, the other a "style."

A consciously picturesque *flirt* . . . but her flirtatiousness rarely goes any further than that—titillation plus elegance, and a slight touch of danger.

When all is said and done she is very practical: she sticks by her husband, Hastings—the "enduring" Englishman.

Hector: The Intelligent Man without Employment in Heartbreak House.

He wants *to get* out—*somehow* . . . but there's no place to go. He cannot see the goal. Therefore he wants everything destroyed! He has no task. For this reason he dreams up exploits, philanders, plays "parts," dresses up (in "crazy" costumes), becomes decorative . . . even in his intelligence.

Like Ellie he's trying to find—port, but he knows of none, foresees none.

"I am deliberately playing the fool," but not out of worthlessness, out of aimlessness.

He's a dilettante—forced to be one—yet he has the energy and intelligence to be something more.

Debonair and cool like a practical madman. A bit of a show-off. This gives him an identity. . . .

But this is his pose . . . the real man is dissatisfied, unhappy.

A pretty woman is a challenge to him: it leads to an activity of flirtation, the semblance of impressive action. He is telling the truth—or part of it—when he says he doesn't like being attracted—for it arouses him without leading anywhere. He is a civilized person, not a lecher. Thus he is a romantic without a cause.

He sees futility in all positions and arguments—even that of the anarchist . . . he hasn't even the confidence to feel superior to anyone.

He curses women because they are the only thing left for him to deal with . . . yet he knows they are only distractions to him.

He wants "beauty, bravery on earth." But he cannot find it around him or in him—except as a senseless activity.

The "saddest" character in the play and he behaves like an ass and a liar . . . though he often speaks honestly and even wisely.

Mangan: The "Strong Man" of Heartbreak House ("Not a well man").

He wants to get in everywhere—and to get the hell out too.

The big "capitalist"; the sharper, the practical man, the man who counts in business and in politics. All of this is the Pose.

The real man is wistful, twisted, rather frightened and a somewhat resentful child . . . the most "cheated" or frustrated person in the house.

He's "aggressive" . . . yet he is always caught off guard. He's sure an aggressive manner is the way to success, but he becomes unsure when his success is challenged or his aggressiveness doesn't impress.

Except in a very limited sphere, he's always out of his element, shaky—unhappy.

So he's always *forced* to pose—except when he believes it's particularly clever of him to tell the truth about himself.

"I don't quite understand my position here"—is the keynote. He never does—anywhere outside his office.

In the end he has a "presentiment" (of death) because he's insecure, a "worrier."

Afraid of women—gullible—an easy prey for them. Shy with Ellie, mooney with Hesione.

Like all lower-class folk who have arrived at the upper middle class he has an excessive sense of propriety—or priggishness.

He's full of unaccountable resentments (a source of comedy in this)—secret and almost ludicrous hostilities. He gets sore and vindictive in spurts. One can hardly discern the source of his irritations.

The craziness (or "unusual circumstances") of this house bursts the bubble of his pose . . . he collapses into tears, a hurt boy.

Mazzini Dunn: The Ineffectual Intellectual in Heartbreak House.

To be helpful to all (in Heartbreak House) is the "spine." Mazzini has "moist eyes," always smiling—except for moments of total consternation, and even then there's a little smile. He is obliging to everybody.

He feels a bit inferior, insufficient, guilty. Thus he wants to make up for it by being helpful. He regards everyone as somehow better, cleverer, stronger than he. He admires everyone.

(From the actor's standpoint: a sweet zany.) Shy and modest because of all this. But sweet: there is nothing cringing or undignified about him. He accepts his humble position.

He loves his wife as he does Ellie but he feels indebted to them—as to everyone else.

He is credulous, gullible . . . the world is always a surprise to him; he smiles with wonder and admiration. He really doesn't understand evil.

He thinks all one has to have are the right influences and inspirations to become good, loyal, strong.

(Key lines: "How distressing! Can I do anything I wonder?" "Think of the risk those people up there are taking"—in reference to the bombers in the air raid. "And the poor clergyman will have to get a new house.")

Randall.

To act as if he were the one proper—immovable—person. The "imperturbably," the superb English gentleman. Ornament of all diplomatic circles.

That is the Pose. Unruffled, exquisite, the last word in smoothness. Narcissistic.

The real man: a bundle of ragged nerves, a spoiled almost hysterical baby.

He believes himself a romantic character, so impressive in bearing that no matter what he does he must somehow appear dashing and right.

He's always play-acting till his "hat" is knocked off . . . then he screams like a helpless kid.

The most absurd of all the characters . . . the most "typically"

British—in the old-fashioned comic sense. A "cultured" dandy, su-
per-sophisticated. He will still look and be a kid at sixty-five.

His nerves will always show through his *sang-froid*.

His eyelids flutter . . . a bit effeminate.

He has no real passions or convictions. Therefore he needs his
adoration for Lady Utterword. All his convictions have been absorbed in his pose—which is his class pattern.

Billy Dunn.

He reverses all values in *Heartbreak House*.

To get out, make out—anyway he can.

Shaw's intention with this character is to illustrate the total top-
sy-turvydom of Heartbreak House. A sense of guilt hovers over
Heartbreak House. Its inhabitants no longer believe in the old justice. The criminal no longer believes in his crime: it's just another
way of earning a living.

Because of all this Dunn behaves like a clown—now contrite,
now shrewd, now crooked, now pious, now immoral, now joking:
for all these poses serve him (A "ham" actor.)

The real man is the poor bloke who couldn't make it either in
Heartbreak House or in Horseback Hall, and therefore preys on
both—preferably on the former, since he would simply be given a
tanning in the latter.

He ends in a terrified attempt to escape—in vain.

Nurse Guinness: The Leveller.

To wait it out—with a minimum of worry.

She's an "anarchist"—she doesn't care because she does get
along.

"Quite unconcerned," says Shaw. She's quietly brazen.

A CONCLUDING STATEMENT[1]

Sitting at the back of the auditorium at a Washington performance of *Heartbreak House*, I was delighted to hear a spectator
whisper to his neighbor, "Shaw certainly wrote wonderful gags."
Why "delighted," why not dismayed? Shaw a gag writer: blasphemy! But I *was* delighted because the spontaneous remark in
ordinary American meant that the person who had made it was
glad to be attending a "laugh show."

Everyone nowadays refers glibly to Shavian wit. But in relation
to *Heartbreak House*—less known because infrequently performed—there is a tendency to become solemn. Shaw himself is

1. Published in the souvenir program sold in the theater a few days after the
opening.

largely responsible for this, first, because he called his play a Fantasia in the Russian Manner on English Themes, and, second, because in his Preface he cited Chekhov's plays as models.

In directing the play the first thing I told the actors was that both the phrase "Russian manner" and the name Chekhov were to be disregarded in connection with Heartbreak House: they were altogether misleading. True, the name *Heartbreak House* signifies in Shaw's words "cultured, leisured Europe before the (First World) War" and Chekhov's plays deal with the educated middle class of the late nineteenth century. It is also true that in Russia Chekhov's plays—despite their melancholy—are construed as comedies, but there most of the resemblance between *Heartbreak House* and Chekhov ends.

The only other parallel between the work of the two playwrights is that Chekhov's world was destroyed by the Revolution of 1917 and the folk in *Heartbreak House* drifted into the First World War and if not destroyed were terribly shaken. Also the emphasis in this Shaw play—as in those of Chekhov—is not on the plot but on character and atmosphere.

What makes *Heartbreak House* utterly different from Chekhov is its unique style. Shaw's play is extravagant, full of capering humor which verges on the farcical. One of the characters refers to the environment he finds himself in as "a crazy house" in which one's mind "might as well be a football." The fact that this "crazy house" is also a truth house—a sort of distorting mirror which exaggerates the features of the people who enter it gives the play its human and social relevance but it does not distract from the topsy-turvy fun that my Washington playgoer enjoyed so much.

Years ago when there was still some resistance to Shaw—as we all know the greatest playwrights of our time encountered resistance as they came on the scene—certain critics complained that Shaw's characters were not people but puppets. There is no need to deny this. Shaw's characters *are* puppets—unnatural only in the sense that they reveal the truth about themselves more directly, more pointedly, more eloquently, more wittily than people in life are able to.

The director's task then was to combine the "fun" aspect of the play—its arch frivolousness—with its basic intent. The setting had not only to disclose a place but make a comment—smilingly suggestive of the author's mood. The clothes had to be costumes. The characterizations had to be tipped from realism to a kind of gay picturesqueness. Gravity had to be avoided—except as fleeting reminders that we were still dealing with a truth about life—our lives. This slight duality—a sort of "gayed up" seriousness—part game, part prophecy—is only a reflection of the text itself which begins as a comedy of mad manners and ends with an air raid by an enemy never named or even hinted at throughout the course of the play.

What was Shaw's purpose and why did he write *Heartbreak House* in this peculiar way? The play exemplifies a typical Shavian "trick." *Heartbreak House* is all carefree talk and horseplay— apparently devoid of dark portent; then it bursts for a moment into a scene of shock and ends ironically on a note of almost languid peace. "Nothing will happen," one of the house guests says. Something does happen and something more fatal may yet happen— expected, almost hoped for, by certain of the characters.

These "charming people, most advanced, unprejudiced, frank, humane, unconventional, free thinking and everything that is delightful" are content to drift. No matter what inner qualms they may have, no matter what emptiness or discontent they occasionally experience, they have settled for the happiness of dreams and daily pastimes. For all his sharp teasing, Shaw is tolerant with them. Only, says he, in earnest jest, if you go on like this without "navigation"—that is without plan, purpose and preparative action—your ship will "strike and sink and split."

The thought or warning which informs the play—stated in a frolic of entertaining word and postures—is wholly appropriate to our day and our theatre. Though the people of *Heartbreak House* are English it is not merely a play about a certain class or a certain country. Time has turned it into a play about practically all of us, everywhere.

LOUIS CROMPTON

Heartbreak House†

Heartbreak House is a curious paradox among Shaw's dramas: it is at one and the same time a novel experiment and a very reactionary play. The experimentalism lies in Shaw's use of Chekhov as a model, a choice he signalized by his subtitle, "A Fantasia in the Russian Manner on English Themes." There is no question of Shaw's enthusiasm for his mentor; he once declared after watching *The Cherry Orchard* that it made him want to tear up his own plays and begin afresh. He had unbounded admiration for the quiet

† In contrast to Clurman's directorial approach, Louis Crompton provides a model of rigorous, adult, philosophic-literary criticism, finding Shaw's roots in Carlyle as well as Chekhov, and tracing the people of the play to some possible prototypes. This is Chapter Ten of Crompton's book *Shaw the Dramatist* (Lincoln, Neb., 1969), pp. 153–168.

realism with which Chekhov dissects his characters' contradictions and futilities, and for his rigorous avoidance of stereotypes and the clichés of conventional comedy and melodrama. Even the secondary characteristics of Chekhov—the naïve self-absorption of his people, the absurd non sequiturs, the tragicomic impasses, and the sense of boredom and frustration that infect his country-house gatherings—attracted Shaw to the extent of leading him to pay the Russian master the compliment of imitation.

Yet the spirit of *Heartbreak House* is at the same time so diverse from Chekhov's that some writers have objected that its Chekhovism is wholly superficial.[1] This is not my view: the whole spirit of the Chekhovian vintage is, I believe, here; what happened is that Shaw has added to it a pungent ingredient to make a much headier brew. Never one to take a simple view of a matter, or to be satisfied with another man's formula, no matter how sophisticated, Shaw has added to Chekhov a strong dash of the nineteenth-century writer who of all writers would appear to most critics to be Chekhov's exact opposite—Thomas Carlyle.

There is more of Carlyle—and, indeed, of the Old Testament—in *Heartbreak House* than in any other of Shaw's plays. This is what I have had in mind in calling *Heartbreak House* a markedly reactionary drama as well as a technically advanced one. To understand the reason for this sudden upsurgence of the stern Victorian prophet in Shaw we need only to consider the change in manners and social outlook that had taken place in the decade since the writing of *Man and Superman*. As the author of that comedy's satiric irreverences, Shaw had looked like the very midwife of the twentieth century, the man best fitted to lay the ghost of the Victorian proprieties. Now, a decade later, Shaw renders his judgment on the era that followed the old Queen's death. The new prospect did not reassure him. The smug philistinism that Arnold and Dickens had pilloried a generation earlier was now in full retreat, but the new age, having thrown off the shackles of Victorian moralism, had also thrown off with them the Victorian sense of purpose. Instead of trying to realize Utopia, it had merely followed the more seductive course of wandering where its sentimental and romantic impulses led it. A narrow world had given way to one that was sophisticated, skeptical, and pleasure-seeking: Bohemia, the devil's kingdom, had superseded Mrs. Grundy's Philistia. But whatever the gain in charm and intelligence, Shaw thought it more than outweighed by the loss of will, social energy, and public conscience. Far from inspiriting him, the spectacle of a country in

1. Cf. Stark Young, *Immortal Shadows*, pp. 207–209. F. P. W. McDowell reviews criticism of the play and also discusses its Chekhovism in "Technique, Symbol, and Theme in *Heartbreak House*," *PMLA*, LXVIII (June 1953), 335–356.

which Edward the *bon vivant* had replaced Victoria the good as the national exemplar aroused his deepest apprehension.

The result was to fire Shaw with a neo-Victorian prophetic ire. In *Heartbreak House*, Shaw visits upon the age of Bloomsbury with its cult of sentimental personal relations the same scorn Carlyle visited upon the age of Brummell with its Byronism and its pococurantism.[2] Hence the paradox already referred to, for *Heartbreak House* is an *avant-garde* drama, designed to titillate the subtle and refined palates of the hedonists and dilettantes at the same time that it is meant to scourge them. Like Carlyle's *French Revolution* and Dickens' *Bleak House*, it is an adaptation to the author's own purposes of the Calvinist–Old Testament theory of history as a series of divine judgments upon human behavior. Shaw is telling us in his tragicomedy that we must be prepared, if not as "sinners in the hands of an angry God," at least as mortals in a world of men, to abide the consequences of our social actions—or negligences— as they issue in war, plague, famine, and revolution. Nowhere else in Shaw's writings does he express such sardonic joy in human misfortune as in the passage in the preface to *Heartbreak House* which begins, "Apostolic Hapsburg has collapsed; All Highest Hohenzollern languishes in Holland," where, in rhythms as mockingly derisive as the choruses in Handel's *Israel in Egypt*, he celebrates the downfall of the Central Empires in the course of World War I.

But if the spirit behind *Heartbreak House* is that of Micah, Jeremiah, and the Book of Exodus, Shaw's avowed literary strategy, as we have seen, was to appeal to the most highly developed taste of the intelligentsia he was attacking. Shaw knew that Captain Shotover, his spokesman in the play, must first of all, like Coleridge's Ancient Mariner, hold his audience spellbound if he was to strike home with his message. As Shaw himself put it, "The funny old captain, having lured them into his ship by his sallies, ties them up to the gangway and gives them a moral dozen."[3] The result is Chekhov reorchestrated, so to speak, with tubas and drums added, to allow for the playing of a *Dies Irae* at the end.

Heartbreak House is thus a redistillation of Chekhov and at the same time a passing beyond him, for Chekhov's world is static and directionless. Though his characters often talk grandly and eloquently about the future of humanity, it is obvious that they are not going to act on their convictions, and Chekhov records their orations with a sympathy that is undercut with humorous skepti-

2. "Beau" Brummell was the leader of fashion in the early nineteenth century, as the so-called "Bloomsbury Group" were the leaders of literary and artistic fashion from 1907 through World War I. Prominent in the Bloomsbury Group were such figures as Leonard and Virginia Woolf, E. M. Forster, and Lytton Strachey. Pococurantism is the studied attitude of being blasé or bored [*Editor*].

3. "Bernard Shaw on 'Heartbreak House,'" *Illustrated Sunday Herald*, October 23, 1921, p. 5.

cism. His aim is to present men and women to us dramatically, not to point the way. As a result some critics have exalted his detachment into an end in itself and attacked Shaw as the perverter of the master. But this is to ignore that fact that Chekhov himself found the lack of commitment in contemporary writing its greatest failure and contemporary nihilism the age's bane. In a letter to the critic Alexei Suvorin written in the first flush of his fame, he put the case sharply enough:

> Science and technology are passing through a great period now, but for our writing fraternity it is a flabby, sour, dull time. . . . Remember that the writers whom we call eternal or simply good and who intoxicate us have one very important characteristic in common: they move in a certain direction and they summon you there too, and you feel not with your mind alone, but your whole being that they have a goal. . . . The best of them are realistic and paint life as it is, but because every line is permeated as with sap, by the consciousness of a purpose, you are aware not only of life as it is but of life as it ought to be, and that captivates you. And we? We! We paint life as it is, and beyond that neither whoa! nor giddap! Whip us and we cannot go a step farther. We have neither immediate nor distant aims and our souls are a yawning void, we have no politics, we don't believe in revolution, we have no God. . . .[4]

Like the clear-eyed medical man he was, Chekhov diagnosed the disease of will-lessness from which cultivated Europe suffered before the war, but he felt powerless to cure it. Shaw agreed with the diagnosis but desired to rouse the sleepwalkers of *The Cherry Orchard* and *The Three Sisters* to a recognition of their plight.

Shaw started writing his play in 1913 in a moment that to the casual observer looked peaceful enough. Europe had not known a continent-wide convulsion since the time of Napoleon. But Shaw saw clearly that behind the calm, the intensification of international hatred, fear, and envy, coupled with the paralysis of the foreign offices, was causing a slow but dangerous drift toward war. Sensing that time was running out, he took up the public advocacy of a triple alliance between Britain, France, and Germany as a way of staving off the disaster. Consequently, though Shaw did not know what the end of his drama would be when he began to write it—he even declared that he did not see one speech ahead but let the play write itself—his premonitions were of the direst, and there is an ominous undercurrent in the Captain's electrically charged warnings from the first scene on.

For all his preoccupation with foreign affairs, Shaw does not set

4. Chekhov to Alexei Suvorin, November 25, 1892, *The Portable Chekhov*, ed. A. Yarmolinsky (New York: Viking, 1947), pp. 624–625.

his play in Whitehall or the Quai d'Orsay. Instead he comments on the situation obliquely by taking us to a country house in
Sussex on a fine September evening when five visitors arrive. Four
of them—Ellie, Ariadne, Mangan, and Randall—suffer some sort
of heartbreak in the course of the evening. Ostensibly, it is these
disappointments that give the play its name. Yet in point of fact,
as Shaw made clear to Trebitsch, it is not this kind of heartbreak
he is really alluding to in his title. The word "heartbreak," he
explained, meant a "chronic complaint, not a sudden shock." Its
real meaning is the despair felt by the social philosopher who has
come to realize that these charming, "advanced, unprejudiced,
frank, humane, unconventional, democratic, free-thinking" men
and women are totally feckless in social matters and quite incapable
of realizing the danger in which they stand. Shaw added that he
was using the word in the way Carlyle had used it when he referred
to the blind faith of nineteenth-century liberalism in the beneficent
effects of laissez faire as "heartbreaking nonsense."

To the Chekhovism of the play Shaw has added his own poetic
symbolism. The shiplike room in which the action takes place is
meant to put us in mind both of England's maritime history and of
the allegory of the ship of state in *The Republic*.[5] Captain Shotover, who designed it, is a very old man who was born in the
1820's. He was thus a contemporary of the great explorers like Sir
John Speke and John Hanning Franklin (whose Arctic adventures
seem to be echoed in his tales), and of those other Victorian navi-
gators such as Ruskin, Mill, Marx, and Tolstoy, who attempted to
chart the course of man's social and spiritual destiny. During his
adventures as a commercial trader he was forced to pretend to sell
his soul to the devil as the only way of striking awe into his crew
of desperadoes. This pretense led to his real damnation, from which
he was only redeemed by an informal marriage to a West Indian
negress, who presumably forced him for the first time to see natives
as fellow humans. The main characteristic of his life, however, has
been his heroic sense of purpose which has led him to brave every
new hardship and danger undaunted. Throughout all his hairsbreadth adventures his code has been, like that of Tennyson's
Ulysses, "to strive, to seek, to find, and not to yield." Above all, he
has lived in fear of happiness, contentment, acquiescence, and pur-
poselessness.

But the warnings of the prophets have gone unheeded. What
Carlyle called the "hog philosophy" of free enterprise has
triumphed in a world that has avowed a faith in the survival of

5. Shaw remarked to Paul Green, of *Heartbreak House*, that "it is a sort of national fable or a fable of national-ism" (*Dramatic Heritage* [New York: Samuel French, 1953], p. 127).

the fittest, the fittest in this case being the greediest and least public-spirited. Worse still has ensued, for the Captain eventually made the mistake of abandoning the humanizing, mundane negress to marry a captivating and seductive Eastern enchantress—a kind of oriental houri who is referred to in the play as a "black witch" of Zanzibar—and from this union has sprung a daughter who combines his vitality and intellectual brilliance with her mother's exotic beauty.[6] Hesione Shotover is of the race of Kundry, Circe, and Astarte.[7] Her appearance and manner are those of Mrs. Patrick Campbell, whose potent spell had fascinated Shaw first over the footlights, and then from much closer range while he rehearsed her for her part in *Pygmalion*. Mrs. Campbell combined a sensitive poetic culture with a feckless charm, an impish sense of humor, and a statuesque Italianate beauty at once classical and Pre-Raphaelite. Edward Burne-Jones, whose style she adopted as her own, was sufficiently struck by her *femme fatale* attractiveness to paint her as a "Vampire," and this painting no doubt provided the epithet which Shaw has Hector hurl at his wife in the play.[8]

Hesione represents a post-Victorian world in which the cultivation of private feeling has superseded an interest in public affairs. Her function is not to create heroes, but to enchant them and minister to their pleasures by realizing in real life their favorite poems and stage romances. But she is no sensual monster; she is a refined, cultivated society hostess whose bohemianism is part of her fashionable smartness. Her aim is to make existence a thing of poetry and sentiment which will find its culmination in happy love affairs. Her faith in this ideal has been bolstered by her own lifelong passion for her dashing and romantically handsome husband, Hector. Their love match has seemed so satisfying to her that she is preoccupied in arranging similar matches or liaisons for others. One result of her highly gratifying marriage has been to remove her far above mere jealousy or possessiveness; indeed, she is willing to connive at latter-day amorous escapades on her husband's part, and even to promote them, since she is sincerely puzzled by the restlessness and discontent that possess him, and sure enough of her own power to risk such experiments.

Shaw complained that the first audiences of the play could not

6. The epithet "black" presumably does not mean Negro here. The reference is more likely to the baleful black magic the tropical beauty exercised.
7. All enchantresses of mythology [*Editor*].
8. On July 28, 1929, Shaw wrote to Mrs. Campbell: "Of course we are a pair of mountebanks; but why, oh why do you get nothing out of me, though I got everything out of you? Mrs. Hesione Hushabye in *Heartbreak*

House, the Serpent in Methuselah, whom I always hear speaking with your voice, and Orinthia [in *The Apple Cart*]: all you, to say nothing of Eliza, who was only a joke. You are the Vamp and I the victim; yet it is I who suck your blood and fatten on it whilst you lose everything! It is ridiculous!" (*Bernard Shaw and Mrs. Patrick Campbell: Their Correspondence*, ed. Alan Dent [New York: Alfred A. Knopf, 1952], p. 334).

make head or tail of Hesione's husband. He sought to enlighten them by explaining that Hector was to be interpreted as a "liar, boaster, hero, stylist, Athos and D'Artagnan rolled into a single passionately sincere humbug."[9] Once more, as in *Arms and the Man*, Shaw is analyzing that strange anomaly, uncommon in literature but not unknown in life, the hero-poseur. To those naïve souls who imagine that men are either strong, silent heroes or simple frauds, Shaw points out that there are in fact brave men (of whom at a later date he might have chosen T. E. Lawrence as an example) with courage, imagination, and dramatic flair, who, though they have had a whole series of amazing real adventures, deprecate these and satisfy their modesty and literary inventiveness at once by making up a series of false ones. Hector is, of course, none other than our old friend Sergius Saranoff, the comedic Hamlet of *Arms and the Man*, making his appearance again after the career of writing and adventuring Bluntschli had recommended to him—and twenty years of marriage. That Shaw once more had the Scottish aristocratic revolutionary author Robert Cunninghame Graham in mind in creating his swashbuckling disillusioned romancer seems clear enough from the pseudonym Darnley that he gives him (with its hint of royal Scots blood), his sheik's costume (Cunninghame Graham had traveled through Morocco disguised in native dress), and Ellie's description of him as a Socialist who "despises rank, and has been in three revolutions fighting on the barricades."

Hesione appreciates and respects her husband's courage even though she recognizes that it is part schoolboy bravado and part fear of being thought a coward. She also understands and forgives him his lies. What she does not understand is his political side, for Hector is a born reformer who has been diverted from his mission by Hesione, to whom revolutionary politics are merely another excuse for risking his life needlessly. She has beguiled him into a life of erotic and social pleasures, and encouraged him to play the picturesque traveler in oriental robes while the burden of supporting the household falls on her aged but still resourceful father. Yet all this cannot hide from Hector that it is Hesione who is the haremkeeper and he who is the sexual ornament or male sultana. Like Shakespeare's Cassio, he is a man "damn'd in a fair wife," and his sense of damnation expresses itself in the scraps of wild poetry and Hamlet-like imprecations he utters—not against his beautiful captress, but against himself. In his analysis of Hector's relation with Hesione, Shaw is following the idea developed by Ibsen in *Little Eyolf* and by Tolstoy in *The Kreutzer Sonata* that marriage may on occasion be the most dangerous and soul destroying of all sexual relationships.

9. "Bernard Shaw on 'Heartbreak House,'" *Illustrated Sunday Herald*, October 23, 1921, p. 5.

What Shaw is trying to say is that happiness, particularly in its most refined, cultivated form, is damnation. By contrast, heartbreak of the sudden-shock type may be a step towards salvation. Unless one grasps this idea he will go hopelessly wrong in trying to understand *Heartbreak House*, and in particular he will be merely baffled by the development of Hesione's young protégée, Ellie Dunn, which forms the chief dramatic action of the play. Desmond MacCarthy, for instance, has denounced Ellie's sudden transformation from a "green girl" into an "acute, collected woman" as a "thundering impossibility."[1] Ellie first arrives at the Sussex country house in a contentedly happy daze, which we soon discover is the consequence of her clandestine but thrilling meetings with a mysteriously romantic gentleman who calls himself Marcus Darnley. It is Ellie's escape from this state first into a condition of hardheaded cynicism and then into discipleship to the Captain that has puzzled critics.

Ellie's two remarkable changes of heart can be fathomed only if we first of all consider her father and her relation to him. Shaw seems to have based the character of Mazzini Dunn on an idealistic entrepreneur of his acquaintance, Ebenezer (later Sir Ebenezer) Howard. Howard was perhaps the exact temperamental opposite of the flamboyant Cunninghame Graham. He was nevertheless an equally unusual personality. As a young man he had come under the influence of Emerson and Whitman in the 1870's during a sojourn in Nebraska and Chicago. He then returned to England to live the life of a high-minded, self-effacing dreamer, all the while cheerfully enduring the dreariest poverty. Yet for all his lack of personal success, he was destined to have a profound influence on the twentieth century as founder of the international city-planning movement. Beginning with Welwyn City near Shaw's home at Ayot, the movement he inspired led to the founding of some score of model towns in England and America. One of his biographers wrote of him:

> Howard's personality was a continual surprise to strangers knowing nothing of his astonishing achievements. He was the mildest and most unassuming of men, unconcerned with personal appearance, rarely giving evidence of the force within him. Of medium height and sturdy build, he was the sort of man who could easily pass unnoticed in a crowd; Mr. Bernard Shaw, who much admired what he did, only overstates a truth when he says that this "amazing man" seemed an "elderly nobody," "whom the Stock Exchange would have dismissed as a negligible crank."[2]

Ellie worships her father and has even become engaged to his fifty-year-old colleague, "Boss" Mangan, who has helped him

1. Desmond MacCarthy, *Shaw's Plays in Review* (New York: Thames and Hudson, 1951), p. 151.
2. F. J. Osborn, preface to Ebenezer Howard, *Garden Cities of Tomorrow* (London: Faber and Faber, 1946), pp. 22–23.

through a financial crisis. The idea of a marriage of gratitude between Ellie and the dull and unattractive financier naturally shocks Hesione, whose favorite pastime, as we have seen, is arranging for other people's sentimental gratification. She is delighted to hear of Ellie's interest in Darnley, and not offended but only sorry on Ellie's behalf when the romantic dream hero turns out to be none other than her own philandering Hector incognito. But Ellie, though she is momentarily shaken, does not in the long run react at all as Hesione expects her to. Among Chekhovians who sigh, agonize, fascinate each other, and laugh and weep at their own follies without changing their ways, Ellie discovers that she is in their world but not of it.[3] Ellie is shocked but she also is brought suddenly to the realization that "heartbreak is not what I thought it must be." She means that she is not a stage Ariadne who bemoans her lost lover and enjoys heartbreak (after the style of Octavius Robinson in *Man and Superman*) for the theatrical and poetic possibilities of that much dramatized condition. Her hurt and chagrin are in fact overborne by her self-scorn, and she becomes hard and clear-eyed, not tearful.

Ellie survives heartbreak. The Captain's second daughter—who actually does bear the name of Ariadne—wants to think of herself as heartbroken but in reality has no heart to break. Ariadne had left home at nineteen and married a hidebound colonial governor named Hastings Utterword in order to escape a family whose easygoing bohemianism irked her. Now, twenty-three years later, she returns to what she imagines will be a sentimental reunion with her father and sister. Shotover, however, receives her woodenly, and Hesione, amazed as she is at Ariadne's reappearance, shows none of the warm interest in her she takes in Ellie. Ariadne is intensely annoyed with this cool reception, but she cannot hide, even from herself, that her chagrin is not really sentimental disappointment, but simply her old exasperation with her family's lack of conventionality. It is her sense of decorum, not her heart, that is bruised. In her frustration she turns to Hector, and he, in his own despite, reacts as spontaneously to his wife's sister's sexual vitality as he does to his wife's. The ironic result is that he finds himself playing Don Juan against his will without the least illusion that he loves or even likes Ariadne. For though she lures Hector on, Ariadne has none of her sister's frank candor, and plays the game of sex after the fashion of one of Blake's "angels," that is, clandestinely, behind a façade of propriety. The situation is rendered one degree more absurd when Ariadne's brother-in-law, Randall Utterword, appears

3. When St. John Ervine objected that Ellie seemed out of place in the play, Shaw replied that he had intended to give such an impression and had emphasized the effect by choosing the Irish actress Ellen O'Malley for the part because he thought she was a strong "Lady Macbeth" type, and not an ingenue or a "sweet little sexual attraction" (unpublished letter, October 28, 1921, Hanley Collection, University of Texas).

and turns out to be an aging *cicisbeo* with the nerves of a lovesick adolescent and a more than husbandly sense of jealousy.

Behind this cat's cradle of amorous intrigues stands the Captain, half dotard and half seer. While the Chekhovians nurse their broken hearts, he keeps the family in money by selling new lethal inventions to the militarists, and ponders the problem of social power. The problem presents itself to him this way: If blindly selfish men like Mangan and Hastings are willing to fight for their private wealth and class privileges, what are the public-spirited to do in the face of such determination? The Captain hopes to create a death ray which will act at the mere will of the benevolent, exactly as the psychological power of awe operates to control tyranny and violence in Shaw's utopian society in *Back to Methuselah*. The Captain is thus a prefiguration of the Ancients of the succeeding play cycle; his quest for the seventh stage of concentration is none other than their quest for godhead through the union of omnipotence and good will and for the inauguration of the rule of the philosopher-king that is the culmination of Shaw's social and political hopes. There is reason in Shotover's madness, even as there is in Lear's. It was this visionary side of the drama that made Shaw commend *Heartbreak House* as his own favorite among his plays on the grounds that "it has more of the miracle, more of the mystic belief in it than any of my others."[4]

The critics' obtuseness to the play's political implications made Shaw complain to St. John Ervine on the occasion of its first production:

> The criticisms are all stupid (except Hope in the New Age) because every situation in my plays has a public interest; and critics, leading a Savage Club life, are incapable of public interests. They grin at the burglar as the latest Gilbertism, and never reflect on the fact that every day malefactors exploit the cruelty of our criminal law to blackmail humane people. They are not interested in Mangan because they are not interested in Lord Devonport. What use are such political imbeciles to me?[5]

The Lord Devonport whom Shaw used as a model for Mangan was Hudson Kearley, the founder of a national chain of grocery stores who became a Liberal member of parliament and in 1907 was appointed first chairman of the Port of London Authority, a post that brought him into acrimonious opposition with the dockers' union. To Shaw he must have appeared as a prime example of a businessman unfitted for public service through his economic and social philosophy, the exact antithesis of the selfless Howard.[6]

---

4. *Dramatic Heritage*, p. 127.
5. Shaw to St. John Ervine, October 28, 1921, Hanley Collection.
6. Later, during the war, Beatrice Webb complained that Lloyd George had handed over each ministry to a special interest: "the Food Controller is a wholesale Grocer"—"the egregious Devonport" (February 22, 1917, *Beatrice Webb's Diaries 1912–1924*, ed. Margaret Cole [London: Longmans, Green and Co., 1952], p. 83).

Mangan proves no match for a clever seductress like Hesione when she employs her wiles to lure him away from Ellie. Unfortunately, however, Hesione's plot backfires, for Ellie makes another surprising discovery about herself. When Mangan tries, under Hesione's influence, to break off the engagement, she comes to realize that his wealth was more than an incidental attraction—she had in fact counted on it to escape from her family's poverty. With this realization she now fights to keep him to his pledge, and he is startled to find what power of will this frail girl has when her mind is made up to a course of action. He squirms and writhes, and even reveals to her that, far from being her father's friend in need, he had made him his own cat's-paw and dupe, but to no avail; she holds him in a grip of steel, meeting each revelation with a counter-revelation and each threat with a counterthreat.

It is the Captain who loosens her grip by warning her that she must not sell her soul. She fences with him by paraphrasing Ruskin and Morris—and Shaw—to the effect that only well-fed bodies are capable of spiritual life, but he relentlessly brushes this sophistry aside: the material happiness she is now pursuing in her mood of cynicism is a far hollower ideal than the sentimental happiness she yearned for before. She must renounce both kinds of happiness as an end of existence if she is to escape damnation and despair. His own philosophy has been one of struggle and self-discipline, not a dream of bliss. The horror of old age is just the fact that it may inevitably bring happiness in its wake—"the happiness that comes as life goes, the happiness of yielding and dreaming instead of resisting and doing, the sweetness of the fruit that is going rotten." To save herself, Ellie must live as a free soul, unenamored and unbought.

Shortly after this, the calm is shattered by the arrival of a pseudo-burglar who purposely lets himself get caught in the act of stealing. The scene of the burglar's intrusion has been repeatedly decried as farcical and irrelevant, but it is really neither. Far from being stock comic relief, the burglar is a thoroughly unpleasant fellow, and the predicament he puts the others in is a genuinely uncomfortable one. In his preface on prisons Shaw explained his intention: "In most cases it costs nothing to let a thief off, and a good deal to prosecute him. The burglar in *Heartbreak House*, who makes his living by robbing people, and then threatening to put them to the expense and discomfort of attending his trial and enduring all the worry of the police enquiries is not a joke: he is a comic dramatization of a process that is going on every day."[7] The point is that the enlightened and sensitive part of our community has not only abdicated its

7. Preface to Sidney and Beatrice Webb, *English Prisons Under Local* *Government* (London: Longmans, Green and Co., 1922), p. xxi.

responsibility for guiding the nation's economic and political affairs; it has also failed to evolve a humane and sensible penal code, so that it is faced with the choice between punitive retaliation based on a superstitious ideal of expiation it no longer believes in, and an irresponsible granting of impunity to offenders.

The final act takes place on the terrace later that evening. Earlier in the play the *crise de coeur* of the various characters have been interspersed with a good deal of comic bustle and fantastical farce. Now as the house party relaxes to hymn the beauty of the moonless night, the mood becomes musical and operatic. Shaw gives an indication of the tone he was aiming at in a note to his French translator correcting the overly prosaic style in which he had at first translated Ellie's speeches—"Après la reveille de Mangan, jusqu'à la fin de la pièce, Ellie est une figure de poésie, rêveuse, lyrique, jamais terre à terre, quoique toujours forte."[8] Musical feeling pervades the scene, and Hesione even detects the sound of a "splendid drumming in the sky." However, as we soon see, this background music has an ominous ambiguity. Shaw first evokes the night of Tristan with its voluptuous languor, but gradually the echoes of Isolde's invocation fade into the drumbeats of *Götterdämmerung*, and the ecstasies of love-pain pass into ecstasies of danger and destruction as *Heartbreak House* comes to judgment.

The idea that it is Tristan's story and not Siegfried's that is the natural prelude to the "Twilight of the Gods" is the central idea of Shaw's play. Victorians like Morris had proclaimed that "love is enough," and moderns like Auden tell us that we "must love one another or die" and then on second thought change it to "love one another *and* die," which is worse. Shaw simply announces the futility of love as a serious value: Ellie nurses love's young dream and sees the bubble burst; Randall represents the tragedy of a man who never achieves his heart's desire, Hector the tragedy of the man who does, Ariadne the comedy of a vigorous woman duped by convention into believing in sentiments she does not feel or even really want to feel. Hesione, the self-appointed patroness of lovers in the play, finally wonders "just how much longer I can go on living in this cruel, damnable world." Much modern pessimism— Jean Anouilh's might be taken as a typical instance—has exactly the same basis. What Shaw does is tell us that such feelings are wasted. He wants us to digest our sentimental disappointments and brace ourselves for nobler and more urgent business. His advice to us is comparable to Carlyle's advice to his age to close its Byron and open its Goethe.

The scene on the terrace now becomes a moment of truth for

8. Manuscript note in typescript of French translation, p. 86, Hanley Collection.

the whole group. Ellie, who has at last won through to salvation, hails the Captain as her soul's natural master and her spiritual husband. Mangan admits his political talent is largely obstructive and reveals that he has no inkling whatsoever of how to steer the ship of state. Lady Utterword counsels abandoning England's sham democracy and putting Hastings at the helm to rule by a colonial governor's methods of brute coercion, but the Captain scoffs at this as "not God's way." The natural leader of the country is the idealistic Hector, but his self-disgust at his enthrallment to women makes him the most Byronic of all. He interprets the sounds in the sky as "Heaven's threatening growl of disgust at us useless futile creatures," and looks forward to the holocaust he expects with the suicidal fervor of the baffled idealist. Hesione, puzzled by the men's discontent and sublimely ignorant of its cause, turns to them and asks despairingly, "Aren't you happy . . . ? Open your eyes: Addy and Ellie look beautiful enough to please the most fastidious man: we live and love and have not a care in the world. We women have managed all that for you. Why in the name of common sense do you go on as if you were two miserable wretches?"

What is remarkable about this scene is that for all its intellectual intentions—here analyzed somewhat nakedly—the dialectical structure remains largely implicit. The characters, as in Chekhov, assert their own convictions and express their feelings very much as if the others were not present. They inhabit separate, self-sufficient worlds and are not here debaters in a Platonic dialogue, as they are in the last act of *Major Barbara*, for instance. The plangent expression of conflicting feeling, musically composed, dominates over abstractions, as the voices interweave symphonically. At last, however, one voice rises above the rest, as Mazzini joins Hesione in rebuking the others. The bohemian informality and casual ease of this country-house week end, he tells them flatteringly, represents all that is most pleasant and charming in English life. At one time, fearing disaster, he had joined socialist societies to fight poverty and avert revolution, and pacifist societies to combat militarism and avert war, but now he is convinced that he took too melodramatic a view of matters. Obviously, there is a Providence that looks out for men and prevents catastrophes.

His willingness to bask in the apparent halcyon calm and savor the sweet life accurately reflects the mood of Asquith in Downing Street and Grey in the Foreign Office on the very eve of World War I. The mood was endemic in Paris and Vienna and St. Petersburg among all but the one per cent of European society that had resolved to pin its hopes on blood and steel. Nothing ever happens, Mazzini assures the company. The Captain, from the depths of his

Victorian conscience, demurs, with the grimmest Carlylean realism: "Nothing but the smash of the drunken skipper's ship on the rocks, the splintering of her rotten timbers, the tearing of her rusty plates, the drowning of the crew like rats in a trap."

A moment later the first bombs fall and we realize that the moonless night has been an invitation to enemy airplanes. The play which Shaw had begun in 1913 was finished in 1916, the year of Verdun. The first zeppelin raids had been greeted with the same amazed delight as a relief from boredom and routine with which Hesione and Ellie greet the bombs at the final curtain. Bombs had fallen near Ayot, and a workman who had wantonly lit a flare in a field to attract aircraft (as Hector lights up the house) had been killed. Shaw declared that his plays were

> interludes, as it were, between two greater realities. And the meaning of them lies in what has preceded them and in what follows them. The beginning of one of my plays takes place exactly where an unwritten play ended. And the ending of my written play concludes where another play begins. It is the two unwritten plays [the critics] should consider in order to get light upon the one that lies between.[9]

It is not too difficult to accept Shaw's challenge and sketch a sequel to *Heartbreak House*. The play ends just as the war begins. Presumably Hesione will organize entertainment for the troops, and Ariadne war drives, while Hector will go to his death as a dashing cavalry officer, and Hastings as a general will blunder into massacres and be quietly relieved of his post. Ellie, in whom the spirit of an Edith Cavell lies latent, will be a nurse in France; Mazzini will work silently and efficiently without acclaim organizing industry and then be swept out of his post when peace with its cry for normalcy returns, while Mangan's surviving counterparts will be put in charge of wartime industries until their incompetence and the necessities of the situation force their replacement. Mangan's own death by bombing at the end of the play parallels the "spontaneous combustion" of the mock Lord Chancellor in Dickens' *Bleak House*, the two deaths symbolizing the final explosion of the false values, commercial and legal, the men are associated with. So the inhabitants of Heartbreak House will enter history and find their fulfillment or doom, not through any will of their own, but through the brute compulsion of political forces they refused to try to control.

Shaw repeatedly called *Heartbreak House* his greatest play. Some critics have agreed with this estimate and placed it high among his achievements; others have dismissed it as mere fantastication. One

9. *Dramatic Heritage*, pp. 125–126.

common reaction has been an initial delight with its surface attractions, followed by a later revulsion.[1] In such cases one is tempted to suspect that the critic did not at first get past the brilliant exterior, and that the response that found the work unpalatable was, if hostile, nevertheless the more profound, since he had at least become aware of what Shaw was opposing and of the weight of social responsibility being laid on his shoulders. I would myself place it among Shaw's best works. If it has not the intellectual brilliance of *Man and Superman* and *Major Barbara* or the heroic *élan* of *Saint Joan*, it is unsurpassed in the Shavian canon for the subtlety of its art, its depth of poetic feeling, and the fascination of its symbolism. On these merits it may be ranked next after his three greatest masterpieces. And, on the realistic side, as a fable of the way civilizations can drift into catastrophes, it is still all too chillingly to the point.

ARTHUR H. NETHERCOT

Zeppelins Over Heartbreak House†

The fact that Shaw based the final episode in his *Heartbreak House* on an actual event that he himself had participated in, or least witnessed, from his home at Ayot St. Lawrence has been generally known for some time,[1] but Shavian scholars have also generally overlooked the fact that in a letter to his friends the Webbs on October 5, 1916, he drew a very graphic picture of the whole incident, in which can be detected the germs of many of the details of the aerial bombing raid with which he ended his play. It is true that he never during the whole play specifically identified England's attackers nor did he ever describe the kind of flying machine from which the bombs were being dropped. As a matter of fact, he does not even use the word "bombs" anywhere. All the audience hears is the repeated word "explosions" and the sound of these explosions offstage, with a reference to "those poor fellows up there." This generalized treatment of a very concrete episode is, of course, intentional and completely in accord with Shaw's purpose of broadening out his picture of the plight of England and her probable catastrophe throughout the play.

* * *

1. Stark Young at first agreed with Edmund Wilson that *Heartbreak House* was "probably the best of the Shaw plays." Reviewing a performance in 1938, however, he attacked it as "garrulous, unfelt, and tiresome" (*Immortal Shadows*, pp. 206–207).
† Arthur Nethercot provides an interesting sidelight on the source material for the dropping of the bombs in the last act in this article from *The Shaw Review*, Vol. 9 (May, 1966).
1. See, for example, Blanche Patch, *Thirty Years with G.B.S.* (New York, 1951), p. 69.

When the real raid came, early in October 1916, Shaw was apparently just finishing his play; as his preface states, he had begun to write some months before a shot had been fired in the war (that is, early in 1914 or late in 1913) and had continued to work on it for two or three years during the war. He had created and established his collection of characters representing the two dominant but useless type of upperclass English people whom he summed up in his preface as Heartbreak House and Horseback Hall. He had allowed these characters to discuss the unhappy condition of England at considerable length, to interact with one another, sometimes seriously and sometimes comically, and to have come to pretty much of a stalemate. What was he going to do? How was he going to end his play? (Shaw always admitted that when he began a new play he very seldom, if ever, knew just how he was going to end it.)[2] As Hector puts it, *"impatiently,"* just before the first "dull distant explosion" is heard, "How is all this going to end?" To Mazzini Dunn's optimistic, soothing, but platitudinous reply, "It won't end, Mr Hushabye. Life doesn't end: it goes on," the newly realistic, even cynical Ellie answers, "Oh, it cant go on forever. I'm always expecting something. I dont know what it is; but life must come to a point sometime." Shaw, too, was always expecting something. He too didn't know what it was to be; but his play had to come to a point sometime.

The Germans and the Zeppelins provided the point—opportunely for Shaw, unhappily for themselves, as shown in the letter to the Webbs, as follows:

> . . . The Potters Bar Zeppelin manoeuvred over the Welwyn Valley for aboout half an hour before it came round and passed Londonwards with the nicest precision over our house straight along the ridge tiles. It made a magnificent noise the whole time; and not a searchlight touched it, as it was the night-out of the Essenden and Luton lights. And not a shot was fired at it. I was amazed at its impunity and audacity. It sailed straight for London and must have got past Hatfield before they woke up and brought it down. The Commander was such a splendid personage that the divisional surgeon and an officer who saw him grieved as for an only son. At two o'clock another Zeppelin passed over Ayot,[3] but we have no telephone, and nobody bothered. I went to see the wreck on my motor bicycle. The police were in great feather, as there is a strict cordon, which means

2. "When I take my pen or sit down to my typewriter, I am as much a medium as Browning's Mr. Sludge or Dunglas Home. . . . When I write a play I do not foresee nor intend a page of it from one end to the other: the play writes itself. I may reason out every sentence until I have made it say exactly what it comes to me to say; but whence and how and why it comes to me, . . . I do not know." (Preface to *Buoyant Billions*. 1947).

3. Ayot St. Lawrence in Hertfordshire was the home of the Shaws from 1906 on [*Editor*].

that you cant get in without paying. The charges are not excessive, as I guess; for I created a ducal impression by a shilling.
Corpses are extra, no doubt; but I did not intrude on the last
sleep of the brave. What is hardly credible, but true, is that the
sound of the Zepp's engines was so fine, and its voyage through
the stars so enchanting, that I positively caught myself hoping
next night that there would be another raid. I grieve to add that
after seeing the Zepp fall like a burning newspaper, with its
human contents roasting for some minutes (it was frightfully
slow) I went to bed and was comfortably asleep in ten minutes.
One is so pleased at having seen the show that the destruction of
a dozen people or so in hideous terror and torment does not
count. "I didn't half cheer, I tell you" said a damsel at the
wreck. Pretty lot of animals we are![4]

Though obviously not all the details in the play coincide exactly
with the details of the actual raid, since the Shaws had no telephone and the Shotovers had one, and the sky over Ayot that night
was full of stars, whereas the sky over Heartbreak House was black,
there are enough correspondencies to show how Shaw transmitted
the exciting and tragic reality into the thrilling but almost stylized
symbolism of the final scene. The "magnificent noise" made by the
first Zeppelin as it passed over the Welwyn Valley became, first,
Hesione Hushabye's "sort of splendid drumming in the sky," then
her "Sh-sh! Listen: do you hear it now? It's magnificent," and,
finally, her "And the sound in the sky: it's splendid: it's like an orchestra: it's like Beethoven." And Ellie, now become a kindred
spirit, responds: "By thunder, Hesione: it is Beethoven." Shaw in
his letter confessed: ". . . I positively caught myself hoping next
night that there would be another raid." Incredible to himself as
this sentiment seemed, he echoed it and broadend it out in the
last two speeches of the play. * * *

Shaw's sympathy for the incinerated crew of the dirigible is
echoed in the anxiety of the humanitarian Mazzini: "Think of the
risks those poor fellows up there are running!" The source of Nurse
Guinness's all-too-human but savage response. "Think of t h e m,
indeed, the murdering blackguards! What next?" is found in the
" 'I didn't half cheer, I tell you' said a damsel at the wreck. Pretty
lot of animals we are!" Shaw's surprise over the absence of search-
lights to pick up the airship over Ayot is perhaps reflected in reverse
in Hector's reckless outcry, "There is not half light enough. We
should be blazing to the skies," in Ellie's impulsive "Set fire to the
house, Marcus" (Mrs. Hushabye only a few minutes before has
ironically inquired of Mazzini, "What's the matter, Mr. Dunn? Is
the house on fire?"), and in Lady Utterword's sarcastic suggestion

4. Archibald Henderson, *George Bernard Shaw: Man of the Century* (New York,
1956), pp. 378–79.

to Randall that he play "Keep the home fires burning" on his flute. From the beginning Hector has always wanted more light, since as the curtain goes down on Act I he has asked the old Captain, "Shall I turn up the lights for you?" and since, when in Act III Nurse Guinness has turned off all the lights in the house at the angry command of the police, Hector cries *"furiously,"* "Who put that light out?" (Afterwards, shouting "It shall be seen for a hundred miles," he dashes into the house to turn on all the lights and tear down the curtains.)

Like Hector, many of the people who had seen, read or studied *Heartbreak House* have asked for more light, especially on the two final speeches of Hesione and Ellie. As I have tried to elucidate Shaw's possible meaning, in my book *Men and Supermen* (p. 72):[5]

> ... when the invading air fleet attacks, Ellie, remembering the England which actually exists, calmly and clear-sightedly, with none of the thrill-seeking emotionalism of Mrs. Hushabye, calls on Hector to set fire to the house so that it will be marked out for the bombs of the raiders. When their bombs miss the main target, blow up the clergyman's house, and kill only the two "burglars," she is acutely disappointed, and prays that the planes [sic] will return the next night.

Several of the characters in the play with whom Shaw seems to sympathize must seem to be suffering from a sort of death wish. But, after all, much as everyone must agree at least theoretically with Shaw's doctrine of the necessity of the elimination of the unfit or dangerous elements and classes of society as one element of Captain Shotover's diagnosis of the situation at the end of the play, bombs dropped from the sky ("The judgment has come") are not generally as selective in their victims as Shaw's are here in removing the two kinds of "burglars" and making it necessary to provide the rector with a new house—or a new religion, such as Creative Evolution. Better instruments for the remaking of society can certainly be devised, as Shaw himself tried to do in other plays—but still without discovering anything at all practical in improving the world situation.

5. New York: Benjamin Bloom, 1966.

On *Saint Joan*

From The Trial of Jeanne D'Arc†

FEBRUARY 24TH. THIRD SESSION.

On the following Saturday, February 24th, we the said bishop repaired to the same room in the castle of Rouen where Jeanne appeared in judgment before us in the presence of many reverend fathers, doctors and masters.

* * *

[There follow the names of sixty-two notables—*Editor.*]

We first of all required the aforementioned Jeanne to speak the simple and absolute truth on the questions put to her, and to make no reservation to her oath; and we thrice admonished her to do this. The said Jeanne answered: "Give me leave to speak" and then said: "By my faith, you could ask things such as I would not answer." She said also: "Perhaps I shall not answer you truly in many things that you ask me, concerning the revelations; for perhaps you would constrain me to tell things I have sworn not to utter, and so I should be perjured, and you would not want that." And she added, "I tell you, take good heed of what you say, that you are my judge, for you assume a great responsibility, and overburden me." She said also that she thought it should be enough to have twice taken the oath.

Moreover, asked if she would swear, simply and absolutely, she answered: "You may well do without it! I have sworn enough, twice"; adding that all the clergy of Rouen and Paris could not

---

† The trial of Joan of Arc, from January through May of 1431, was recorded in French by the notary Guillaume Manchon. The original minutes do not survive, but an authenticated translation into Latin was made some years later, and at least three copies of this translation are extant. From 1841 to 1849 the French scholar J. E. J. Quicherat assembled all the documents of Joan's trial and later rehabilitation, and published them with commentary in five volumes. Shaw says he based his play directly on these records, though he indicates in the extended preface to the play that he knew well the other Joans of literature from Shakespeare through Andrew Lang and Mark Twain.

A complete rendering of the trial record into English was not made until 1932, nine years after Shaw completed his play. Nevertheless the following translation by W. P. Barrett may be taken as a sample of the source material from which the play emerged. *The Trial of Jeanne D'Arc*, translated into English from the original Latin and French documents by W. P. Barrett, was published by Gotham House in 1932. The following selections are from pages 48–56 and 341–351.

condemn her, but by law. She said that of her coming to France she would willingly speak the truth, but not the whole truth; and a week would not be enough for that.

But we, the aforementioned bishop, told her to take the advice of the assessors, whether or not she should swear. To that she replied that of her coming she would willingly speak the truth, and not otherwise; and that we must not speak of it to her any more.

We said that she lay herself open to suspicion if she would not swear to speak the truth. She replied in the same way as before. Again we required her to swear, precisely and absolutely. Then she answered that she would willingly say what she knew, but not all. She said also that she came from God, and that there is nothing for her to do here, and asked to be sent back to God, from whom she came.

Required and admonished to swear, under pain of being charged with what was imputed to her, she answered: "Continue."

A last time we required her to swear, and urgently admonished her to speak the truth in matters concerning the trial, telling her she exposed herself to great danger by her refusal. Then she answered: "I am ready to swear to speak the truth of what I know concerning the trial." And in this manner she took the oath.

Then, at our order, she was questioned by the distinguished doctor Jean Beaupère above-mentioned, who first asked her when she had last taken food and drink. She answered that since yesterday noon she had not taken either.

Asked when she had heard the voice come to her, she answered: "I heard it yesterday and to-day."

Asked at what hour yesterday she had heard this voice, she answered that she had heard it three times: once in the morning, once at vespers, and once when the *Ave Maria* was rung in the evening. And often she heard it more frequently than she said.

Asked what she was doing yesterday morning when the voice came to her, she said she was sleeping and the voice awakened her.

Asked if the voice woke her by touching her on the arm, she answered that it was without touching her.

Asked if the voice was actually in the room, she said she did not know, but it was in the castle.

Asked if she did not thank it and kneel down, she answered that she thanked it, but she was sitting on the bed, and she put her hands together; and this was after she asked counsel of it. Whereupon the voice told her to answer boldly.

Asked what the voice had said when she was awakened, she answered that she asked the voice to counsel her in her replies, telling the voice to beseech therein the counsel of Our Lord. And the voice told her to answer boldly and God would comfort her.

Asked if it had not spoken certain words to her before she questioned it, she replied that the voice spoke certain words, but she did not understand them all. However, when she awakened from her sleep, the voice told her to answer boldly.

Then she said to us, the aforementioned bishop: "You say that you are my judge; take good heed of what you do, because, in truth, I am sent by God, and you put yourself in great peril," in French 'en grant dangier.'

Asked if the voice sometimes varied in its counsel, she answered that she had never found it utter two contrary opinions. She said also that that night she had heard it tell her to answer boldly.

Asked whether the voice had forbidden her to answer everything she was asked, she said: "I will not answer you that. I have revelations concerning the king which I shall not tell you."

Asked if the voice had forbidden her to tell of the revelations, she answered: "I have not been advised upon that. Give me a fortnight and I will answer you." And as she had again asked for a delay in her reply, she said: "If the voice forbade me, what would you say?"

Asked again if that had been forbidden her [by the voice], she replied: "Believe me, it was not men who forbade me." She said that she would not answer that day; and that she does not know if she ought to reply, or not, until it has been revealed to her. She said she firmly believes, as firmly as she believes in the Christian faith and that the Lord redeemed us from the pains of hell, that this voice comes from God, and by His command.

Asked whether this voice, which she says appears to her, comes as an angel, or directly from God, or whether it is the voice of one of the saints, she answered: "This voice comes from God; I believe I do not tell you everything about it; and I am more afraid of failing the voices by saying what is displeasing to them, than of answering you. For this question, I beseech you to grant me a delay."

Asked if she believes it displeasing to God to speak the truth, she answered: "My voices told me to say certain things to the king, and not to you." She saw that that night the voice told her many things for the good of the king, which she wished he might know forthwith, even if she had to go without wine till Easter! For, as she said, he would eat the more happily for it.

Asked if she could not so influence the voice that it would obey her and take news to her king: she answered she did not know whether the voice would obey her, unless it were God's will, and God consented thereto. "And if it please God," she said, "He will be able to send revelations to the king; and with this I shall be well pleased."

Asked why this voice no longer speaks with the king, as it did when Jeanne was in his presence, she answered that she did not know, if it were not the will of God. And she added that but for the will of God she could do nothing.

Asked if her counsel revealed to her that she should escape from prison, she answered: "Must I tell you that?"

Asked whether that night the voice had not counseled and advised her upon what she should reply, she said that if the voice revealed such things she did not understand them.

Asked whether, on the last two days that she had heard the voices, she had seen a light, she answered that the light comes in the name of the voice.

Asked if she saw anything else with the voices, she answered: "I will not tell you everything: I have not leave, nor does my oath touch on that. This voice is good and worthy; and I am not bound to answer you." She asked that the points on which she did not straightway answer should be given her in writing.

Asked whether the voice, of which she asked counsel, had sight and eyes, she answered: "You will not learn that yet"; and said that there was a saying among little children, "Men are sometimes hanged for telling the truth."

Asked if she knows is in God's grace, she answered: "If I am not, may God put me there; and if I am, may God so keep me. I should be the saddest creature in the world if I knew I were not in His grace." She added, if she were in a state of sin, she did not think that the voice would come to her; and she wished every one could hear the voice as well as she did. She thought she was about thirteen when the voice came to her for the first time.

Asked whether in her youth she had played in the fields with the other children, she answered that she certainly went sometimes, but she did not know at what age.

Asked if the people of Domrémy sided with the Burgundians or the other party, she answered that she only knew one Burgundian; and she would have been quite willing for him to have his head cut off, that is if it had pleased God.

Asked if at Maxey the people were Bungundians or enemies of the Burgundians, she answered they were Burgundians.

Asked if the voice told her in her youth to hate the Burgundians, she answered that since she had known that the voices were for the king of France, she did not like the Burgundians. She said the Burgundians will have war unless they do as they ought; she knows it from her voice.

Asked if it was revealed to her in early years that the English should come to France, she answered that the English were already in France when the voices began to come to her.

Asked if she was ever with the children who fought for her party, she answered no, as far as she remembered; but she sometimes saw certain children from Domrémy, who had fought against those from Maxey, returning wounded and bleeding.

Asked whether in her youth she had any great intention of defeating the Burgundians, she answered that she had a great desire and will for her king to have his kingdom.

Asked if she had wanted to be a man when it was necessary for her to come to France, she said she had answered elsewhere.

Asked if she took the animals to the fields, she said that she had answered elsewhere; and that since she had grown up, and had reached understanding, she did not generally look after the beasts, but helped to take them to the meadows and to a castle called the Island, for fear of the soldiers; but she does not recall whether or not she tended them in her youth.

Then she was questioned about a certain tree growing near her village. To which she answered that, fairly near Domrémy, there was a certain tree called the Ladies' Tree, and others called it the Fairies' Tree; and near by is a fountain. And she has heard that people sick of the fever drink of this fountain and seek its water to restore their health; that, she has seen herself; but she does not know whether they are cured or not. She said she has heard that the sick, when they can rise, go to the tree and walk about it. It is a big tree, a beech, from which they get the fair May, in French *le beau may*; and it belongs, it is said, to Pierre de Bourlemont, knight. She said sometimes she would go playing with the other young girls, making garlands for Our Lady of Domrémy there; and often she had heard the old folk say (not those of her family) that the fairies frequented it. And she heard a certain Jeanne, the wife of mayor Aubery of Domrémy, her godmother, say that she had seen the fairies; but she herself doesn't know whether it is true or not. As far as she knew, she said, she never saw the fairies at the tree. Asked if she saw them elsewhere, she does not know at all. She had seen the young girls putting garlands on the branches of the tree, and she herself sometimes hung them there with the other girls; sometimes they took them away, and sometimes they left them there.

She said that since she learned that she must come to France, she had taken as little part as possible in games or dancing; and did not know whether she had danced near the tree since she had grown to understanding. Although on occasions she may well have danced there with the children, she more often sang than danced. There is also a wood, called the oak-wood, in French *le Bois-chesnu*, which can be seen from her father's door; not more than half a league away. She does not know, nor has she ever heard, that the fairies repair there; but she has heard from her brother that in the country around it is said she received her message at the tree; but she says she did not, and she told him quite the contrary. Further, she says, when she came to the king, several people asked her if there were not in her part of the country a wood called the oak-wood; for there was a prophecy which said that out of this wood would come a maid who should work miracles; but Jeanne said that she put no faith in that.

Asked if she wanted a woman's dress, she answered: "Give me one. I will take it and go: otherwise I will not have it, and am content with this, since it pleases God that I wear it."

Whereupon we put an end to all interrogation for this day, and assigned for the next session the following Tuesday, so that at the same hour and in the same place the whole convocation should assemble and proceed to the subsequent interrogations.

[Three months elapse, during which Joan is subjected to more than twenty sessions with her priestly accusers, many of them in her prison cell—*Editor*.]

THURSDAY, MAY 24TH. THE PUBLIC SERMON. JEANNE RECANTS. THE MITIGATED SENTENCE IS PRONOUNCED.

On Thursday after Whitsuntide, May 24th of the same year, we the said judges repaired in the morning to a public place, in the cemetery of the abbey of Saint-Ouen at Rouen, where the said Jeanne was present before us on a scaffold or platform. First we had a solemn sermon pronounced by master Guillaume Erart, a distinguished doctor of sacred theology, for the salutary admonition of the said Jeanne and of the great multitude of people present. . . .

* * *

[There follow the names of forty-one notables, ending with "and many others"—*Editor*.]

The said doctor began his sermon by taking for his text the word of God in the fifteenth chapter of St. John: "A branch cannot bear fruit of itself except it abide in the vine." Then he solemnly explained that all Catholics must abide in the true vine of Our Holy Mother Church which Our Lord planted with His right hand: he showed how this Jeanne had cut herself off from the unity of our Holy Mother Church by many errors and grave crimes, and how she had frequently scandalized the Christian people. He admonished and exhorted her and the multitude of people by salutary doctrines.

When the sermon was over he addressed Jeanne in these terms: "Behold my Lords your judges who have repeatedly summoned and required you to submit all your words and deeds to Our Holy

Mother Church, showing and pointing out to you that in the opinion of the clergy many things are to be found in your words and deeds which it is good neither to affirm nor uphold."

To which Jeanne replied: "I will answer you. Touching my submission to the Church, I have answered them on this point. Let all that I have said and done be sent to Rome to our Holy Father the Pope to whom after God I refer myself. As for my words and deeds, they were done at God's command." She said that she charged no one with them, neither her king nor any other; and if there were any fault it was hers and no other person's.

Asked whether she would revoke all her words and deeds which are disapproved of by the clergy, she answered: "I refer me to God and to our Holy Father the Pope."

Then she was told that this would not suffice, that it was not possible to seek Our Holy Father the Pope at such a distance: that the ordinaries were each in his own diocese competent judges. Therefore she must needs submit to Our Holy Mother Church, and hold as true all that the clergy and other authorities had said and decided concerning her words and deeds. Whereupon she was admonished by three admonitions.

Then, as this woman would say no more, we the said bishop began to read the final sentence. When we had already completed the greater part of the reading, Jeanne began to speak, and said she would hold all that the Church should ordain, all that her judges should say and decree, and would obey our ordinance and will in all things. She said repeatedly that inasmuch as the clergy had pronounced that her revelations and apparitions were not to be upheld or believed, she would not maintain them; but would refer in all things to her judges and our Holy Mother Church.

Then in the presence of the aforenamed and before a great multitude of people and clergy, she made and pronounced her recantation and abjuration, according to the formula of a certain schedule written in French which was then read, which she uttered with her own lips and signed with her own hand. The tenor thereof follows.

JEANNE'S ABJURATION

"All those who have erred and been at fault in the Christian faith and have by God's grace returned to the light of truth and unity of Our Holy Mother Church, should vigilantly prevent the Enemy of Hell from driving them back and causing their relapse into error and damnation. Therefore, I, *Jeanne*, commonly called *The Maid*, a miserable sinner, recognizing the snares of error in which I was held, and being by God's grace returned to Our Holy Mother Church, in order to show that my return is made not feignedly but with a good heart and will, I confess that I have most grievously sinned in falsely pretending to have had revelations and apparitions from God, His angels, St. Catherine and St. Margaret; in seducing others; in believing foolishly and lightly; in making superstitious divinations, in blaspheming God and His Saints; in breaking the divine law, Holy Scripture, and the canon laws; in wearing a dissolute, ill-shaped and immodest dress against the decency of nature, and hair cropped round like a man's, against all the modesty of womankind; also in bearing arms most presumptuously; in cruelly desiring the shedding of human blood; in declaring that I did all these things by the command of God, His angels and the said saints, and that to do so was good and not to err; in being seditious and idolatrous, adoring and calling up evil spirits. I confess also that I have been schismatic and in many ways have erred from the path. These crimes and errors, I, being by God's grace returned to the way of truth through the holy doctrine and good counsel of yourself and the doctors and masters whom you sent me, unfeignedly and with a good heart abjure and recant, renouncing and cutting myself off from them all. Upon all the aforesaid things I submit to the correction, disposition, amendment and entire decision of Our Holy Mother Church and of your good justice. And I vow, swear and promise to you, to my lord Saint Peter, Prince of the Apostles, to Our Holy Father the Pope of Rome, his vicar and his successors, to you, my lords, to the lord bishop of Beauvais and the religious brother Jean Le Maistre, vicar of the lord Inquisitor of the faith, my judges, that I will never through exhortation or other means return to the aforesaid errors, from which it has pleased God to deliver and remove me; but will always dwell in the unity of Our Holy Mother Church and the obedience of our Holy Father the Pope of Rome. This I say, affirm and swear by God almighty and the holy Gospels. In sign whereof I have signed this schedule with my mark."

Signed "JEHANNE ✠."

Here follows the tenor of this abjuration in Latin [an exactly similar document].

SENTENCE AFTER THE ABJURATION

And lastly, after we the judges had received her recantation and abjuration as is set forth above, we the said bishop pronounced our definitive sentence in these terms:

"In the name of the Lord, amen. All pastors of the Church who desire and endeavor to lead the Lord's flock faithfully must, when the perfidious sower of errors laboriously attempts with great cunning to infect the flock of Christ with virulent poisons, assemble their whole strength in order to combat the assaults of the Evil one with greater vigilance and more urgent solicitude. This is particularly necessary in these dangerous times in which the words of the apostle announced that many false prophets would come into the world and introduce sects of perdition and error, which by their varied and foreign doctrines might seduce Christ's faithful people, if our Holy Mother Church with the aid of healthy doctrine and canonical sanctions, did not struggle to overthrow these erroneous inventions. Therefore before us, your competent judges, namely Pierre by divine mercy bishop of Beauvais and brother Jean Le Maistre, vicar in this city and diocese of the notable master Jean Graverent, Inquisitor of Heretical Error in the kingdom of France, especially appointed by him to officiate in this cause, you, Jeanne, commonly called *The Maid,* have been arraigned to account for many pernicious crimes and have been charged in a matter of faith. And having seen and examined with diligence the course of your trial and all that occurred therein, principally the answers, confessions and affirmations which you made; after having also considered the most notable decision of the masters of the Faculties of Theology and of Decrees in the University of Paris, in addition to that of the general assembly of the University, and of the prelates, doctors and men learned in theology and both canon and civil law who were met together in a great multitude in this town of Rouen and elsewhere for the discussion and judgment of your statements, words and deeds; having taken counsel and mature conference with those zealots of the Christian faith, and having seen and weighed all there is to see and weigh in this matter, all that we and any man of judgment and law could and should observe: we, having the honor of the orthodox faith before our eyes, so that our judgment may seem to emanate from the face of Our Lord, we say, decree and pronounce that you have gravely sinned by falsely simulating revelations and apparitions, by seducing others, by lightly and rashly believing, by uttering superstitious prophecies, by blaspheming God and His saints, by prevaricating to the law, the Holy Scripture, and the canonical sanctions, by despising God in His sacraments, by fomenting seditions, by apostasy, by falling into the crime of heresy and erring on many points in the Catholic faith. But inasmuch as you have, after repeated charitable admonitions, by God's help through a long delay returned into the bosom of Our Holy Mother Church, and with contrite heart unfeignedly, as we would fain believe, have openly renounced your errors, which since they have lately been reproved in a public sermon, you have with your own lips publicly abjured along with all heresy: according to the form appointed by ecclesiastical sanctions we unbind you by these presents from the bonds of excommunication which enchained you, on condition that you return to the Church with a true heart and sincere faith, observing what is and shall be enjoined by us. But inasmuch as you have rashly sinned against God and the Holy Church, we finally and definitely condemn you for salutary penance to perpetual imprisonment, with the bread of sorrow and water of affliction, that you may weep for your faults and never henceforth commit anything to occasion weeping."

THE AFTERNOON OF THE SAME DAY, MAY 24TH. JEANNE PUTS ON WOMAN'S DRESS.

In the afternoon of the same day we, brother Jean Le Maistre, vicar aforementioned, accompanied by the noble lords and masters Nicolas Midi, Nicolas Loiseleur, Thomas de Courcelles, and brother Ysambard de La Pierre, and several others, repaired to the prison where Jeanne then was. We and our assessors explained to her how God had on this day been most merciful to her, and how the clergy had shown her great mercy by receiving her into the grace and pardon of our Holy Mother Church: how therefore it was right that she, Jeanne, should humbly submit to and obey the sentence and ordinance of the lord judges and ecclesiastics, and should altogether abandon her errors and her former inventions, never to return to them; how, if she did return to them, the Church would not receive her to clemency, and she would be wholly abandoned. Moreover, she was told that she must put off her male costume and take woman's dress, as the Church had commanded.

Jeanne answered that she would willingly wear woman's dress, and in all things obey and submit to the clergy. She was given woman's dress which she put on immediately she had take off the male costume: she desired and allowed her hair, which had hitherto been cut short round the ears, to be shaved off and removed.

The Trial for Relapse

MONDAY, MAY 28TH. JEANNE RESUMES MAN'S DRESS.

On Monday following, the day after Holy Trinity Sunday, we the said judges repaired to Jeanne's prison to observe her state and disposition. We were accompanied by the lords and masters Nicolas de Venderès, William Haiton, Thomas de Courcelles, brother Ysambard de La Pierre, Jacques Le Camus, Nicolas Bertin, Julien Flosquet, and John Grey.

Now because the said Jeanne was wearing a man's dress, a short mantle, a hood, a doublet and other garments used by men (which at our order she had recently put off in favor of woman's dress), we questioned her to find out when and for what reason she had resumed man's dress and rejected woman's clothes. Jeanne said she had but recently resumed man's dress and rejected woman's clothes.

Asked why she had resumed it, and who had compelled her to wear it, she answered that she had taken it of her own will, under no compulsion, as she preferred man's to woman's dress.

She was told that she had promised and sworn not to wear man's dress again, and answered that she never meant to take such an oath.

Asked for what reason she had assumed male costume, she answered that it was more lawful and convenient for her to wear it, since she was among men, than to wear woman's dress. She said she had resumed it because the promises made to her had not been kept, which were to permit her to go to Mass and receive her Saviour, and to take off her chains.

Asked whether she had not abjured and sworn in particular not to resume this male costume, she answered that she would rather die than be in chains, but if she were allowed to go to Mass, if her chains were taken off and she were put in a gracious prison [and were given a woman as companion], she would be good and obey the Church.

As we her judges had heard from certain people that she had not yet cut herself off from her illusions and pretended revelations, which she had previously renounced, we asked her whether she had not since Thursday heard the voices of St. Catherine and St. Margaret. She answered yes.

Asked what they told her, she answered that they told her God had sent her word through St. Catherine and St. Margaret of the great pity of this treason by which she consented to abjure and recant in order to save her life; that she had damned herself to save her life. She said that before Thursday they told her what to do and say then, which she did. Further her voices told her, when she was on the scaffold or platform before the people, to answer the preacher boldly. The said Jeanne declared that he was a false preacher, and had accused her of many things she had not done. She said that if she declared God had not sent her she would damn herself, for in truth she was sent from God. She said that her voices had since told her that she had done a great evil in declaring that what she had done was wrong. She said that what she had declared and recanted on Thursday was done only for fear of the fire.

Asked if she believed her voices to be St. Catherine and St. Margaret, she answered "Yes, and they came from God."

Asked to speak truthfully of the crown which is mentioned above, she replied: "In everything, I told you the truth about it in my trial, as well as I could."

When she was told that when she made her abjuration on the scaffold or platform before the judges and the people, she had admitted that she had falsely boasted that her voices were St. Catherine and St. Margaret, she answered that she did not mean to do or say so.

She said she did not deny or intend to deny her apparitions, that is that they were St. Catherine and St. Margaret; all that she said was from fear of the fire. She recanted nothing which was not against the truth. She said she would rather do penance once and for all, that is die, than endure any longer the suffering of her prison. She said that whatever they had made her deny she had never done anything against God or the faith: she did not understand what was in the formula of abjuration. She said she did not mean to revoke anything except at God's good pleasure. If the judges wished, she would once more wear women's dress, but for the rest she would do no more.

After hearing these declarations we left her to proceed further according to law and reason.

LUIGI PIRANDELLO

Bernard Shaw's *Saint Joan*†

The audience bewildered me.

At the première of *Saint Joan,* by George Bernard Shaw, I felt myself a real foreigner, suddenly brought face to face with this mysterious America of yours. Though it was not altogether bewilderment, I felt, as I went home from the play, that I had learned something interesting and unexpected about the psychology of the American.

During the first three acts of *Saint Joan* I noted with great satisfaction the rapt attention, the shrewd and intelligent smiling, the hearty laughter and the sincere applause with which every shaft of wit or irony in this admirable and inimitable Shavian dialogue was welcomed by an audience keenly aware of the artistic treat that was spread before it. But then came the fourth act, which seemed to

† The premiere of *Saint Joan* was presented by the Theatre Guild in New York three months before its London opening. It happened that the great Italian playwright Luigi Pirandello attended the premiere, and the *New York* *Times* naturally asked him for comment. The response of the Italian genius to the Irish one (and to the American audience) appeared in the magazine section of the *Times* on Sunday, January 13, 1924, pp. 7–12.

me the best in the whole play—the trial and condemnation of the Maid—where Shaw's dramatic power rises to its height, and where he really succeeds in awakening a deep and intense emotion. I had been expecting, in view of the preceding cordiality of the audience, to see people jump to their feet and break into unrestrained applause. Nothing of the kind! I looked around the theatre in surprise. It was as though I had been suddenly transported into a world wholly unknown and incomprehensible to me. The spectators sat for the most part in silence.

For a moment or two I was oppressed with a sudden sense of mortification at my own incompetence. But then my own feelings were so great that I could not help asking a question that was a question half of protest to the friends about me. Had that scene been a failure? Had no one been moved by that almost divine explosion of passion in the Maid just before she was dragged away to the stake? I received in reply a suggestion that few had applauded for the very reason that the emotion in the audience was so great. And then, indeed, I was more surprised than ever.

I am sure that, had an act as powerful as the fourth act of *Saint Joan* been produced on any one of the numerous Italian stages, all the people present would have jumped to their feet, even before the curtain fell, to start a frenzied applause that would have called the actors, and possibly the author, to the footlights, not once, but many times, to receive the gratitude of the audience for the anguish it had suffered, and its joy for having witnessed such a triumph of art. But here, on the other hand, a certain sense of modesty seemed to be uppermost. A certain sense of shame at being deeply moved, a need of hiding emotion, and of getting rid of it as soon as possible. To applaud would have meant confessing this emotion to one's self and then publicly to others; and few seemed willing thus to betray themselves.

But then, to tell the truth, I was not as well satisfied as I had been at the applause during the three preceding acts, though these, in a somewhat different way, were just as deserving. As an Italian, I could not think it fair that an author should be applauded when he makes us laugh, and rewarded with silence when he brings tears to our eyes. Perhaps the reason is that it is harder to make an Italian laugh than it is to make him weep.

At any rate, I have a strong impression that for some time past George Bernard Shaw has been growing more and more serious. He has always believed in himself, and with good reason. But in a number of plays, after his first successes, he did not seem to believe very much in what he was doing. This, at least may properly be suspected, since it cannot be denied that in his eagerness to defend his own intellectual position against the so-called 'bourgeois morality', he not infrequently abandoned all pretensions to seriousness as an artist. Now, however, he seems to be believing less in himself, and more in what he is doing. From the epilogue of this drama on Joan of Arc we may gather almost explicitly the reason for which Shaw wrote it. This world, he seems to say, is not made for saints to live in. We must take the people who live in it for what they are, since it is not vouchsafed them to be anything else.

In fact, as we look carefully and deeply at this work of Shaw, taken as a whole, we cannot help detecting in it that curious half-humorous melancholy which is peculiar to the disillusioned idealist. Shaw has always had too keen a sense of reality not to be aware of the conflict between it and his social and moral ideals. The various phases of reality, as they were yesterday, as they are today, as they will be tomorrow, come forward in the persons who represent them before the ideal phantom of Joan (now a Saint without her knowing it). Each of these type persons justifies his own manner of being, and confesses the sin of which he was guilty, but in such a way as to show that he is unable really to mend his ways—so true is it that each is today as he was yesterday, and will be tomorrow as he is today. Joan listens to them all, but she is not angry. She has for them just a tolerant pity. She can only pray that the world may some time be made beautiful enough to be a worthy abode for the saints!

This new tolerance and pity rise from the most secret depths of poetry that exist in Shaw. Whenever, instead of tolerating, instead of pitying, he loses his temper at the shock of reality against his ideals, and then, for fear of betraying his anger—which would be bad mannered—begins to harass himself and his hearers with the dazzling brilliancy of his paradoxes, Shaw, the artist properly speaking, suffers more or less seriously—he falls to the level of the jeu d'esprit which is amusing in itself, though it irremediably spoils the work of art. I may cite in point a passage in the second act of *Saint Joan* where the Archbishop expatiates on the differences between fraud and miracles. 'Frauds deceive,' says he. 'An event which creates faith does not deceive, therefore it is not a fraud but a miracle.' Such word play is for amusement only. A work that would do something more than amuse must always respect the deeper demands of art, and so respecting these, the witticism is no longer a witticism but true art.

In none of Shaw's work that I can think of have considerations of art been so thoroughly respected as in *Saint Joan*. The four acts of this drama begin, as they must begin, with Joan's request for soldiers of Robert de Beaudricourt to use in driving the English from 'the sweet land of France'. And they end, as they must end, with the trial and execution of Joan. Shaw calls this play a chronicle. In fact, the drama is built up episode by episode, moment by moment some of them rigorously particular and free from generality—truly in the style of the chroniclers—though usually they tend to be what I call deliberate 'constructiveness'. The hens have not been laying, when suddenly they begin to lay. The wind has long been blowing from the east, and suddenly it begins blowing from the west. Two miracles! Then there are other simple, naïve things, such as the recognition of the 'blood royal' in the third act, which likewise seems to be a miracle.

But these moments are interspersed with other moments of irony and satire, of which either the Church or the English are the victims. However, this attempt to present the chronicle inside what is really history does not seem to me quite as happy as it was in *Caesar and Cleopatra*. In *Saint Joan*, history, or rather character historically conceived, weighs a bit too heavily on the living fluid objectivity of the chronicle, and the events in the play somehow lose that sense of the unexpected which is the breath of true life. We know in advance where we are going to come out. The characters, whether historical or typical, do not quite free themselves from the fixity that history has forced upon them and from the significant rôle they are to play in history.

Joan herself, who is presented to us as a fresh creature of the open fields, full of burning faith and self-confidence, remains that way from the beginning to the end of the play: and she makes a little too obvious her intention not to be reciting a historical rôle and to remain that dear, frank, innocent, inspired child that she is. Yes, Joan, as she really was in her own little individual history, must have been much as Shaw imagined her. But he seems ot look on her once and for all, so to speak, quite without regard for the various situations in which she will meet life in the course of the story.

And she is kept thus simple and unilinear by the author just to bring her airy, refreshing ingenuousness into contrast with the artificial, sophisticated—or, as I say, 'deliberate' or 'constructed'—complexity of her accusers. There is, in other words, something mechanical, fore-ordained, fixed, about her character. Much more free and unobstructed in his natural impulses, much more independent of any deliberate restraints, and accordingly much more 'living' (from my point of view) is the Chaplain, de Stogumber, the truly admirable creation in this drama, and a personage on which Shaw has surely expended a great deal of affectionate effort.

At a certain moment Joan's faith in her 'voices' is shaken. And this charming little creature, hihterto steadfastly confident in the divine inspiration which has many times saved her from death i⟨

battle, is suddenly filled with terror at the torment awaiting her. She says she is ready to sign the recantation of all that she has said and done. And she does sign it. But then, on learning from her judges that the sentence of death is only to be changed into a sentence of life imprisonment, she seizes the document in a sudden burst of emotion and tears it to pieces. 'Death is far better than this!' she cries. She could never live without the free air of the fields, the beauty of the green meadows, the warm light of the sun. And she falls fainting into the arms of the executioners, who drag her off to the stake.

At this moment Shaw carries his protagonists to a summit of noble poetry with which any other author would be content; and we may be sure that any other author would have lowered the curtain on this scene. But Shaw cannot resist the pressure and the inspiration of the life he well knows must be surging in such circumstances in his other character—the Chaplain. He rushes on toward a second climax of not less noble poetry, depicting with magnificent élan the mad remorse, the hopeless penitence of Stogumber, thus adding to our first crisis of exquisite anguish another not less potent and overwhelming.

Rarely has George Bernard Shaw attained higher altitudes of poetic emotion than here. There is a truly great poet in Shaw; but this combative Anglo-Irishman is often willing to forget that he is a poet, so interested is he in being a citizen of his country, or a man of the twentieth century society, with a number of respectable ideas to defend, a number of sermons to preach, a number of antagonists to rout from the intellectual battlefield. But here, in *Saint Joan*, the poet comes into his own again, with only a subordinate rôle left, as a demanded compensation, to irony and satire. To be sure *Saint Joan* has all the savor and all the attractiveness of Shaw's witty polemical dialogue. But for all of these keen and cutting thrusts to left and right in Shaw's usual style of propaganda, *Saint Joan* is a work of poetry from beginning to end.

This play represents in marvellous fashion what, among so many elements of negation, is the positive element, indeed the fundamental underpinning, in the character, thought and art of this great writer—an outspoken Puritanism, which brooks no go-betweens and no mediations between man and God; a vigorous and independent vital energy, that frees itself restlessly and with joyous scorn from all the stupid and burdensome shackles of habit, routine and tradition, to conquer for itself a natural law more consonant with the poet's own being, and therefore more rational and more sound. Joan, in fact, cries to her judges: 'If the Church orders me to declare that all I have done and said, that all the visions and revelations I have had were not from God, then that is impossible. I will not declare it for anything in the world. What God made me do, I will never go back on; and what He has commanded, or shall command, I will not fail to do, in spite of any man alive. That is what I mean by impossible. And in case the Church should bid me do anything contrary to the command I have from God, I will not consent to it, no matter what it may be'.

Joan, at bottom, quite without knowing it, and still declaring herself a faithful daughter of the Church, is a Puritan, like Shaw himself—affirming her own life impulse, her unshakable, her even tyrannical will to live, by accepting death itself. Joan, like Shaw, cannot exist without a life that is free and fruitful. When she tears up her recantation in the face of her deaf and blind accusers, she exemplifies the basic germ of Shaw's art, which is the germ also of his spiritual life.

ALICE GRIFFIN

The New York Critics and *Saint Joan*†

When Shaw's *Saint Joan* had its world premiere in New York in December of 1923, although it was a popular success, its reception by the New York critics did not indicate that within three decades it would come to be recognized as one of the world's dramatic masterpieces. As a matter of fact, it was not even elected by Burns Mantle as one of the "ten best" plays of the 1923–4 season for inclusion in his annual volume.

There having been two Broadway revivals since that time, and a third, starring Jean Arthur, having toured several Eastern cities last fall, it might be interesting to trace the history of *Saint Joan* on our professional stage to determine how a great play comes to be acknowledged as such by those whose reactions have come to determine the fate of a production—the Broadway critics. And in passing, through their words and Shaw's own, some indication of the type of production given the play may also be gained. Like those of many a lesser work, the first reviews of *Saint Joan* were "mixed"; in the Katharine Cornell revival in 1936, it was beginning to be cautiously accepted as an outstanding work, and by 1951, when Uta Hagen was starred, the play was generally acknowledged as a modern masterpiece, with the reviewers highly critical because the production did not equal the play in excellence.

† Alice Griffin's examination of the record in 1955 by no means brings the stage history of *Saint Joan* up to date, but it does place journalistic criticism in the proper perspective of time. It is from the *Shaw Bulletin* (later *The Shaw Review*), January, 1955, pp. 10–15.

The presentation by the Theatre Guild in 1923 was preceded by the usual production problems posed by every play, even and perhaps especially—by the great ones. As recounted by Lawrence Langner, co-director of the Guild, in his book *The Magic Curtain* (New York, 1951, pp. 174–183), the first and continuing difficulty was with the length of the script. To Langner's first plea Shaw replied with his now-famous cable: "Begin at eight or run later trains. . . ." Another problem was that the Guild cast started rehearsing with the first script Shaw had sent to Langner; then the Guild learned that the author was sending a revised version. When they protested, Shaw replied: "When I heard that you were actually rehearsing from a copy which you knew to be an unrevised first proof I tore my hair. I should not have trusted you with it . . . and if the stoppage of the rehearsals (not that I have any hope that you really stopped them) cost you £400, which is great nonsense, my only regret is that it did not cost you £4,000, an all-too-slender penalty for such criminal recklessness. . . ."

Finally the play opened, on December 28th at the Garrick Theatre, and had the power of the critics been as great then as it is today, one wonders whether *Saint Joan* would have made the grade. As it was, it was so successful that it had to be moved to a larger theatre to take care of capacity crowds. But Percy Hammond of the *Tribune* was not much impressed. "Mr. Shaw's chronicle of Joan of Arc makes the life and works of that sainted maiden duller though more probable than legends have taught us to believe," he said, calling the work "just another example of Mr. Shaw's gift for interminable rag-chewing."

Although Alexander Woollcott in the *Herald* admitted that it was "a play that has greatness in it," he also complained that "certain scenes grew groggy for want of a blue pencil . . . others falter and go raucously astray. . . ." However, he also called it "beautiful, engrossing, and at times exalting," while Frank Lea Short in the *Christian Science Monitor* found it "very near to being [Shaw's] best work." Said Short, "Shaw's 'Joan' bids fair to be the Joan of the theatre of our time. It may even live far into the future." He was, however, critical of what he called its "local gags." Writing in *Theatre Arts Monthly* for March, 1924, Kenneth Macgowan felt that Shaw had passed his prime: "Personally I am thoroughly annoyed by the play. It isn't half Shavian enough. Age seems to be withering the scorn of this iconoclast, tarnishing the perverse brilliance of his mind, and taming his wit." The talk was not brilliant, Mr. Macgowan asserted, and "the inspiration and divinity of Shaw have departed."

As contrasted with the analyses of Katharine Cornell's portrayal in 1936, not too much space was devoted to Winifred Lenihan, who enacted Joan. Macgowan commented that "Winifred Lenihan plays Joan with not very great spiritual vision, but within her limits she is simple, earnest, and vigorous; her faults are never positive." Percy Hammond saw Miss Lenihan's interpretation as "a smug and self-satisfied flapper, eager for excitement."

From the very first production, the epilogue, here as abroad, was greeted with much adverse comment. Woollcott felt that Shaw himself would probably cut some of the scenes "when he sees the play outrun itself in London, especially that final scene which says the same thing several times." And Hammond did not even stay for the epilogue: "I left, as many others did, before the dreamy epilogue, and so I can report only through hearsay that it, too, was tiresome."

Yet from the first the play aroused much thought and discussion on the part of critics and others. Writing of the new play, Walter Prichard Eaton pointed out that "Shaw is not only one of the keenest minds in the world today; he is one of the most religious of men . . . *Saint Joan* is the work of a religious soul." Luigi Pirandello, asked to write his impressions of the play for the New York *Times*, stated that he puzzled at the silence of the audience attending the play: "Had an act as powerful as the fourth act of *Saint Joan* been produced on any one of the numerous Italian stages," he asserted, "all the people present would have jumped to their feet, even before the curtain fell, to start a frenzied applause." In New York audiences, he noticed, "a certain sense of modesty seemed to be uppermost. A certain sense of shame at being deeply moved, a need of hiding emotion and getting rid of it as soon as possible."

Shaw was not too concerned with the American reviews, but he seemed much impressed that Pirandello had written about *Joan*. Writing to Lawrence Langner about the reviews and about publicity for the play, he said: "I am not at all anxious about *Joan*; but I am somewhat concerned about you. You could hardly have been rattled by Heywood Broun and Alan a Dale *et hoc genus omne* if you had not been rattled already . . . The great press feature of the production was the notice by Pirandello, which you never even mentioned."

When he received photographs of the production, Shaw commented in detail about the casting, the costumes, the sets, and the direction:

> . . . both Baudricourt and Poulengy should be in half armor and be obviously soldiers and not merchants. This is important, as it strikes the note of France in war time. As it is, Poulengy's coat should not be belted . . . In the second act . . . at the end of the act [Joan] should be in front of all the rest, in command of the stage in the good old fashioned way from the point of view of

the audience, and not beautifully composed in the middle of the picture with all the other people turning their backs to the spectators. Why don't you carry out my directions and get my effects instead of working for pictorial effects ... The Bishop looks about right for the Inquisitor and the Inquisitor for the Bishop ... The altar and candles in the middle of the cathedral scene are feebly stagy, and do not give the effect of a corner of a gigantic cathedral as my notion of one big pillar would. And it leads to that upstage effect, with a very feminine operatic-looking Joan in the centre, which I wanted to avoid. The drag towards the conventional is very evident; and is the last word in operatic artificiality ... but still, it is all very pretty in the American way, and might have been worse.

Since the London productions are not within the scope of this article, it can be noted only in passing that the play there equalled its American success. Desmond MacCarthy, in the *New Statesman and Nation* for April, 1924, called it " ... I think, the greatest of Shaw's plays." In discussing the theme of the play, he wrote: "As the epilogue, to which several dramatic critics have objected, shows, the essence of the theme is the struggle of religious inspiration against established religions, against the patriot, the statesman, and the indifferent. ..." Of Sybil Thorndike's Maid he stated: "Her distress, her alertness, her courage, she does drive home, but whether the fault lies in the part itself or in the interpretation, 'the angelic side' of the Maid is obscured."

Concerning the London production Shaw wrote to Langner that "the Play has repeated its American success here: it is going like mad; and everyone, to my disgust, assures me it is the best play I have ever written. Sybil Thorndike's acting and Charles Rickett's stage pictures and costumes have carried everything before them. I am convinced that our production knocks the American one into a cocked hat. ..."

By the time *Saint Joan* was revived on Broadway, in March of 1936, with Katherine Cornell starring, and directed by Guthrie McClintic, even Percy Hammond had revised his opinion of the play and certainly of the epilogue. Although he found the play this time "a bit loquacious," he said of the final scene: "When in the epilogue [Joan] vanished in a happy ending tableau ... I said to myself, here is the Theatre in one of its most consecrated moments." And he had high praise, as did all the critics, for Miss Cornell's Joan, played, he said, "with all the magic and vigor known to the stage and to one of its ablest apostles."

At this production a Shavian comment on the epilogue was printed in the program, as follows: "Without the epilogue the play would be only a sensational tale of a girl who was burnt, leaving the spectators plunged in horror, despairing of humanity. The true tale of *Saint Joan* is a tale with a glorious ending; and any play that did not make this clear would be an insult to her memory." Shaw's attitude about the epilogue in the printed version of the play is the same, but somewhat differently expressed, it may be recalled: "It was necessary by hook or crook to shew the canonized Joan as well as the incinerated one; for many a woman has got herself burnt by carelessly whisking a muslin skirt into the drawing room fireplace, but getting canonized is a different matter, and a more important one."

Brooks Atkinson, writing of the Cornell production in the New York *Times*, declared that a "generous share of the modern theatre's grandeur is now on display." He was critical of some of the scenes as being "no more than competent" and of the "manner and verbosity of the epilogue" which "snatch a fine play back into the theatre tedium." "But," he concluded, "if *Saint Joan* offered nothing except the solemn trial scene and the compassionate wisdom of the inquisitor's speech, it would still rank with the best in the modern theatre."

As contrasted to 1923, a greater percentage of the reviewers were praiseful, but not all. John Anderson, writing in the *Evening Journal*, felt that, despite the program explanation, "it needs a better epilogue," while Richard Lockridge of the New York *Sun* was ecstatic about Miss Cornell but more reserved about the play: "Except when she is on stage, it is a trifle wan and wordy, and rather too much given to lengthy speeches, not all of which are in Shaw's best vein." He felt that, as a production, the first one had been better, "more of a piece, and served better to disguise the fact that the author's reflections are not invariably profound." Burns Mantle of the *News* agreed that Miss Cornell was better than the play, for whenever she was in command, he said, the scene was an inspired one, but whenever "Mr. Shaw took it over . . . it went temporarily a little sluggish." His opinion about the epilogue was that it "was attractively realized . . . and seemed less a foolish appendage than it has before." Robert Garland, in the New York *World-Telegram*, felt that "such verbiage as this self-styled 'chronicle play' quite obviously possesses is to be blamed directly on the playwright," and Arthur Hornblow of *Theatre Magazine* also protested at the "superabundance of Shavian talk," and was critical too of the familiarity with which Joan addressed the Dauphin, "taking unwarranted liberties with history." But he, like almost all of the others, agreed that this was Shaw's greatest play.

Gilbert W. Gabriel, in the New York *American*, expressed the effect of the passage of time on *Joan* in this manner: "Thirteen years have not caused the best play Bernard Shaw ever wrote to dwindle at all, to blanch or turn dim, dull or puny. These same years have only confirmed his masterpiece." And John Mason Brown, in the New York *Evening Post*, reflected that "of all Shaw's plays *Saint Joan* seems to have upon it the most enduring marks of greatness." Brown found it "a play that in spite of its . . . length is a masterpiece that has moral grandeur to it, and above which hovers a light that is similar to the one which Joan sees dancing above Robert de Baudricourt's head."

Edith Isaacs, writing in *Theatre Arts Monthly* for May, 1936, reflected the general critical praise for Katharine Cornell's interpretation:

> The qualities that mark Katharine Cornell's conception of the part of Saint Joan are all in Shaw's portrait: the joyous, simple faith in the voices and her humble dedication to their service; her blatant pride before men, the vanity that makes her love her youth's clothes and her uniform, the boyishness that demands an equal association with soldiers and their commanders. Out of these elements Katharine Cornell builds up her Joan from the inspired village girl . . . through the leadership of the King's forces and the hour of triumph, to the tragic final day of trial as a sorcerer and heretic. Through the scenes of the trial . . . she weaves all these elements of character like counterpoint against the fears, the bitterness and revenge, the narrowness of her opponents, lifting the scene up and up so that when she is finally led forth to the burning in the public square you are there with her, and at the same time she is still there with you in the hall of the castle, the scene of the trial, where Joan remains alive in spirit to this day.

By the time of the 1951 revival, in October of that year, presented by the Theatre Guild, directed by Margaret Webster, and with Uta Hagen in the lead, the play's status was assured, as far as the critics were concerned, with only one dissenter. As is always true of the revival of a classic, the major portion of each review was devoted to comments on the production, just the reverse of the 1923 reviews. While the play was acknowledged to be a masterpiece, there was a majority of unfavorable opinion concerning the production. Brooks Atkinson of the New York *Times* was the most kindly disposed toward the production, stating: "The play is inspired. Neither Miss Hagen nor her associates let it down." But Bert McCord, in the *Herald-Tribune*, after asserting that "it is great theatre and should be witnessed by all who are interested in the theatre and believe that it can be great," went on to assert that the production did not realize the effort of the playwright, and that Miss Hagen's Joan was only "workmanlike." John Chapman of the *Daily News* felt that Miss Hagen's performance was "intelligent" but did not "convey the passion and zeal of a true saint." And Chapman believed the epilogue to be "tiresomely overwritten."

Robert Garland, as Percy Hammond had before him, found that the play impressed him more than it had on its previous trip to Broadway. Writing in the *Journal-American*, Garland stated: "Now, more than before, it is evident that the playwright wrote better than we know," but he did not like Miss Hagen's performance. The dissenter regarding the play was Robert Coleman of the *Daily Mirror*. Whereas Brooks Atkinson and said that the play "makes the theatre something worth venerating again," Coleman could see in it only "run-of-the-mill, pedestrian Shaw." He complained that "over the years we were under the impression that this was by all odds the best of the modern master's scripts. But now we aren't so sure."

Possibly Richard Watts Jr. of the New York *Post* best summed up one of the conclusions of this consideration of the reception of *Saint Joan* on Broadway. It is a point which can be stated very simply: a great play needs a great production to realize itself fully. After calling *Saint Joan* "a noble and magnificent play, the most distinguished dramatic work of its eminent author, and one of the greatest achievements of modern writing for the theatre," Watts stated that this production was "curiously lacking in distinction." "Unless it is superbly done, it can seem incredibly wordy," he said. "It merely happens that, in addition to its perversities, it possesses a true magnificence of thought, emotion, and creative imagination. It requires unusual excellence in a large number of parts to bring out its very genuine greatness." This was the same play that had premiered in 1923, and which had probably been given the same quality of production. But in twenty-eight years, *Saint Joan* had become a world masterpiece.

On *Too True to Be Good*

KATHERINE HAYNES GATCH

The Last Plays of Bernard Shaw:
Dialectic and Despair†

The low esteem in which Shaw's last plays are held when they
are compared with those of his prime may in the long view be justified, but their reputation is in some measure the result of a failure
to establish the critical bases on which these plays may be assessed
as Shaw's peculiar contribution to English stage comedy in the
second quarter of this century. That Shaw himself termed *Heartbreak House*, written on the eve of the First World War, "the
most extraordinary" of his plays challenges his critics to examine
closely the later comedies, which go still further in attempting new
modes for an era that Shaw said made democracy "a fantasy acted
by people in a dream." *Heartbreak House* Shaw had subtitled *A
Fantasia in the Russian Manner on English Themes; The Apple
Cart* (1929) he called *A Political Extravaganza*. The implication is
strong that he had felt compelled to invent a genre to suit the inevitably political themes and the distorted human values of the world
between two wars. To capture his vision of terrifying possibilities,
Shaw, like other modern artists, relied on extravagance of manner
and an atmosphere that sometimes suggests the absurdity of
dreams.

The revival of *The Apple Cart* for the coronation year, 1953,
indicates some of the misconceptions of Shaw's artistic and political premises still persisting at the mid-century. If this play is inter-

† From *Saint Joan* to his death in 1950
Shaw wrote fourteen more plays, in
quantity a full lifetime's output for
many a playwright. However, the quality of these later plays has been much
questioned. Certainly they are in a different mode from the plays of his middle years. They are not easily dismissed as the brilliant garrulities of an
old genius. There is lately the strong
suspicion that they may even be stageworthy.

Katherine Gatch was among the first
to direct serious critical attention to
these later works. This article was one

of the *English Institute Essays* for
1954. It is included in *English Stage
Comedy*, edited by W. K. Wimsatt, Jr.
(New York: Columbia University
Press, 1954), pp. 126–147.

We have included Professor Gatch's
critical estimates of the plays that fol-
low *Too True to Be Good*, and we
commend the plays to those who wish
to fill in Shaw's last two decades:
*On the Rocks, The Apple Cart, The
Simpleton of the Unexpected Isles, The
Millionairess, Geneva, In Good King
Charles's Golden Days*, and *Buoyant
Billions*.

459

preted as praising monarchy in the person of King Magnus, then *The Apple Cart,* like *Candida* and *Saint Joan,* enjoys popular success for quite un-Shavian reasons. Actually, Shaw is using the king only as his symbol for the supreme aristocrat in the classic sense of the person best fitted to rule because he has been disciplined for public office and is willing to undertake its responsibilities with "the high republican conscience." *The Apple Cart* makes political the ironic pattern that Shaw had acknowledged a generation earlier as basic to his work. "I deal," he said, "in the tragi-comic irony of the conflict between real life and the romantic imagination. . . ." The grotesque spectacle of real life after 1918 required a tonality very different from that of the comedies written in the traditions of Shakespeare, of Molière, and even of Ibsen. Yet Shaw did not, like some artists in this age, go so far as to disintegrate the inherited techniques of his craft, because to the last he hoped that the meaningless fragmentation of democratic society was not the promised end. Hope and belief gave Shaw his dramatic structure, but in the last plays fear and disgust created the tone; and where hope wavers, the structure is weak.

The most tiresome commonplace in the criticism of Shaw's plays, early and late, is that they are all talk and no plot. Why, if these plays are not plays, should they behave on the stage as if they were? The question is not answered by saying that Shaw, while avowing his debt to the comedy of manners, cunningly concealed it by inverting the conflicts and resolutions of that comedy to make his conversation pieces viable for the stage. Chesterton early pointed out the crucial importance of "conversion" in the typical Shavian story; Edmund Wilson declared but did not demonstrate that the Marxian analysis of society gave the plays structure; Eric Bentley has mentioned dialectic and warned critics to watch for the "synthesis" in the working out of Shaw's comic situations, illustrating his meaning of synthesis in a valuable commentary on *Major Barbara.*

I wish to suggest that Shaw often used a dialectical structure derived from Hegel and Marx, but beguilingly modified by his own temperament, observations, and convictions. By dialectic, for want for a pleasanter term, I mean the tripartite pattern in which Hegel envisaged historical change and which Marx and Engels turned to their own uses: thesis, antithesis, and synthesis. It should be said at once that Shaw's use of the triad is not unrelated to his more personal and Socratic dialectic, the search for truth out of half-truths and differing opinion; but for the discussion of plot the dialectic process must be understood as divisible into three phases. The essence of the Hegelian dialectic is change, just as the essence of the Socratic dialectic is progression through contraries. Whatever the condition of a Shavian play, it is not static. Like Hegel and like Marx in their treatment of historical change, Shaw opens his come-dies with a social situation temporarily well consolidated. Hegel's illustration was republican Rome; Marx's eye was fixed on the bour-geois society of his own century; and there too was Shaw's begin-ning. From within republican Rome (thesis) Caesar broke away (antithesis) and ultimately effected the synthesis of the empire. But where Hegel brought the process to rest in the Prussian state, and Marx could not seem to imagne anything beyond the classless society which he fancied would follow the revolution, Shaw as a Creative Evolutionist conceived of unending change. At the close of *Back to Methuselah* Lilith says, "It is enough that there is a beyond."

The reading of Marx had awakened the young Shaw to the importance of the economic bases of society, but he could no more be a consistent dialectical materialist than he could as a Creative Evolutionist be a scientific determinist. The comic spirit is inimical to the rigid mental habits of the ideologue. Shavian laughter springs from the common sense that Bergson describes as "the mobility of the intelligence conforming exactly to the mobility of things . . . the moving continuity of our attention to life." The Shavian dialectic uses in its synthesis the solvent of the comic spirit and corrects both the Prussianism of Hegel and the proletarian ideology of Marx by the humanity of the great comic tradition.

When in 1897 Shaw, at the top of his form as a critic, reviewed Meredith's long-unpublished *Essay on Comedy and the Uses of the Comic Spirit,* he seized upon Meredith's thesis that comedy civilizes and responded gratefully to Meredith's praise of the mas-ters of the comic spirit as an intellectual aristocracy. "Look there for your unchallengeable upper class," Meredith said. "He should know," Shaw commented, "for he certainly belongs to it." In Meredith,[1] Shaw found his prophet. Disavowing any taste for Nor-wegian gloom, Shaw hinted that his own comedies, awaiting publi-cation in the next year, would claim spiritual kinship with Shake-speare and Molière. In the very year in which Shaw praised Mere-dith's essay he created General Burgoyne of *The Devil's Disciple,* a brilliant aristocrat in the eighteenth-century manner, who person-ifies at once the spirit of comedy and Shaw's own temperament. Of him Shaw says in his notes to the play:

> Burgoyne . . . is a man who plays his part in life, and makes all his points, in the manner of a born high comedian. . . . His pecu-liar critical temperament and talent, artistic, satirical, rather his-trionic, and his fastidious delicacy of sentiment, his fine spirit

1. George Meredith, 1828–1909. Shaw held this high estimate of Meredith in spite of the fact that Meredith, as a publisher's reader, flatly turned down Shaw's early novels [*Editor*].

and humanity, were just the qualities to make him disliked by stupid people because of their dread of ironic criticism.[2]

And one might add, these are just the qualities needed to modify the humorless excesses of the doctrinaire.

Certainly the heroes and heroines of Shavian comedy are for the most part the wellborn, readily articulate, and self-directing people of traditional high comedy. They serve as the antithetical agents when the dialectic operates in the plot, for Shaw trusted his observation that revolutionary leaders do not spring from the proletariat. A Barbara Undershaft (or a Beatrice Webb as Shaw had observed in real life) breaks away from the security of the ancestral mansion to carry salvation to the world of slums and dark satanic mills. Lady Cicely Waynefleet, with seemingly inconsequent charm, converts the dispossessed Captain Brassbound to her view that hatred and violence on his part will make him as bad as his oppressors, and cannot right the injustice done to his dead mother. John Tanner, author of "The Revolutionist's Handbook," confers on himself the degree MIRC—Member of the Idle Rich Class—and acknowledges his chauffeur, Henry Straker, as the new and unillusioned man. Vivie and Fanny are graduates of Cambridge. The Roman Lavinia, who leads the martyrs to the arena for the god whom her free mind will not let her name or localize, is a patrician with a fine scorn for the irresponsible members of her class and deep pity for the oppressed. The aristocratic principle in Shavian comedy operates in the critical intelligence, the cultivated sensibilities, and above all in the acceptance of responsibility. In Shaw's late plays, as in his early ones, these qualities of mind and character constitute the hope for society. But in the late plays the hope that they can be made to function politically is so deferred as to suggest despair.

To make this aspect of the late plays clear it is necessary to consider a few early ones where by contrast the dialectic works with precision and confidence. I am sorry to have to mention *Candida*, but Shaw's only explicit statement about his use of thesis and antithesis relates to that play and has been overlooked by the Candidamaniacs:

> The time was ripe for a modern pre-Raphaelite play. Religion was alive again, coming back upon men, even upon clergymen, with such power that not the Church of England itself could keep it out. . . . To distil the quintessential drama from pre-Raphaelitism, medieval or modern, it must be shewn at its best in conflict with the first broken, nervous, stumbling attempts to formulate its own revolt against itself as it develops into some-

2. *Three Plays for Puritans*, pp. 79–80 [*Editor*].

thing higher. A coherent explanation of any such revolt . . . can only come when the work is done. . . .[3]

The tell-tale phrases here are *revolt against itself* and *develops into something higher*. Of Eugene Marchbanks and his conflict with the Christian Socialist clergyman Morell, Shaw says pointedly:

> Here, then, was the higher but vaguer and timider vision, the incoherent, mischievous, and even ridiculous unpracticalness, which offered me a dramatic antagonist for the clear, bold, sure, sensible, benevolent, salutarily short-sighted Christian Socialist idealism.[4]

Obviously this is a statement of thesis and antithesis. Candida's maiden name was Burgess. Christian Socialism is wedded to and dependent upon bourgeois comfort. Significantly, although Eugene, the wellborn, hates to see Candida peel onions, he hates even worse to see her break Morell's spirit, for his instincts are those of high breeding, and he recoils from cruelty. The synthesis—which is the secret in the playwright's heart—will fuse Morell's Christianity, Candida's practicality, and Eugene's critical intelligence.

Major Barbara demonstrates the Shavian dialectic very clearly and it is an invaluable aid to the understanding of the late plays. Mr. Bentley is right, I think, in seeing its hero in Adolphus Cusins, the professor of Greek. He is also right in thinking that Undershaft is the false Nietzschean Superman who fancies himself beyond good and evil. The humorous and scholarly Cusins nicknames Undershaft "Mephistopheles," calling attention to the fact that like Goethe's antagonist he does good with evil intentions. I should like to place even greater emphasis on the professor of Greek as the true protagonist. Not only does the conclusion represent the synthesis of Barbara's love and faith with her father's practical genius; Cusins functions as the humanist whose knowledge of the past is needed to give right direction to the future. It is inexcusably literal minded to see the Undershaft gunpowder as anything but a symbol for power. You can't have power for good without risking power for evil, as Cusins says. The responsible intellect must control power, as it must also light the way for Barbara's faith, lest it become fanaticism. The aristocratic principle operates in Barbara, too, and she is both comically and heroically the noblewoman when, catching Cusins' vision, she cries:

> I have got rid of the bribe of bread. I have got rid of the bribe of heaven. Let God's work be done for its own sake: the work he had to create us to do because it cannot be done except by living

3. Preface to *Plays Pleasant and Unpleasant*, Vol. II, pp. vi–vii [*Editor*].   4. P. viii [*Editor*].

men and women. When I die, let him be in my debt, not I in his; and let me forgive him as becomes a woman of my rank.

The dialectic is part of the joke in *Fanny's First Play*. The critics whom Fanny's father summons utter every cliché that has dogged Shaw's reputation, but they fail to understand the dynamics of the plot. The play presents two bourgeois households, both alike in dignity, long associated in business, and now about to be further consolidated by marriage. The houses of Gilbey and Knox are redolent of the atmosphere of the dissenting Protestant sects, which, according to one reading of history, aided capitalism in disintegrating the medieval synthesis. Bobby Gilbey is rebellious against the strictness of home and against the pietism of a Catholic tutor, who has been hired because his brother, a monsignor, is a customer of the family business. Bobby's marriage contract with Margaret Knox is threatened by his preference for Dora Delany, daughter of joy and of the proletriat. After a too joyful evening Dora lands herself and Bobby in jail for disorderly conduct. Meanwhile, Margaret, on her way home from an evangelistic meeting, with spirit set free, picks up a French naval officer and goes dancing with him. In a police raid, Margaret, like Bobby, goes to jail. The dialectical farce is brought to a hilarious synthesis when a way is found for a happy future by the Gilbeys' monumental butler, Juggins, who reveals at the crisis that he is the brother of a duke, and that he is doing penance by servitude for having insulted a member of the working class. The noble Juggins, heretofore useful only as arbiter of taste to the bourgeoisie, will now be united with the group, for he has fallen in love with Margaret Knox, who appeals more than ever to his aristocratic tastes for having lost her middle-class conventionality in Holloway Gaol. Bobby and Dora will complete the synthesis in a classless society where "like will to like"—and the brother of a duke will teach Dora table manners. The final Shavian trademark is the moment of real feeling when Mrs. Knox, a sincerely religious woman who understands both penitence and joy, transfers her belief in converison to a social context. *Fanny's First Play* stands to Shaw's first plays in the self-critical relation of *A Midsummer Night's Dream* to early Shakespearean comedy. It demonstrates that Shaw's comic sense saved him from the rigidity of pattern.

After this *tour de force*, *Androcles and the Lion* begins a new phase and looks toward the deepening moods of *Heartbreak House* and *Saint Joan*. While *Major Barbara* treated sincere but youthful religious enthusiasm with propriety in the atmosphere of social comedy, *Androcles and the Lion*, where the odor of blood rises from the arena, could preserve comic tone only by recourse to fantasy. The ridiculous Antonine Emperor marks the decline of Rome, but the truly antithetical force within the state, the force that can set Caesars at naught, is the Christian humility of Androcles and the blood of the martyrs, the seed of an organization mightier than Caesardom. Androcles and his lion go waltzing off together in symbolic synthesis. The lion, like the Undershaft gunpowder, is power, an authentic Christian symbol. The lion must be uncaged but controlled by Androcles. Counterpointed against the ineffable humility of Androcles is the intellectual integrity of Lavinia, whose patrician distinction of mind defines the values which Androcles and his lion must maintain. This is essentially the same synthesis as in *Major Barbara*: faith and power must be directed by responsible mind.

Heartbreak House is the hinge between Shaw's early and late plays and records crisis for the playwright as for the world. In Captain Shotover, Shaw grasped the exasperation of aging genius with the mass of "practical" men who will not take a disinterested view of human destiny. "There is enmity between our seed and their seed," says Shotover. ". . . When we believe in ourselves we shall kill them." To which Hector, with deeper humanity, replies, "It is the same seed. . . . We are members one of another." Writing of *The Master Builder*,[5] Shaw commented on "the sublime delirium that sometimes precedes bodily death . . . and the horror that varies the splendor of delirium." His last plays may have been called extravaganzas because Shaw felt in his own art something of that delirium and of that horror. "Why should not old men be mad?"

After the war, the Hegelian reading of history was rendered obsolete by the theories of Petrie and Spengler, which better suited the postwar temper. As a Creative Evolutionist, accustomed to the long view, Shaw easily adapted himself to the cyclical concept of history in *Back to Methuselah*, his first postwar play. But *The Tragedy of an Elderly Gentleman*[6] and *Saint Joan* both bear witness to the emotional experience which separated the postwar Shaw from the hopeful Fabian who had once gaily adapted dialectic to comedy.

Too True to Be Good (1932), written when Shaw was almost as old as Captain Shotover and King Lear, reveals both his humanity toward a younger generation drowning in despair and his own desperate clinging to the raft of dialectic. Like *The Apple Cart*, this play is subtitled *A Political Extravaganza*, although it presents its meaning in terms of private lives rather than cabinet crises and puts its emphasis on the spiritual ills of the postwar world. The maladies are those incident to the children of nineteenth-century parents, and there are no simple remedies. In a new key of extravagant absurdity, Shaw enters a realm of multiple suggestion and complexity of mood, yet the three acts and their settings afford recognizable dialectic symbolism.

5. One of Ibsen's later plays (1892), a discussion of which Shaw appended to his *Quintessence of Ibsenism* in the later editions [*Editor*].

6. Part 4 of the five-part *Back to Methuselah* [*Editor*].

Act I opens in the fetid atmosphere of a sickroom where every window is sealed against fresh air and where lavish appointments intensify the feeling of bad ventilation. Clearly Shaw's disgust with the ill health of capitalist society is very different from the mood in which, a quarter of a century earlier, he had depicted the stodgy comfort of Lady Britomart Undershaft's drawing room. But the action, the revolt of a sick daughter from the career of invalidism which her managing mother has organized for her, parallels Barbara's flight from Mayfair to the work of the Salvation Army. Both young women have made "the revolt from within." In order that the extravaganza should at once establish itself as a dramatic type, the play opens with a fantasy of a monstrous microbe, possibly a warning to the literal minded that the play may make them quite, quite ill. To prevent this misfortune, the Theatre Guild persuaded Beatrice Lillie to play the role of Sweetie, the nurse, and encouraged her to steal the show. The Shavian action, however, involves the stealing of a necklace which belongs to the Patient. That unappetizing invalid is an unconscious fraud who needs only an object in life to enable her to spring from the bed, join the eloquent burgler, Aubrey Bagot, and the nurse who is his accomplice, in the theft of her own jewels, and take off with them for a spree in primitive places.

Escape from the sickroom takes the Patient, in the second act, into the unbearable glare of a sandy and tropical terrain, where the primitve is too suddenly substituted for the overcivilized. Beneath the absurd incidents, the substructure of the classic antithesis is visible in mock violence suggestive of the end of an era of imperialism. The trio find themselves involved with Colonel Tallboys, numskull and water-colorist, in charge of the military post, who provokes an attack from the native tribe by his total ignorance of the ways of the desert. All the Europeans owe their lives in the end to the common sense and common humanity of Private Meek—the character with more than a touch of genius who is likely to turn up in any typical Shavian comedy. The scenes involving Meek and Tallboys are lovely farce in Shaw's early manner, and Private Meek is Shaw's gay tribute to his friend Lawrence of Arabia, who by this time was calling himself T. E. Shaw. Meek's knowledge of dialects, his ingenuity and omnipresence, his motorcycle, his headgear, and his habit of demoting himself to the ranks are Lawrence to the life. The satire on the military mind of Tallboys, who aggravates the dangerous friction between the white and dark races, is integral to the scheme of this political extravaganza. The intellectual grasp of international relations, as Shaw understands it, amounts to common sense and humanity raised to the degree of genius in experts like Lawrence—but the numskulls and water-colorists remain in command.

The third act, which in strict accord with dialectic should effect a synthesis, is strangely set in a surrealistic waste land where we may make what we can of the narrow gap, the symbolic grottoes suggestive of outworn cultures, and the beach with its sand and stones. The atmosphere of this scene is a far cry from the shining efficiency of the Undershaft works and the model town of the last act of *Major Barbara*. As in that play, the high point of the last act is the intellectual clash between an older man, product of nineteenth-century philosophy, and a younger one. But whereas Adolphus Cusins and Andrew Undershaft find a way to work together, and a hopeful future lies before Barbara and her learned lover, in *Too True to Be Good* the clash is never resolved. Aubrey, the erstwhile burglar, and his father, who appears here as the Elder, denounce each other, and Aubrey and the Patient separate, he to be swallowed up in a fog of intellectual despair, the girl to find practical work.

Aubrey Bagot's father, the Elder, is a nineteenth- century atheist and scientific determinist from whose relentless moral sternness the boy had long since taken refuge in religion, getting himself ordained while at Oxford. During the war, Aubrey became an ace with a brilliant record for bombing civilians. In the morbidity of self-loathing afterward, he took up with Sweetie, the nurse, and completed his experiments in degradation by turning burglar. Sweetie is a promiscuous vulgarian who, on the expedition in the second act, masquerades as a countess. She is a Shavian inversion of the postwar women of high social position and promiscuous habits, like Lucy Tantamount of *Point Counter Point*.[7] Aubrey attributes his despair and depravity to the determinism of his father, but he also resembles the intellectuals of the lost generation who under the tutelage of D. H. Lawrence discovered the mystique of the lower centers. Aubrey's relation to the nineteenth-century Elder, his twentieth-century associates, his return to religion, and his eloquent despair suggest that his real name was Aldous, that the Elder's name was Thomas, and that Shaw felt tragicomedy in the plight of both generations of Huxleys. For the Elder, Newton's universe, which was the "stronghold of rational Determinism . . . has crumbled like the walls of Jericho before the criticism of Einstein," and "the calculable world has become incalculable." The illusion of design in the universe which had been an esthetic substitute for theology now mocks the neo-Darwinian. When he goes to a museum of natural history he sees "nothing in those grotesque monsters of the deep but the caricatures of some freakish demon artist. . . . " Rushing out of the museum lest he go mad, and demanding a solid footing in dogma, he is made dizzier still by realizing that "the only trustworthy dogma is that there is no dogma." His son, brought up

7. The novel by Aldous Huxley [*Editor*].

to be "an incorruptible God-fearing atheist," has become a scoun-
drelly religious burglar. The Elder bids him to go drown himself. At
the end Aubrey holds the stage alone. As the others sneak away
from his preaching, he says,

> They are too absurd to be believed in; yet they are not fictions:
> the newspapers are full of them: what storyteller . . . would dare
> to invent figures so improbable as men and women with their
> minds stripped naked? . . . The horror of the naked mind is still
> more than we can bear.

At this point, however, the critics of *Too, True to Be Good*
missed their cue. They leapt to the conclusion that Aubrey's
despair was Shaw's despair and quoted maliciously:

> I am by nature and destiny a preacher. I am the new Eccle-
> siastes. But I have no Bible, no creed: the war has shot both out
> of my hands. . . . I am ignorant: I have lost my nerve; . . . all I
> know is that I must find the way of life, for myself and all of us,
> or we shall surely perish. And meanwhile my gift has possession
> of me: I must preach and preach and preach no matter how late
> the hour and how short the day, no matter whether I have noth-
> ing to say—

and the fog from the sea envelops him. That Shaw's critics crowed
to find these signs of pessimism in him was perhaps the nemesis visited upon one who had used Macbeth's nihilism as evidence of
Shakespeare's own philosophical bankruptcy. But Shaw could talk
back to his critics. In one of the Malvern Festival programs he sin-
gled out Mr. Krutch for punishment:

> I find it hard to forgive him for saying that I announced, in . . .
> *Too True to Be Good*, that world affairs are now irremediable,
> and that mankind is damned beyond hope and redemption. . . .
> The despair of the shell-shocked young gentleman-burglar-
> clergyman, who made such a pitiful attempt to be happy by
> spending a lump of unearned money, is not my despair. . . . I
> made him a good preacher to warn the world against mere
> fluency, and the result was that his talking took Mr. Krutch in.
> He must be more careful next time.

The eloquence which Shaw has always generously lent even to
characters of whom he disapproved has often taken critics in.
Aubrey's prototype is the Devil of *Man and Superman*. The clue to
meaning lies always in the character who goes off at the end to *do*
something. Here the recovered Patient is the hopeful case. Debili-
tating as her sickroom has been, the girl has standards. Though she
learns to be frank in speech, her taste is offended by Sweetie. After
a brief fling with Aubrey she is bored, and wants a good hard job of
practical work to do. In the end she makes an amusing alliance

with her mother. The old lady, Mrs. Mopley, has had a blow on her head from Colonel Tallboys for disturbing him at his watercolors, and it does her good. Shaw may be indicating that the stupidity and brutality of the war knocked sense into many left-over Victorians. Mrs. Mopley fails to recognize her coddled and cosseted daughter in the bronzed and athletic Patient whom she really likes. Now, the awakened mother and the rebellious daughter go off together "to found a sisterhood of service, like St. Teresa, with the mother as cook-housekeeper." This alliance of energetic mother and daughter is faintly reminiscent of the rapprochement of Lady Britomart and Barbara on the houskeeping level. They are perhaps the Intelligent Women for whom Shaw wrote the *Guide to Socialism and Capitalism*[8] in his despair at fallacious argument among men.

The title of *On the Rocks* echoes Captain Shotover's warning to irresponsibles as to the fate of the drifting ship; and twenty years after *Heartbreak House* it seemed that the democracies were indeed drifting onto the rocks of fascist or proletarian dictatorship. The tone of *On the Rocks* is dread. Vestigal remains of the dialectic are visible only in a eugenic farce, almost as obvious as *Fanny's First Play*. The farce has to do with the love affairs of the Prime Minister's children. His overbred son, David, is to marry one. Aloysia Brollikins, a bounding daughter of the proletariat, winner of many scholarships and politically more literate than the Prime Minister. Miss Brollikins comes onto the scene with the working class delegation. Flavia, the Prime Minister's daughter, who has yearned for the rough masculinity of a working man, settles for a radical peer, the Earl of Barking, fresh from Oxford. He is a strident tough in a turtlenecked pullover, in which disguise he is expiating the sins of class pride, like Juggins the butler in *Fanny's First Play*. Shaw strikes off the emergent radical types of the thirties brilliantly, but because they are ideological fanatics, he finds them thoroughly unlovely when compared with Barbara Undershaft and her Oxford professor. In this play the dialectic is adventitious farce.

The real meaning of *On the Rocks* inheres in the character of Sir Arthur Chavender, the Prime Minister whose week-end conversion to a radical philosophy satirizes political amateurs during the depression. With the ship almost on the rocks the gentleman amateur is not a figure of fun, and the hilarious Cabinet meetings here, as in *The Apple Cart*, are really appalling. The satire never deals so sharply with the Prime Minister, however, as by implication it deals with the audience who votes for him. Thirty years earlier Shaw had said, "What our voters are in the pit and gallery, they are in the polling booth." At the prescription of a fashionable lady

8. *The Intelligent Woman's Guide to Socialism and Capitalism*, 1928 [*Editor*].

psychiatrist, Chavender makes a Friday to Tuesday retreat, accompanied by volumes of Marxist literature instead of his customary detective stories and copy of Wordsworth. Returning from his retreat with the fresh ardor of the convert, he sets the politicians in an uproar by his proposals for radical change. Then, with his customary charm, he declines responsibility and resigns. But the farce evaporates from the last moments of the play when he explains to his wife why he is not the man for the job: "I shall hate the man who will carry it through for his cruelty and for the desolation he will bring on us and our like." This is one of those quick transitions to genuine feeling which everyone versed in Shavian comedy will recognize. The Chavender type, whose good will the early Fabians had hoped might be taken up into the new synethesis, has not acquired political acumen. The curtain falls on the sound of shattering glass and the singing of the unemployed, "England, arise! the long, long night is over"; but in ironic counterpoint comes the thwacking sound of police batons.

The real horror implied in the ending of *On the Rocks* is expressed in the formidable title of its preface, "Extermination." Critics have shuddered in alarm at this preface without seeing that it modulates from irony to direct appeal and back again without warning, in the manner of Swift. Had Shaw called it "A Modest Proposal for the Extermination of the Politically Irresponsible," readers might have heard the overtone of the first subheading, "Killing as a Political Function." The opening paragraph ends with one of Swift's matter-of-fact sentences: "Extermination must be put on a scientific basis if it is ever to be carried out humanely and apologetically as well as thoroughly." The seeming approval of cold-blooded Russian methods is given the lie by the moving plea, in the later part, for the sacredness of criticism. "Beware," Shaw says, "how you kill a thought that is new to you." That anyone could read to the end of the preface and still not understand his intention is a risk that as professional ironist he must have been willing to take. Bernard Shaw could not, like the rigid Hegelian or Marxist, countenance cruelty. He balances his acceptance of historical necessity by an impassioned plea for tolerance—the political theme of *Saint Joan*. With a flash of his invincible faith in the future, he directly answers Yeats's despair in "The Second Coming" with a deft verbal echo of the horrendous beast slouching toward Bethlehem to be born. "The beast of prey," Shaw said, "is not striving to return: the kingdom of God is striving to come."

The theme which links *On the Rocks* to *The Simpleton of the Unexpected Isles* is the coming up to judgment of the irresponsibles. Edmund Wilson has called *The Simpleton* Shaw's only really silly play, and there is no denying the afflicting ineptitude of its allegory. Although Shaw may be credited with having intended *The Simpleton* to provoke a revulsion against silliness, this play must be counted an experiment that brought art to the vanishing point. *The Simpleton* closes with the suggestion that the future belongs to the learners and that western man is no longer capable of learning. A civilization rotten with illusions is judged and discarded. The survivors are an ambiguous pair of orientals. Significantly, there is no vestige of the dialectic. *The Simpleton of the Unexpected Isles* has no structure, and it conveys the feeling that the failure of this civilization is a farce of simple-minded folly, not a twilight of the gods.

In *The Millionairess* (1936) Shaw returned, with reservations, to the hopeful synthesis. The heroine has the galvanic energy that marked the conductors of the Life Force in the early comedies; but she is, in the words of the man she is about to marry against his will, "a terrible woman," and Shaw means it. The Egyptian doctor has explained quite clearly all the reasons for *not* renouncing the ascetic bachelorhood of his dedicated life, but as Epifania extends her wrist he automatically puts his finger on her pulse and takes out his watch. "You are a terrible woman . . . but I love your pulse and I cannot give it up." The Egyptian doctor represents the holy wisdom, which may or may not be garnered in the East, but which the West with its megalomanic energy certainly lacks. Epifania, the millionairess, has an unholy and appalling vitality, a pulse "like a slow sledge hammer," but she is mean, bullying, avaricious, and a law unto herself. She makes money by instinct and bosses everyone. I fear Shaw meant her for the United States of America. Although Katharine Hepburn in her recent revival of *The Millionairess* lacked the vitality to realize those terrifying energies, the play proved stageworthy, if only as farce. *The Millionairess* is actually a morality play, in which the doctor speaks the last word, warning that "the wrath of Allah shall overtake those who leave the world no better than they found it." Epifania, like the Undershaft symbol, is power. The hope is that the Egyptian doctor, an intellectual aristocrat, like the professor of Greek, will use power for good; for he accepts responsibility and is indifferent to personal success. He shares Barbara's dedication to service and its religious motivation, but not her humanity. In *The Millionairess*, the familiar Shavian dialectic takes on larger dimensions. The synthesis is no longer a fusion of classes. It is no less than the vision of one world in the union of East and West.

Geneva (1938), the play in which the farcical dictators, Battler, Bombardone, and Flanco, are summoned to a court of pure justice, shows a world synthesis to be very far off. The machinery for international cooperation is in the hands of superpatriots like Begonia

Brown. Begonia, the proliferating plant of the suburbs, is passionately loyal to Camberwell, and has no conception of abstract justice. There is some faint hope for the world, however, because the nations answer the summons to court. Shaw was to write two more plays, *In Good King Charles's Golden Days*, on the eve of the Second World War, and *Buoyant Billions* after it was over. In *King Charles* he abandoned the dialectic to let the Merry Monarch look down the centuries to come and see a melancholy vista of conflict. In *Buoyant Billions*, the playwright in his nineties found hope only in mathematical abstraction and ended with the marriage of an heiress to a young man who will devote his life to research for the mathematical hormone.

In all Shaw's late plays the ironic relationship between the magnitude of the themes and the triviality of the treatment is calculated; the political extravaganzas are tragicomedies, concerned with the grotesque disproportion between the gigantic problems and the pygmies who deal with them. Thomas Mann has said:

> The striking feature of modern art is that it has ceased to recognize the categories of tragic and comic, or the dramatic classifications, tragedy and comedy. It sees life as tragicomedy, with the result that the grotesque is its most genuine style—to the extent, indeed, that today that is the only guise in which the sublime may appear. . . . The grotesque is the genuine anti-bourgeois style.[9]

Whatever the ultimate verdict about the artistic success of Shaw's late plays, as an aging man he was not unresponsive to the compulsions upon the artist to find new modes for our time.

STANLEY WEINTRAUB

The Two Sides of "Lawrence of Arabia": Aubrey and Meek[†]

In his usual fashion of concealing information by revealing information, Bernard Shaw told reporters at the opening of his play *Too True to Be Good* in 1932 that one of the leading characters was modelled upon his friend "Lawrence of Arabia." Few were interested in the revelation as "copy," because they failed to understand Shaw's play, which, in the style of his later years, was complicated

9. H. T. Lowe-Porter, trans., *Past Masters* (London, 1933), p. 240. (Mann's Preface to the German version of Conrad's *The Secret Agent*).
† Dr. Weintraub has written more exhaustively of the relationship between the Shaws and Lawrence of Arabia in his book *Private Shaw and Public Shaw* (New York: Braziller, 1963). This article is from *The Shaw Review*, Vol. 7. (May, 1964), pp. 54–57.

and discursive. Still, there has never been any doubt that the play's "Private Meek" was T. E. Lawrence in his post-Arabian incarnation as Private (later Aircraftman) Shaw.

Lawrence, who enjoyed the caricature of himself as Meek (never was a man less so), let his guard down about another aspect of the play when, before its first production, he wrote to Mrs. Shaw, asking her to tell G.B.S. that it was "probably the finest acting thing" G.B.S. had ever done. The slip came in a worried afterthought—that Cedric Hardwicke, a fine actor who had already created the difficult role of King Magnus in Shaw's political play *The Apple Cart* (1929), would let T. E.'s own conception of Aubrey in the play "frantically down. He will never understand what he represents. I shall dread seeing the play acted, for fear it does not come up to what it is. . . ." The implication is that Lawrence himself did. And Lawrence, it seems, understood what may have been an unspoken secret he shared with the Shaws—that *Too True to Be Good* was too true to be comfortable, an analysis of his motives and nature far beyond the obvious implications of Private Meek and Private Shaw.

In *Private Shaw and Public Shaw* (New York and London, 1963) I first probed into this suspected secret. Since writing the book it has become clear to me that although I had not been wrong, there were subtleties and complexities in the character of Aubrey, the confidence man, which I had not sounded. These make Meek, the happy warrior of the play, almost a reverse image of the troubled Aubrey.

Whether G.B.S. recalled (or consulted) Lawrence's *Seven Pillars of Wisdom*[1] for any of the raw material from which he molded his gay caricature of Private Meek is now only a matter of conjecture. Shaw hardly needed to go back to the book, since his familiarity with its contents included having edited it for publication. Although there are some parallels to *Seven Pillars*, we find rather an evocation of some of the many sides of the younger Lawrence, who loved to make a game of war and military customs and proprieties, who could dominate as well as enrage helpless superiors—and who could get his job done. Definitive details of Colonel Lawrence—Aircraftman Shaw—appear in the script of the play: his appearance, authentic in physical particulars and in insignificant stature; his pseudo-meek quick-wittedness, combined with modest omniscience; his voluntary shifting down the ladder of rank from colonel to private; his knowledge of dialects and tribal psychology as in his suggestion that his commanding officer keep an offered

1. Lawrence's great work on the revolt of the Arabs during World War I, which was also a personal memoir, was privately printed in 1926—five years before Shaw wrote the play—but not published for general circulation until 1935 [*Editor*].

bribe, because the chieftain "won't believe you have any authority unless you take presents"); his charismatic leadership qualities; his technical facility with mines, in blowing up bridges and trains (the mines replaced farcically by colored flares in the play); his freedom from need for woman or wife; his unseen but ear-shattering motor-cycle.

This is Lawrence at his happiest, the incarnation as Private Meek displaying all the facets of Arabian, Army and Air Force life in which Lawrence found satisfaction in the employment of his peculiar talents. He found additional pleasure in surveying this side of himself from the perspective of the finished play, and suggesting ways in which the affectionate caricature could be improved, and married even more closely to military reality. He made nearly two dozen specific recommendations for alterations in the text, and G.B.S. adopted all of them—a turnabout from the days when T. E. meekly accepted G.B.S.'s wholesale alterations and excisions in *Seven Pillars of Wisdom*.

Although Lawrence feared that mere actors might not be able to comprehend and convey—as he phrased it—"my conception of Aubrey," he made no attempt to alter, clarify or simplify Shaw's characterization, as he had done with Meek. Possibly he realized that he had already said too much. He may not even have wanted G.B.S. to realize that Aubrey was a private secret between them.

It was always an open secret that Private Meek, complete to the long head adorned with Wellingtonian nose, was a portrait of Private Shaw, but it has not been as easy to see that Aubrey Bagot, ex-R.A.F. combat officer, represents another aspect of that complex personality—the "Colonel Lawrence of Arabia" side. Here is the young officer plucked from civilian innocence (and recently out of college) and thrust into the horrors of military necessity so graphic-ally described in *The Seven Pillars*, from the murder of helpless prisoners and the execution of offenders at point-blank range to the mercy-killing on the field of battle of mortally wounded friends, and the massacre of civilians in mined railroad cars. Lawrence had left Oxford and a promising career as a scholar-archeologist, but he could not return to it on demobilization. "Digging up old civilizations"—as G.B.S. later put it—was deprived of meaning by a war which demonstrated how precarious our own civilization and its values really were. The seeming irrationality of Lawrence's postwar be-havior seems, from this perspective, almost inevitable.

Shaw's Aubrey Bagot, who had left behind his university educa-tion, and his recent ordination in the Church of England, to join a combat service, is warped by his wartime experience to such an extent that he cannot resume his life at the point war interrupted it, and lapses, like Lawrence (but in his own way), into irrational behavior. "I was hardly more than a boy," Aubrey recalls, "when I first dropped a bomb on a sleeping village. I cried all night after doing that. Later on I swooped into a street and sent machine gun bullets into a crowd of civilians: women, children and all. I was past crying by that time. And now you preach to me about stealing a pearl necklace!" He had been awarded (in his description) "a very poorly designed silver medal" for the wartime deeds for which his conscience tormented him. "What am I?" he asks: "A soldier who has lost his nerve, a thief who at his first great theft has found honesty the best policy. . . . Nature never intended me for soldiering or thieving: I am by nature and destiny a preacher. . . . But I have no Bible, no creed: the war has shot both out of my hands. . . ."

Had Aubrey been too closely parallel to Lawrence's wartime and postwar experience, Shaw would have both given the game away and destroyed Aubrey's independence as a dramatic character. Yet Aubrey Bagot's surname suggests the British commander of what was then the Transjordanian Army of the Desert Area, General John *Bagot* Glubb, known familiarly as "Glubb Pasha." (T. E. had been called "El Aurens" and "Emir Dynamite," among other things. And he had helped negotiate Transjordan into existence while with the Colonial Office in 1921.) Could G.B.S. have provided this clue unconsciously?

Aubrey Bagot bears aditional resemblances to Lawrence which are more clearly identifiable, and only partially disguised by differences in detail. Aubrey, for example, loses a brother in the war, and recalls bitterly the waste of his death; while Lawrence was shocked when his brothers Will and Frank were both killed in action. Aubrey is contemptuous of his silver medal, while Lawrence, summoned at the end of the war to an audience with King George V to receive a decoration, refused to accept it, leaving the startled monarch with the box in his hands. Further, Aubrey, who has lost his faith, confesses to his father that the war only completed the religious deterioration begun at home when he was a boy. His father ("The Elder")—an unbeliever—insists that this could not be true, for he had shielded Aubrey from a religious education. "You thought you did . . .," Aubrey replies, "but you reckoned without my mother. . . . You forbade me to read the Bible; but my mother made me learn three verses of it every day, and whacked me if I could not repeat them without misplacing a word. She threatened to whack me still worse if I told you."

The "incorrigibly superstitious mother" (the Elder's term) seems almost ceratinly to have had her origin in Lawrence's own mother, who overcompensated for her marriage and family being without benefit of clergy (Lawrence's father Sir Thomas Chapman having left his wife and four daughters to live with her). "Mrs.

Lawrence" had had a strict Calvinist upbringing, and became so overwhelmed by her sense of sin and guilt that she strove for atonement in the only way her background allowed—by extremities of religious devotion, including attempts to make her children intensely religious. T. E. was profoundly—but negatively—affected, something we may see in Shavian exaggeration in the evangelical passion of the lengthy oration with which Aubrey ends the play, seeking affirmations to preach, and in his disillusion not being able to find them. It is possibly an ironic pun, therefore, that Aubrey's postwar existence has been that of confidence man. "I shall spend another six years on the make," he tells his father, "and then I shall retire and be a saint." The mood and the terminology, incidentally, seem like parodies of Lawrence's repeated references to his diminishing term of enlistment, his retirement and proposed ascetic withdrawal from active life.

Too, True to Be Good, nevertheless, is more than a discreet probing into the motives for Lawrence's behavior, disguised slyly as a caricature of his "Private Shaw" side. It is a play, G.B.S. warns, about politics, religion and economics in a world whose values, rendered obsolete by war, will only lead to greater catastrophes. And there is more than a little of G.B.S. himself in Aubrey, who has a compulsion to "preach and preach and preach." Yet, because we appreciate the play as comedy or as polemic, we lose sight of the fact that one of the most enigmatic personalities of our century is partly hidden it it—oddly enough, because he is also so obvious in it, in another role. A review of the "Lawrence of Arabia" film concluded that the film did not catch "an answer to the fundamental enigma of Lawrence. . . , a glimpse of the secret spring that made him tick." But, continued the review in afterthought, "People who knew Lawrence did not catch it. Lawrence himself did not seem to know what it was. Perhaps it did not exist." This play, by G.B.S., who knew Lawrence as well as anyone, and who, with Charlotte, became T. E.'s surrogate parent, may be an overlooked clue to that enigma, in the already split personality G.B.S. split into Aubrey and Meek.

FREDERICK P. W. McDOWELL

[The "Pentecostal Flame" and the "Lower Centers"]†

Criticism of Shaw's later plays has emphasized that they are structurally weak, tend to sprawl, and possess little unity in action

† Dr. McDowell here carries Katherine Gatch's thesis to a complete exegesis of *Too True To Be Good*, uncovering hidden structural elements. This article appeared in *The Shaw Review*, Vol. 2 (September, 1959). pp. 27–38.

and development.[1] In comparison with the plays written in his prime, this stricture possesses some validity, to the extent that these later works lack a number of commanding individuals who dominate—and develop in—personally significant situations. The somewhat loose accretion of character and incident in *Too True to Be Good* may be partly justified, however, by considering one of Shaw's purposes in writing it: the attempt to register the chaos of the powstwar age through the somewhat amorphous structural lines of the work.[2] It is possible, therefore, to interpret positively Desmond MacCarthy's negatively presented view of this play as a "series of snapshots taken from different angles of a postwar state of mind."[3]

If the figures in *Too True to Be Good* exert less pressure on the imagination and appeal less to our sympathy than do those in the plays written before *Heartbreak House*, still the characters are clearly defined and implicated in varying degrees in the pressures of the post-World War I era. Except for the central figures, most of them were not meant to be fully rounded: in the symposium technique wherein the participants exchange ideas, it is enough if the ideas animate the characters and if the characters, at least intermittently, convey symbolically the writer's values. In contrast to *Getting Married* and *Misalliance*, the earliest examples of the true symposium in Shaw (if the Hell scene[4] is excepted), the problems argued in Shaw's work after *The Apple Cart* are political and social rather than predominantly ethical, and public rather than private in scope. In these later plays the ideas explored are more abstract than those analyzed in the earlier symposia; one result is that the characters who expound these ideas and who are so fully identified with them become more abstract and allegorical. Characters are, therefore, sometimes less incisively drawn than in the earlier discussion plays, whereas the ordering of ideas shows an increasing virtuosity and stylization. The full truth is more difficult for Shaw to present in these late works, at the same time that it is more difficult for the reader to grasp entirely.

In responding to the sense of disorder in the age reflected in *Too True to Be Good*, most critics have, I feel, overlooked those aspects of the work which give it considerable unity. A loose, even capricious, ordering of materials need not mean a total absence of organization; in *Too True to Be Good* a minimal framework exists and gives direction and force to the play. Shaw himself may have misled his critics by having "the Microbe" at the end of Act I contend

1. See A. C. Ward, *Bernard Shaw* (New York and London, 1951), p. 173; Edmund Fuller, *George Bernard Shaw* (New York, 1950), p. 99; and St. John Ervine, *Bernard Shaw* (New York, 1956), p. 526.
2. See Shaw's statements in the *Mal-*

vern Festival Book, 1932 in E. J. West, ed. *Shaw on Theatre* (New York, 1958), pp. 214–217.
3. *Shaw's Plays in Review* (New York, 1951), p. 190.
4. Act III of *Man and Superman*, 1903 [*Editor*].

that the work is now over but that the characters will spend two more acts discussing it. Actually, *Too True to Be Good* coheres remarkably in the analysis which Shaw accords its central characters, the Patient and Aubrey Bagot, who develop and show a certain complexity. The involutions of their psychology provide a focus for the actions and the thoughts of the other characters whose appearance on the scene is sometimes arbitrary and contrived. The conversion of the Patient, which begins in Act I and is completely worked out in Act III, and the continuous revelation of the varied facets of Aubrey Bagot's character firmly, if somewhat tenuously, hold together this play. Some of the more simply conceived figures in the play, such as Colonel Tallboys and Mrs. Mopply, also show a similar capacity for growth and help keep the play from becoming that mere accretion of episodic material which Shaw's hostile critics have deemed it to be. An air of fantasy, moreover, permeates the play, and gives it a remarkable unity of mood and atmosphere, and supports Shaw's contention that a genuine reality is almost certain to possess strange and bizarre aspects.

The Patient's quest for reality begins with her rejection of psychically induced illness and her rebellion against the falseness of the mores of her society when Aubrey Bagot—a lapsed clergyman, a wartime aviator, and an army chaplain now turned burglar—reveals to her the artificiality of her life. He proposes that she sell her jewels and allow herself to be kidnaped by him and his female assistant and former mistress, the amoral Sweetie, who has been hired as nightnurse by the Patient's anxious mother, Mrs. Mopply. In Act II after brief and disillusioning contact with Aubrey, the Patient decides that she needs more than satisfaction of the senses to achieve self-definition. In Act III she attains her positive philosophy, a Shavian harmonizing of contemplative and active elements in personality.

Contrapuntally with the Patient's consistent progress toward the light, Shaw presents Aubrey's fumbling journey toward self-realization. In Act I Aubrey perfervidly lectures the Patient on the need for her to live vitally and dangerously: "Have you no conscience, that you waste God's gifts so shamefully?" In Act II she goes too far in exposing hypocrisy for his comfort; he is a more conventional person than he ordinarily cares to admit. In fact, her plain speaking disturbs even Sweetie, who continually seeks, but with increasing disillusionment, for fulfillment through sex alone. As a result of reaction against his newly-found father's restrictive influence, Aubrey in Act III recovers his spiritual independence and admits anew his responsibility to face reality even when it is disconcerting.

In the relationships among the Patient, Sweetie, and Aubrey in

Acts II and III, there develop many amusing and paradoxical situations. The characters are now in primitive surroundings in a British dependency, possibly somewhere on the African coast. Sweetie, unconventional with respect to sex, is emotionally a slave to convention and wants only romance from the men she has known; for her a love affair must be a perpetual honeymoon. As to personal behavior, Sweetie is the least inhibited person in the play; as to underlying motivation, she is the most impervious to suggestion from without, and is possibly, therefore, the most conservative. For the Patient, Sweetie's harsh candor in confessing her past vagaries is at this point profoundly disturbing, even though the Patient had previously deflated her associate by calling her a "silly bitch." The Patient has not yet completely attained the regenerate state of confident self-possession so greatly valued by Shaw in which she will be able to face with serenity even the most brutal aspects of experience. The result is that she is now distressed by Sweetie's cynical utterances as to the animalism of sex.

Upsetting as Sweetie is to her equanimity, the Patient is forced to admit that Sweetie is real since she does more than talk and has had the courage to test her convictions. We know that Shaw in the 1930's favored action instead of theorizing about it; something then is even to be said for action which is, as in Sweetie's case, in accord with the dictates of her "lower centers." One basic form of reality, then, albeit not the highest form, is that manifested by the unconscious self. Its irrational urges are frequently more genuine than the articulate ideas in our conscious minds, ideas that are often the result either of an unadmitted hypocrisy or of an unperceptive conformity to convention. Since the war the "lower centers," Aubrey remarks, have become "vocal" and have told us new and startling truths: as a result, he perceives that established institutions are violently disintegrating, "rocking, and splitting and sundering." When the lower centers erupt, there is, accordingly, little left to hold by that is fixed or absolute: "They [the lower centers] leave us no place to live, no certainties, no workable morality, no heaven, no hell, no commandments, and no God." The disruptive effects of these "lower centers"—now frankly acknowledged for what they are—extend even to the conventionally organized five act play and make it an inadequate vehicle for the presentation of our modern problems, which are not always susceptible to ordered formulation in a universe where the only immutable law is that of change. Even the higher centers in their most articulate and inspired manifestation as "right reason," cannot countermand completely the influence of our unconscious selves. As a relativist in outlook, Shaw welcomed that aspect of modernism which disint grated inhibiting custom; as a philosopher with some aspira toward the ideal and the eternal, he was made somewhat uneasy by the too ready denial of all absolutes by "advanced" spokesmen of the time who regarded as significant only those realities emanating from the aggressive instincts.

Somewhat later in Act II, the Patient—previously the person shocked—becomes the shocker, and those who have previously been outrageously vociferous are in their turn discomposed by a person exhibiting a still more radical candor. The Patient's ideas and attitudes are authoritative, since they derive from the "higher centers" rather than the lower. These "higher centers" are ambivalent in nature: if they can speak negatively through "respectable conversation" they can also be commandingly evinced through "the great poetry and literature of the world," through inspired utterance of any sort. Sweetie and Aubrey are therefore disarmed by the Patient's consciously assumed mask of vulgarity, when she describes purposeless human beings as nothing more than "inefficient fertilizers" who "convert good food into bad manure." The Patient's frankness seems far more brutal to Aubrey than Sweetie's; once the Patient achieves spiritual light, her hold upon reality is strong and her remarks are the more damaging to all pretense because of the inescapable truth they embody. Later, when in Act III the Patient declaims against being devoured by the "parasites" of the rich, Aubrey recoils from such evocative, figurative language and again feels wounded in spirit by the Patient's "intellectual coarseness."

As a result of her experiences in Act II, the Patient finds an inner regeneration and becomes well, strong, and emotionally cleansed. Dressed "en belle sauvage," she has ostensibly been vitalized by an appreciation of wild nature and has come to appreciate fully the wonders of the universe. More important still, she has attained a knowledge of her own inner resources and a sense of social responsibility. If she now knows that her past life has been unreal, her present life is not so genuine as she wishes it to be; and she still yearns for some sort of projection for her sacred self within, which it does not yet have. For this reason she wishes to be vigorous and positive—to beat or even to kill as her "lower centers" might dictate, if that should be necessary—in order that her break with her respectable past may be conclusive. By the exertions of the will, we must achieve a modicum of order from the chaos of our li--   effects of the lower centers upon them. This
                        ble light by the Patient has its counterpart in
                        his materials in the play: its structure becomes
                        he Patient assumes spiritual control of her des-
                        he end still a seeker may be inferred from the
                        ver becomes so taut as those written by Shaw
                        In those earlier works, the central characters

found more positive answers to their problems than the Patient manages to achieve.

In Act III the Patient realizes still more firmly that a cleansed spirit is only a preliminary—if an indispensable one—to assertive activity in the world outside. Shaw was evidently projecting through the Patient a favorite idea of his, that "until the heart and mind of the people is changed"[5] there is little possibility of political progress. The glories of nature are not enough for the Patient who craves "something sensible to do" and who feels "utterly miserable"—like a "lost dog"—without a well-defined purpose in her life. For a time, she feels that she is spiritually adrift, just as Sweetie is emotionally adrift. But her revived self is soon impatient of aimlessness; and she feels herself compelled to become a housekeeper to the world and to set it in order. It is as if she had in mind Shaw's own statement in "The Revolutionist's Handbook" appended to *Man and Superman*: "If there be no will, we are lost."[6] Despite its order and beauty, the cruelties and vastness of the universe lead her, in metaphysical self-defense, to affirm—at least tentatively—humanistic and spiritual values. In Act I, she has not found reality among the enervating luxuries of civilization; in Act II she does not find it in primitive nature; in Act III she finds some degree of truth within her own soul as that provides her with the impetus to discover purposes outside and larger than herself.[7]

Exerting an almost religious consecration to these ends, the Patient wishes to organize a sisterhood which will first withdraw women from the world and then allow them to return to it fortified with a genuine wisdom. This order will appeal to the aspirations of all women, once they have been liberated—as the Patient herself has been—from the tyrannies of the family and sex and once they perceive, then, that family affection and sexual fulfillment are only aspects, sometimes quite nugatory, of self-realization. The sisterhood, the Patient avers, need not even be a nunnery, if the men will enter it without spoiling things—without, that is, obtruding emotional irrelevancies into a program of social betterment. In getting beyond the disillusionments of romance to responsible selfhood, the Patient recalls the Ellie Dunn of *Heartbreak House*, whose infatuation with Hector Hushabye of course went deeper than the Patient's for Aubrey.

Sergeant Fielding, who is not introduced until Act III, combines aspects of the Patient's direct spiritual progress and Aubrey's spiritual vacillation. He is a young man whose moral seriousness has been consistently developed by close study of the Bible and *Pil-*

5. "The Revolutionist's Handbook," *Man and Superman*, p. 180.
6. *Ibid.*, p. 204.
7. I am indebted to Katherine H.

Gatch's discussion of this play in "The Last Plays of Bernard Shaw: Dialectic and Despair," *English Stage Comedy*. [See above—*Editor*.]

grim's Progress; he used to believe these books implicitly since they seemed to describe as an actuality a divine world far removed from life. They seem to have an even greater relevance, now that he has found in these repositories of God's wisdom an implicit commentary upon the present and a spiritual depth apparently absent from his immediate world. The war itself and the postwar age seen trivial to the Sergeant (as they also seemed in some moods to a disillusioned Shaw) in comparison with the prophetic intensities which pervade the Bible and Bunyan. The prospect of terror and violence which unnerves Christian when he describes to his wife the overthrow of their city by fire from heaven has its modern counterpart: European capitals, which recall the "Falling towers" of Eliot's "The Waste-Land," are on the verge of being destroyed by manmade fire from heaven; and governors, with their helpless burdens "of corpses and debts on their backs," echo Christian's plaint, "What shall I do to be saved?" This last question sounds antiphonally throughout the whole of Act III: the Patient and Aubrey are concerned with it and the Elder later uses the phrase. The insecurity and latent violence in the postwar age are, of course, mirrored in the dissolving perspectives which characterize the shifting, yet fully articulated, structual lines of the play. The haphazard tensions and the incertitudes of the age are again adroitly suggested by another parallel from Bunyan: we are all concerned, says the Sergeant, with "fleeing from the wrath to come," yet have no "shining light" to guide us.

Although the Sergeant reverences the Bible, he is repelled—as Shaw was—by those parts of it which celebrate the arrogance and self-righteousness of a chosen race and their assumed rights of pillage and slaughter. The Great War has conclusively shown, he says, how pernicious such an assumption of ethnic superiority can become, both as a national philosophy and as a practical means of solving international problems. Even in a world distrustful of absolutes, the less militant portions of the Scripture, the Sergeant believes, still have spiritual immediacy. Just as Shaw continued to reverence the ethical content of the Bible, so the Sergeant commends as workable ideals those set forth by the Prophet Micah: to "do justice; love mercy; and walk humbly before your God."

As a moralist the Sergeant is inferior to the Patient whose resources, self-discipline, and sense of reality are fully realized by the end of the play. He adopts a Shavian view that minds as well as bodies figure in sexual relationships; but in his personal life he fails to live up to the implications of this principle. He is unable to resist the appeal of Sweetie who is essentially mindless and without spirituality. A romanticism which he could only exercise through his critical intellect is in abeyance where Sweetie is concerned; it deflects him from his aspirations and interferes with the forward progression of his inner life. The momentary blindness which overcomes Aubrey during the war when he first saw Sweetie and endowed her with "not only every charm, but every virtue," thus afflicts in more aggravated form the seriously religious Sergeant. The three principal foci of intellectual interest in the play—the Patient, the Sergeant, and Aubrey—thus parallel and complement one another in their development; Shaw's unfolding the destinies of people with somewhat similar yet divergent characteristics provides another structural principle in the play. Introduced early in Act III, the Sergeant is, moreover, a link between Sweetie who predominates in Acts I and II and Aubrey whose inspired prophecies close the action in Act III.

At the end of the play the Sergeant concludes that sex is "one of the facts that religion has to make room for." At this point he perhaps too readily assumes that association with Sweetie will represent completion for him: life, he perceives, is complex and varied, and can no more ignore Sweetie's sexual hedonism than his own spiritual conscientiousness. The direction of Sweetie's development away from sex to the impersonal is reversed in the Sergeant: if Sweetie is converted in some degree to a more spiritual life, the Sergeant is in some sense deconverted from it. In sex, Shaw implies, extremes meet and influence one another, sometimes positively, sometimes disastrously.

The Patient's mother, Mrs. Mopply, having persecuted Colonel Tallboys for dereliction of duty in failing to rescue her child from brigands, also undergoes a forcible regeneration in Act III, when the Colonel, forced beyond his endurance, strikes her with an umbrella. With this sudden blow, she sees how deadening her own existence, based upon the lifeless aspects of Victorianism, has been. She now finds out that life is the opposite of what she had been told; she agrees with the Elder when he describes her, along with the others, as "falling through the bottomless abyss"; and she admits that now she does not "know my head from my heels." Violence can become, than, a needed preliminary to spiritual light: perhaps this truth is implied in the somewhat contorted presentation of events and people in this play. After some momentary confusion at seeing life with changed eyes, Mrs. Mopply accepts the constructive aspect of modernism: one's responsibility of knowing oneself and of acting to some purpose.

The hold of convention over an individual's free life is also amusingly revealed in Colonel Tallboys. If it were not for his wife, he says, he would be glad to give up his commission and become a genuine man like Private Meek. Meek is the all-competent soldier, whose attributes are those of Shaw's friend, Colonel T. E. Lawrence, who subsequently had a career as private in the Royal Air Force. At first reluctantly and then willingly, Tallboys resigns the conduct of the expedition to a better man who is his inferior in prerogatives. Genuine authority, distinction, and flexibility of mind like Meek's do not need the external support of rank to be effective, Shaw implies: it is possible as a private soldier to possess the talents of a Caesar. It is only when the Colonel gives over his scorn and envy of Meek and treats him as a human being that he becomes a human being himself. After he turns over his command to Meek and devotes himself to water-coloring, he becomes a better man as an artist than he had ever been as a soldier. Shaw implied, moreover, that imperial power administered by a stupid man like Tallboys, with his slavish adherence to routine, can hardly last.

Although he does not have the stature of Captain Shotover in *Heartbreak House*, Aubrey Bagot resembles him in being at once a great soul and its caricature. Aubrey's character is, therefore, richly ambiguous throughout the play—he is at times contemptible and at other times supernally wise. Conflicting impressions of Aubrey are registered through the disparate episodes of the play and unite to form a charater of considerable complexity. Near the point in Act II, for example, where the Patient shocks his prudish sensibility, he yet shows that he is in significant communion with the Life-Force. Commenting upon Harry Smiler, who gratuitously murdered a policeman after the war for the thrill of the thing, Aubrey says that Harry went wrong because he was totally insensitive to "the miracles of the universe" and to "the problems of human destiny". Thus Aubrey implies that he is appreciative of these larger aspects of existence, as Shaw himself was. Previously, in Act I, Aubrey had been aware of the commanding significance to the Patient of his counsel to revolt: "the aspiring soul escapes from home, sweet home . . . the girl's prison and the woman's workhouse." Accordingly, he reflects not only Shaw's philosophy of creative evolution but his Nietzschean gospel of living experimentally. At this point, Aubrey sees the need for "the innermost uppermost life" in the Patient to assert itself, he senses that this unsure and challenging world is important only as a field for the adventures "of the life everlasting," and he decries as a primary aim in life the search for security: "They who cry safety first never cross the street: the empires which sacrifice life to security find it in the grave."

If the Patient shocks him in Act II and early in Act III (he decides she does not have "the instincts of a lady"), Aubrey, who has the last speech in the play, recovers his balance and comments philosophically upon the modern obsession induced by "the iron lightning of war," of stripping our souls of their "angelic veils." Aubrey's words in this last speech have the ring of sincerity.

Yet we do not forget that the Patient had loved Aubrey, found him wanting, and dismissed him as unworthy of her affection. He had previously in Act III decided opportunistically to be a popular "saint"—to acquire a halo "as large as Sweetie's sun hat" by making money, endowing hospitals, and contributing to party funds—in contrast to the Patient with her sincere quest for sanctity. Even here, however, Aubrey should not be misjudged: he is surely not the Shavian saint in the sense that Father Keegan[8] is one, yet Aubrey does possess some of Keegan's saintly short-range impracticality and some of his saintly long-range sureness of vision.

If the rending of deceptive appearances as described by Aubrey means the loss of some desirable amenities and the revelation "too keen . . . to bear" of a concealed life, still we may come to see that the idealisms of the past, comforting as they once were, are no longer quite applicable to the present. In theory Aubrey approves of the modern determination to seize the truth beneath appearances, but in actuality he is dismayed by some of the more violent manifestations of this tendency. Even when he discerns the need at all cost to identify himself with "the pentecostal flame" of the Life-Force, he is still somewhat imperfectly emancipated. Aubrey's timorousness concering revolutionary modernism exceeds that revealed by Shaw. Yet Aubrey's reservations about an extreme iconoclasm may well reflect Shaw's skepticism of the absolutely confident younger generation of the 1920's.

The constructive side to present unrest is this: if our souls now go in rags, if their former trappings have been seen to be specious, still knowledge of how things stand is salutary and bracing—Carlyle's point made long ago in *Sartor Resartus*.[9] At least Aubrey realizes that with the "fiery forcing house" of the war the old standards have gone and life is confusing, chaotic, and disorderly. Accordingly, he finds that the war has bereft him of Bible and creed. Instead of revelling in our "nudity," we must realize that new affirmations are needed to supersede the remnants of outmoded beliefs. New values are needed lest the unimaginative men of action, who do not think and feel, totally prevail, now that "we have outgrown our religion, outgrown our political system, outgrown our own strength of mind and character." We must, Aubrey insists, find "the way of life" or perish; and he realizes that the "lower centers" of Sweetie—which are directionless—do not comprise all of reality. In so far as he identifies himself with the pentecostal flame, he transcends, then, the chaotic aspects of his own

8. From *John Bull's Other Island*. See John Gassner's reference at the conclusion of *Bernard Shaw and the Making of the Modern Mind* [*Editor*].
9. Written in 1833, the title means "The Tailor Reclothed." Shaw's relationship to this earlier iconoclast and prophet of the doctrine of work is noted also in Louis Crompton's treatment of *Heartbreak House*, above [*Editor*].

life. The Patient's achievement of light, the Sergeant's incursion of human feeling, and Aubrey's vision of spiritual fire are varying aspects of the positive direction of Act III, and provide an appropriate end to the circuitously unfolding action of the play.

Aubrey's sensitivity and sincerity in his most impassioned moments render too extreme, I think, William Irvine's judgment that Aubrey combines "a facility for words with no capacity for faith and action."[1] Aubrey does possess faith, but is tragically unable to express it outwardly by meaningful action. He is to be aligned with those other talkers of intelligence in the Shavian drama who are disorganized or ineffective in their personal lives: Charteris, Valentine, John Tanner, Cusins, Larry Doyle, and Hector Hushabye.[2] If, as Shaw remarked in his preface, Aubrey is a "scoundrel" without "conscience," he still has on occasion insight so deep as to carry unmistakably the burden of the Shavian ethos. In so curtly dismissing Aubrey, Shaw himself may have forgotten his own conviction expressed many times: "It is generally admitted that even good men have their weaknesses: what is less recognized is that rascals have their points of honor."[3]

In Aubrey Shaw admits that spiritual humility before the ultimate mystery of creation is all-important; yet he feels that earnest social energies, directed by the wisdom accorded us when we are in harmony with ultimate reality, count for still more. The last word may not be with the Patient, but she has had the courage to be forthright in action and to approach the pentecostal flame without fear of being "shrivelled up." Despite his clear appreciation at times of the nature of the ineffable, Aubrey's hesitations in his progress toward the light become emblematic of the difficulties experienced by many intellectuals in the modern age in achieving philosophical clarity and self-definition.

The unexpected, the unpredictable, the indeterminate, and the paradoxical determine the conditions of modern life and by implication underlie the quest undertaken by the Patient, by Aubrey, and by Sergeant Fielding. As far as salvation is concerned, the Sergeant disagrees with Bunyan that the way is straight before us. A straight road would not in itself get us to heaven; the way to redemption may be circuitous; and in any event the road will have to be opened up by strenuous effort.

In this play Shaw delighted thus in presenting certain distortions. Truth is so strange that fiction pales beside it; the unusual, the far-fetched, and the fantastic alone give us the key to reality. Through the means of fantasy, Shaw emphasized the unusual, not

1. *The Universe of G.B.S.* (New York, 1949), p. 371.
2. From the plays (in order): *The Philanderer, You Never Can Tell, Man and Superman, Major Barbara, John*

Bull's Other Island, Heartbreak House [*Editor*].
3. *Everybody's Political What's What* (New York, 1944), p. 191.

to say the grotesque, aspects of life in the twentieth century. As social, political, and moral commentator, Shaw could imply that his own standards were close to the opposite of those inherent in the absurd situations he presented; or else he could show that the absurd situations he presented had more reality than those ordinarily accepted without cavil by the conventional. As satirist he also exposed as absurd those influences which interfered with the flexible functioning of the state and with the comprehending relationships between individuals in it.

The Patient goes beyond the normal expectations of the Burglar and the night-nurse when she suddenly and unexpectedly jumps out of bed and manhandles those who are threatening to overpower her with violence. One does not ordinarily expect a burglar to be a lapsed clergyman nor for him to have been ordained furtively by the deviousness of his mother, so as to avoid the wrath and opposition of his father, an uncompromising atheist. It is, of course, a fantastic enterprise for the Burglar and the Nurse to kidnap the Patient in Act I and have her consent to it, but not so fantastic after all if we consider the blankness of her previous existence. When Aubrey challenges her, her response is ambivalent: she feels she is in a dream but does not wish the dream to end.

One of the chief characters in Act I, the Microbe, is a creature of Shaw's whimsical fancy through whom he can present some of his opinions upon medicine, disease, and physicians. The most important point made by the Microbe is that illness is often psychosomatic. For comic effect Shaw inverted accepted theories upon the cause of disease by presenting the Microbe-monster as having been made ill by the hypochrondriac Patient, instead of his causing her to be sick. Since the play opens with the plaints of the Microbe, the fantastic aspects of the play—its partial divorce from the completely probable—are established from the very outset. In Shaw's view, doctors are not often the healers they are purported to be; they sometimes make a sickly person yet more ill. At least the physician in this play has the honesty to admit that he is a hypocrite. When the Patient recovers from her hypochrondria, the Microbe who had been made ill by her excesses recovers. The doctor had previously told the Microbe that it is faith in oneself and in "that mysterious power which gives us our life and which none of us knows anything about" rather than science which makes one well; but a doctor customarily ascribes his cures to "science" because that is what people believe in.

In the situations involving Aubrey and his father, Shaw reversed stereotyped characters and incidents so completely that the play once again acquires the startling quality we associate with the unique fabrications of fantasy. In the Elder, Shaw satirized the somnolence with which the Victorian intellectual in literature and life lost his faith in traditional Christianity and exchanged for the inscrutable workings of an anthropomorphic creator a faith in scientific reality. Accordingly, Shaw presented a new phenomenon in literature, the athiest who in the twentieth century has lost irretrievably his faith in the "new" orthodoxy of nineteenth-century science which had erected deterministic natural law into an absolute. In the twentieth century the "infallible" laws of nature have only a contingent validity, as a result of "indeterministic" theorizing which stresses probability rather than uniformity in the workings of the universe. The Elder does not know what to do to be saved now that his dogmatic philosophy of science has been questioned, now that the dynamic "Purpose and Design" basic to Shaw's theory of creative evolution may be rising "from the dead" to cast down the sway of impersonal natural law. He can only feel a sense of violent overthrow, a sense of forces at work which he cannot understand, an overpowering sense of disintegration in nature and society.[4] The Elder cannot see that purpose and design exist, but that their workings in life are inscrutable, episodic, and unpredictable. Shaw may actually have thought that he could best embody his Einsteinian indeterminism and relativity in a somewhat "photographic" representation of the external formlessness of nature and society. Pattern in the natural and human world is thus concealed but intermittently asserts itself strongly; just so does Shaw's sense of dramatic structure, in apparent abeyance in the play, firmly support its somewhat miscellaneous groupings of characters and incidents.

The Elder fails to see that his intellectual rigidity and his sentimentalizing of a liberal creed have resulted in a departure from a desirable norm of values. What had been sophistication in the Victorian era has come to be intellectual immaturity, if not timidity, in the modern age. If the Elder's intellectual foundations have mouldered and if he does not quite possess the imaginative force to formulate a new philosophy, he has painfully acquired a Shavian insight into the reasons for the failure of deterministic science, as a myth or religion, to provide spiritual light and life for the present age: "The science I pinned my faith to is bankrupt: its tales were more foolish than all the miracles of the priests, its cruelties more horrible than all the atrocities of the Inquisition. Its spread of enlightenment has been a spread of cancer: its counsels that were to have established the millenium have led straight to European suicide."

The fantastic elements of the play shade off into allegory. People and incidents take on overtly symbolic value as a result of being

4. In this regard, see Shaw's statement in *Everybody's Political What's What*, p. 361: "Mr. Everyman is often as credulous and bigoted in his modern scientific scepticism as his grandfather was in his Evangelicalism."

several removes from average reality. Aubrey, himself no exception to his own statement, says of these people in his concluding speech: "There is something fantastic about them, something unreal, and perverse, something profoundly unsatisfactory." The Patient, both unregenerate and regenerate, is emblematic of the modern age. On the one hand, she is symbolic in her sickness, in her self-pity, and in her self-indulgence of those aspects of the age which Shaw felt should be ridiculed. On the other hand, she also possesses productive energies which at first lie fallow but which the present-day individual may utilize to achieve a modicum of order out of disorder. Accordingly, the Patient has used her own resources to achieve regeneration and to develop a secular idealism, and she has shown unexpected strength, physical and moral, when the Burglar challenges her. The directionless younger generation as a whole is epitomized in Sweetie who is fickleness incarnate and who is characterized by her inconstancy and her complete lack of moral sense. Colonel Tallboys is symbolic as a survivor from the Victorian Age which produced him, in his earlier conventionality, in his sense of frustration over men and women who lack direction and faith, and in his recourse to nature and art—the solace of the spiritually shaken Victorian—when, in his later more perceptive phase, humanity still seems to fail him.

The ills of the modern age can be measured in terms of Aubrey's futile life as petty criminal after the war. His life of crime had its origin in the bombings in which he participated: as he says, the theft of a pearl necklace is nothing in comparison to the things which he did during the war with his father's implied approval. It is not valid, Aubrey says, to divide himself into a war self and a peace self, as some would still urge him to do. Our evil impulses are part of our whole psychology and cannot be separated from it; our sinful natures, as well as our potential idealism, argue our common humanity. Even sincere impulses may be pernicious if they are not rationally examined. Mrs. Bagot's uncritical enthusiasm for the war forced Aubrey's reluctant brother into it—the result was that he was killed and she died of remorse.

The irritating optimism and bluster in his father's prewar agnosticism caused Aubrey in revulsion to become a clergyman in the established church. However, Aubrey discerns during his wartime career as army chaplain certain hypocrisies which disillusion him with organized religion as strongly as his father had been disillusioned with it: "When I was wounded and lost my nerve for flying, I became an army chaplain. I then found myself obliged to tell mortally wounded men that they were dying in a state of grace and were going straight to heaven, while as a matter of fact they were dying in mortal sin and going elsewhere." Aubrey's disillusionment with the Christianity he has embraced is radical and represents, at least in part, Shaw's own distrust of the latent hypocrisy he saw in many of the official formulations of Christian values. When his father accuses him of being a scoundrel, Aubrey says that his religious education (engineered by his mother without the Elder's knowledge) has taught him that if he is "bold, unscrupulous, acquisitive, successful and rich," only then will he be admired and respected, and only then can he afford to be honest.

The Elder, figure of ridicule as he sometimes is, betrays too much urgency in his conviction that all of us are falling into a "bottomless abyss" for this assertion to seem only the timorous utterance of an idiosyncratic man. The stridency of his statements is in itself an indication that the modern age is in chaos, and there is truth as well as hysteria in his contention that, having fallen into this abyss, "our dizzy brains can utter nothing but madness." The Sergeant at least agrees with the Elder that in the war the bottom not only came out of soldiering but out of everything: the war, he says, was not devilment but damnation. With the Elder's rejoinder that we are only "lost souls, all of us," the Patient agrees in part, she says, that in fact "we are only lost dogs" and that, despite our present drifting, we may like lost dogs, find our way home again—if we but achieve command of ourselves. In his concluding speech Aubrey understands the sharp but limited insights of his parent, the Elder, and declares, echoing him, that the people in the play "are all . . . falling, falling, falling endlessly and hopelessly through a void in which they can find no footing." The latent violences in the period erupt in catastrophe: see the sudden onset of the Great War, which was, in part, the result of the unimaginative application to human affairs of the Elder's positivistic science.

In *Too True to Be Good* Shaw acutely balanced the positive with the negative. If Aubrey and the Patient at the end of the play are optimistic, still one must admit that their optimism is only tentative. Tone and texture of the play, on the other hand, aptly mirror the chaotic post-war age to which Shaw, as an intellectual conditioned in part during another period, had to adjust himself. The presence in conjunction in *Too True to Be Good* of the objective critical spirit, of a strong subjective sympathy with the characters, of a sense of the underlying tensions of the 1920's, and of an inventive fancy consistently expressing itself in richly symbolic situations provides this play with greater distinction, I feel, than it has ordinarily been thought to possess.

The Plays of Bernard Shaw

The date given is the date of the completion of the play, not necessarily the date of first publication, as recorded in Mander and Mitchenson's *Theatrical Companion to Shaw*. Except as noted, the titles of the plays are listed as they appear in the Standard Edition.

Widowers' Houses 1892
The Philanderer 1893 ⎫ (in *Plays Pleasant and*
Mrs Warren's Profession 1894 ⎬ *Unpleasant*, Volume I)

Arms and the Man 1894 ⎫
Candida 1895 ⎪ (in *Plays Pleasant and*
The Man of Destiny 1895 ⎬ *Unpleasant*, Volume II)
You Never Can Tell 1896 ⎭

The Devil's Disciple 1897 ⎫ (in *Three Plays for*
Caesar and Cleopatra 1898 ⎬ *Puritans*)
Captain Brassbound's Conversion 1899 ⎭

The Admirable Bashville 1901 (in *Translations and Tomfooleries*)

Man and Superman 1903

John Bull's Other Island 1904

How He Lied to Her Husband 1904

Major Barbara 1905

Passion, Poison, and Petrifaction, OR *The Fatal Gazogene* 1905 (in *Translations and Tomfooleries*)

The Doctor's Dilemma 1906

*The Interlude at the Playhouse** 1907

Getting Married 1908

The Shewing-up of Blanco Posnet 1909

Press Cuttings 1909 (in *Translations and Tomfooleries*)

The Fascinating Foundling 1909 (in *Translations and Tomfooleries*)

* not included in the Standard Edition

The Glimpse of Reality 1909 (in *Translations and Tomfooleries*)

Misalliance 1910

The Dark Lady of the Sonnets 1910

Fanny's First Play 1911

Androcles and the Lion 1912

Overruled 1912

Pygmalion 1913

Great Catherine 1913

The Music-Cure 1913 (in *Translations and Tomfooleries*)

O'Flaherty, V. C. 1915 (in *Playlets of the War*)

The Inca of Perusalem 1916 (in *Playlets of the War*)

Augustus Does His Bit 1916 (in *Playlets of the War*)

Annajanska, the Bolshevik Empress 1917 (in *Playlets of the War*)

Heartbreak House 1919

Back to Methuselah 1920

Jitta's Atonement 1922 (in *Translations and Tomfooleries*)

Saint Joan 1923

The Apple Cart 1929

Too True to Be Good 1931

Village Wooing 1933

On the Rocks 1933

The Simpleton of the Unexpected Isles 1934

The Six of Calais 1934

The Millionairess 1935

Cymbeline Refinished 1937

Geneva 1938

In Good King Charles's Golden Days 1939

Buoyant Billions 1948

Shakes Versus Shav 1949

Farfetched Fables 1950

*Why She Would Not** 1950

* not included in the Standard Edition

Selected Bibliography

Bellamy, Edward. *Equality*. New York, 1897.
———. *Looking Backward*. Boston, 1941.
Bentley, Eric. *Bernard Shaw, 1856–1950*. Amended Edition, New York, 1957.
———. *The Playwright as Thinker*. *New York*, 1946.
Bergson, Henri. *Creative Evolution*. Translated by Arthur Mitchell. New York, 1944.
Brustein, Robert. *The Theatre of Revolt*. Boston, 1964.
Carpenter, Charles A. *Bernard Shaw and the Art of Destroying Ideals*. Madison, Wis., 1969.
Chesterton, G. K. *George Bernard Shaw*. New York, 1949.
Colbourne, Maurice. *The Real Bernard Shaw*. New York, 1949.
Crompton, Louis. *Shaw the Dramatist*. Lincoln, Neb., 1969.
Ervine, St. John. *Bernard Shaw; His Life, Work and Friends*. London and New York, 1956.
Fergusson, Francis. *The Idea of a Theatre*. Princeton, N. J., 1949.
Fremantle, Anne. *This Little Band of Prophets: The British Fabians*. New York, 1960.
Henderson, Archibald. *George Bernard Shaw: Man of the Century*. New York, 1956.
Irvine, William. *The Universe of G.B.S.* New York, 1949.
Joad, C. E. M. *Shaw*. London, 1949.
———, ed. *Shaw and Society*. New York, 1953.
Kaye, Julian B. *Bernard Shaw and the Nineteenth-Century Tradition*. Norman, Okla., 1958.
Kronenberger, Louis, ed. *George Bernard Shaw: A Critical Survey*. New York, 1953.
Langner, Lawrence. *G.B.S. and the Lunatic*. New York, 1963.
MacCarthy, Sir Desmond. *The Court Theatre, 1904–1907*. London, 1907.
———. *Shaw*. London, 1951.
———. *Shaw's Plays in Review*. New York, 1958.
McCarthy, Lillah. *Myself and My Friends . . . With an Aide by Bernard Shaw*. London, 1934.
Mander, Raymond, and Mitchenson, Joe. *Theatrical Companion to Shaw*. London, 1954.
Meisel, Martin. *Shaw and the Nineteenth-Century Theater*. Princeton, N. J., 1963.
Nethercot, Arthur H. *Men and Supermen: The Shavian Portrait Gallery*. Cambridge, Mass., 1954.
Patch, Blanche. *Thirty Years with Bernard Shaw*. London, 1951.
Pearson, Hesketh. *Bernard Shaw: His Life and Personality*. London, 1942.
———. *G.B.S.: A Postscript*. New York, 1950.
Rattray, Robert F. *Bernard Shaw: A Chronicle*. London, 1951.
Shaw, George Bernard. *An Autobiography, 1856–1898*. Selected from his writings by Stanley Weintraub. New York, 1969.
———. *Bernard Shaw and Mrs. Patrick Campbell: Their Correspondence*. Edited by Alan Dent. New York, 1952.
———. *Collected Letters, 1874–1897*. Edited by Dan H. Laurence. New York, 1965.
———. *Ellen Terry and Bernard Shaw, A Correspondence*. Edited by Christopher St. John. New York, 1931.
———. *Essays in Fabian Socialism*. In the Standard Edition of *The Works of Bernard Shaw*. London and New York, 1932.
———. *Everybody's Political What's What*. Standard Edition. London and New York, 1944.
———. *Letters to Granville Barker*. New York, 1957.
———. *Major Critical Essays (The Quintessence of Ibsenism, The Perfect Wagnerite, The Sanity of Art)*. Standard Edition. London and New York, 1932.
———. *Platform and Pulpit*. Edited by Dan H. Laurence. New York, 1961.
———. Preface to *Three Plays by Brieux*. New York, 1911.
———. *Shaw on Theatre*. Edited by E. J. West. New York, 1958.
———. *Plays*. Standard Edition. London and New York, 1930–1950.

————. *Shaw on Religion*. Edited by Warren Sylvester Smith. London and New York, 1967.

————. *Sixteen Self Sketches*. Standard Edition. London and New York, 1949.

————. *The Adventures of the Black Girl in Her Search for God and Some Lesser Tales*. Standard Edition. London and New York, 1934.

————. *The Intelligent Woman's Guide to Socialism and Capitalism*. Standard Edition. London and New York, 1928.

————. *The Religious Speeches of Bernard Shaw*. Edited by Warren Sylvester Smith. University Park, Pa., 1964.

Smith, Warren Sylvester, *The London Heretics*. London, 1967, New York, 1968.

Strauss, E. *Bernard Shaw: Art and Socialism*. London, 1942.

Weintraub, Stanley. *Private Shaw and Public Shaw*. New York, 1963.

West, Alick. *George Bernard Shaw, "A Good Man Fallen Among Fabians."* New York, 1950.

Winsten, Stephen. *Days with Bernard Shaw*. New York, 1949.

————. *G.B.S. 90*. London and New York, 1946.

————. *Jesting Apostle: The Life of Bernard Shaw*. London, 1956.

————. *Salt and His Circle*. London, 1951.